SOUTH AMERICA

From Machu Picchu to the Amazon rainforest

Claudia Martin

amber
BOOKS

First published in 2026

Published by
Amber Books Ltd
United House
London N7 9DP
United Kingdom
www.amberbooks.co.uk
Facebook: amberbooks
YouTube: amberbooksltd
Instagram: amberbooksltd
X(Twitter): @amberbooks

ISBN: 978-1-83886-698-3

Project Editor: Anna Brownbridge
Design: Keren Harragan
Picture Research: Adam Gnych

Printed in China

Contents

Introduction

A continent of superlatives and extraordinary diversity, South America stretches from Colombia's arid, sunbaked Punta Gallinas to Chile's wind-whipped Tierra del Fuego. Reaching all the way from Colombia and Venezuela to Chile is the continent's jagged spine: the planet's longest above-ocean mountain range, the Andes. This chain of snow-capped mountains, volcanoes and plateaus extends for 8,900km (5,500 miles). The Andes are the cradle of the world's biggest river by volume, the Amazon, its basin nourishing the world's largest rainforest, covering 6 million sq km (2.3 million sq miles). This forest is the most biodiverse place on Earth, holding 10 per cent of known species, from fierce, muscular jaguars to tiny but equally deadly frogs. Despite the formidable terrain, the Andes were also one of the birthplaces of civilization. It was here, from 3500 BCE, that complex societies blossomed, known for their monumental architecture and sophisticated crafts. Yet later waves of migration, colonization and enslavement have all left their mark on the continent, from its soaring cathedrals to its tango dancers, its carnivals to its gauchos.

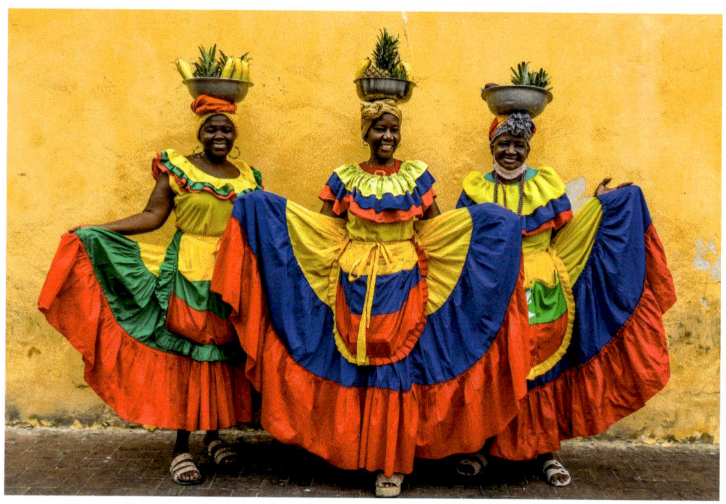

ABOVE:
***Palenqueras*, Cartagena, Colombia**
Now a tourist-friendly symbol of Colombia, women of San Basilio de Palenque, such as these fruit vendors, were at the forefront of the struggle against slavery.

OPPOSITE:
Machu Picchu, Peru
Occupied from 1420, this Inca citadel lies on an Andean ridge.

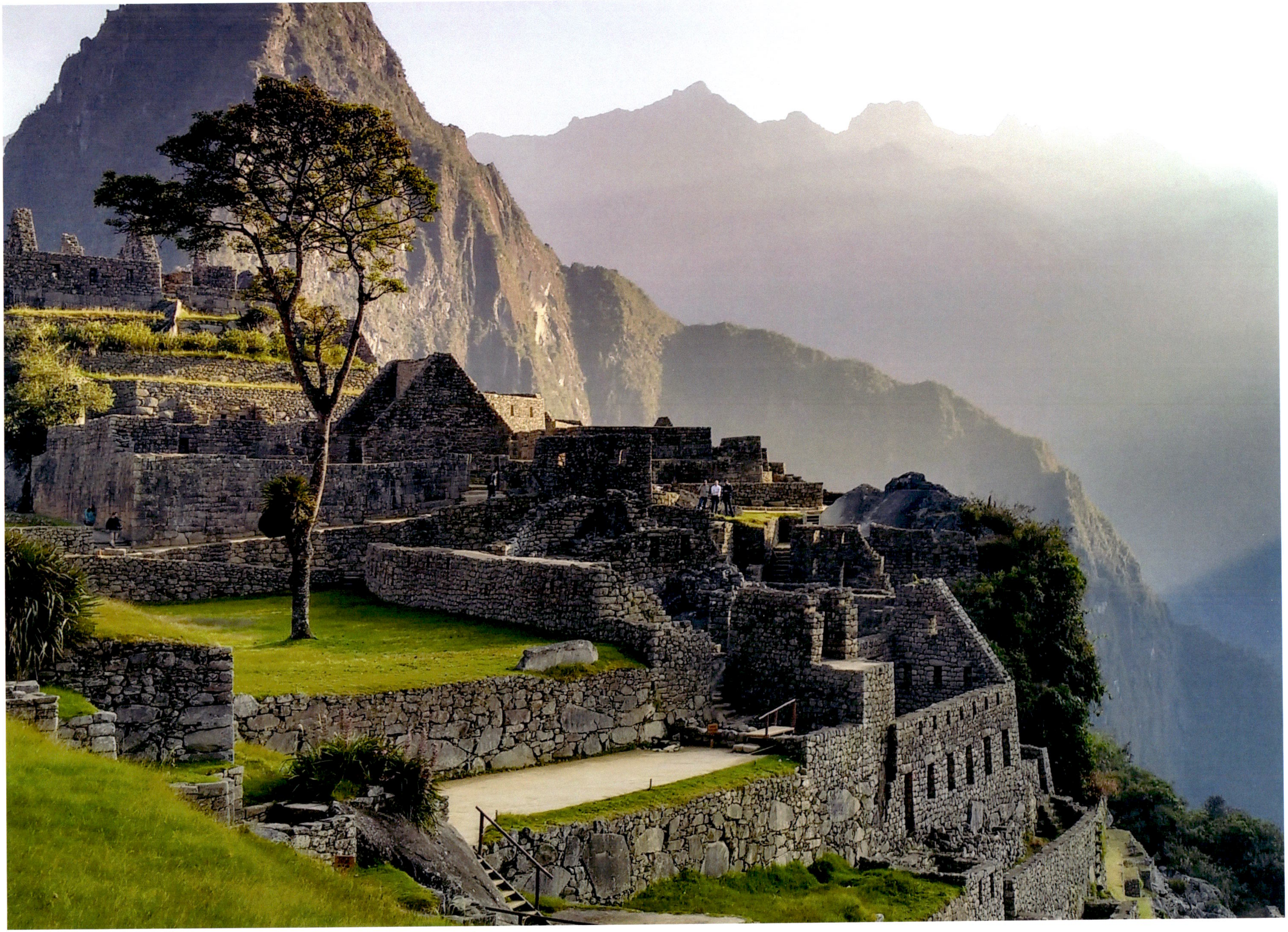

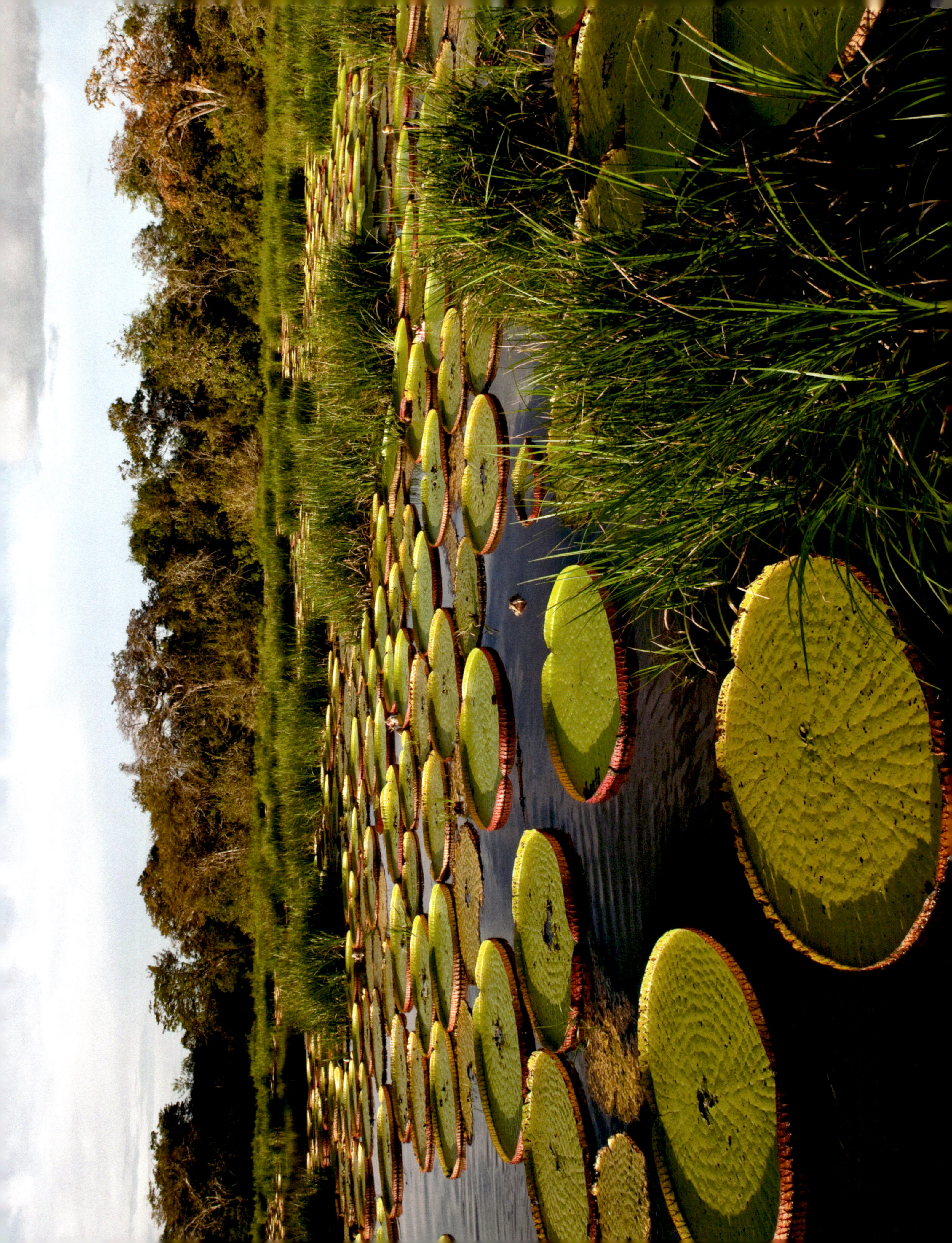

Guyana, Suriname and French Guiana

This region, often known as the Guianas, is home to two independent nations and French Guiana, the largest overseas department of France. The Guianas have a small population, of just 1.7 million, which clusters along the coast due to the rainforest to the south. Before the arrival of Europeans, this region was inhabited by Arawaks and Caribs, who had also populated the Caribbean islands. The region is still home to many speakers of Arawakan and Cariban languages. One of the most widespread is Arawakan Lokono, spoken in eastern Venezuela, Guyana, Suriname, French Guiana and Trinidad and Tobago. Yet, due to the Guianas' history of colonization, slavery and indentured labour, it is one of the most linguistically diverse regions of South America. Since Guyana was an English colony from 1814 to 1966, its official language is English, but most people speak Guyanese Creole, an English-based creole with African, Indian, Cariban and Arawakan influences, while older members of the Indo-Guyanese community speak Guyanese Hindustani. A former Dutch colony, Suriname is the only independent country outside Europe with Dutch as an official language. Its second most spoken language is Sranan Tongo, an English-based creole that developed among enslaved Africans. In French Guiana, French is the official language, but the many other languages include a French-based creole, known as Créole Guyanais, as well as several distinct Maroon creoles, which developed among communities who escaped from slavery.

OPPOSITE:
***Victoria amazonica*, Rupununi, Guyana**
Guyana's national flower, the giant water lily, has leaves, called pads, up to 3m (10ft) wide. The briefly blooming, fruity-smelling flowers are female on their first night, becoming male on their second night. The flowers close around their pollinators, *Cyclocephala* scarab beetles, to coat them in pollen – and then open to let the beetles fly to a nearby flower in its female phase.

RIGHT:
Male Guianan Cock-of-the-Rock, Guyana
While the female of this species has brown plumage, the male is vivid orange and sports a large crest. In mating season, these features are displayed during leks, when males perch on a branch, puff their feathers, dance and call to females, who watch from the forest floor.

OPPOSITE:
Kaieteur Falls, Guyana
In Kaieteur National Park, the Potaro River plummets 226m (741ft), creating one of the world's most powerful waterfalls, with an average flow rate of 663 cu m (23,400 cu ft) per second. Protecting a moist forest ecosystem, the national park is the home of many endemic species, such as Beebe's rocket frog, just 2cm (0.8in) long.

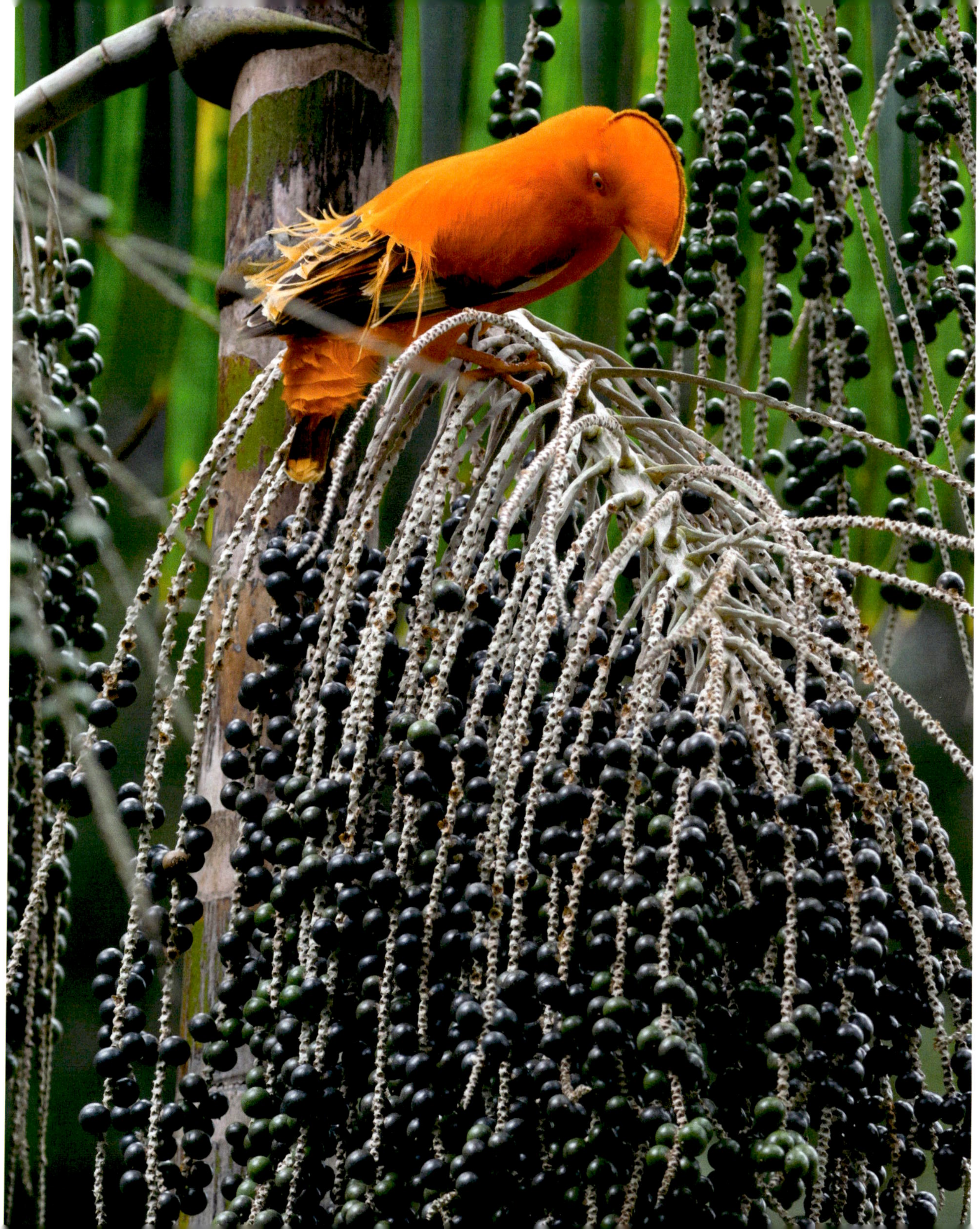

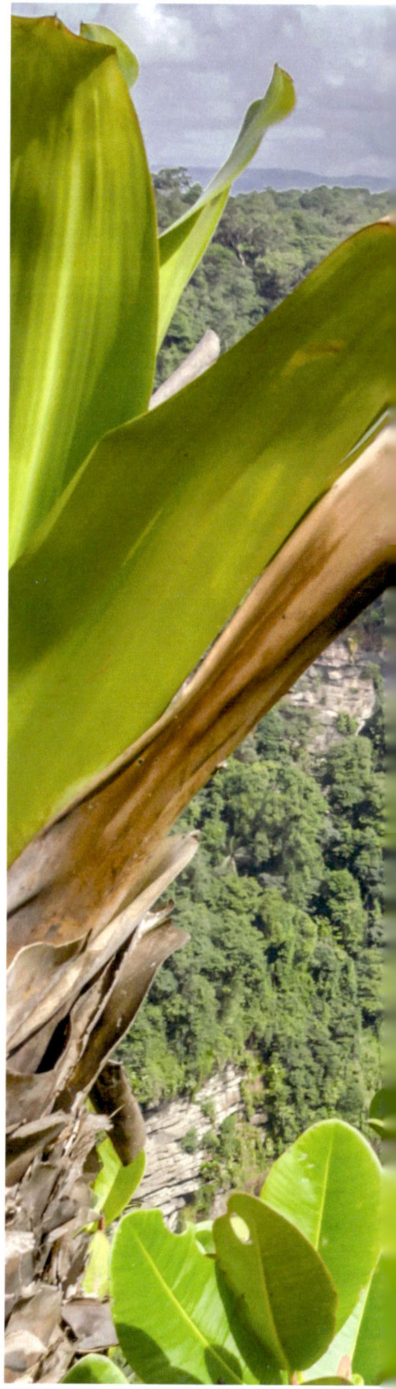

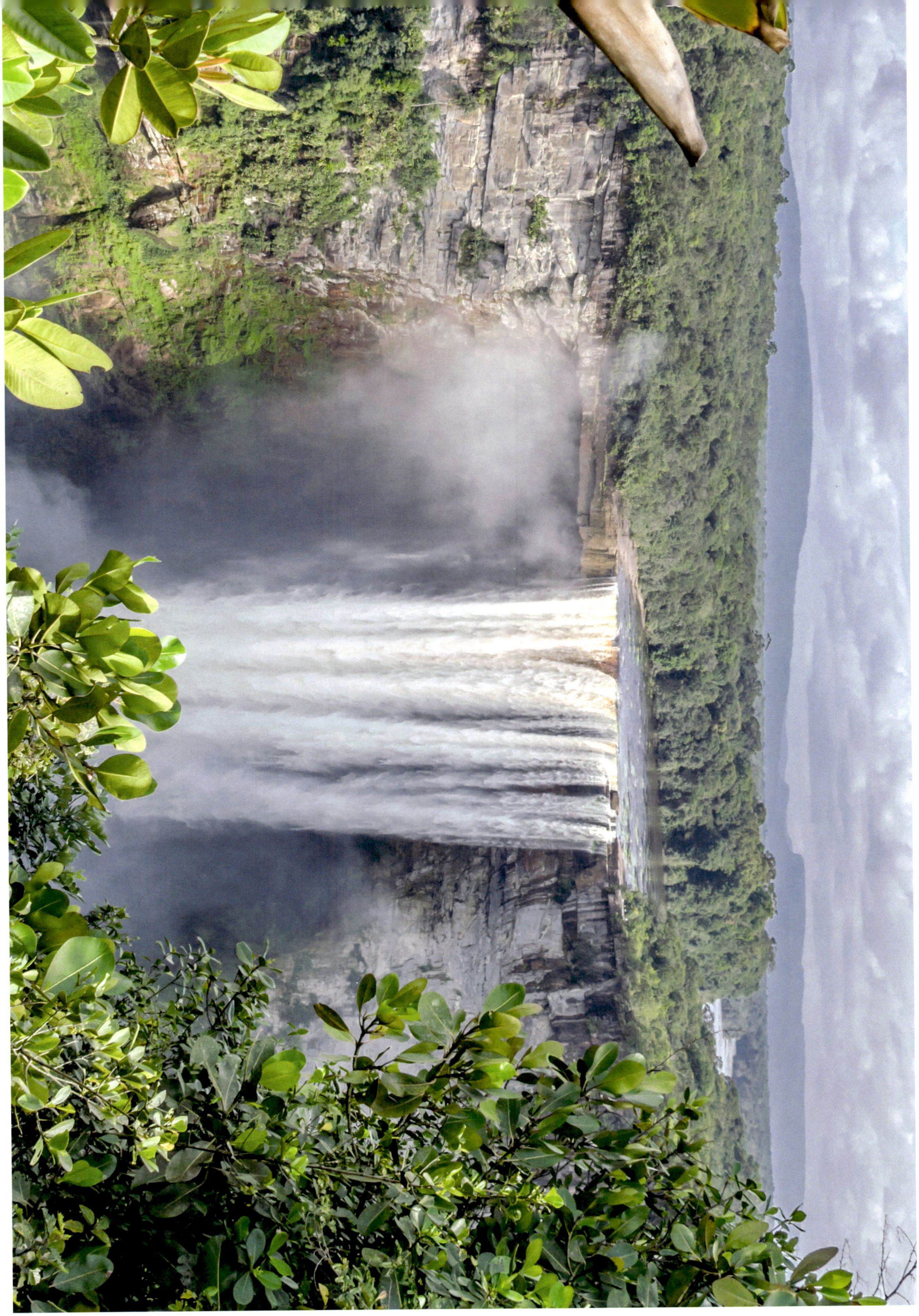

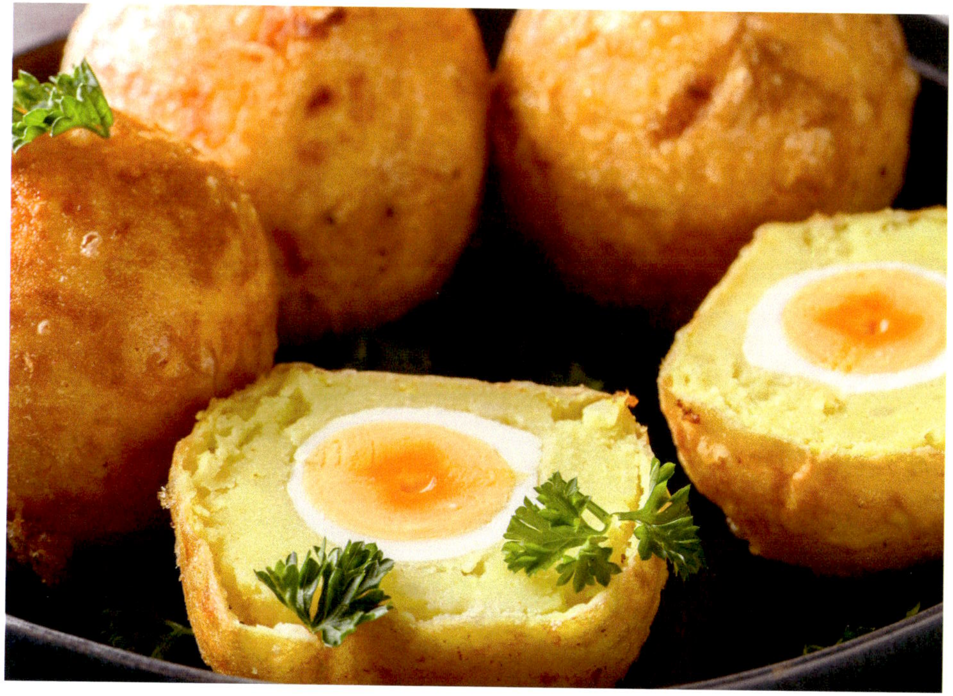

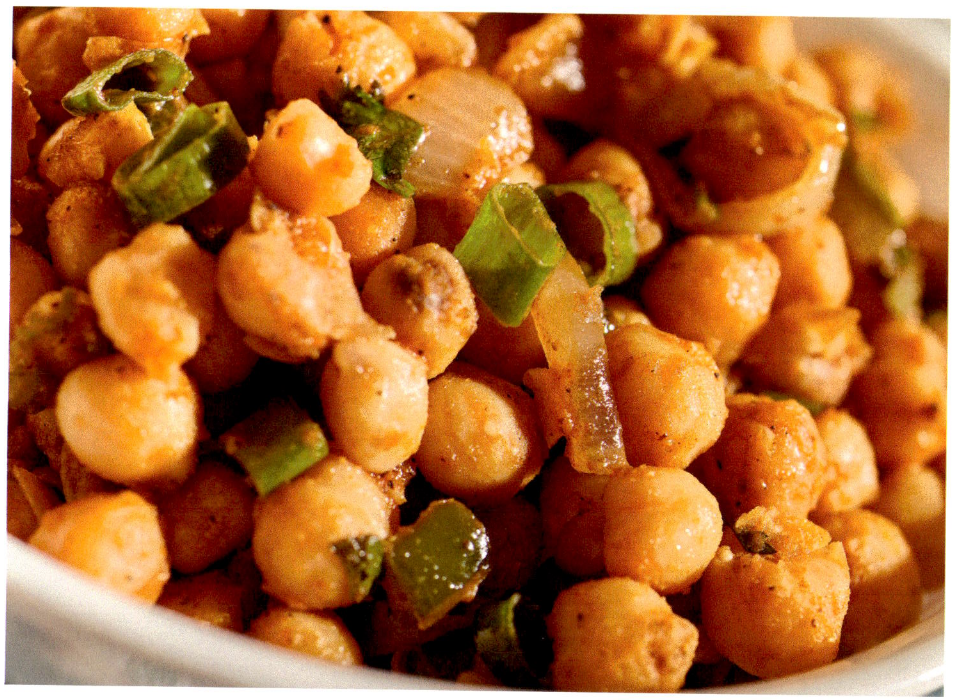

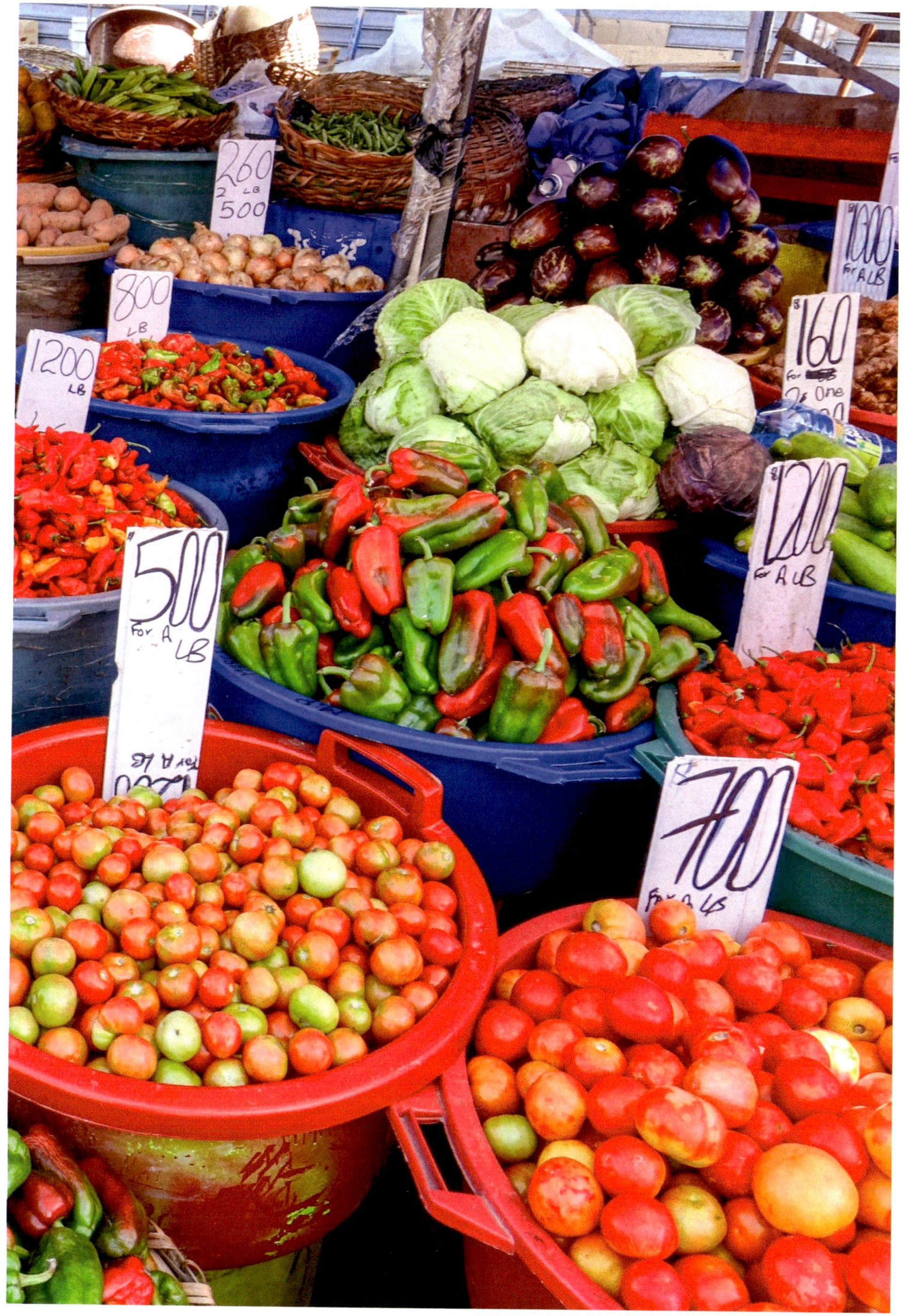
500 for A LB
1200 LB
800 LB

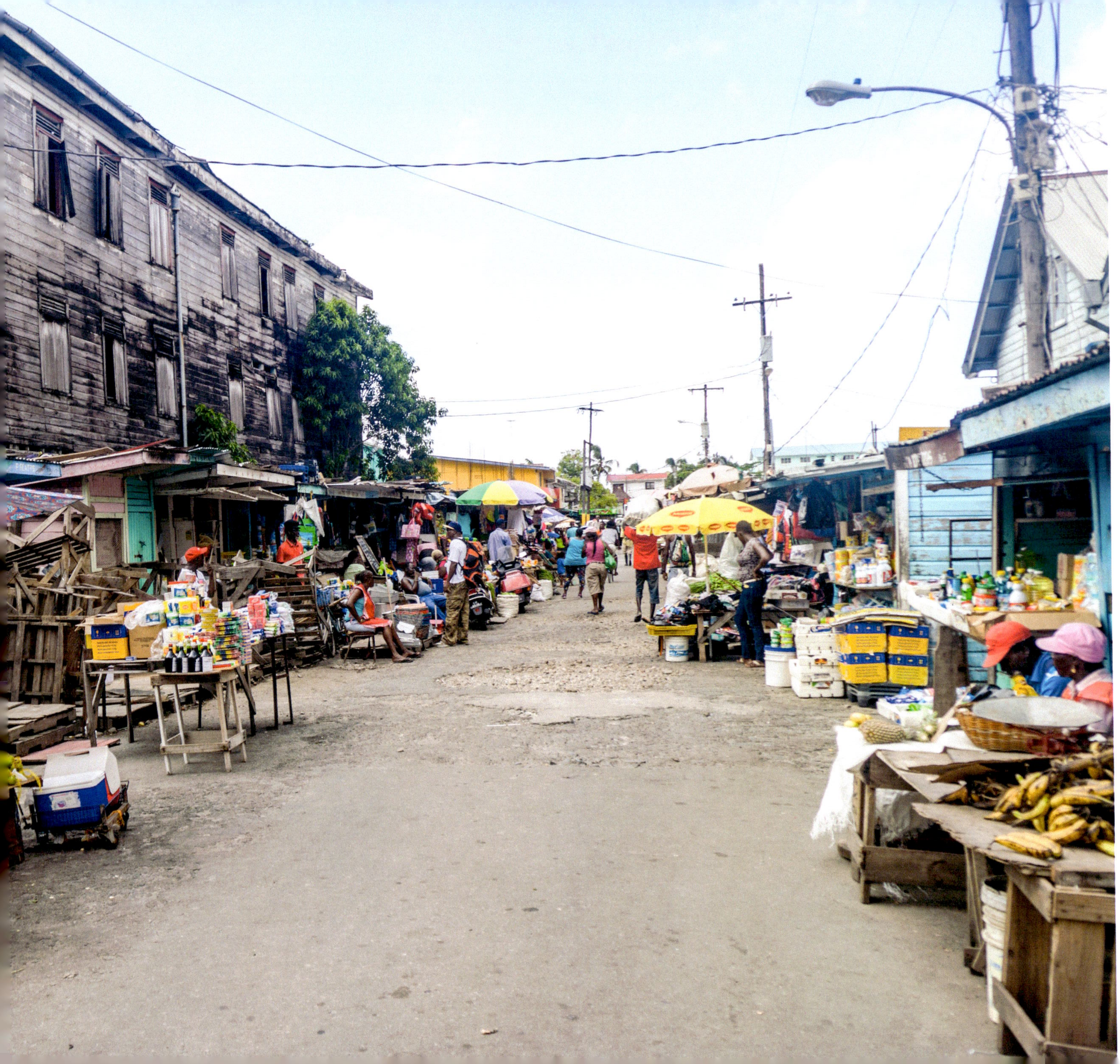

OPPOSITE LEFT TOP AND BOTTOM:
Street Food, Georgetown, Guyana
A popular snack in Guyana's capital and largest city is cassava balls, made from seasoned cassava wrapped around a hard-boiled egg, coated in batter and fried until crispy. No less tasty and filling is *channa*: boiled chickpeas, fried with onions, garlic, peppers and cumin.

LEFT AND OPPOSITE RIGHT:
Bourda Market, Georgetown, Guyana
One of the capital's largest markets, Bourda has stalls selling handicrafts, fruit and vegetables, fish and meat, and staples such as the ubiquitous cassareep sauce, a sweet and spicy syrup made from cassava juice. The market was named after the eighteenth-century Dutch sugar plantation-owner and slaver Joseph Bourda, who was governor of the Dutch colony of Demerara, which was centred on Georgetown.

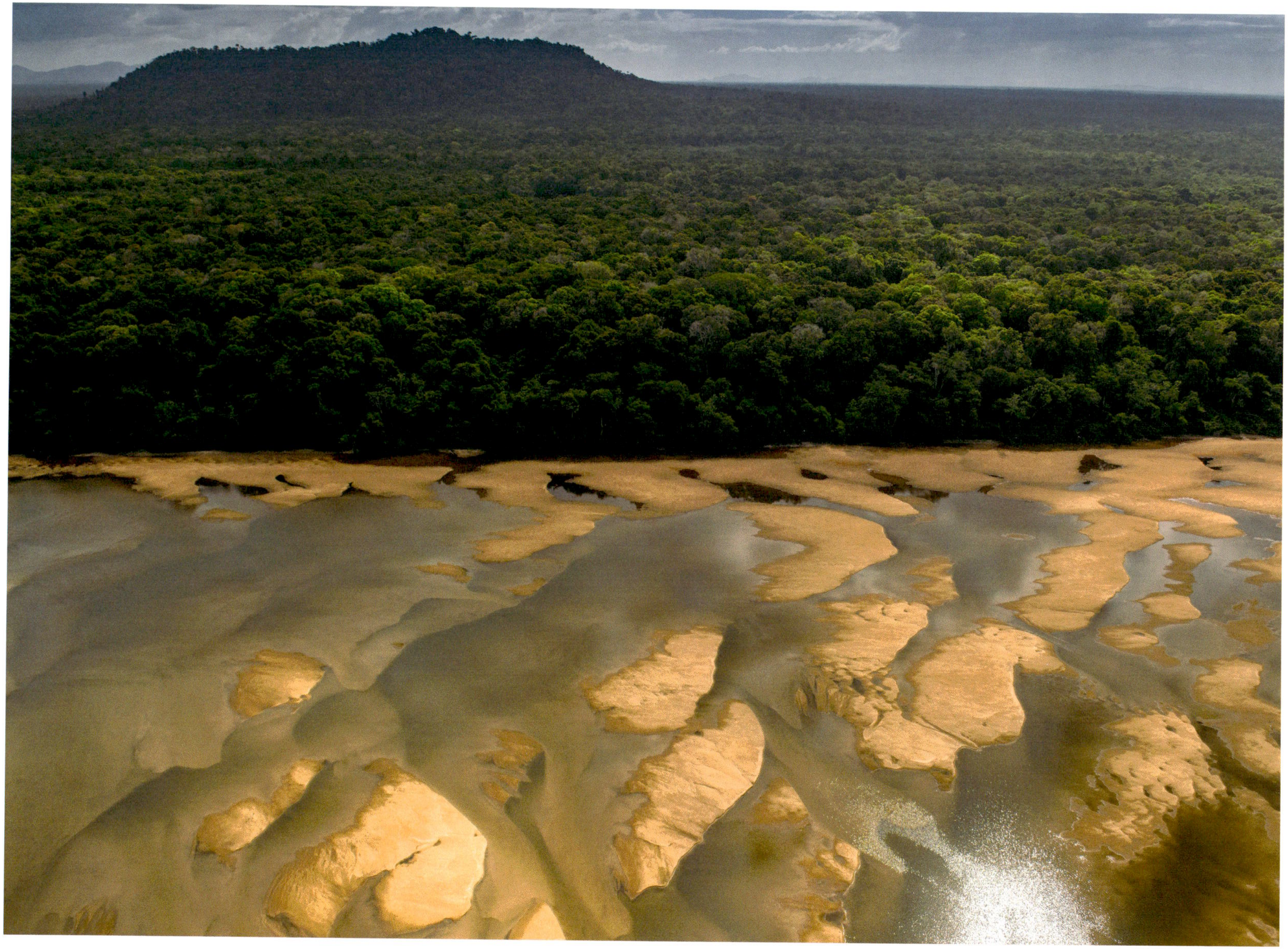

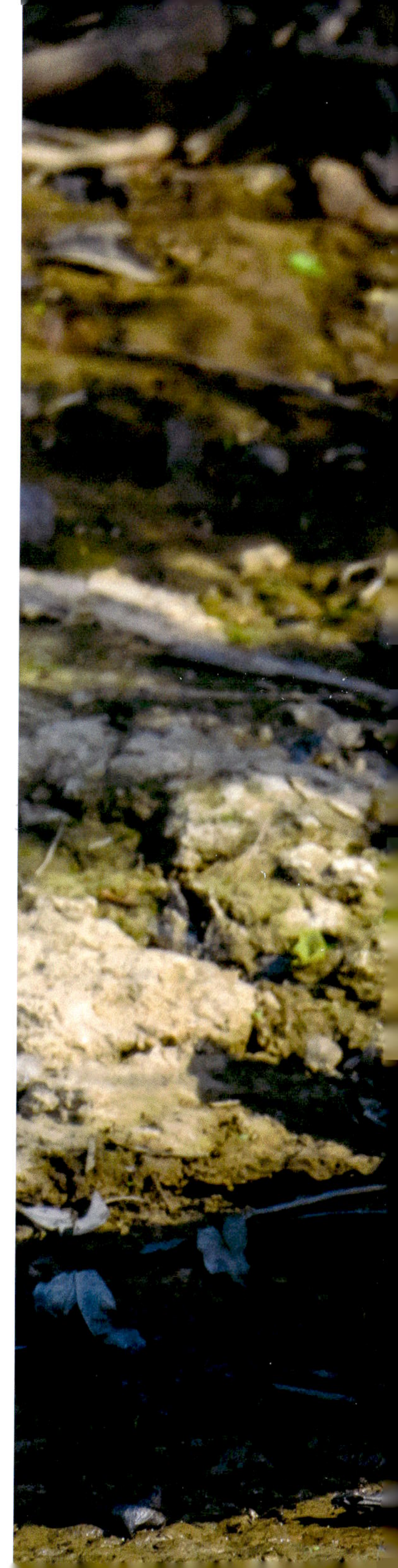

ABOVE:

Essequibo River, Iwokrama Forest, Guyana

The Essequibo River forms the eastern boundary of the Iwokrama reserve, a region of lowland tropical forest and wetland. The forest's super-sized species include jaguars, giant anteaters, giant river otters, giant river turtles, anacondas and arapaima, which are among the largest freshwater fish at 3m (9.8ft) long.

RIGHT:

Black Caiman, Rupununi, Guyana

Growing up to 6.5m (21.3ft) long, the black caiman is the apex predator of southern Guyana's rivers and lakes. It preys on large fish, such as piranha, as well as waterbirds, turtles, smaller caimans and land mammals as big as capybara, agouti and domestic pigs.

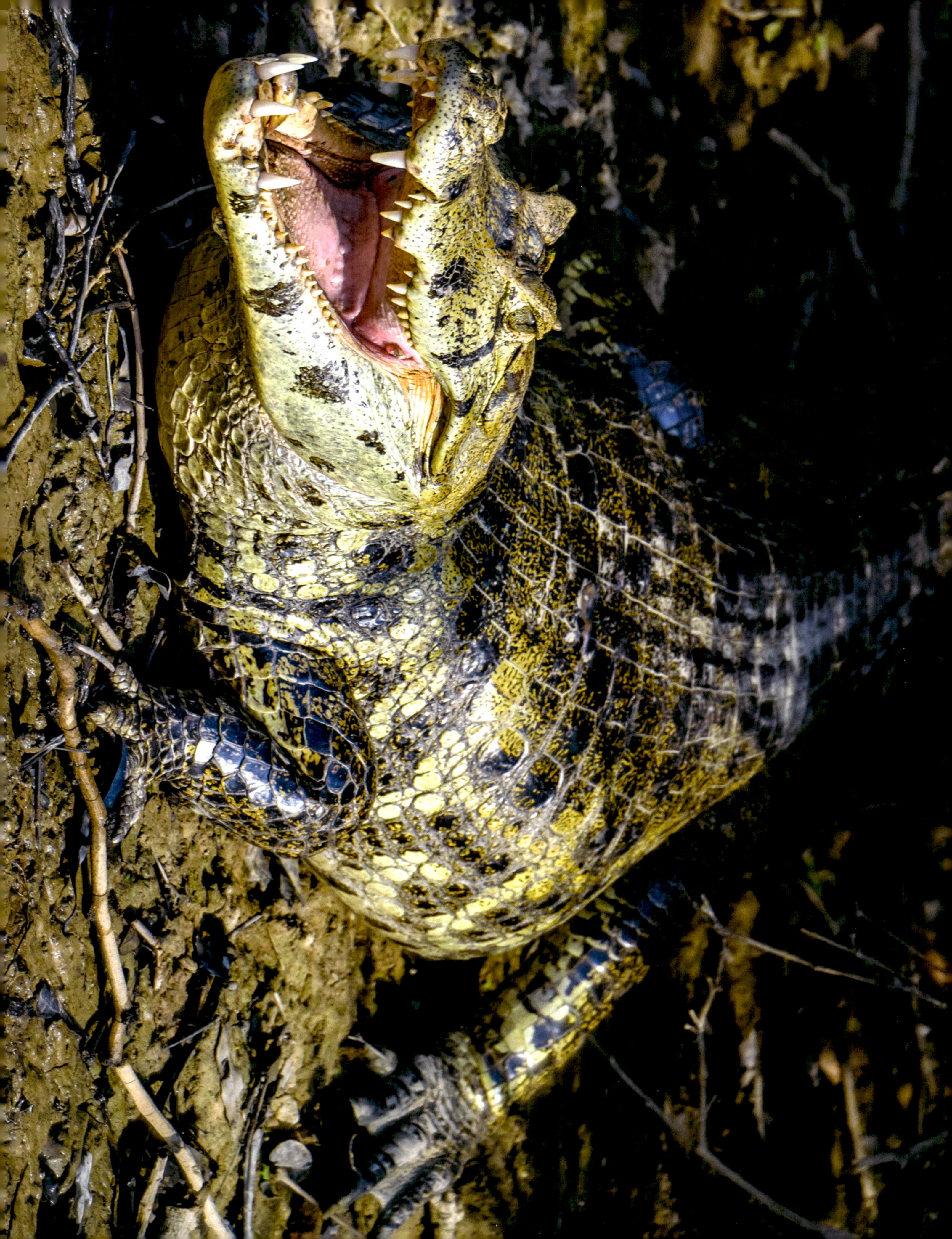

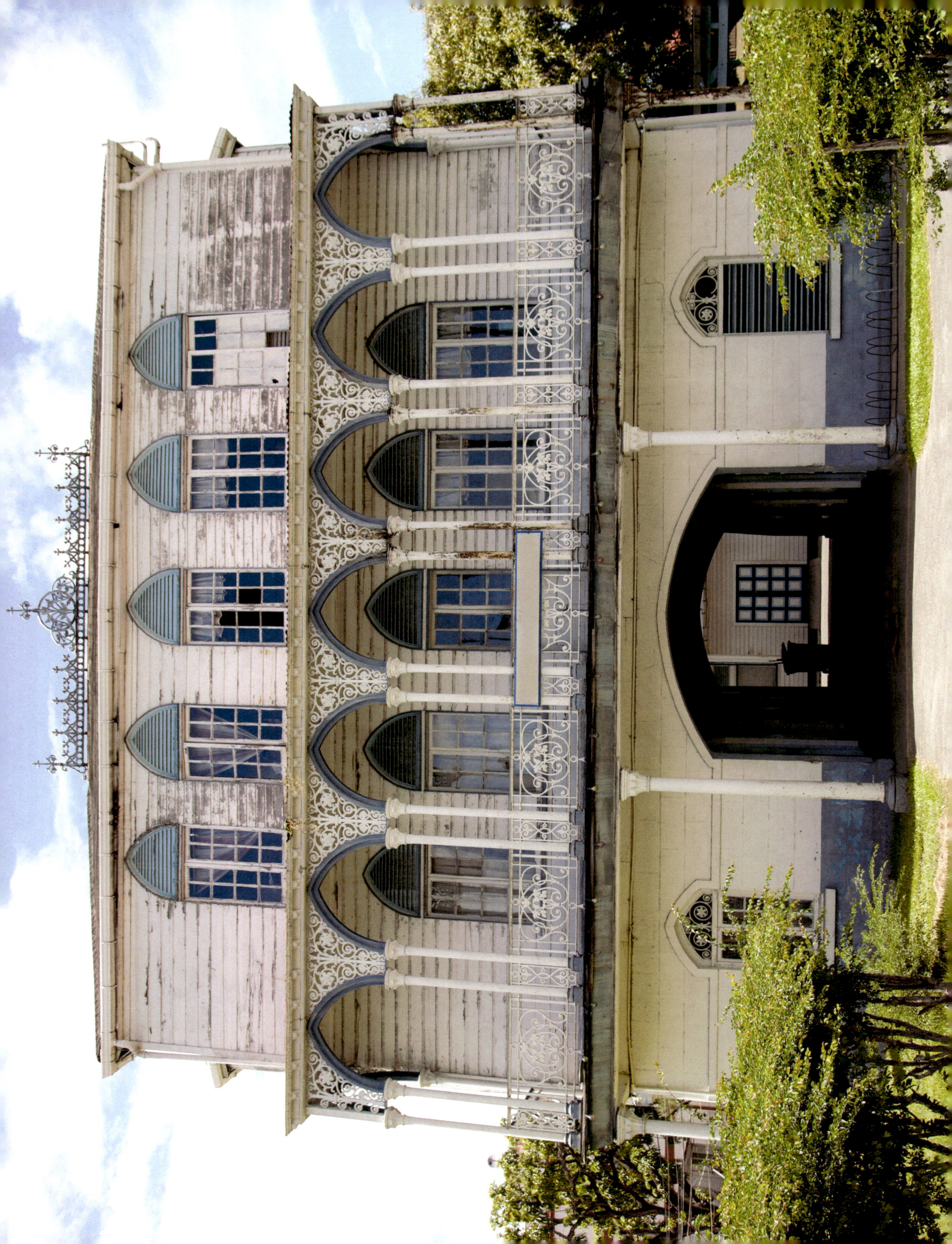

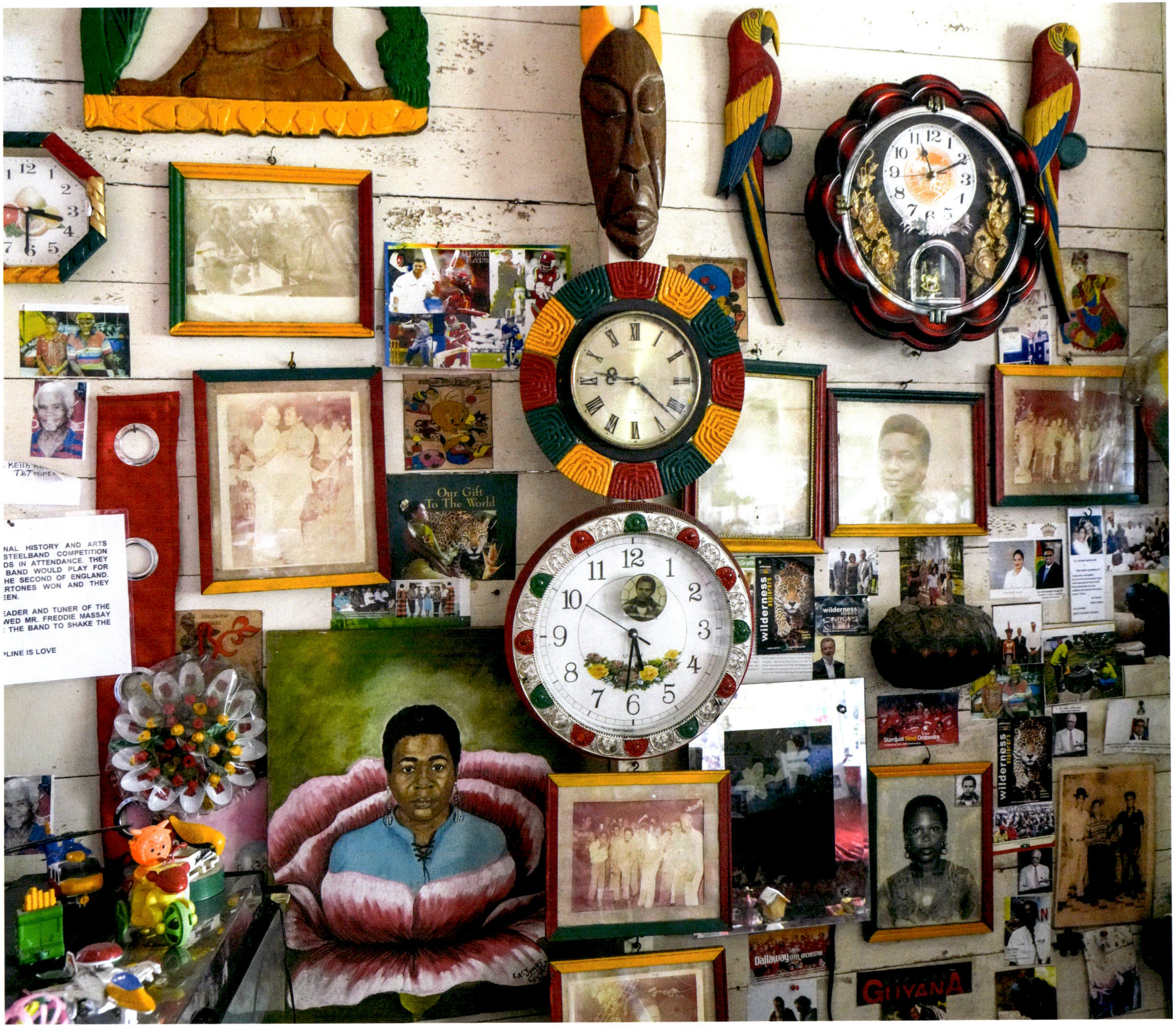

OPPOSITE:
City Hall, Georgetown, Guyana
Completed in 1889, this Gothic Revival building is constructed of wood and sinuous wrought iron. It was designed by English architect and Jesuit priest Ignatius Scoles, who was offered $50 for his building plan, but turned down the payment.

LEFT:
Roy Geddes Steel Pan Museum, Georgetown
This unique museum is in the home of Roy Geddes, who toured the world with his band, the Silvertones. Among the personal mementos, visitors can discover the history of Guyanese steel pan and how the drums are made.

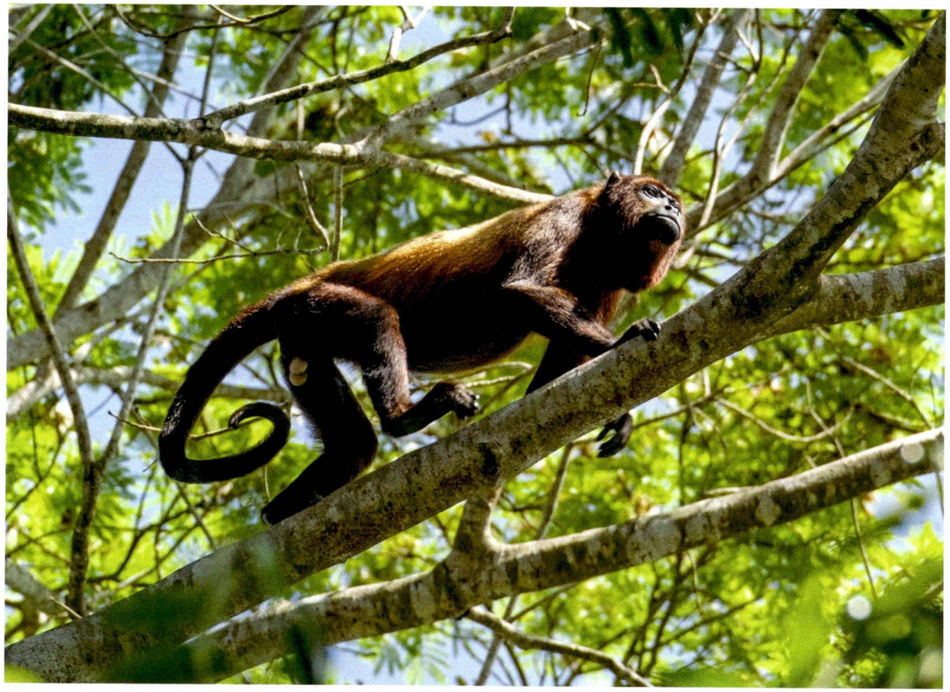

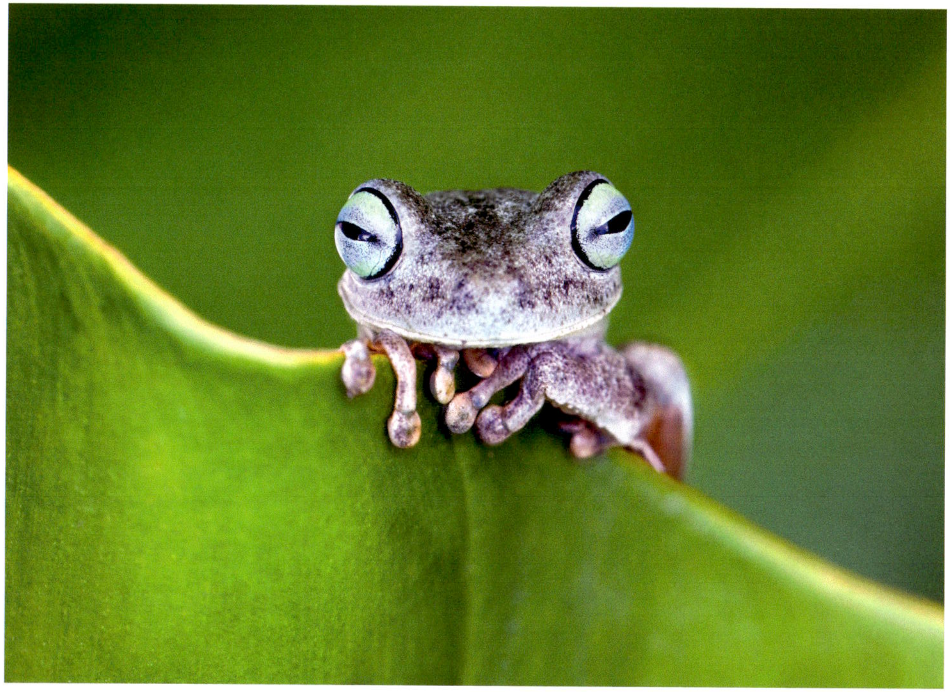

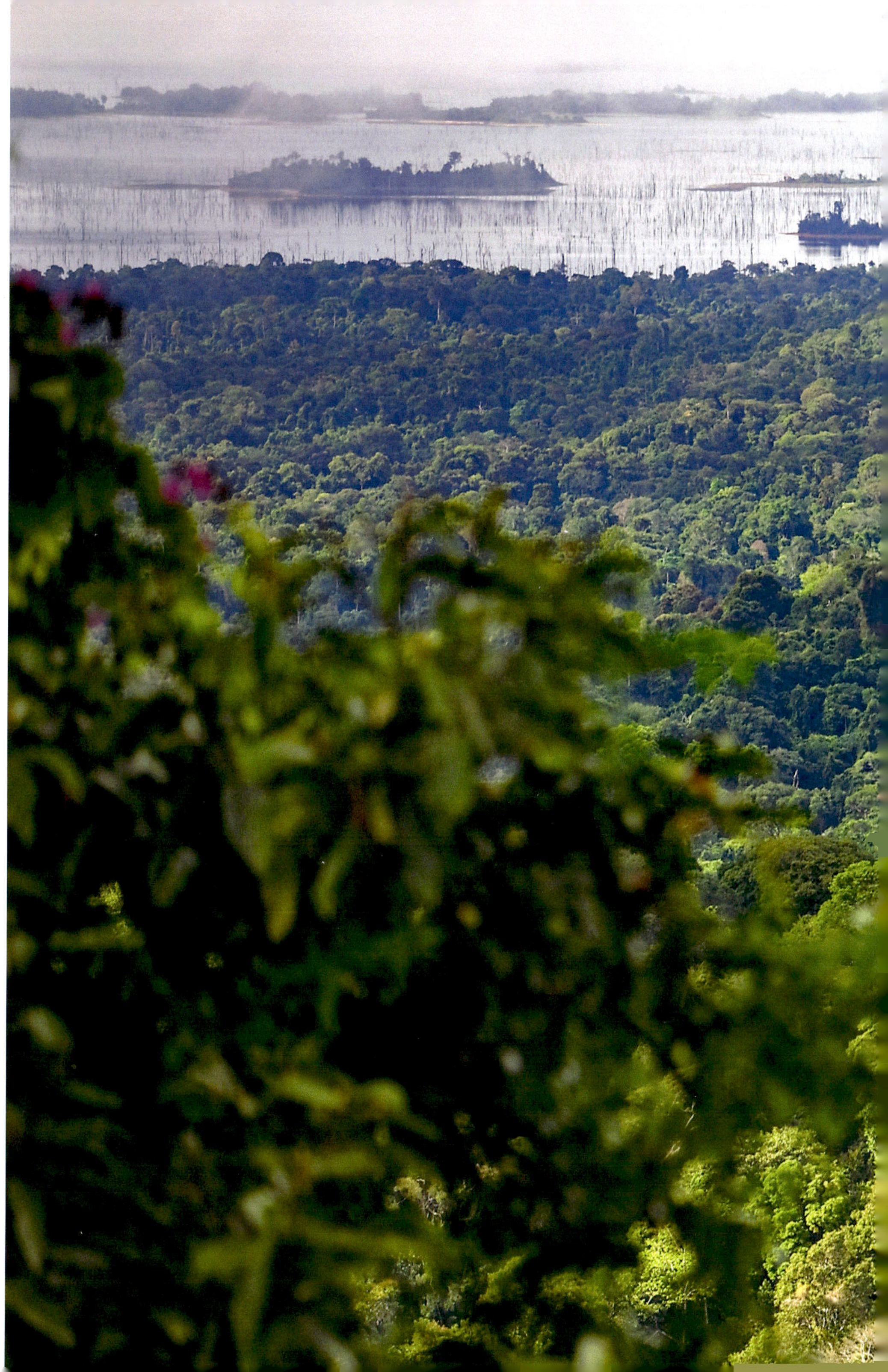

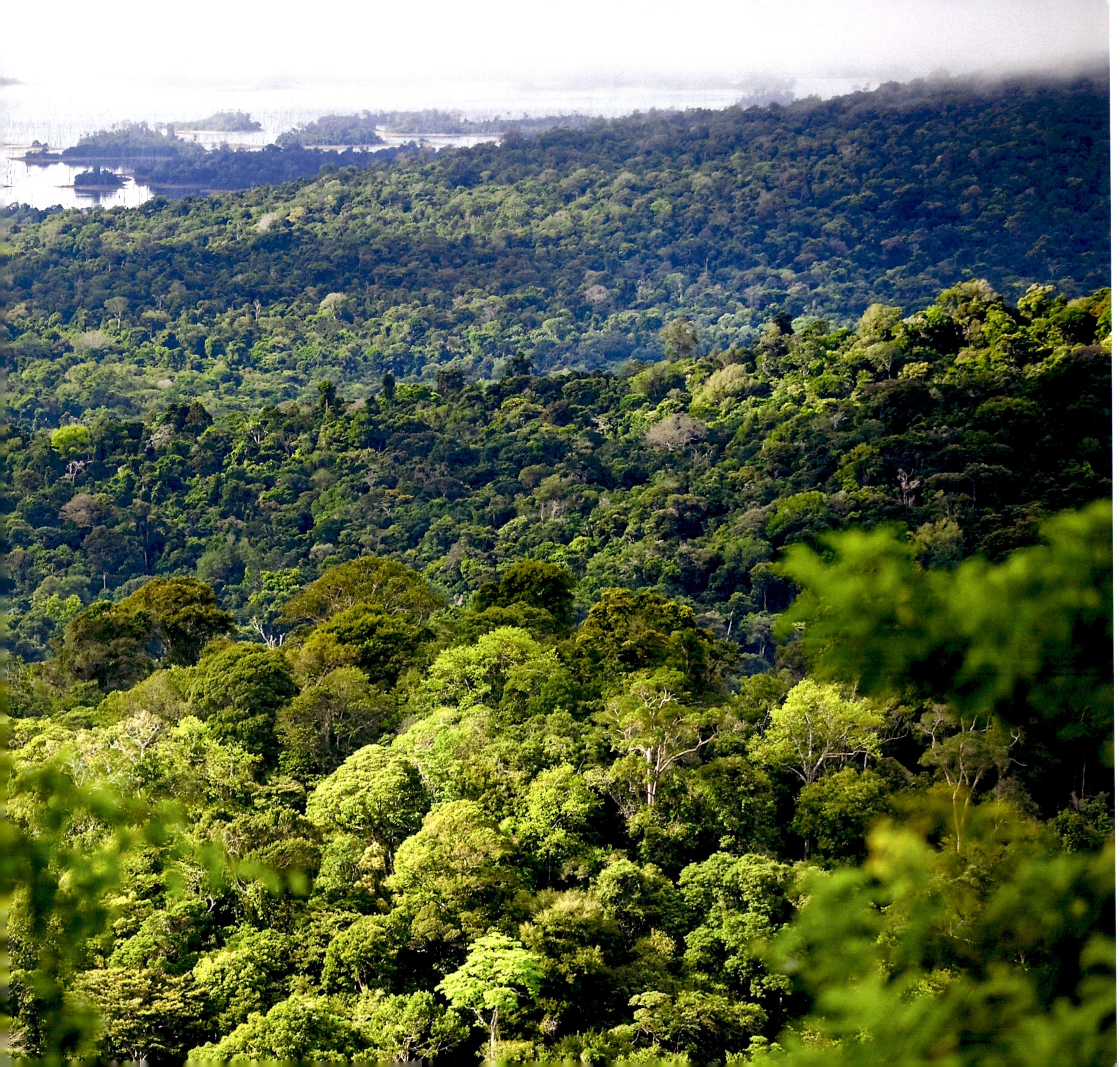

OPPOSITE TOP:

Guyanan Red Howler Monkey, Brownsberg Nature Park, Suriname

This monkey spends most of its time in the canopy of rainforest and swamp forest, where it eats leaves and fruit. Howling sessions, usually involving whole family groups, can be heard up to 2km (1.2 miles) away.

OPPOSITE BOTTOM:

Orange-legged Leaf Frog, Brownsberg Nature Park

Around 5cm (2in) long, this nocturnal frog lives in vegetation in damp forests and seasonally flooded grasslands. The female lays her eggs on a leaf overhanging a puddle or pond. After hatching, the tadpoles drop into the water.

LEFT:

Brownsberg Nature Park

Covering 120 sq km (45 sq miles), this rainforest nature park is home to 1450 species of plants, including countless Brazil nut and cacao trees. At the park's centre is Brownsberg Mountain, named after nineteenth-century gold prospector John Brown.

RIGHT:
Irene Falls, Brownsberg Nature Park, Suriname
This waterfall is a popular day trip from Paramaribo. Its refreshing plunge pool is reached by a short trek through the rainforest, accompanied by the calls of howler monkeys, after a three-hour drive from the city. The last, rough and twisting, stretch of road is best attacked by four-wheel drive.

FAR RIGHT:
Centrum, Paramaribo, Suriname
The capital's old centre, around Waterkant, is a UNESCO World Heritage Site due to its many nineteenth-century buildings. A fusion of Dutch style and local techniques, the buildings were constructed from wood due to the shortage of stone and clay in the area.

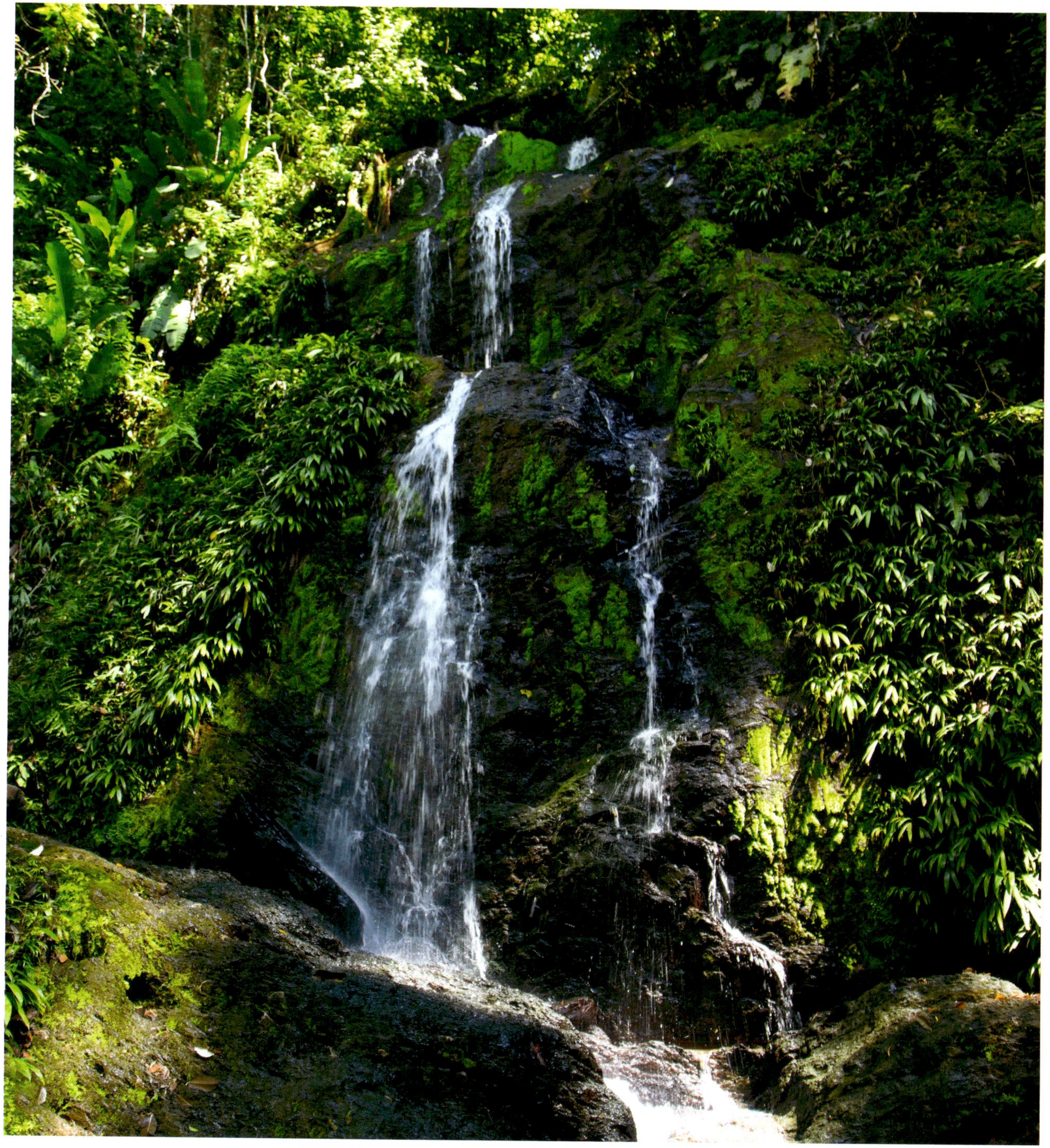

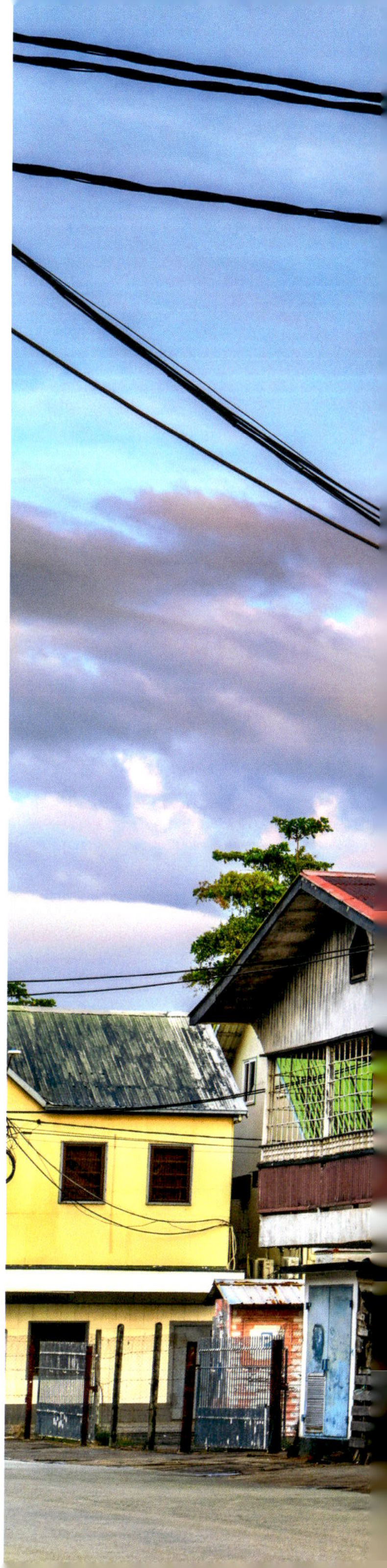

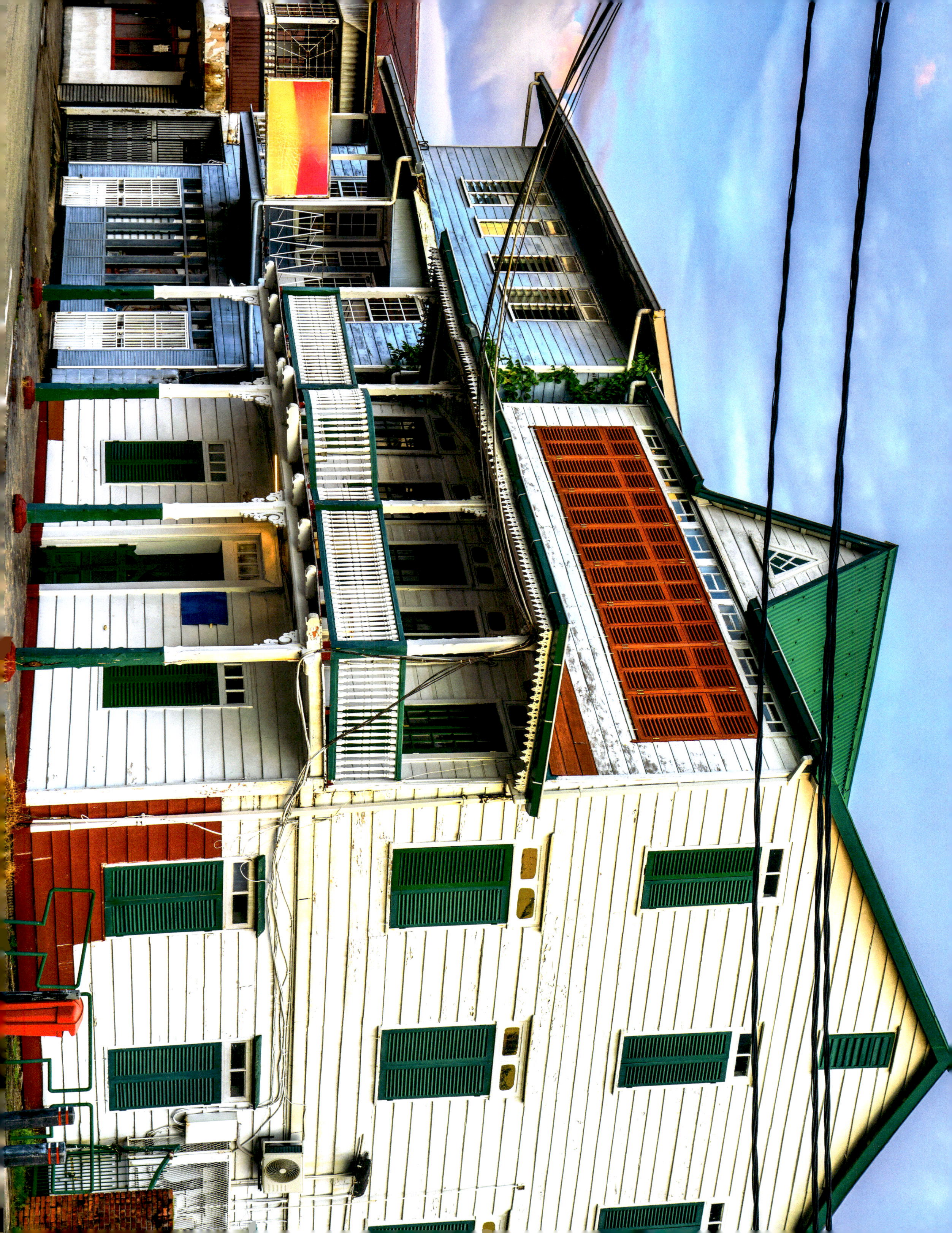

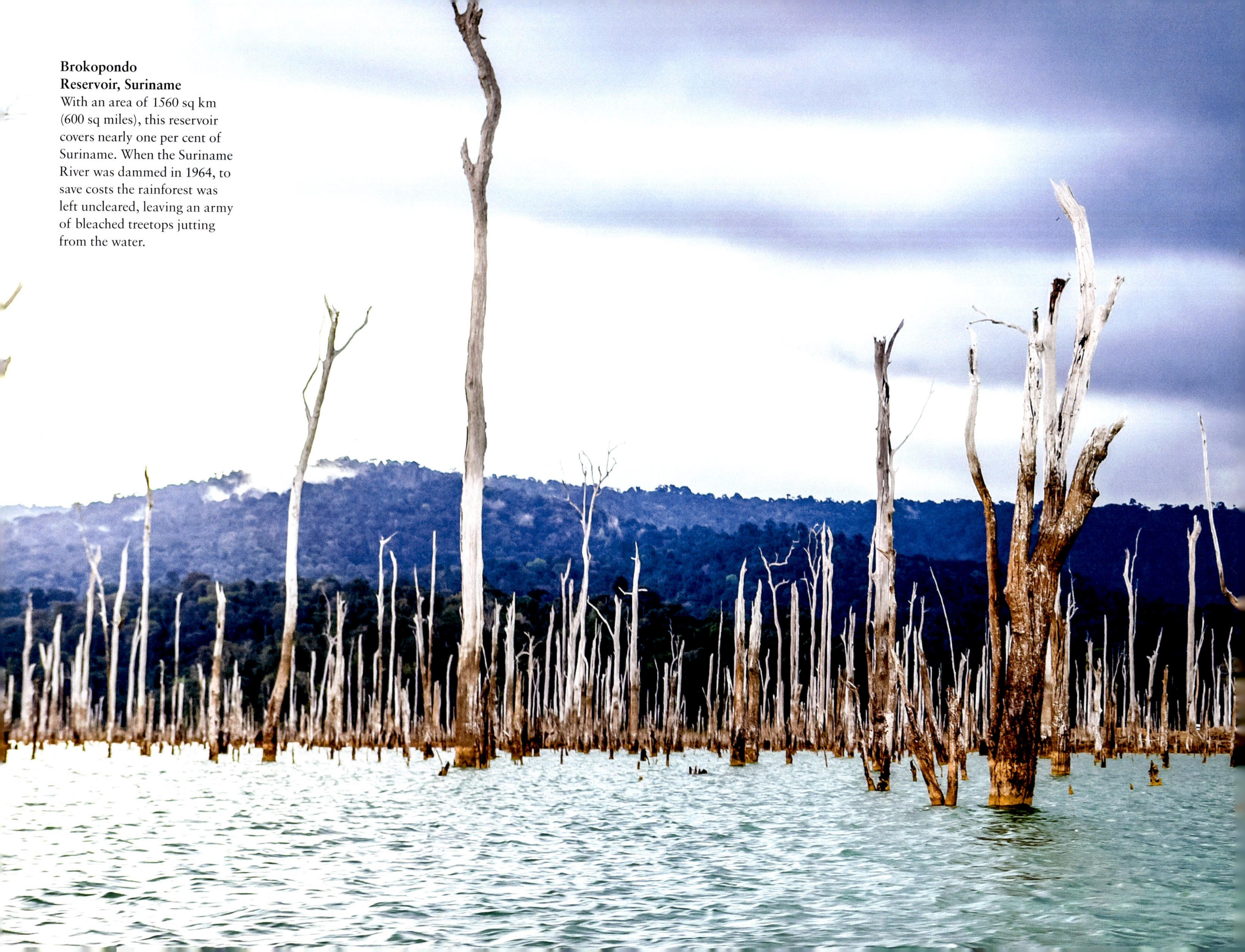

Brokopondo Reservoir, Suriname
With an area of 1560 sq km (600 sq miles), this reservoir covers nearly one per cent of Suriname. When the Suriname River was dammed in 1964, to save costs the rainforest was left uncleared, leaving an army of bleached treetops jutting from the water.

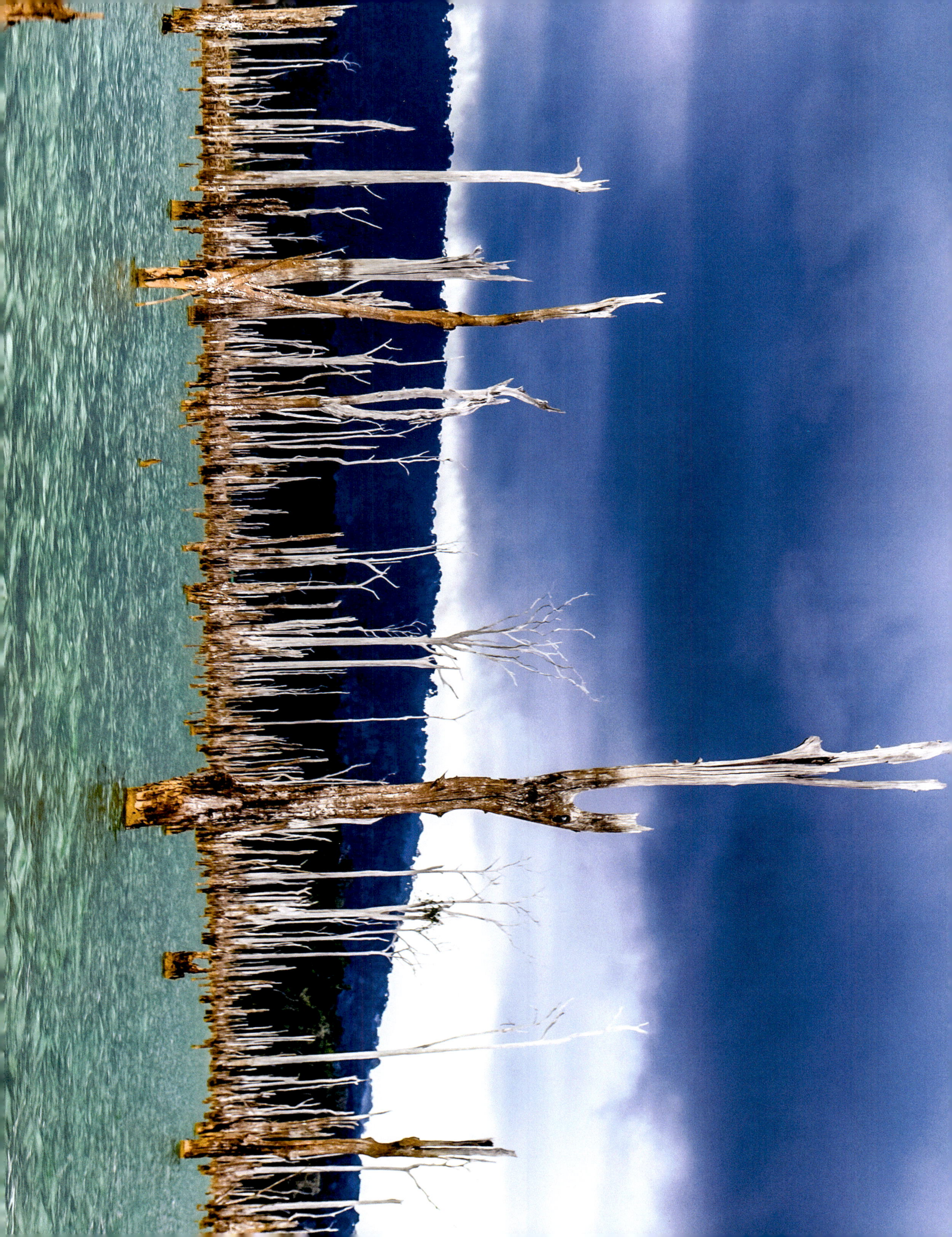

BOTH PHOTOGRAPHS:

St Peter and Paul Basilica, Paramaribo, Suriname

One of the largest wooden structures in the western hemisphere, this cathedral was built between 1883 and 1901, when its early congregation included many contract labourers and freedmen and -women. The interior glows with honeyed light due to its curved surfaces of unpainted cedar.

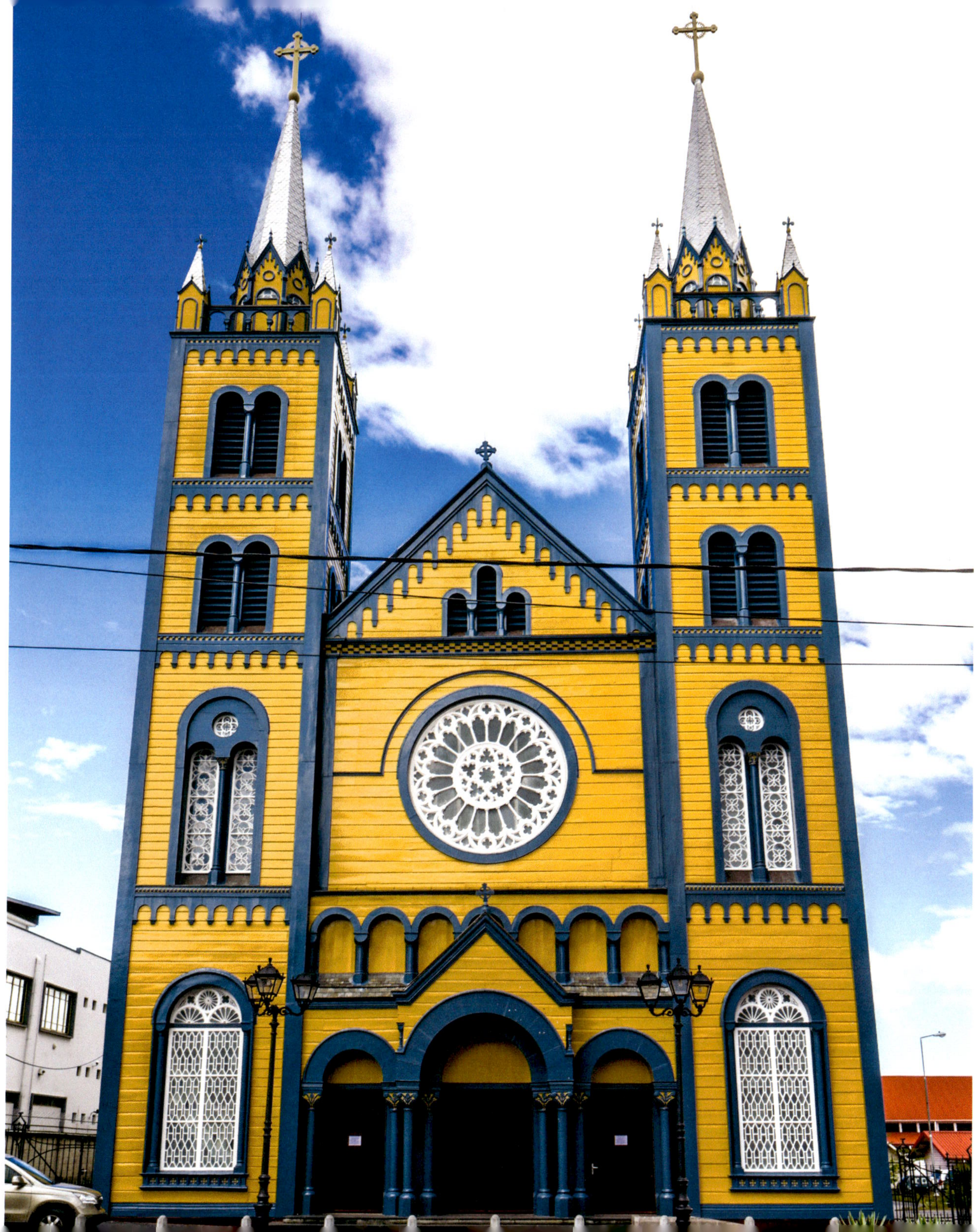

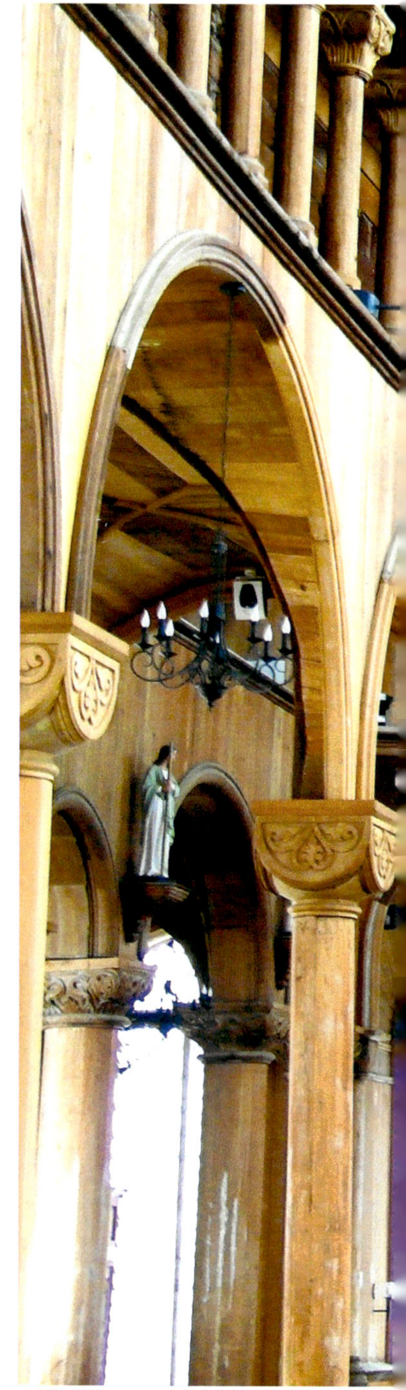

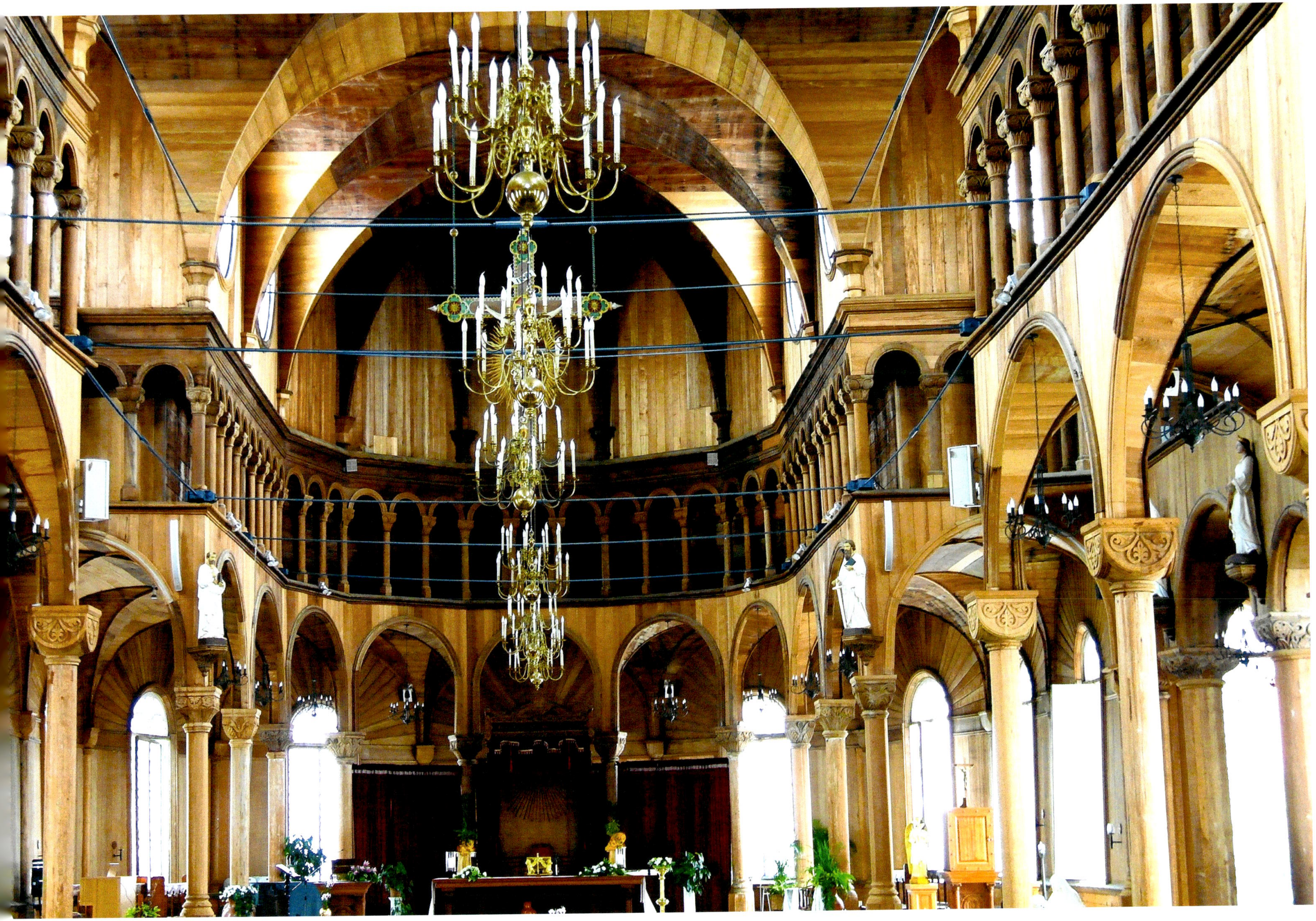

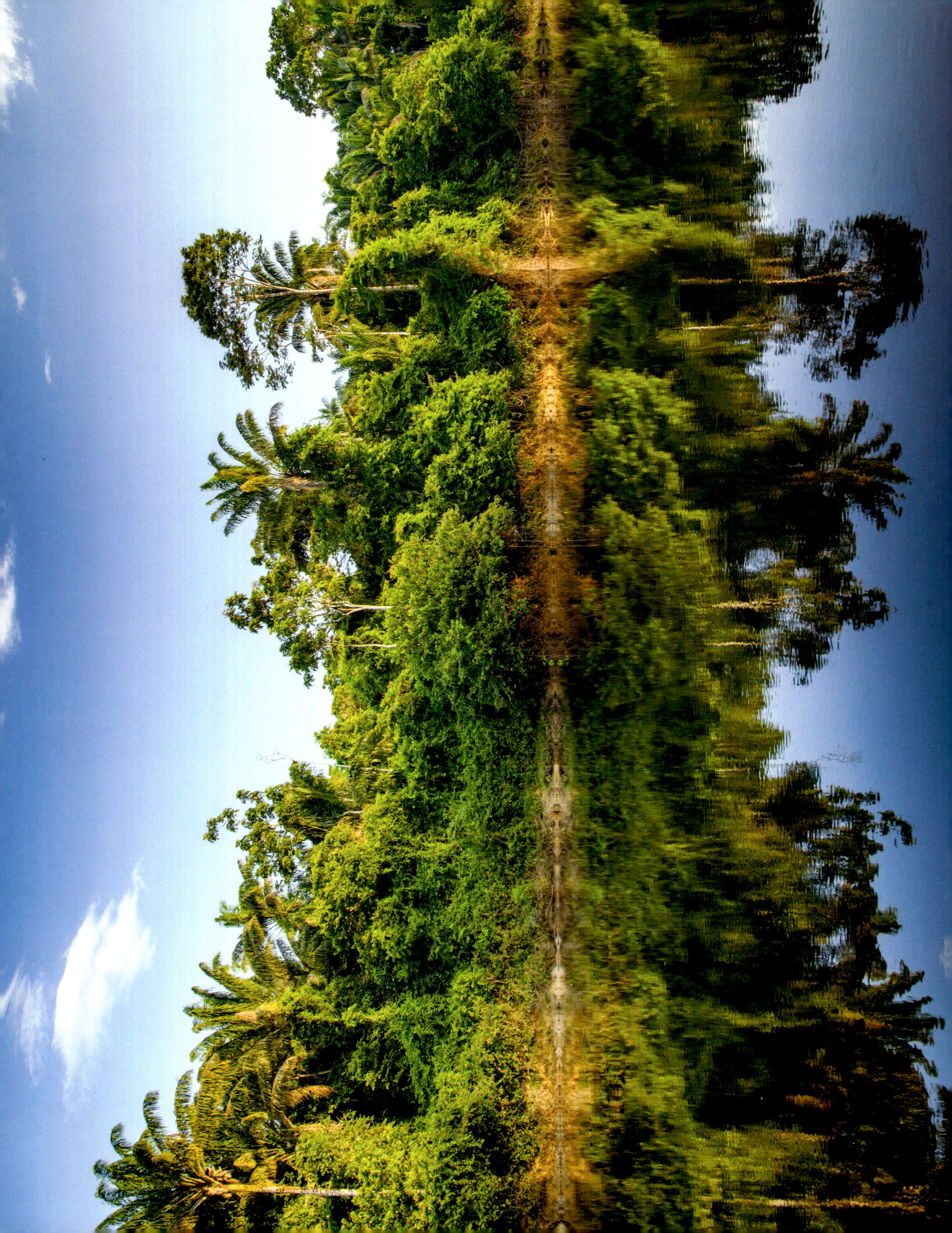

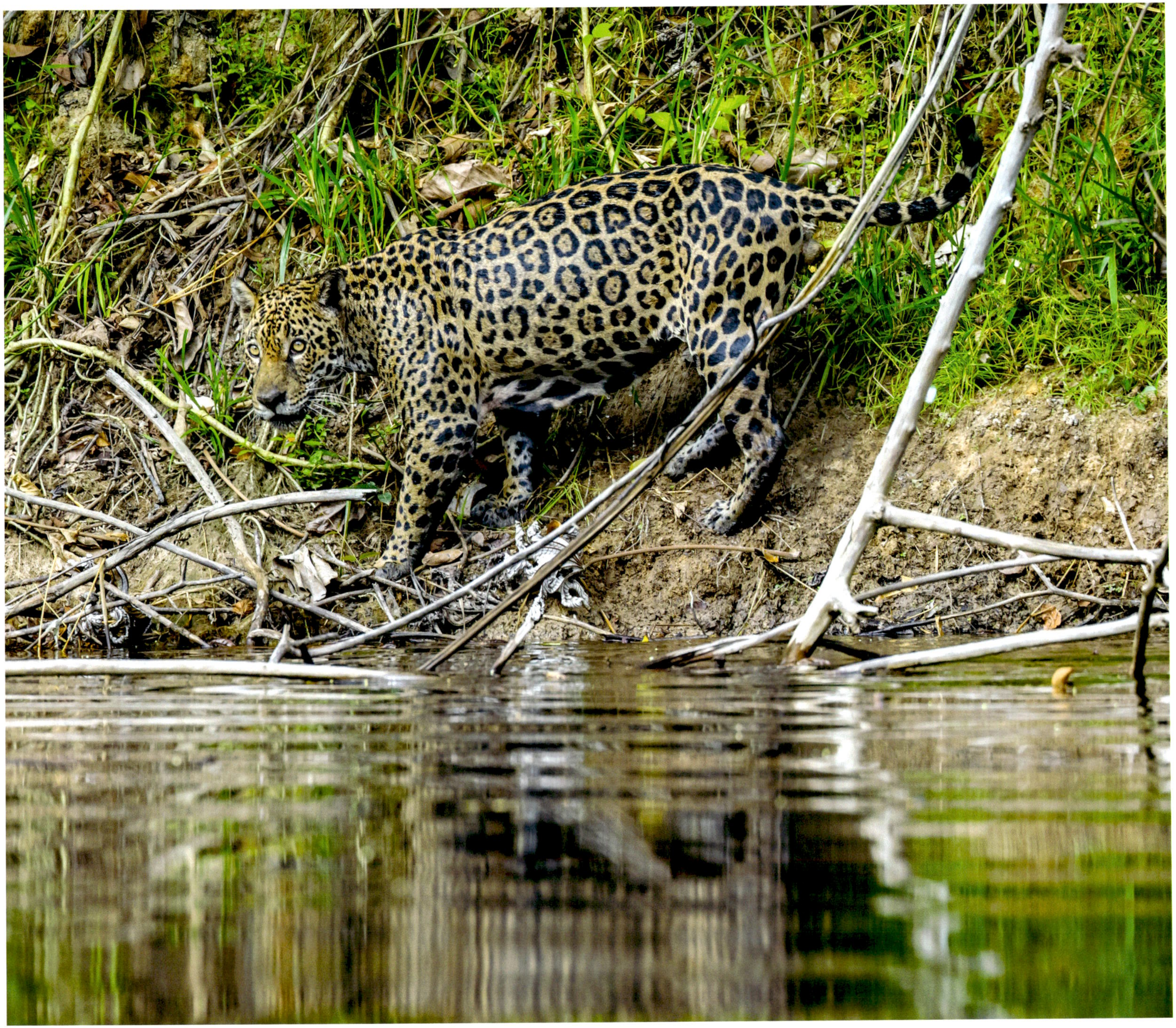

BOTH PHOTOGRAPHS:
Central Suriname Nature Reserve, Suriname
This reserve is a swathe of lowland and montane rainforest, dotted with barren granite domes. The park's terrestrial apex predator is the jaguar, which reaches 1.85m (6ft) long, excluding its muscular tail. On land, the jaguar's preferred prey is capybara and giant anteaters, but this excellent swimmer also dives in pursuit of green anacondas and caimans.

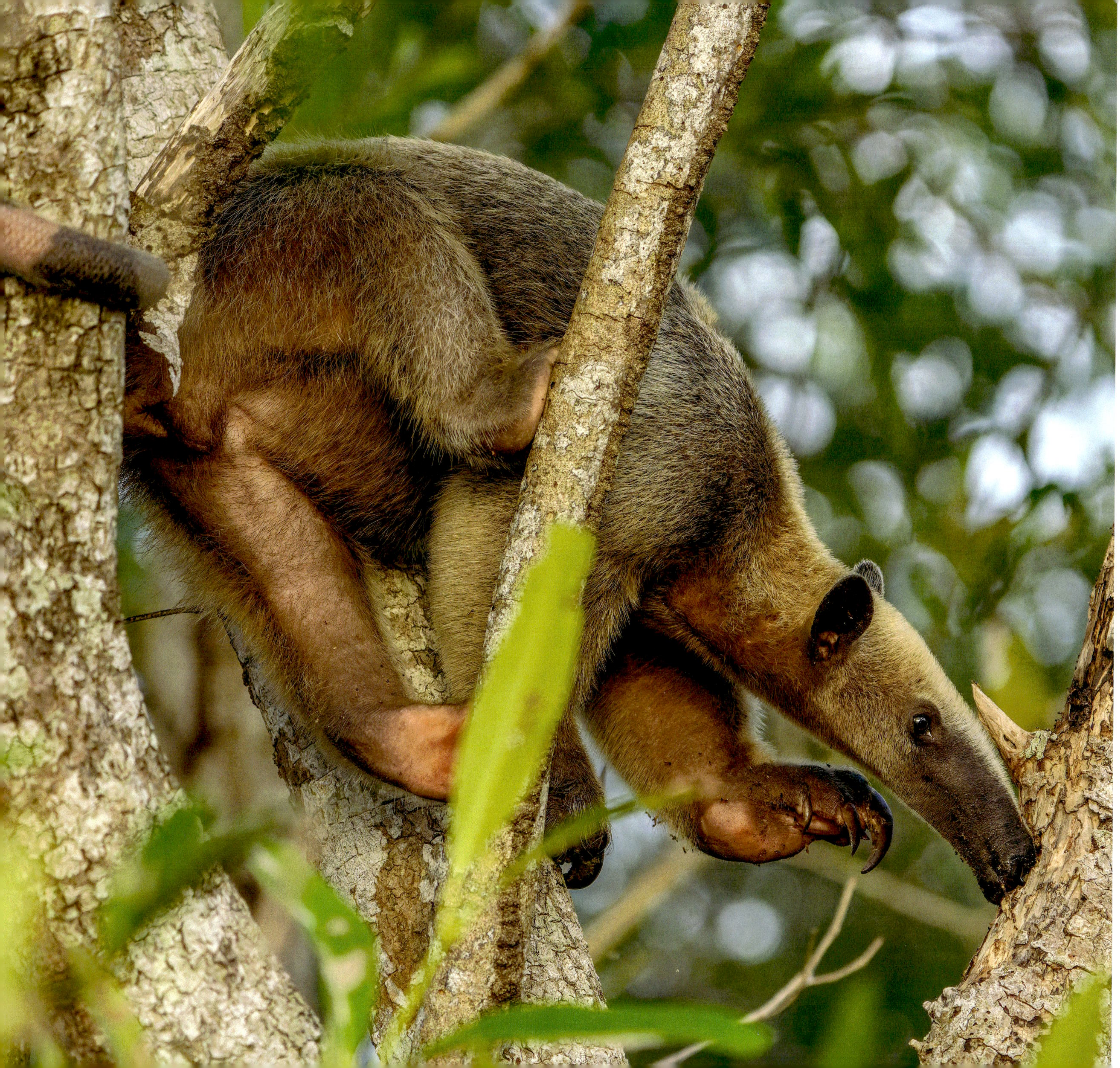

LEFT:
Southern Tamandua, Bigi Pan, Suriname
This semi-arboreal anteater uses its prehensile tail and sharp claws to climb trees, where it hunts for ant and termite nests as well as fruit. It breaks open nests with its claws, then pokes in its long snout, lapping up prey with its sticky tongue, which reaches 40cm (16in) long.

RIGHT:
Green Sea Turtle, Matapica, Suriname
Between February and August, green, leatherback, olive ridley and hawksbill turtles crawl ashore to nest here. The near-deserted beach can be reached only by boat, through a labyrinthine mangrove swamp where spectacled caimans abound.

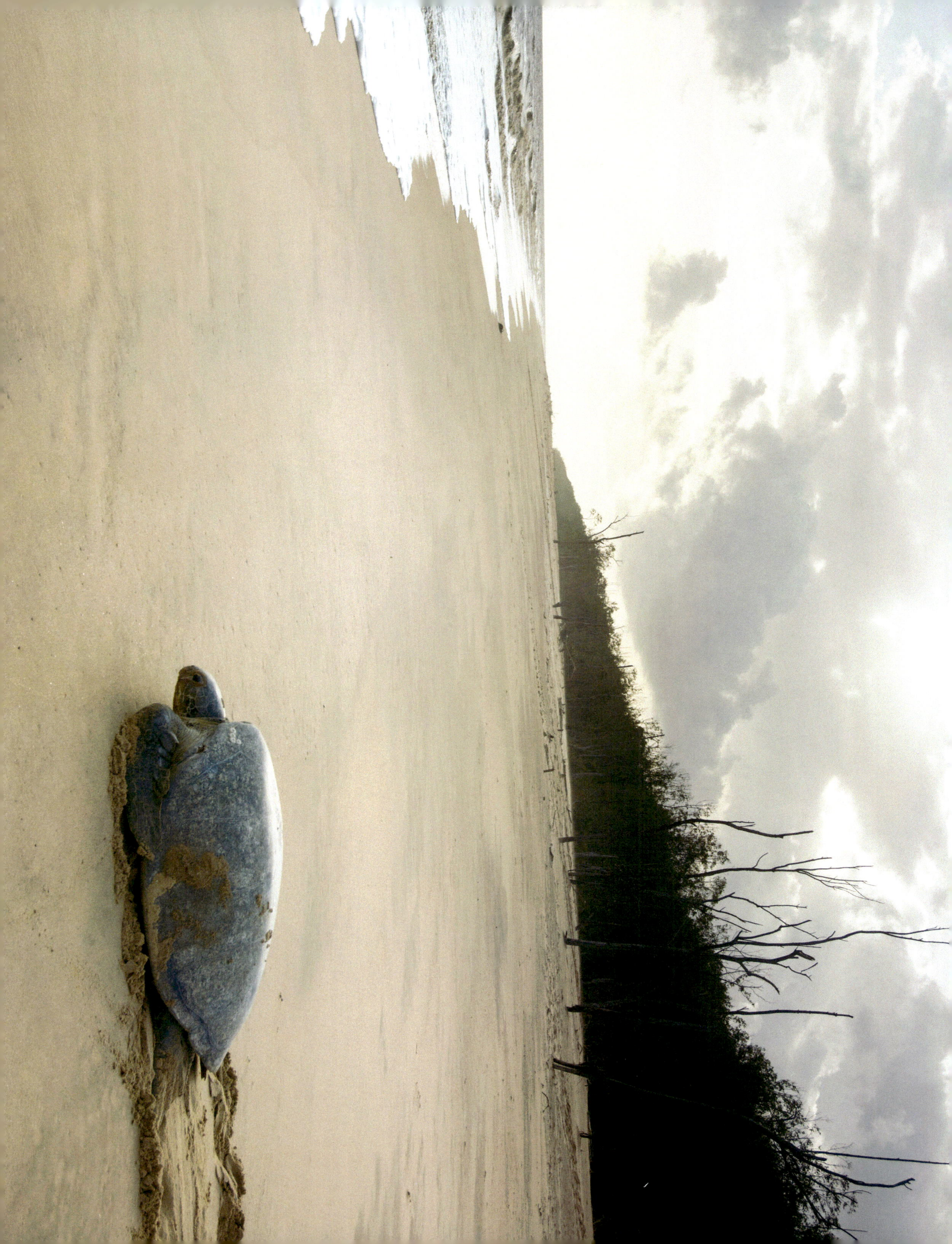

RIGHT:
Guiana Space Centre, French Guiana
Owned by the European Space Agency and French Centre National d'Etudes Spatiales, this spaceport hosts uncrewed missions, including launches of the Galileo James Webb Space Telescope. Its coastal location ensures that discarded rocket stages fall safely into the ocean rather than onto land, and its proximity to the equator provides an extra boost for eastward launches, taking advantage of Earth's equatorial rotation speed of 1,670km/h (1,040mph).

OPPOSITE:
Camp de la Transportation, St-Laurent-du-Maroni, French Guiana
The city of St-Laurent-du-Maroni was founded in 1858 as part of France's largest penal colony, which closed in 1946. Today, there are tours of some remaining prison buildings, including a visit to a cell bearing the graffiti 'Papillon', said to have been written by prisoner Henri Charrière, author of the 1969 novel *Papillon*.

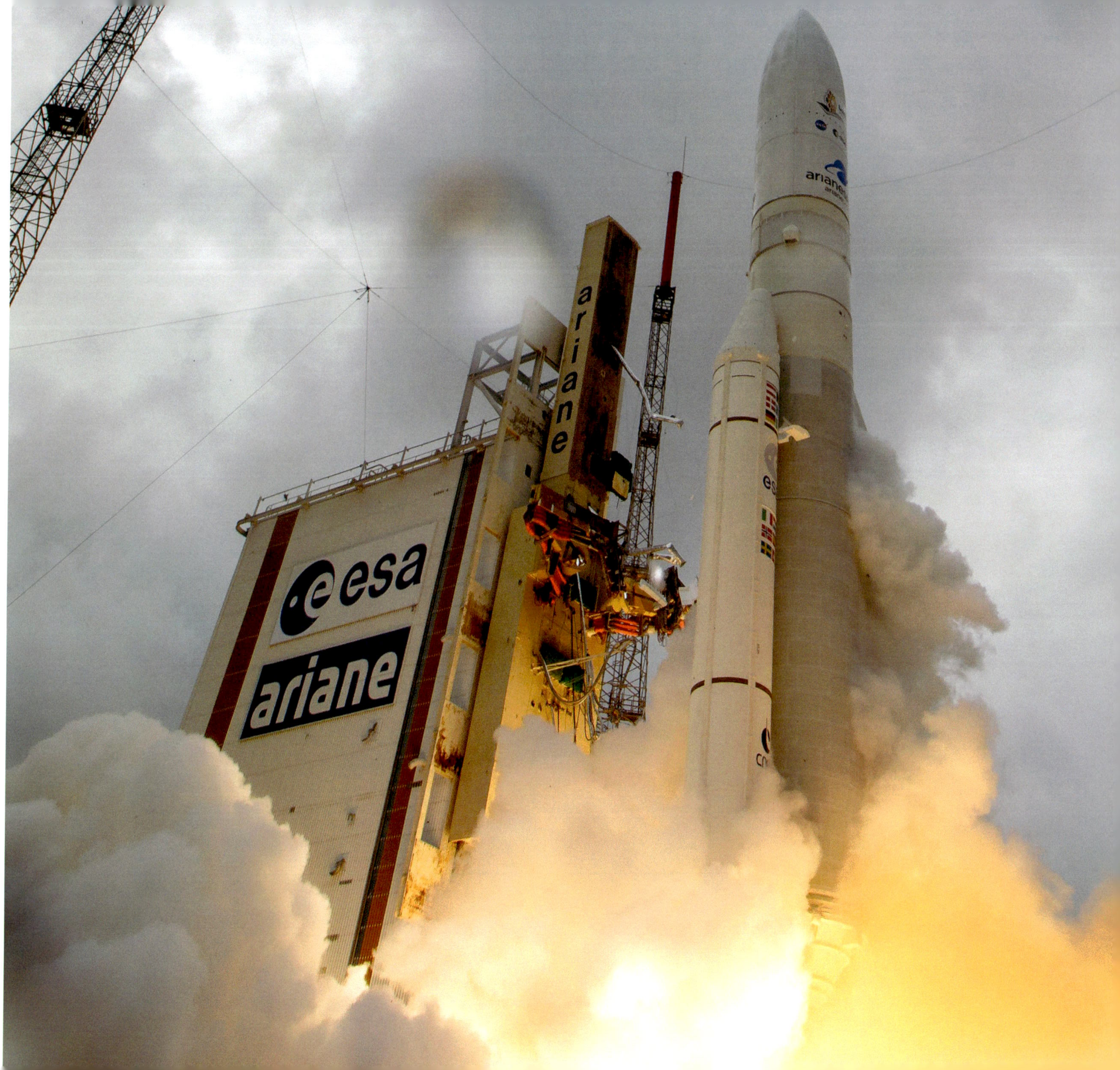

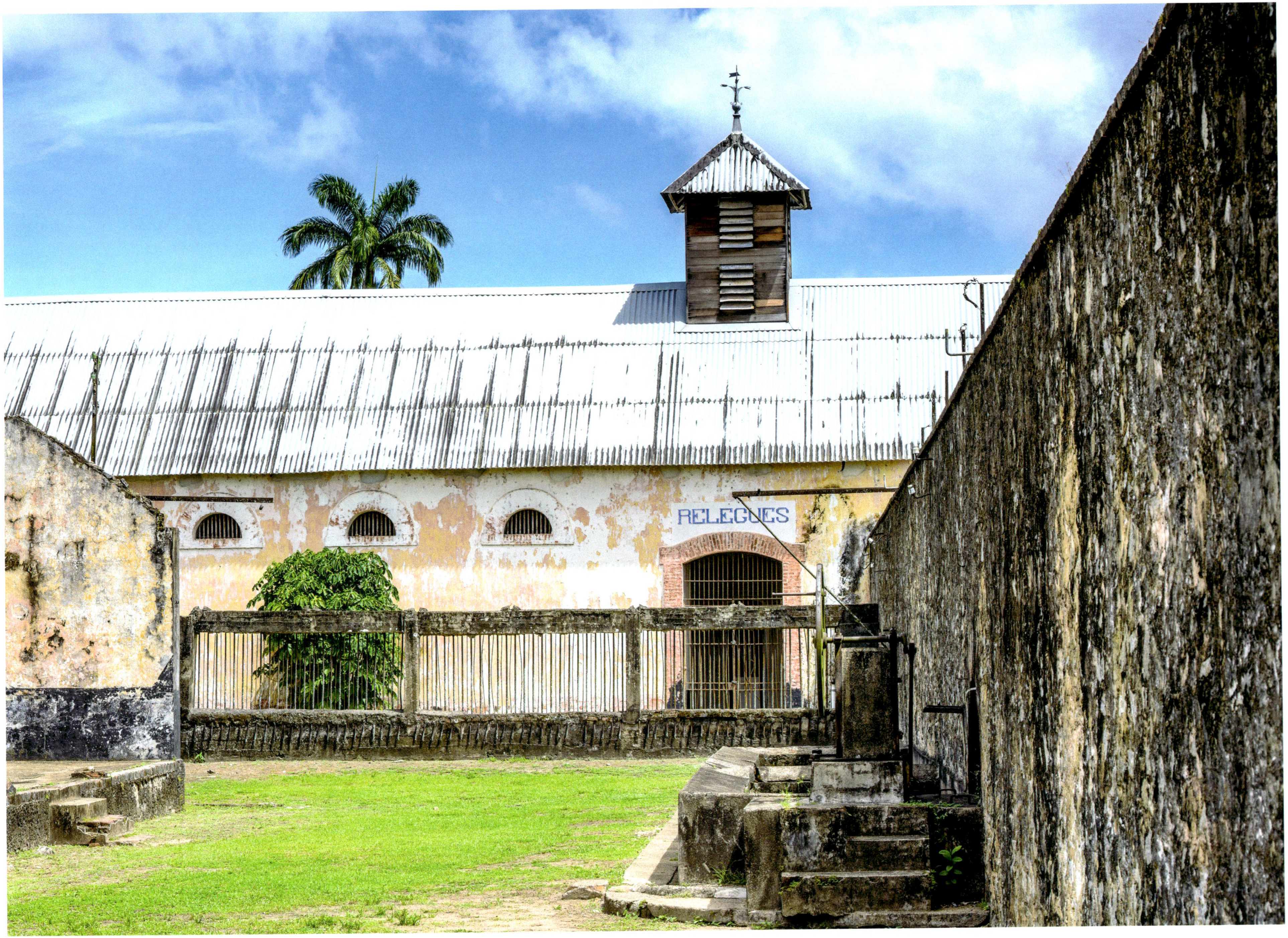
RELEGUES

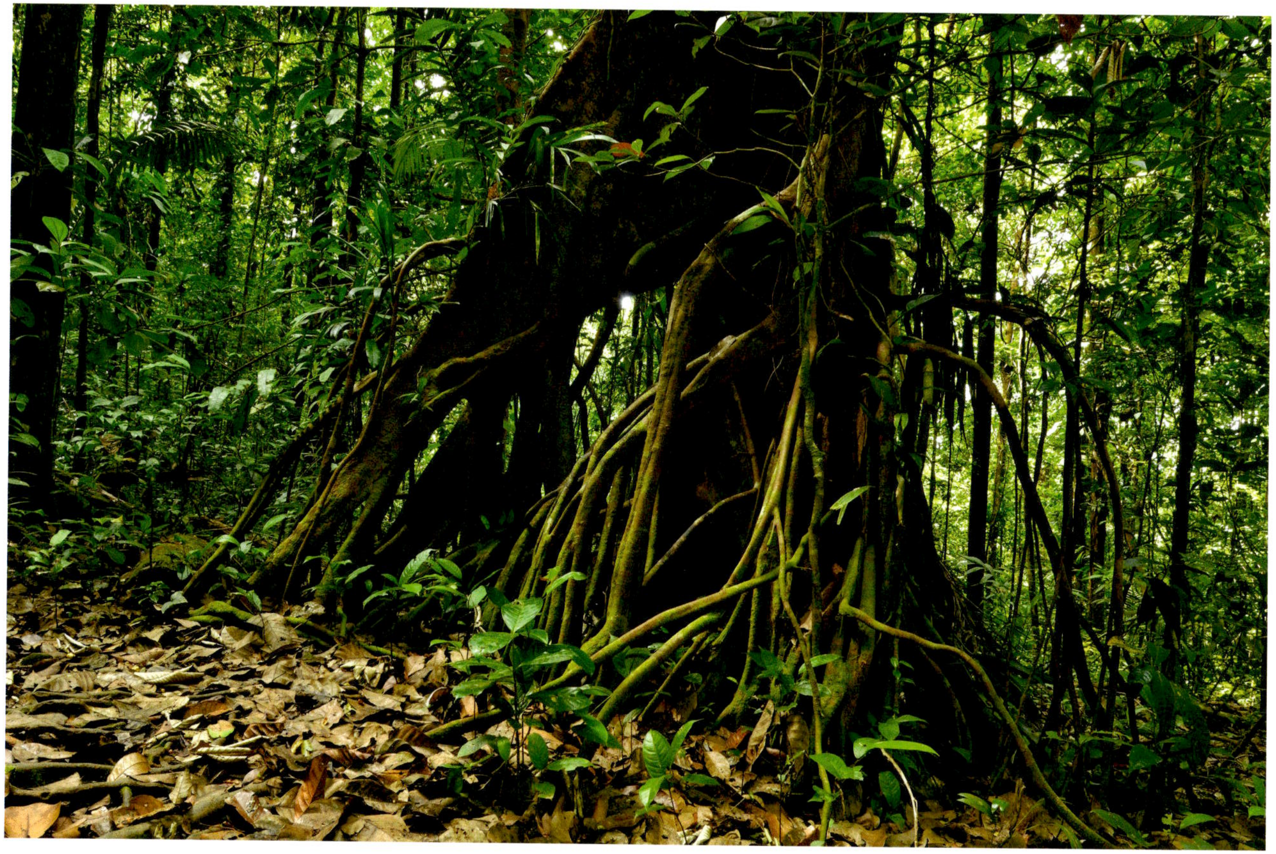

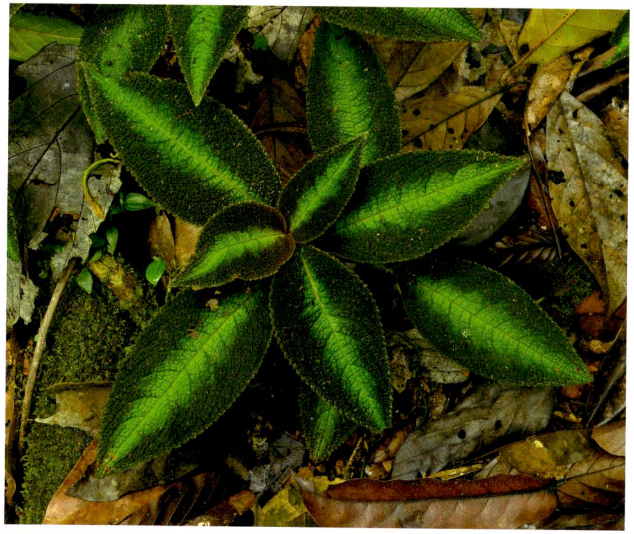

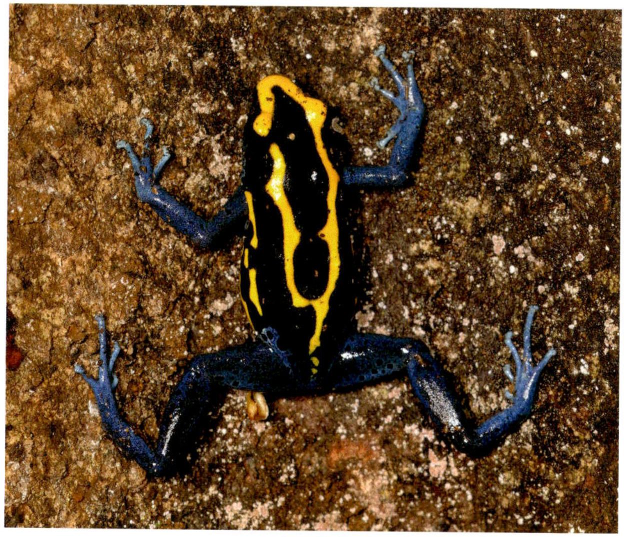

LEFT AND BOTTOM:
Trésor Regional Nature Reserve, French Guiana
In this reserve's vast marsh forest, many tree species have stilt roots, an adaptation that anchors the plants in unstable soil and also takes oxygen from the air rather than the waterlogged ground. The damp ecosystem boasts dozens of frog species, including the dyeing poison dart frog, one of the most variably coloured of poison dart frogs, with 30 morphs. If touched, the frog's toxins cause pain, cramping and muscle stiffness.

RIGHT:
Maroni River, French Guiana
Flowing 612km (380 miles) from the Tumuk Humak Mountains to the Atlantic, the Maroni forms the border between French Guiana and Suriname. More than 250 species of fish swim in the river, including rare tetras such as the Maroni jupiaba.

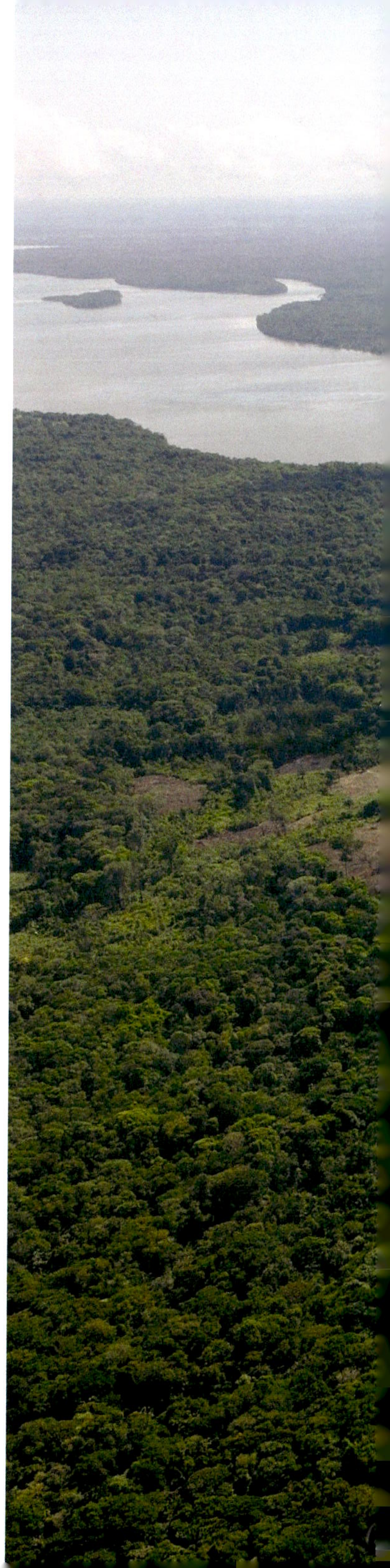

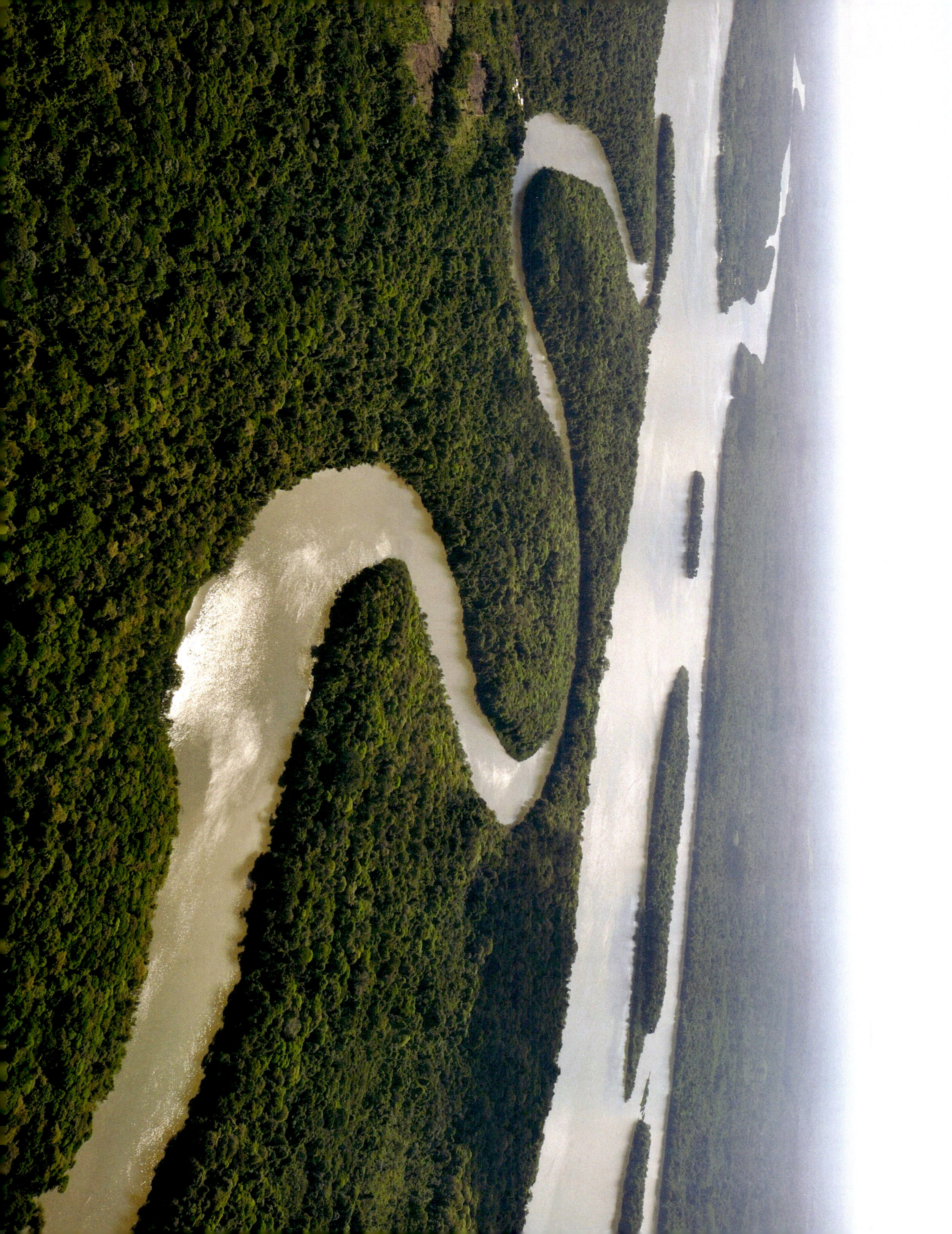

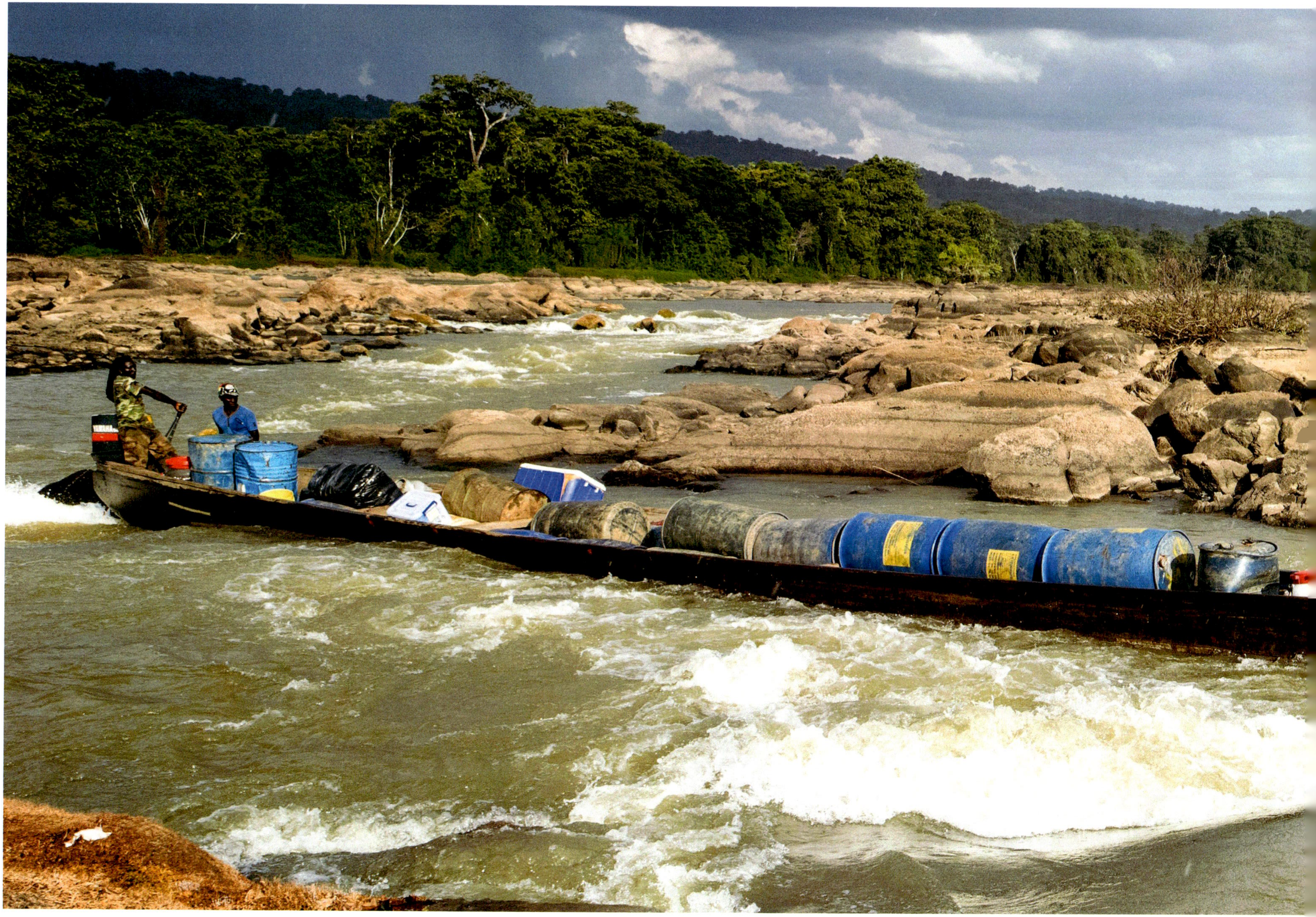

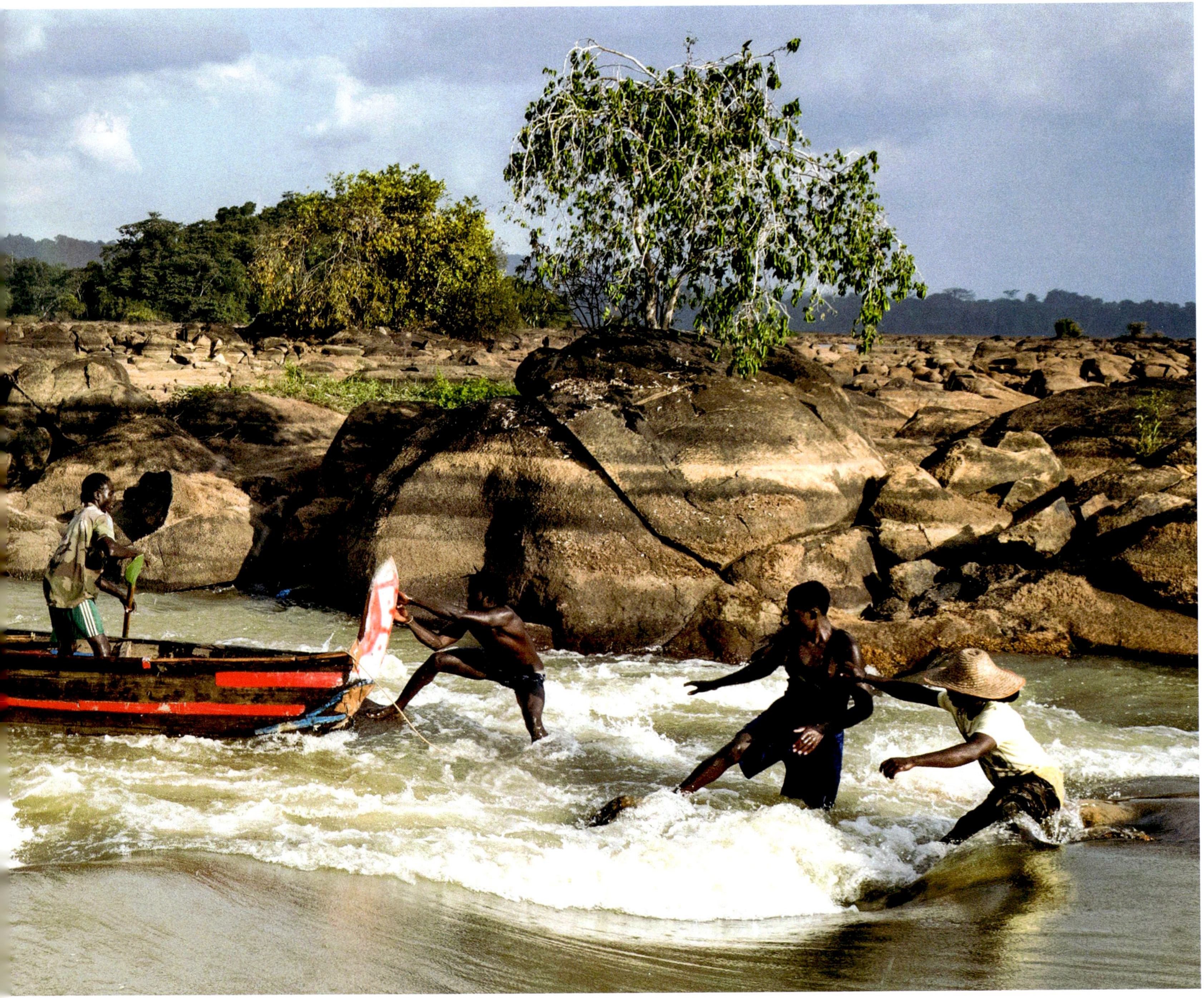

Abattis Cottica, Maroni River, French Guiana
A series of rapids makes canoe transport dangerous in this stretch of the Maroni River, where it surges between countless islets. During the Maroon Wars of the eighteenth century, this area became the boundary between the lands of the Aluku and Ndyuka, both communities of African descent who had escaped from slavery.

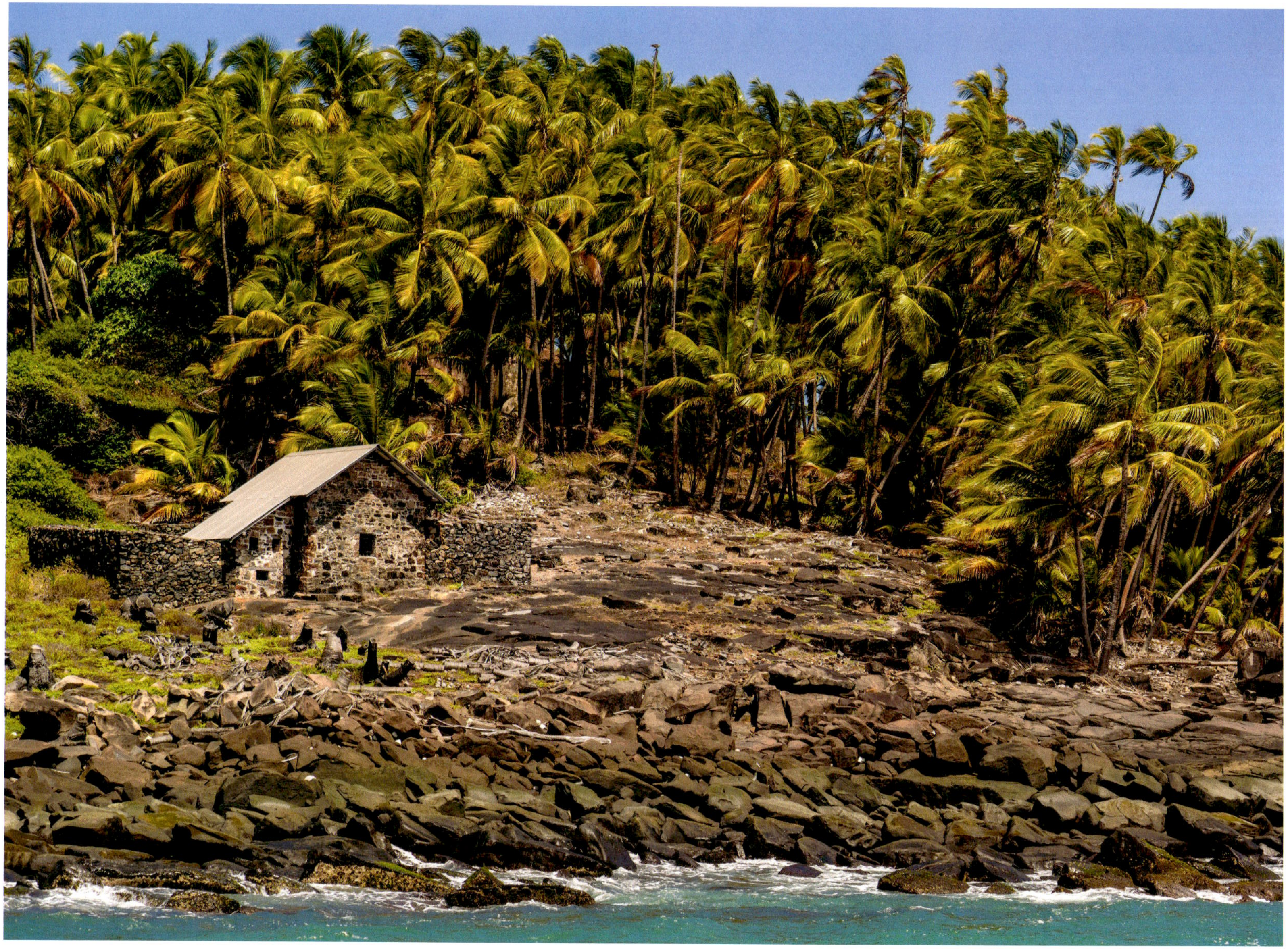

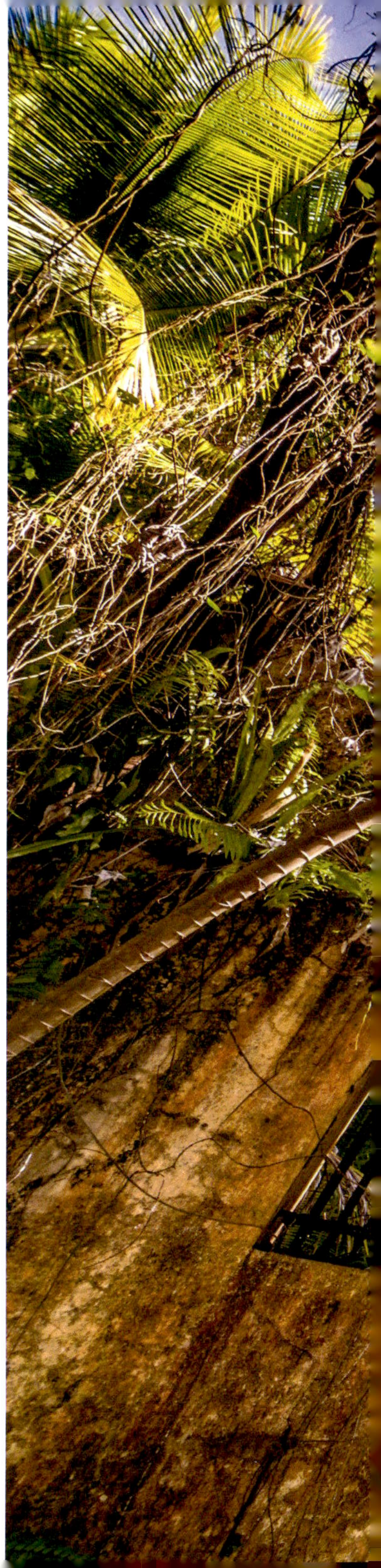

ABOVE:
Cabin of Alfred Dreyfus, Devil's Island, French Guiana
In 1894, French army officer Alfred Dreyfus was imprisoned in this hut in the penal colony of Cayenne after being falsely convicted of being a German spy. In 1899, long after evidence emerged that Dreyfus had been scapegoated for being Jewish, he was pardoned.

RIGHT:
Saint-Joseph Island, French Guiana
While Devil's Island often housed political prisoners, nearby Saint-Joseph Island was reserved for inmates of the penal colony who were sent into solitary confinement for attempted escapes or other rule breaking. Today, this 'prison within a prison' is being reclaimed by the jungle.

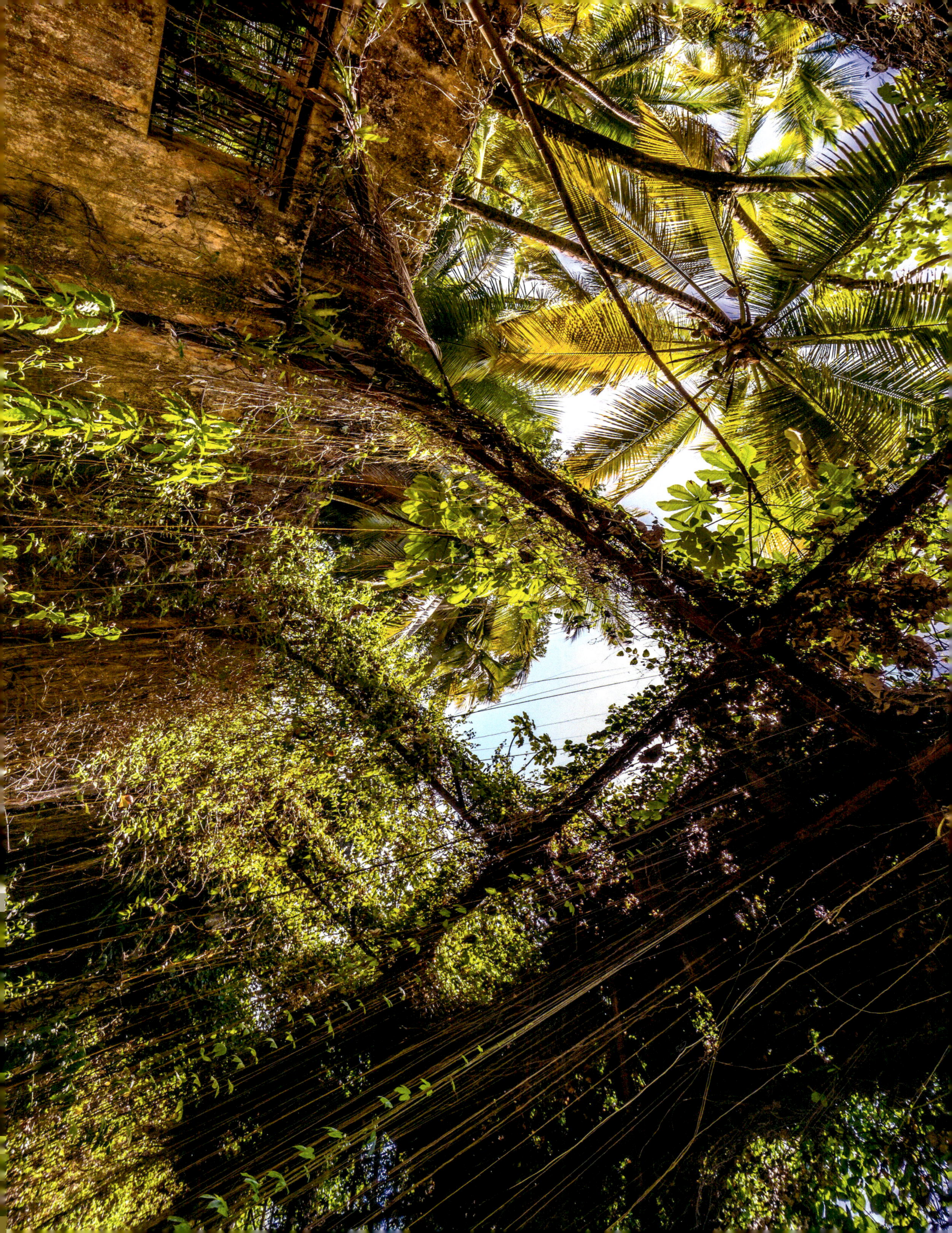

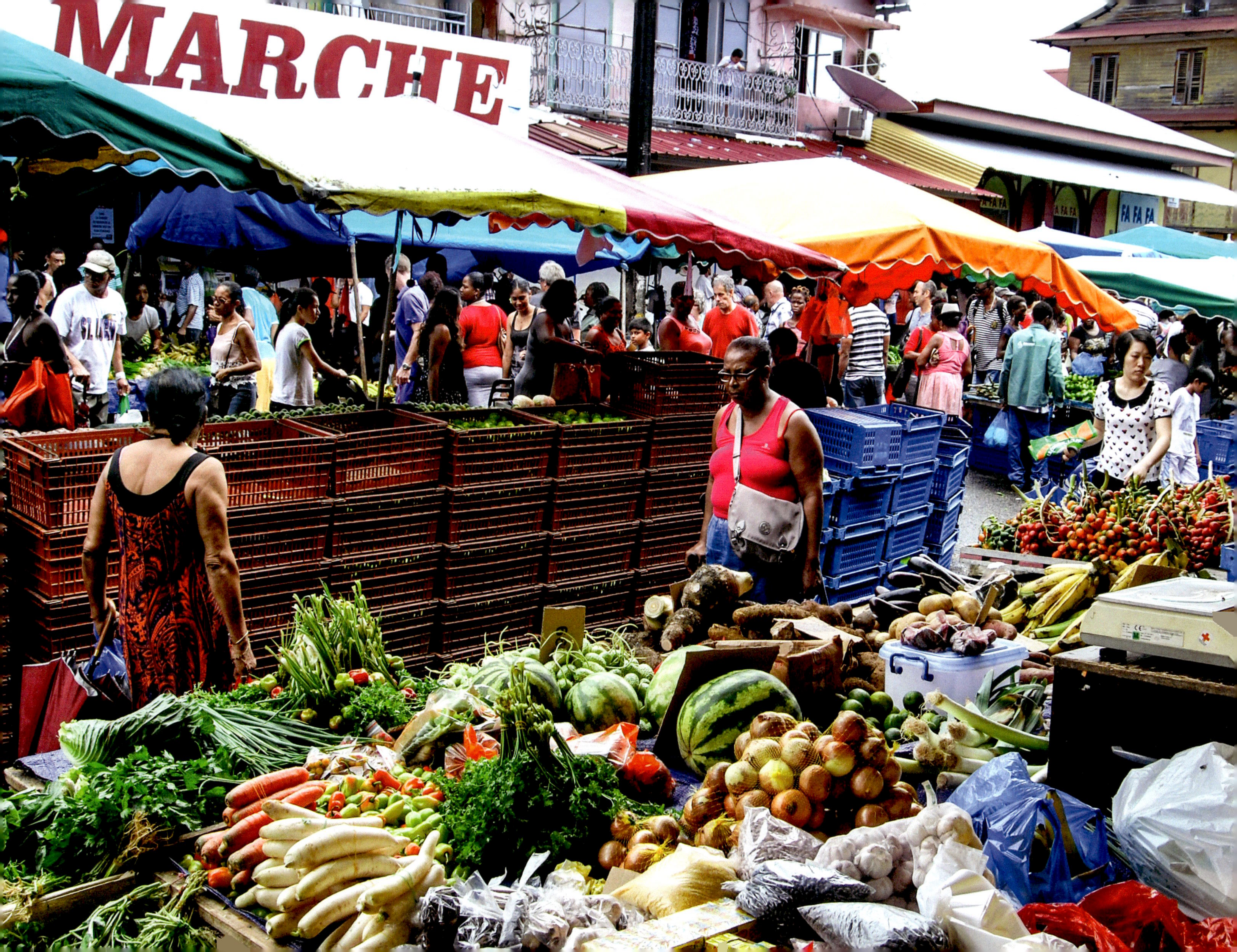
MARCHE
FA FA FA

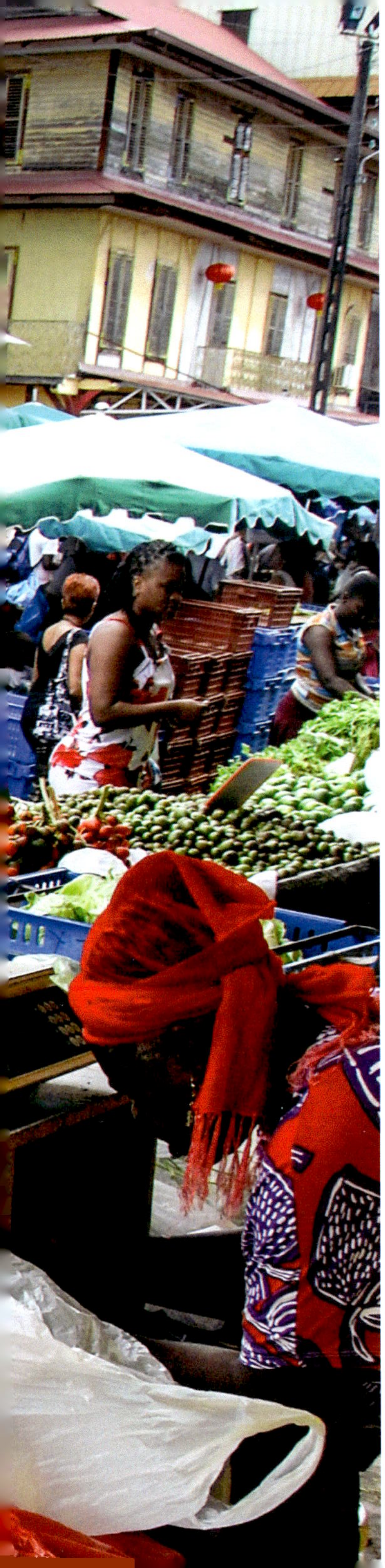

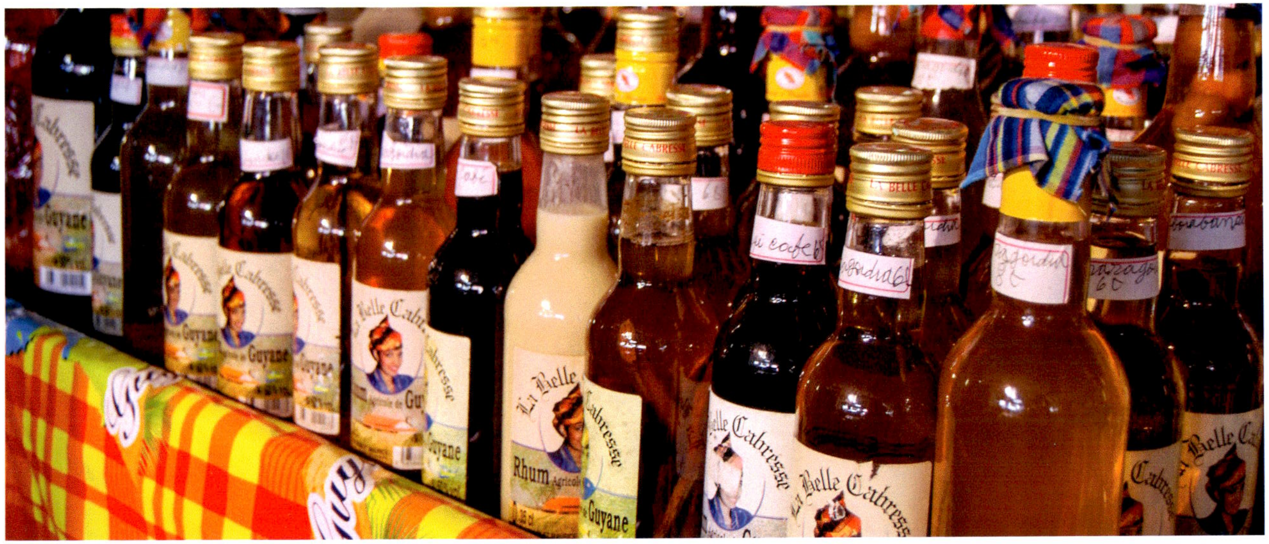

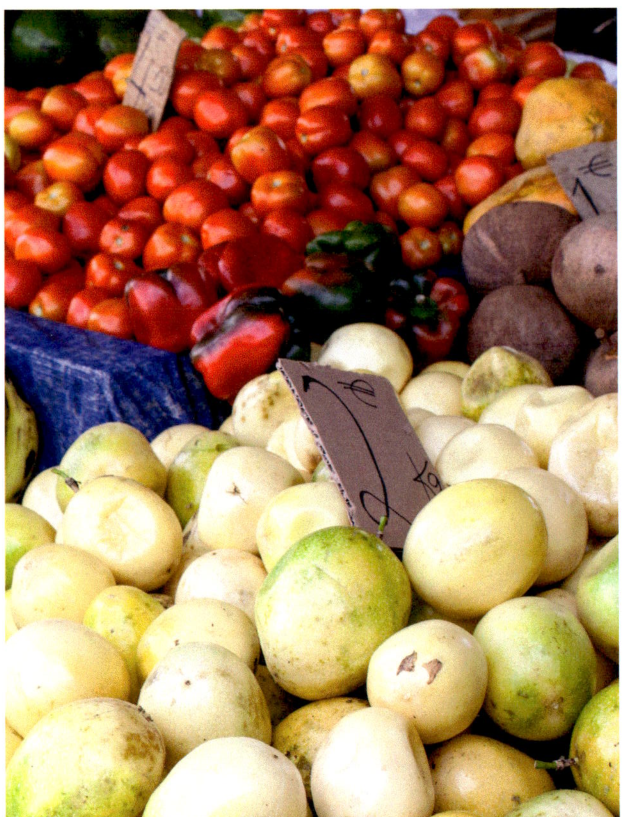

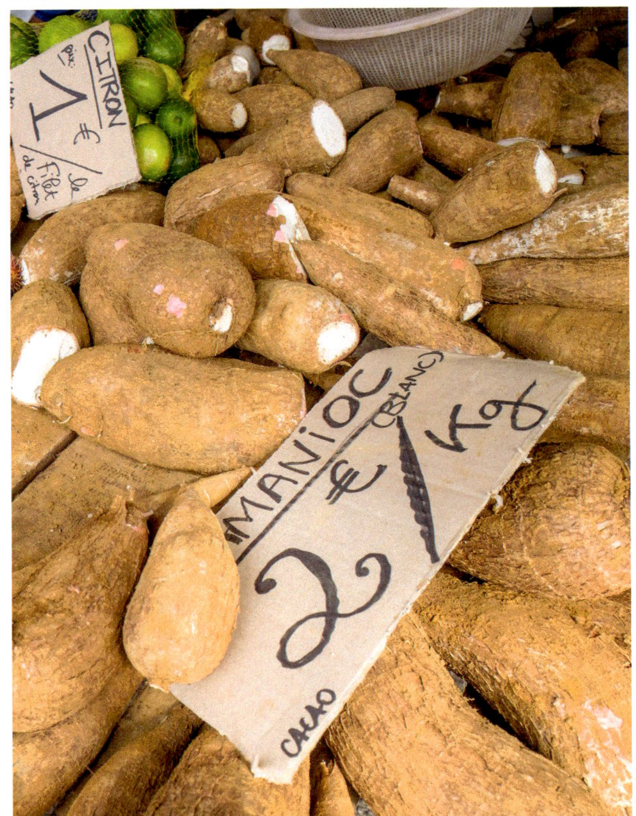

ALL PHOTOGRAPHS:
Central Market, Cayenne, French Guiana
In addition to fresh produce, the capital's busy market offers Wayapi basketry, African-style carvings and Belle Cabresse rum. This famous local *rhum agricole* is distilled from sugarcane juice rather than molasses. It is often used to make the popular tipple known as ti' punch, along with a dash of cane syrup and lime.

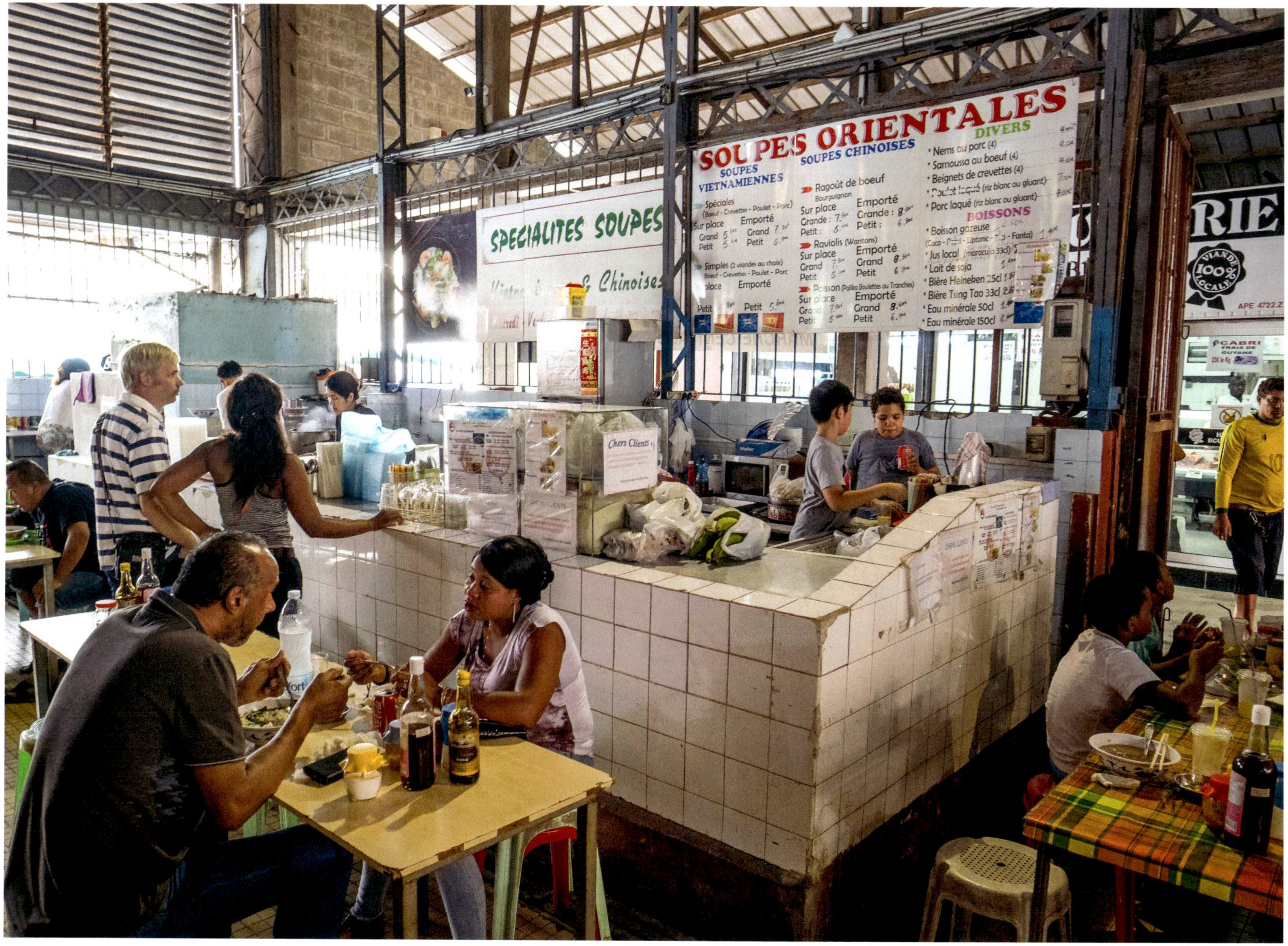

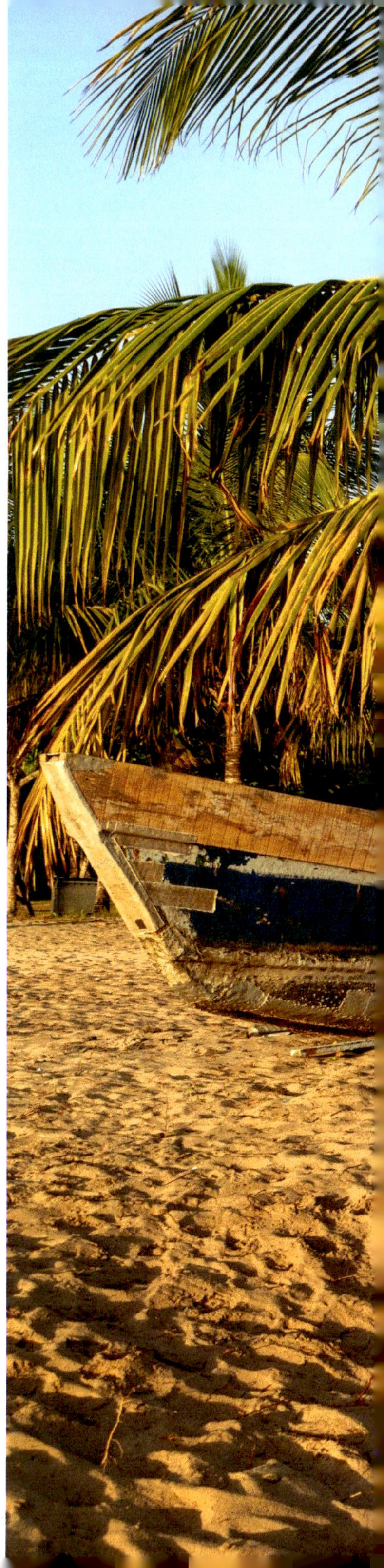

ABOVE:
Central Market, Cayenne, French Guiana
Stalls and restaurants in the capital's market offer Vietnamese, Chinese and Hmong food including *nam van*, a delicious, dense dessert drink made of tapioca pearls and coconut milk. The large Hmong community arrived as refugees from Laos, resettled by France in the 1970s.

RIGHT:
Plage des Hattes, French Guiana
At the mouth of the Maroni River, this 5km (3-mile) beach is a major nesting site for leatherback turtles. Females dig their nests in the sand, above the high-water mark, from April to July, laying 80 to 100 eggs in each clutch. The hatchlings make their perilous dash for the sea between July and September.

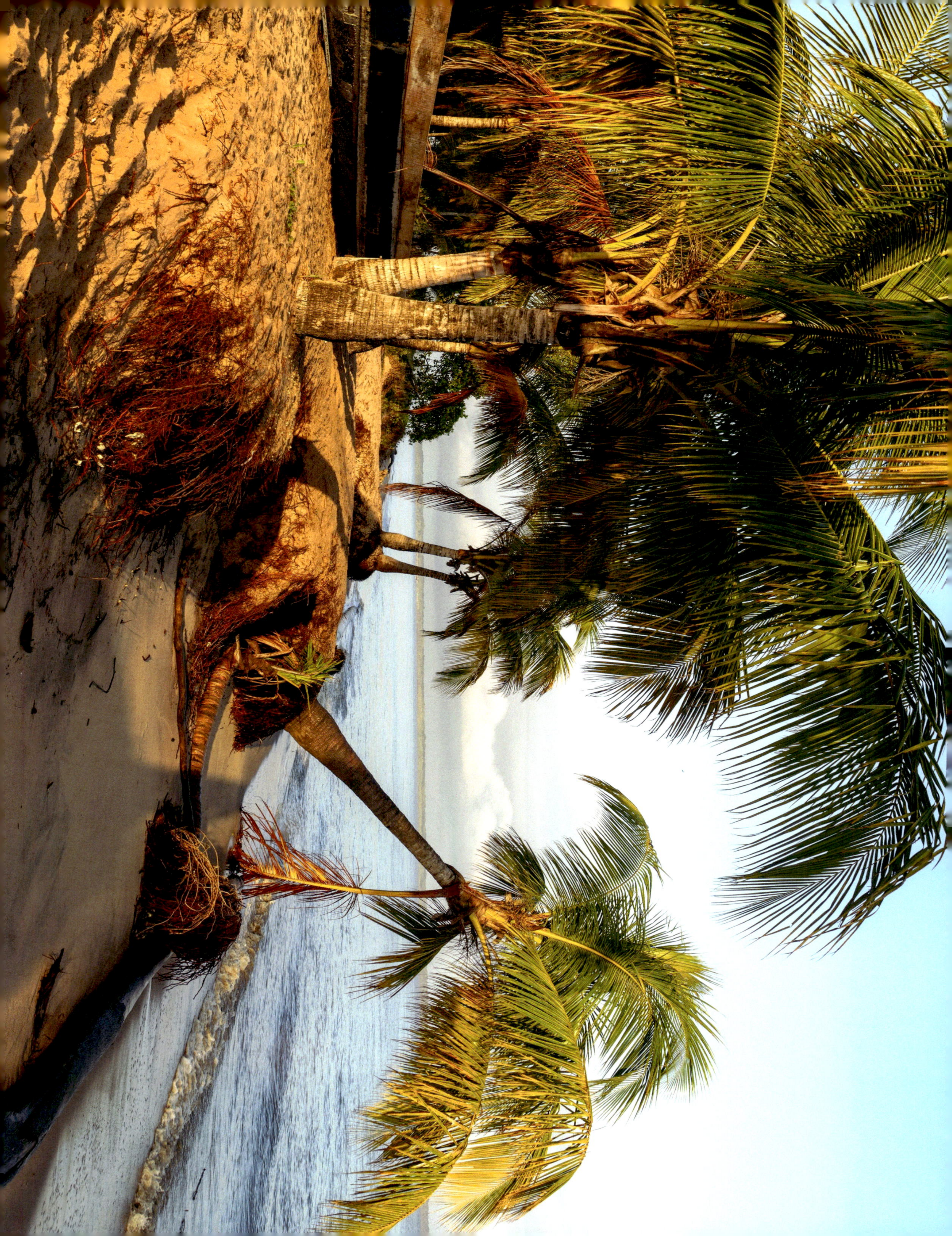

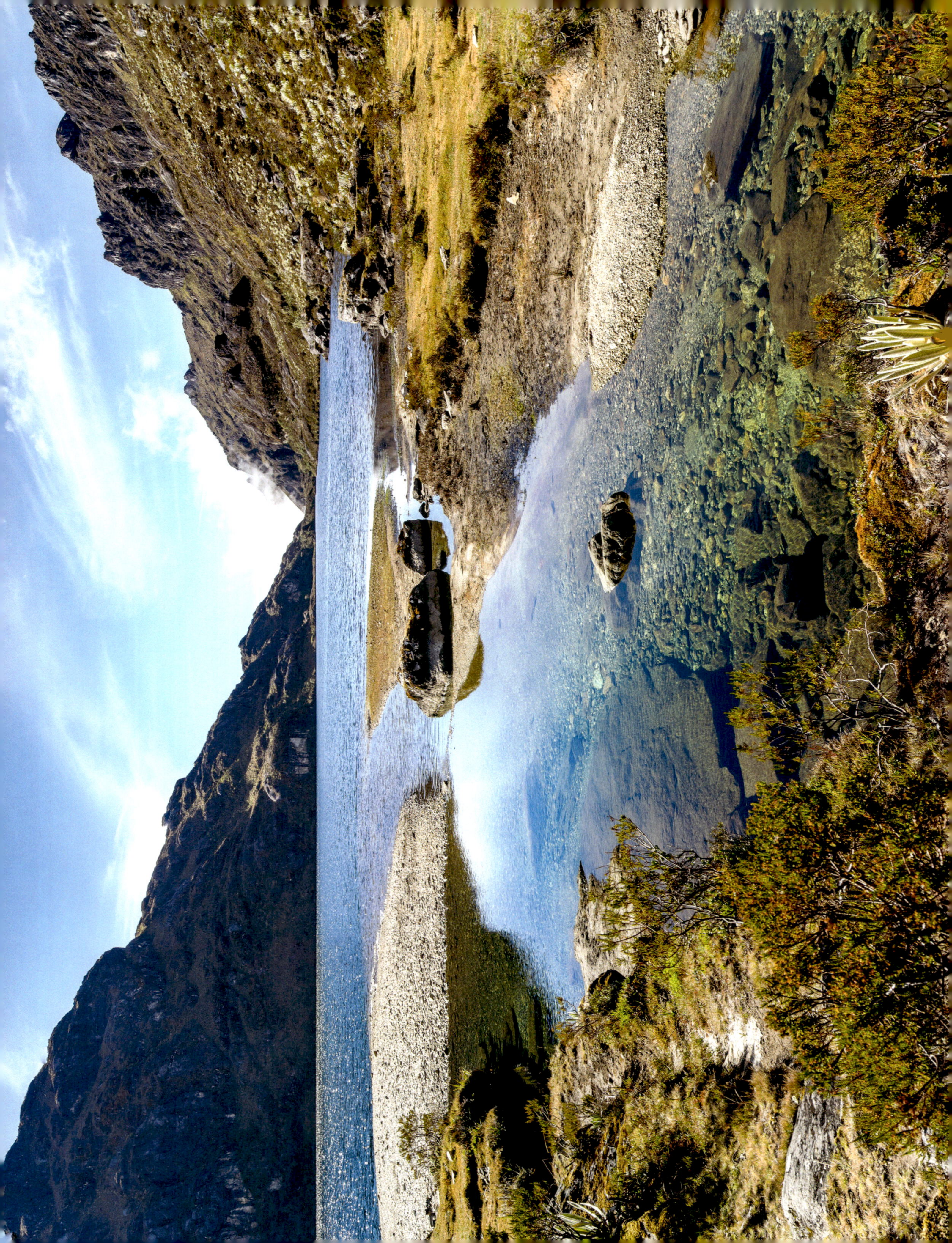

Venezuela, Colombia and Ecuador

Before the arrival of the Spanish from 1498, this region was called by many names by many peoples, from the Timoto–Cuica of today's Venezuela to the Muisca in present-day Colombia and the Incas, who had expanded into what is today Ecuador from their base in Peru. We can learn a little about the region's colonization – and the near-erasure of its existing cultures and communities – from the two competing myths surrounding how Venezuela gained its modern name. The most popular story tells us that, in 1499, Spanish conquistador Alonso de Ojeda's expedition came across the stilt houses around Lake Maracaibo. The scene reminded Ojeda's Italian navigator Amerigo Vespucci (after whom, incidentally, America is named) of Venice, leading him to name the region Veneziola ('Little Venice'). However, one member of the expedition, Martín Fernández de Enciso, told a story that the name, in fact, came from local people who called themselves the Veneciuela. There is no such debate around the naming of Colombia, since it honours the Italian explorer Christopher Columbus, who led a Spanish-backed expedition to the northern coast of South America in 1498. After the region gained independence from Spain, in 1819 the name was adopted by the fairly short-lived republic of Gran Colombia, which was composed of modern-day Colombia, Venezuela, Ecuador, Panama and northwest Brazil. In 1824, the República del Ecuador ('Republic of the Equator') was established as a division of Gran Colombia, with its capital at Quito, just south of the equator.

OPPOSITE:
Santo Cristo Lake, Sierra Nevada National Park, Venezuela
At a height of 3900m (12,800ft) in the Andes, this is one of Venezuela's largest glacial lakes. The surrounding national park contains the country's highest mountain, 4978m (16,332ft) Pico Bolívar, named after the nineteenth-century Venezuelan hero Simón Bolívar, who led Bolivia, Colombia, Ecuador, Panama, Peru and Venezuela to independence from Spain.

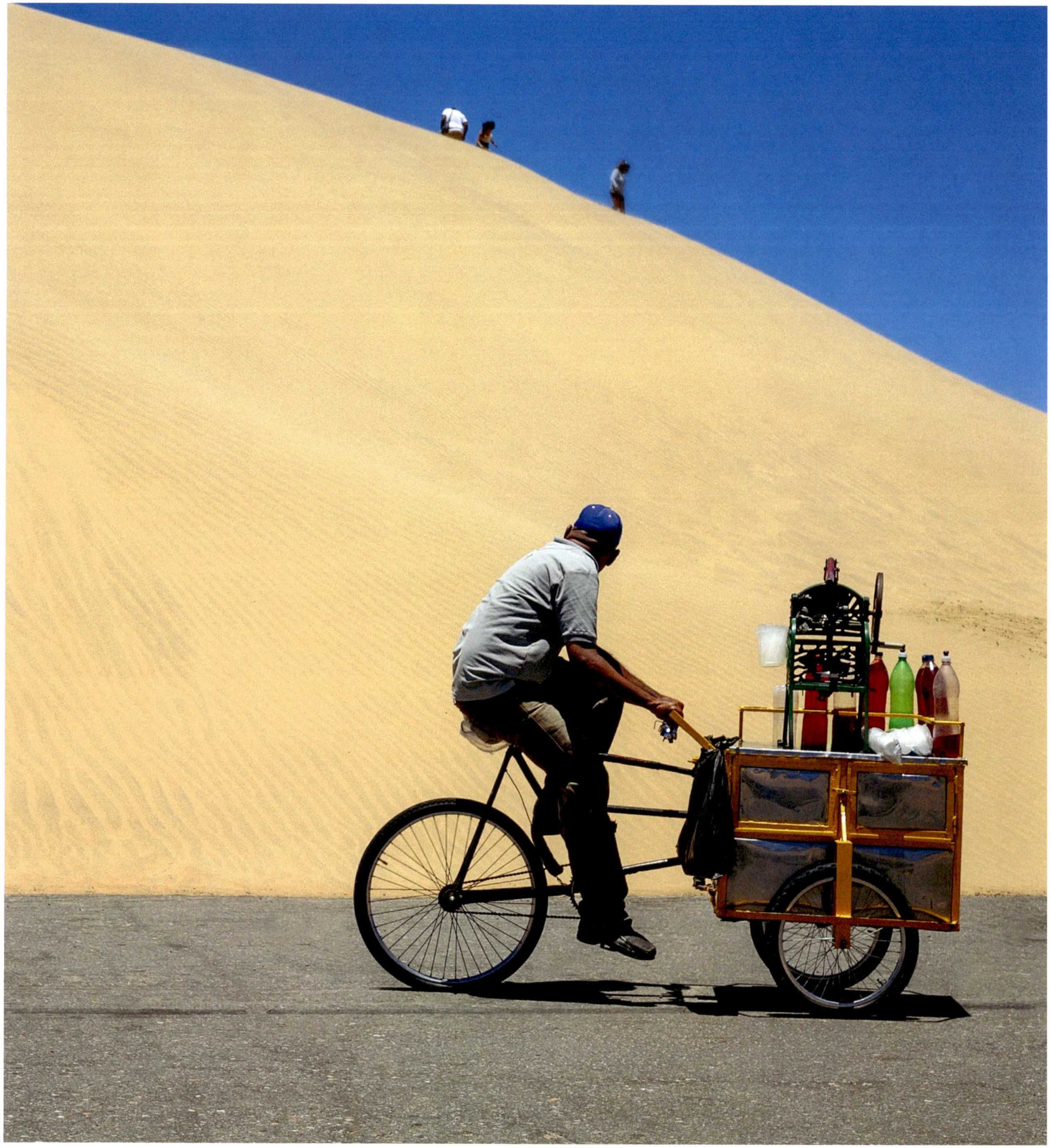

LEFT:
Médanos de Coro National Park, Venezuela
Up to 40m (130ft) high, the sand dunes near Coro cover an area of 150 sq km (58 sq miles). Located in a dry, barren, wind-whipped coastal region, the dunes constantly move and transform. They are formed of both beach and river sediment.

RIGHT:
Angel Falls, Canaima National Park, Venezuela
This is the world's tallest uninterrupted waterfall, with a longest plunge of 807m (2648ft) and a total height of 979m (3212ft). Its' European name honours the American aviator Jimmie Angel, who famously crashed his plane nearby in 1933. The waterfall formed where the Korepa River flows off Auyán-tepui, a vast sandstone outcrop.

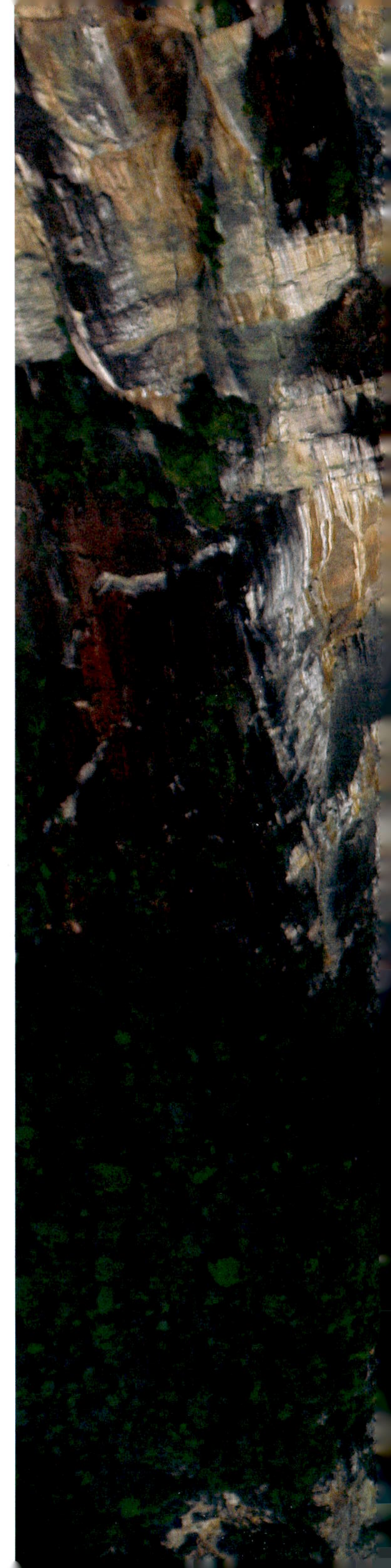

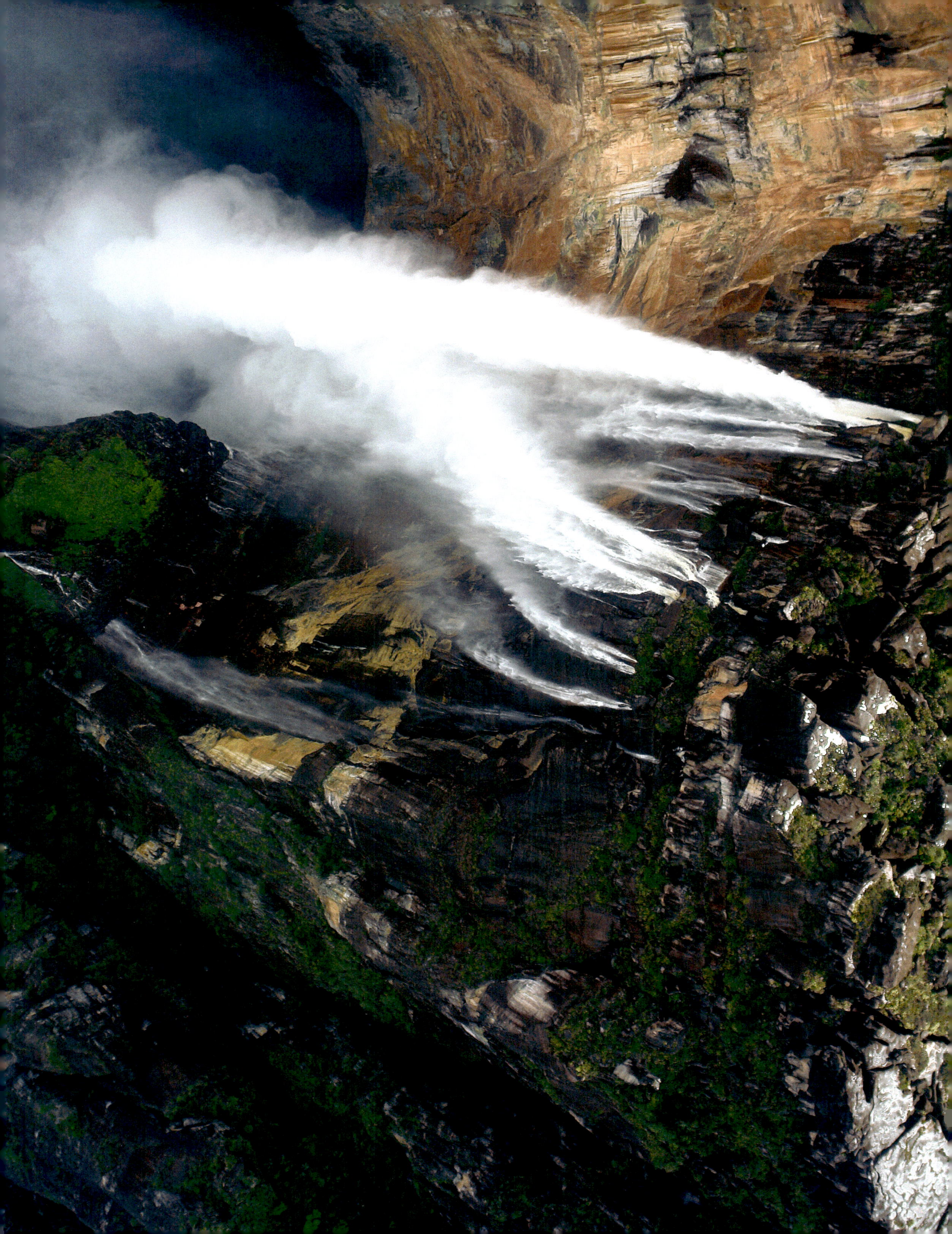

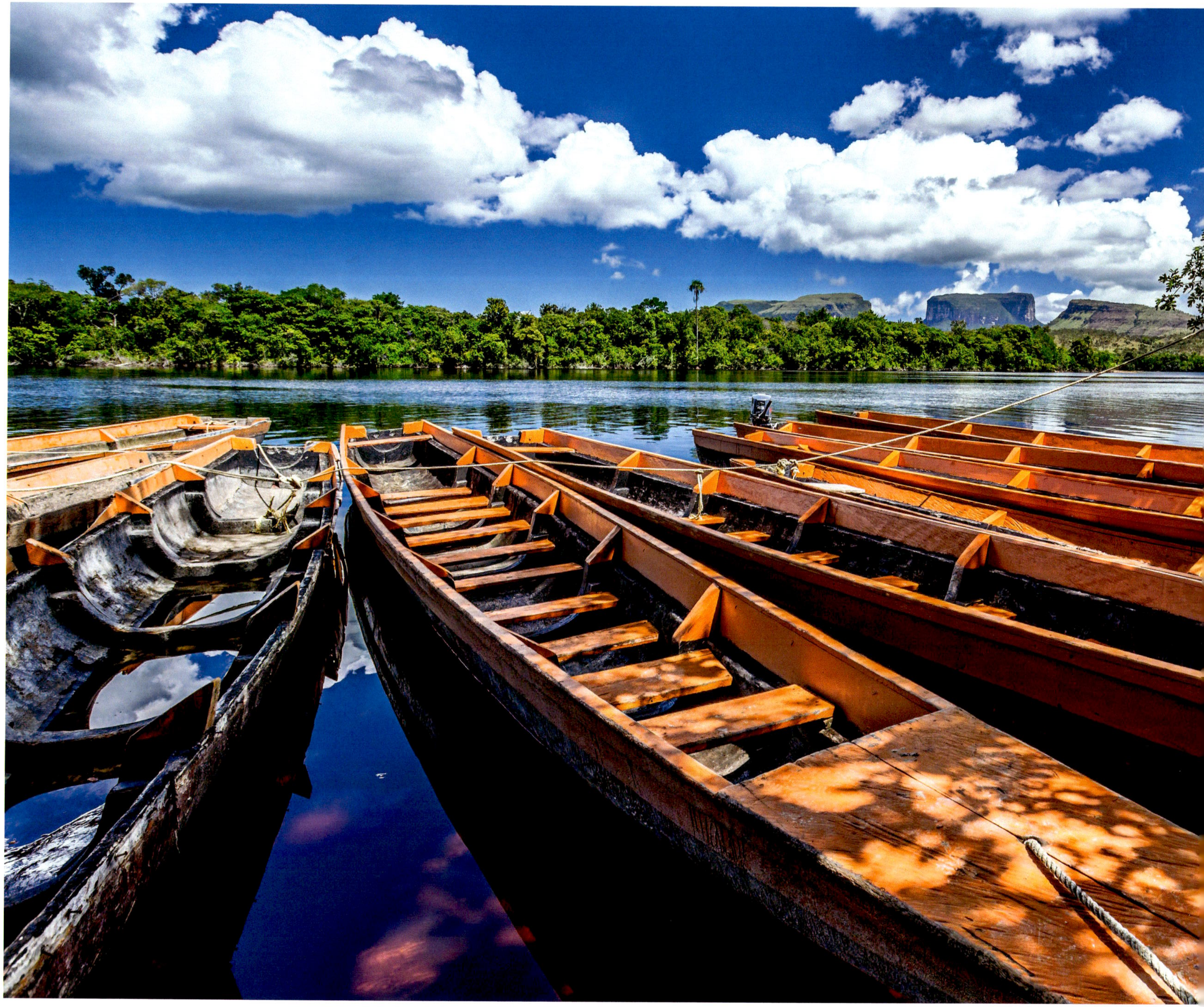

RIGHT:
Carrao River, Canaima National Park, Venezuela
With its source in Canaima National Park, the Carrao flows into the Coroní, which in turn joins the Orinoco. Local people journey along these rivers by canoe, some of them in traditional dugouts called *curiaras*. In the distance, are the Kurun, Kusari and Kuravaina tepuis.

OPPOSITE:
Roraima Tepui, Canaima National Park
On the borders of Venezuela, Guyana and Brazil, Roraima is the highest tepui of the Pacaraima Mountains, reaching a height of 2810m (9220ft). The tepuis are flat-topped mountains, the remains of a sandstone plateau that eroded between 300 million and 70 million years ago. The mountaintops are home to species that evolved in isolation, such as the Roraima mouse and Roraima toad.

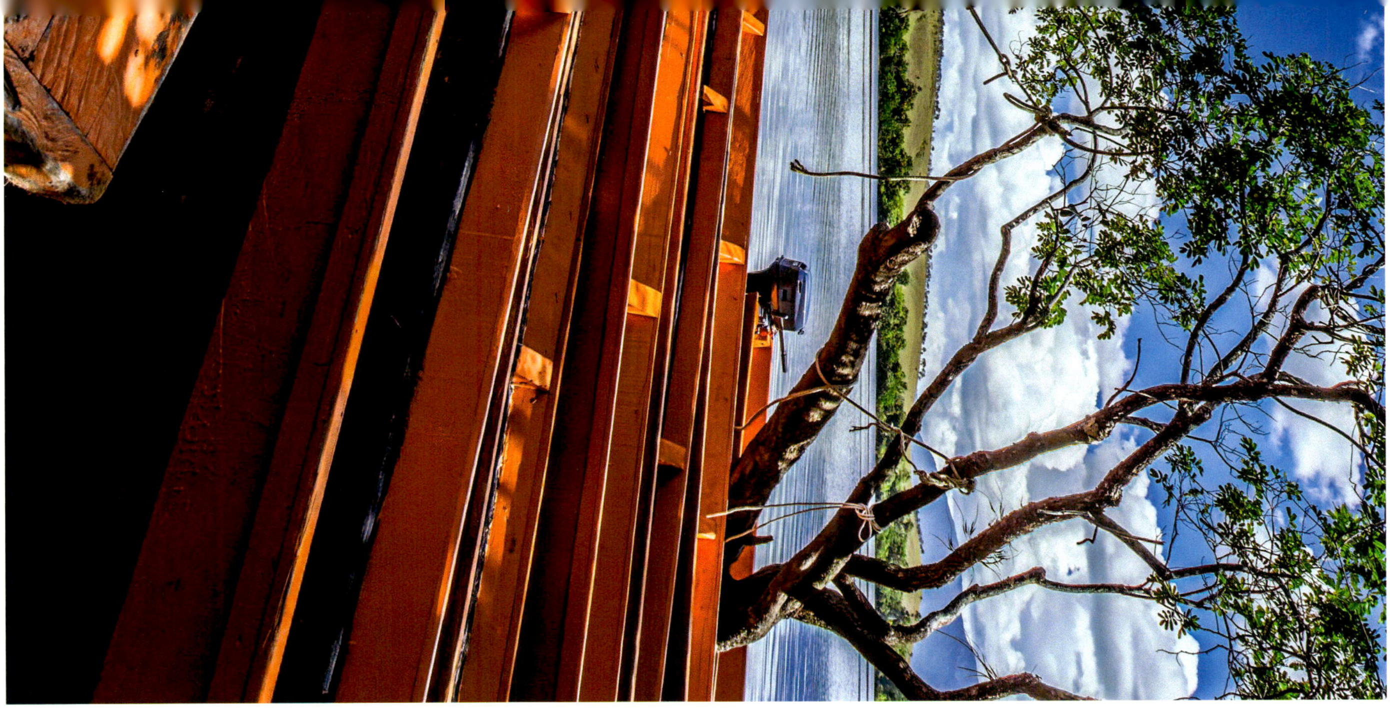
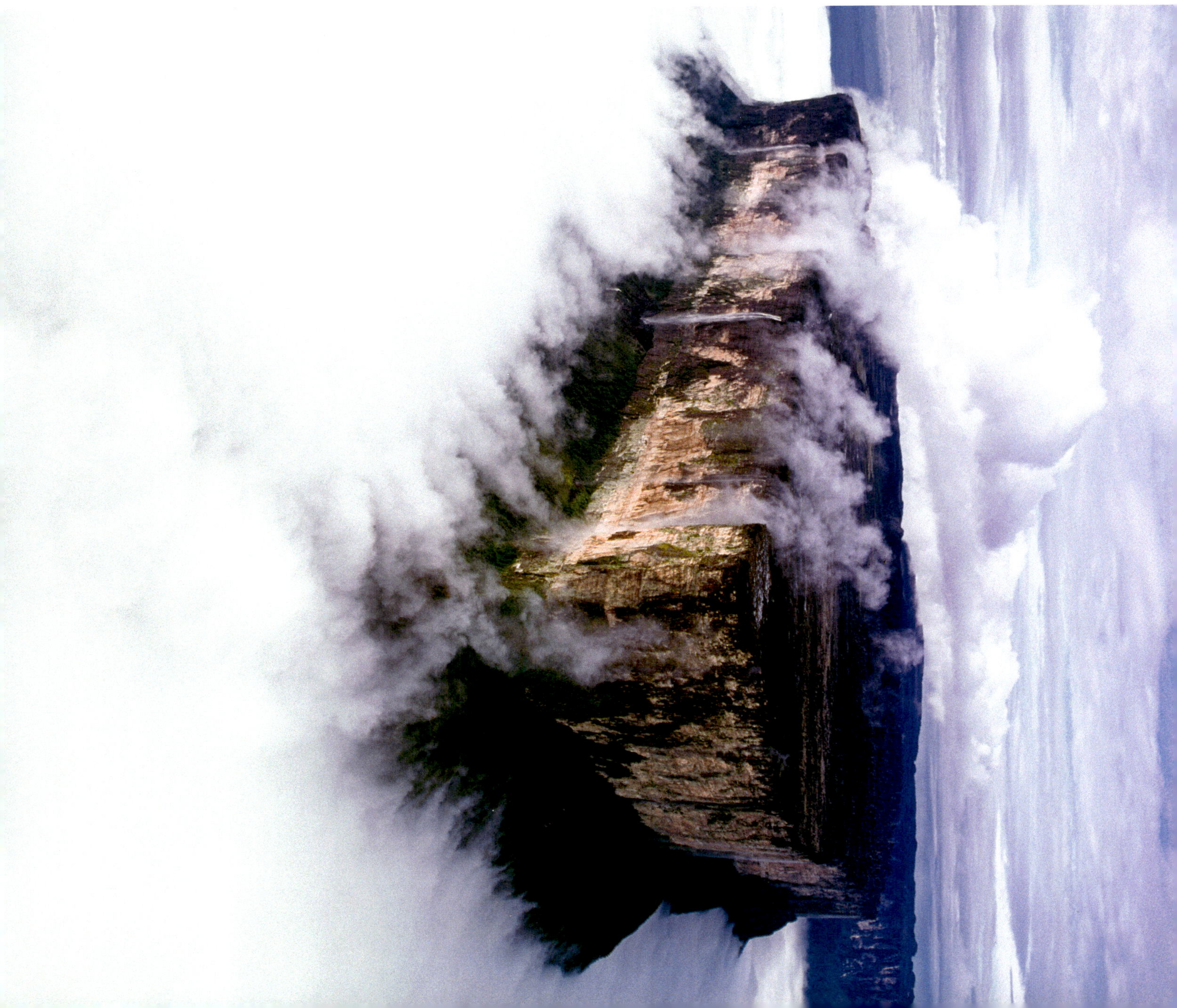

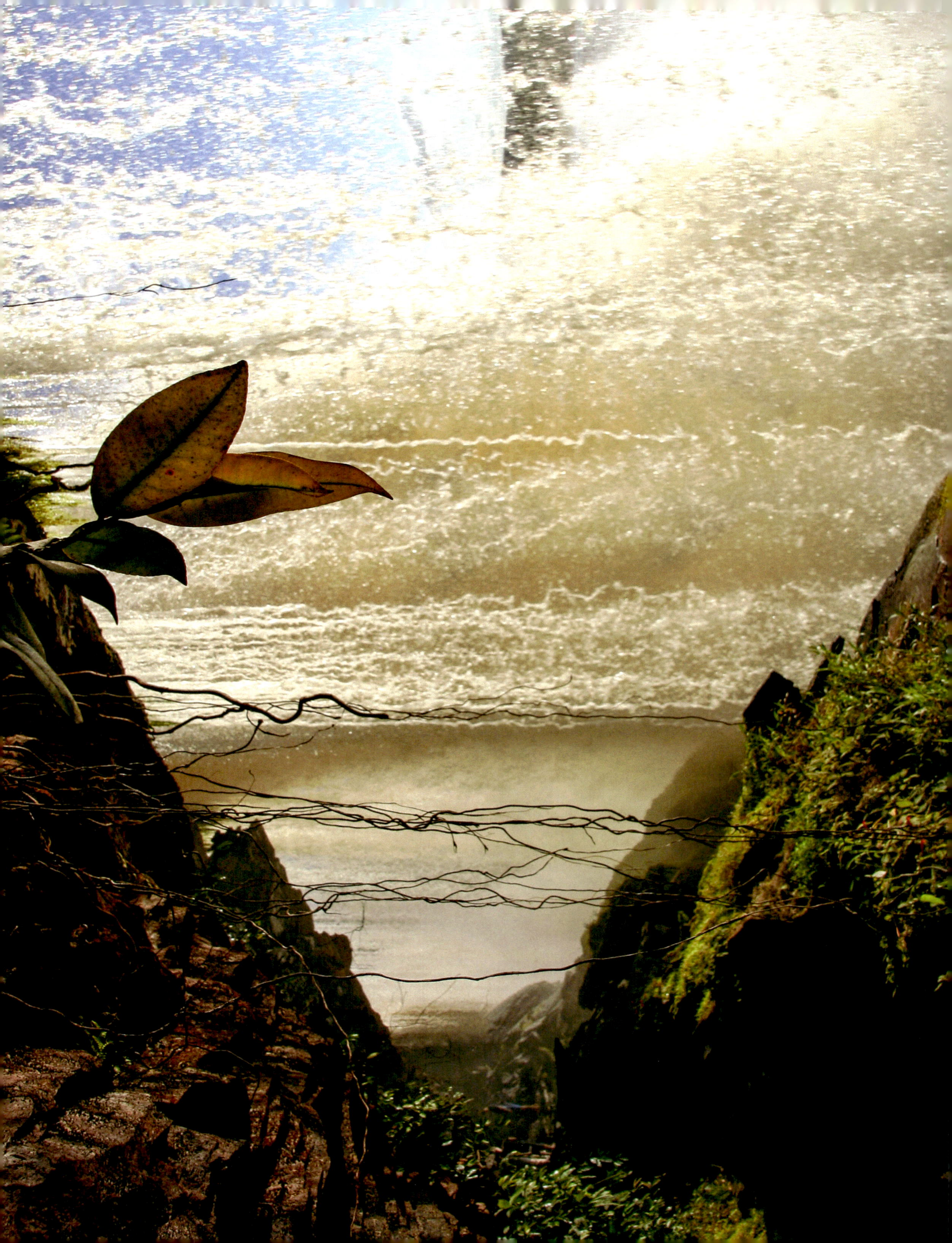

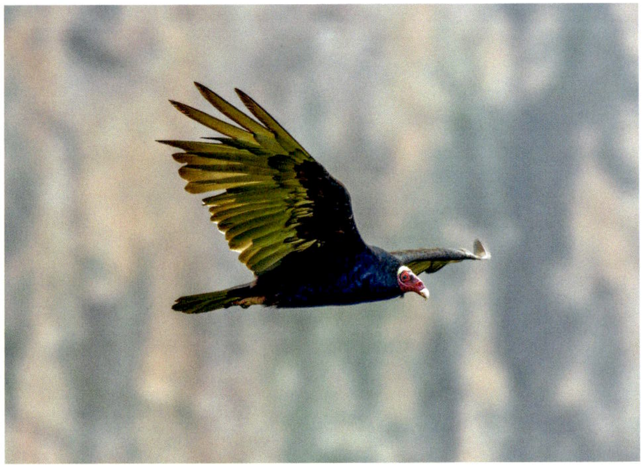

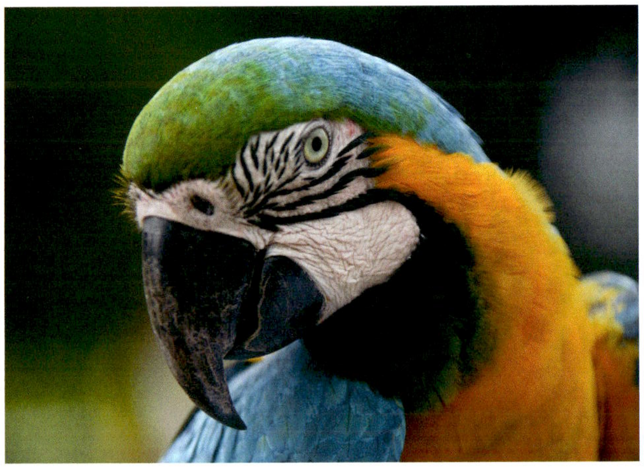

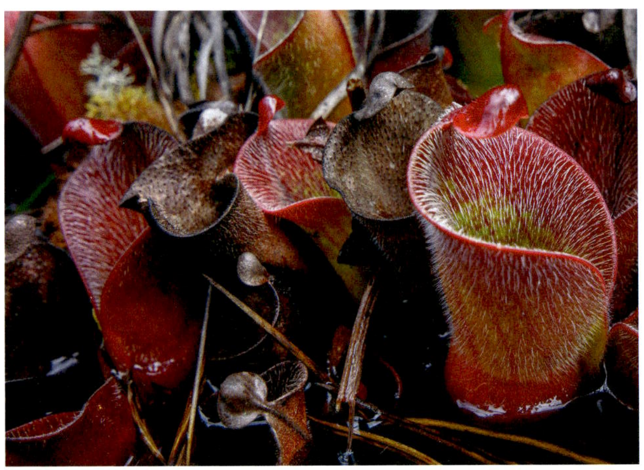

OPPOSITE:
Hacha Falls, Canaima National Park, Venezuela
Hikers can step behind the curtain of water where the Carrao River plunges into Canaima Lagoon. The nearby Canaima village is reached by small plane from Caracas.

LEFT TOP:
Turkey Vulture, Canaima National Park
A turkey vulture makes use of the thermals around Mount Roraima, as it scans the ground for the carcasses of mice, agoutis and foxes.

LEFT MIDDLE:
Blue-and-Yellow Macaw, Canaima National Park
Up to 90cm (35in) long, this parrot lives in tropical forests, where it uses its strong beak for cracking the shells of nuts.

LEFT BOTTOM:
***Heliamphora minor*, Canaima National Park**
Endemic to the summit of Auyán-tepui, this pitcher plant digests insects that fall into its water-filled pitcher. Around a quarter of the plants on a tepui summit are found nowhere else on Earth.

RIGHT:
Canaima Lagoon, Canaima National Park
This lagoon is known for its pink beaches, tinted by pink quartz grains. Its many waterfalls range in shade from tea to coffee due to their blackwater rivers.

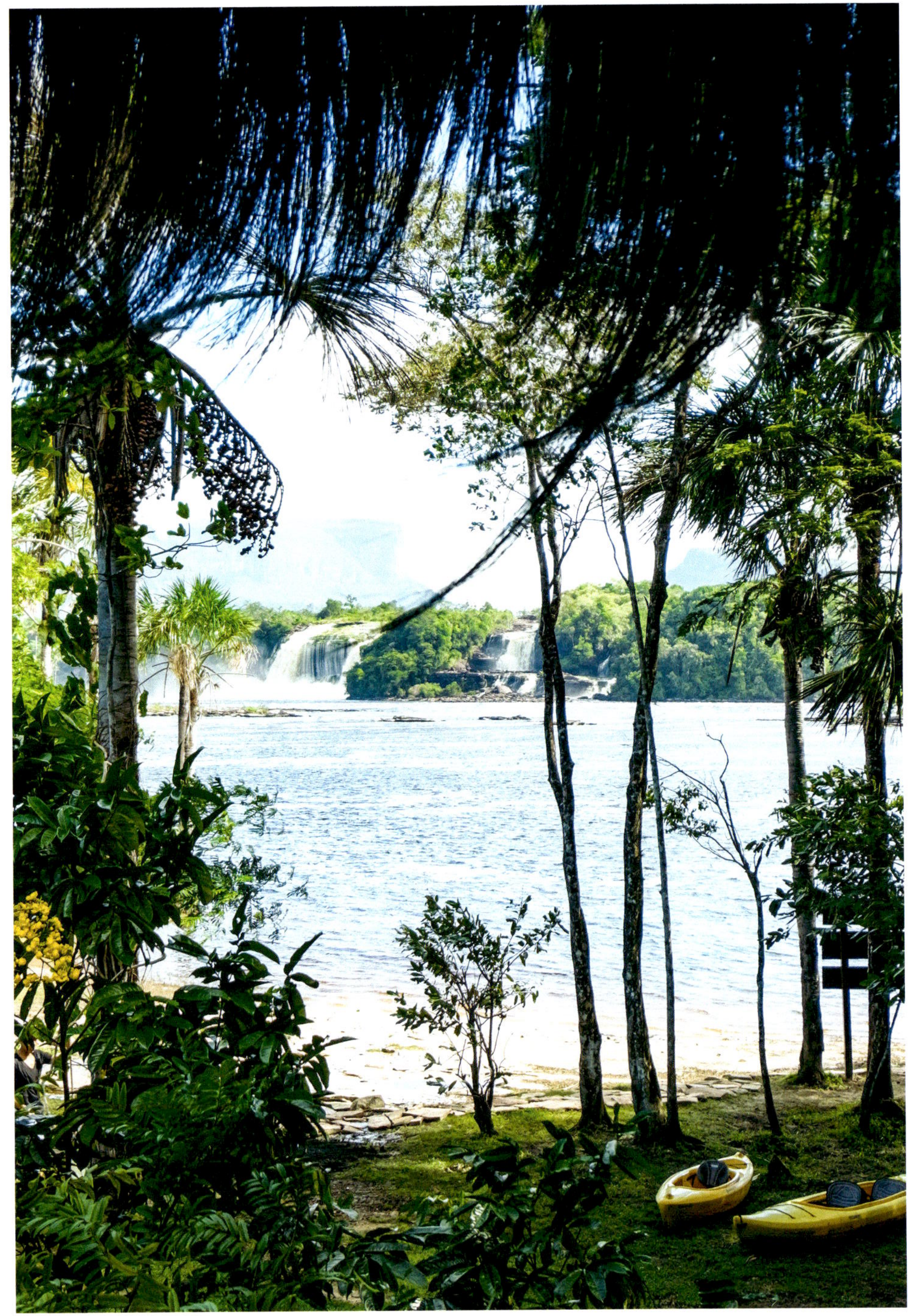

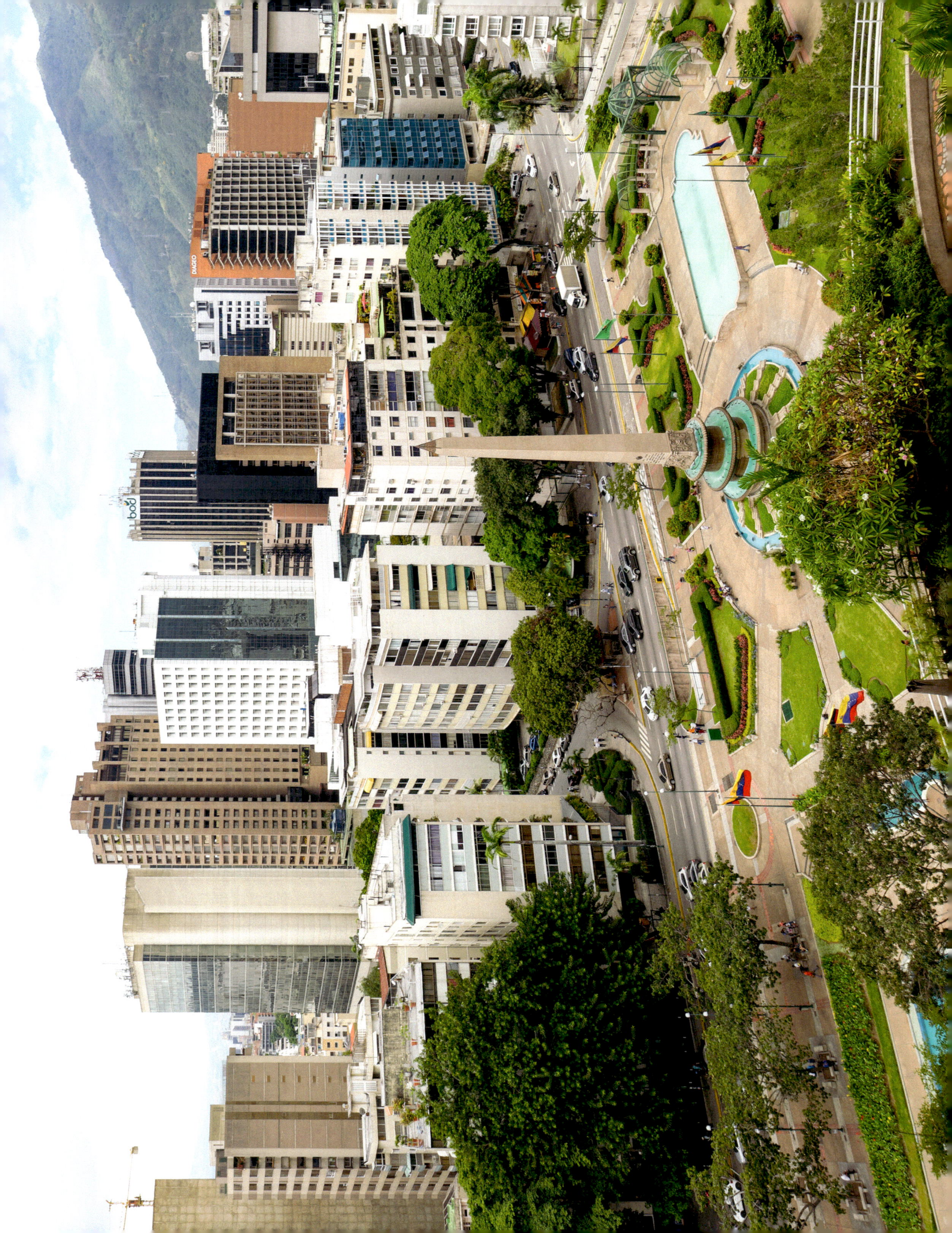
DIAGEO
bod

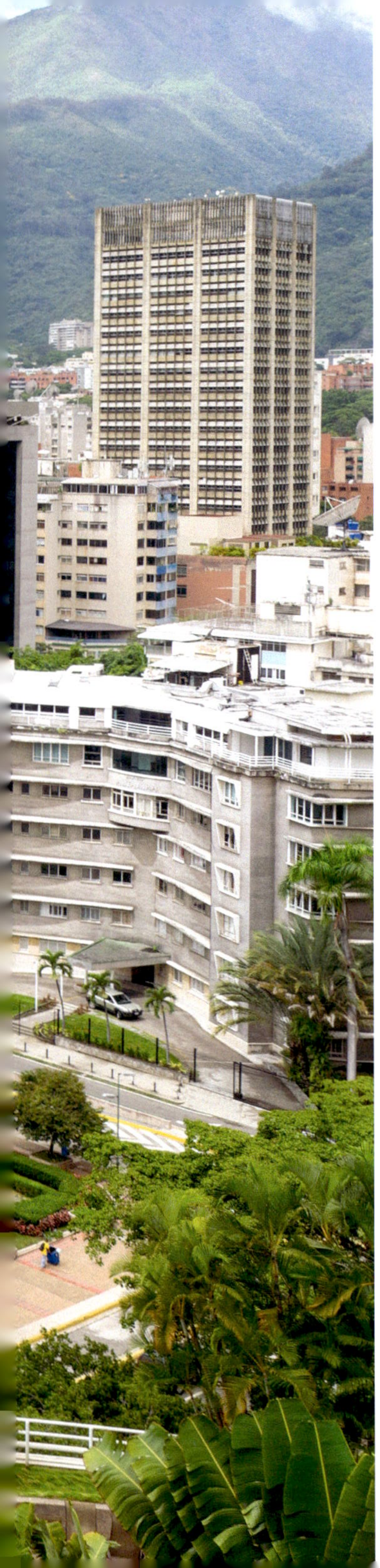

LEFT:
Plaza Francia, Caracas, Venezuela
Originally named Plaza Altamira, this square in the wealthy Altamira neighbourhood was designed in the 1940s. Its name was later changed to 'France Square', at the same time as Paris's Place du Venezuela took its current name, due to an agreement between the two countries.

RIGHT:
National Pantheon of Venezuela, Caracas
Built in 1874, the Pantheon houses the remains of great Venezuelans, including the painter Cristóbal Rojas and poet and politician Andrés Eloy Blanco. Behind the Pantheon is the wave-like façade of the Mausoleum of Simón Bolívar, completed in 2013, which now houses the statesman's remains.

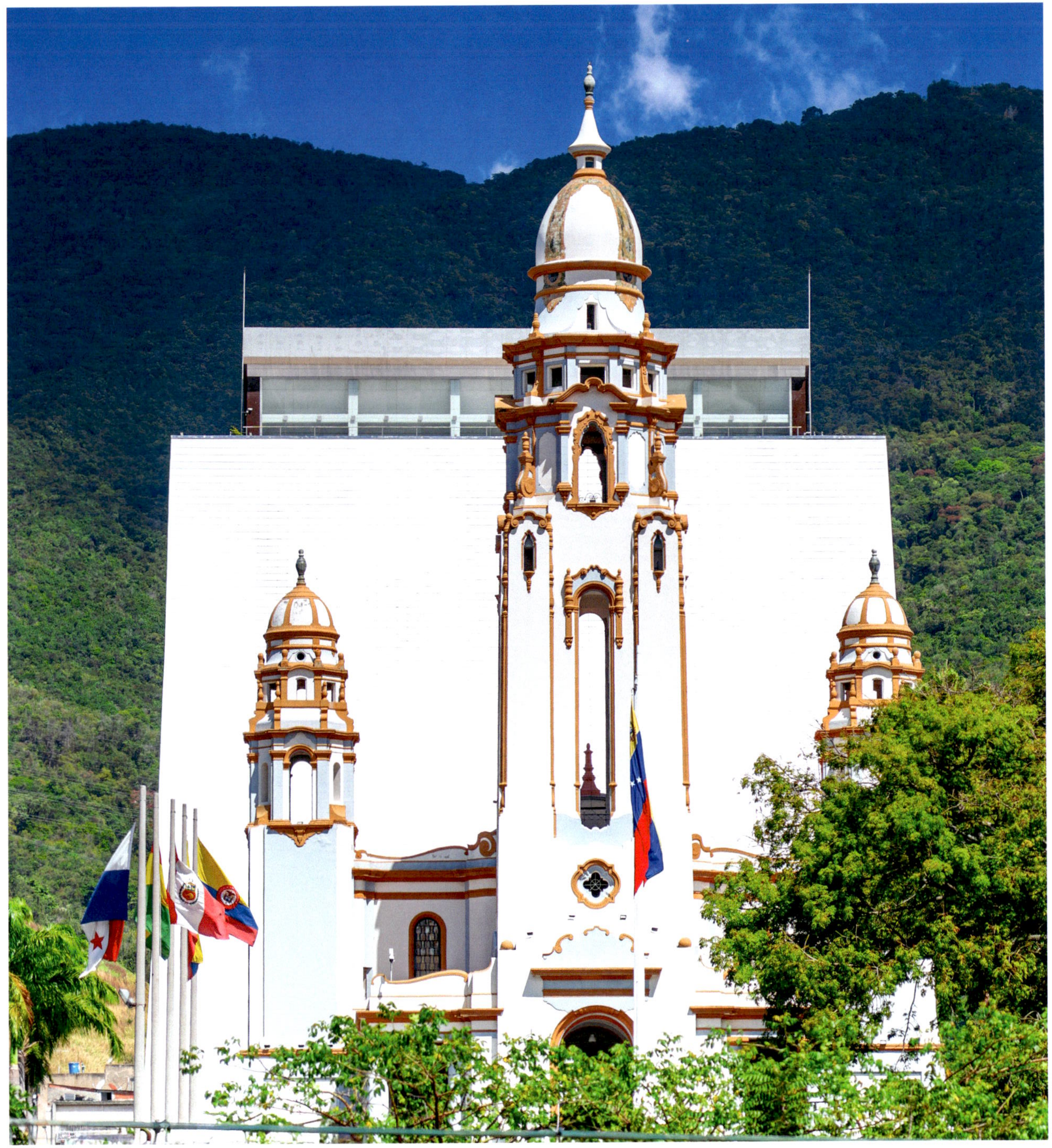

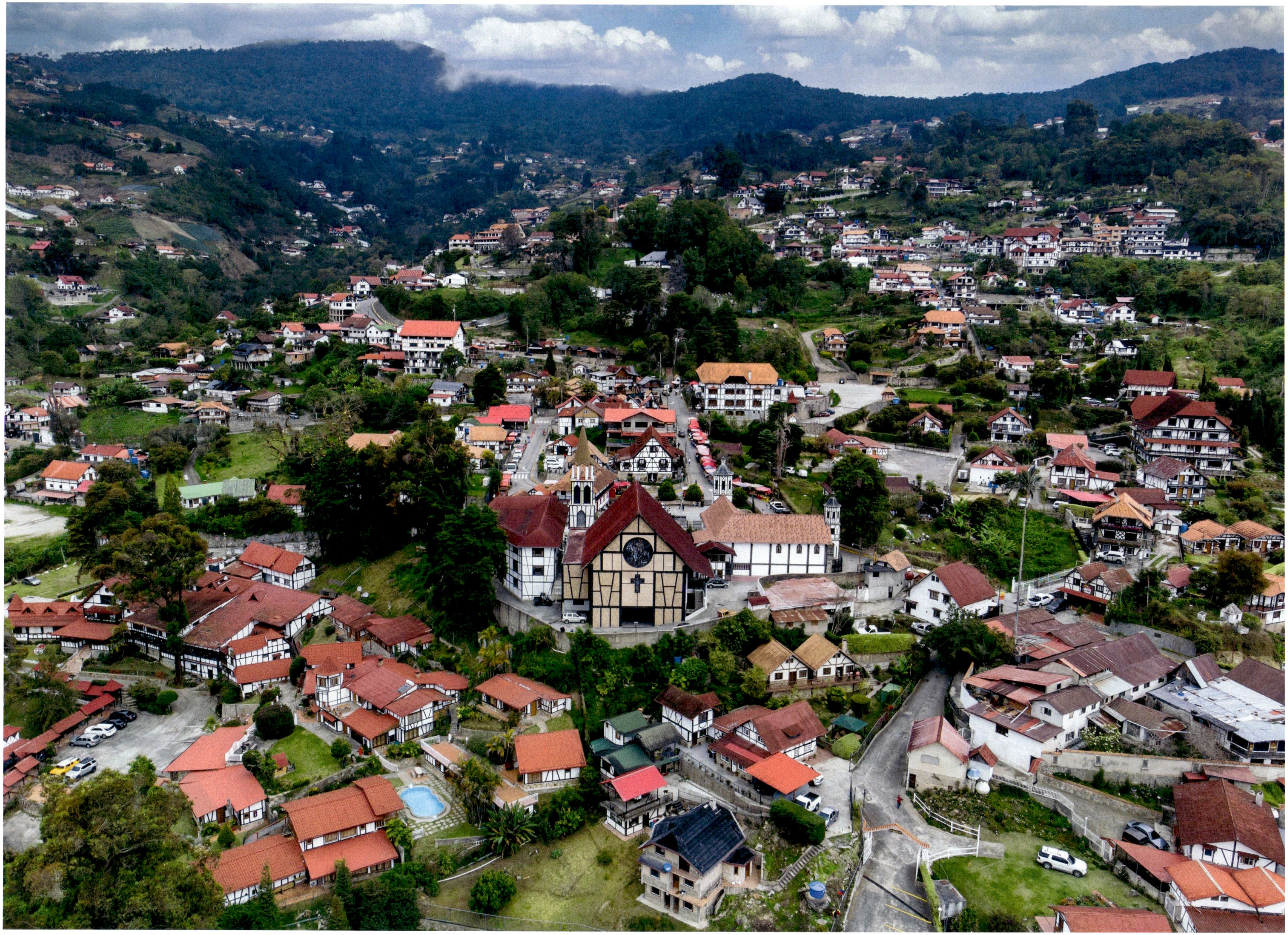

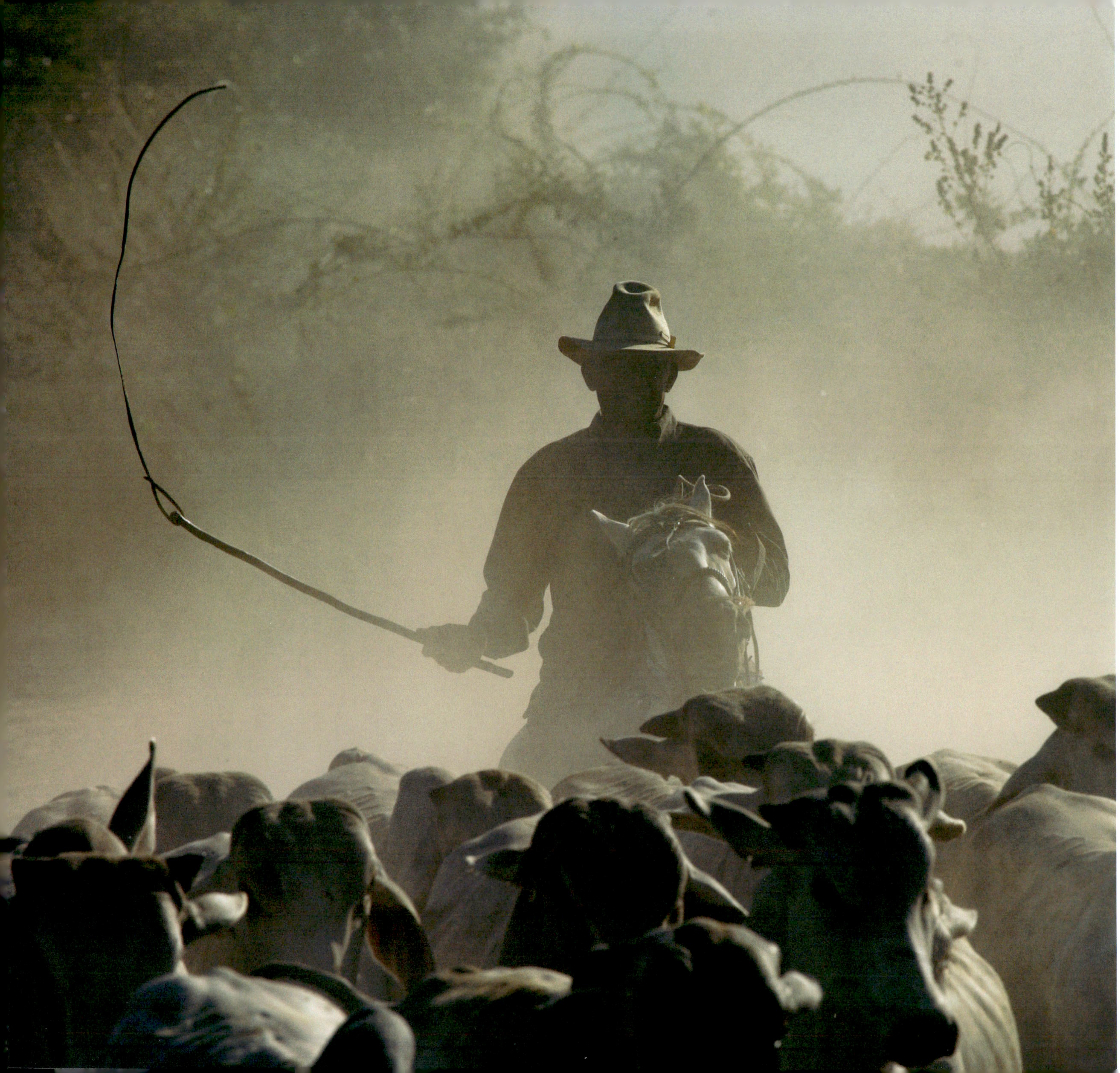

OPPOSITE:
La Colonia Tovar, Venezuela
This mountain town was founded in 1843 by a group of immigrants from the Baden region of Germany. They constructed a settlement of *fachwerk* (half-timbered) houses in the style of their home region. Even today, some inhabitants speak a German dialect, called Alemán Coloniero.

LEFT:
Los Llanos, Venezuela
Stretching across the low plains of Colombia and Venezuela, Los Llanos is a tropical grassland. Since the arrival of the Spanish, the primary industry here has been cattle farming. Traditionally, cowboys called *llaneros* drive the huge herds to higher ground in the wet season and down onto damp areas during the dry season.

RIGHT:
**Brown Pelican,
Los Roques, Venezuela**
In the Caribbean Sea, Los Roques Archipelago consists of more than 300 islands, islets and coral cays. There are few terrestrial animals, but the reef supports 280 species of fish, and the islands are visited by birds such as brown pelicans, red-footed boobies and American flamingos.

FAR RIGHT:
**Cayo de Agua,
Los Roques, Venezuela**
At low tide, a sandbar connects two islets of Cayo de Agua. In the surrounding turquoise shallows, snorkellers can swim alongside French angelfish, foureye butterflyfish and green sea turtles.

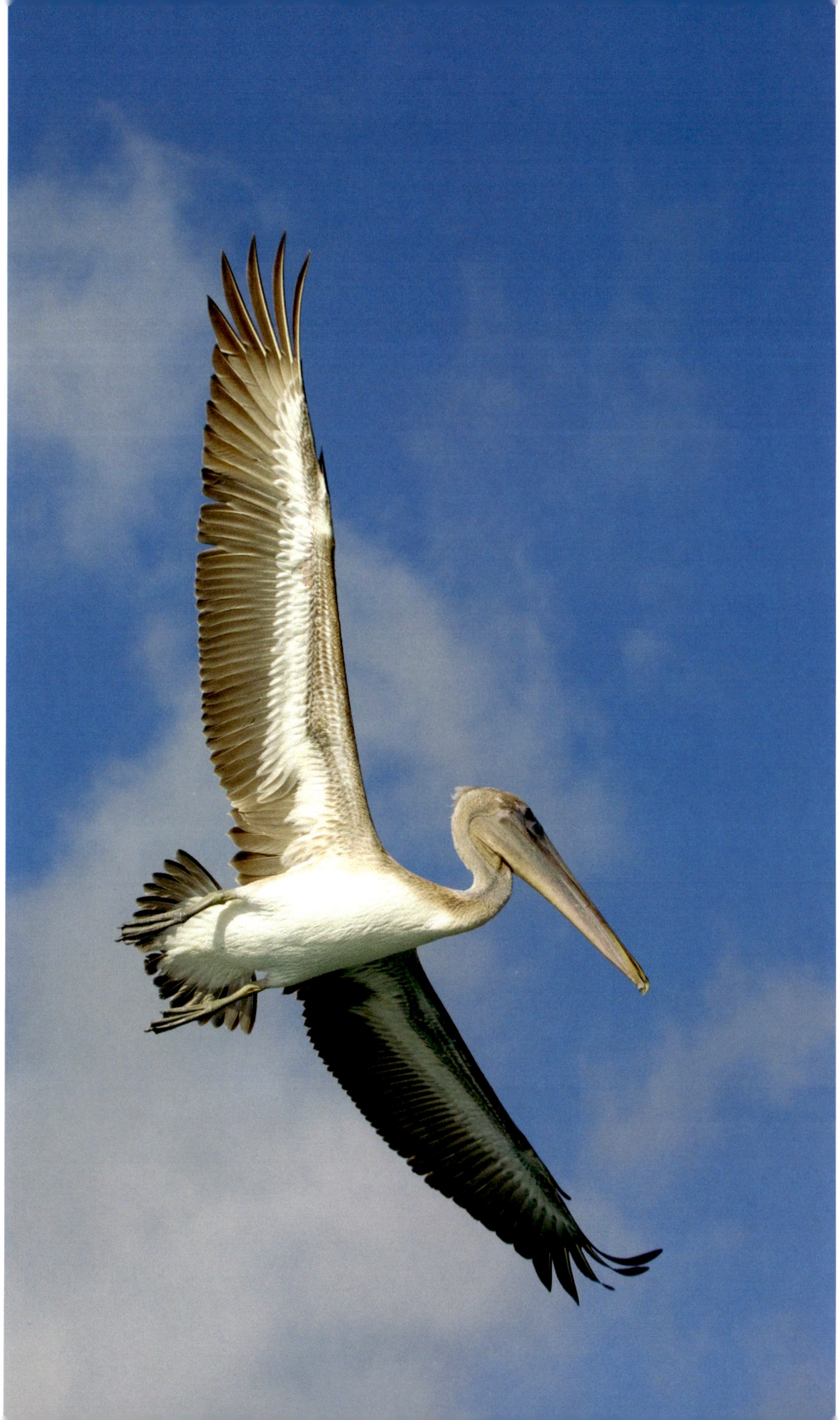

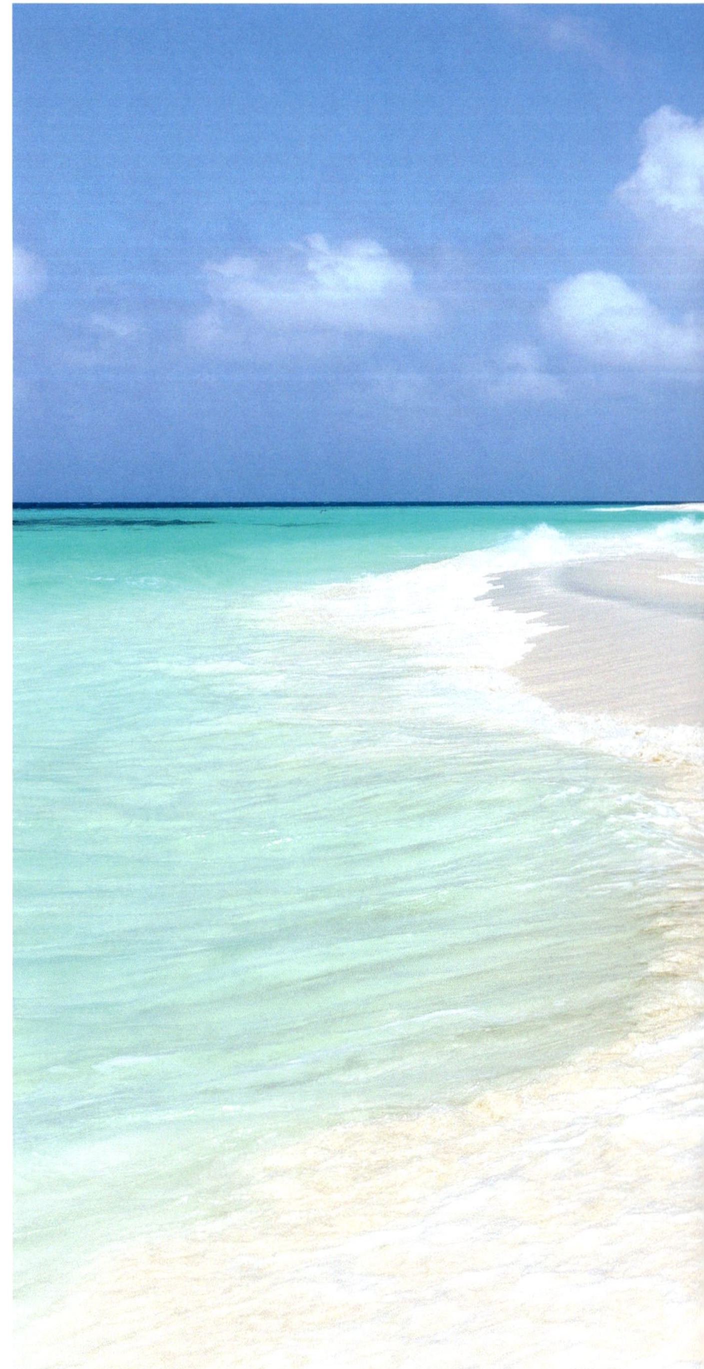

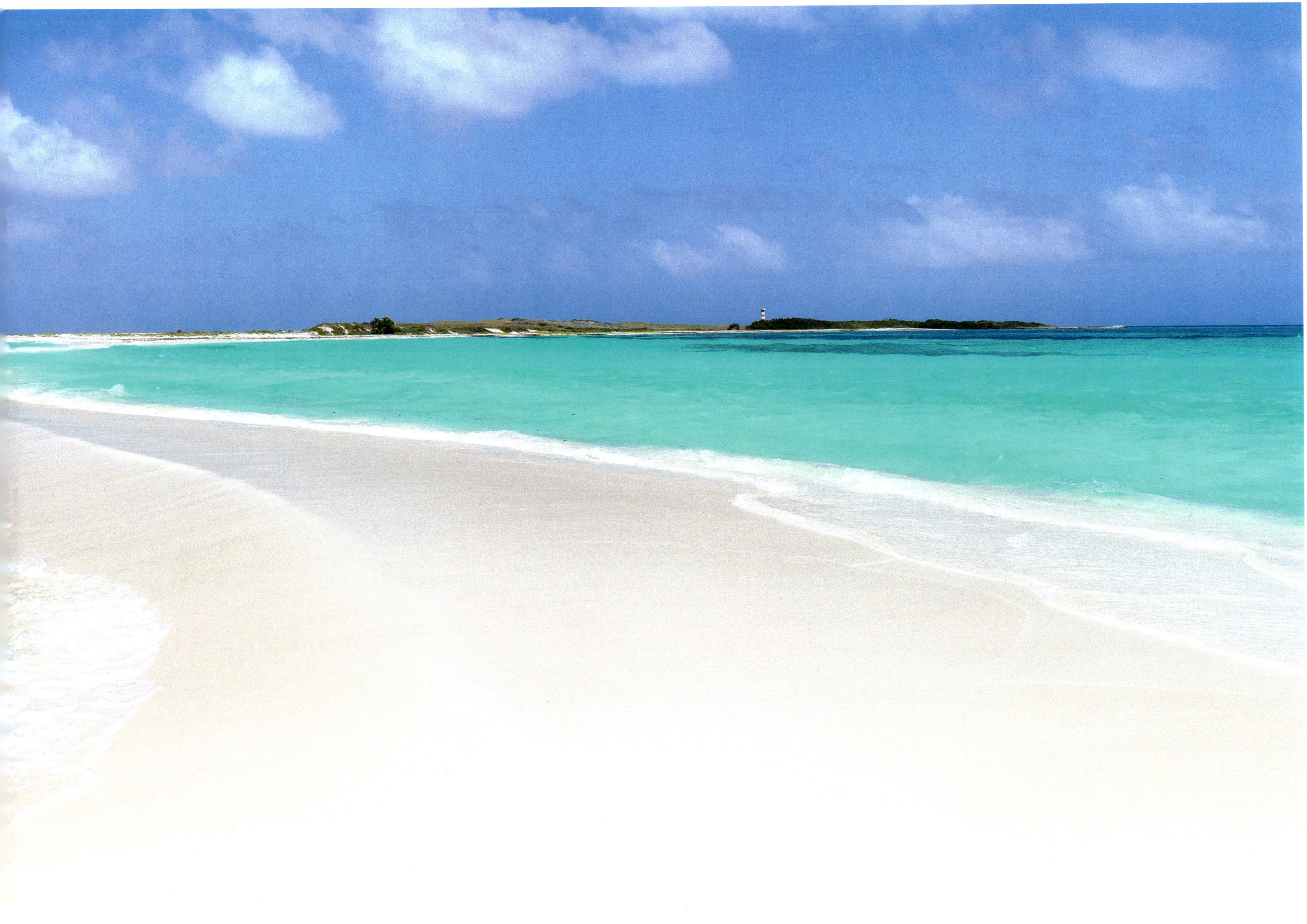

RIGHT:

Playa Pedro Gonzalez, Isla Margarita, Venezuela

Venezuela's largest island, Margarita lies 40km (25 miles) north of the mainland. It attracts tourists with its 70 beautiful beaches and duty-free shoping, but is sadly a hub for drug trafficking.

OPPOSITE LEFT:

Faro de Punta Zaragoza, Isla Margarita, Venezuela

This iconic lighthouse overlooks the beach of Puerto Cruz, which is popular with nature-lovers and families due to its less-crowded white sand, calm waters and mountainous backdrop.

OPPOSITE TOP RIGHT:

Hoatzin, Mariusa National Park, Venezuela

Found in swamps, mangroves and riparian forests of the Orinoco and Amazon basins, this leaf-eating bird is known for its manure-like odour. This smell is caused by the bacterial fermentation of leaves in the bird's large crop.

OPPOSITE BOTTOM RIGHT:

***Palafitos*, Orinoco River, Venezuela**

Stilt houses known as *palafitos* are traditionally built by the Warao (meaning 'people of the canoe') of the Orinoco Delta. The homes have roofs made of palm leaves and are open-sided, providing ventilation and proximity to the water.

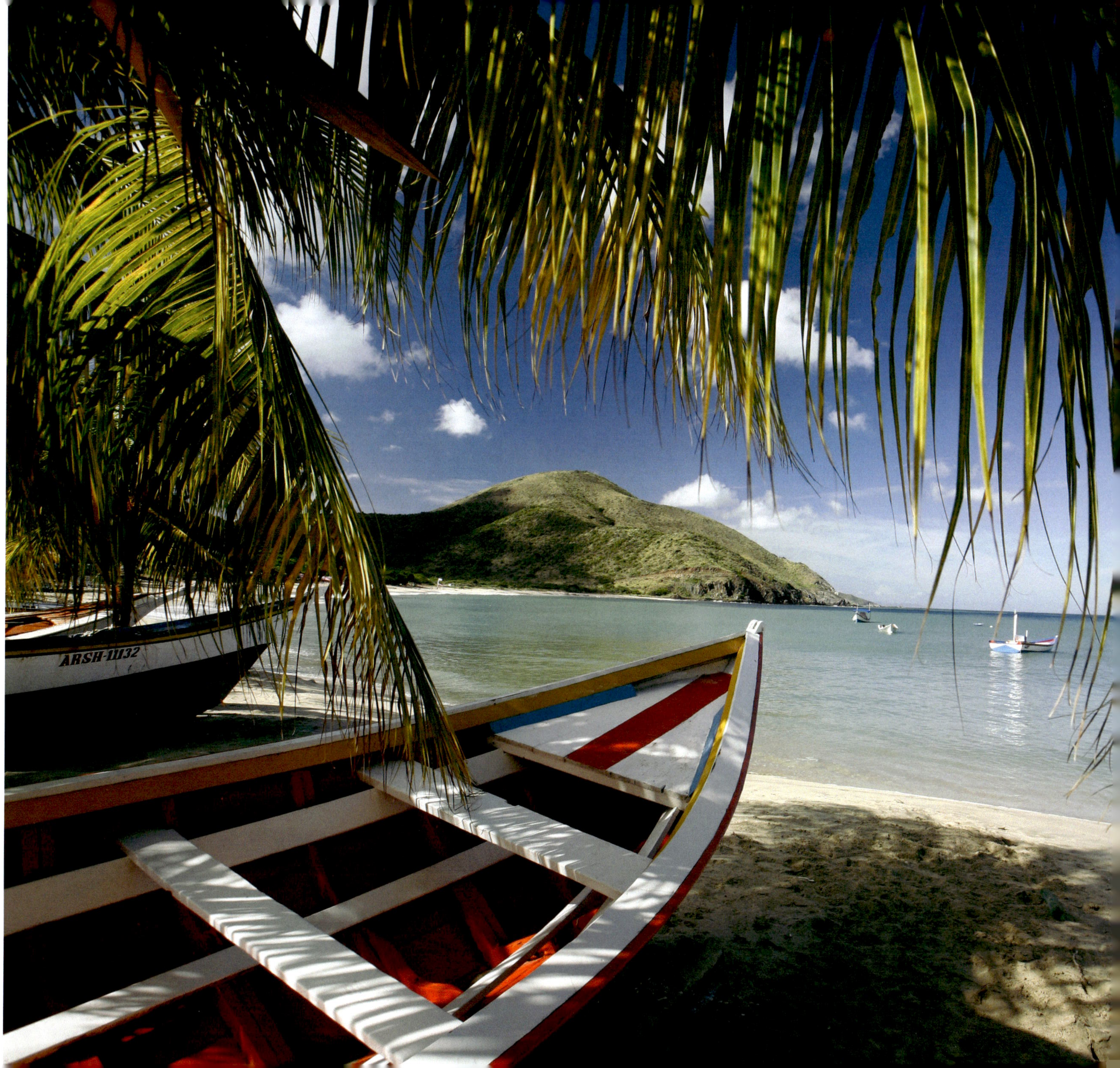

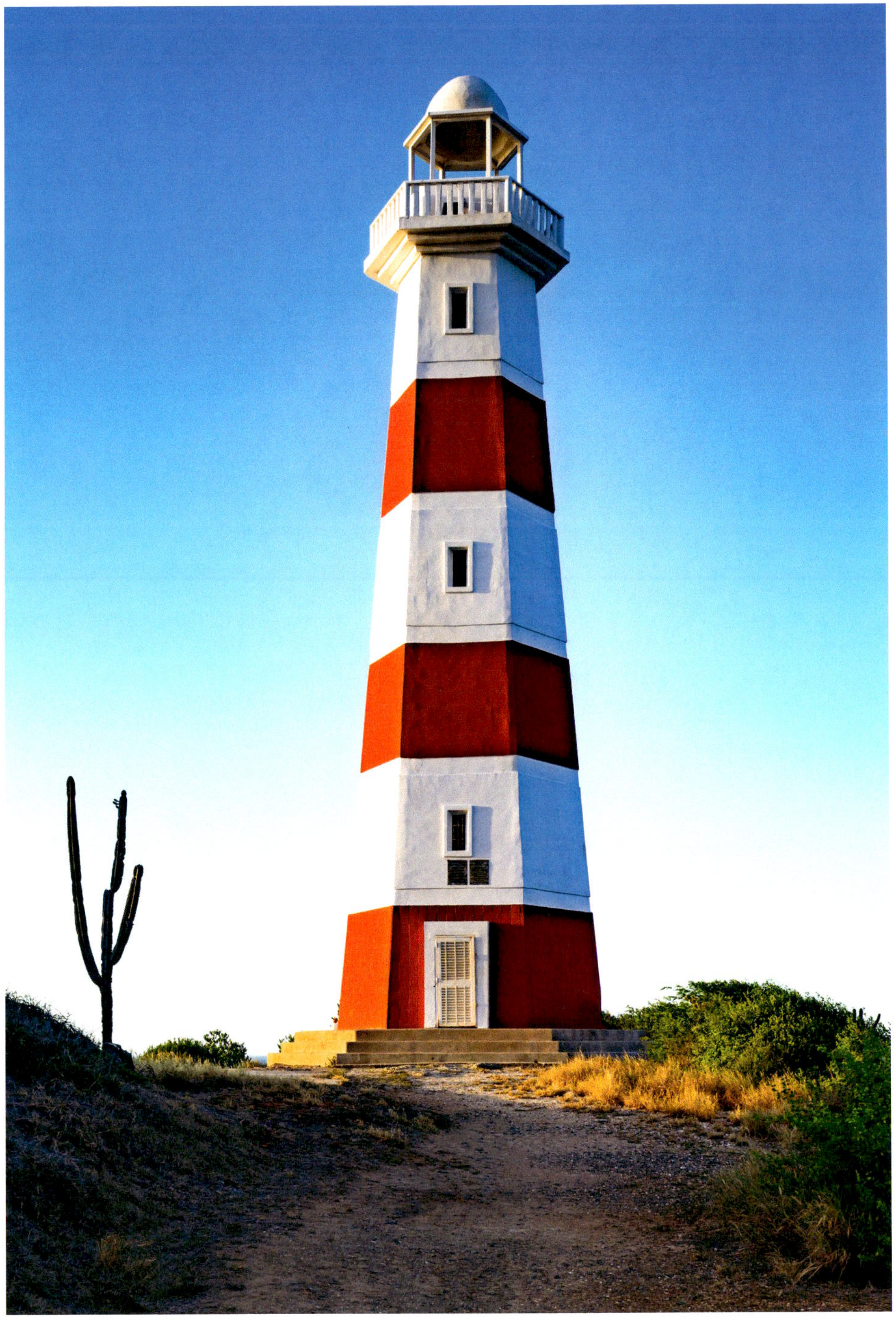
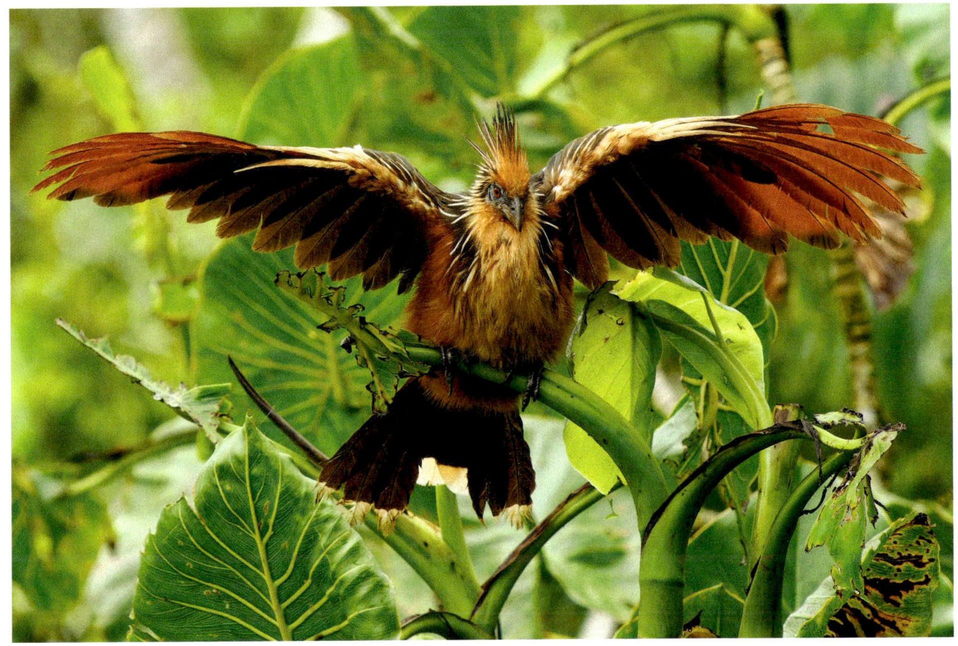
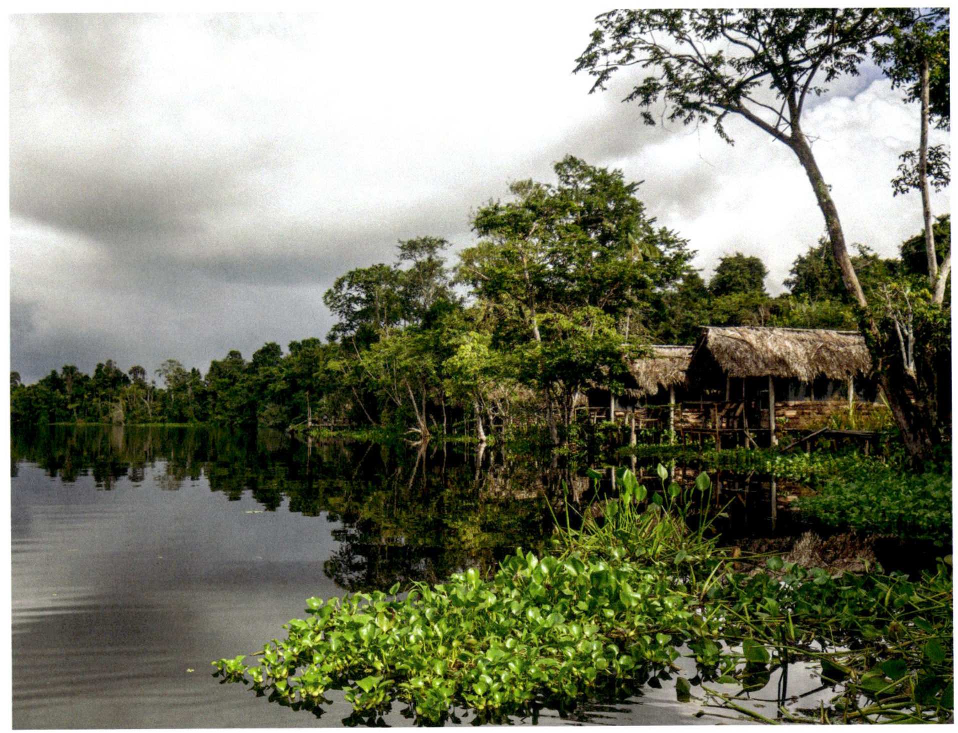

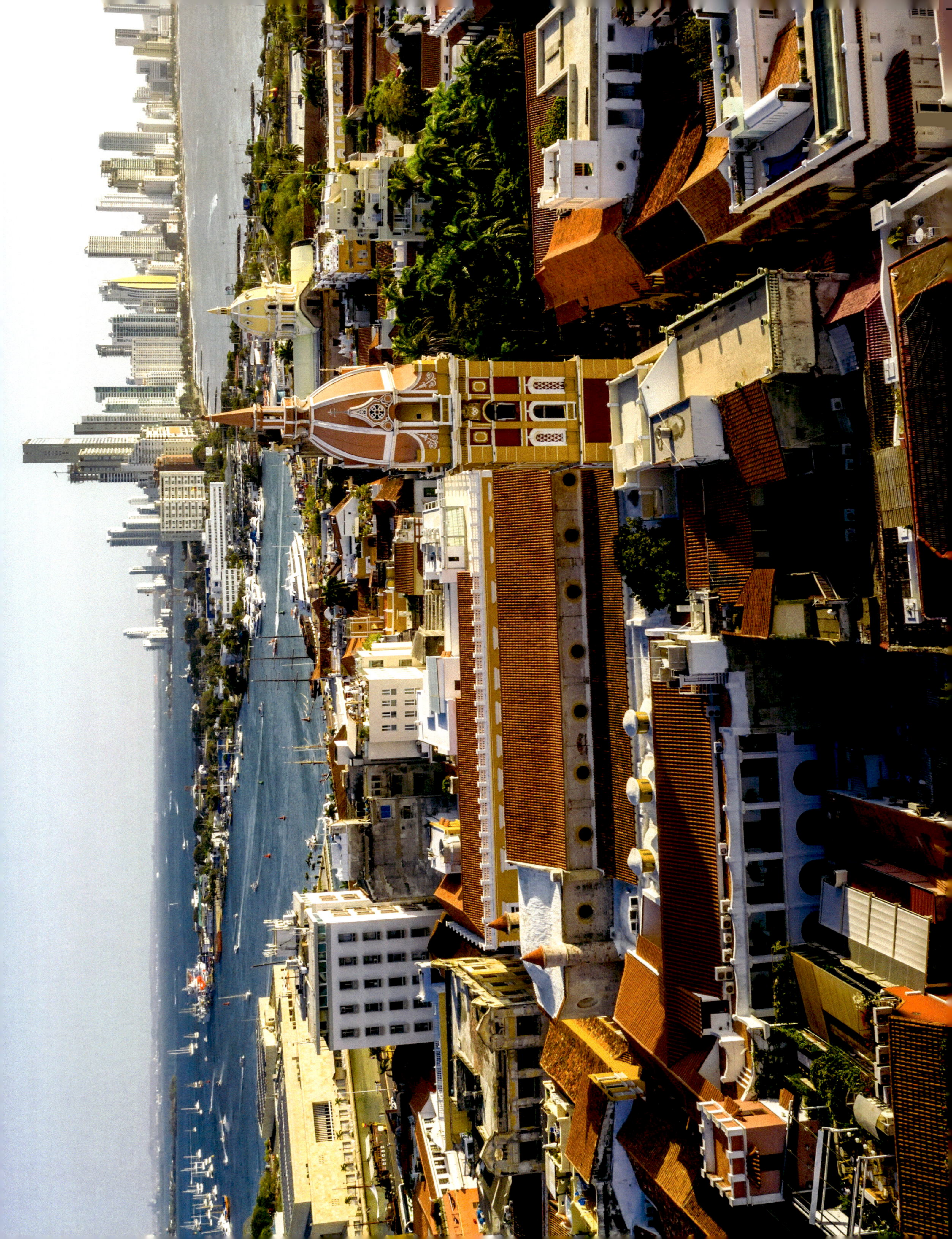

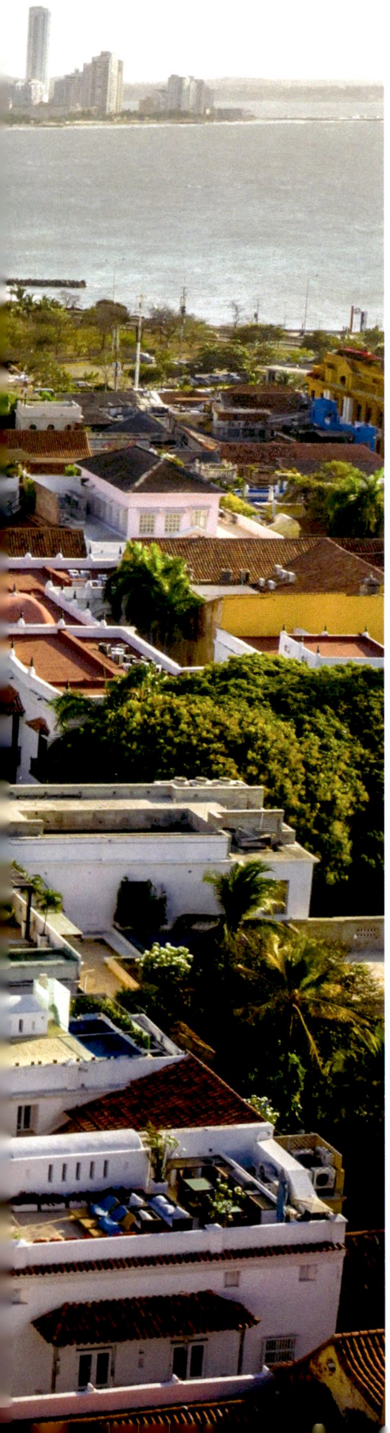

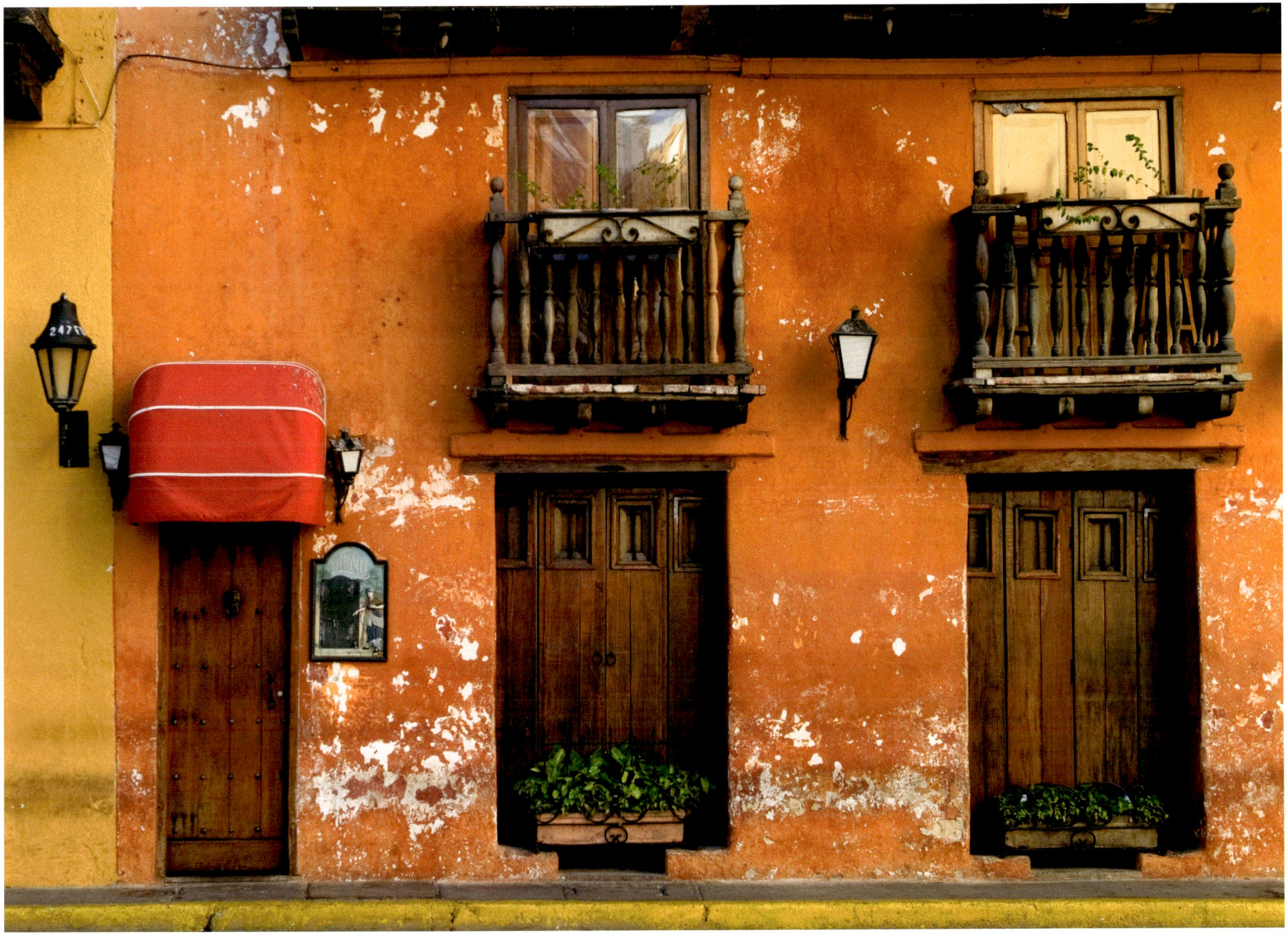

LEFT:

Cathedral of Cartagena de Indias, Cartagena, Colombia

At the heart of Cartagena's walled city, this saffron-coloured cathedral was built between 1577 and 1612. In 1586, the English pirate Francis Drake attacked the city, reducing parts of the growing cathedral to rubble. Eventually, the Cartagenians paid off Drake with the huge sum of 110,000 silver ducats.

ABOVE:

Ciudad Amurallada, Cartagena, Colombia

Founded in 1533 by Spanish conquistadors, Cartagena's walled city is a UNESCO World Heritage Site. The city was named after Spain's Cartagena, which was named after Tunisia's Carthage by Carthaginian leader Hasdrubal. The colourful colonial buildings are still protected by coral stone ramparts.

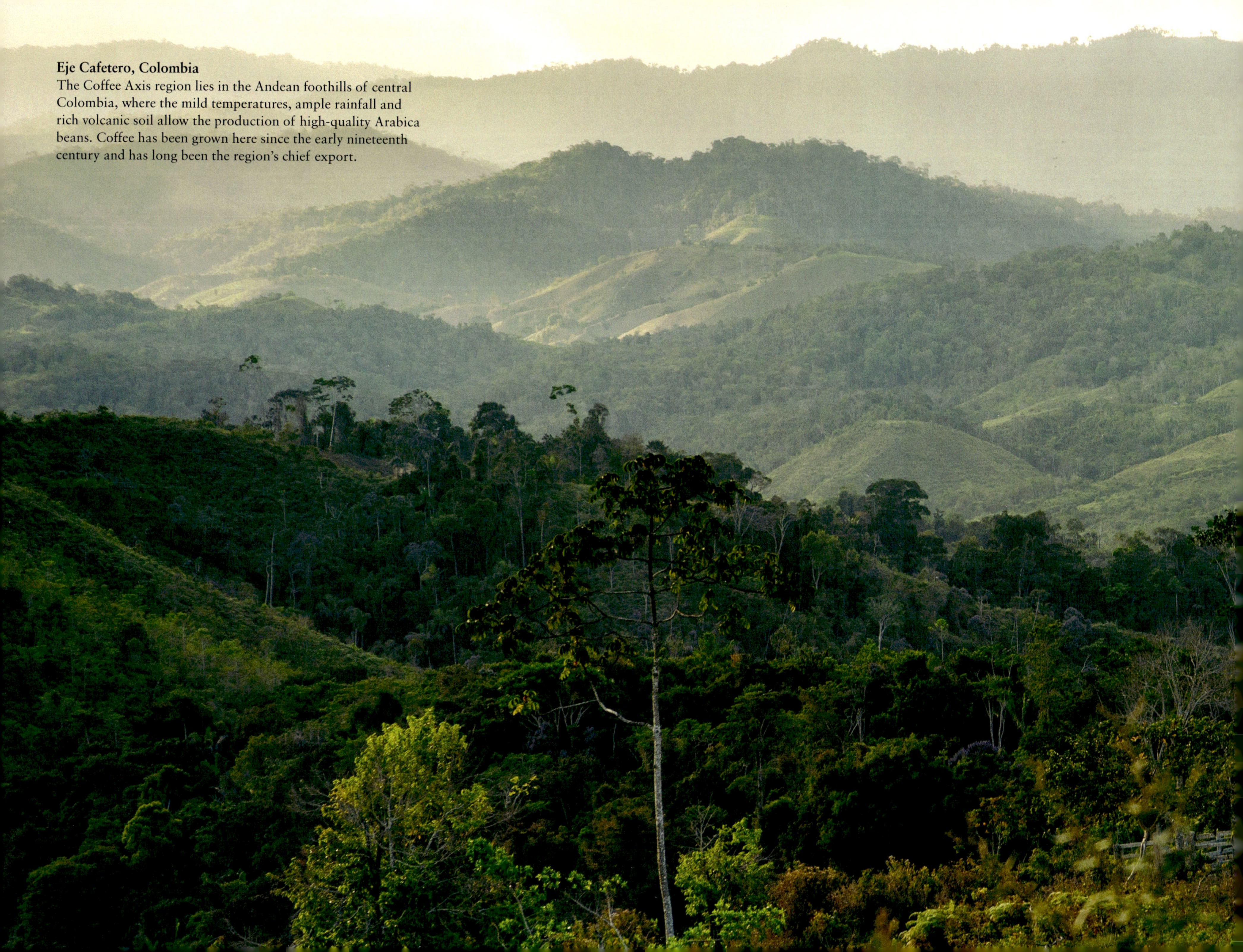

Eje Cafetero, Colombia
The Coffee Axis region lies in the Andean foothills of central Colombia, where the mild temperatures, ample rainfall and rich volcanic soil allow the production of high-quality Arabica beans. Coffee has been grown here since the early nineteenth century and has long been the region's chief export.

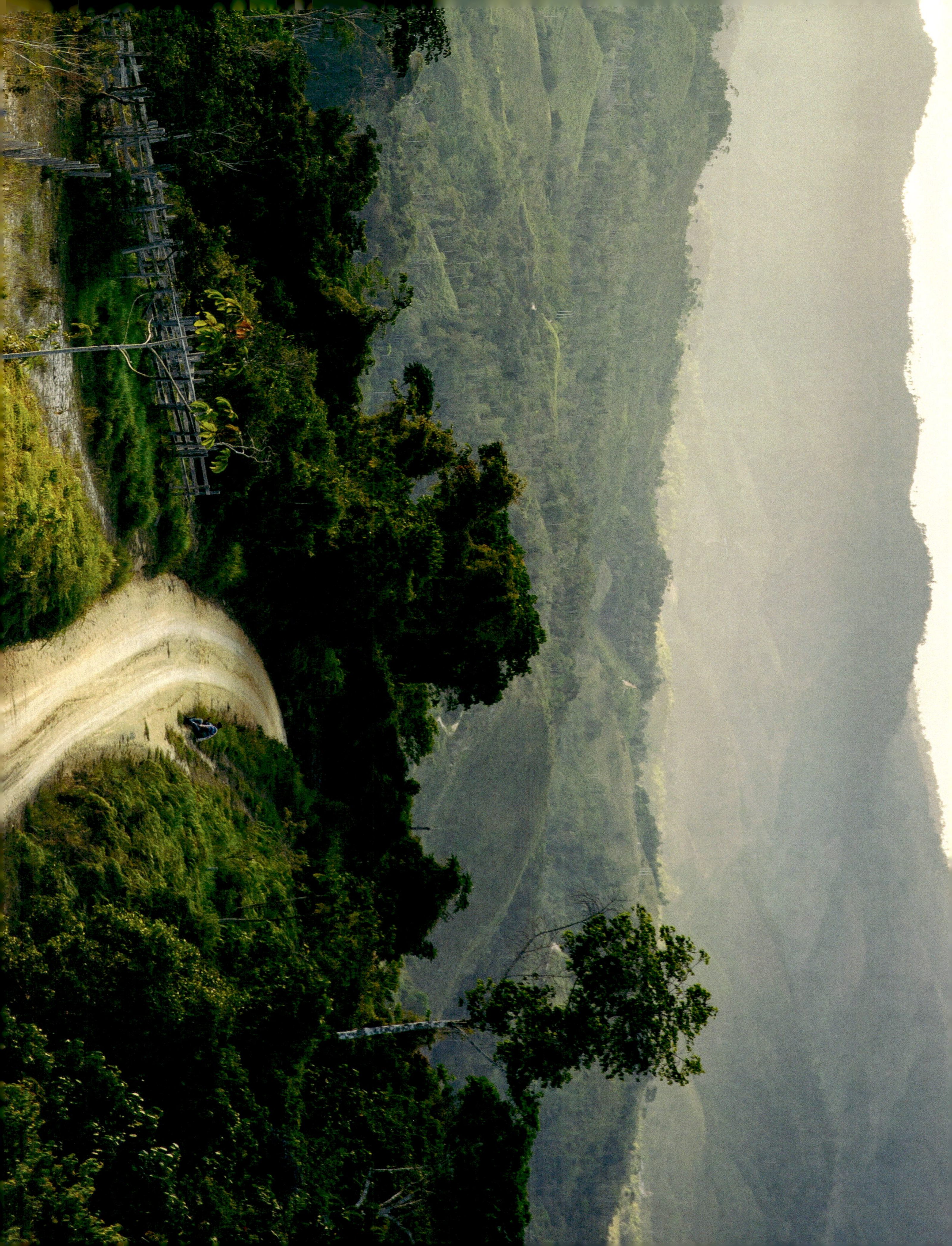

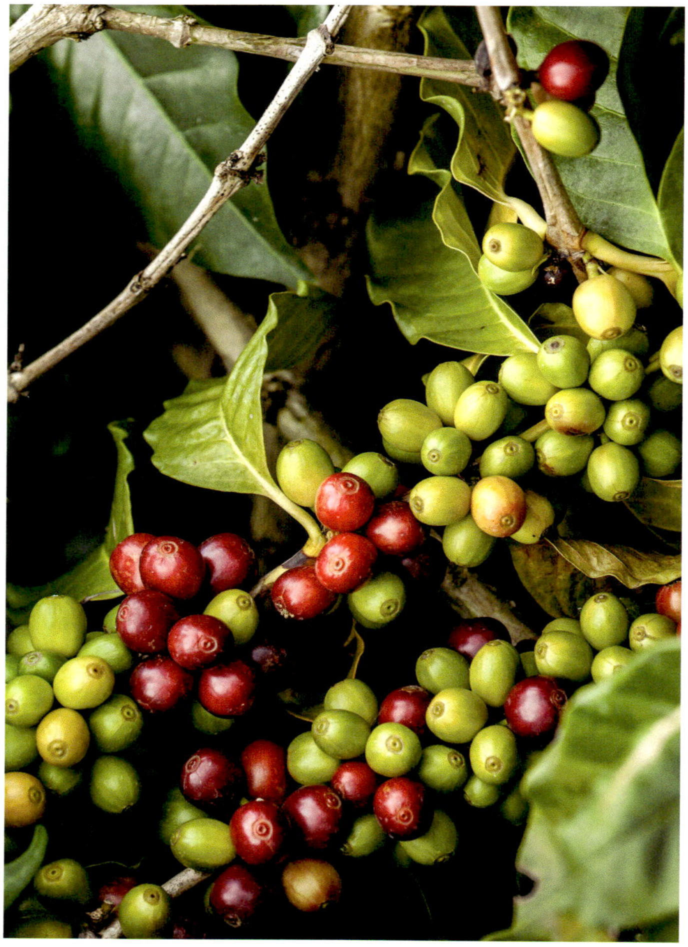

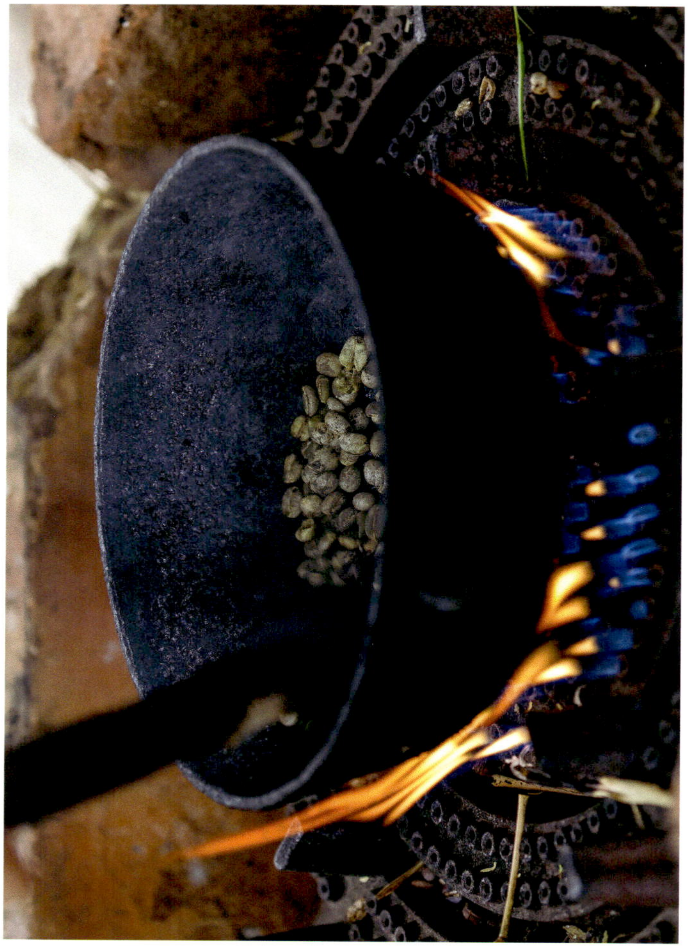

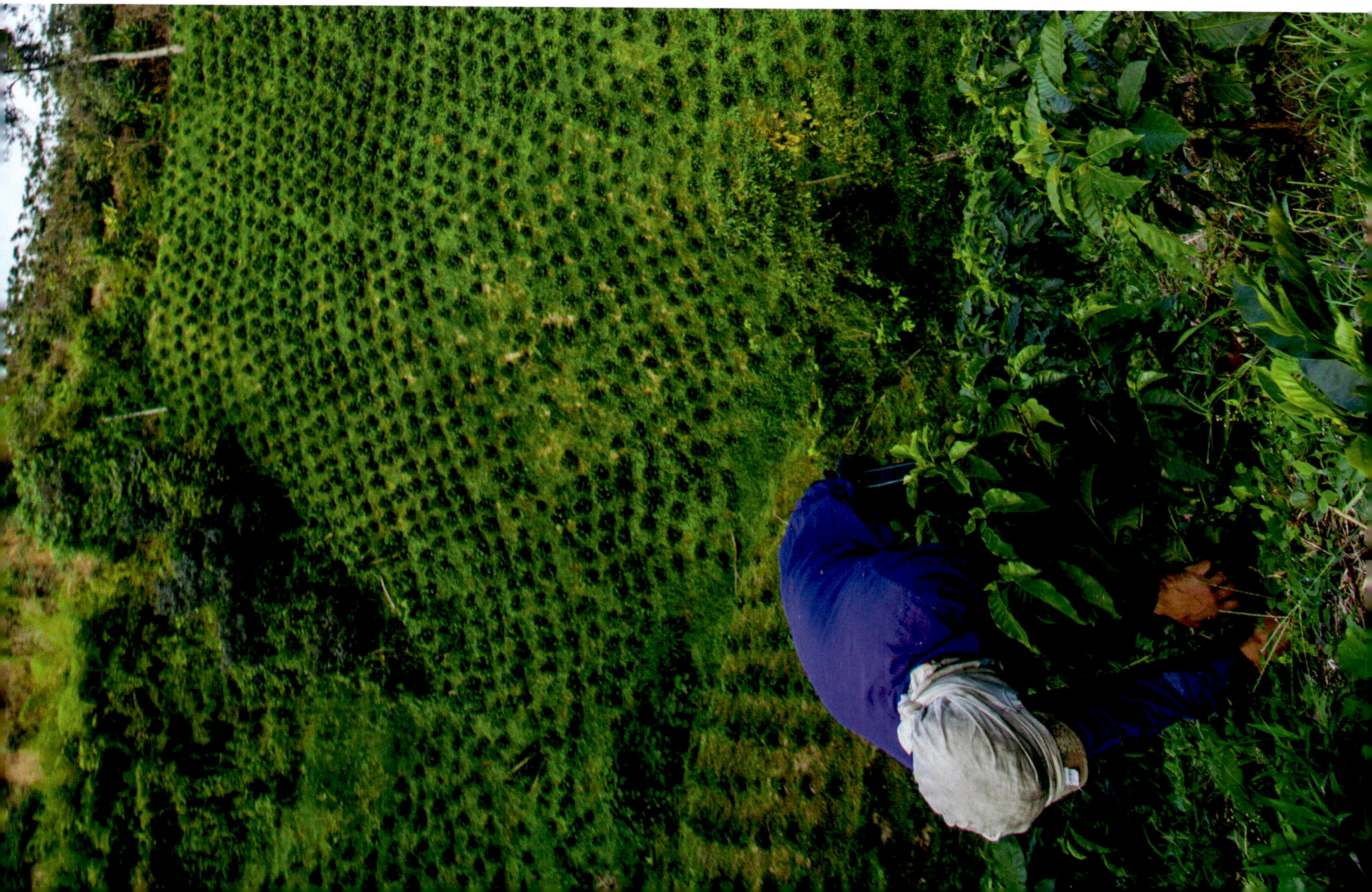

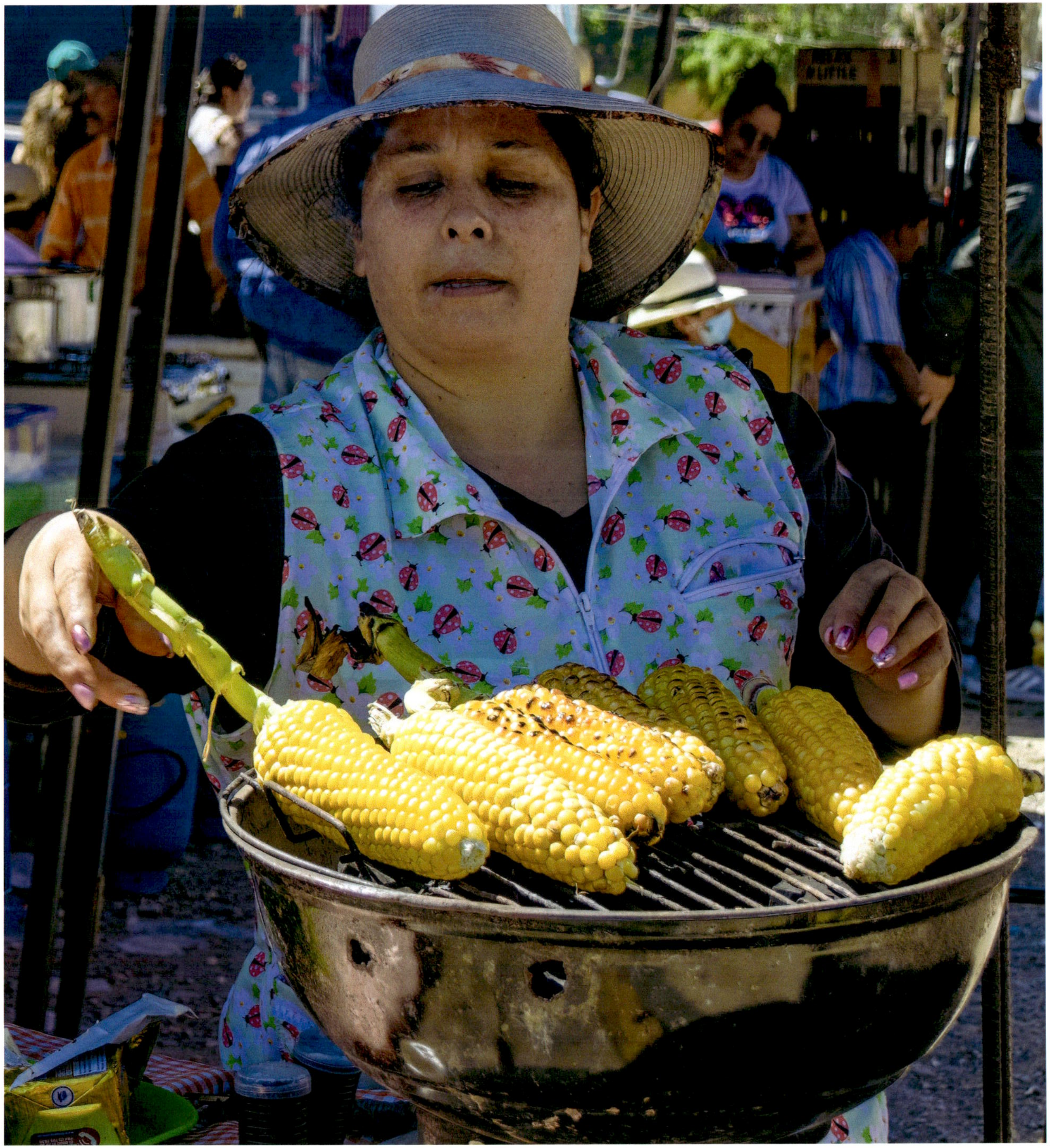

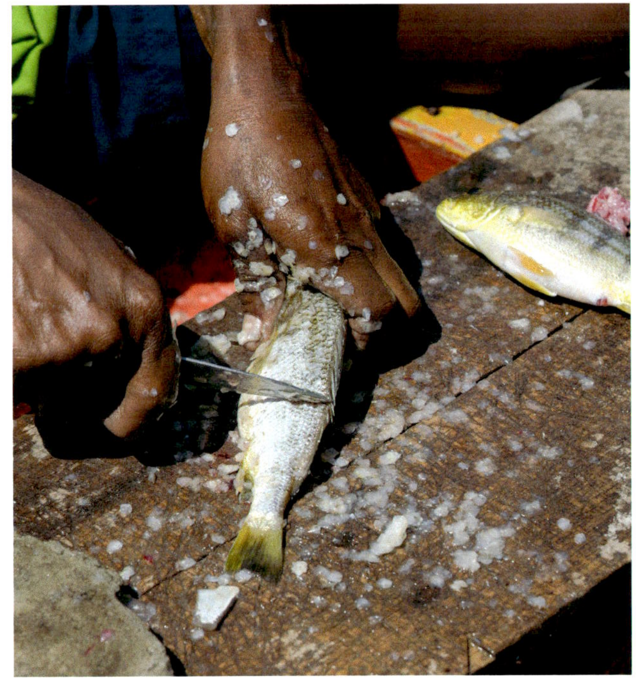

OPPOSITE ALL PHOTOGRAPHS:
Arabica Coffee, Eje Cafetero, Colombia
Coffea arabica plants are harvested by hand to ensure that only ripe, red cherries are chosen. These fruits typically contain two seeds, commonly called coffee beans. The cherry pulp is removed, then the beans are fermented, washed and dried. Finally, they are roasted to develop their flavour and aroma.

LEFT AND ABOVE:
Villa de Leyva, Boyacá, Colombia
On Saturdays, this town's Plaza de Mercado is taken over by a market where stallholders sell snacks, fresh produce and clothes. A stroll away is Plaza Mayor, said to be the largest cobblestone square in South America and an ideal spot to enjoy local wines, their grapes grown on the surrounding slopes.

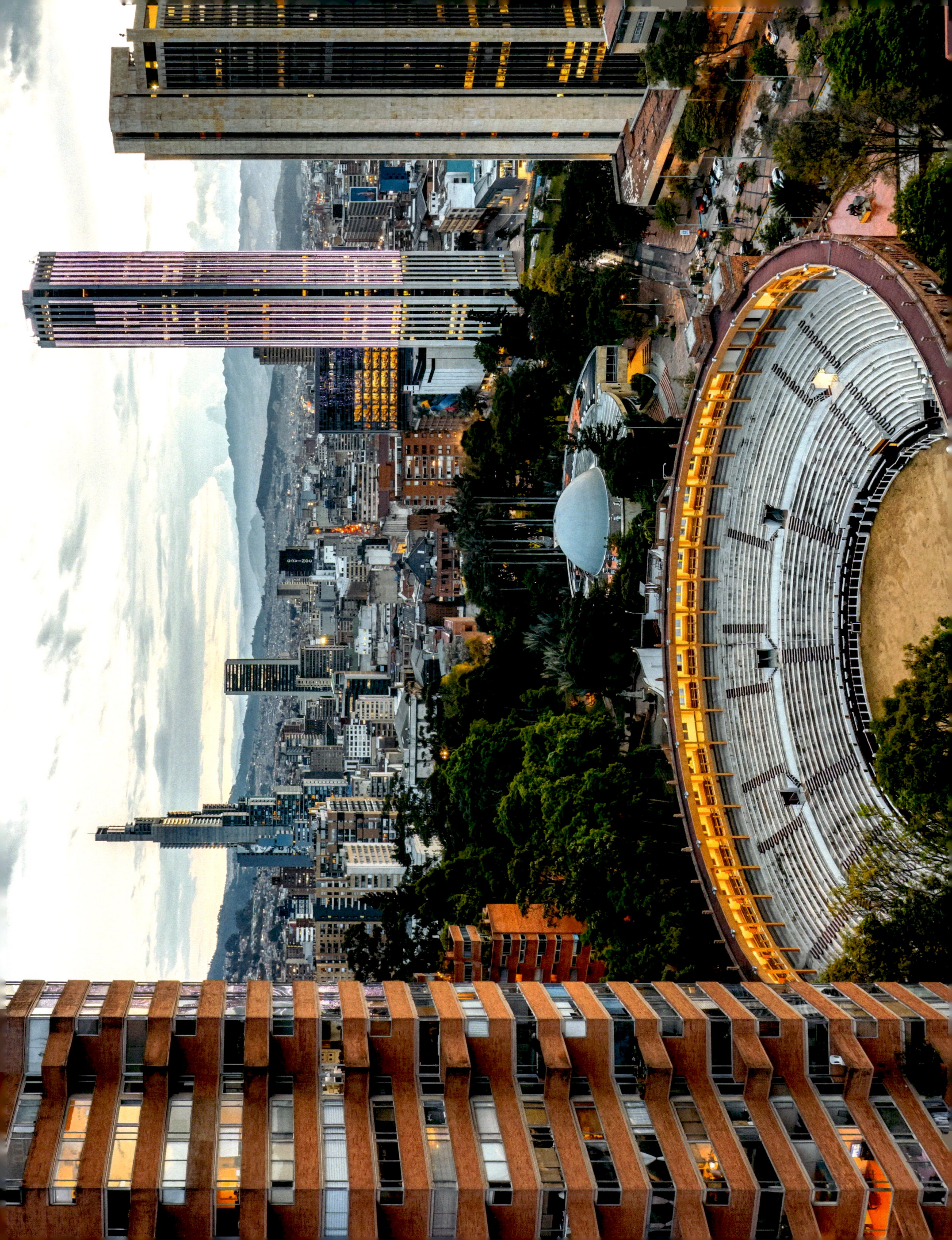

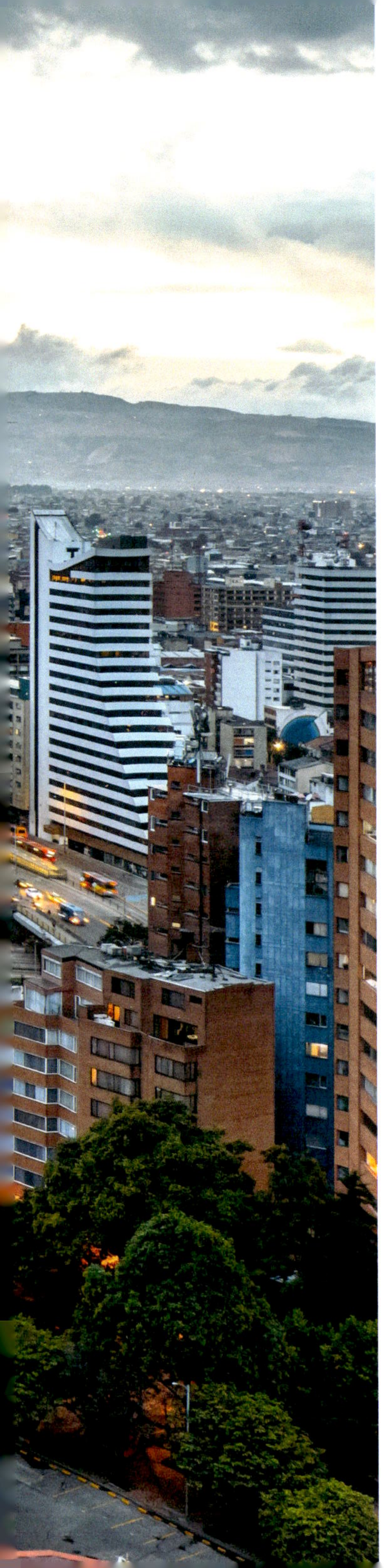

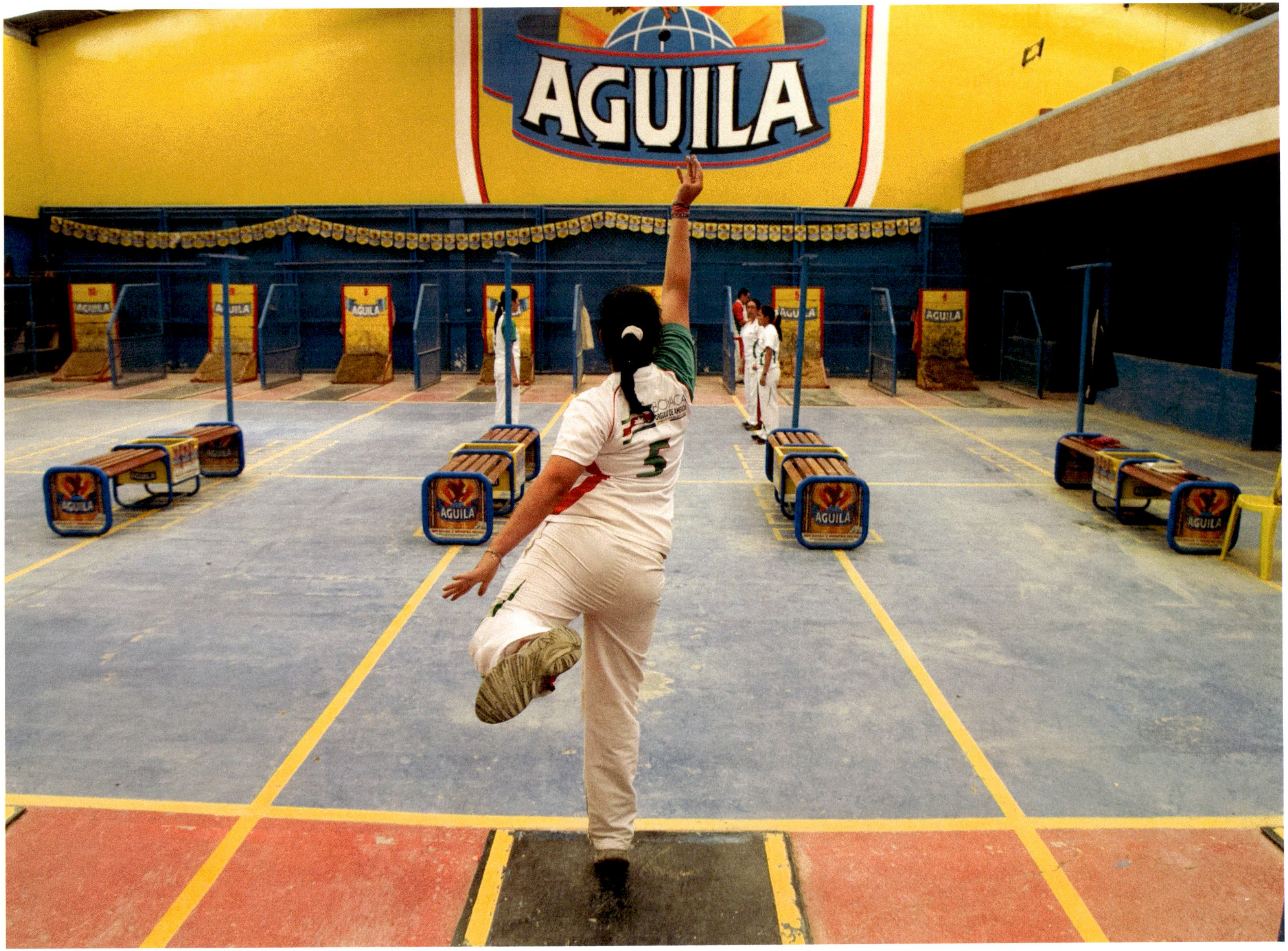

LEFT:
Santamaría Bullring, Bogotá, Colombia
Colombia's capital and largest city, Bogotá is home to 8 million people, making it South America's third largest city, after Brazil's São Paulo and Peru's Lima. The city was founded by Spanish conquistador Gonzalo Jiménez de Quesada in 1538, after his forces had conquered the Muisca people.

ABOVE:
Playing *Tejo*, Bogotá
This pre-Columbian sport is played across Colombia in cantinas and specialized clubs. It involves throwing a metal disc at a clay-covered board, which sits at a 45-degree angle. If the disc hits the board's target, called a *mecha*, correctly, a small gunpowder-fuelled explosion is set off.

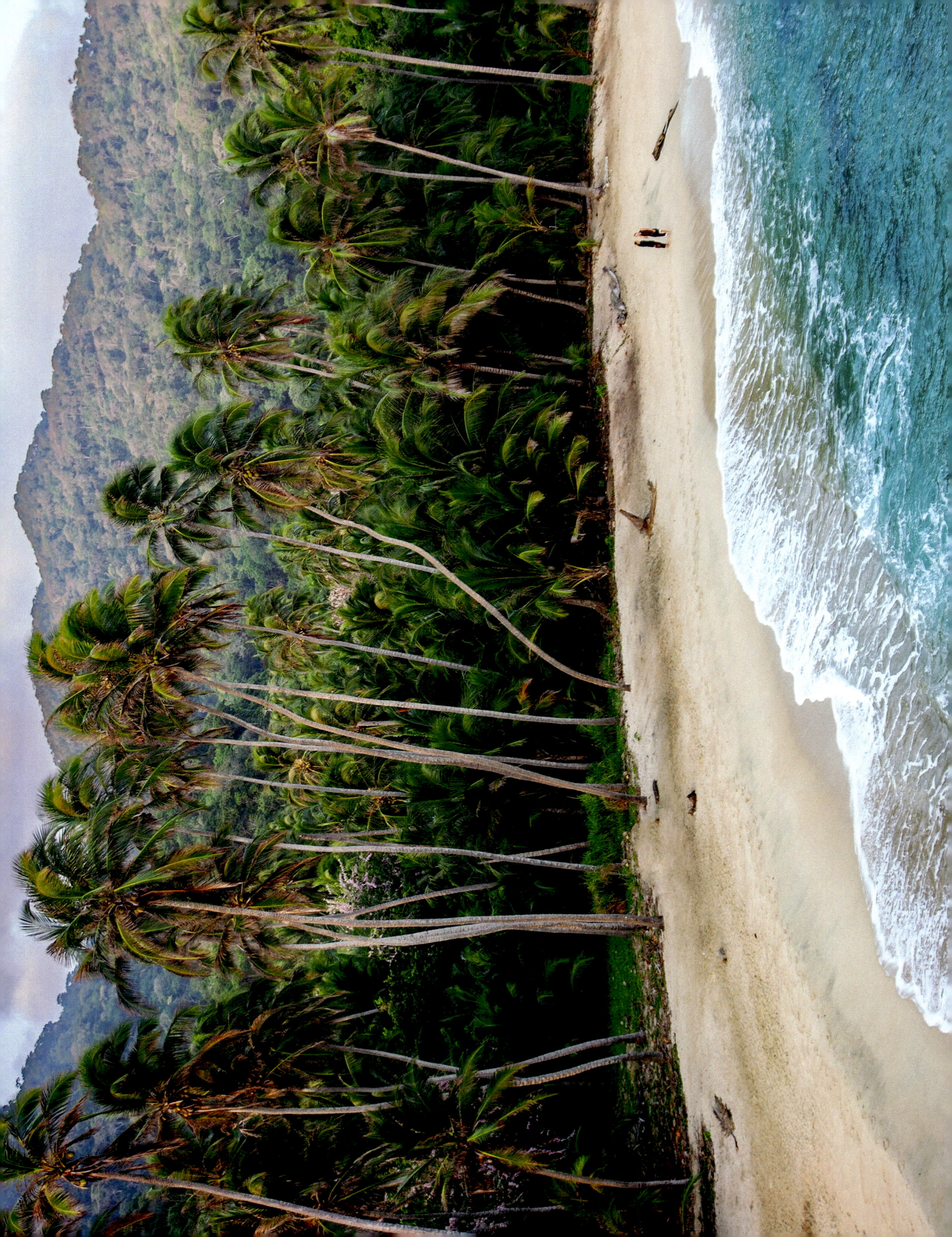

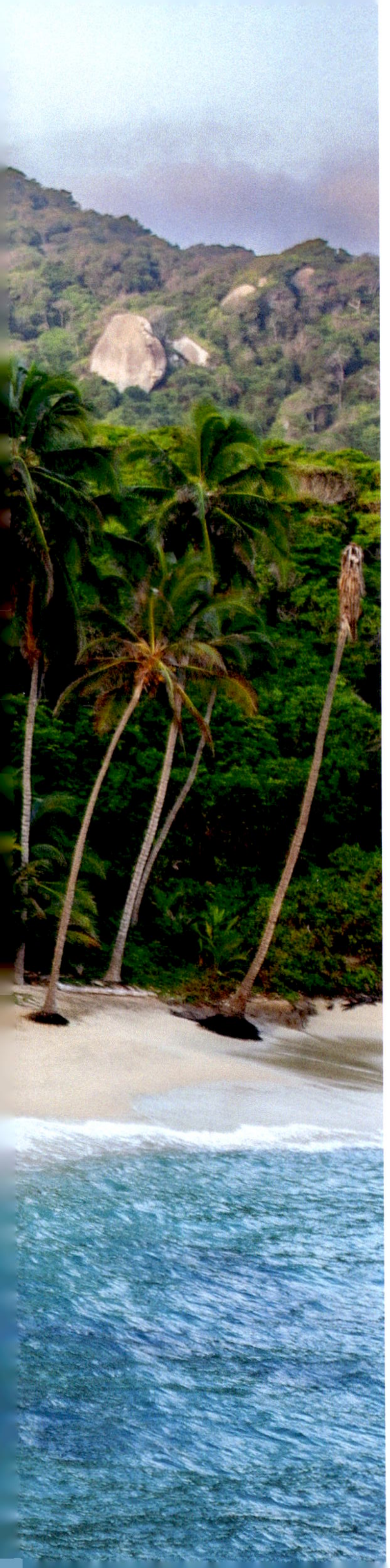

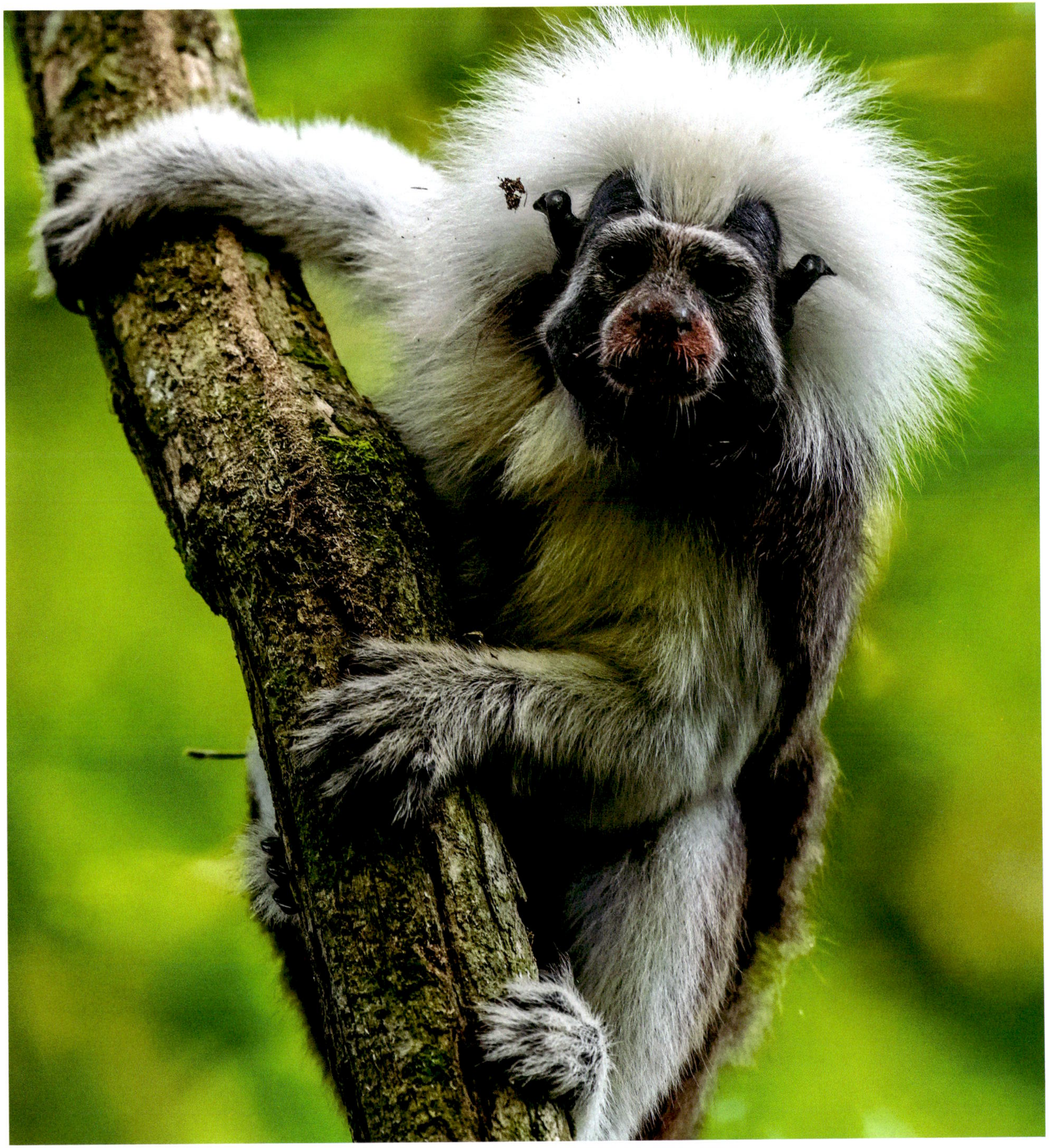

FAR LEFT:

Tayrona National Natural Park, Colombia

Covering both land and sea, this national park encompasses coral reef, beach, tropical dry forest, tropical rainforest and cloud forest. There are more than 770 species of plants here, ranging from iraca palms and coconut palms to mango and fig trees, as well as many *Ceiba pentandra* trees, which produce large seedpods containing the cotton-like fibre kapok.

LEFT:

Cotton-top Tamarin, Tayrona National Natural Park

This critically endangered monkey is dusted with red pollen after feeding on the nectar of orange flame vine flowers. It also eats fruit, gum sap, insects and occasionally small frogs and lizards. One of the littlest primates, this tamarin weighs less than 0.5kg (1.1lb). It lives in a family group of up to 13 members, feeding, sleeping, grooming and playing together.

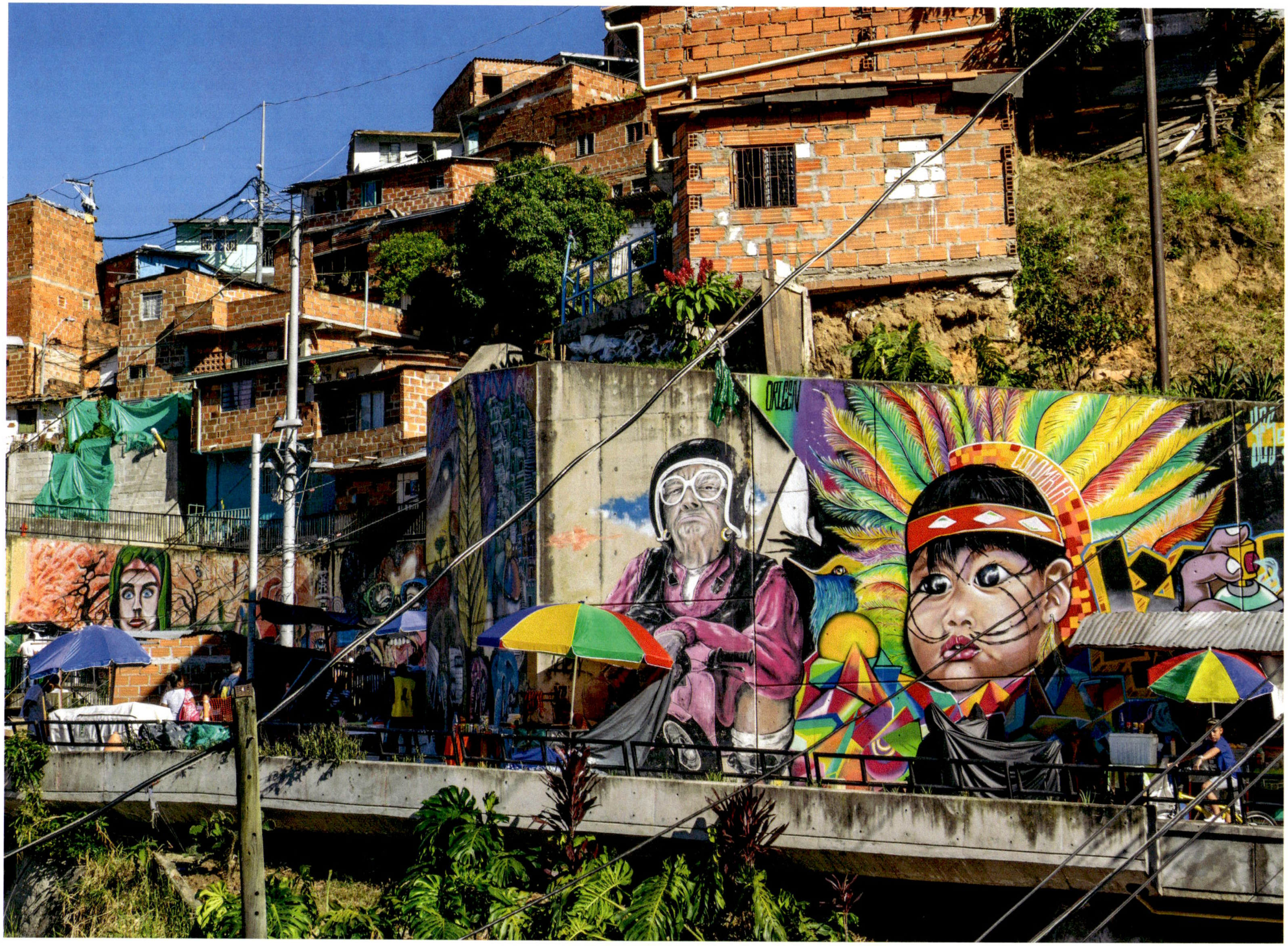

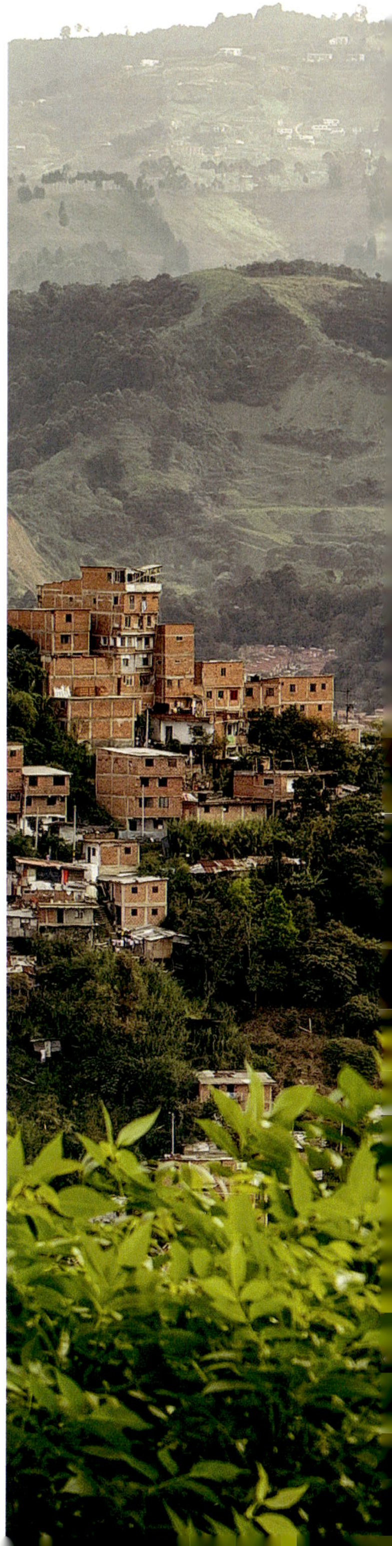

ABOVE:

Comuna 13, Medellín, Colombia

On Medellín's western hills, this community was once deeply troubled by drugs, paramilitary groups and violent government interventions. Today, the *comuna* has transformed itself through community projects and investment in services, while tourists have arrived to see the street art and breakdance performances.

RIGHT:

Metrocable, Medellín

This cable-car network runs from the hillside barrios into the central valley, using six lines and 16 gondolas. The system has transformed life for many inhabitants of the barrios, who – due to the steep terrain, little served by buses – might previously have spent up to five hours travelling to and from work.

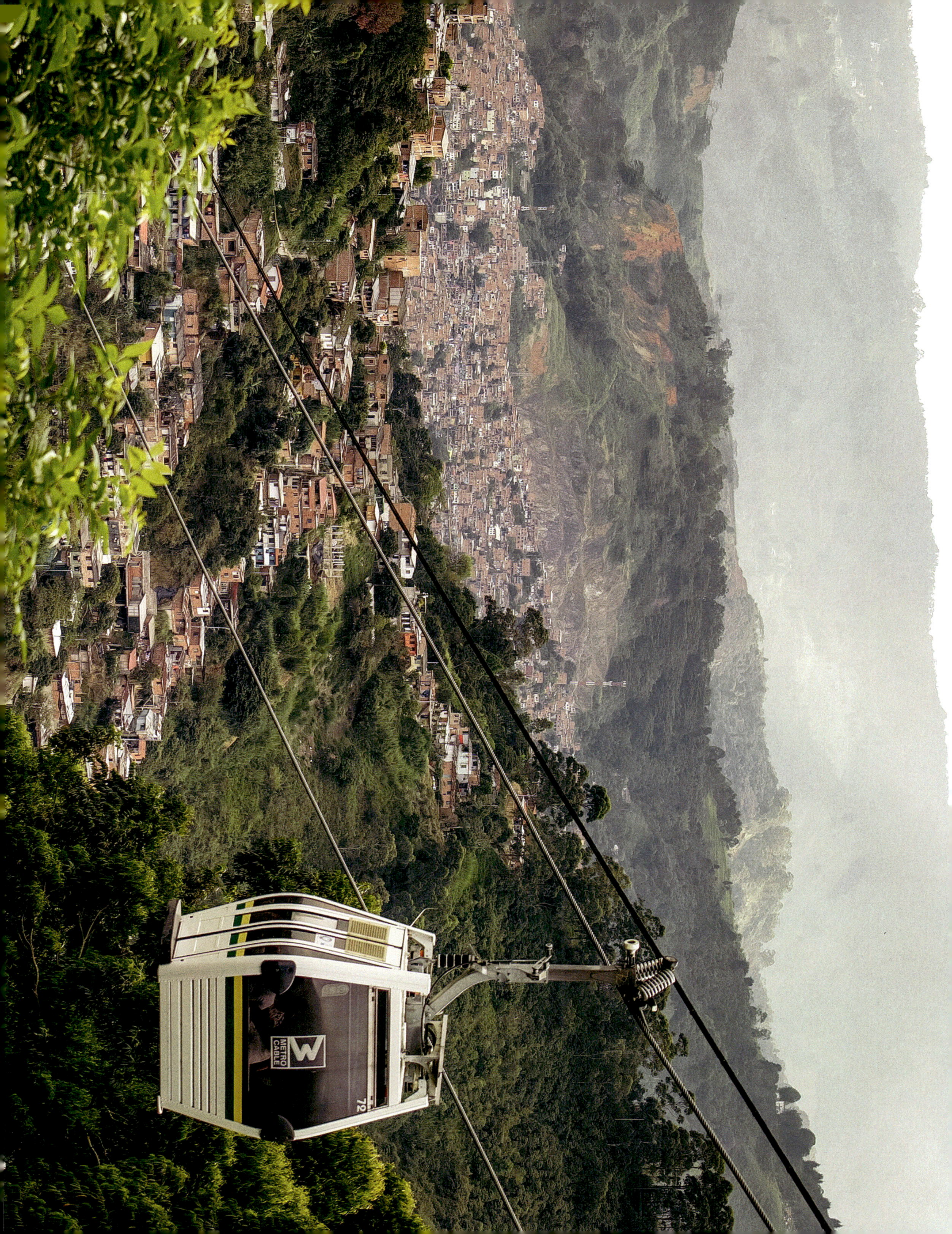
METRO CABLE
72

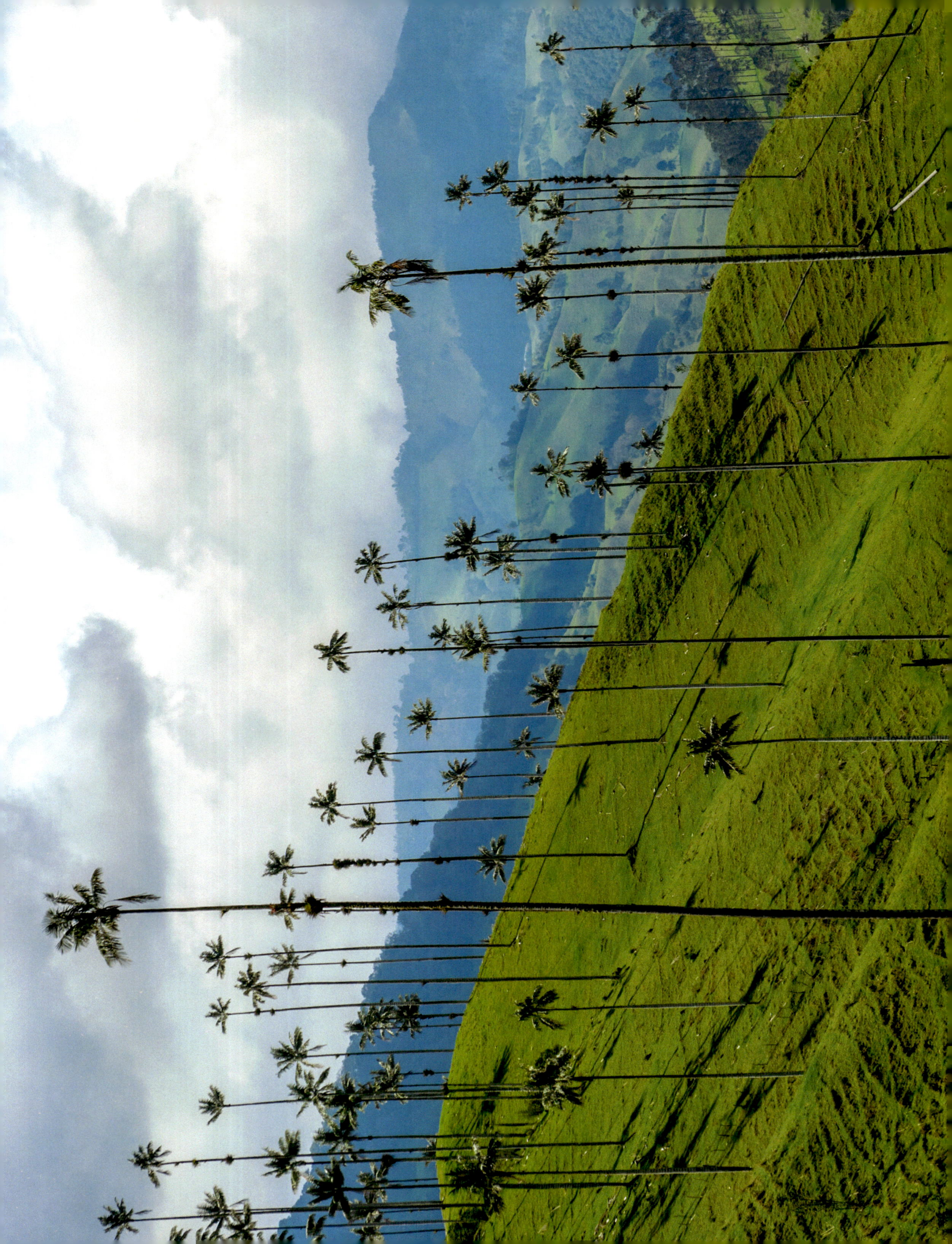

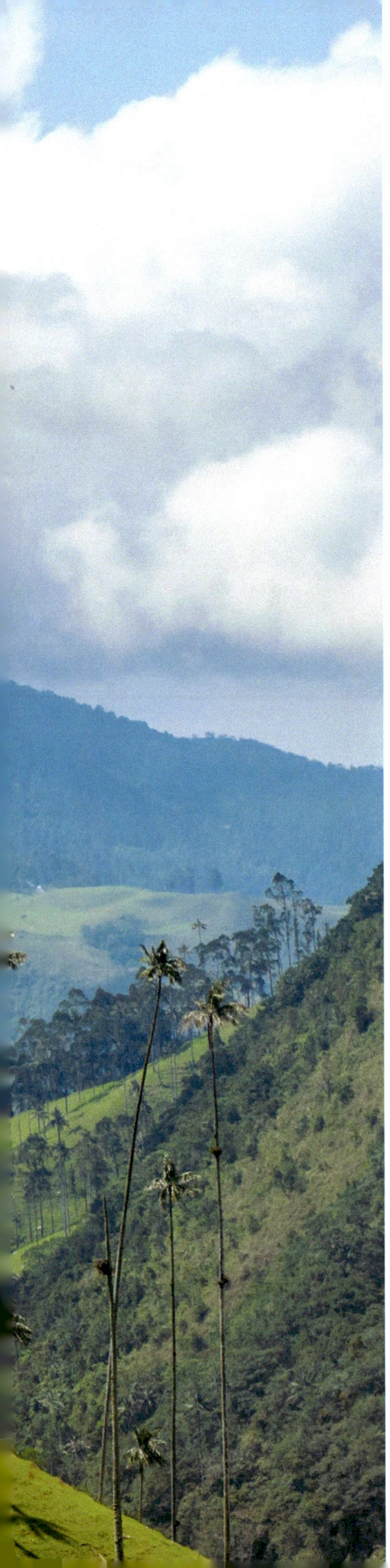

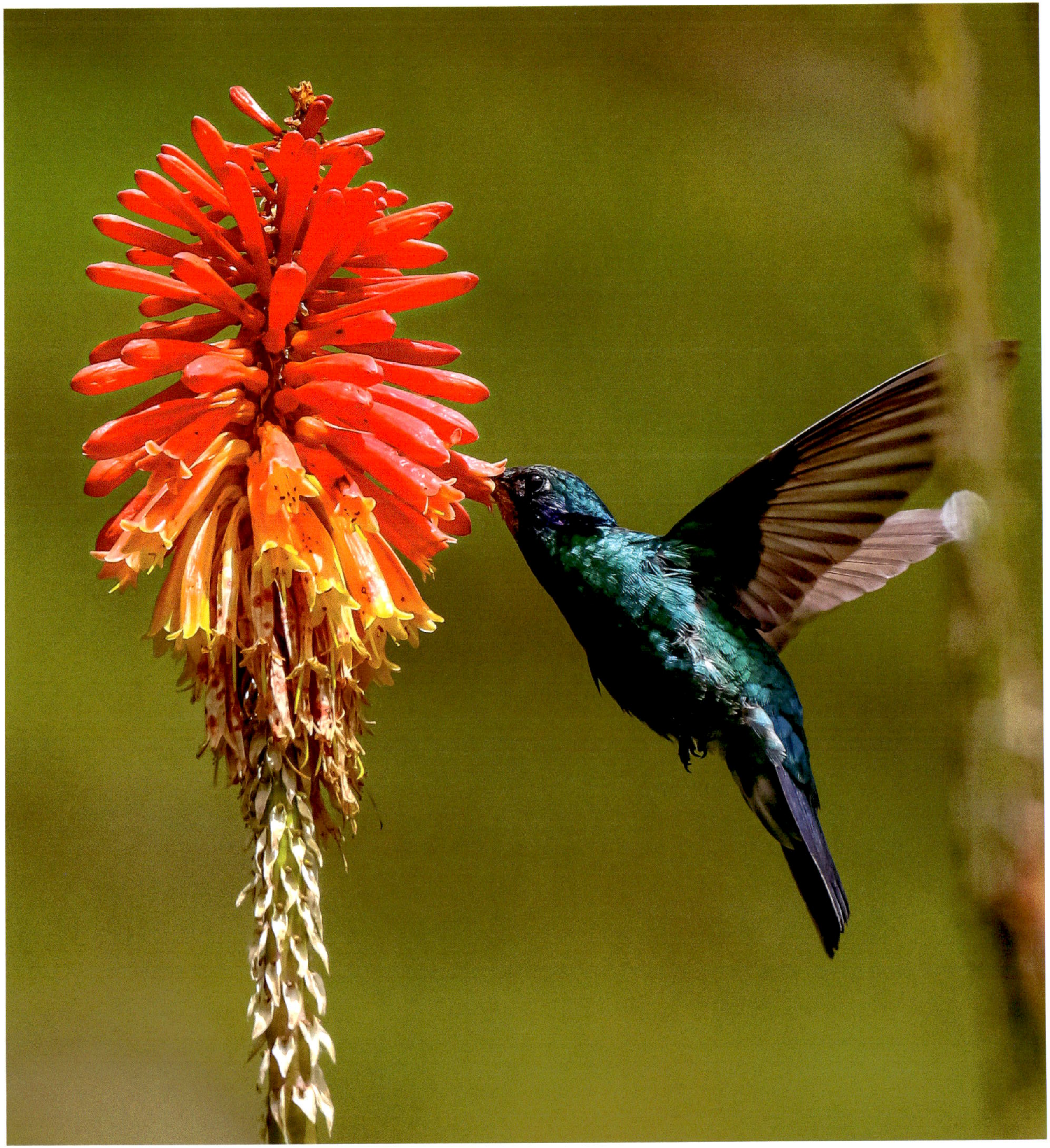

FAR LEFT:
Quindío Wax Palms, Valle de Cocora, Colombia
Up to 60m (200ft) tall, the national tree of Colombia is found in humid regions of Colombia and Peru at between 2000 and 3100m (6600 and 10,200ft) above sea level. The Quindío's wax was once used to make candles, while its fibre was employed in building, but the vulnerable tree is now a protected species.

LEFT:
Sparkling Violetear, Valle de Cocora
Found in the highlands of northern and western South America at heights of 1000 to 4500m (3300 to 14,800ft), this hummingbird reaches 14cm (5.5in) long. It is named for the long, erectile violet feathers that cover its ears. The bird feeds on nectar and catches small insects in flight.

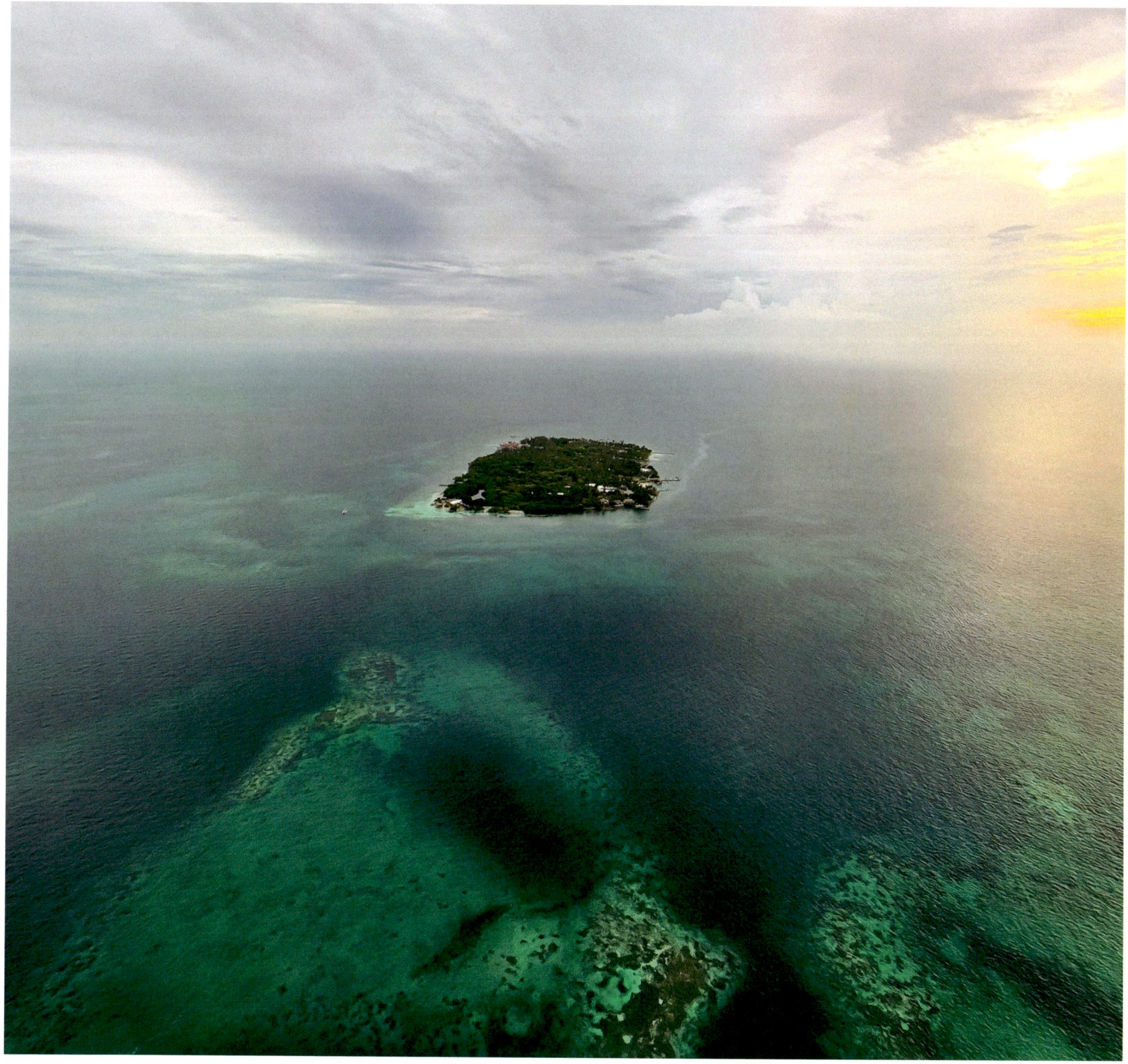

ABOVE:
Múcura Island, Archipelago of San Bernardo, Colombia
In the Gulf of Morrosquillo, the San Bernardo Archipelago consists of nine coral islands and one artificial island. The latter, Santa Cruz del Islote, was constructed in the nineteenth century by fishermen, using found materials to extend a coral platform.

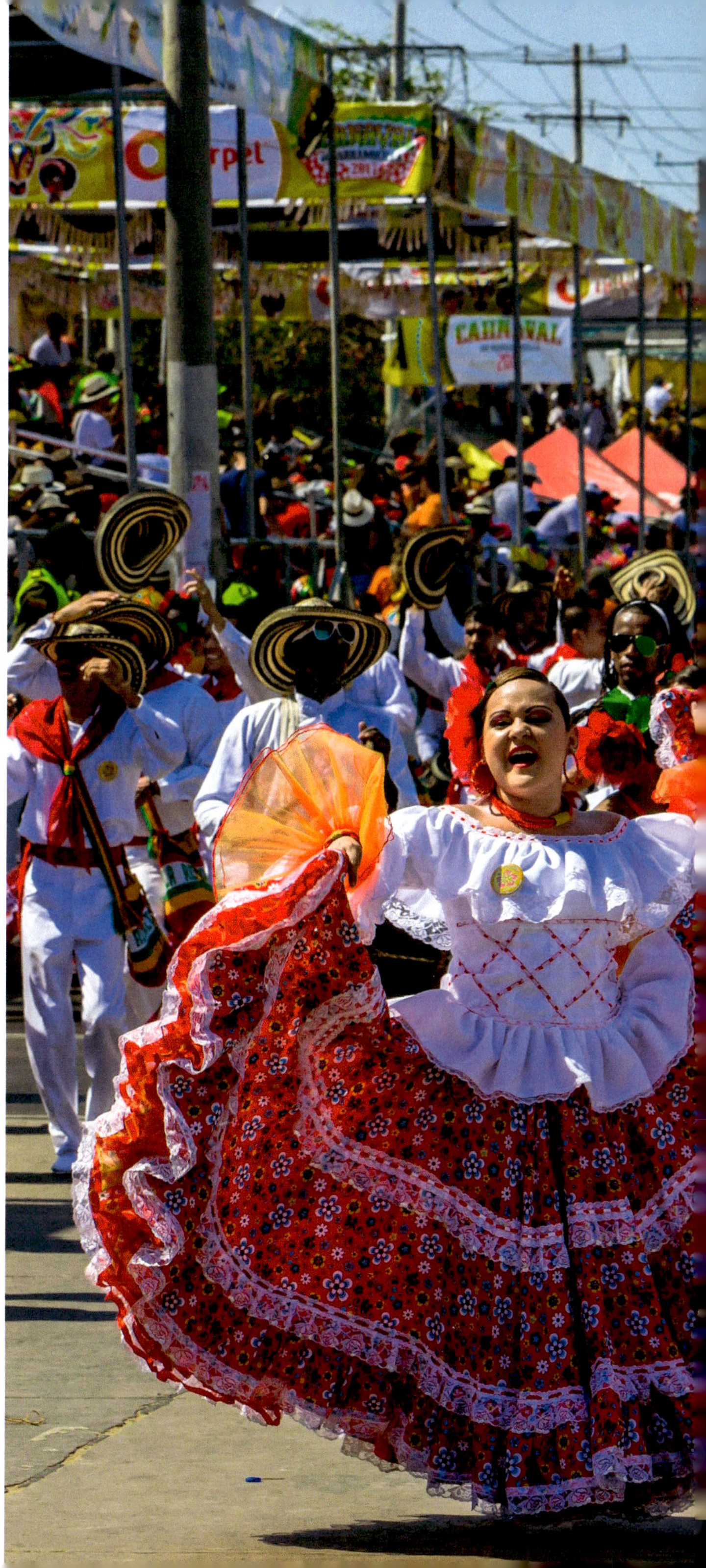

RIGHT:
Carnaval de Barranquilla, Colombia
Attended by up to 5 million people, Barranquilla's carnival takes places over the four days before Lent. Colombian music and dance are performed, including *porro*, *mapalé* and *mice y micas*, revealing Indigenous, African and Spanish influences.

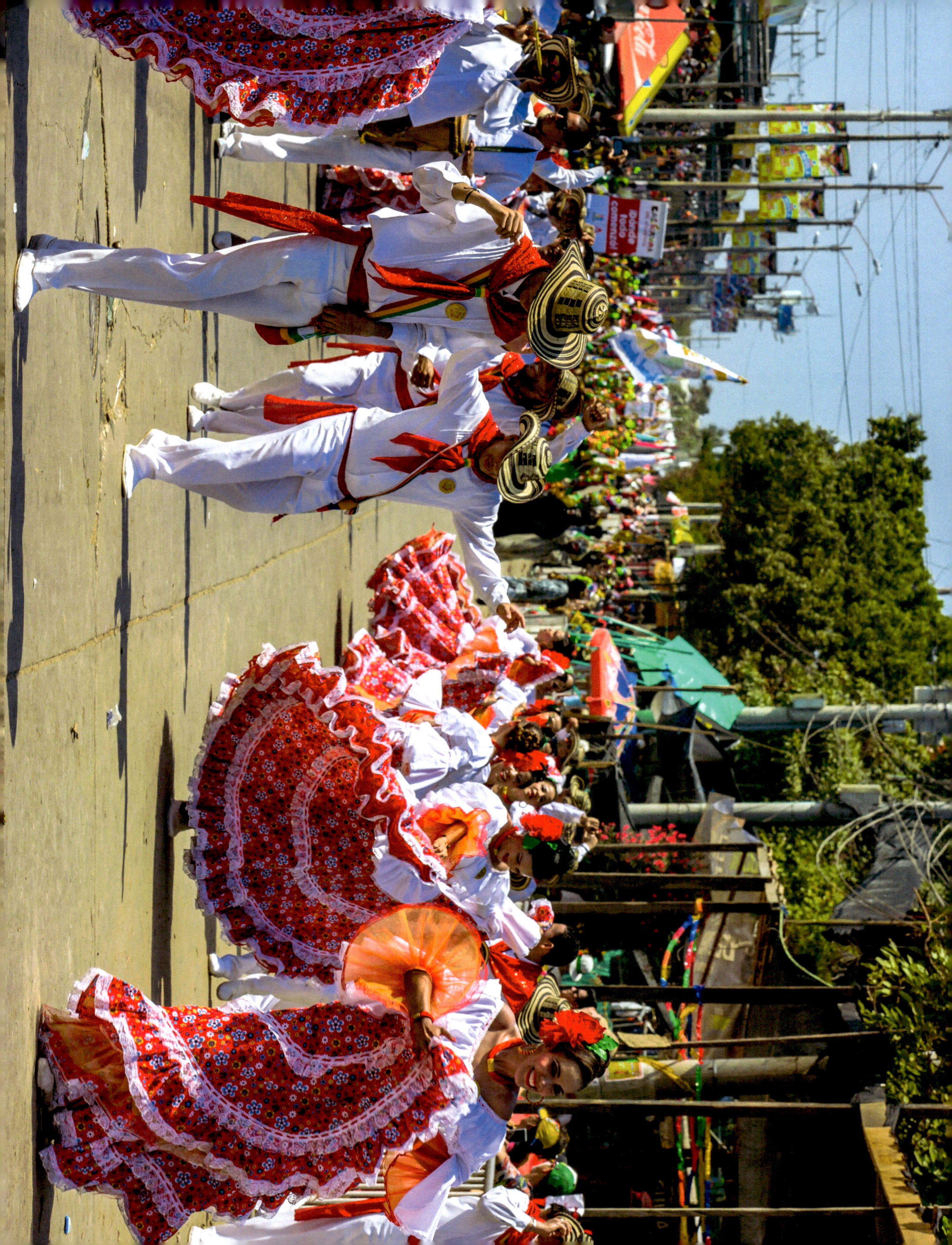

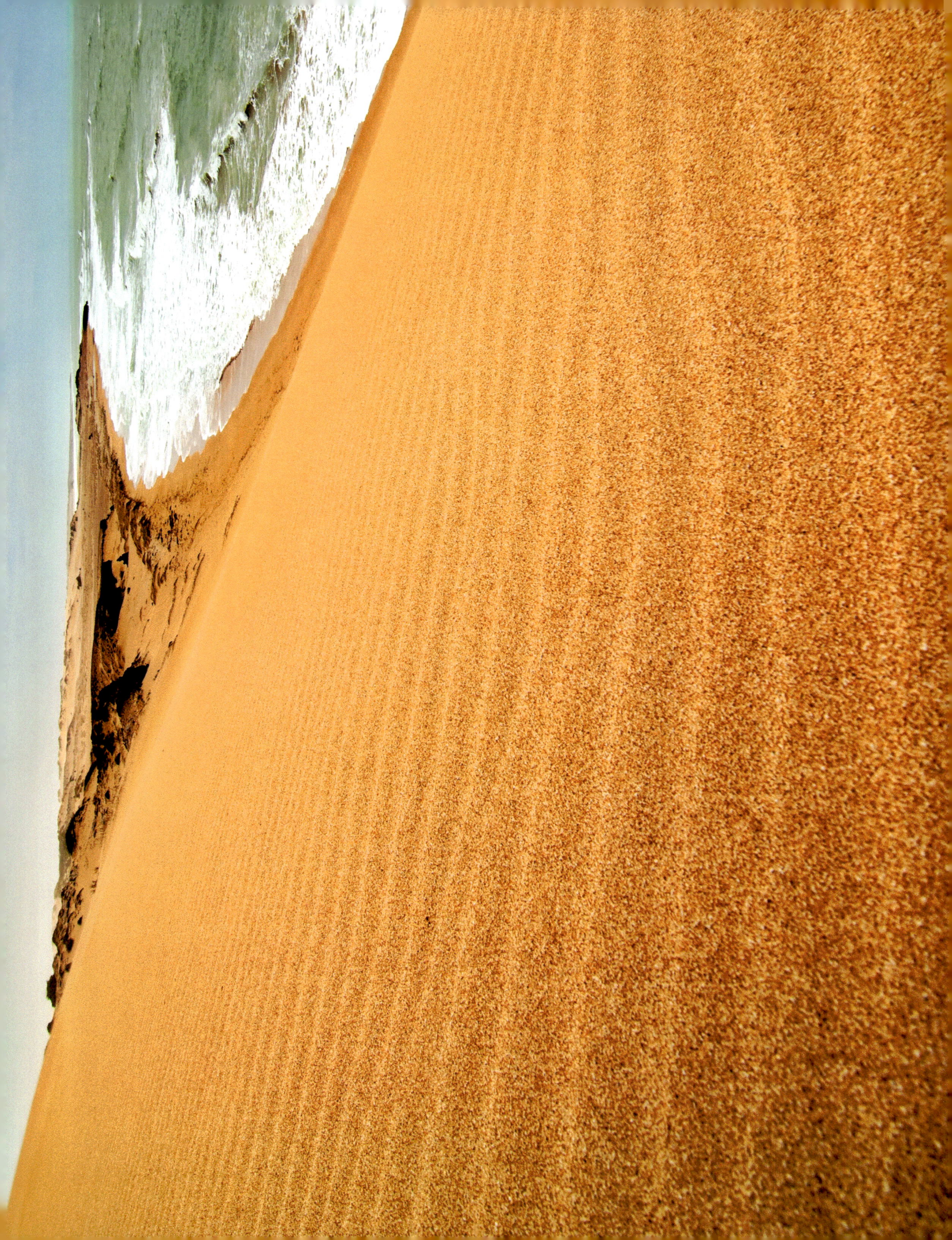

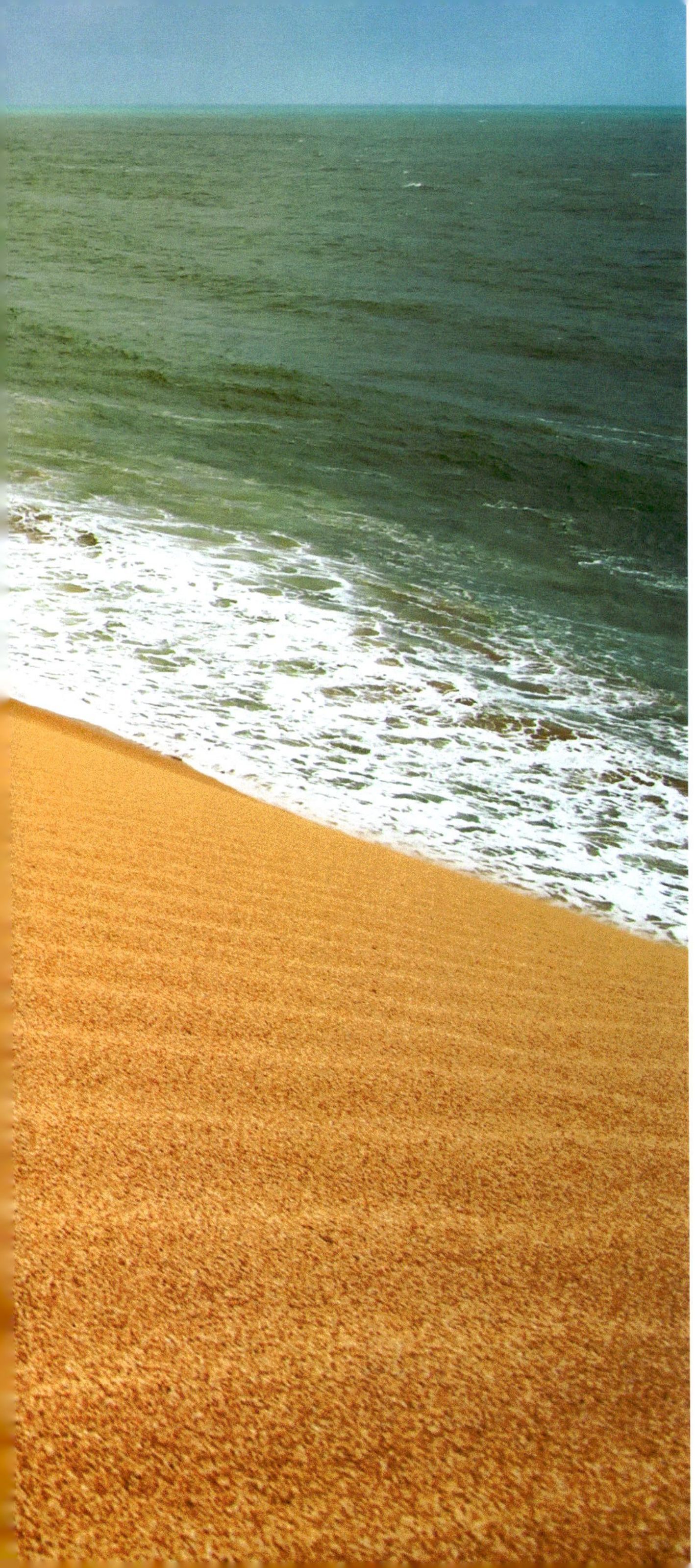

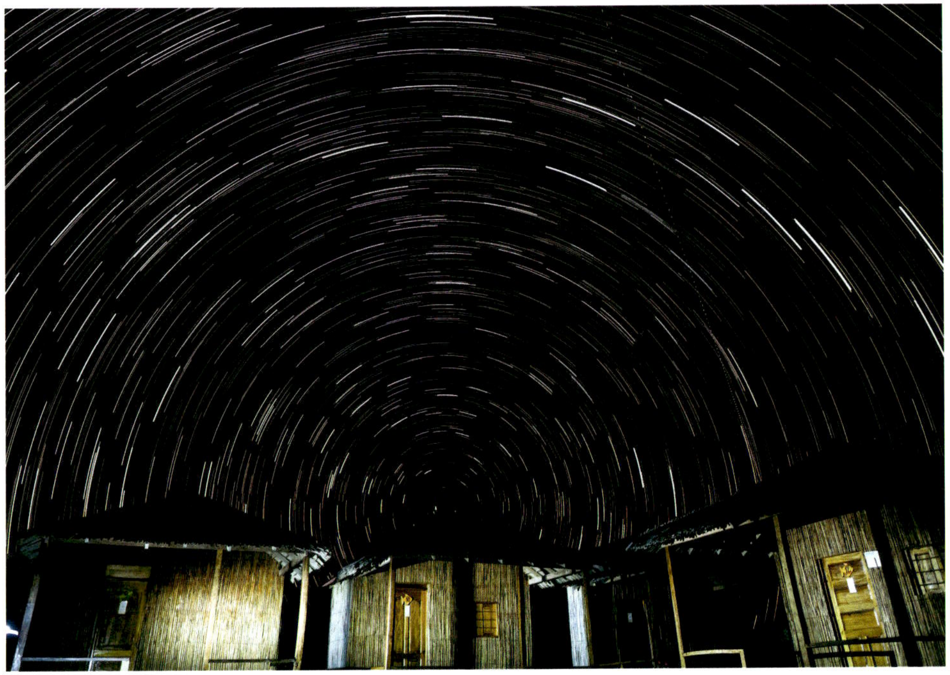

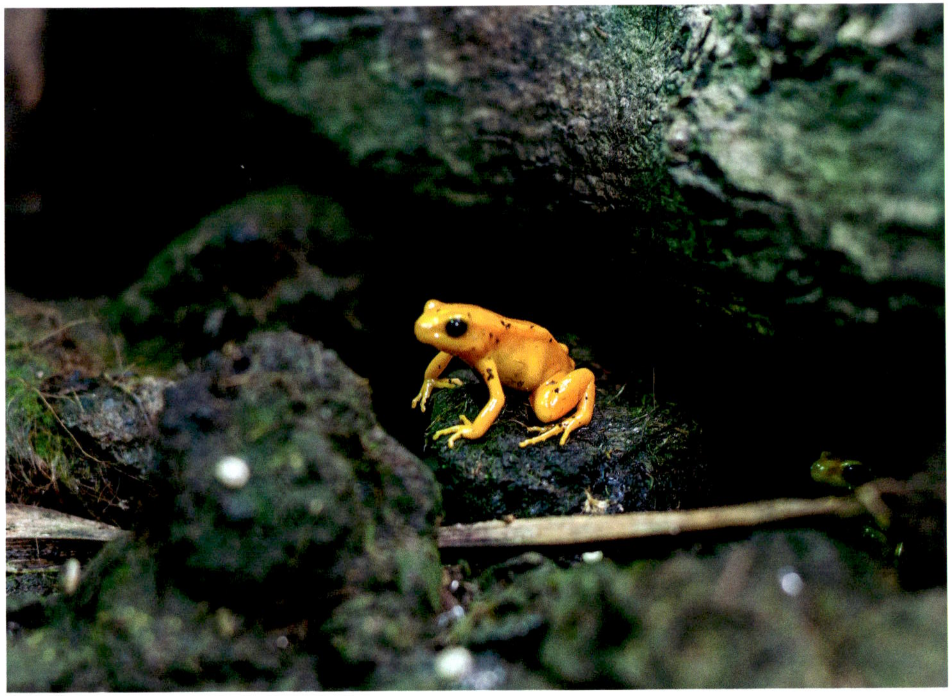

FAR LEFT:

Punta Gallinas, Colombia

The northernmost point of mainland South America, Punta Gallinas is where the La Guajira Desert meets the Caribbean Sea. The region's aridity is due to the rain shadow of the Sierra Nevada de Santa Marta mountain range.

LEFT TOP:

Cabo de la Vela, Colombia

A popular ecotourism destination, this fishing village nestles on a headland on the western coast of the Guajira Peninsula. The spot is sacred to the Wayuu people, since in traditional belief it is a gateway to the afterlife.

LEFT BOTTOM:

Golden Poison Frog, Valle del Cauca, Colombia

Found only in the Chocó Rainforest of western Colombia, where the rainfall is exceptionally high, this frog is endangered due to habitat loss. The female lays her eggs on damp ground, then the male transports the hatched tadpoles to pools. One of the world's most poisonous animals, the frog produces batrachotoxins.

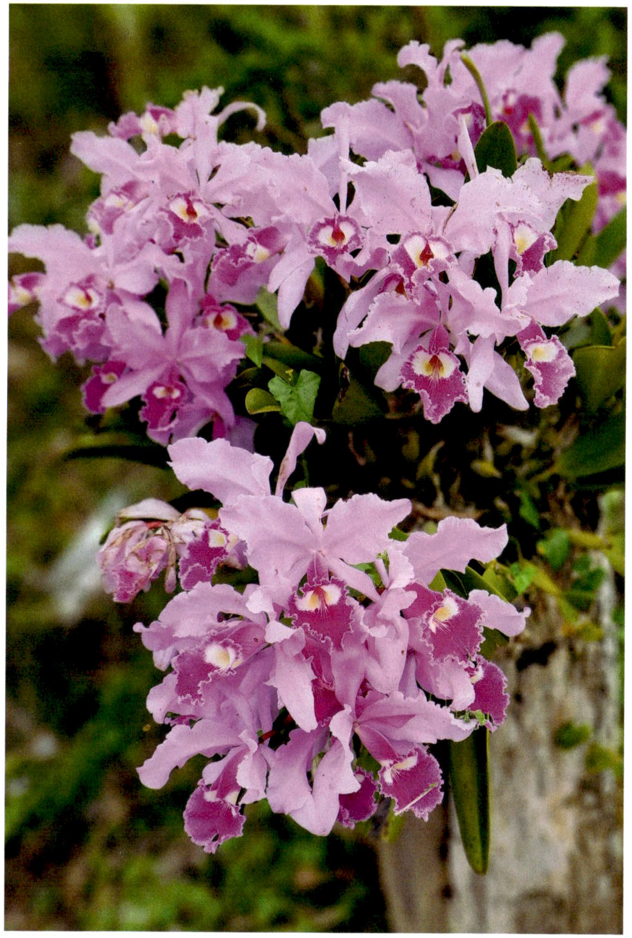

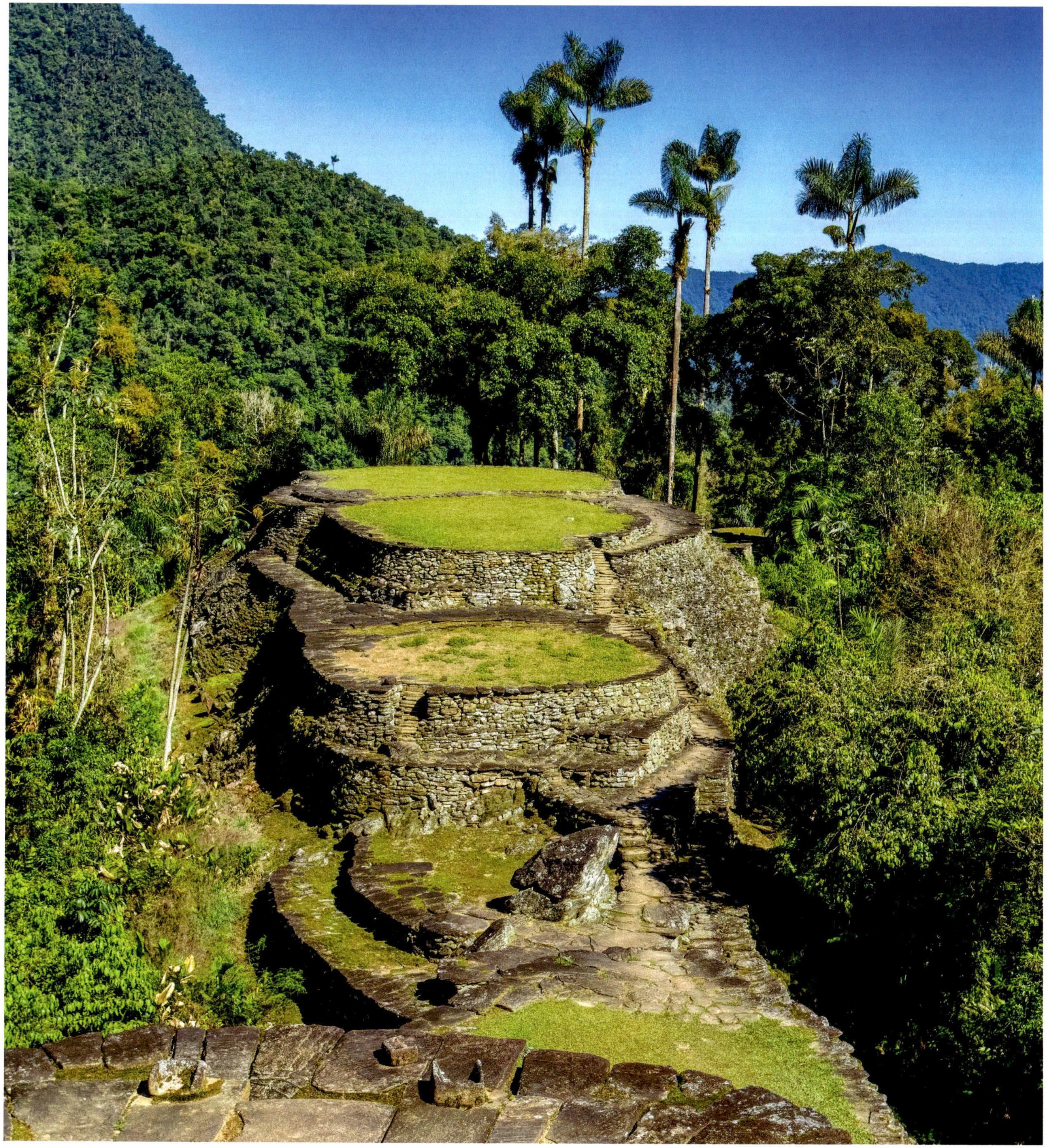

ABOVE:
***Cattleya Trianae*, Magdalena, Colombia**
Colombia's national flower is an epiphytic orchid often called the *flor de Mayo* ('May flower'), found only in Colombian cloud forests.

RIGHT:
Ciudad Perdida, Colombia
This city was built in around 800 CE by the Tayrona people. Excavated so far are 170 circular stone terraces.

OPPOSITE:
San Agustín Archaeological Park, Colombia
This necropolis contains around 300 statues of human figures, often with animal features, which were carved by members of the San Agustín culture between 5 and 400 CE.

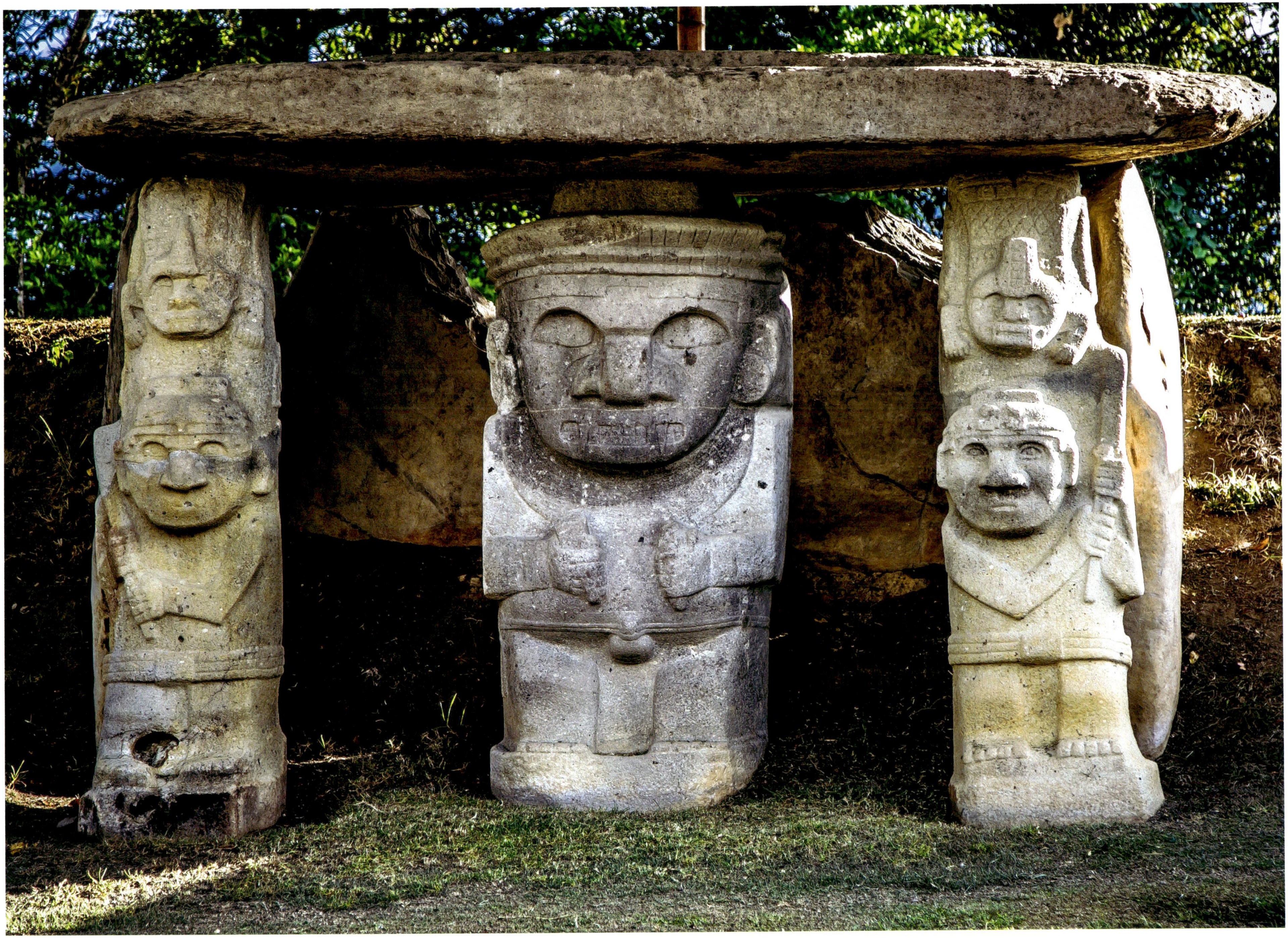

RIGHT:
Andean Condor, Colombia
The national bird of Colombia, the Andean condor is the world's largest bird of prey, with a wingspan of up to 3.3m (10.8ft). It is primarily a scavenger, feeding on dead livestock, armadillos and white-tailed deer.

OPPOSITE LEFT TOP:
Tierradentro Valley, Colombia
This region of the Colombian Andes is famed for its pre-Columbian archaeological sites and striking scenery, its green-cloaked peaks sculpted from volcanic tuff.

OPPOSITE LEFT BOTTOM:
Hypogeum, Tierradentro, Colombia
The Tierradentro culture is known for its hypogea, or underground tombs. Built mainly from the sixth to ninth centuries CE, these have a spiral staircase leading to a small subsurface complex, where the rooms are painted with geometric, human and animal designs.

OPPOSITE RIGHT:
Tatacoa Desert, Colombia
In central Colombia, in the rain shadow of the surrounding Andes Mountains, lies the 330 sq km (130 sq mile) Tatacoa Desert. Its clay formations, featuring maze-like gullies, have been sculpted and resculpted by water and wind.

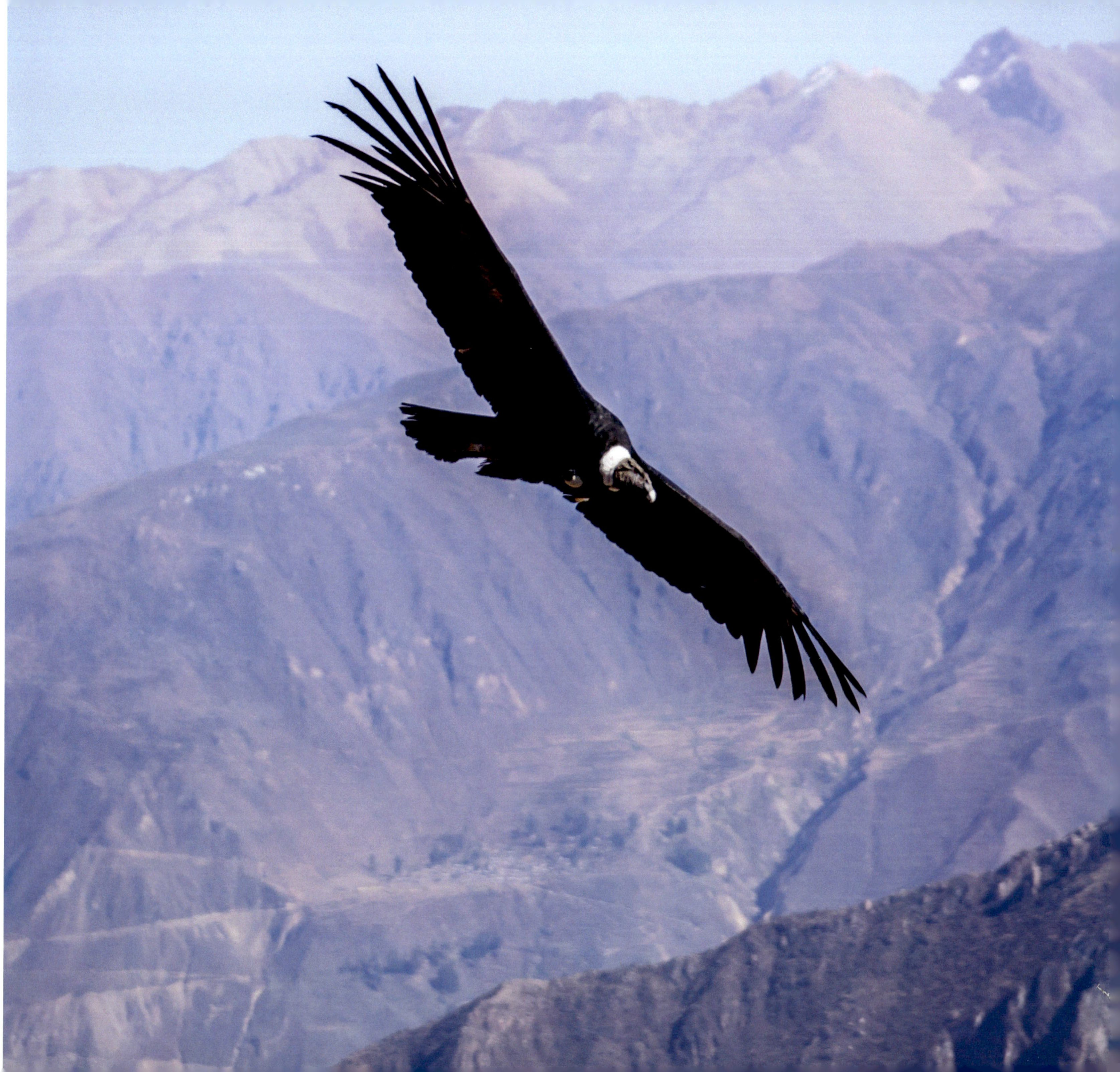

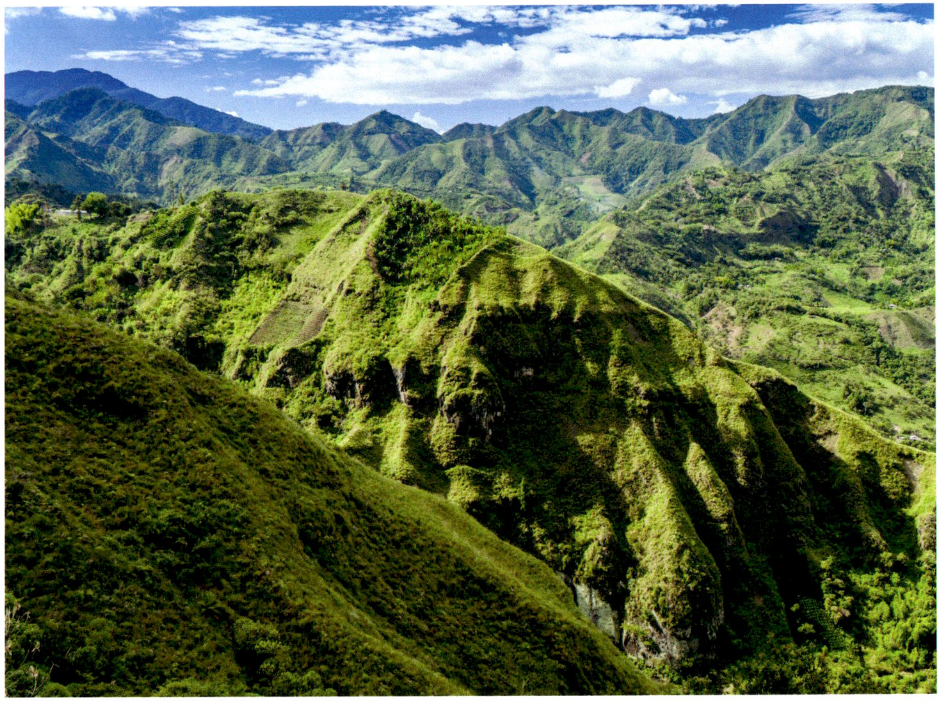

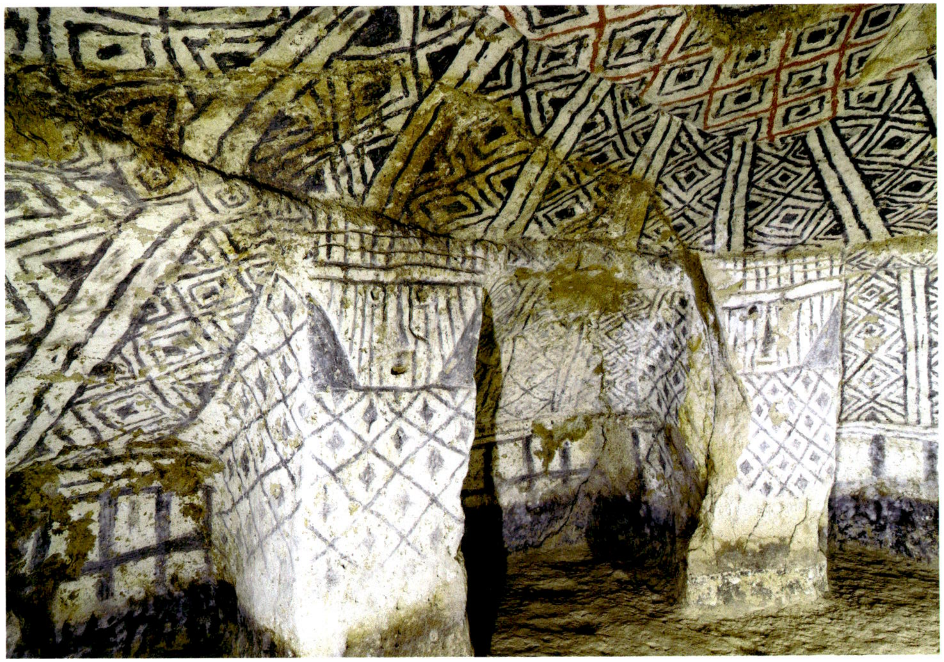

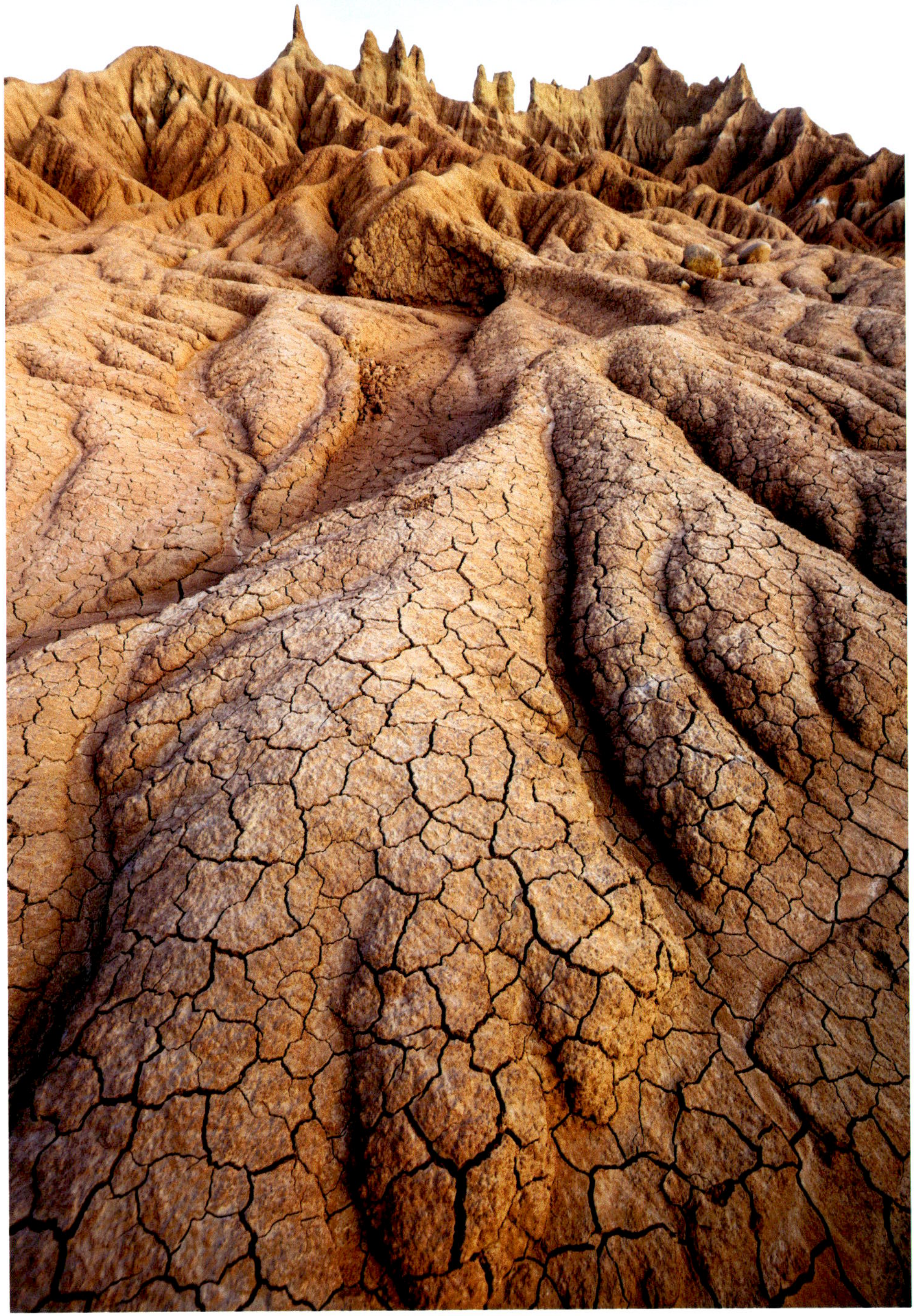

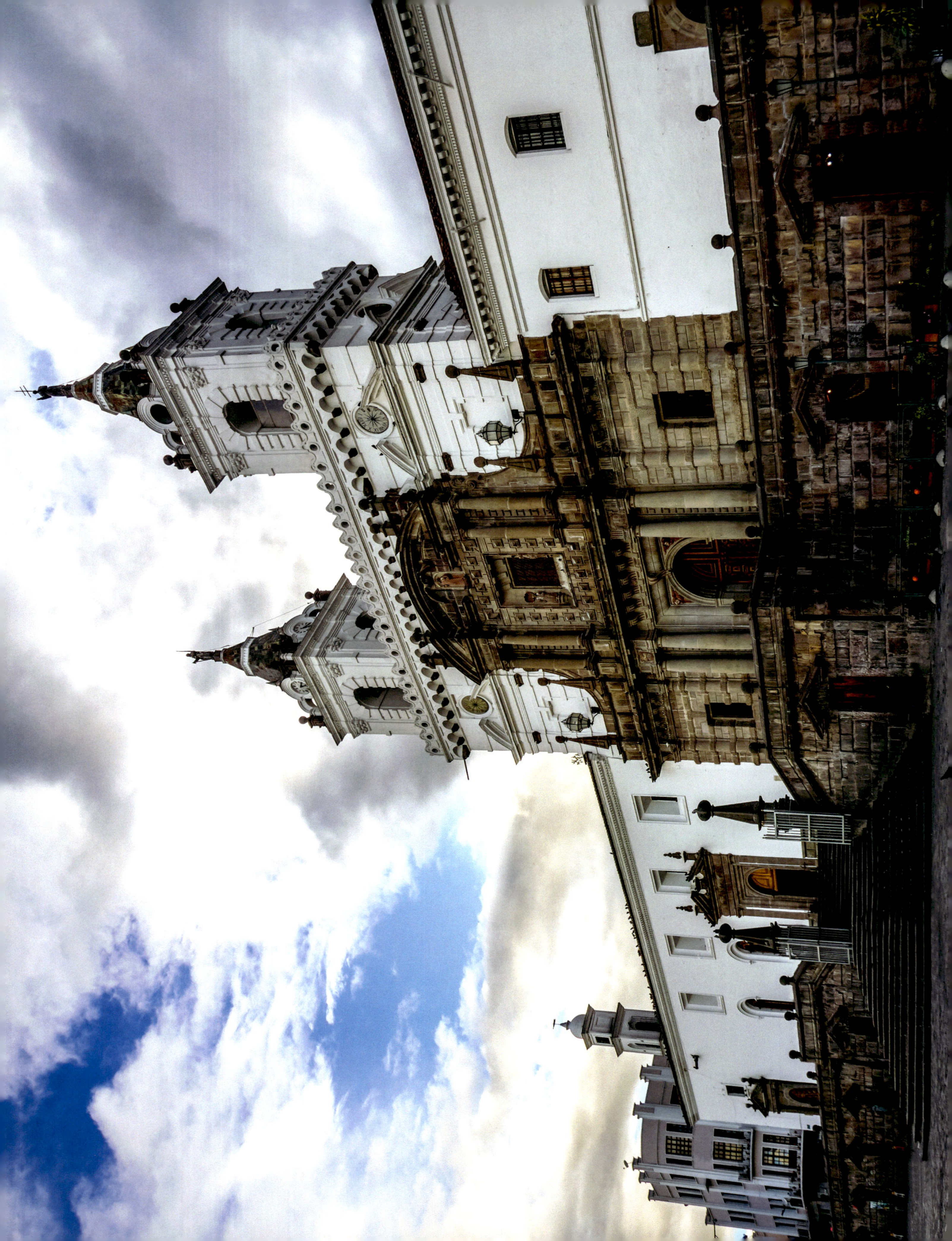

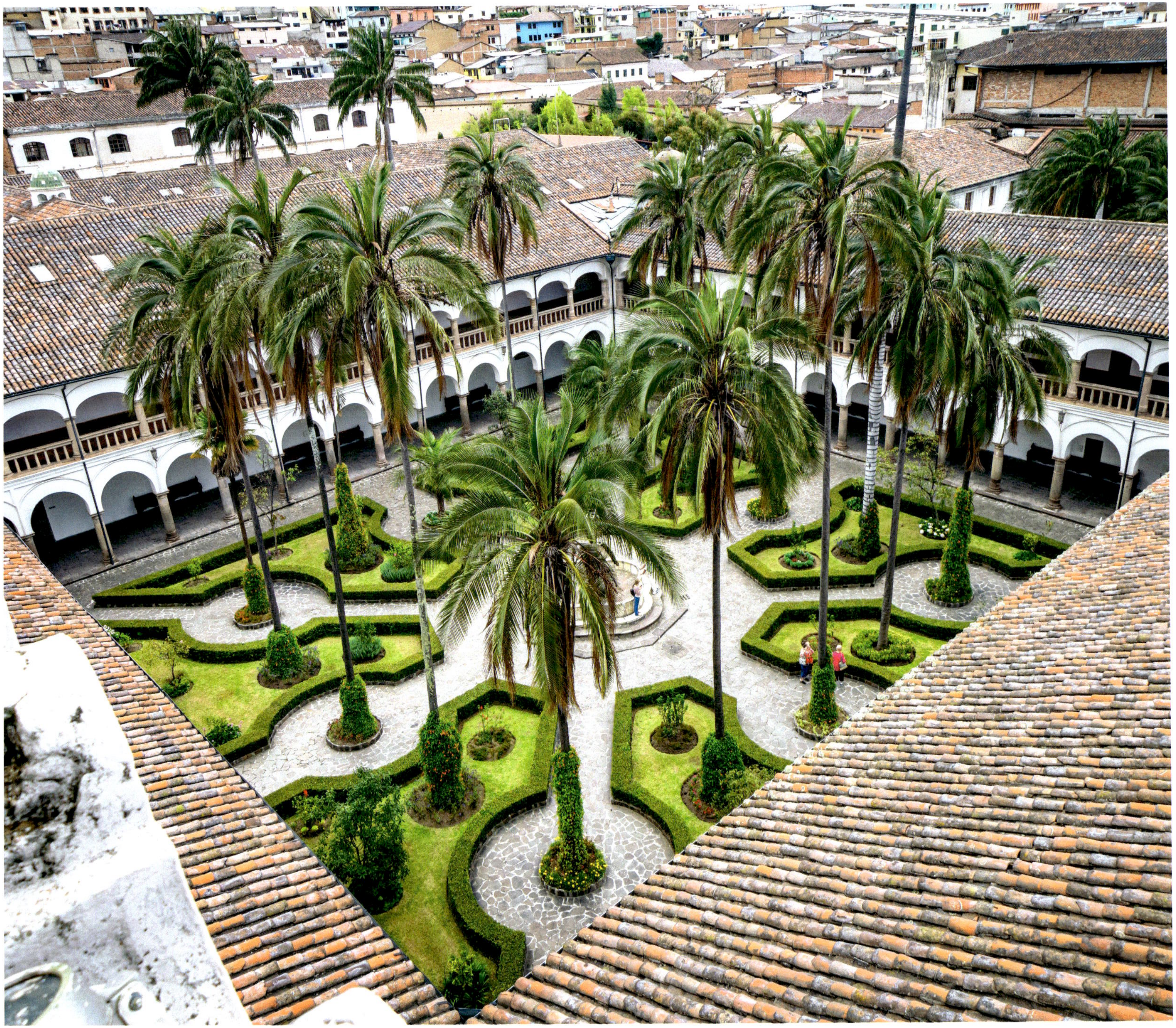

BOTH PHOTOGRAPHS:
Basilica and Convent of San Francisco, Quito, Ecuador
Built between 1535 and 1660, this cathedral combines a harmonious Mannerist exterior with a richly decorated Mudéjar and Baroque interior. The Mudéjar elements include the remarkably beautiful, geometrically patterned *artesonado* ceilings. The interior also houses numerous works of the Quito School, including the 1734 *Virgin of Quito* by Bernardo de Legarda. The main cloister (pictured left) was built between 1573 and 1581, features Mudéjar-style arches on Doric columns.

RIGHT TOP:
***Hornado*, Quito, Ecuador**
A whole roast pig, known as *hornado*, is a staple of Ecuadorian cuisine. Prior to roasting, the meat is usually marinated in lime juice, beer and seasonings such as garlic, cumin, salt and pepper.

RIGHT BOTTOM:
***Llapingachos*, Quito**
Hornado is often served with potato patties called *llapingachos*. The cooked and mashed potatoes are seasoned with onions, cumin and annatto (an orange food colouring from seeds of the achiote tree), then stuffed with cheese and fried until crispy.

FAR RIGHT:
Palacio Arzobispal, Quito
On the Plaza Grande, the sixteenth-century archbishop's palace has been taken over by shops and restaurants, including the popular Hasta La Vuelta, Señor. The surrounding historic centre is a UNESCO World Heritage Site for its Spanish-style colonial architecture and vernacular building techniques.

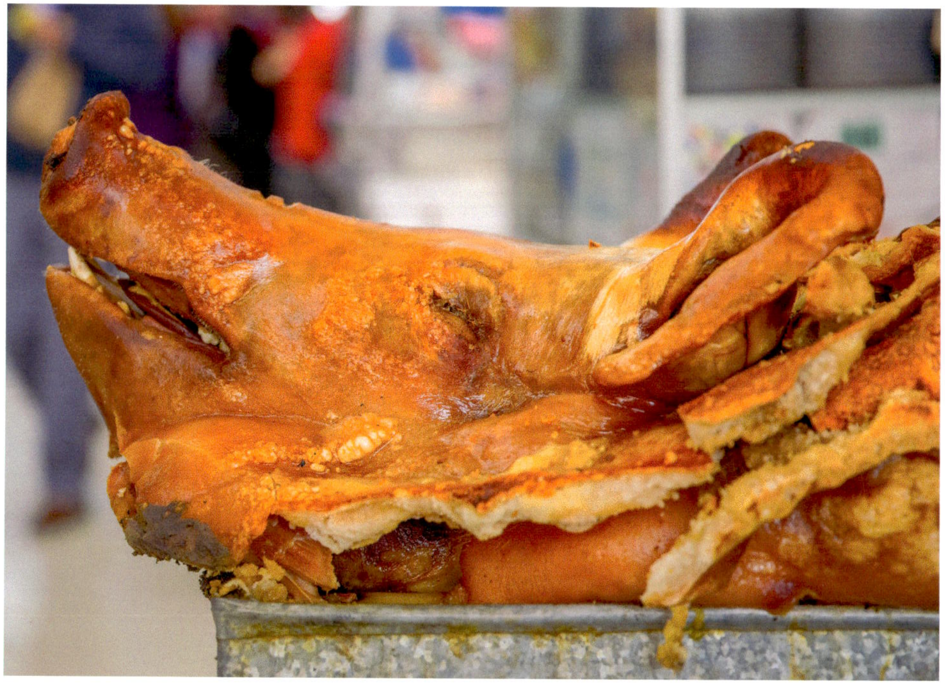

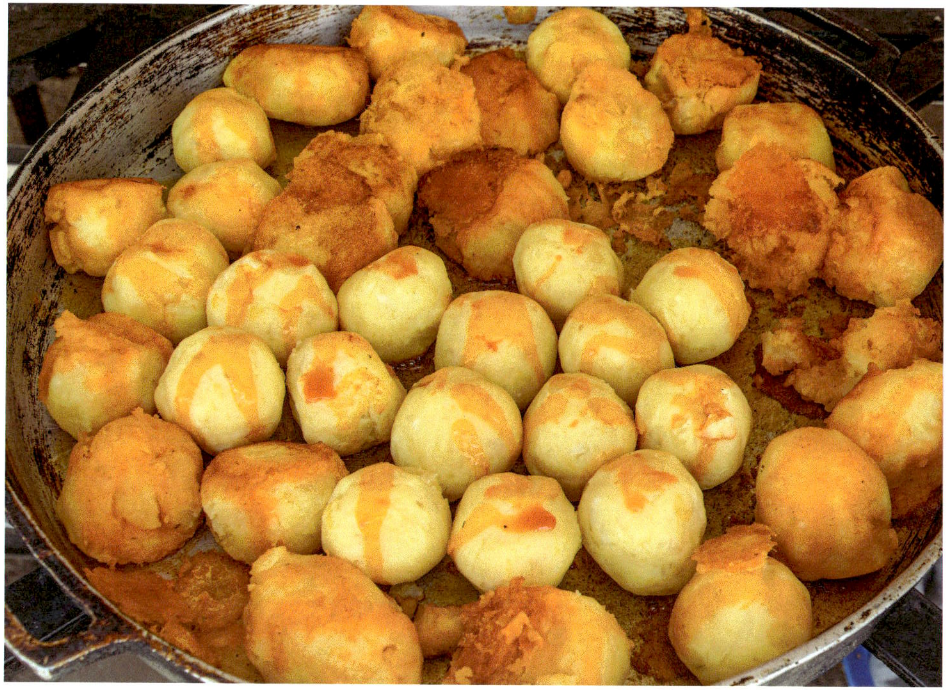

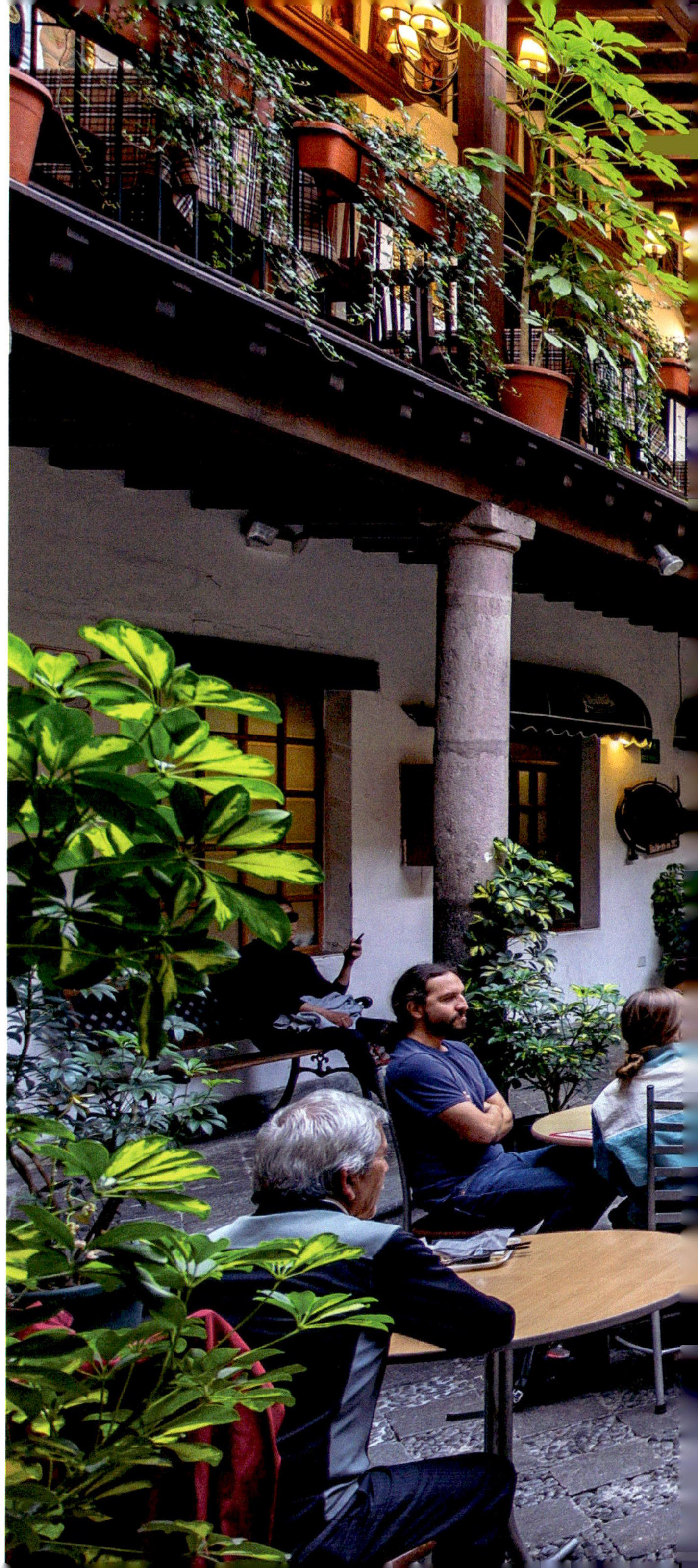

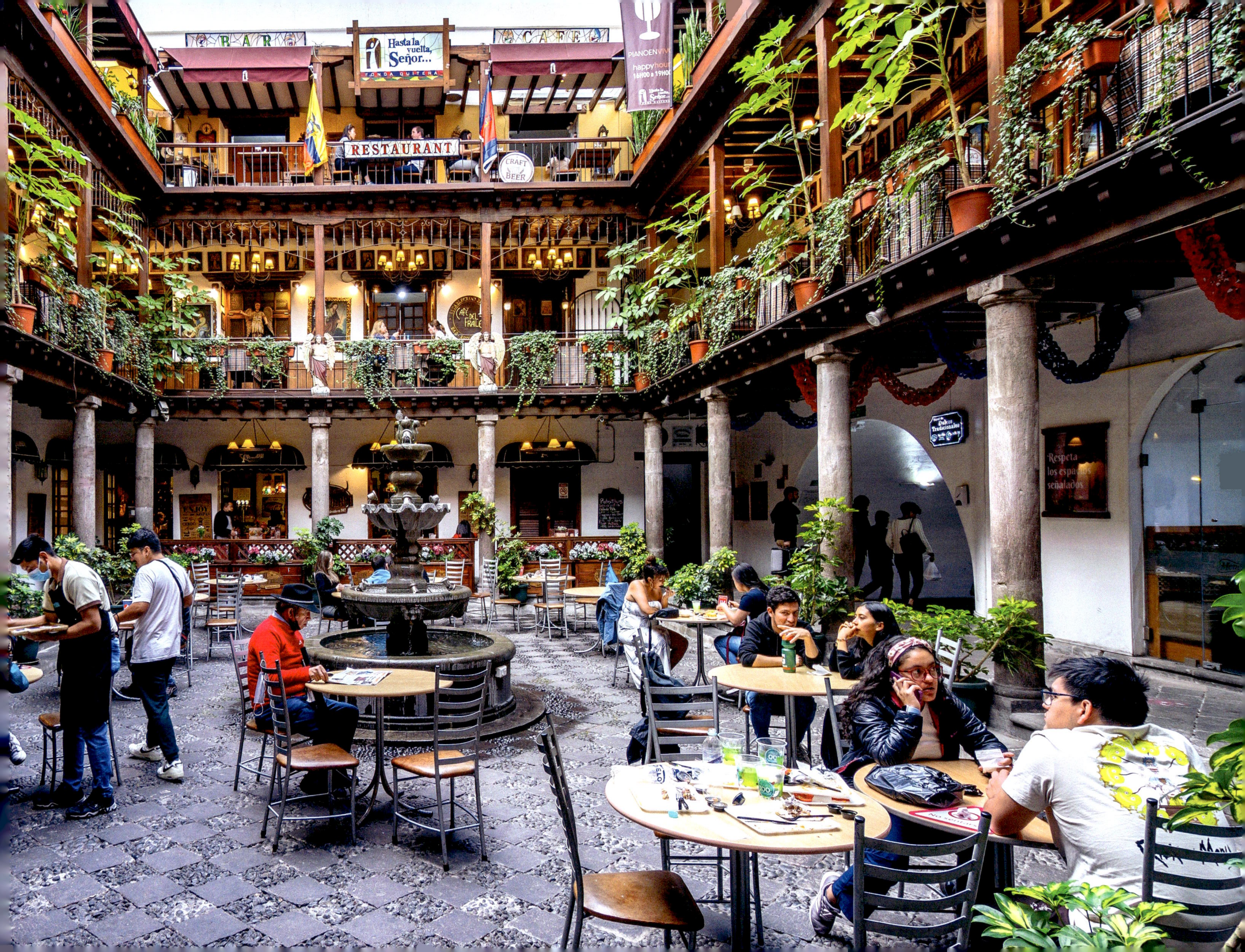
BAR
Hasta la vuelta, Señor...
CAFE
RESTAURANT
CRAFT BEER
happy hour
Respeta los espacios señalados

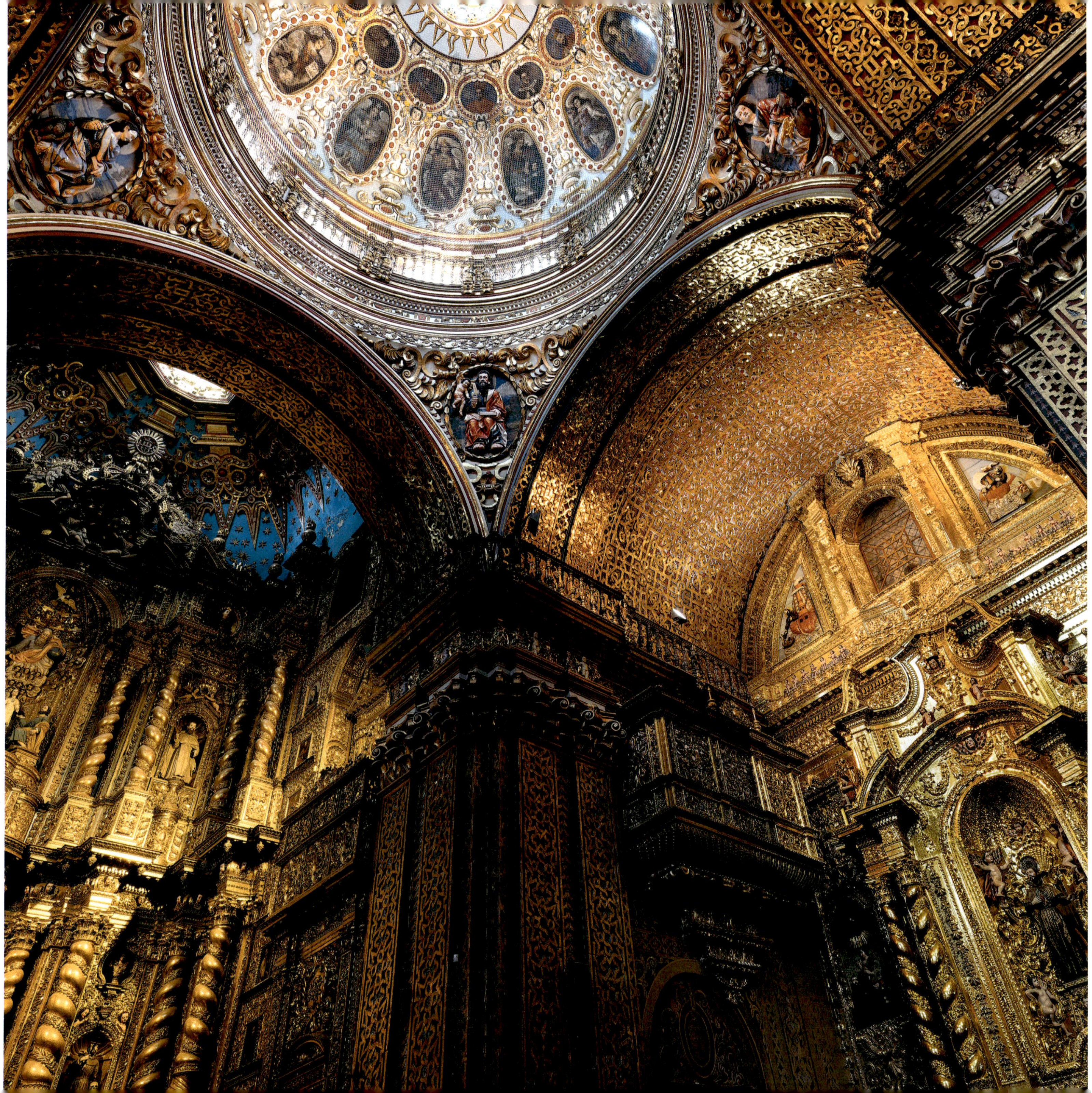

RIGHT:
Church of La Compañía, Quito, Ecuador
Intricately carved from cedar, this church's lavish Baroque interior is coated in gold leaf. The jewel-like effect was intended to awe and inspire worshippers. Capped by green and gold domes, the building was constructed between 1605 and 1765.

OPPOSITE:
Ciudad Mitad del Mundo, Ecuador
Around 26km (16 miles) north of Quito's centre is Ciudad Mitad del Mundo, a park that contains the 1982 *Monument to the Equator*, positioned on the believed location of the equator. The yellow line along one of the garden's paths was intended to separate the northern and southern hemispheres. In fact, modern satellite measurements have revealed that the equator lies about 240m (790ft) north of the line.

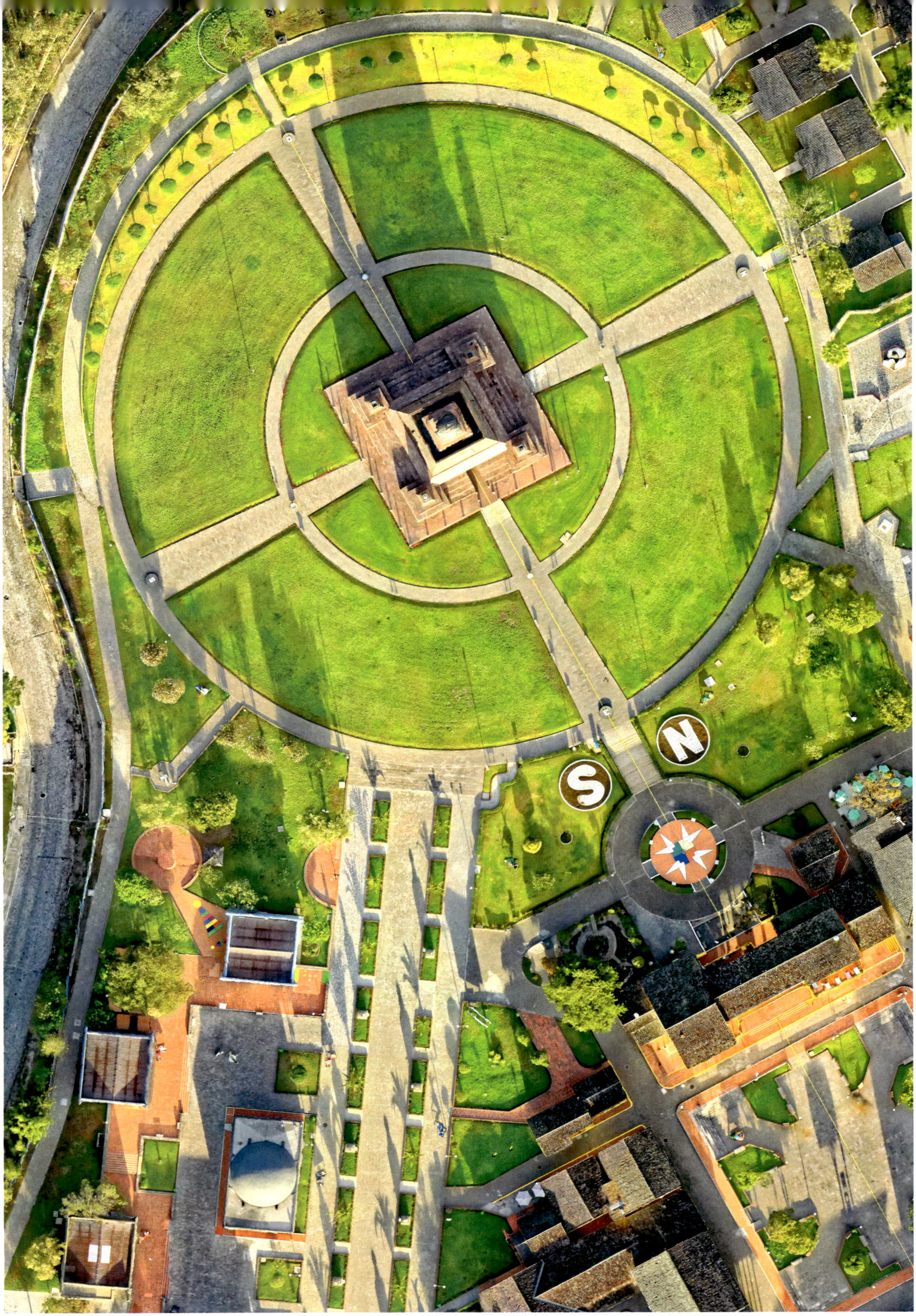
S
N

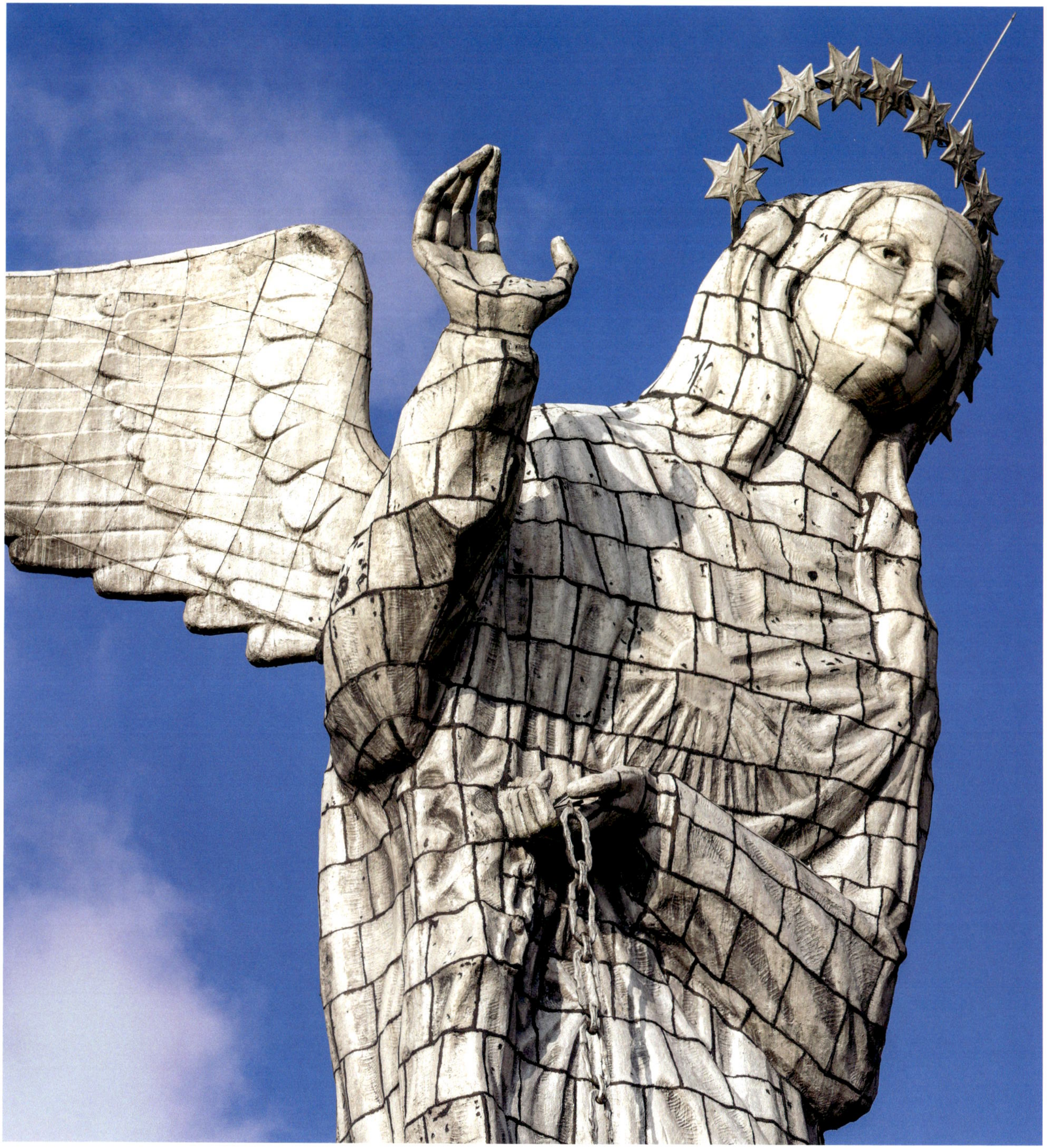

LEFT:
***Virgin of El Panecillo*, Quito, Ecuador**
Located on Quito's El Panecillo hill, 3016m (9895ft) above sea level, this statue was completed in 1970. It is inspired by Bernardo de Legarda's *Virgin of Quito* (see page 81). At 41m (135ft) tall including its base, this monument is the tallest aluminium statue in the world, taller than Brazil's *Christ the Redeemer*, and the highest statue in Ecuador.

RIGHT:
TeleféríQo, Quito
Opened in 2005, this cable car runs from the northern edge of the city up Pichincha, an active stratovolcano that last erupted in 2002. The TeleféríQo is one of the world's highest cable cars, travelling from 3117 to 3945m (10,226 to 12,943ft) above sea level. With an average elevation of 2850m (9350ft), Quito is the world's second highest capital city, after Bolivia's La Paz (3650m; 11,975ft).

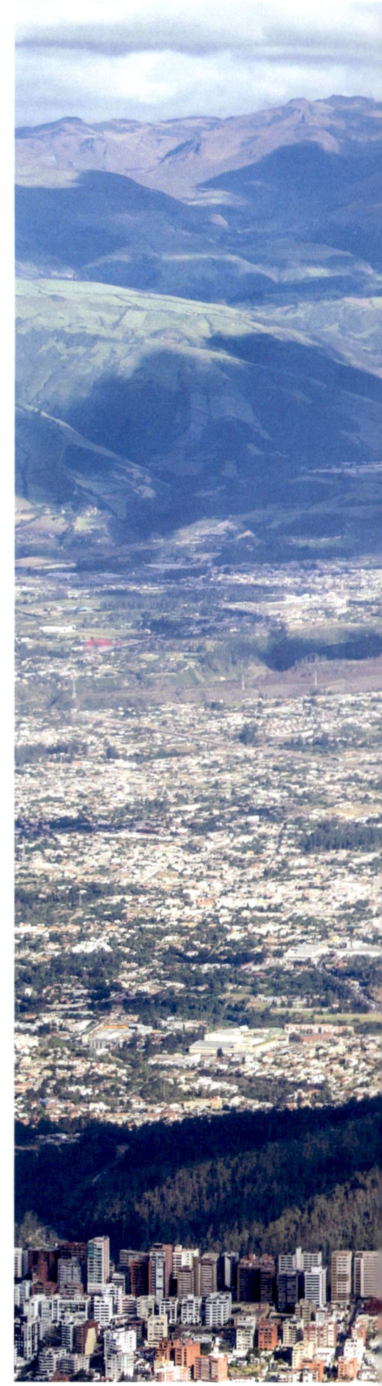

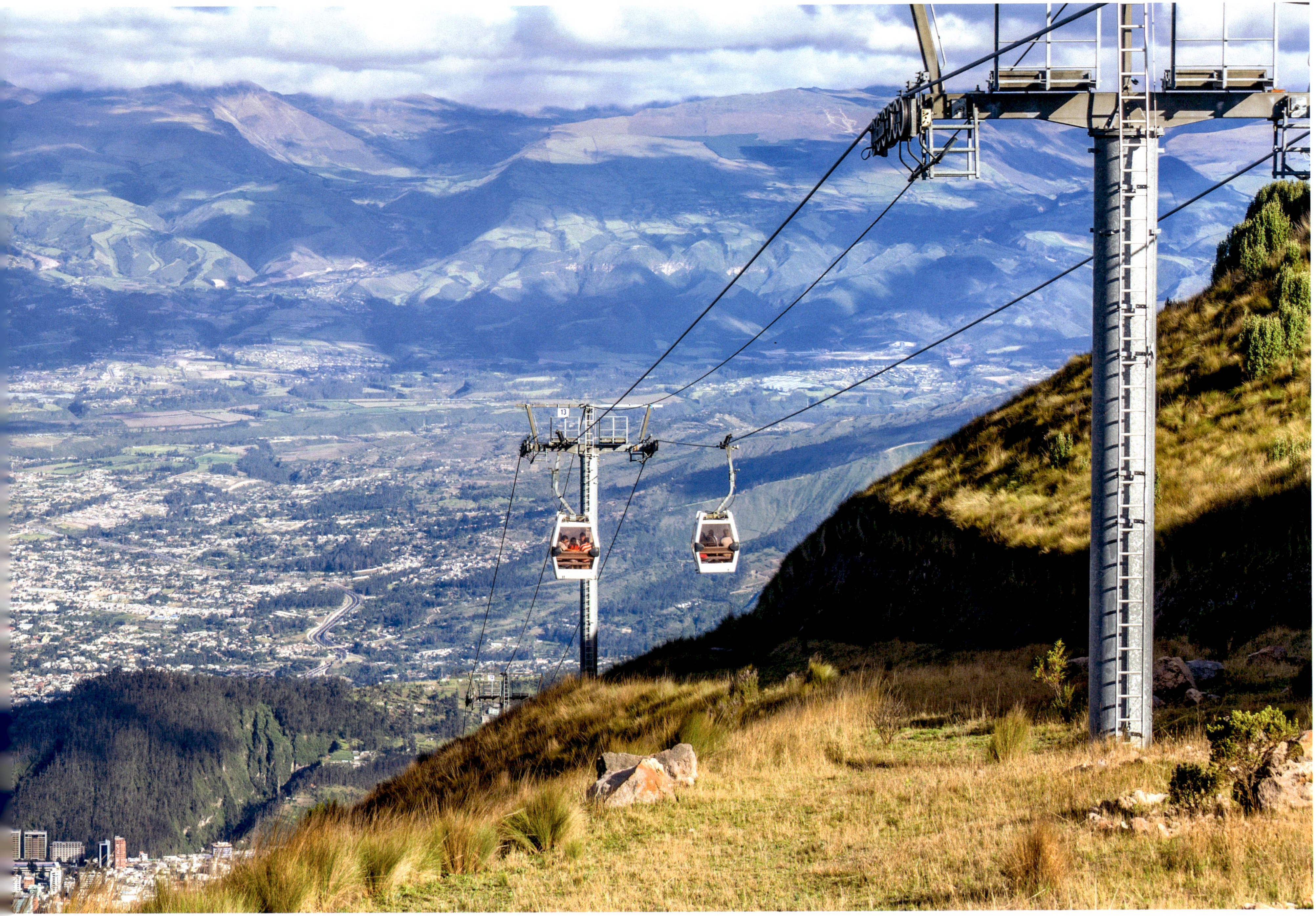

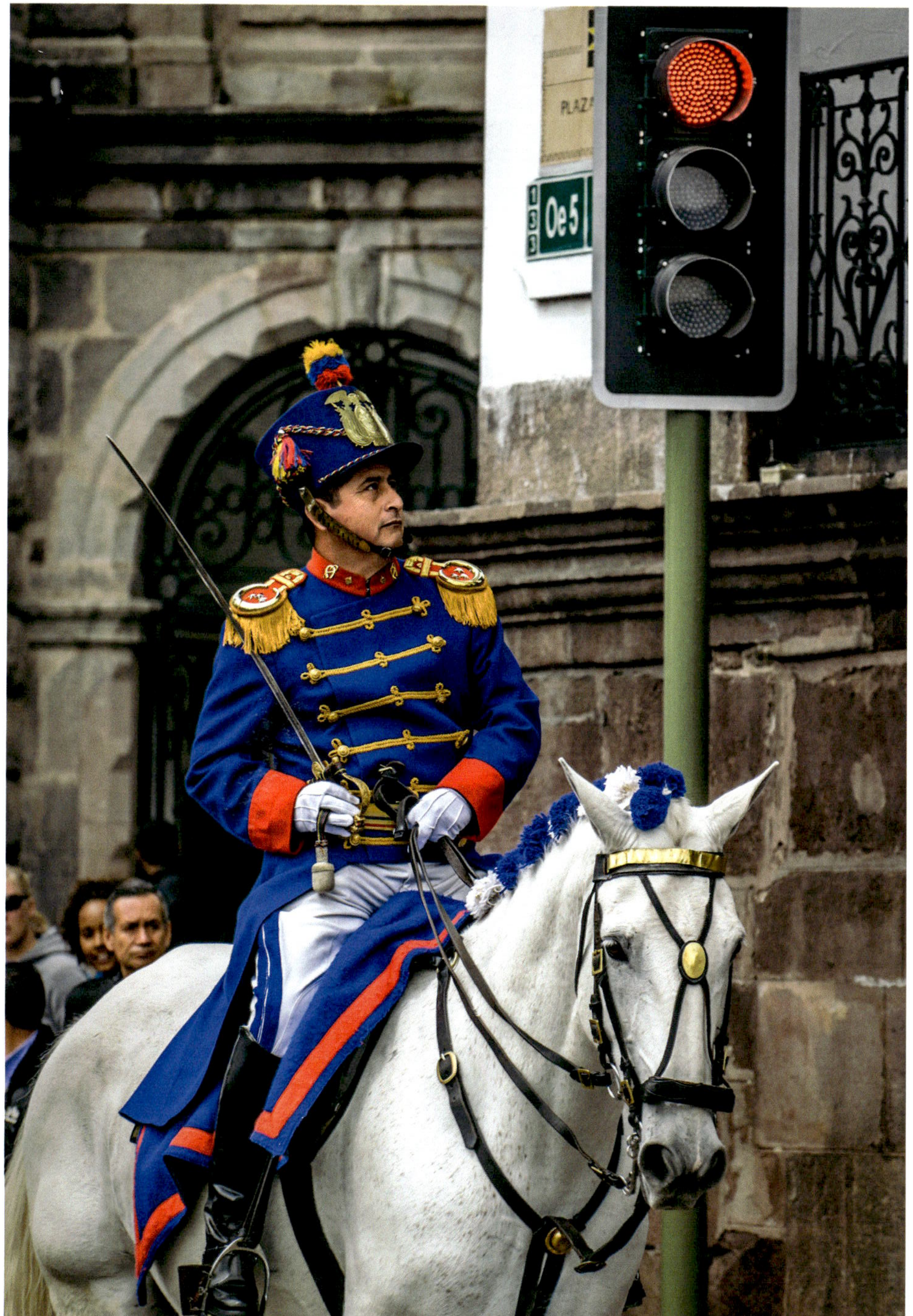
Oe5

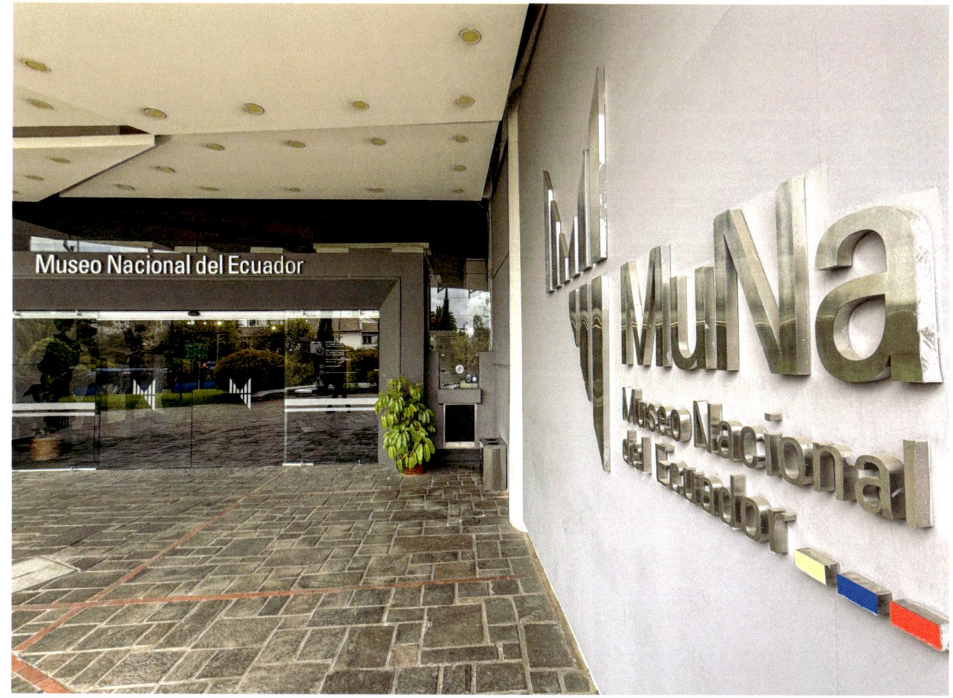
Museo Nacional del Ecuador
MuNa
Museo Nacional
del Ecuador

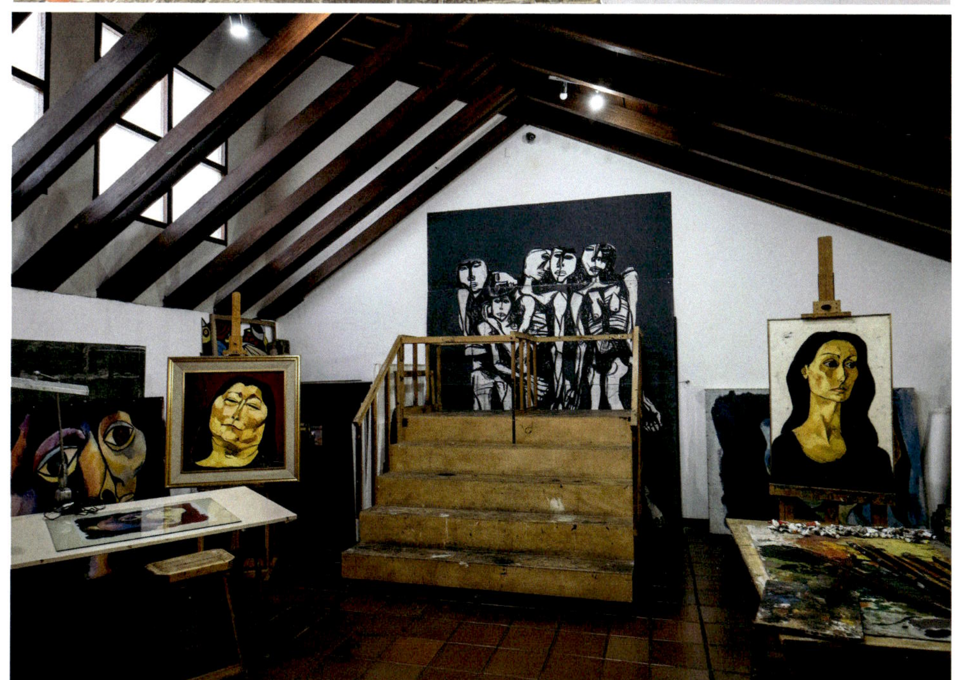

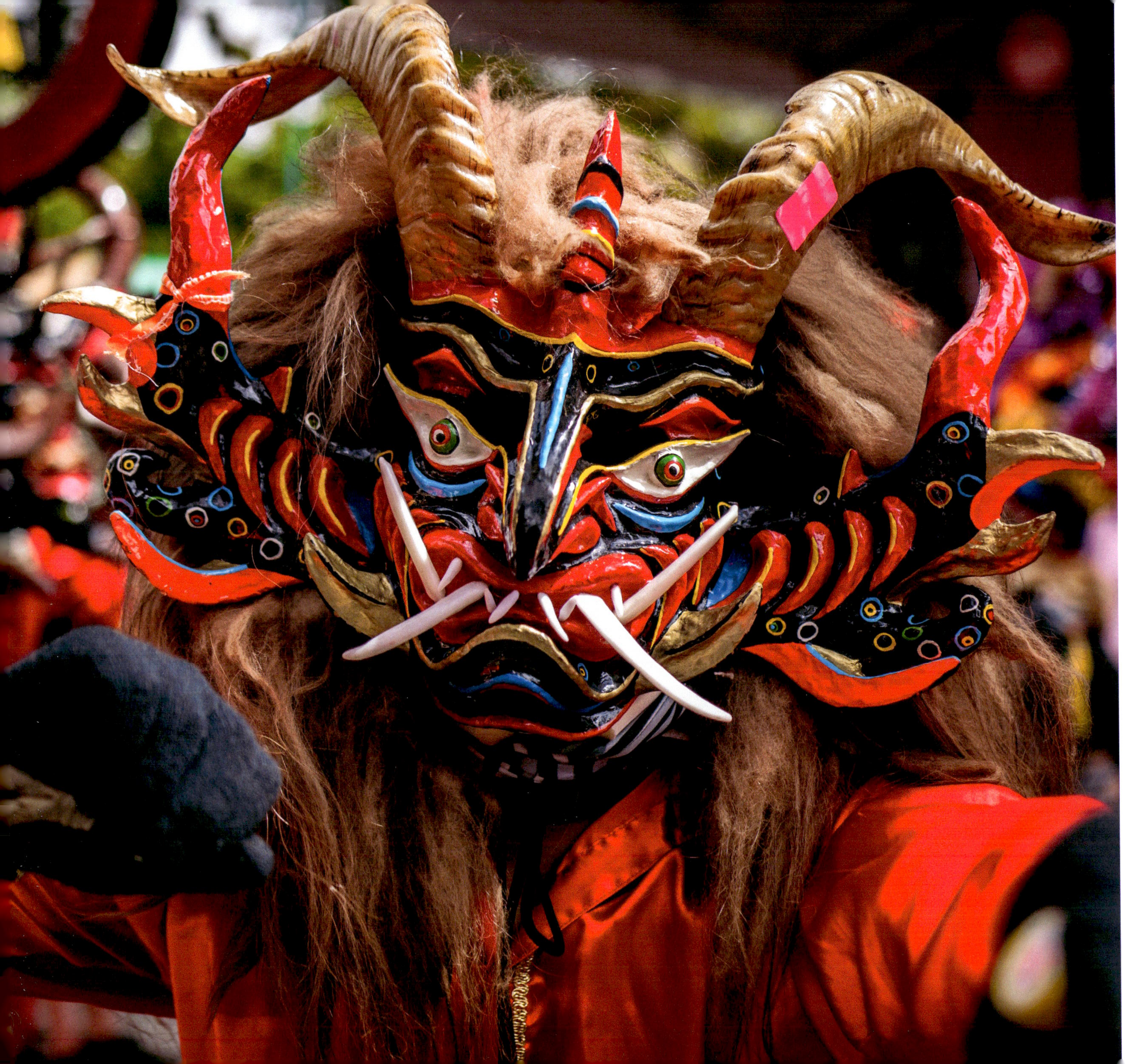

OPPOSITE LEFT:
Granadero de Tarqui, Quito, Ecuador
The President of Ecuador's honour guard is known as the Granaderos de Tarqui. The regiment takes its name from the troops commanded by Antonio José de Sucre, which won a decisive victory against the Spanish in the 1822 Battle of Pichincha, and also fought in the 1829 Battle of Tarqui.

OPPOSITE RIGHT TOP:
National Museum of Ecuador, Quito
This museum's collection includes 70,000 objects, only one per cent of them on display. Visitors can see art from the Quito School and Valdivia and Tumaco-La Tolita cultures.

OPPOSITE RIGHT BOTTOM:
Casa Museo Guayasamín, Quito
In the home of Ecuadorian Kichwa painter Oswaldo Guayasamín is a collection of the painter's own Expressionist works, as well as pre-Columbian artefacts including burial masks.

LEFT:
Diablada de Píllaro, Tungurahua, Ecuador
During this six-day festival, performers wearing devil masks dance through the streets. The event has its roots in pre-Columbian traditions, which absorbed Christian elements while evolving into a channel for rebellion against the Spanish and Catholic Church.

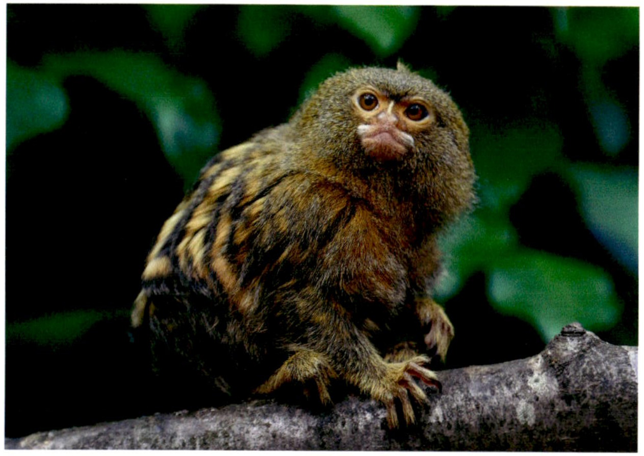

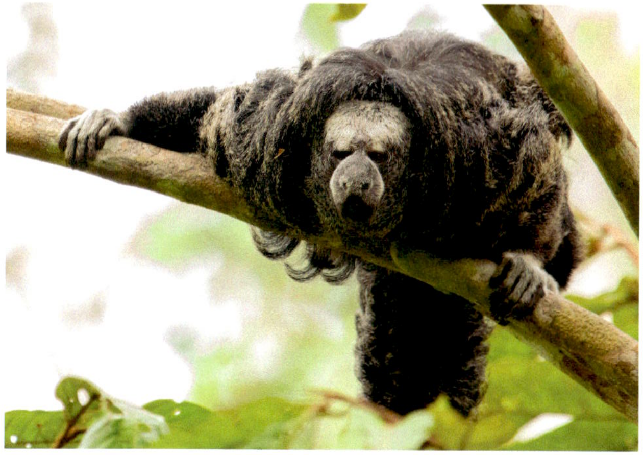

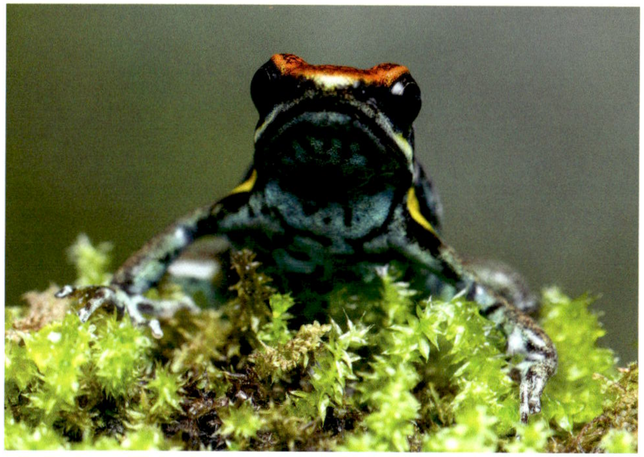

LEFT TOP:

Pygmy Marmoset, Yasuní National Park, Ecuador

Covering 10,000 sq km (3900 sq miles), this rainforest park is one of the most biodiverse areas on the planet, with a dozen monkey species, including the smallest true monkey, the pygmy marmoset, with a head and body length of 12–15cm (4.6–6in). It feeds on tree gum, gnawing holes in bark with its incisors.

LEFT MIDDLE:

Napo Saki, Yasuní

An arboreal fruit-eater, this saki monkey is found around the Napo River. Unlike other New World monkeys, it does not have a prehensile tail so travels through the trees on all fours.

LEFT BOTTOM:

Ecuador Poison Frog, Yasuní

The bright colours of this frog are aposematic, warning predators that its skin glands produce deadly toxins. The male makes a loud two-pulse call to attract a female.

RIGHT:

Quilotoa Lake, Ecuador

This water-filled caldera was created about 800 years ago, when the volcano partially collapsed during a massive eruption. The water's vivid shade is created by the interplay of sunlight and dissolved minerals. The lake forms part of the popular multi-day hike known as the Quilotoa Loop.

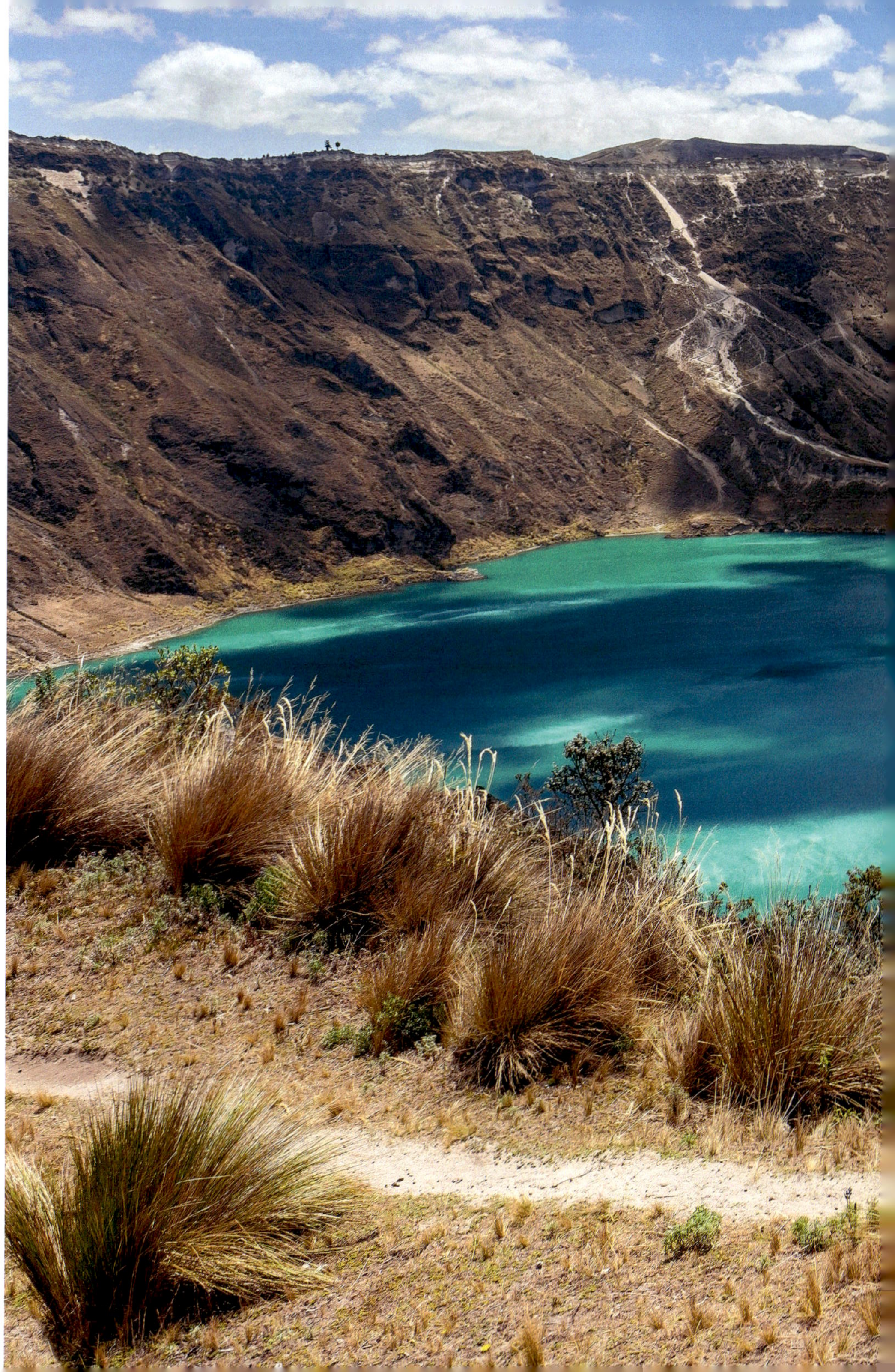

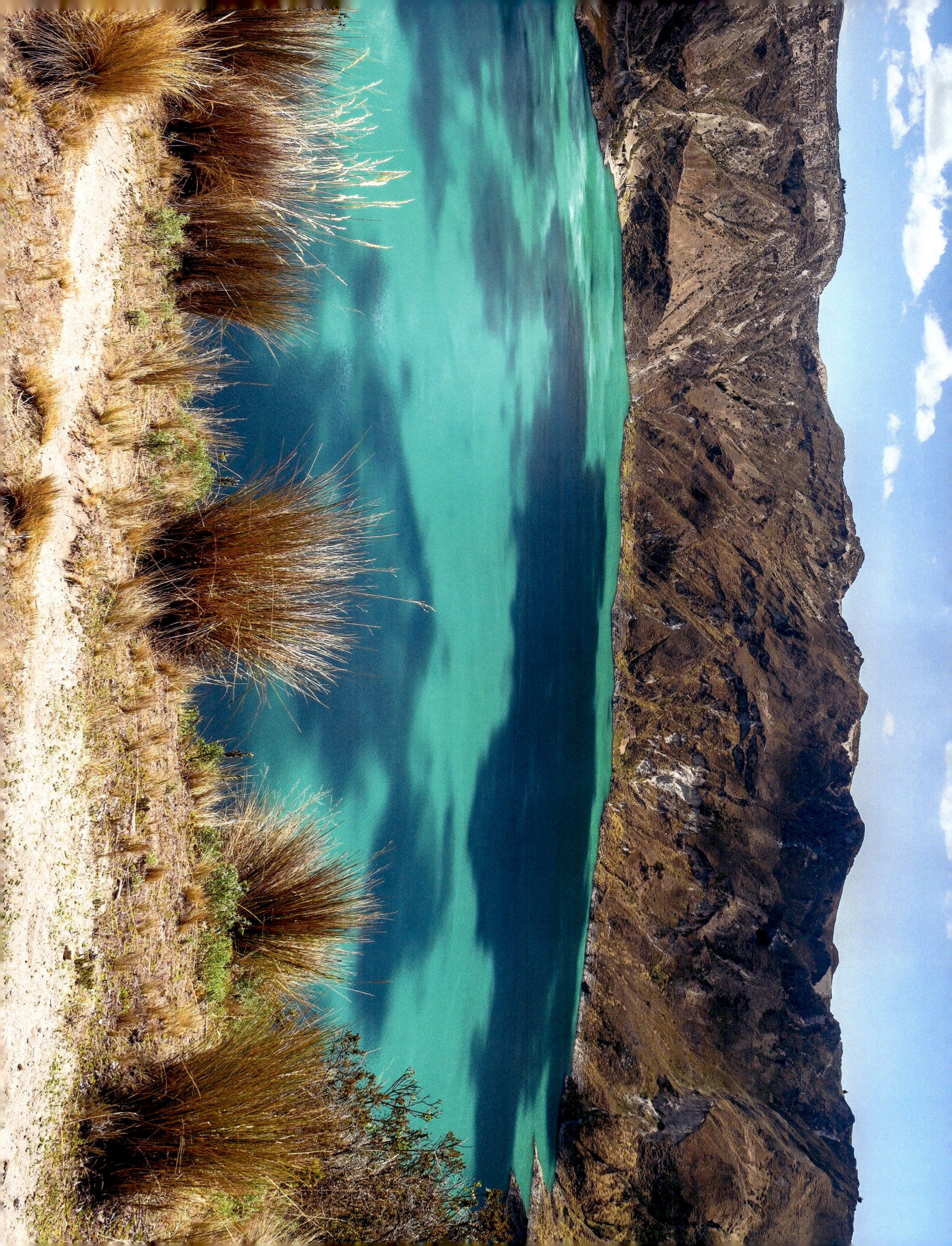

RIGHT:
Seminario San Luis and Nueva Catedral, Cuenca, Ecuador
The three tiled domes of the New Cathedral overlook the courtyard of a former seminary. Construction of the largely Romanesque Revival New Cathedral began in 1885 but continued until 1975. Founded in 1557 on the ruins of an Inca city, Cuenca's historic centre is a UNESCO World Heritage Site.

OPPOSITE LEFT:
Pan Flute, Cuenca
Played throughout the Andes, the pan flute is the national instrument of Ecuador. It is typically made from bamboo stems, closed at the bottom and blown across the top.

OPPOSITE RIGHT TOP:
Charango, Cuenca
This small Andean stringed instrument may have descended from lutes brought to the region by the Spanish. Traditionally, the *charango* was made from an armadillo's shell, but the modern instrument is wooden.

OPPOSITE RIGHT BOTTOM:
Toquilla Hat, Cuenca
Although often called a Panama hat in English, this traditional straw hat has its roots in Ecuador, where it is woven from the leaves of the toquilla palm (*Carludovica palmata*). The Cuenca-style weave has a herringbone pattern.

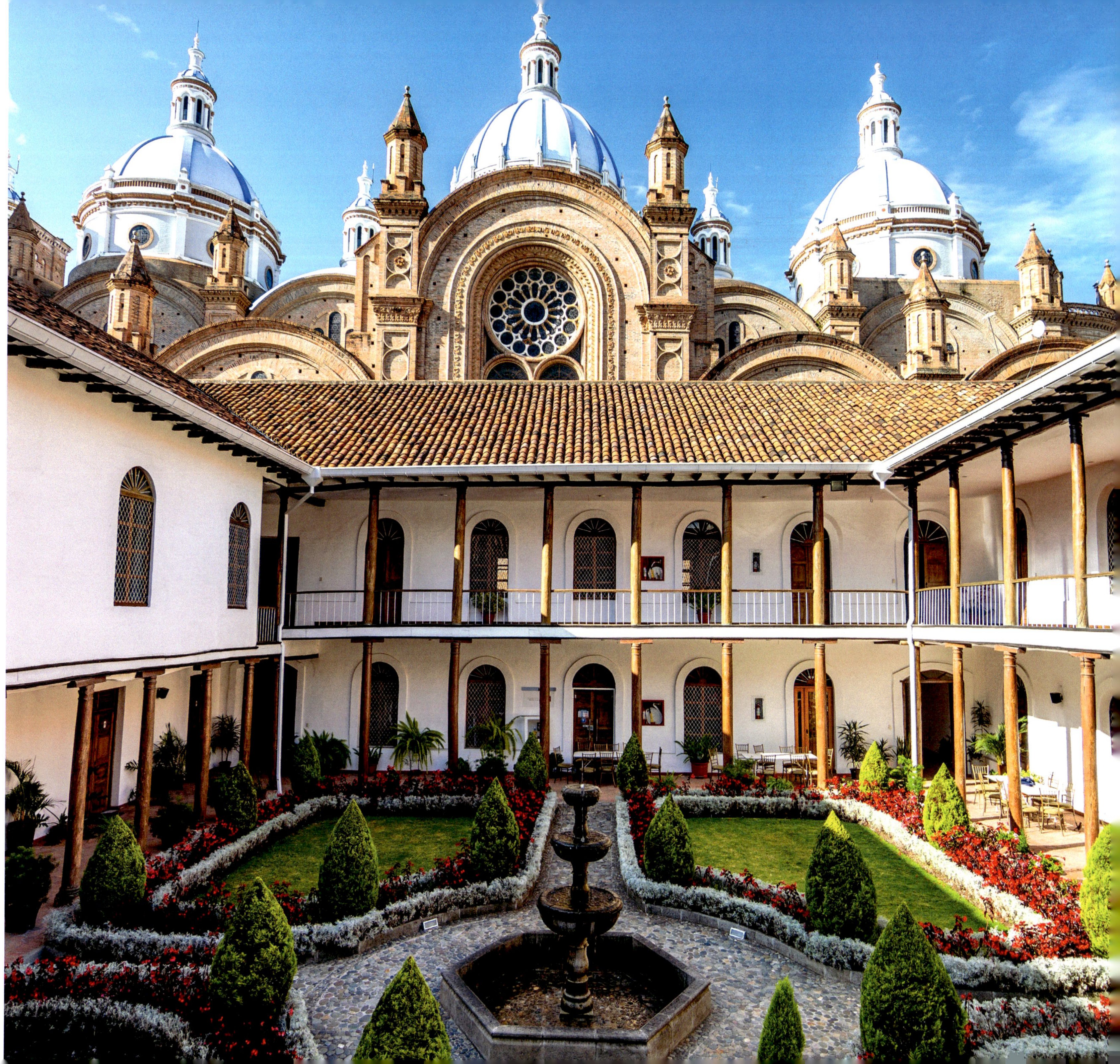

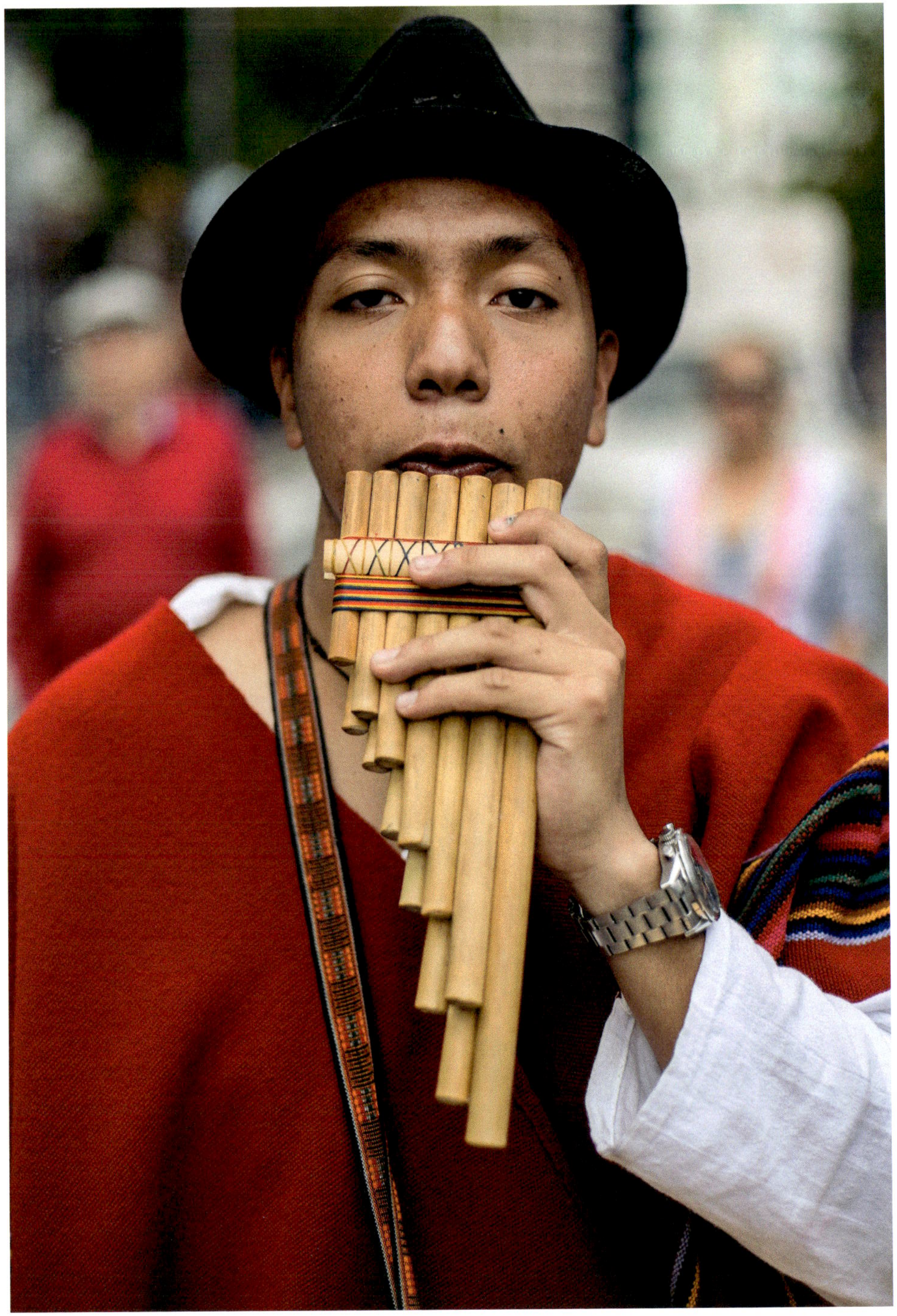

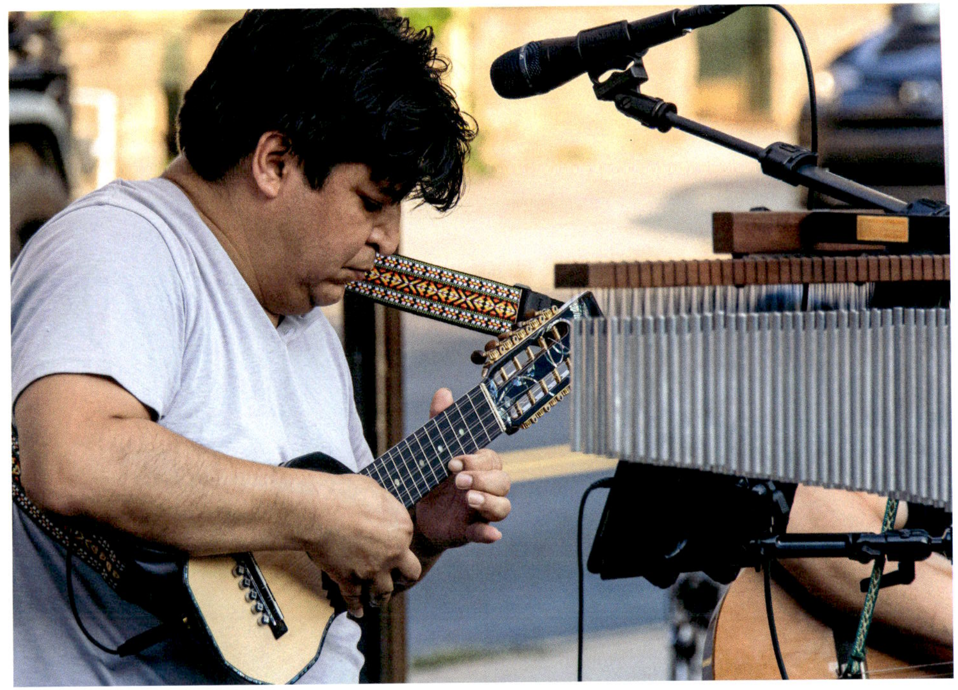

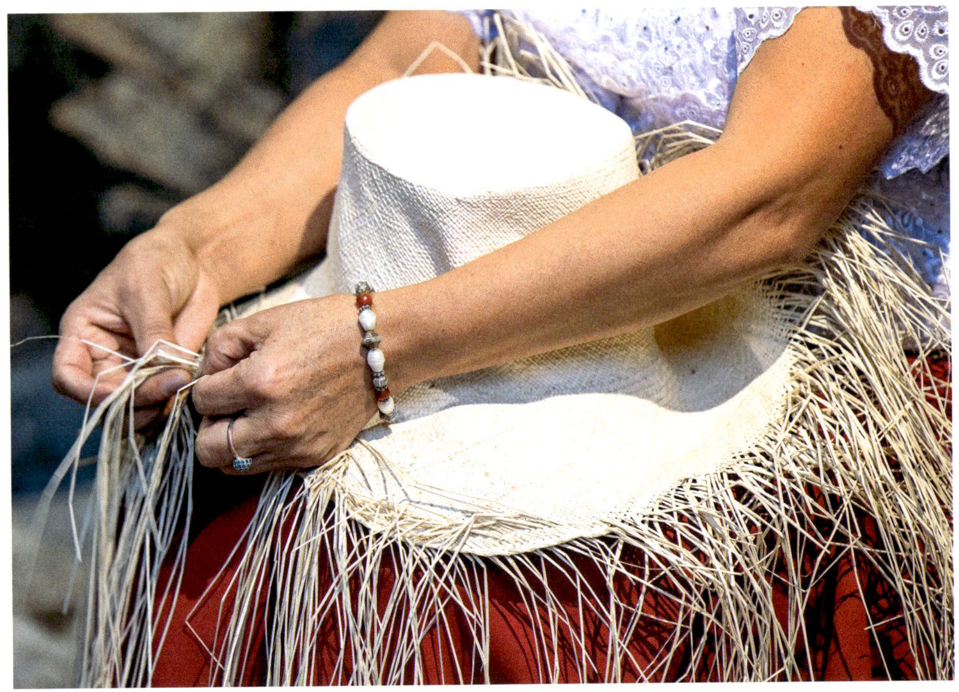

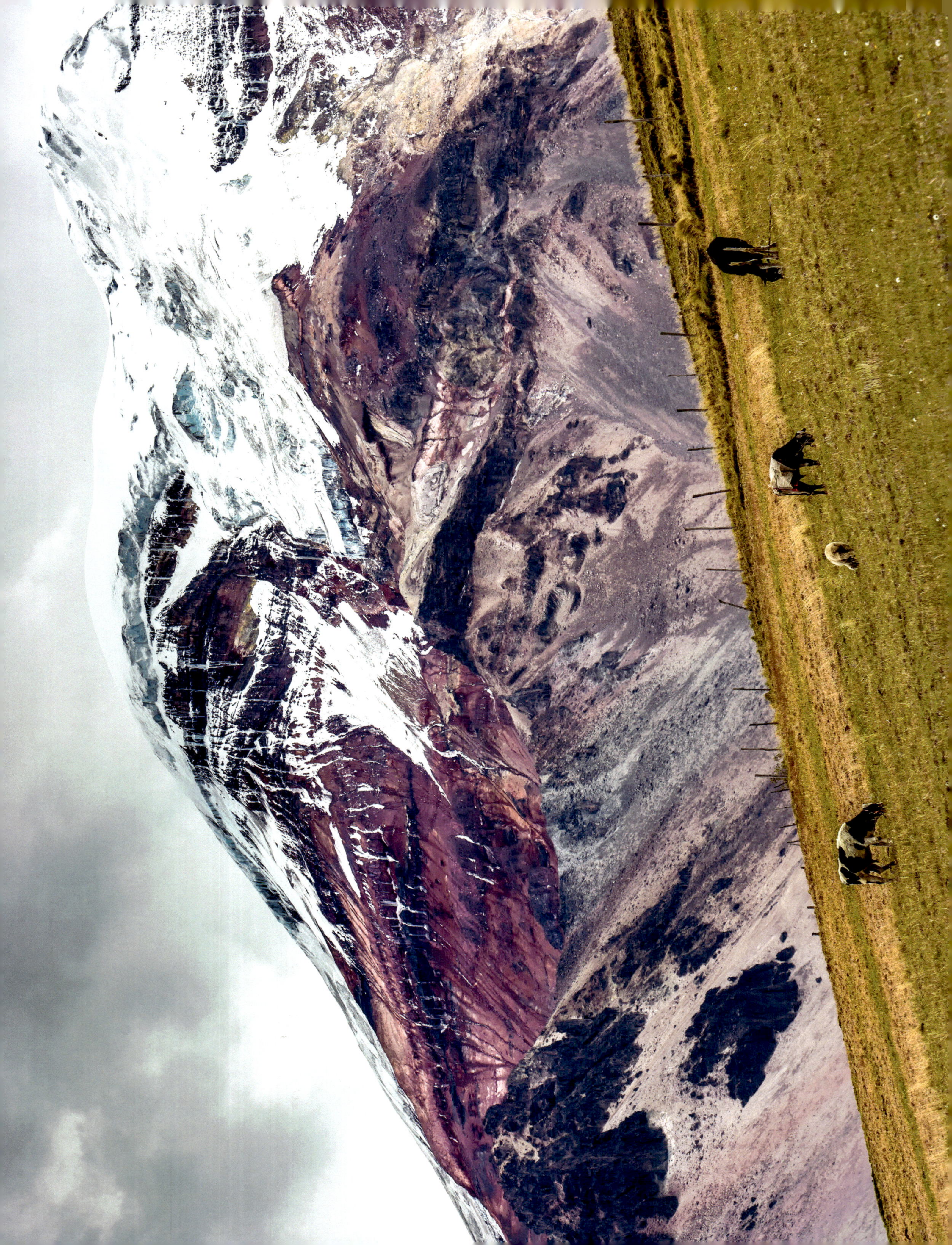

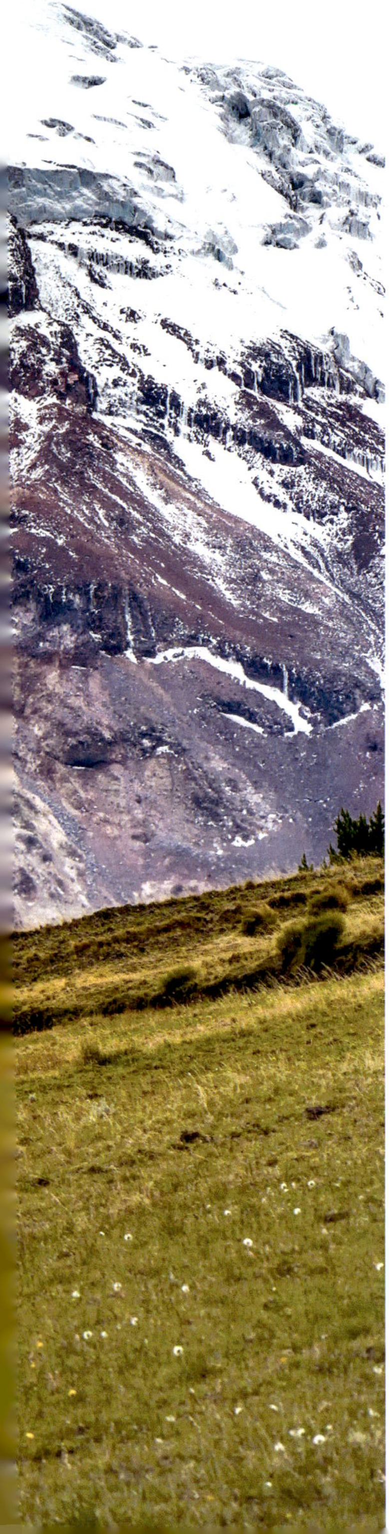

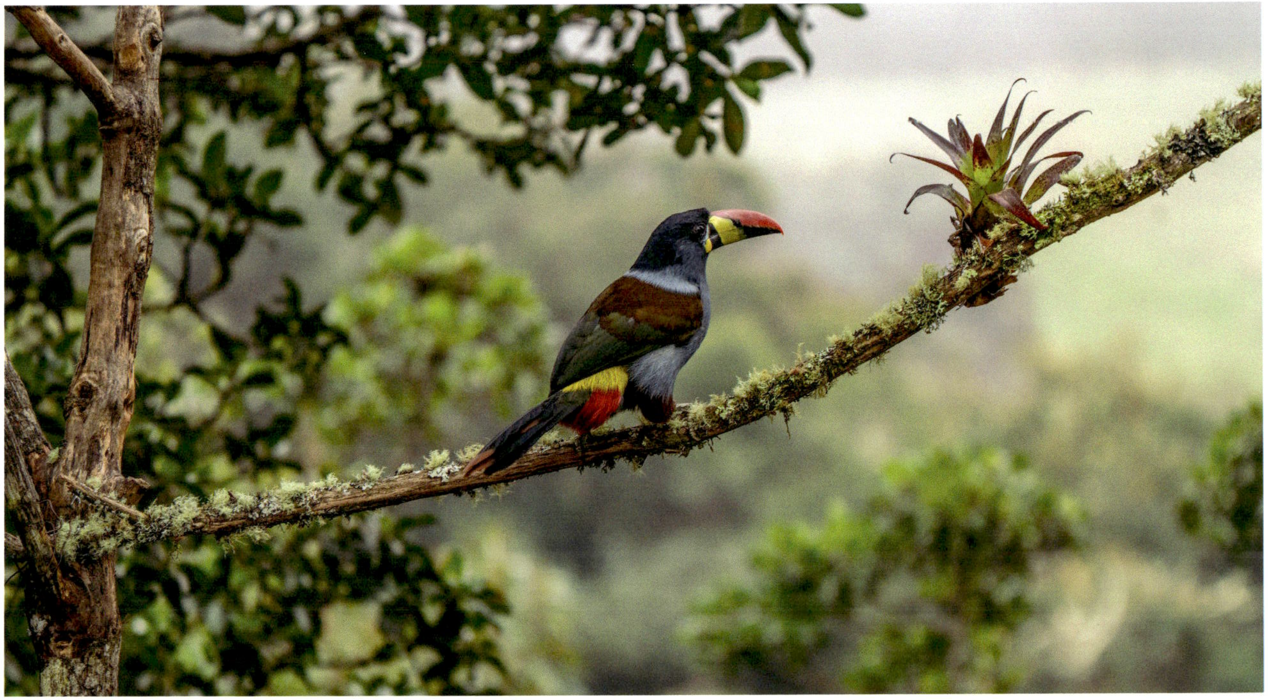

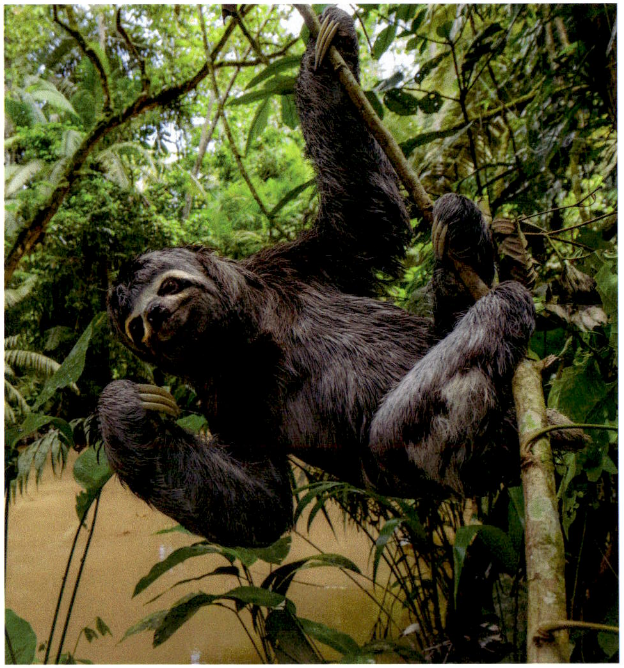

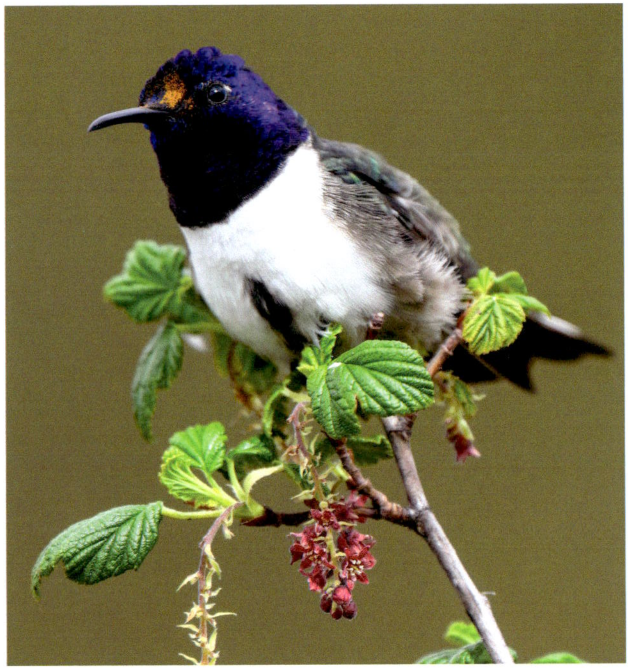

FAR LEFT:
Chimborazo, Ecuador
At 6263.47m (20,549ft) tall, this stratovolcano is Ecuador's highest mountain. Although it is not among the world's 200 tallest mountains when measured from sea level, its summit is the furthest point from the planet's centre due to being on the equatorial bulge.

LEFT TOP:
Grey-breasted Mountain Toucan, El Cajas, Ecuador
This toucan lives in temperate montane forests of the Andes, where it uses its large bill to pluck fruit. The bill is lightweight for its size, since it is composed of a bone lattice, filled with foam-like keratin.

BOTTOM LEFT:
Brown-throated Sloth, Yasuní, Ecuador
Three of the six species of sloths are found in Ecuador, the most common of them the three-toed brown-throated. Due to its low-energy diet of mainly leaves, the sloth sleeps for 15 to 18 hours daily and usually moves slowly.

BOTTOM RIGHT:
Male Ecuadorian Hillstar Hummingbird, Cotacachi Cayapas Reserve, Ecuador
About 12cm (5in) long, this hummingbird lives in Andean grassland at up to 5200m (17,000ft). Unlike most hummingbirds, it perches rather than hovers to feed on nectar, which conserves energy in its cold habitat.

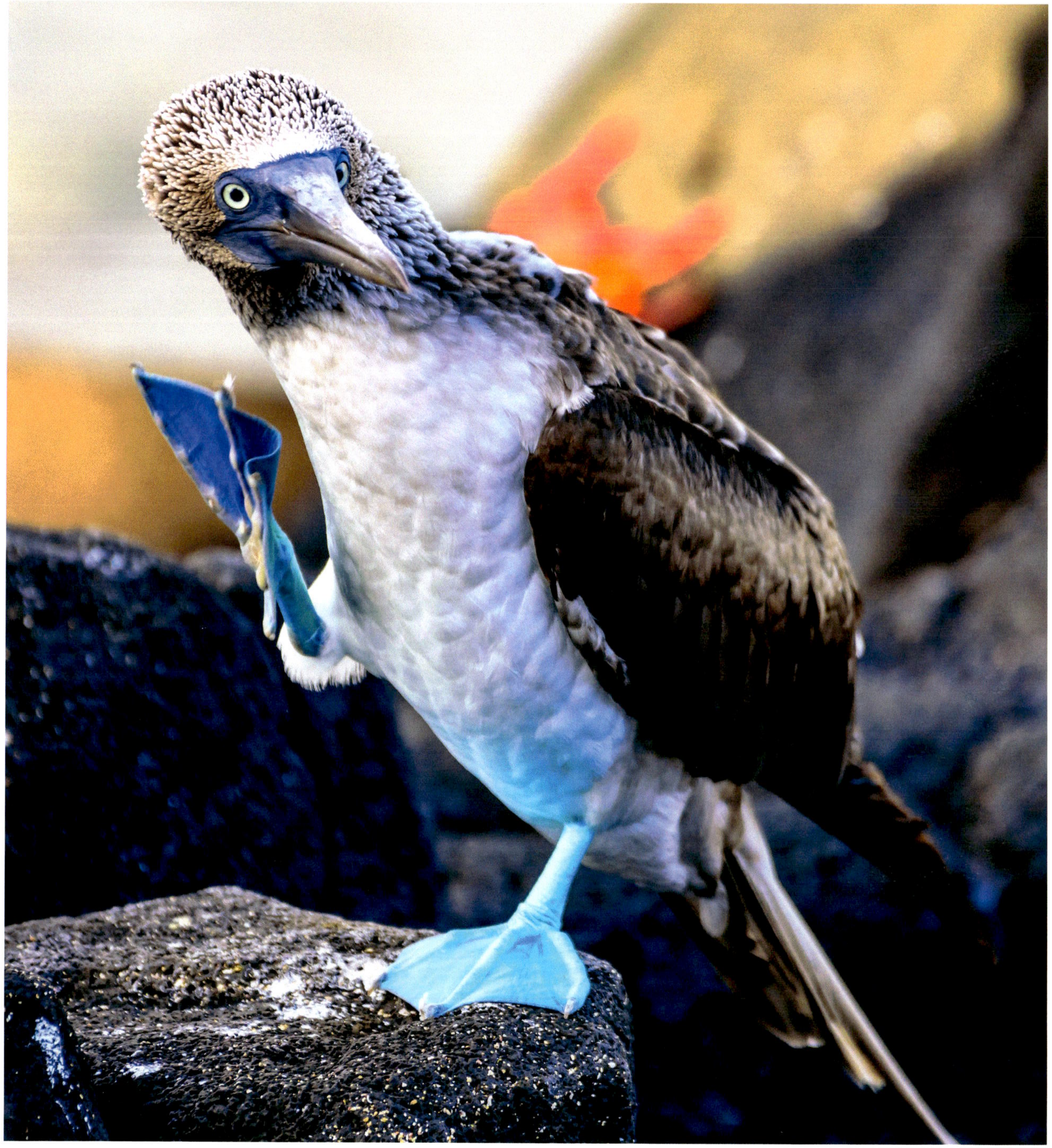

LEFT:
Blue-footed Booby, Galápagos Islands, Ecuador
Half of all breeding pairs of blue-footed boobies nest on the Galápagos Islands. To attract a mate, the male shows off his feet by lifting them while strutting. The feet's bright shade is a sign of fitness to mate. The underlying colour of the skin is purplish, but it turns turquoise if the bird has eaten well, due to carotenoid pigments in its diet of sardines and anchovies.

RIGHT:
Marine Iguana, Galápagos Islands
Up to 97 per cent of the reptiles on the Galápagos Islands are endemic due to their geographical isolation. This island endemism inspired Charles Darwin's theory of evolution after he visited in 1835. One endemic species is the marine iguana, the world's only ocean-going lizard, which dives for algae in shallow coastal water.

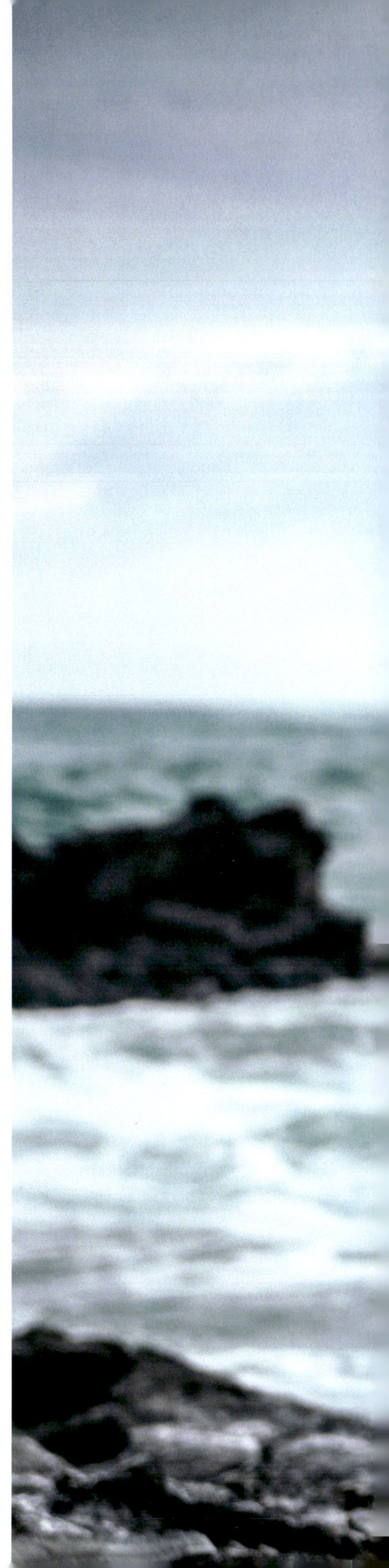

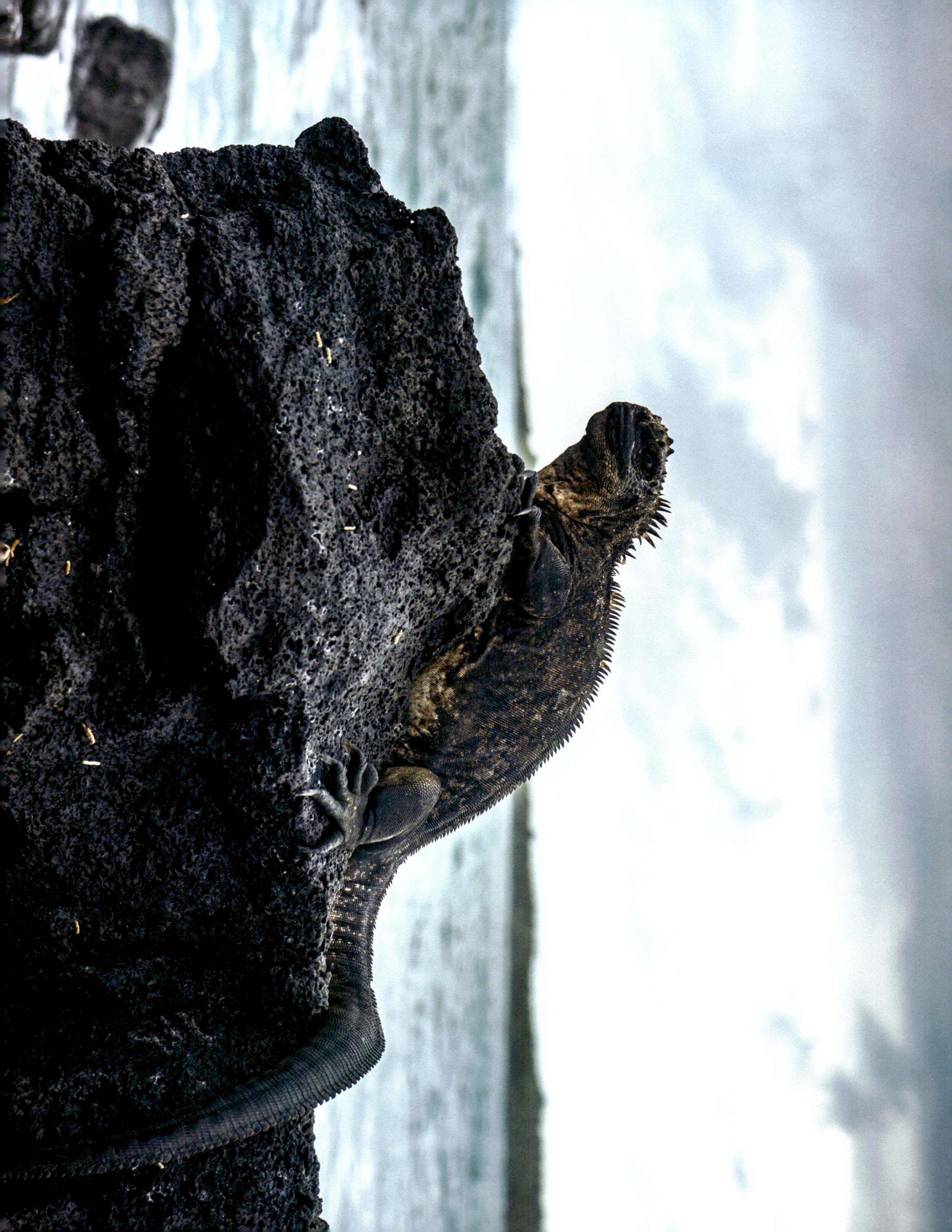

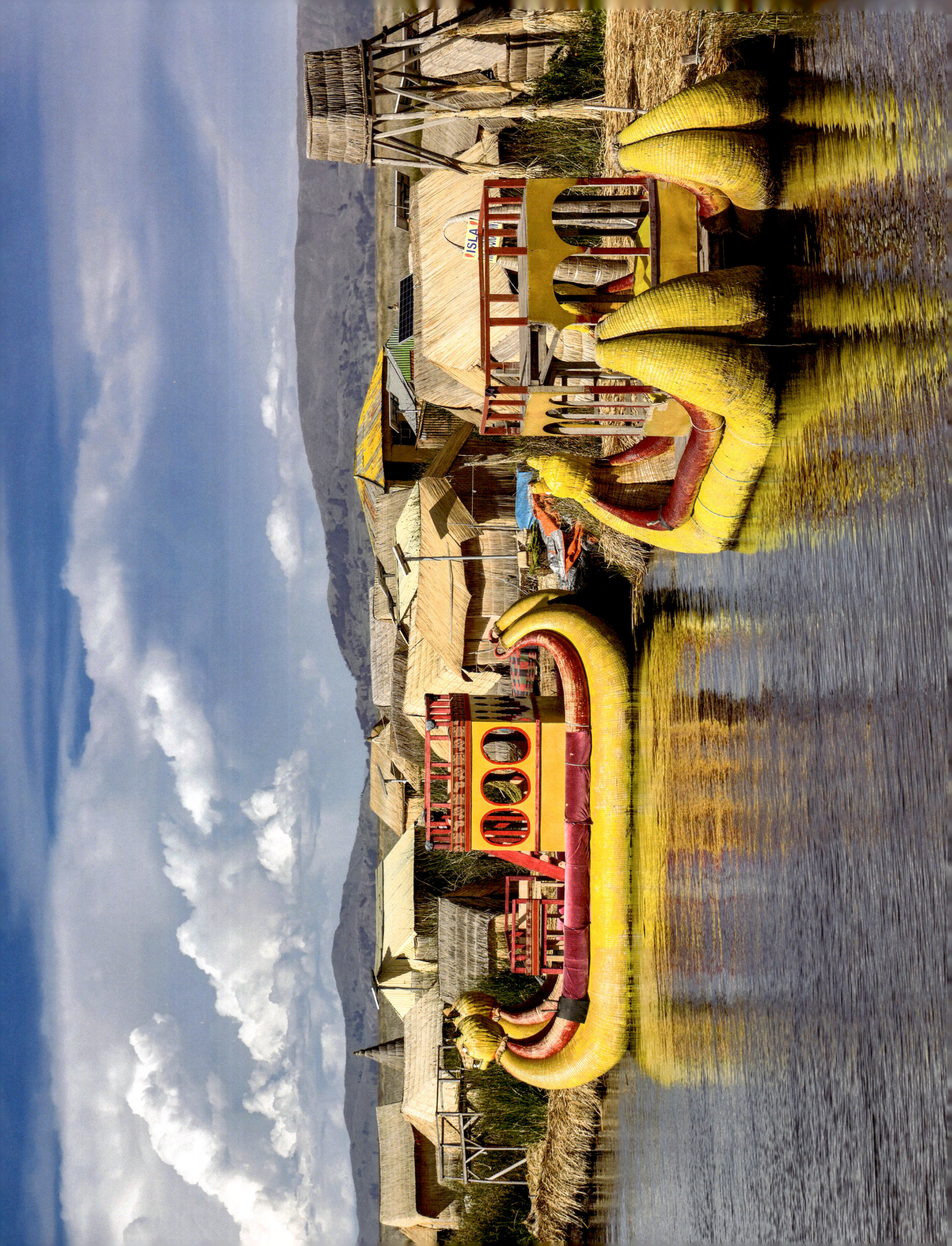

Peru and Bolivia

Peru and Bolivia are megadiverse countries, since they are home to a vast number of Earth's species, many of them endemic. Peru boasts at least 21,000 species of plants and animals, nearly 6000 of them endemic, while Bolivia has more than 20,000 species, at least 3000 endemic. This extraordinary diversity is caused in large part by the countries' tropical location, but is helped along by their extreme range of biomes. Sandwiched between the Pacific Ocean and the Andes, Peru's narrow western strip is largely desert, punctuated by river valleys. The aridity is caused by the cold Humboldt ocean current, which cools the air and limits evaporation, while the towering Andes block moisture-laden air arriving from the Amazon Basin. The Andes themselves form Peru's central *sierra*, where the country's highest peaks are found, at least a dozen active stratovolcanoes and the northern portion of the alpine grassland known as the Altiplano. In Peru's east is Amazonia, a world of highland and lowland rainforest, flooded forest and rivers. South America's largest landlocked country, Bolivia is divided between the Andean highlands of its west, and the tropical lowlands of its north and east. The highland region encompasses snow-capped peaks, Altiplano and temperate, fertile inter-Andean valleys. The Bolivian lowlands are cloaked by the Amazon Rainforest in the east and north, while in the southeast is the Gran Chaco, a vast semi-arid region covered mainly by dry forest, savanna and thorn scrub.

OPPOSITE:

Lake Titicaca, Peru–Bolivia

South America's largest lake straddles the border between Peru and Bolivia, high on the Altiplano. Hundreds of years ago, the Uros people moved onto the lake to escape territorial disputes. Today, some still live on Titicaca on 120 floating islands made from totara roots and reeds. Their homes and boats, used for fishing and hunting waterbirds, are also woven from reeds.

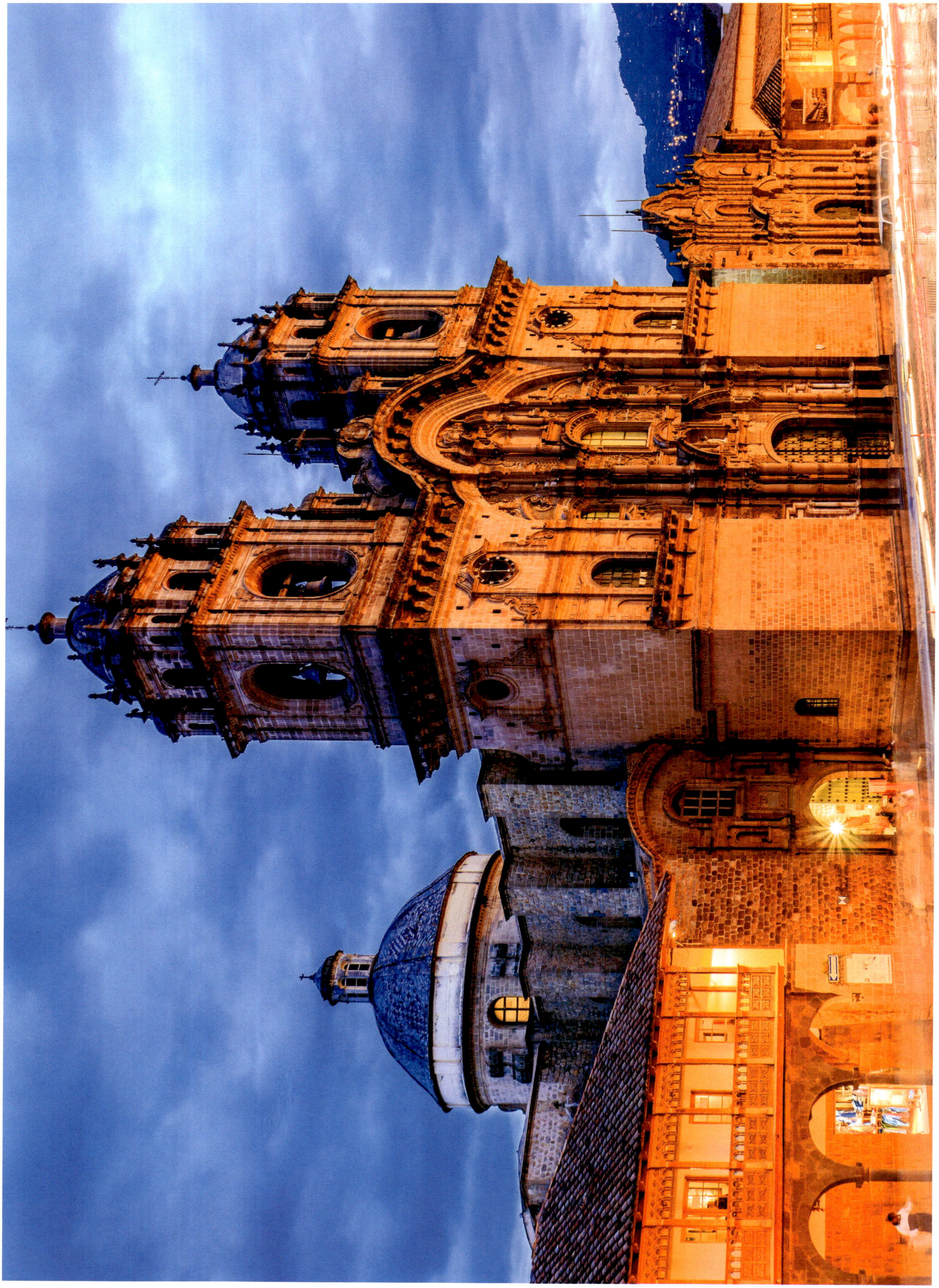

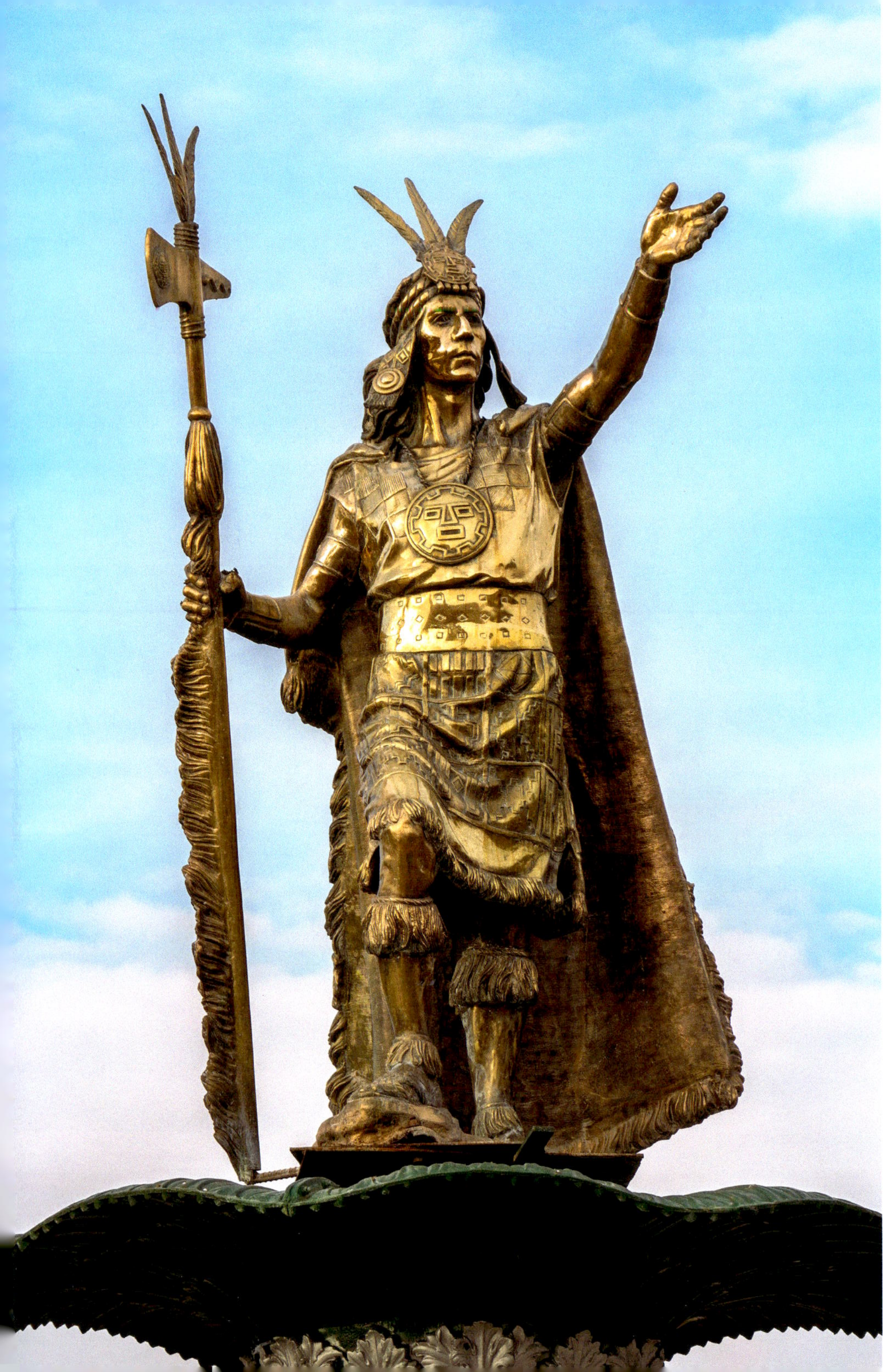

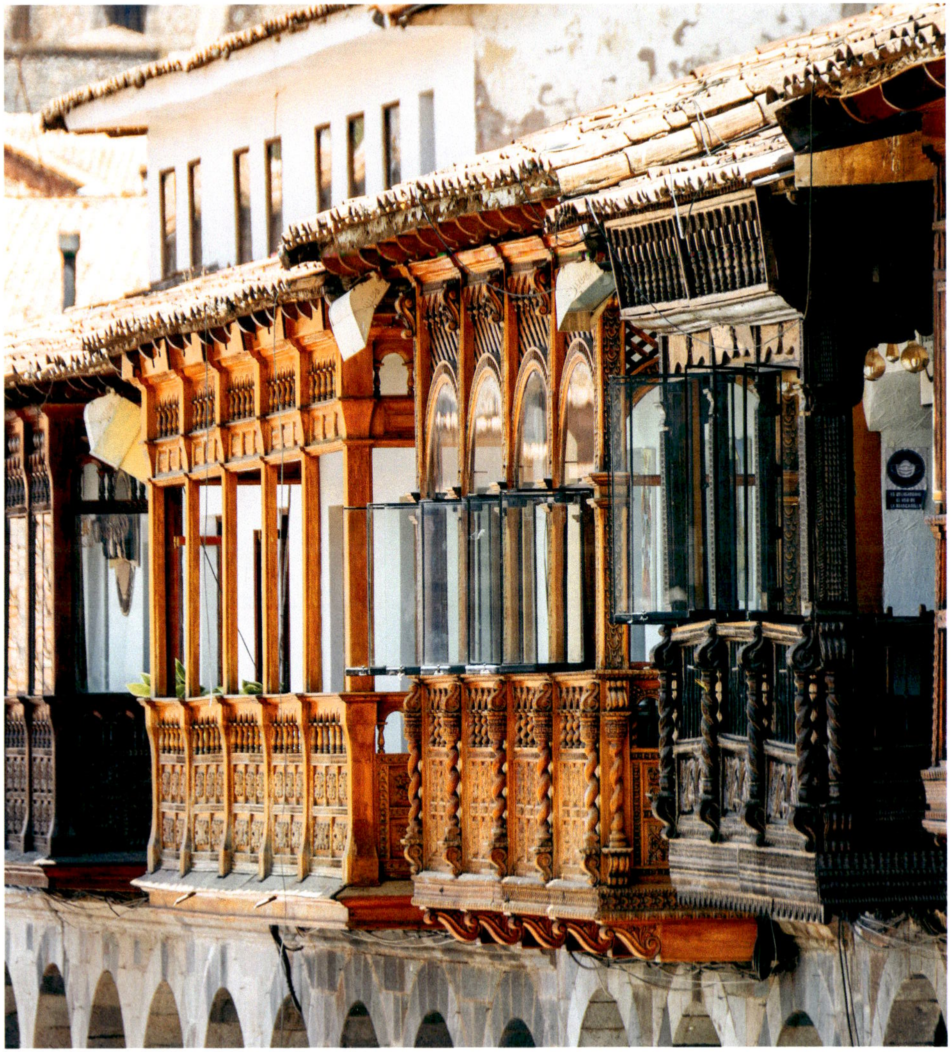

OPPOSITE:
Iglesia de la Compañía de Jesús, Cusco, Peru
Built on the site of an Inca palace, this Jesuit church was completed in 1673. It is a masterpiece of Spanish Baroque, its pink façade featuring a trilobe awash with Corinthian columns and intricately carved niches.

LEFT:
Monument to Pachacuti, Plaza de Armas, Cusco
Pachacuti was the ninth ruler, called the Sapa Inca, of the Kingdom of Cusco. During his reign (c. 1438–71), Inca warriors and diplomats conquered neighbouring territories, starting the rapid expansion of the Inca Empire.

ABOVE:
***Miradores*, Plaza de Armas, Cusco**
Known as *miradores*, balconies carved from cedar or mahogany are a feature of Cusco's colonial architecture. Their open design allowed cooling airflow, while providing privacy for watching the plaza below.

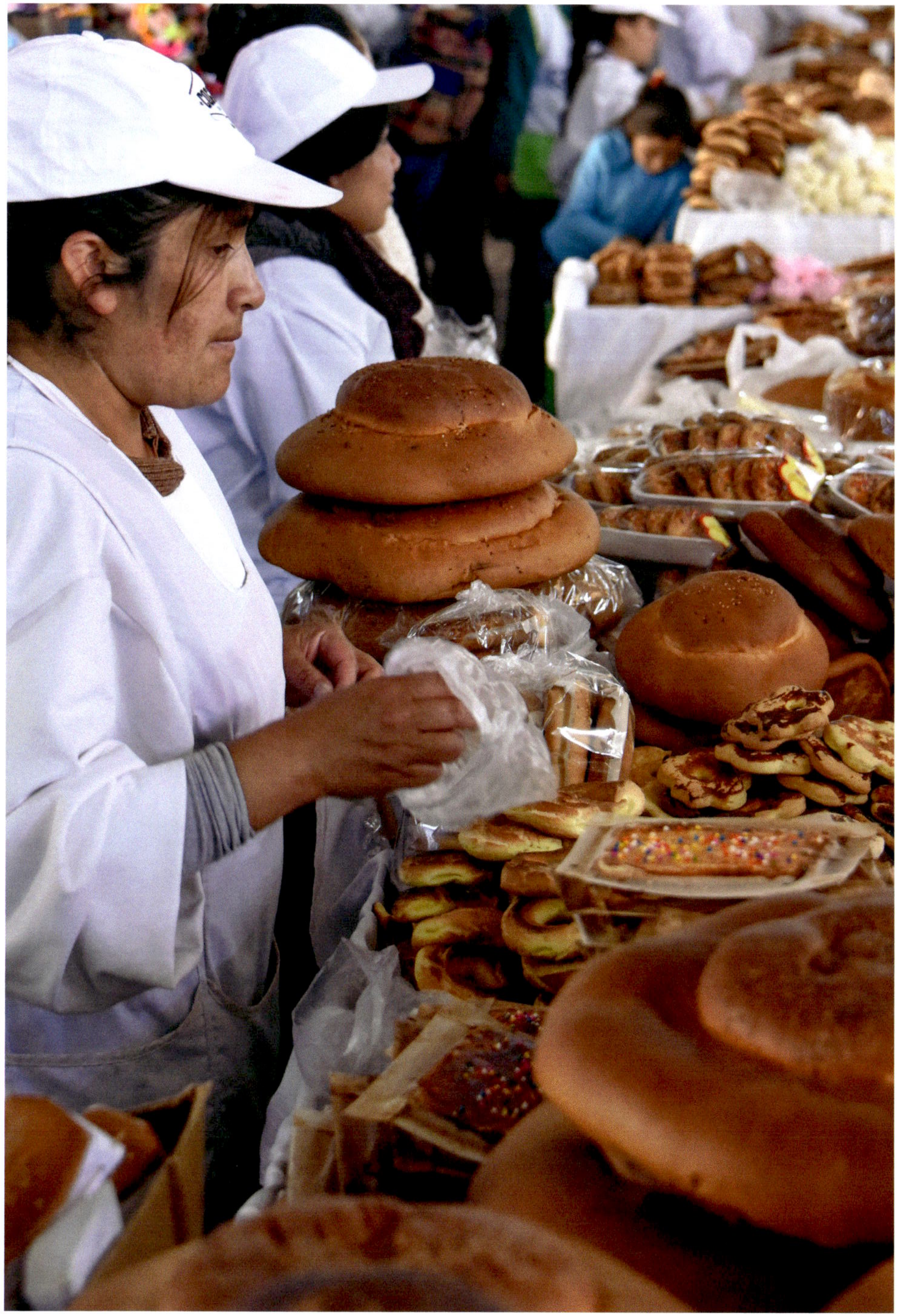

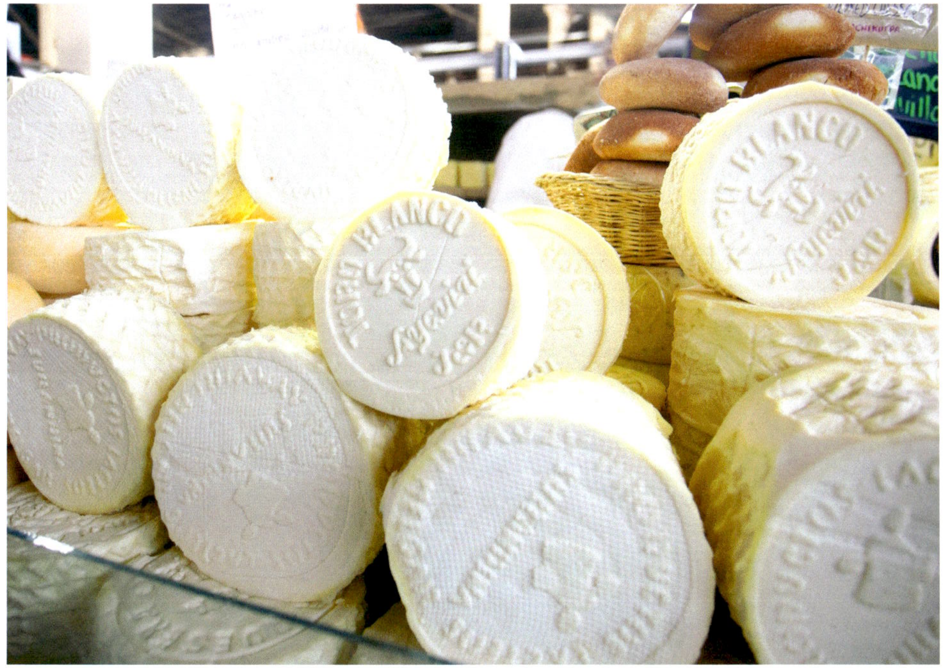
TORO BLANCO

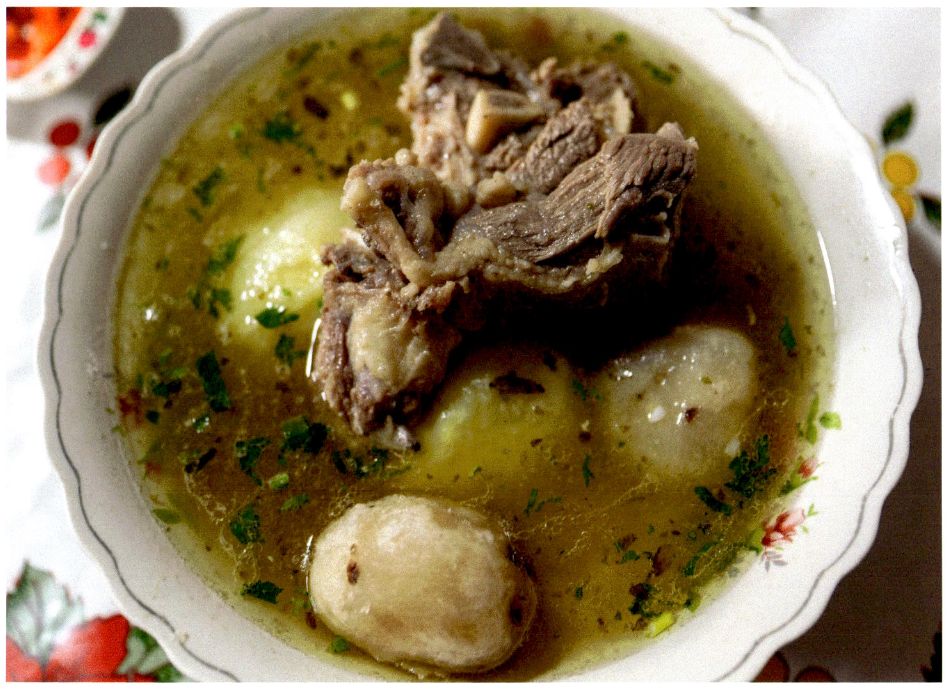

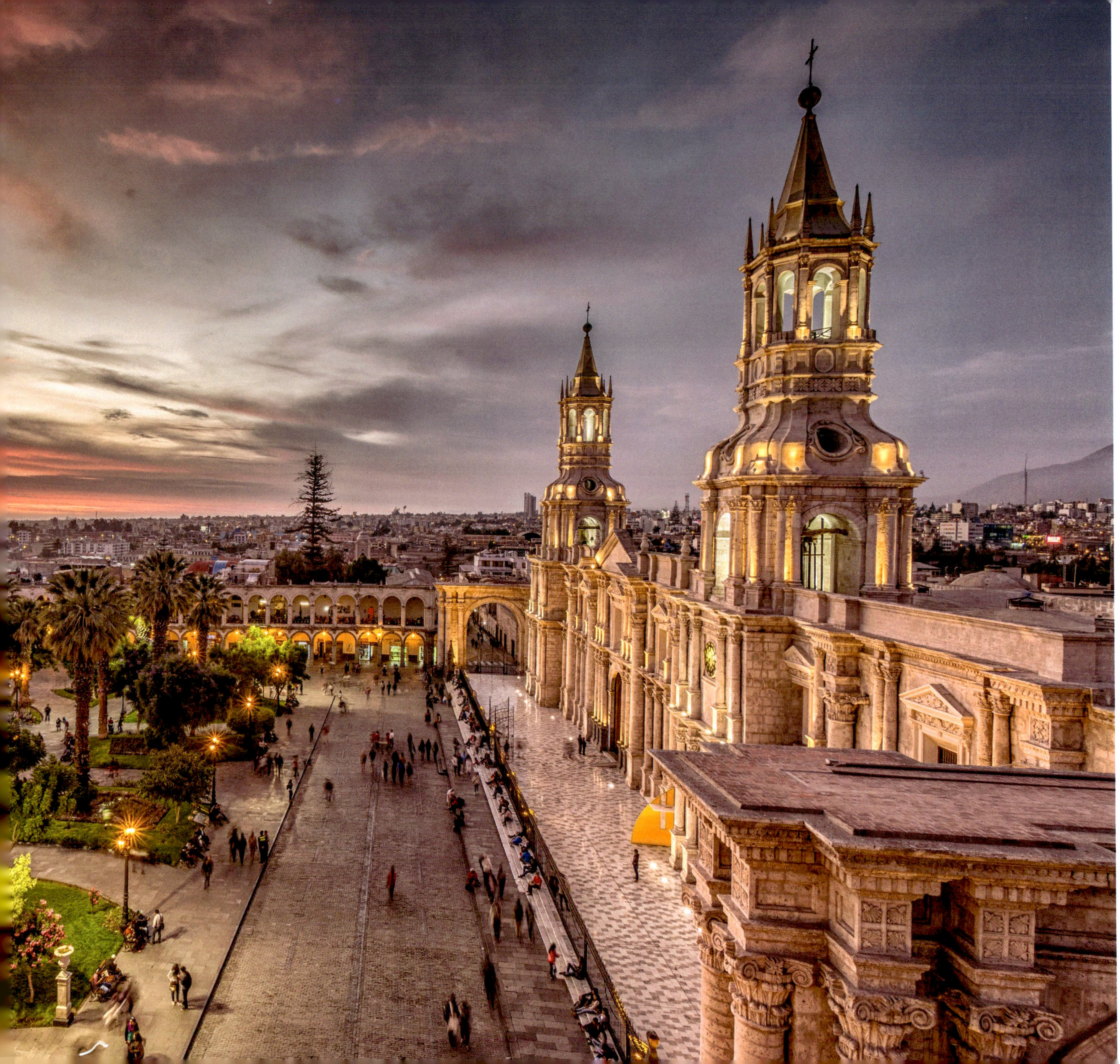

OPPOSITE LEFT:
***Pan Chuta*, Mercado Central de San Pedro, Cusco, Peru**
Stallholders sell local breads, including *pan chuta*, a large, round flatbread from the nearby town of Oropesa. It has a slightly sweet flavour, due to anise seeds, and sometimes a caramel filling.

OPPOSITE TOP RIGHT:
***Queso Fresco*, Mercado Central de San Pedro**
White, soft cheeses are a staple in Peru. They are eaten with corn and used to make sauces such as Huancaína, which also contains spicy ají amarillo peppers.

OPPOSITE BOTTOM RIGHT:
***Caldo de Cordero*, Cusco**
This lamb broth contains freeze-dried potatoes called *chuño*. Traditionally, this Inca method of preservation makes use of frost-resistant potatoes, which are frozen in the cold Andean night air, then dried in intense daytime sunlight.

LEFT:
Basilica Cathedral, Arequipa, Peru
This Neo-Romanesque cathedral, with Gothic touches, was built between 1540 and 1656 from a pale volcanic stone called sillar. The use of this material in its historic centre earned Arequipa the nickname of Ciudad Blanca ('White City').

RIGHT TOP:
***Taulli Macho*, Huascarán National Park, Ancash, Peru**
This giant lupin grows in the Cordillera Blanca, part of the Andes range, as high as 4500m (14,760ft) on Mount Huascarán. The plant's edible but bitter-tasting beans have been eaten by Andean peoples for millennia.

RIGHT BOTTOM:
Pastoruri Glacier, Huascarán National Park
One of the last glaciers in South America's tropics, Pastoruri is retreating rapidly. Currently around 8 sq km (3 sq miles), it lies in a bowl-shaped depression, called a cirque, at an altitude of 5250m (17,200ft).

FAR RIGHT:
Mount Huascarán
At 6768m (22,205ft), Huascarán is the tallest mountain in Peru and the fourth highest in South America after Argentina's Aconcagua (6967m; 22,858ft), Argentina–Chile's Ojos del Salado and Argentina's Monte Pissis. Huascarán has two main summits, with the southern the taller.

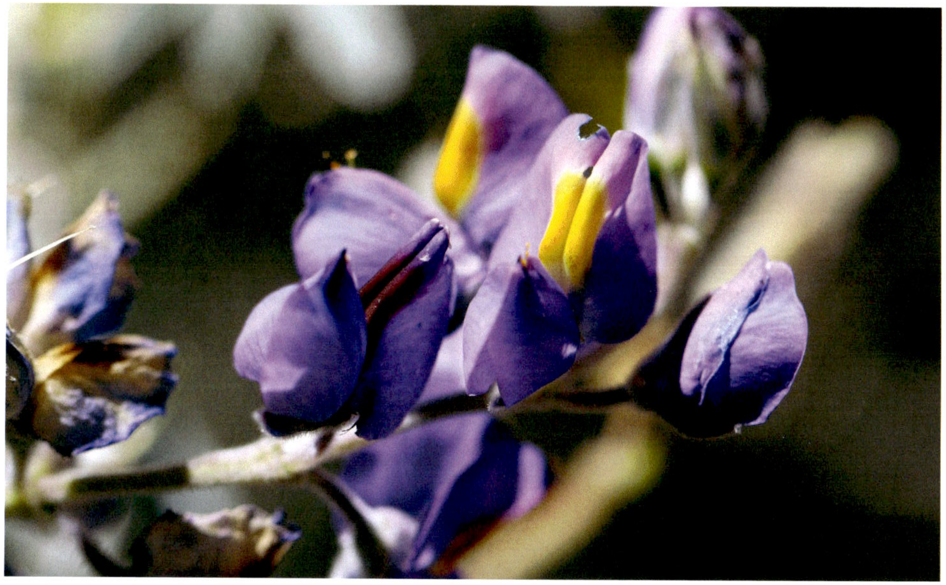

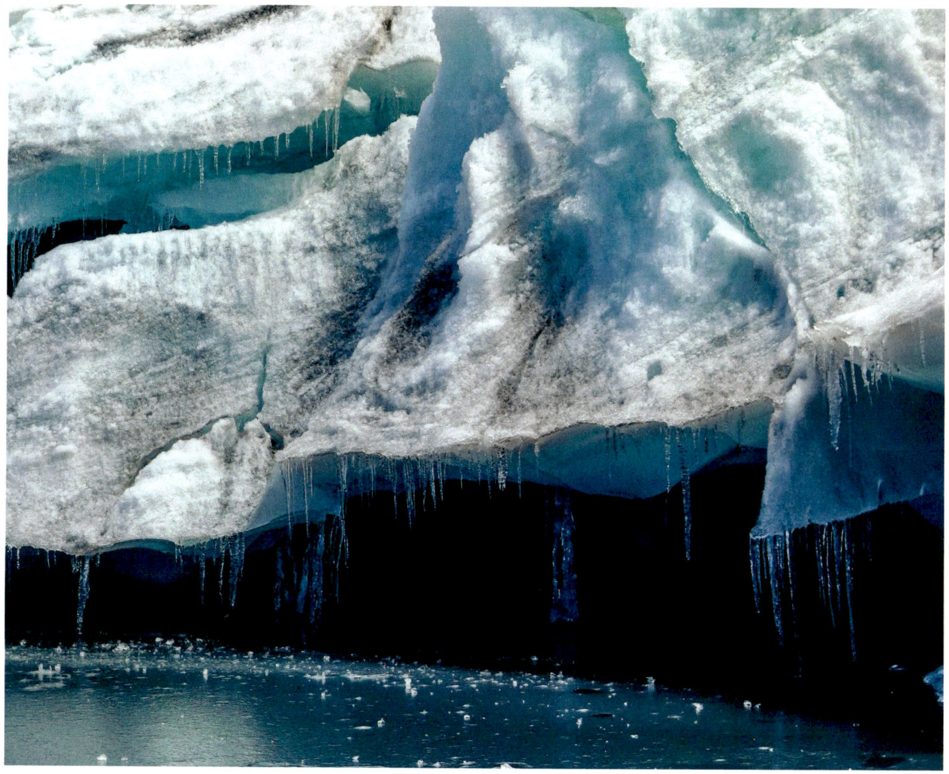

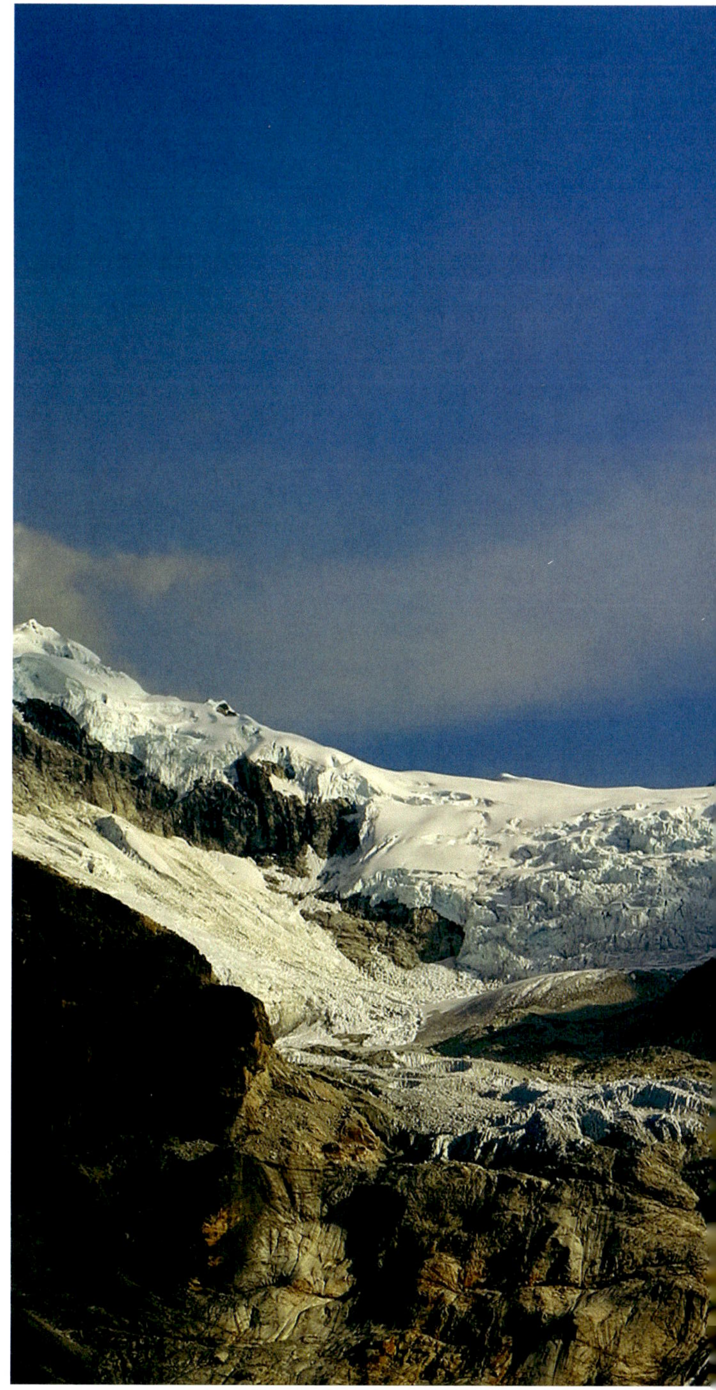

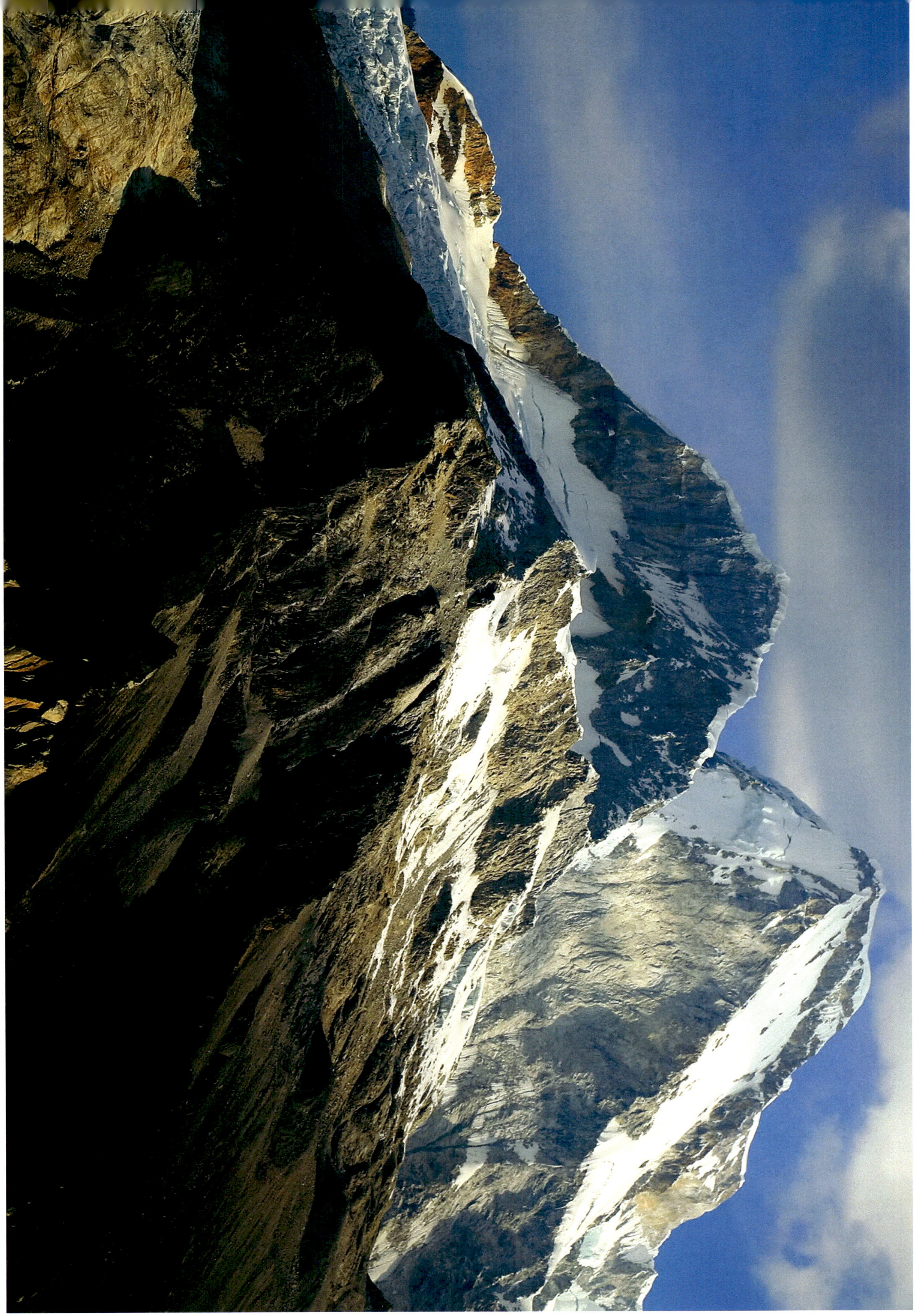

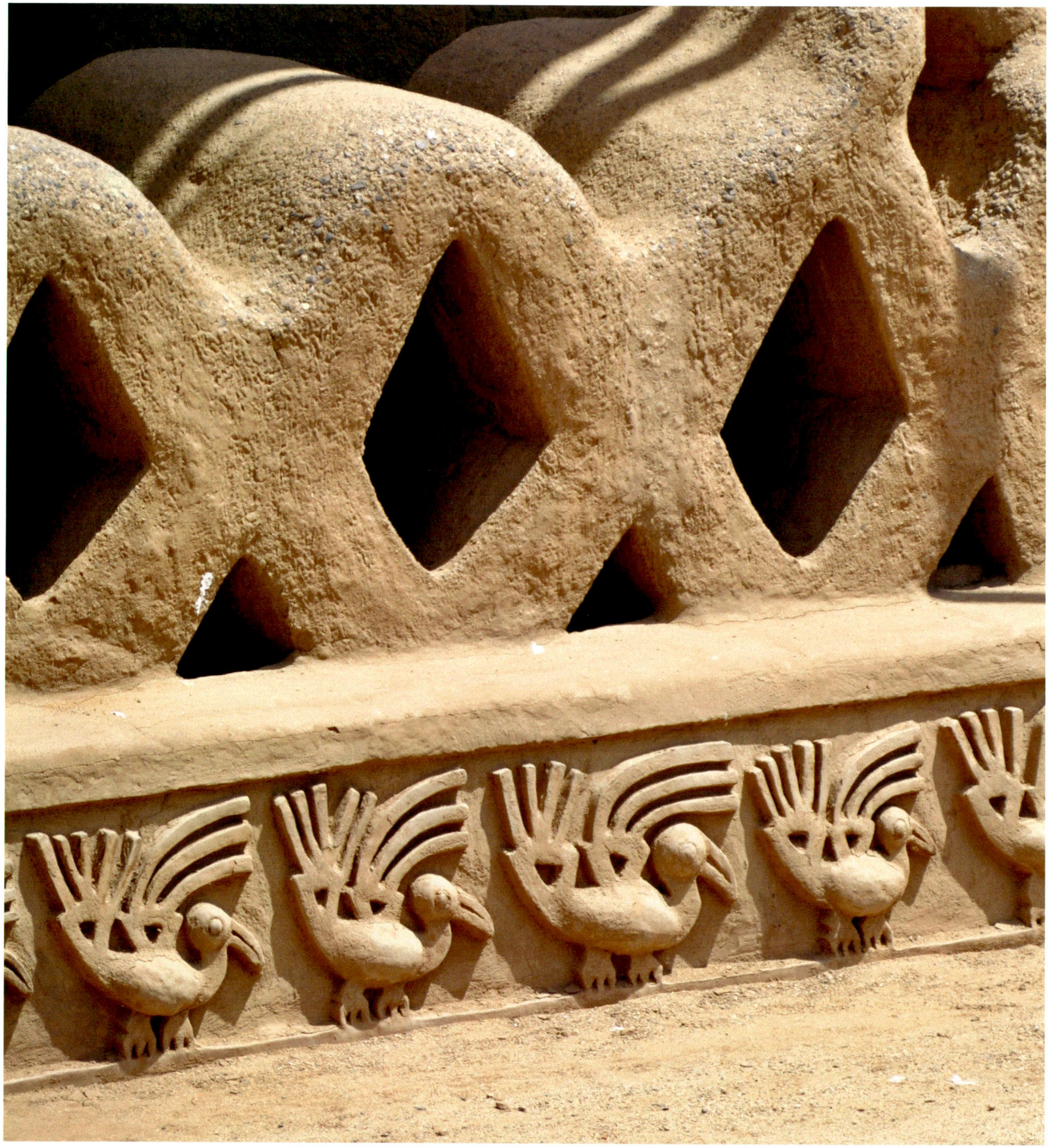
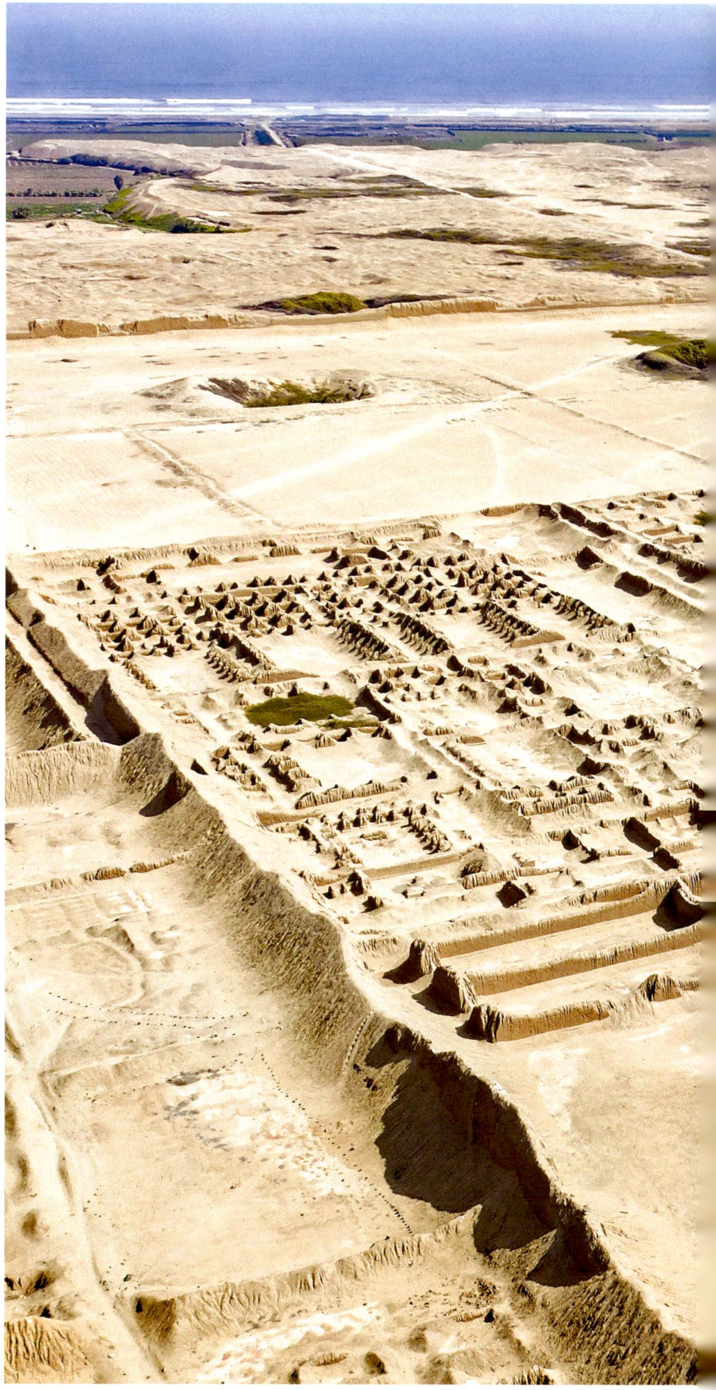

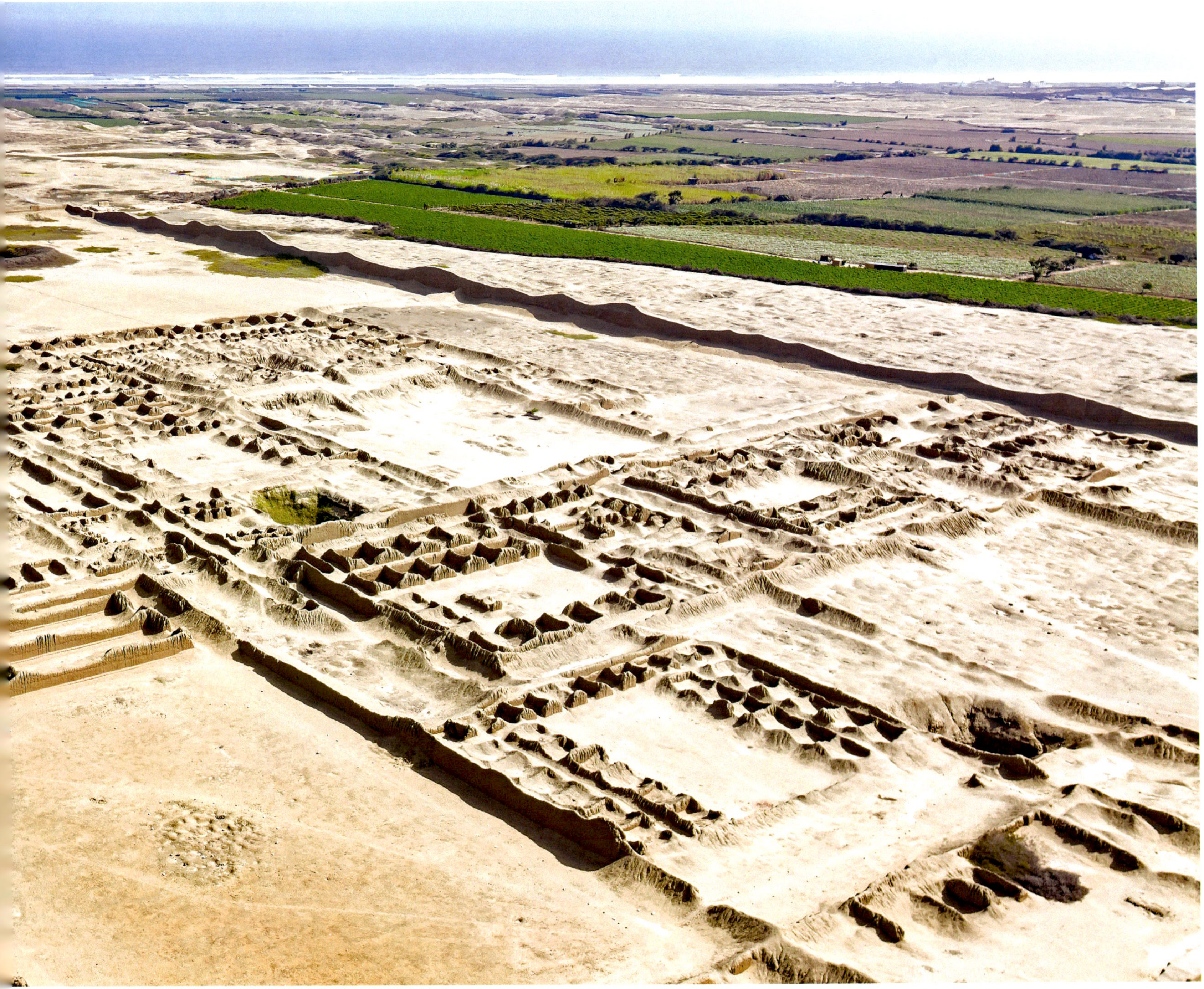

OPPOSITE:

Adobe Frieze, Chan Chan, Peru

Chan Chan was capital of the Chimor Kingdom from around 900 to 1470 CE, with 50,000 inhabitants at the city's peak. The temples, warehouses, palaces and craftspeople's homes were built of sun-dried mud bricks. Many walls were carved with designs of birds, fish, humans and waves.

LEFT:

City Plan, Chan Chan

Located in the coastal Sechura Desert, the walled city of Chan Chan relied on deep wells and on irrigation canals that carried water from the Moche River, which lies 30km (20 miles) away. This was a vulnerability for the inhabitants: in around 1470, the Incas cut off the canals, killing crops and conquering the city.

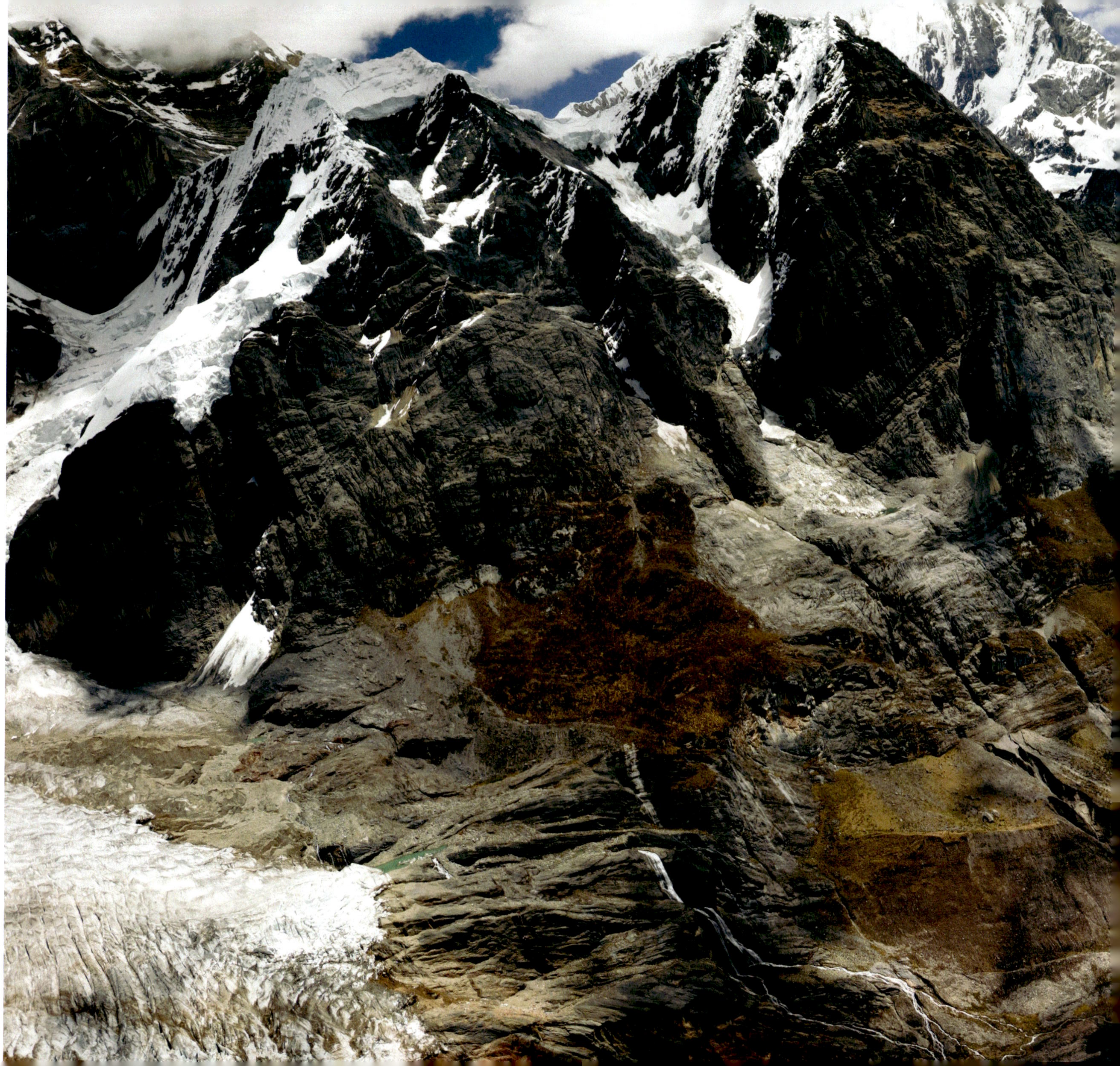

Tres Lagunas, Cordillera Huayhuash, Peru
These three glacial lakes – Cangrajanca, Siula and Quesillucocha – lie on the Huayhuash Circuit, a challenging 130km (80-mile) hiking trail through this Andean range. The range's highest peak is Yerupajá (6617m; 21,709ft), but the most internationally famous is Siula (6344m; 20,814ft) due to Joe Simpson's 1988 book *Touching the Void*, in which he described being left for dead after falling into one of the mountain's crevasses.

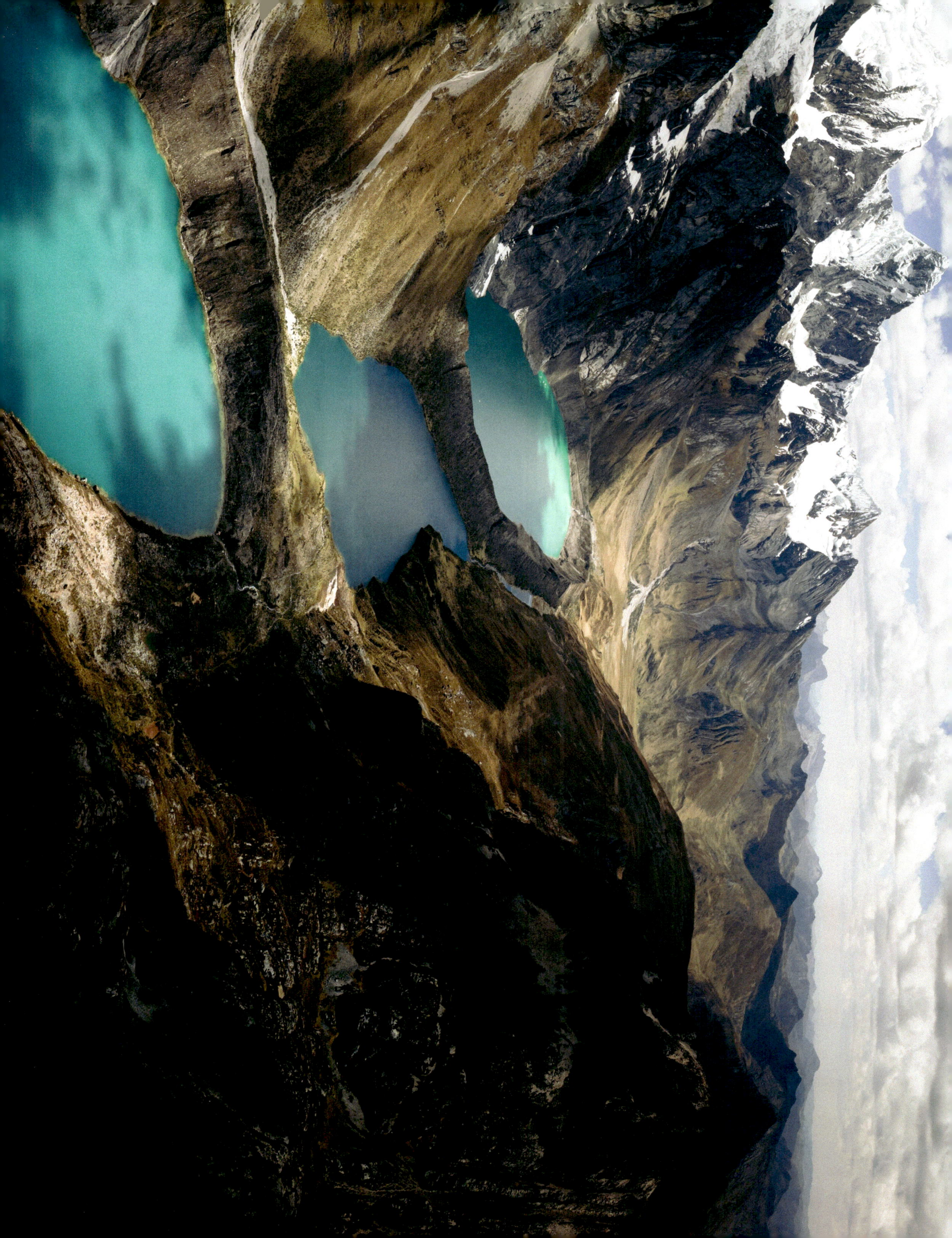

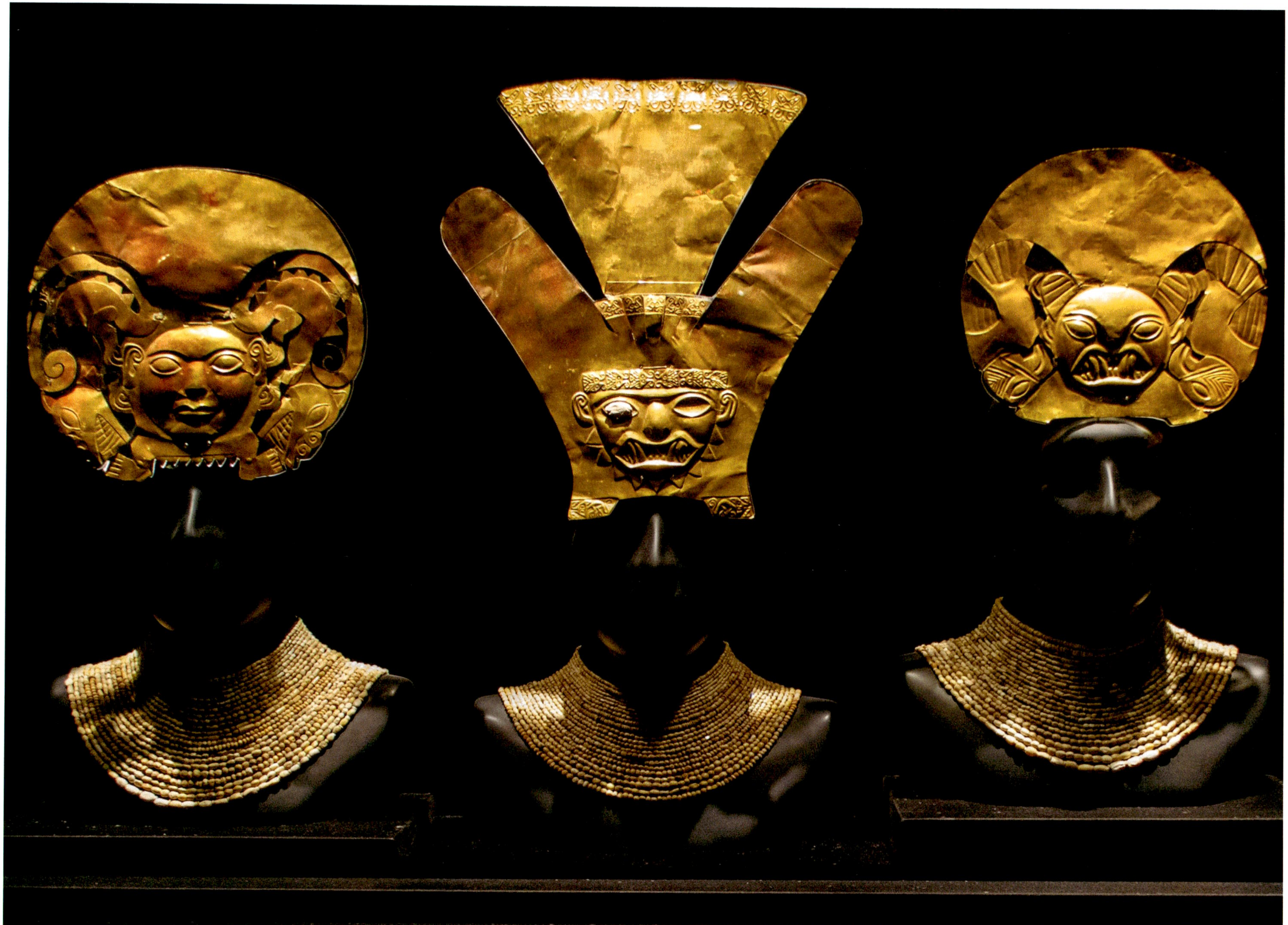

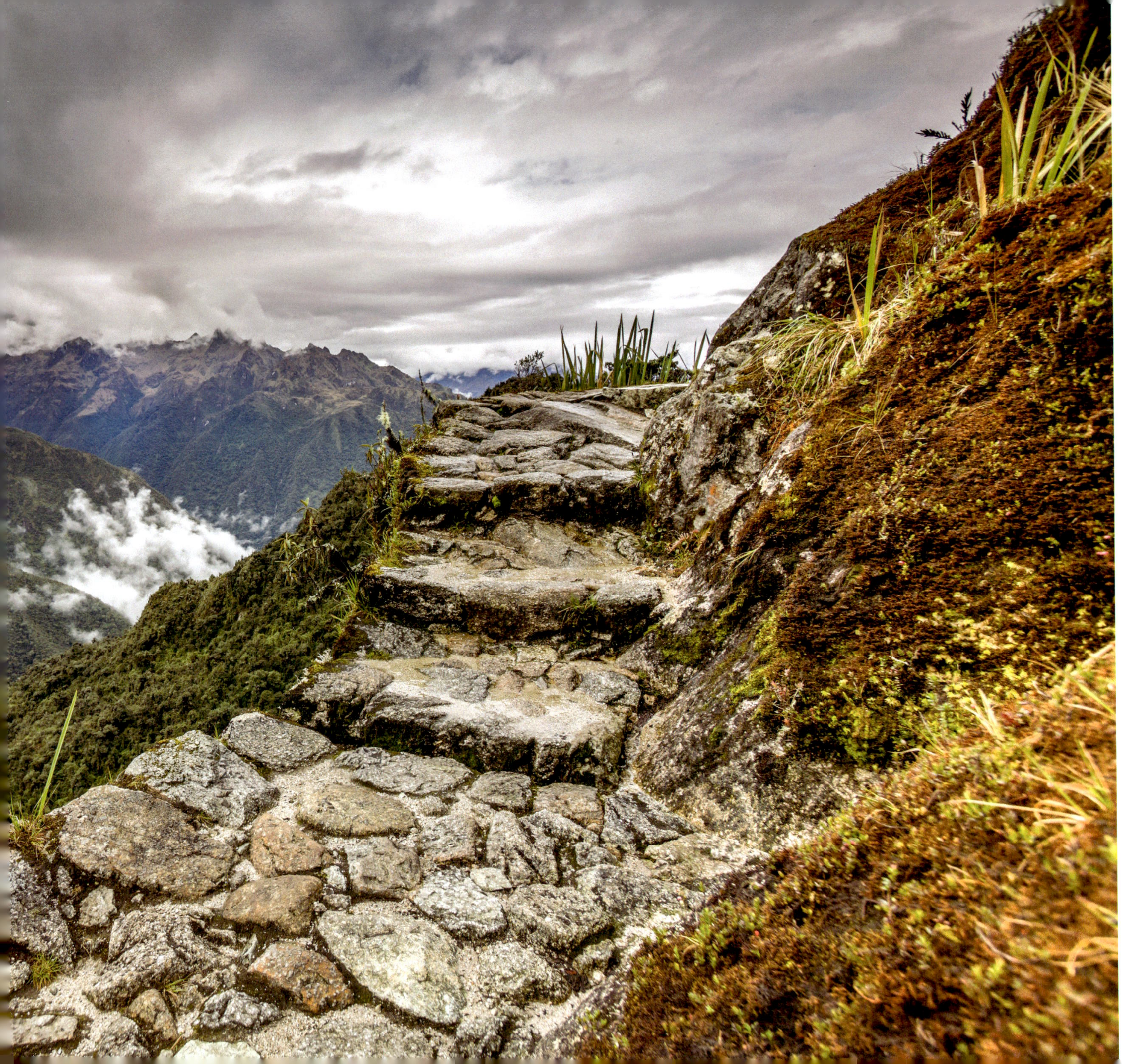

OPPOSITE:
Museo Larco, Lima, Peru
This museum holds 45,000 pre-Columbian artefacts, including these gold headdresses from the Moche civilization, which flourished along the coast of northern Peru from around 100 to 800 CE. Such headdresses were often found among the grave goods of political rulers and warrior-priests.

LEFT:
Inca Trail to Machu Picchu, Cusco Region, Peru
Peru's most popular multi-day hike is the 'Classic' Inca Trail, which covers around 43km (27 miles) over four days. It travels past Inca sites such as Runkuraqay and Sayacmarca, and winds through cloud forests and over mountain passes. Due to the high altitude, reaching 4215m (13,796ft), the hike is challenging despite the option for full porterage.

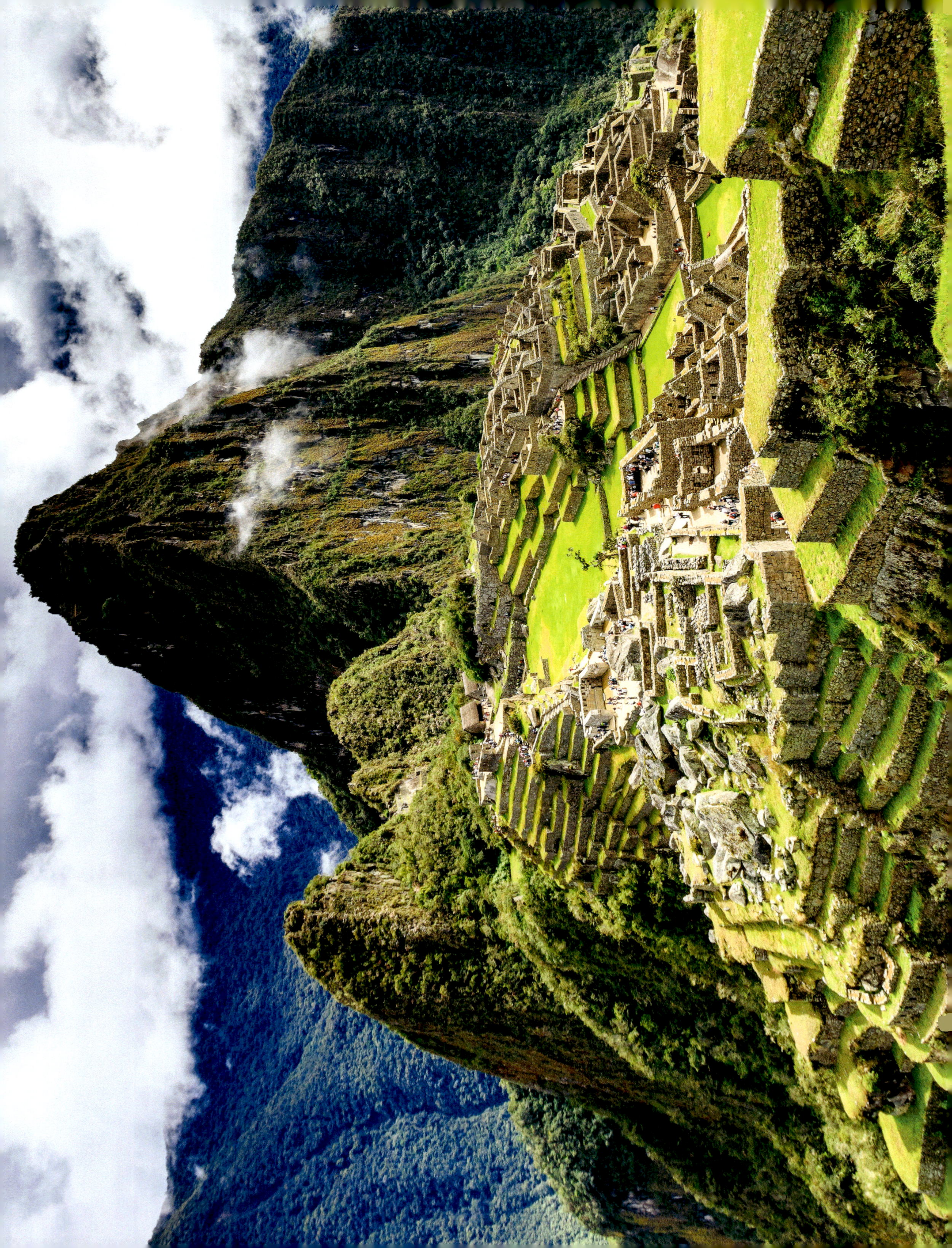

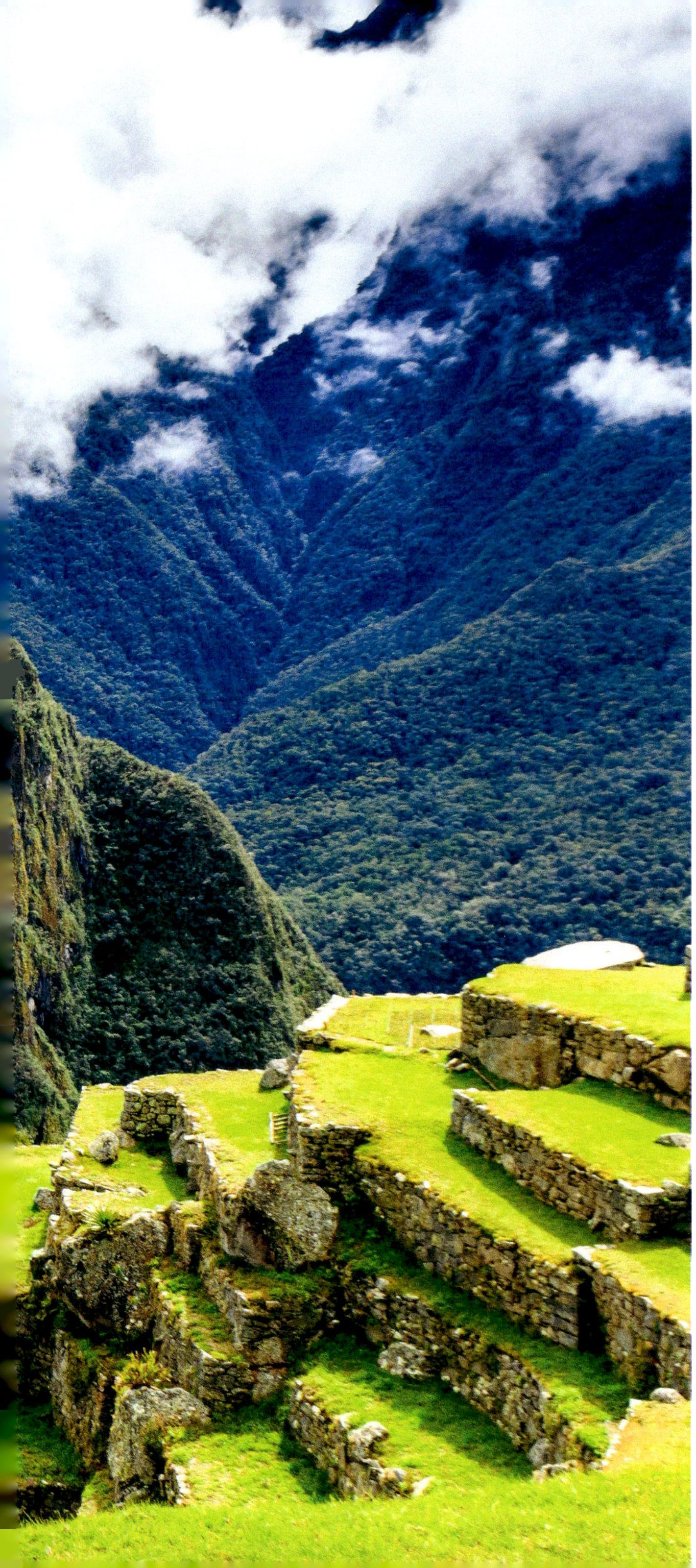

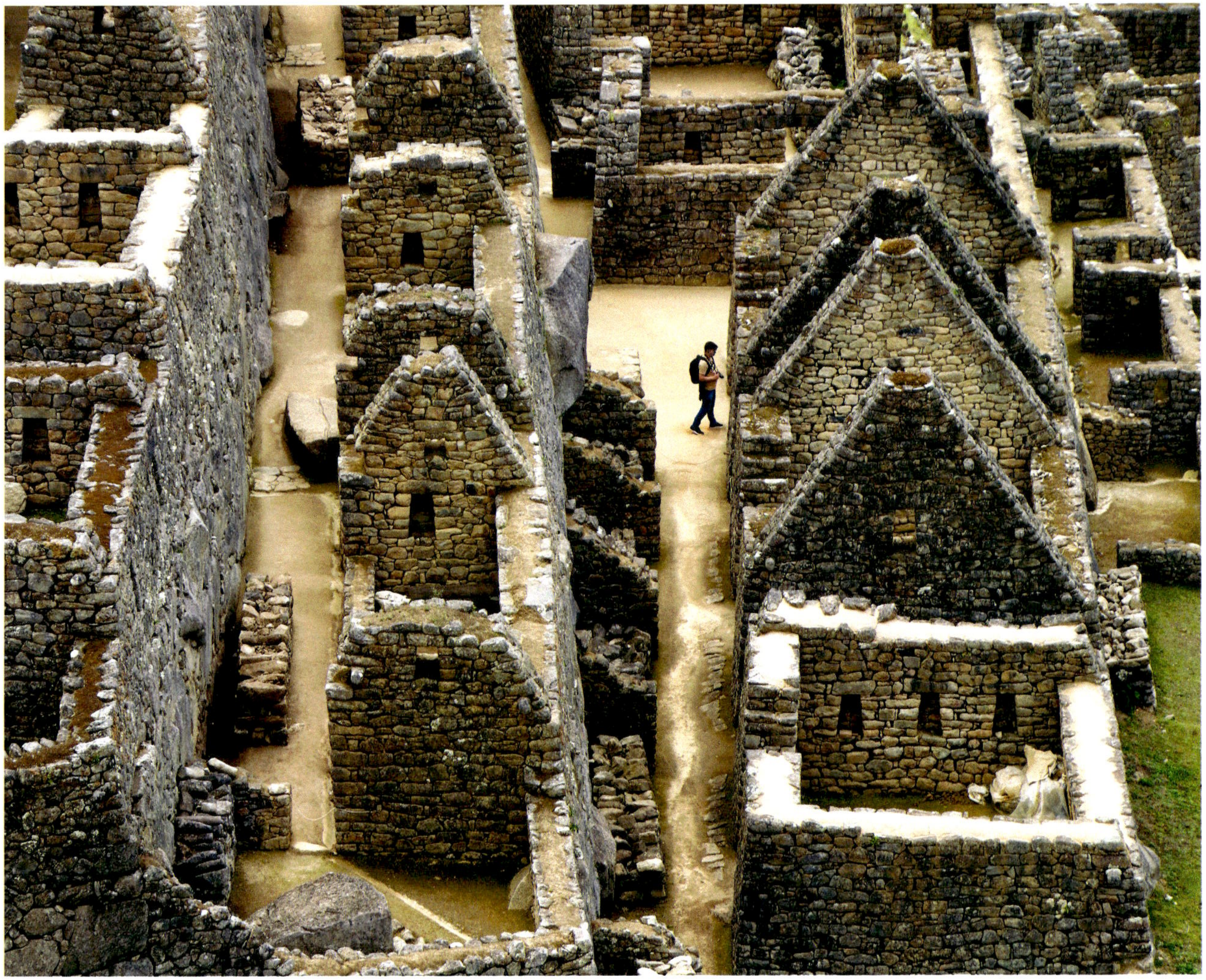

LEFT:

Machu Picchu, Cusco Region, Peru

This citadel was built in around 1450, probably as an estate for Sapa Inca Pachacuti (see page 101). It lies on a ridge between the mountains Machu Picchu and Huayna Picchu, 2430m (7970ft) above sea level. The estate consisted of a royal palace, temples, warehouses, workshops and workers' homes.

ABOVE:

Machu Picchu

Most buildings in Machu Picchu had steep roofs, made from thatched grass over wooden beams, to shed heavy rain. Like other Inca buildings, the walls were built without mortar, using blocks of granite and andesite cut with exceptional precision.

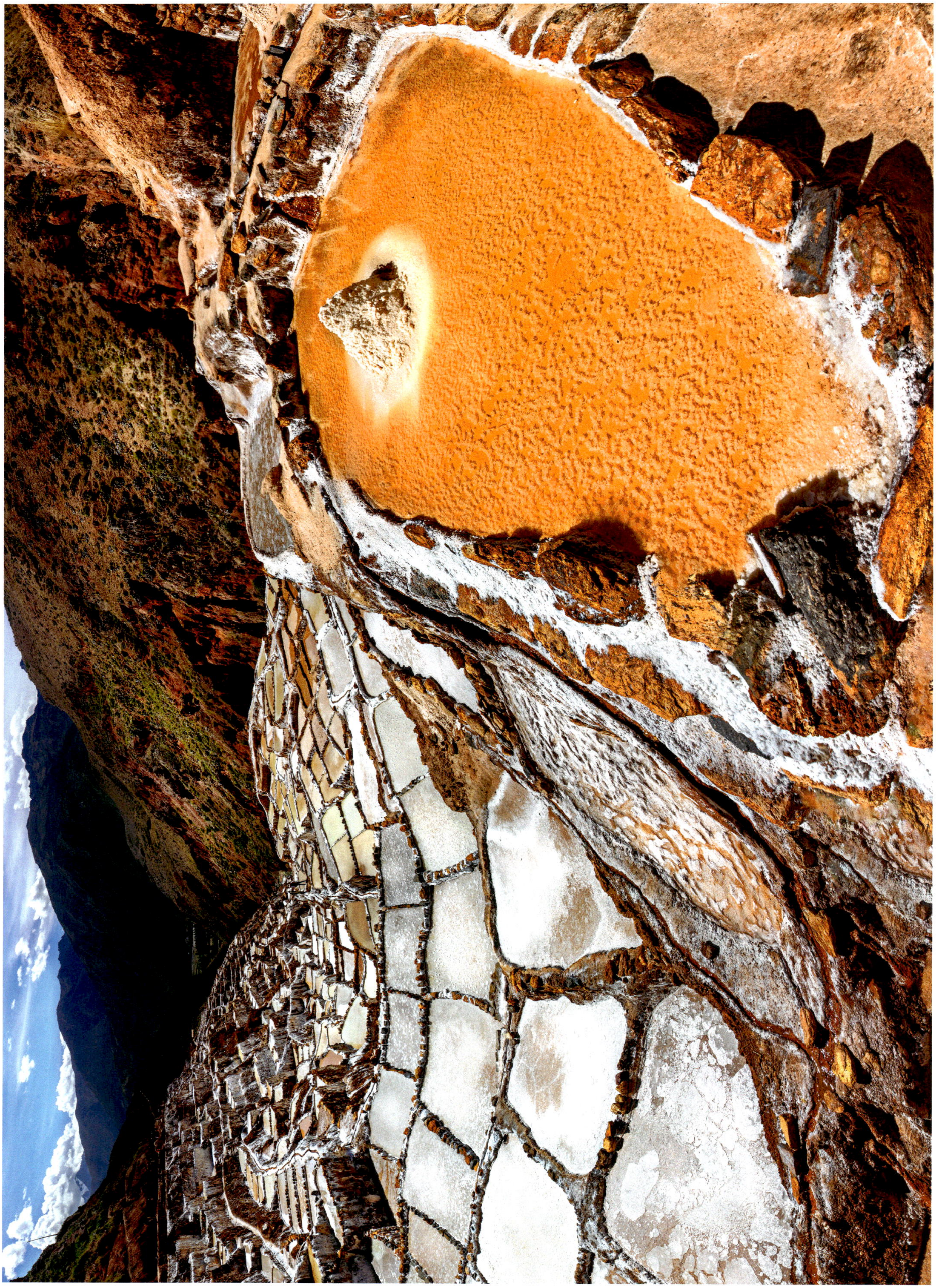

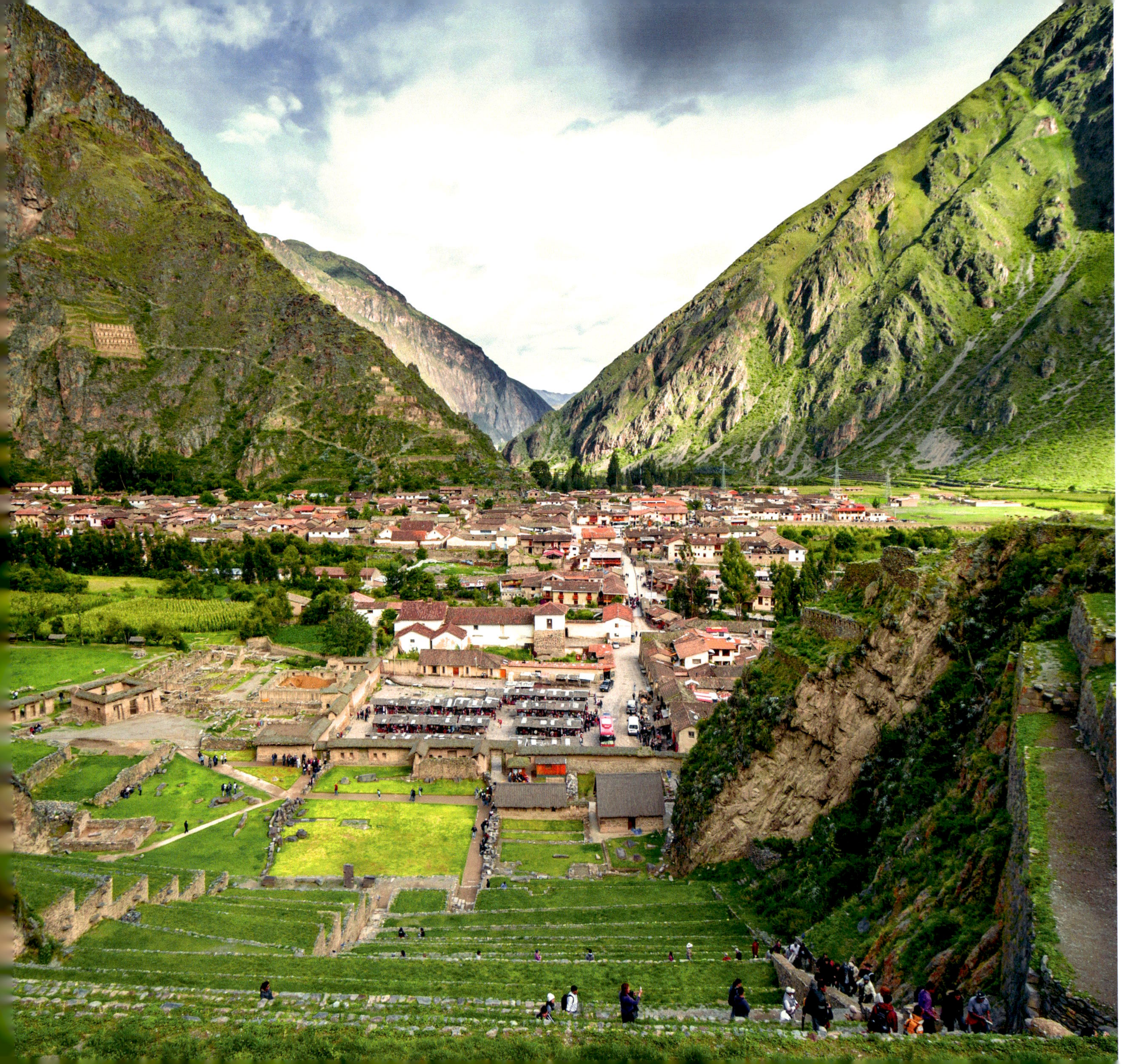

OPPOSITE:

Salineras of Maras, Sacred Valley, Peru

In use for perhaps the last 2000 years, these salt pans are near Urubamba in the Sacred Valley of the Incas. They extract salt from a hot spring at the top of the valley, with the salt left behind as the shallow pools evaporate.

LEFT:

Ollantaytambo, Sacred Valley

In the mid-fifteenth century, the town of Ollantaytambo was conquered by the Inca, who razed then rebuilt it and extended the farming terraces. Some buildings here have been in use since that time. On the left of this photo, on the hillside, are the Inca grain storehouses known as Pinkuylluna, situated at an elevation and well ventilated so that cool mountain winds could preserve the contents.

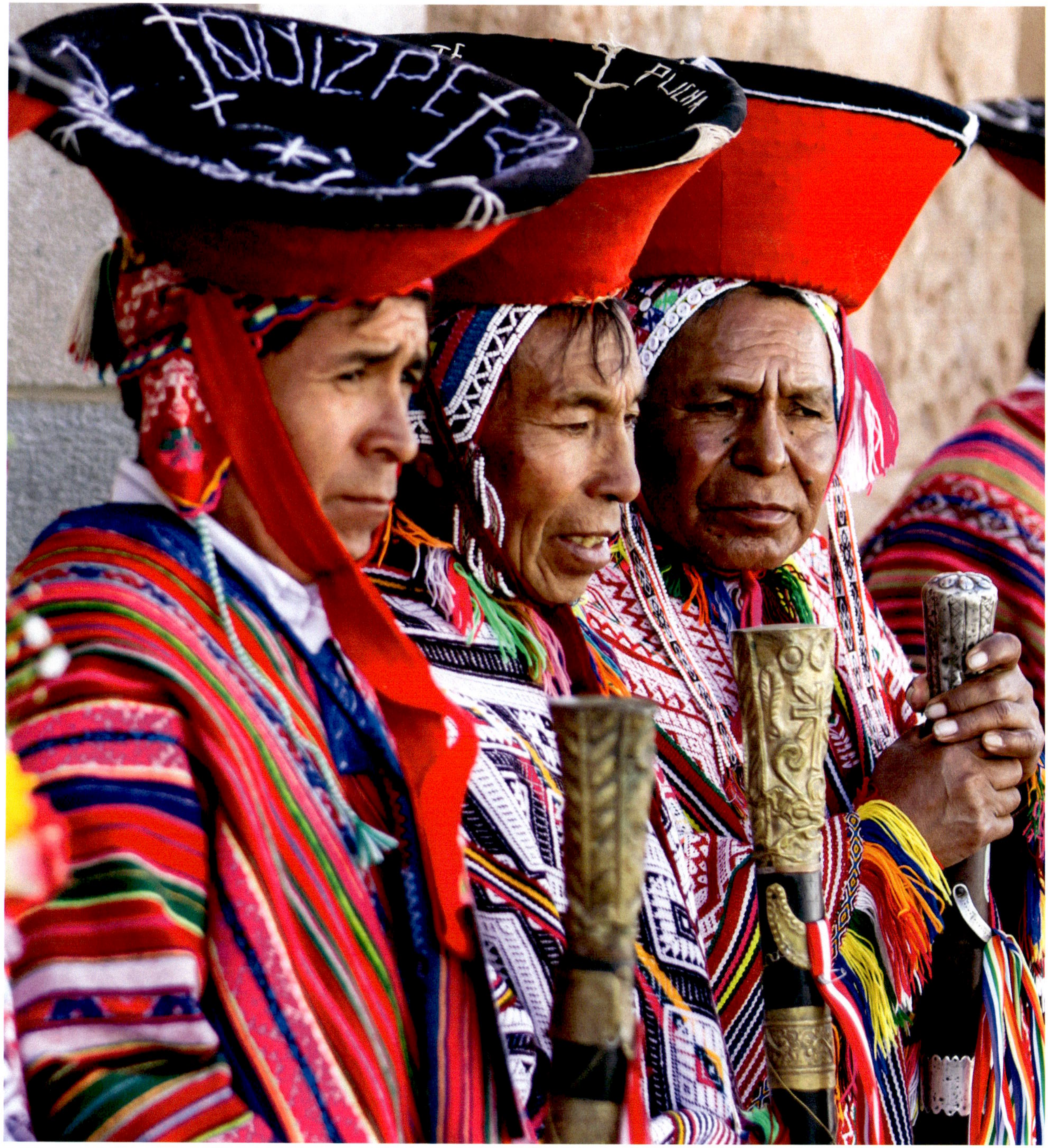

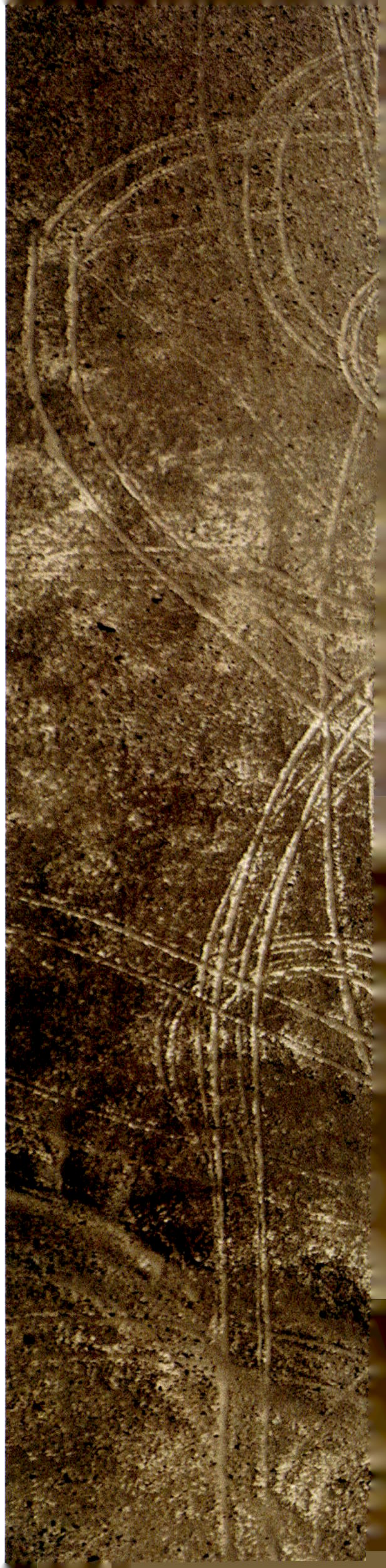

RIGHT:
Pisac, Sacred Valley, Peru
On market days, local Quechua people (descendants of the Incas) arrive in Pisac to sell their produce and buy supplies. Worn by women, the red-felt-covered *montera* hat is believed to date to Inca times, with its particular style and decoration identifying the village and marital status of the wearer.

FAR RIGHT:
Nazca Lines, Nazca Desert, Peru
Created by local people between around 400 BCE and 500 CE, the Nazca lines consist of hundreds of geoglyphs, some over 100m (330ft) long. They were made by scraping away the top layer of reddish pebbles to reveal the paler subsoil, and have been preserved by the dry, windless climate. Visible from the surrounding hillsides and the air, the designs consist of geometric shapes and animals such as a spider, hummingbird and monkey.

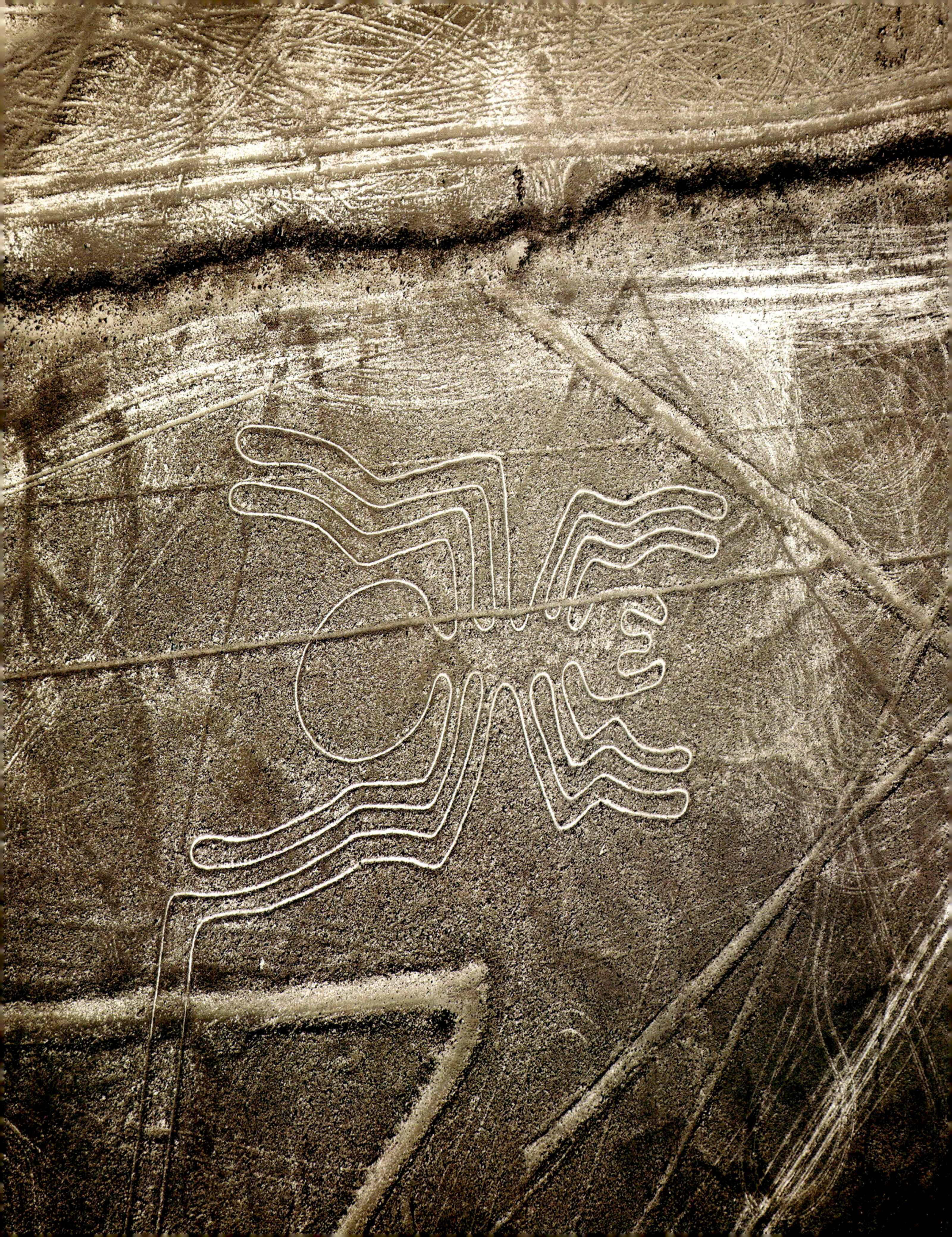

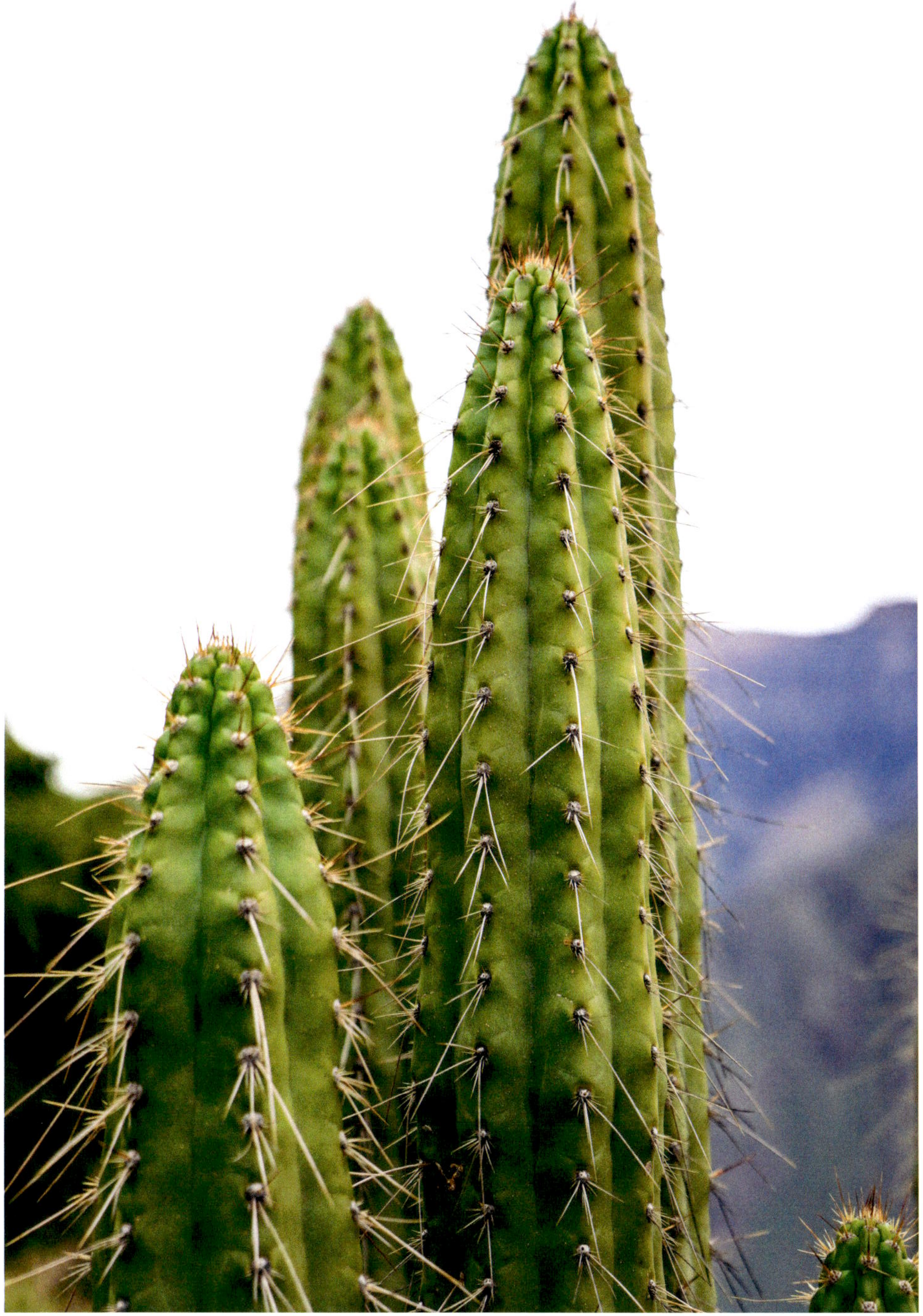

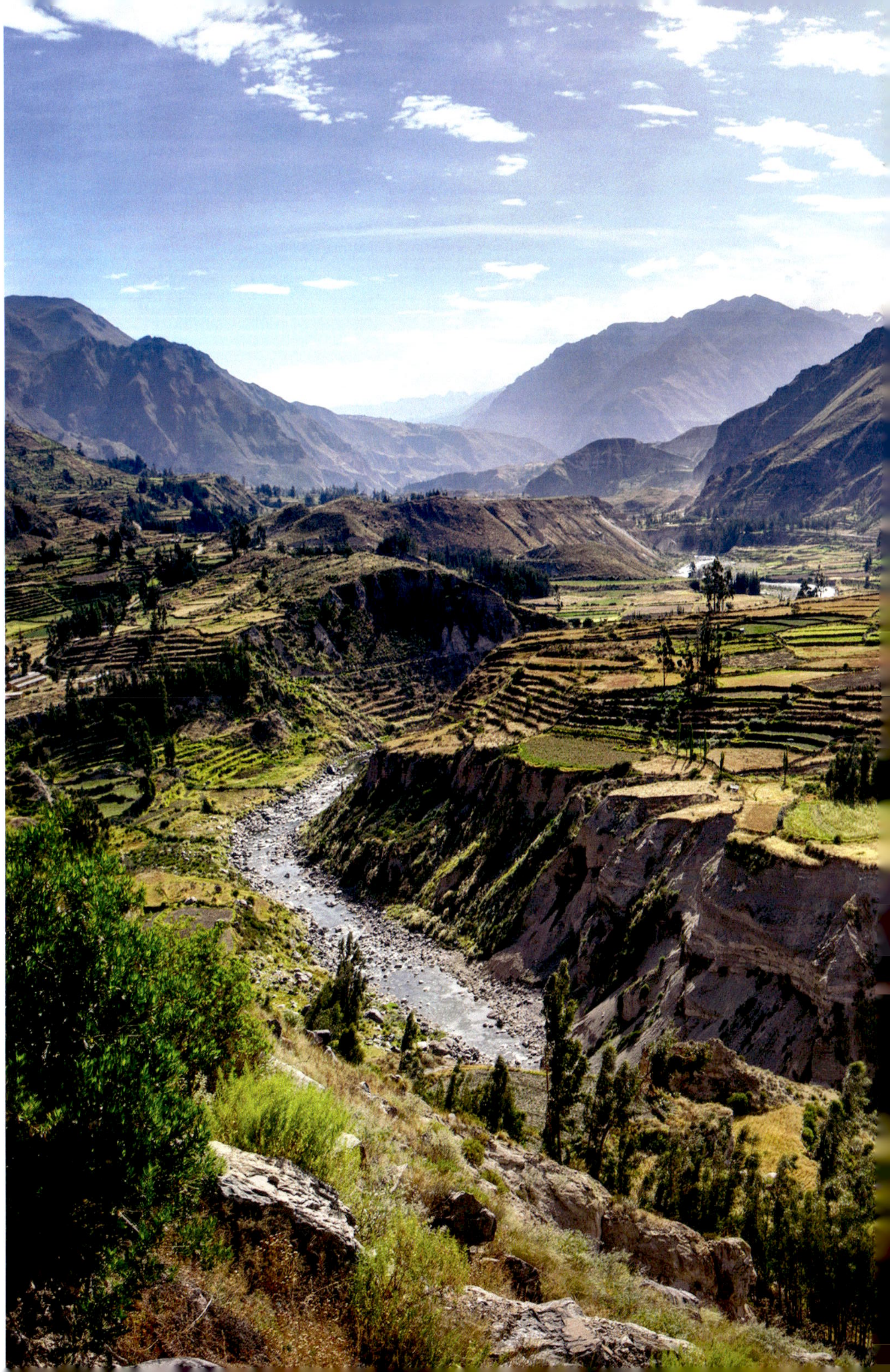

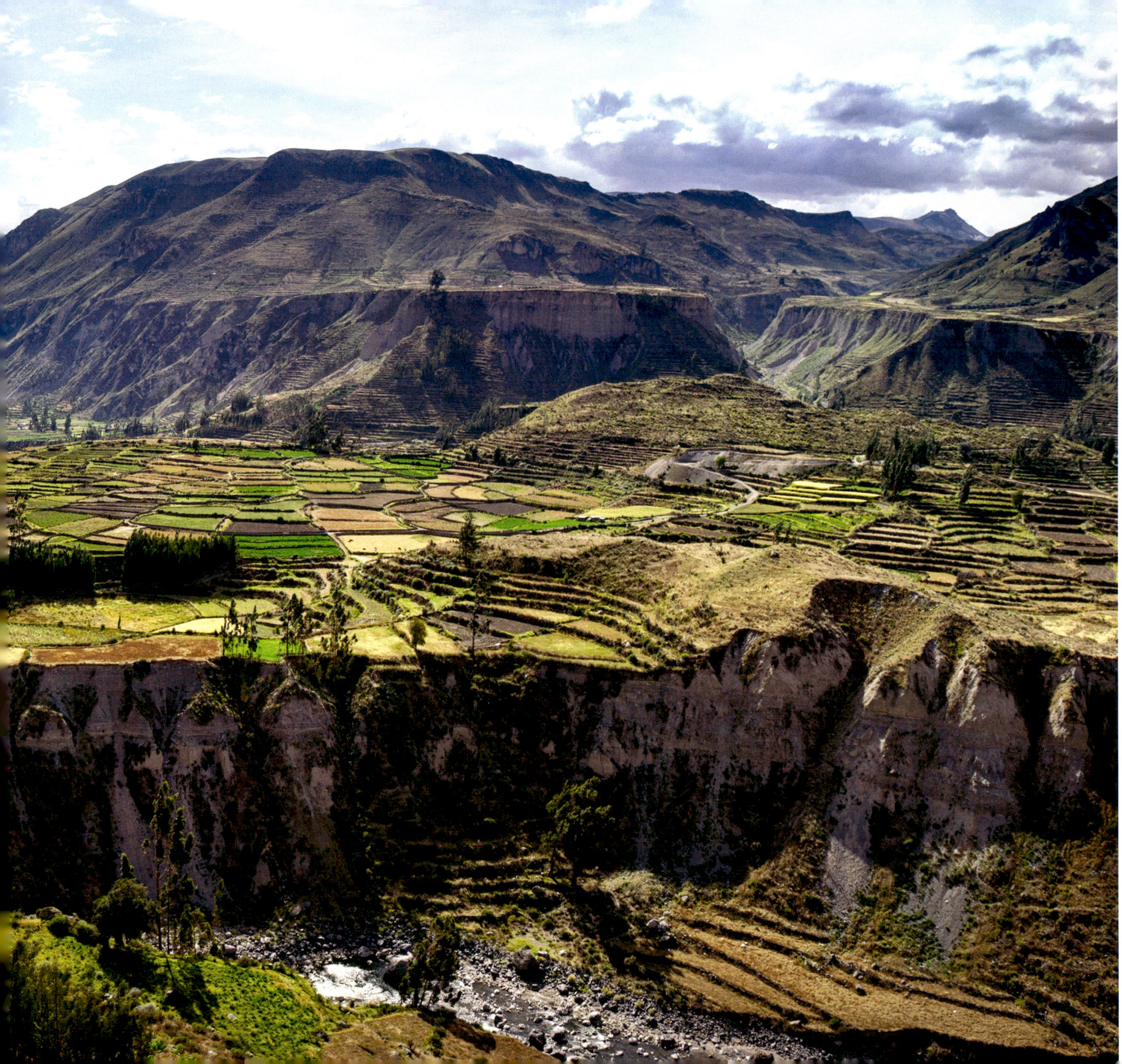

BOTH PHOTOGRAPHS:
Colca Canyon, Arequipa Region, Peru
Carved by the Colca River, this canyon is inhabited mainly by speakers of Aymara and Quechuan languages. Many of the farming terraces here, called *andenes*, have survived since pre-Inca times. The *andenes* allow the use of steep slopes for growing crops such as potatoes, corn, quinoa and beans, while controlling soil erosion and maximizing exposure to sunlight. Cacti in the canyon, such as the Peruvian apple cactus, are used for their edible fruits, while the San Pedro cactus is employed in traditional medicine.

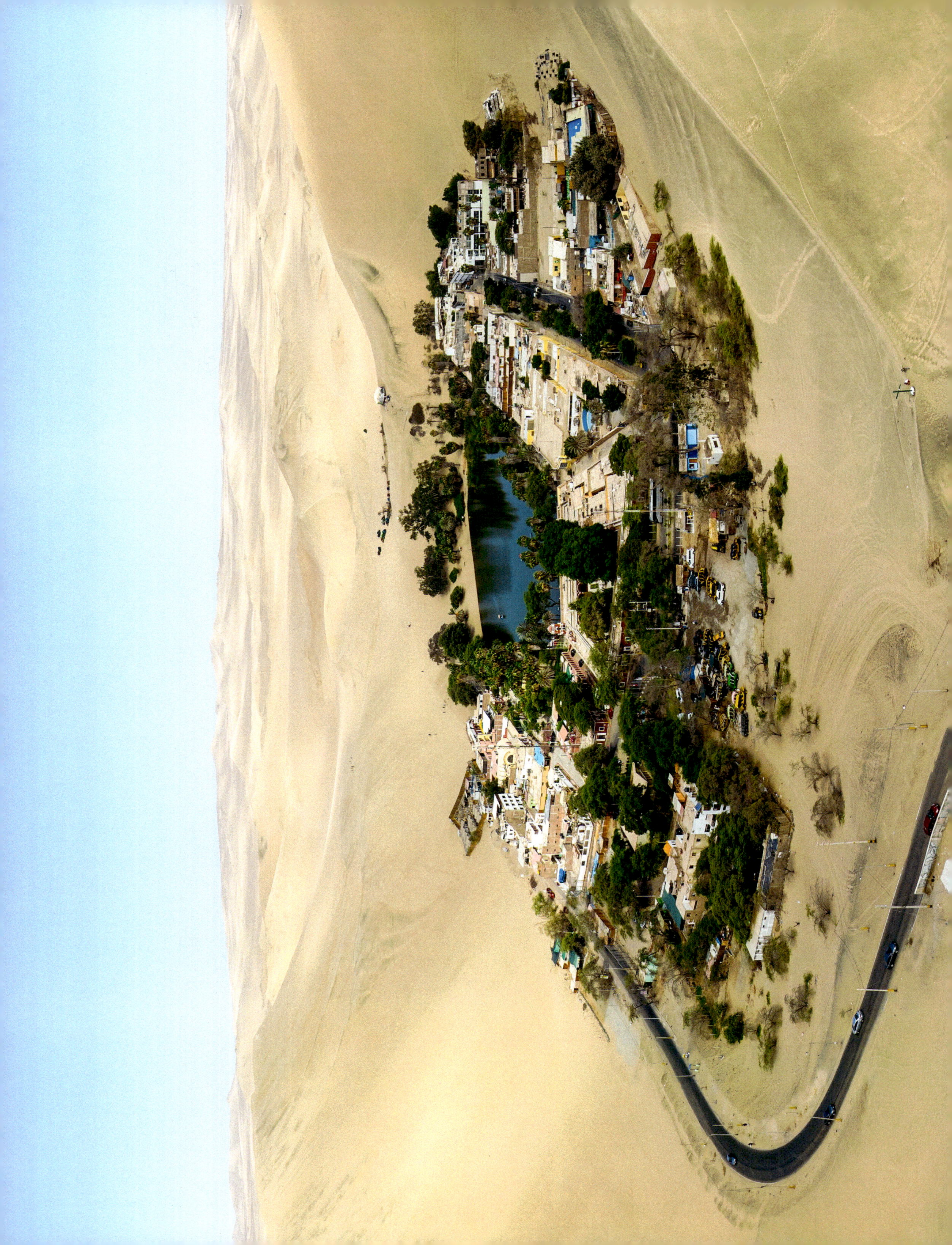

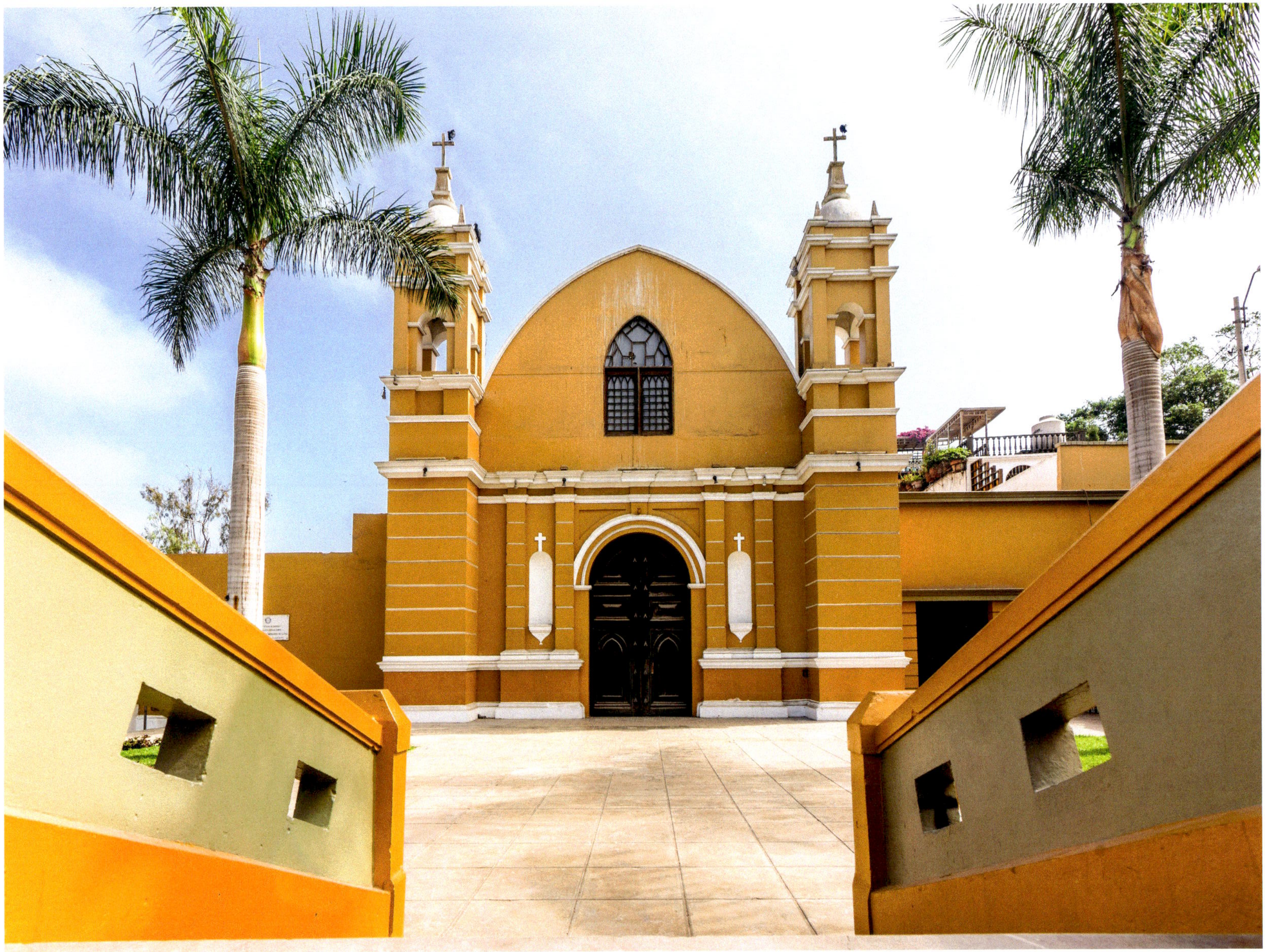

LEFT:
Huacachina, Ica Desert, Peru
This oasis in Peru's coastal desert was created by springs from the underlying aquifer. Today, due to excessive well-drilling, the oasis is artificially maintained. It is a destination for sandboarding on the surrounding dunes.

ABOVE:
La Ermita de Barranco Church, Lima, Peru
Built in the mid-eighteenth century, this Gothic Revival church is in the capital's bohemian seaside neighbourhood of Barranco. The church has been closed since being damaged by the 8.1-magnitude 1974 Lima earthquake.

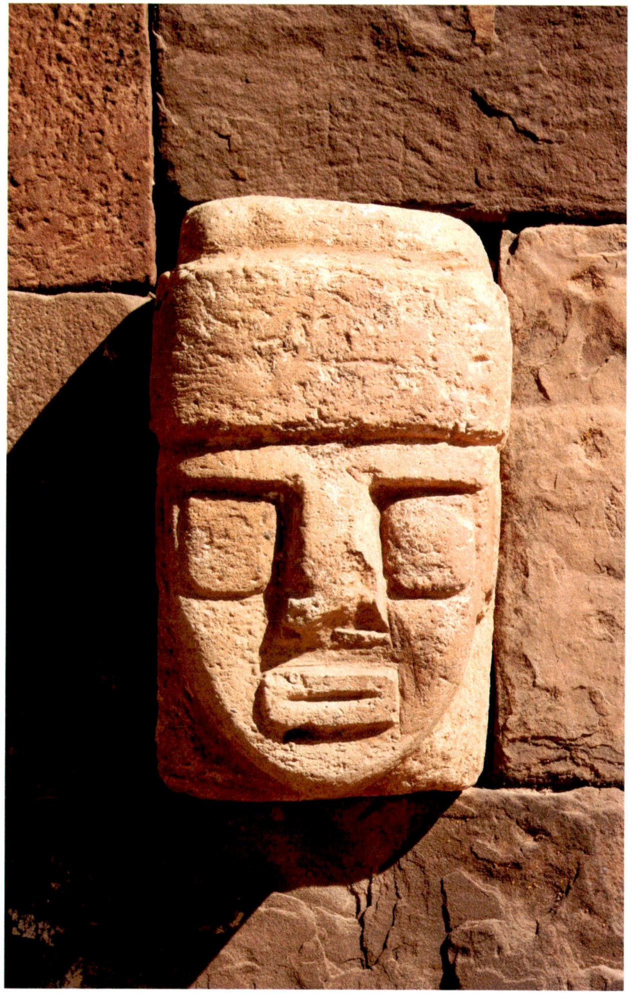

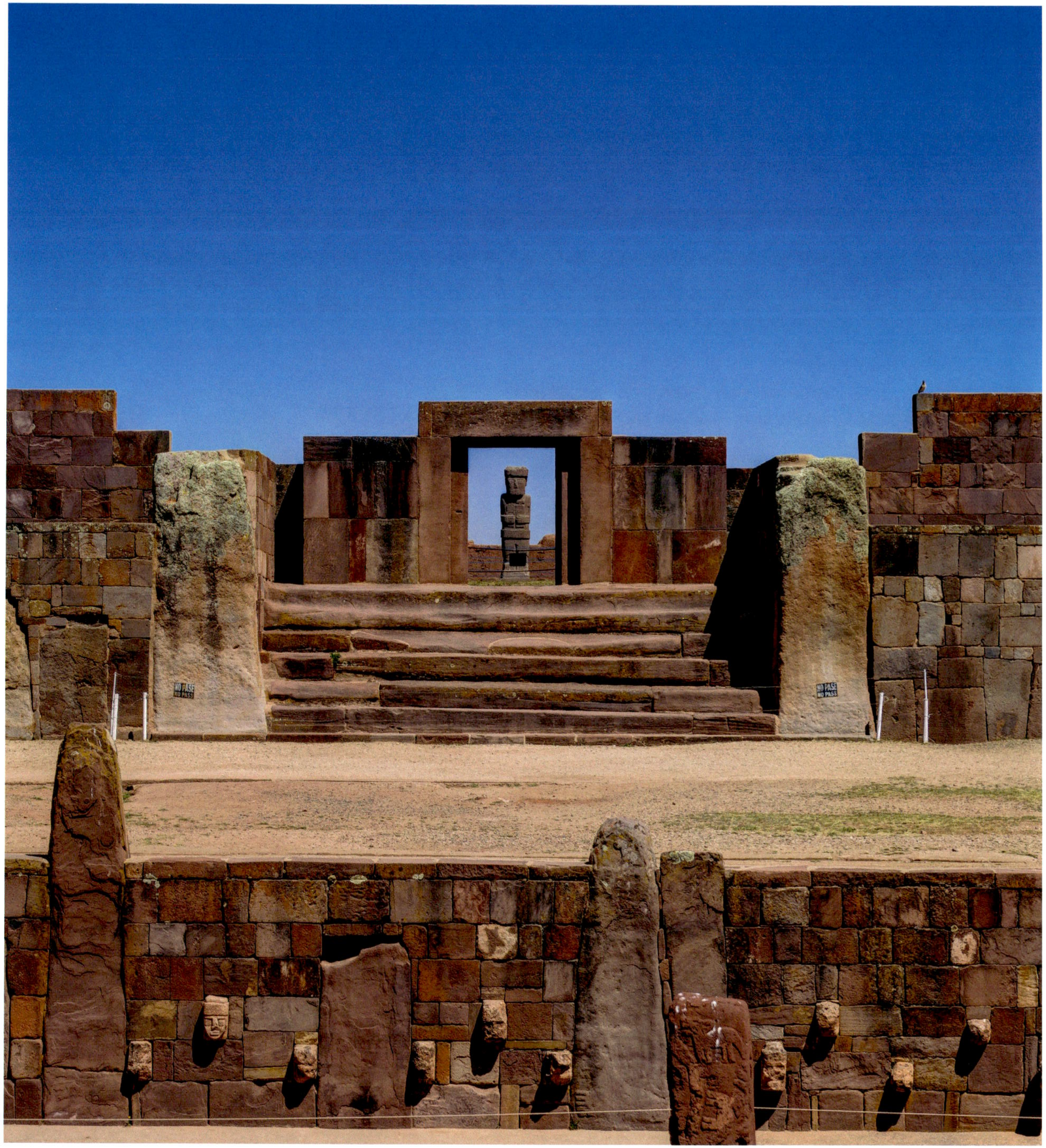

ABOVE AND RIGHT:

Tiwanaku, Bolivia

Founded in around 110 CE, this city was home to 10,000 people at its peak, around 800 CE. Its inhabitants, members of the so-called Tiwanaku polity, worshipped or gathered on platform mounds and in a courtyard called the Kalasasaya (pictured right), surrounded by masonry walls with carved tenon heads.

OPPOSITE:

Potosí, Bolivia

One of the highest cities in the world at around 4067m (13,343ft), Potosí grew quickly after silver was found in Cerro Rico ('Rich Mountain'; pictured) in 1545. Coins were produced in Potosí's mint until 1951. Today, most silver veins have been depleted, but tin, zinc, lead and copper are still mined.

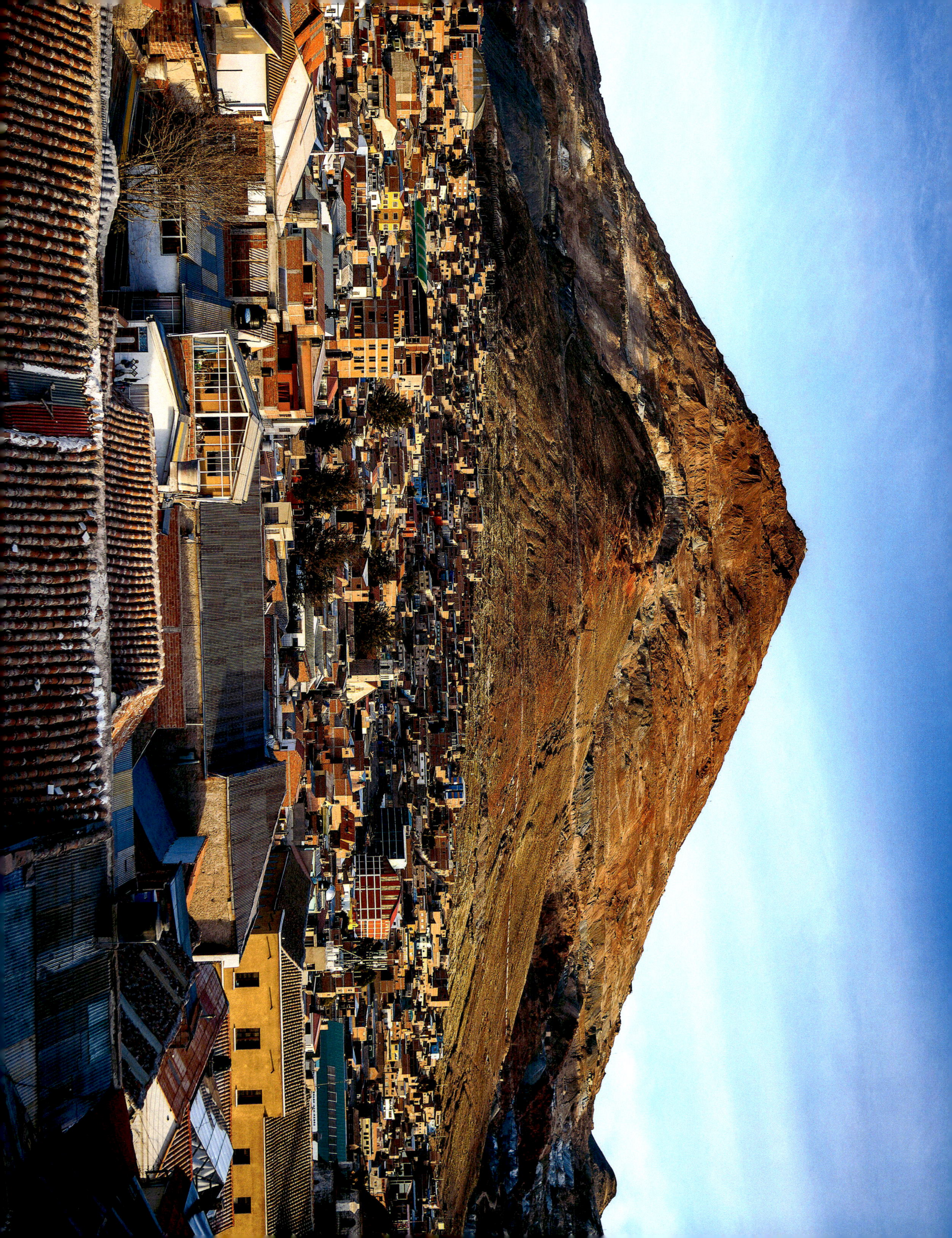

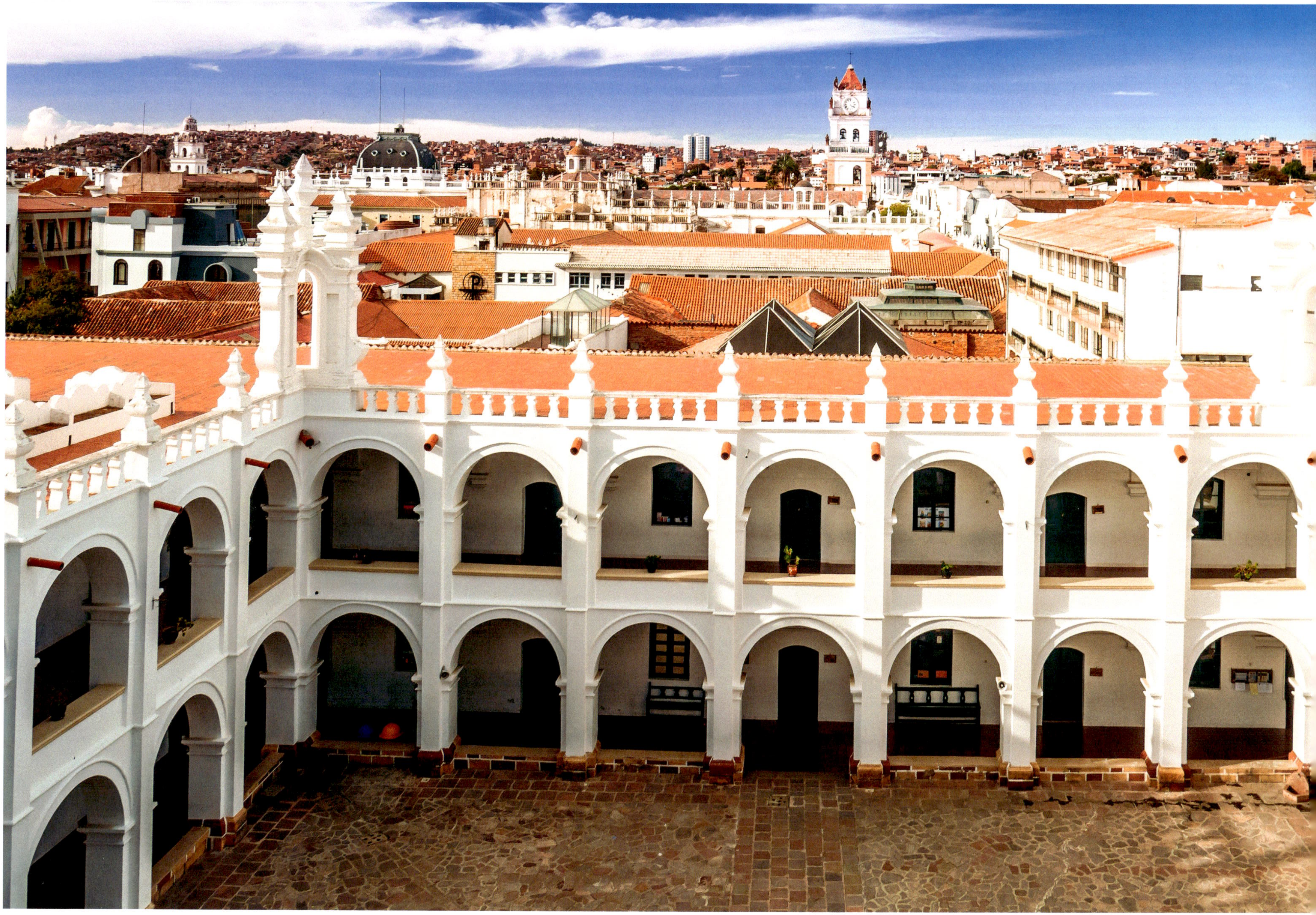

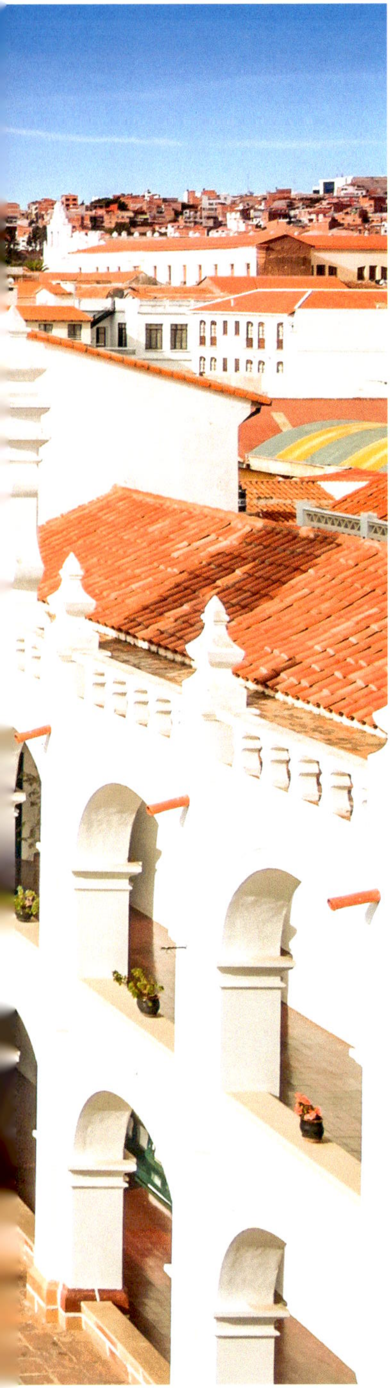

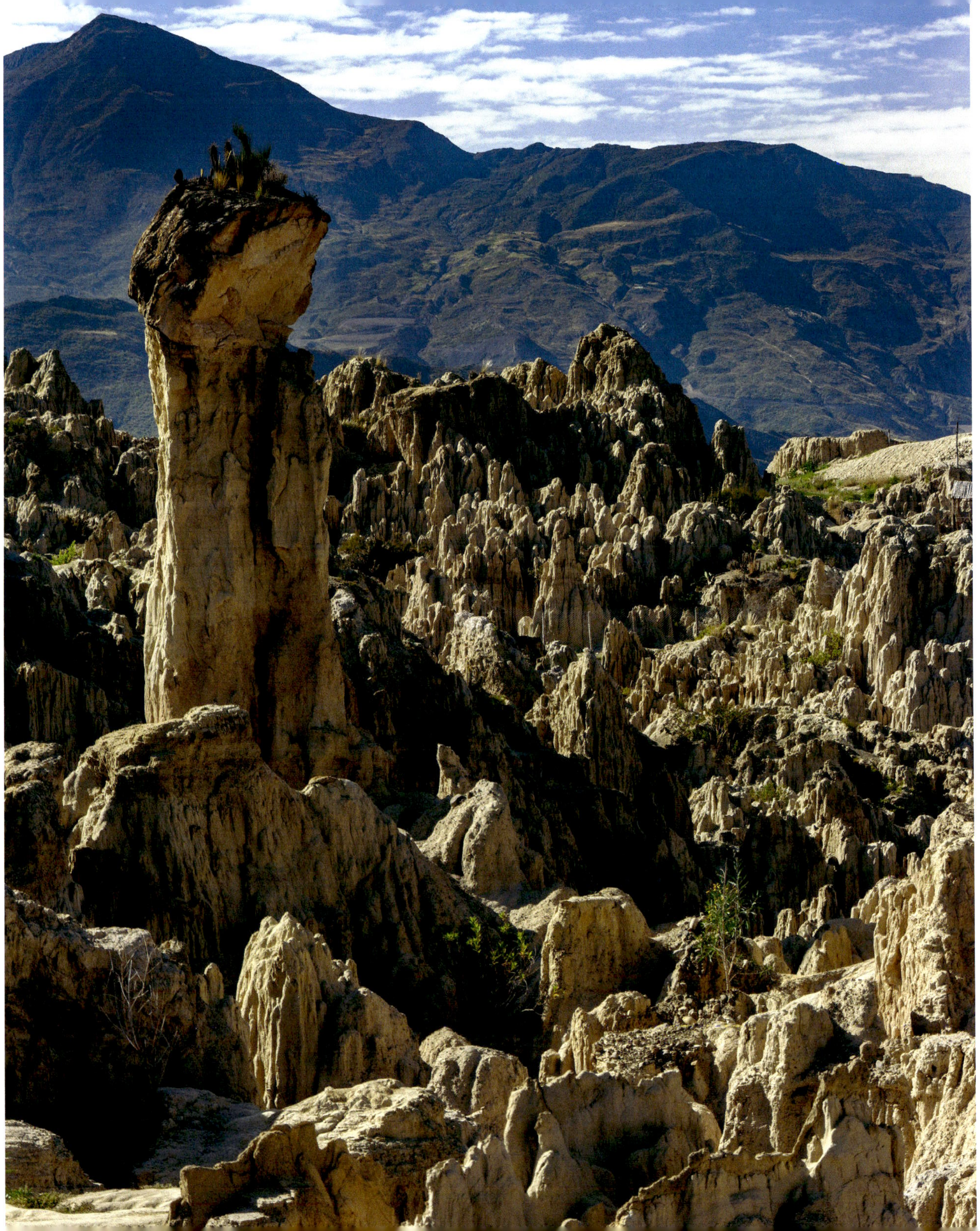

FAR LEFT:

Convento de San Felipe Neri, Sucre, Bolivia

The constitutional and judicial capital of Bolivia (while La Paz is the seat of government), Sucre is located at 2798m (9180ft) in the inter-Andean valleys, between the Altiplano and the Gran Chaco plains. The historic centre is a UNESCO World Heritage Site for its colonial buildings, including this elegant late eighteenth-century monastery.

LEFT:

Valle de la Luna, near La Paz, Bolivia

Rain and streams have worn away the majority of a clay outcrop here, leaving pinnacles and deeply rutted ramparts. The outcrops range from dark red to beige, depending on the clay's mineral content.

BELOW:

James's Flamingo, Laguna Colorada, Altiplano, Bolivia

This flamingo filter-feeds in Andean lakes by dipping its large, slightly open beak underwater, upside down, trapping microscopic algae and diatoms inside its comb-like structures. Like other flamingos, the James's gets its pink plumage from carotenoid pigments in its diet.

RIGHT:

Laguna Colorada

This shallow lake is hypersaline due to being endorheic (having no outlet) and the intense evaporation, causing a build-up of minerals such as borax, sodium chloride and sulphates. The water gets its red shade mainly from salt-adapted red algae, such as *Dunaliella salina*.

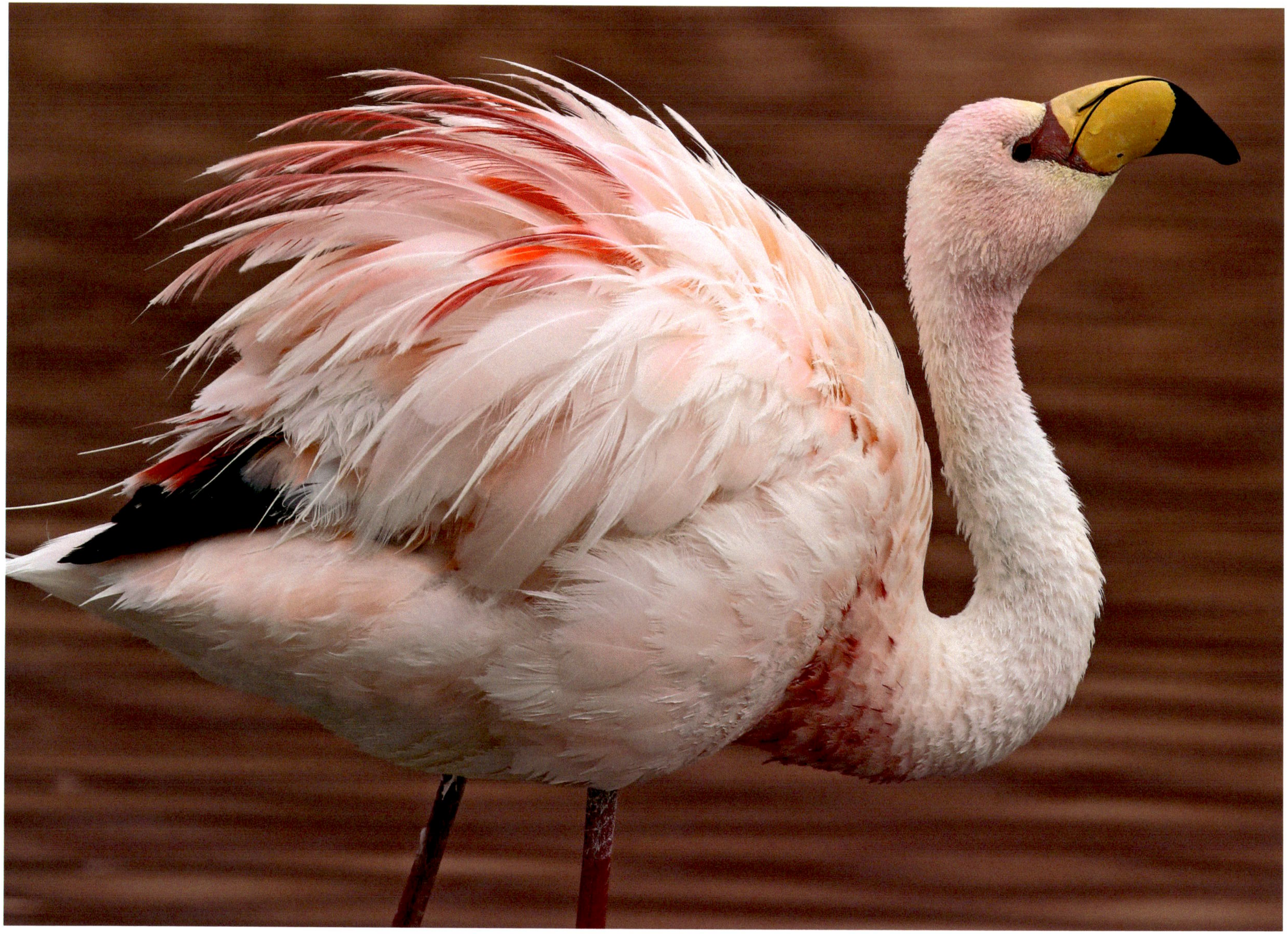

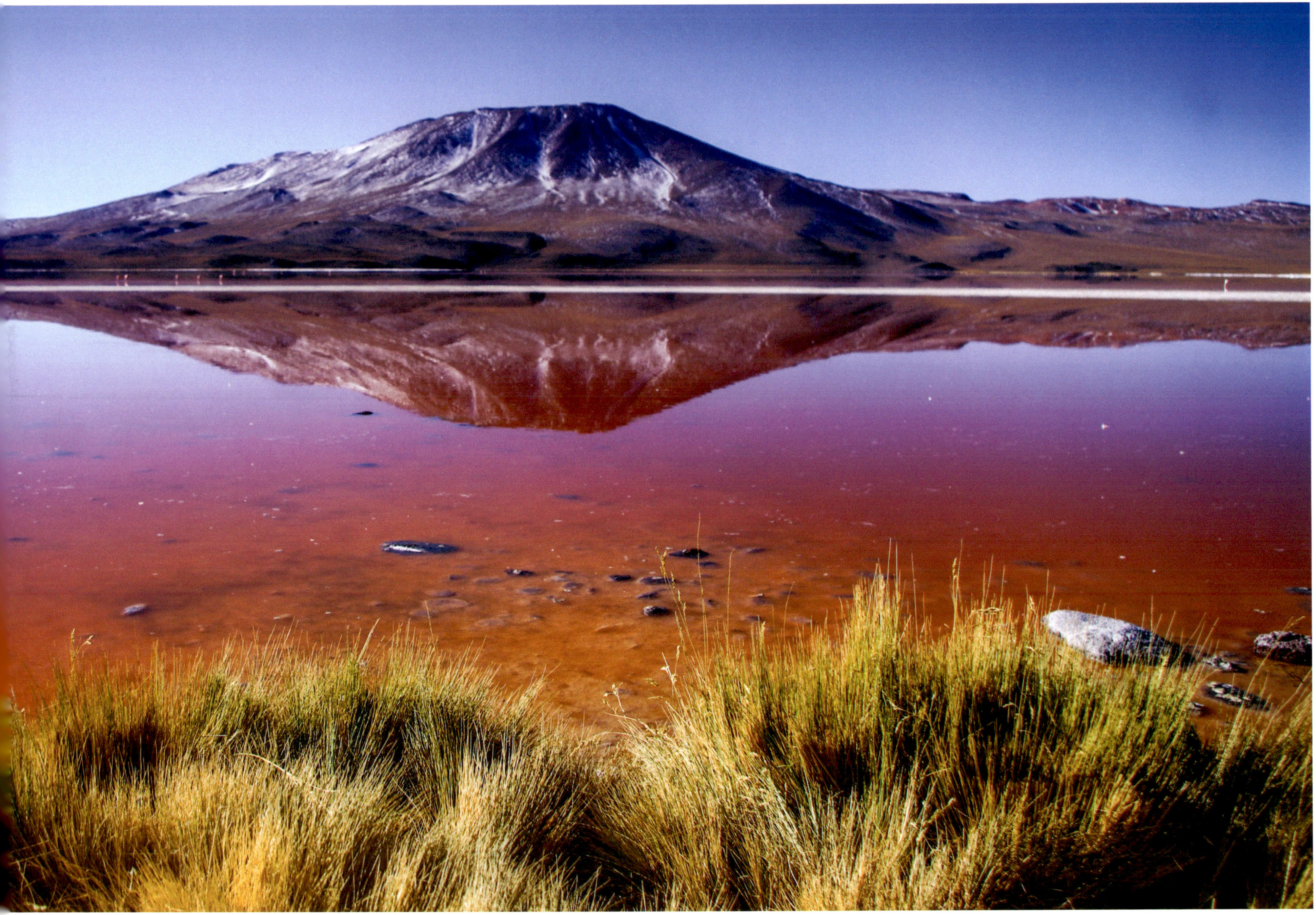

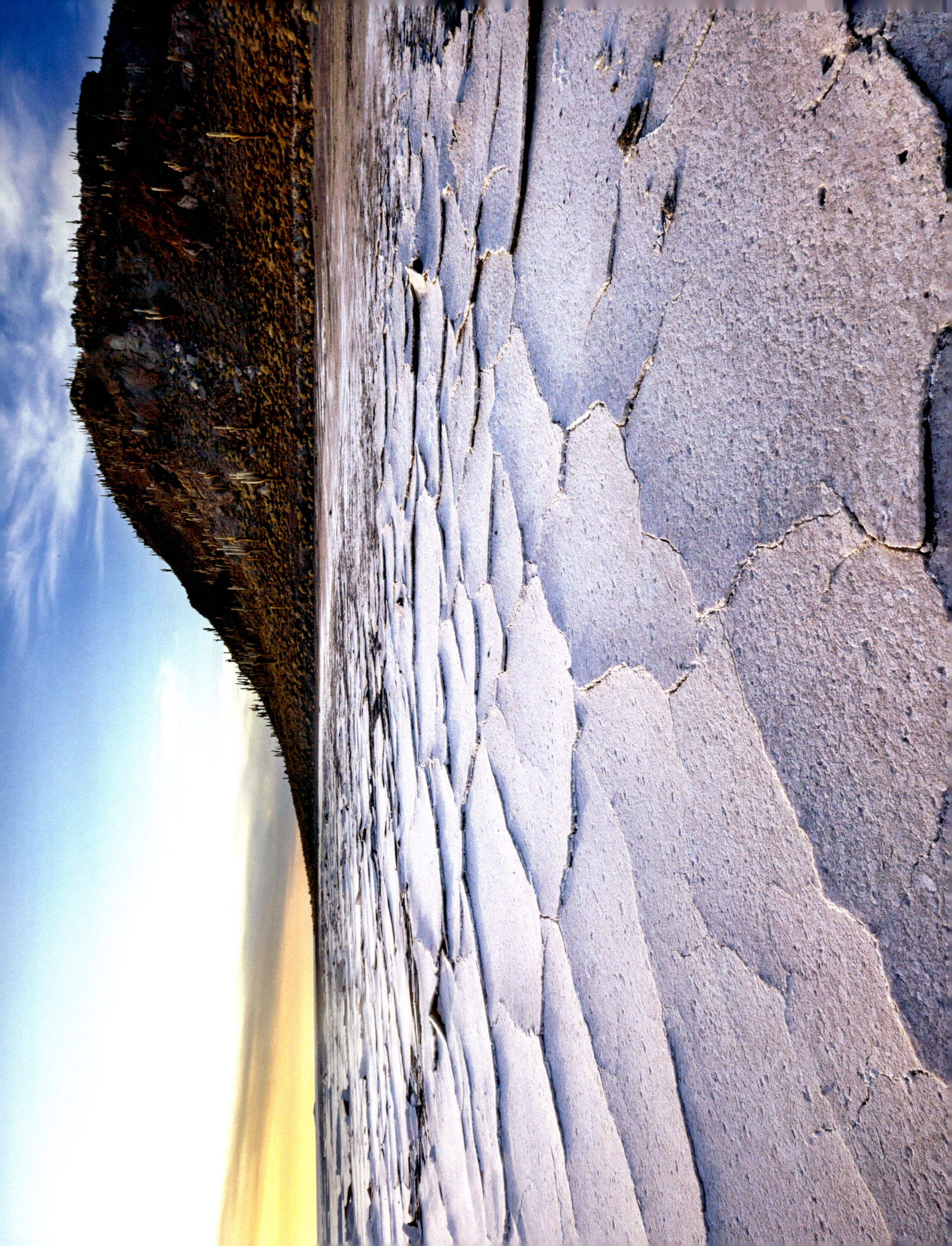

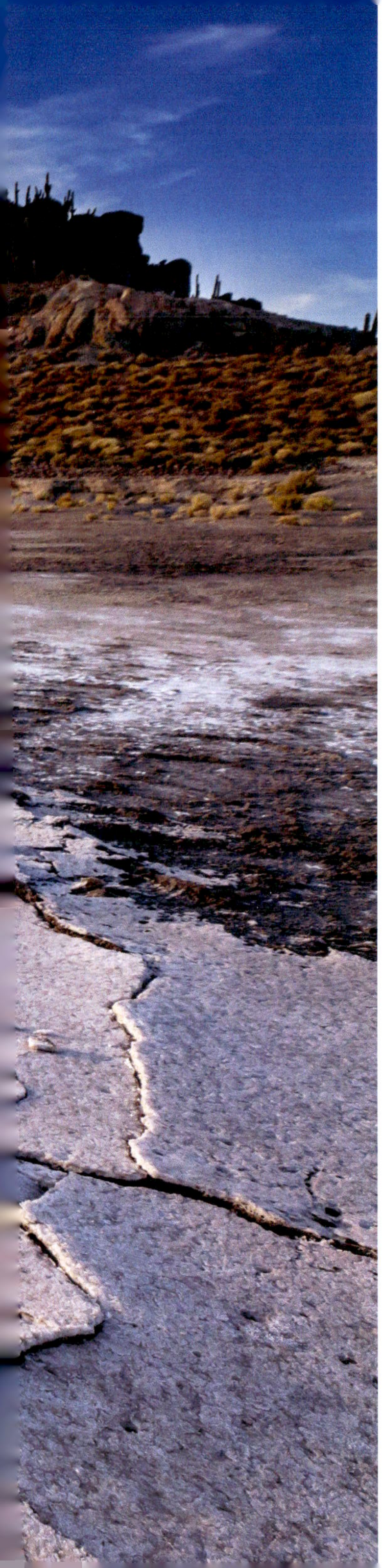

LEFT:
Salar de Uyuni, Altiplano, Bolivia
At 3656m (11,995ft) above sea level, this salt flat was created by the evaporation of prehistoric lakes, leaving behind a brine-mud pool saturated with minerals such as lithium chloride and covered with a salt crust up to 8m (26ft) thick. The salt flat is the world's largest, covering 10,582 sq km (4086 sq miles).

RIGHT:
Llamas, Sajama National Park, Bolivia
In this national park, herds of llamas can be seen alongside two other camelids, alpacas and vicuñas. Of these, vicuñas are the only truly wild animals, with alpacas their domesticated descendants. Llamas are primarily domesticated descendants of another camelid: the guanaco. The park's llamas are owned by Aymara communities, who keep them for wool and meat.

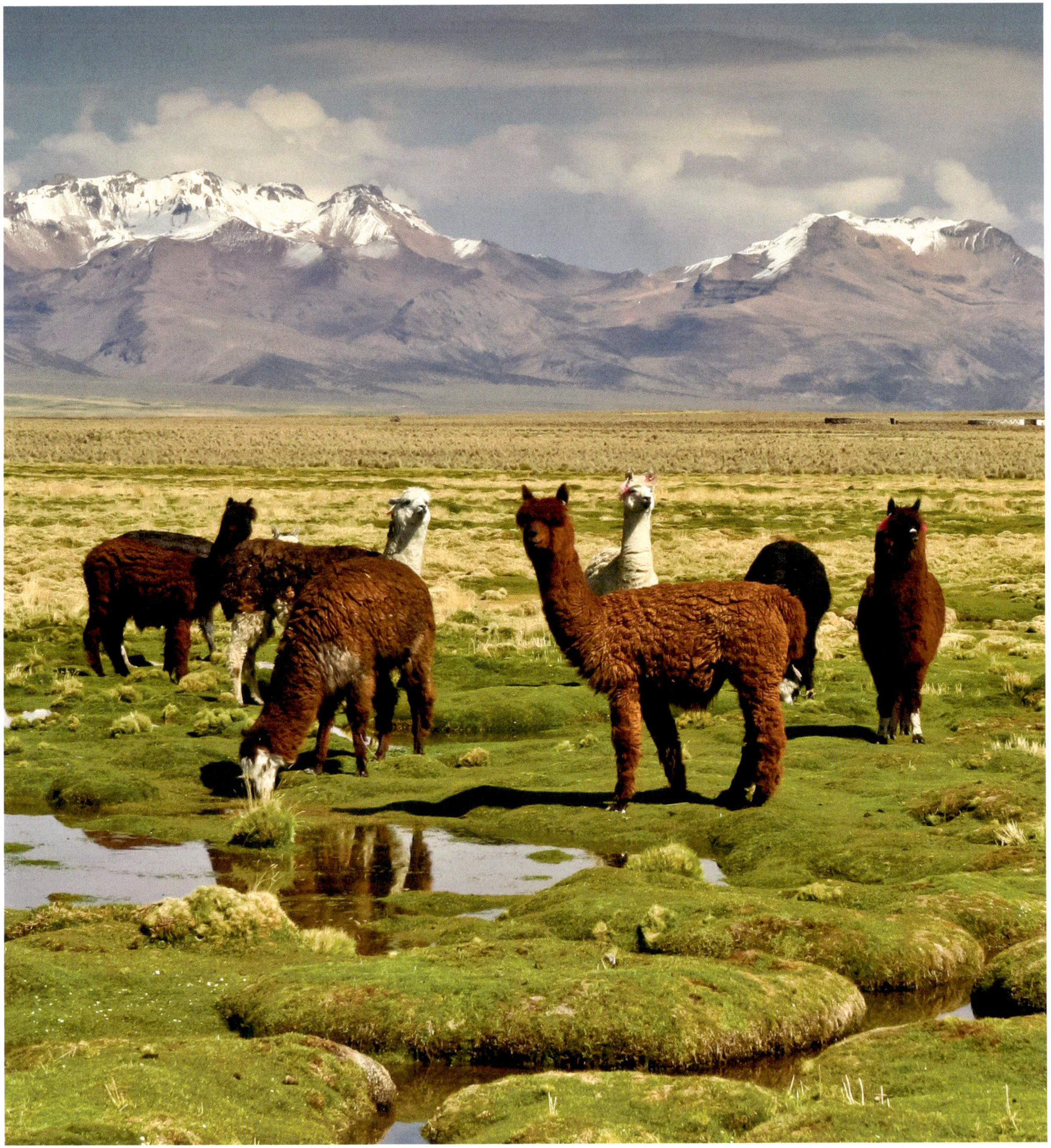

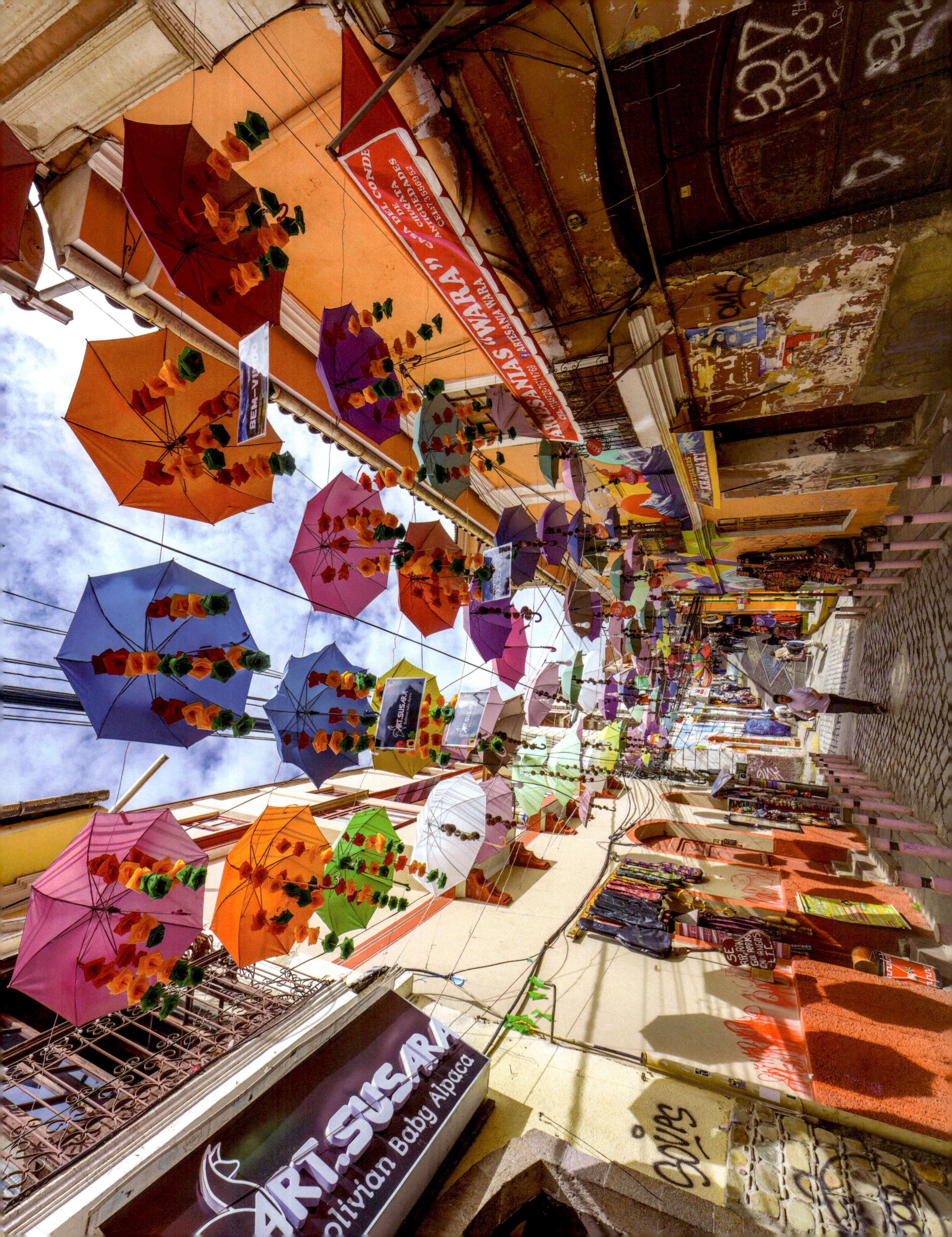
ARTESANIAS "WARA"
CASA DEL CONDE
ART.SUSARA

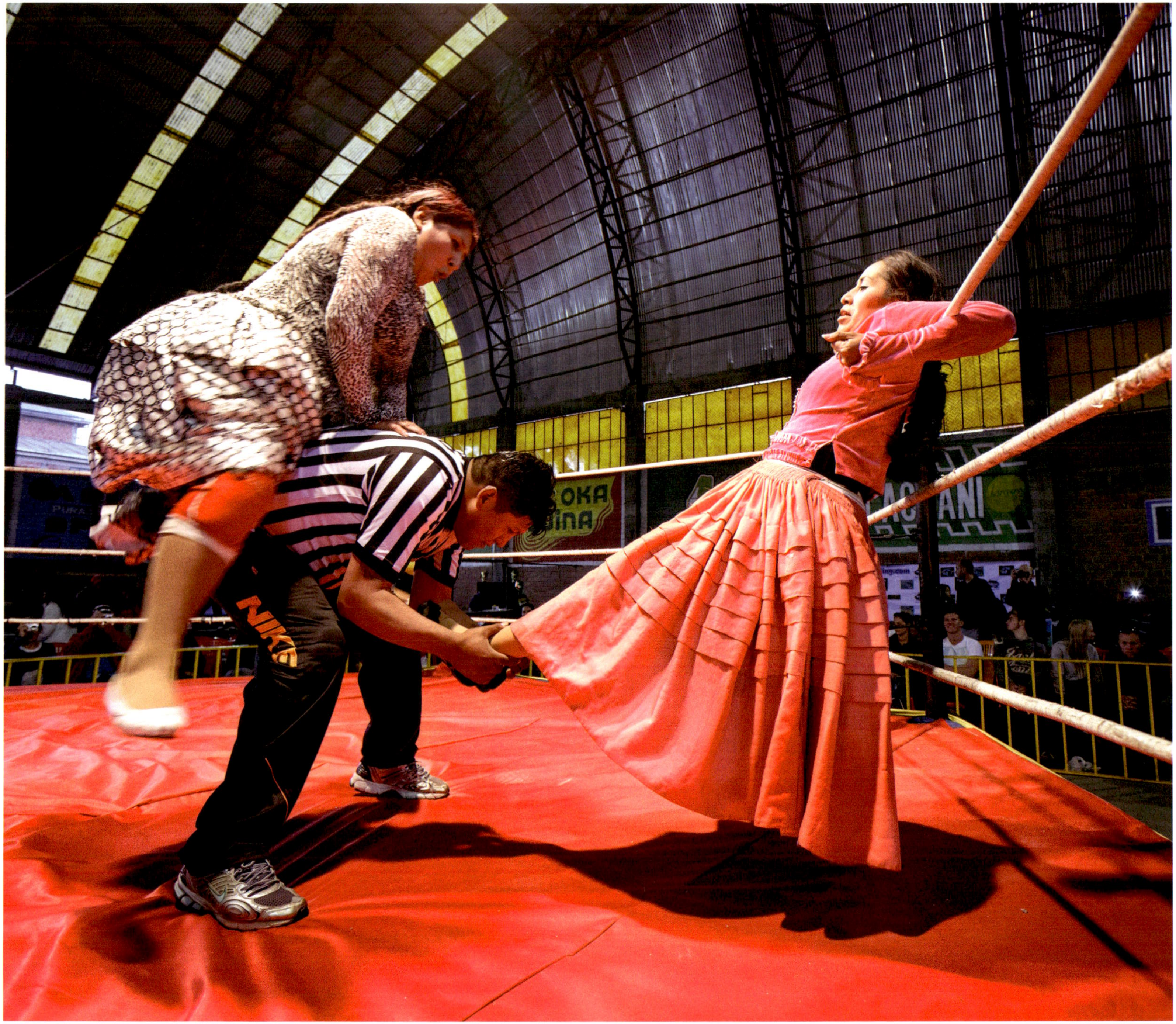

OPPOSITE:
La Calle de los Paraguas, La Paz, Bolivia
Lined with shops selling Andean musical instruments, jewellery and alpaca textiles, this street is in the old San Sebastian neighbourhood of the de facto capital. Alpaca wool is softer, warmer and more durable than sheep wool.

LEFT:
***Cholita* Wrestling, La Paz**
This theatrical, choreographed form of wrestling features female Aymara fighters who wear traditional costume, including the layered skirts called *polleras*. By naming themselves *cholitas*, the wrestlers are reclaiming the pejorative term for young Indigenous women.

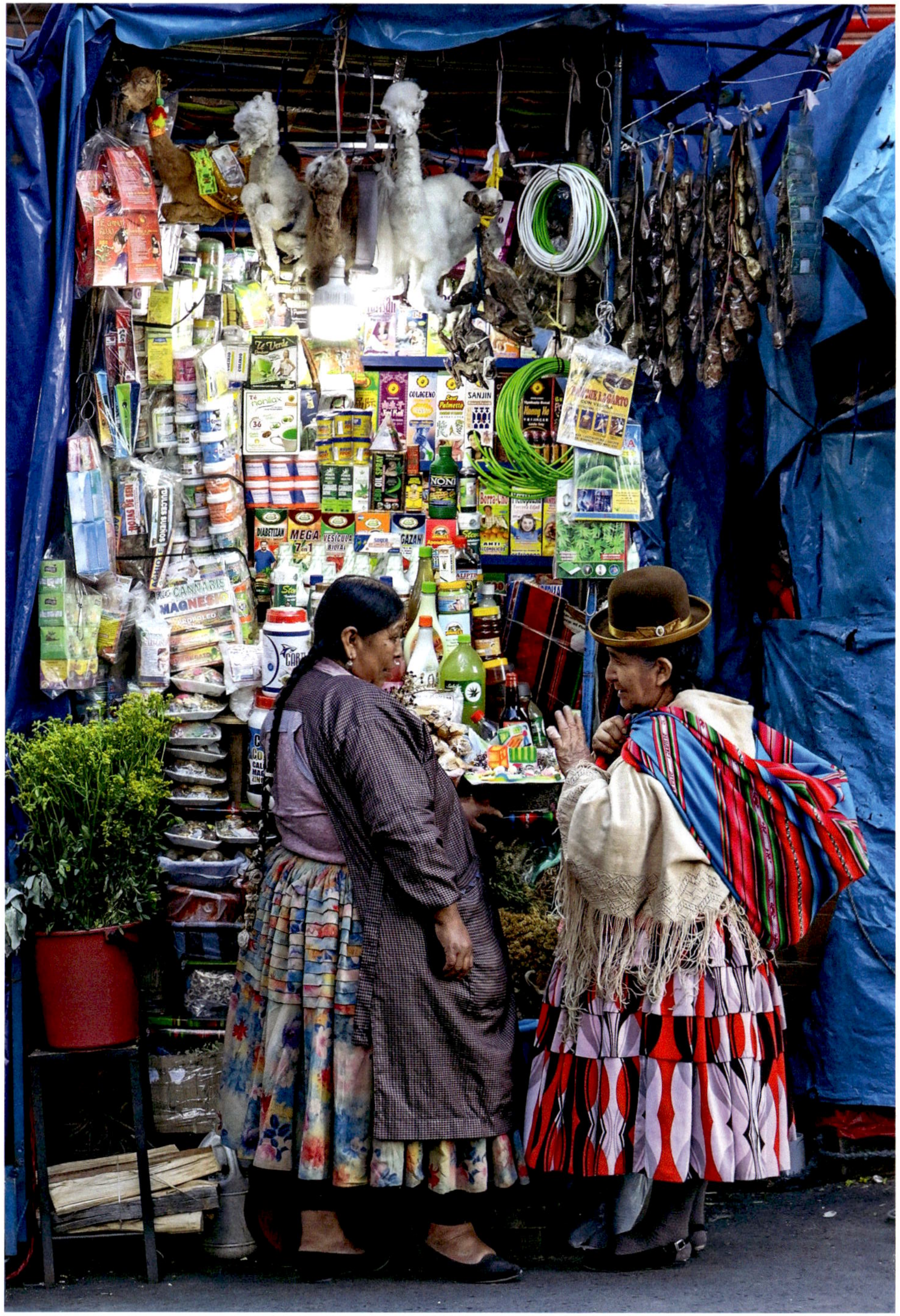

LEFT:
Mercado de las Brujas, La Paz, Bolivia
The 'Witches' Market' is where stallholders and Aymara healers called *yatiris* sell potions and medicinal plants. Among the wares are dried llama foetuses, which are buried under new buildings for good luck.

RIGHT:
Estadio Hernando Siles, La Paz
The world's highest administrative capital at 3650m (11,975ft), La Paz lies in a river-carved canyon on the Altiplano. The city was founded in 1548 by Spanish conquistadors, who named it Nuestra Señora de La Paz ('Our Lady of Peace'). The Estadio Hernando Siles is Bolivia's largest stadium, with 41,143 seats.

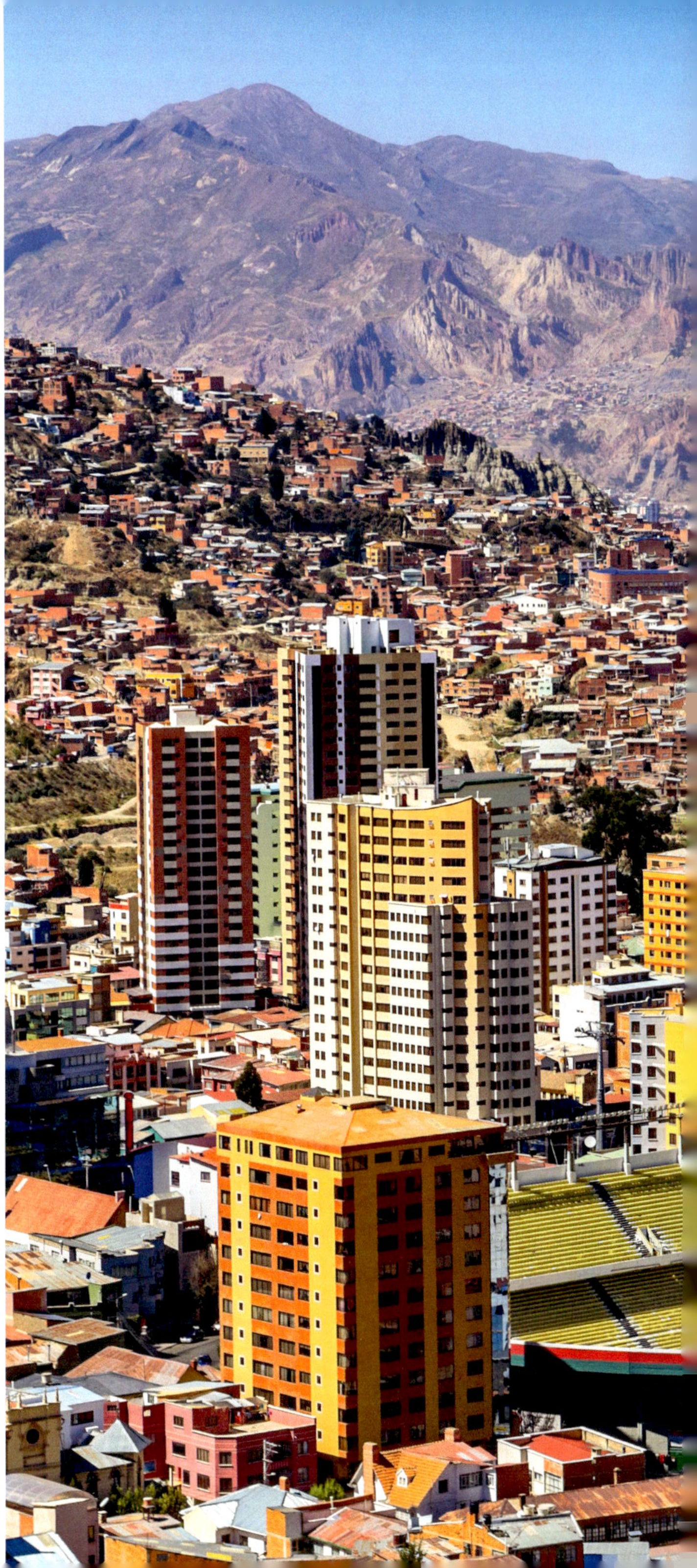

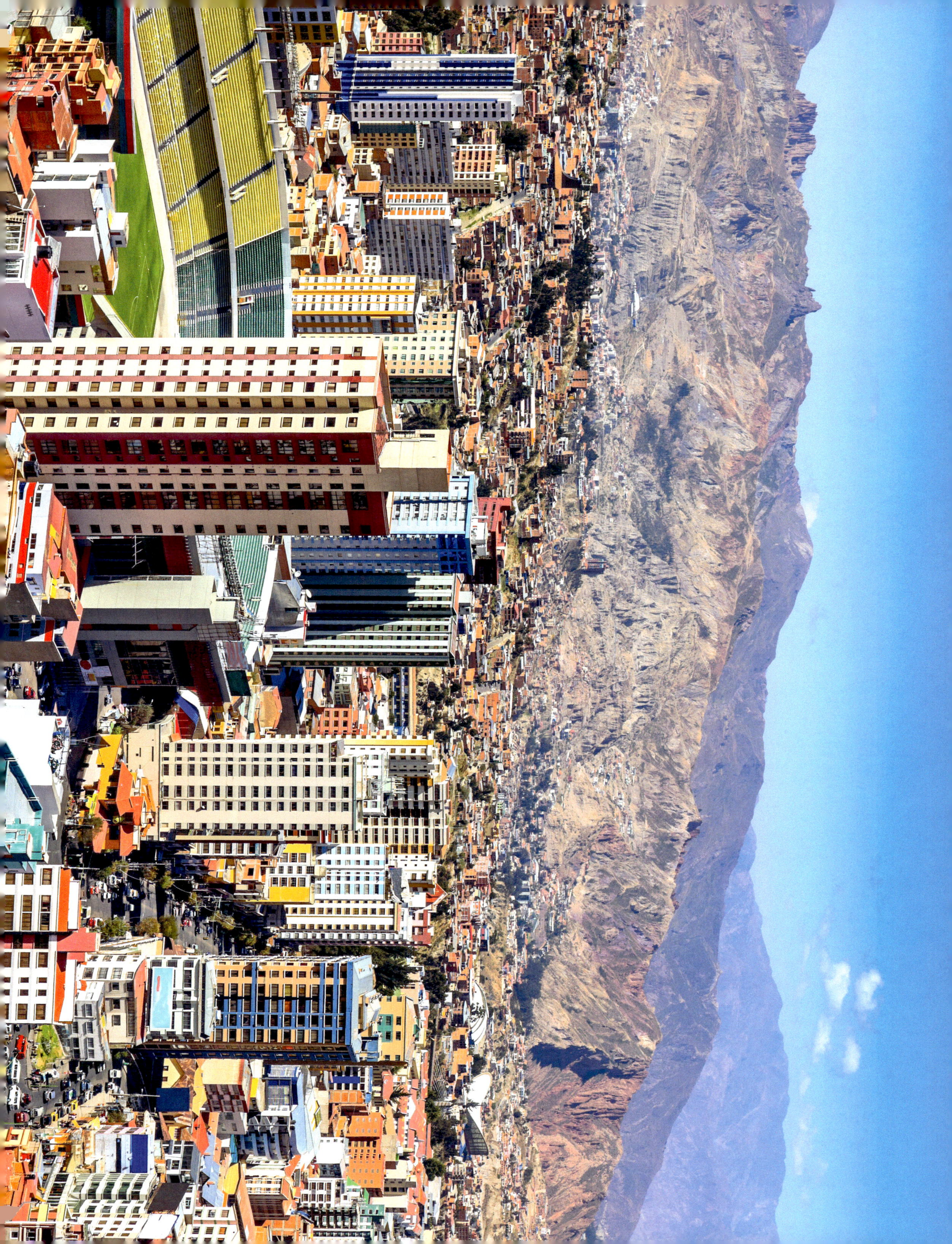

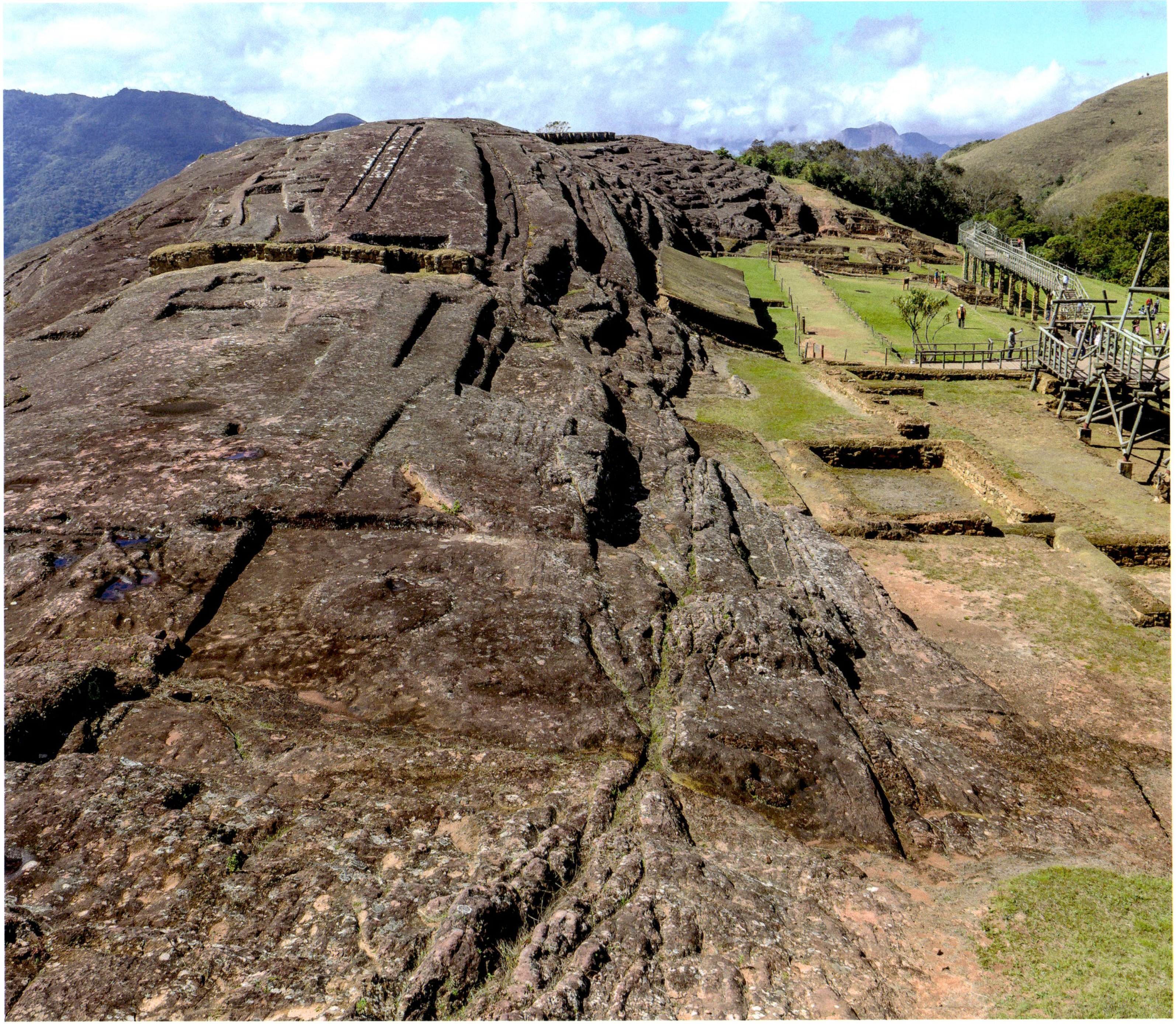

LEFT:
El Fuerte de Samaipata, Florida Province, Bolivia
The fort at Samaipata was held by the Chané, Inca and Spanish. The ceremonial sector (pictured) today consists of an outcrop carved mainly by the Chané, from around 300 CE, with geometric shapes, niches and animals.

OPPOSITE LEFT:
***Patujú*, Santa Cruz, Bolivia**
A national flower of Bolivia, *Heliconia rostrata* grows in the Amazonian lowlands, its red, yellow and green echoing the striped national flag. The plant's claw-like bracts hold flowers that are a vital source of nectar for hummingbirds.

OPPOSITE RIGHT TOP:
Yungas Road, Bolivia
Nicknamed the 'Death Road' for its many accidents, this narrow, cliff-side, foggy road links La Paz with Yungas. Although now replaced with a safer road, it still draws thrill-seeking mountain bikers from around the world.

OPPOSITE RIGHT BOTTOM:
***Yareta*, Eduardo Avaroa National Reserve, Bolivia**
Azorella compacta is a hardy, extremely slow-growing cushion plant that is found in the puna grassland of western Bolivia, at heights of 3200 to 5250m (10,500 to 17,220ft). The oldest plants are estimated to be 3000 years old, making them among the oldest living organisms on Earth.

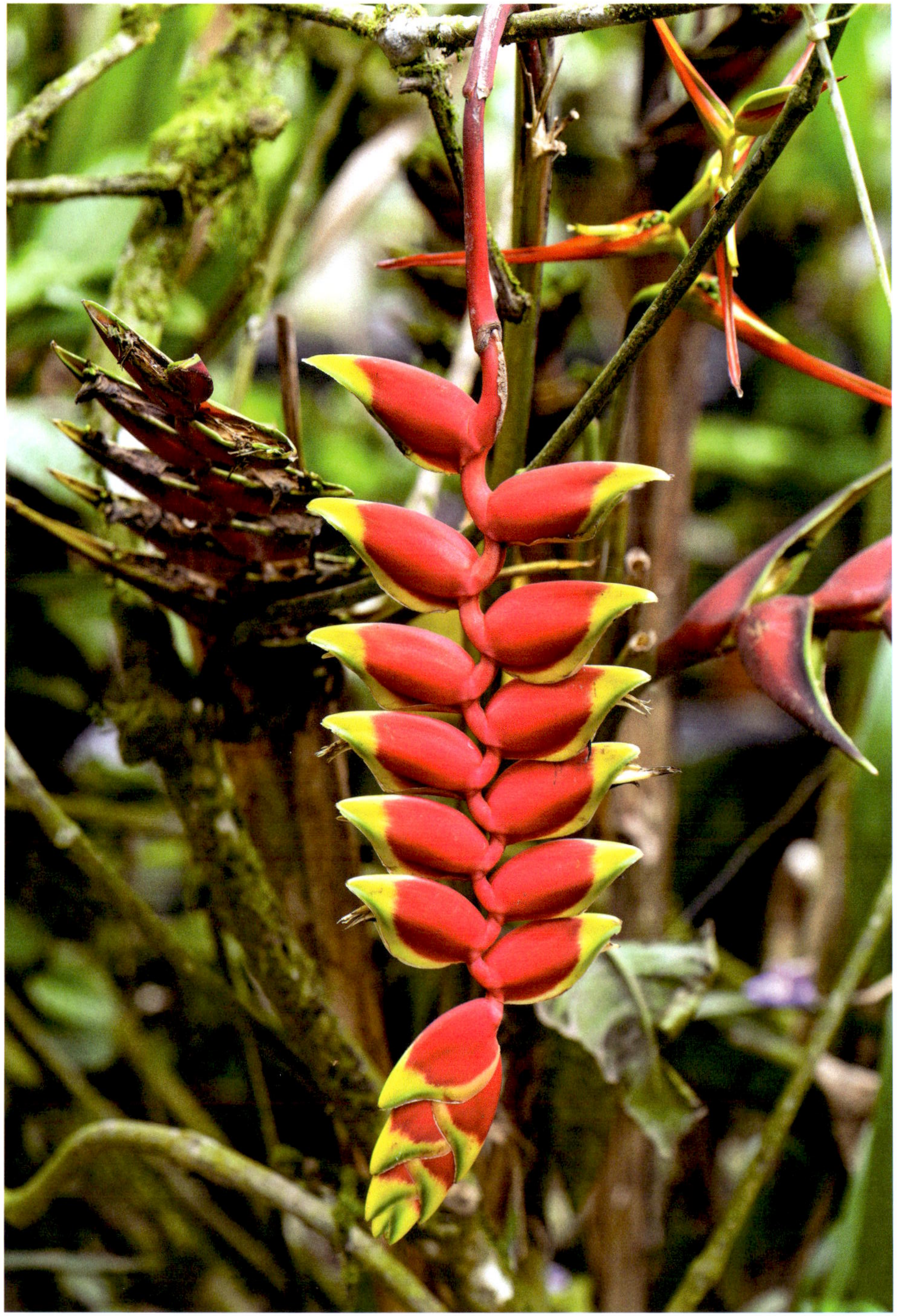

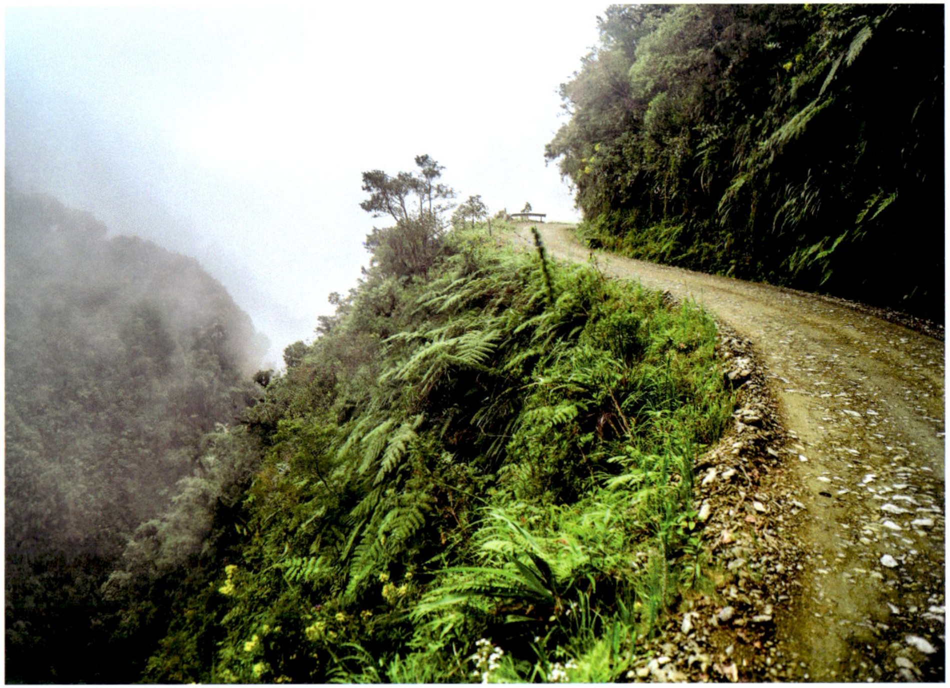

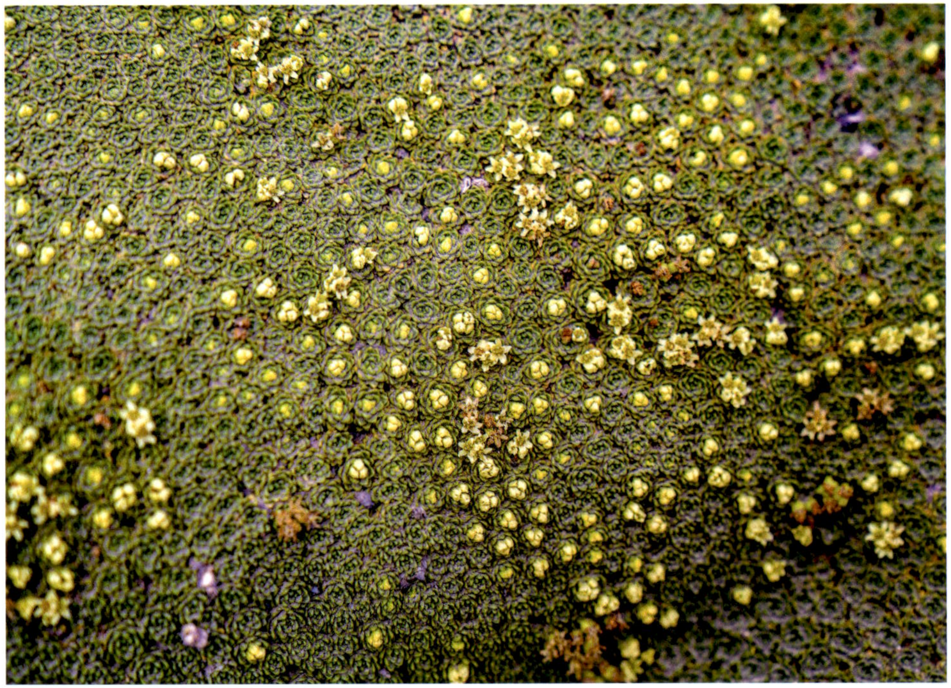

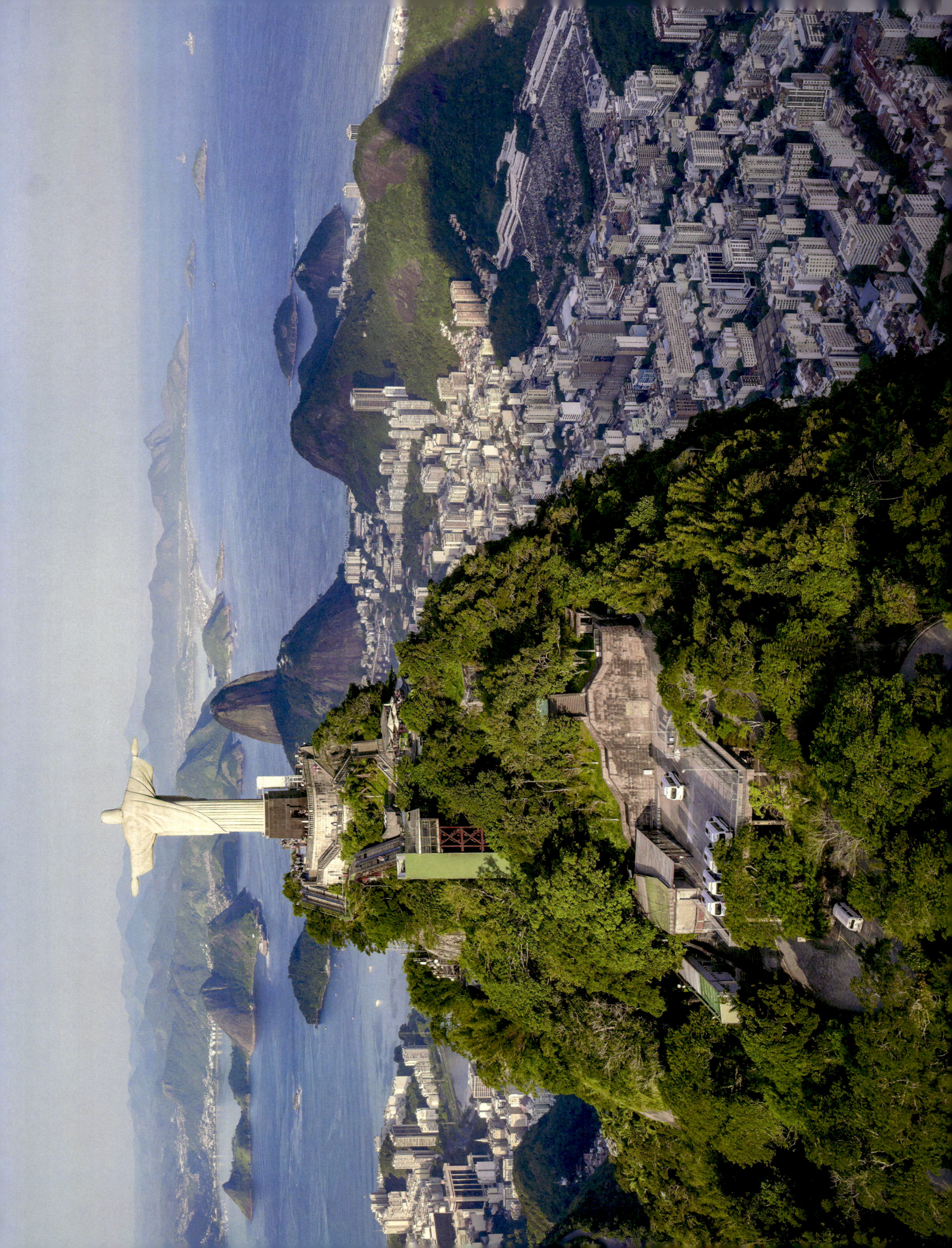

Brazil

The only country in South America with Portuguese as an official language, Brazil takes its name from the Portuguese words for *Paubrasilia echinata*, known in English as the brazilwood tree, which is endemic to the country's Atlantic Forest. When Portuguese explorers first saw these trees in 1500, they recognized them as a relative of the sappanwood, already used in Europe for extracting a valuable red dye for fabric, paint and ink. They named the tree *pau-brasil*, with *pau* meaning 'wood' and *brasil* meaning 'ember-coloured', and set up a hugely lucrative trade in the tree's blood-red, dye-producing heartwood. Soon the region was known as Terra do Brasil, and the tree – once abundant – was in sharp decline. Today, the endangered brazilwood tree has disappeared from most of its range, but replanting and conservation efforts are ongoing. It is apt that Brazil takes its name from a tree, since this is the South American country with the most of them: more then 300 billion. This record is in part due to Brazil's immense size, since it covers 8.5 million sq km (3.3 million sq miles), making it by far the continent's largest country. Forests, including the Amazon Rainforest, cover half of Brazil's land. In the famous Amazon, the most common trees include the well-known and commercially useful kapok, rubber and Brazil nut tree, as well as the less recognizable huasai, murumuru and walking palm. Mass deforestation of the Amazon began in the 1960s, with a quarter lost so far. Led by Brazil's Indigenous peoples, the battle to save the Amazon is on.

OPPOSITE:
***Christ the Redeemer*, Rio de Janeiro, Brazil**
Created by a team led by French-Polish sculptor Paul Landowski, this statue is 30m (98ft) tall, not including its pedestal. It stands on Corcovado, a granite peak just west of the city centre. Built from reinforced concrete, with outer layers of erosion-resistant but easy-to-carve soapstone, the sculpture took nine years to complete, from 1922 to 1931.

RIGHT:
Sugarloaf Mountain, Rio de Janeiro, Brazil
This 396m (1299ft) granite peak is a bornhardt, named after the German geologist Friedrich Bornhardt. A bornhardt is a domed granite outcrop formed through the weathering of granite along fractures, followed by the stripping away of the surrounding softer rock.

OPPOSITE:
Cathedral of Brasília, Brazil
The cathedral of Brazil's capital city was built between 1958 and 1970. Like most of Brasília's public buildings, it was designed by Brazilian Modernist architect Oscar Niemeyer. The roof's concrete struts stretch toward heaven, while the stained glass by French-Brazilian artist Marianne Peretti creates rippling, wave-like movement.

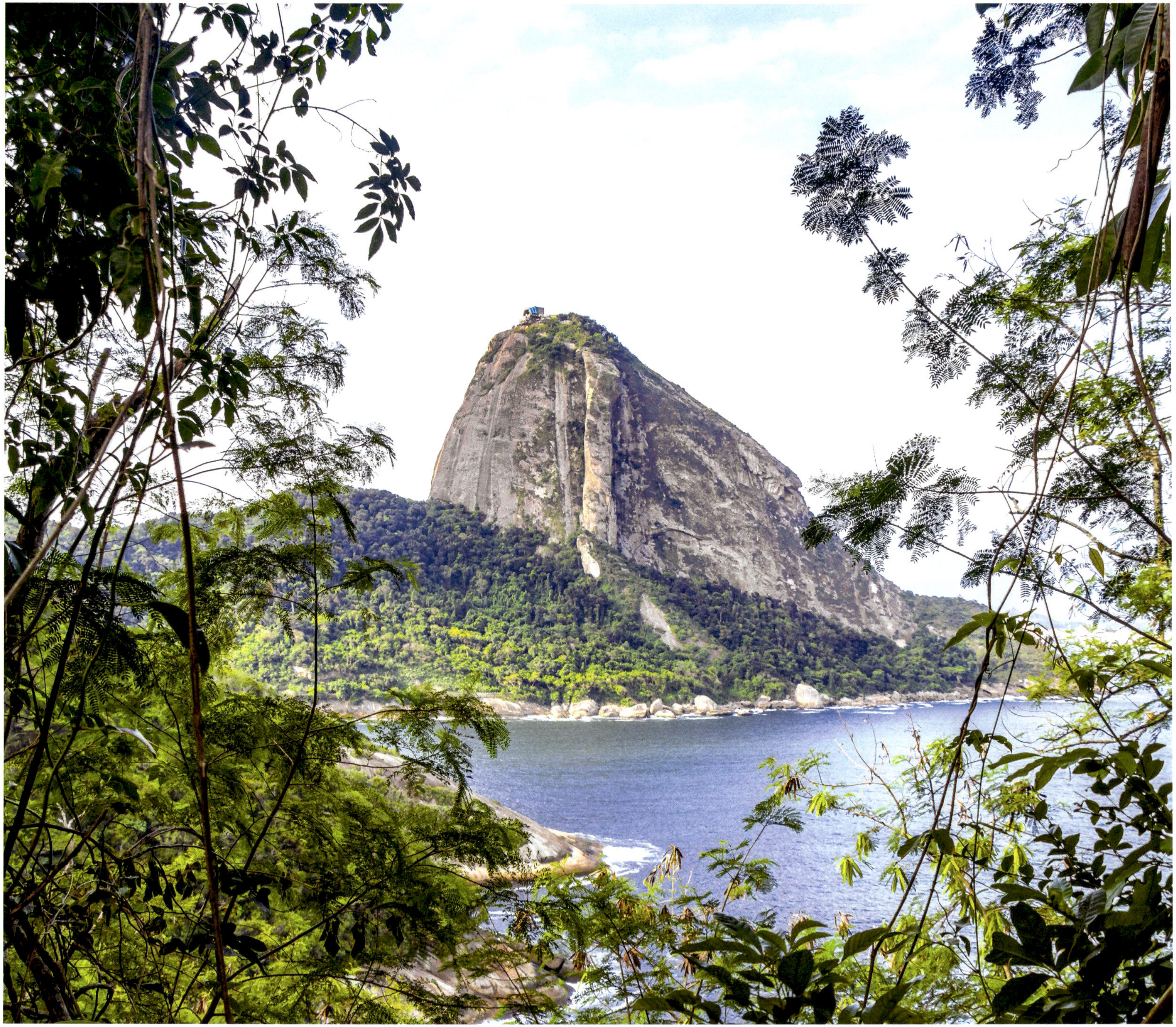

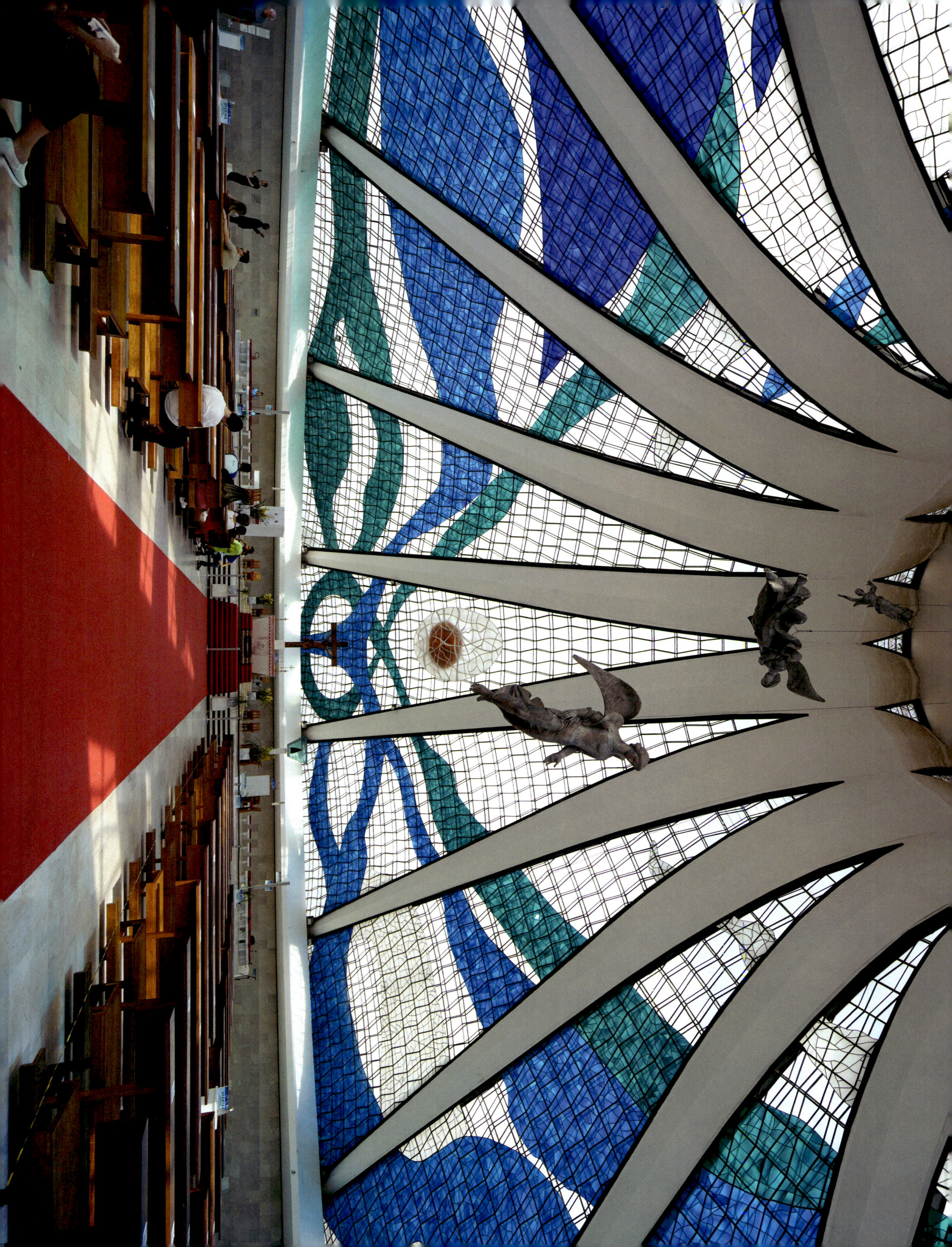

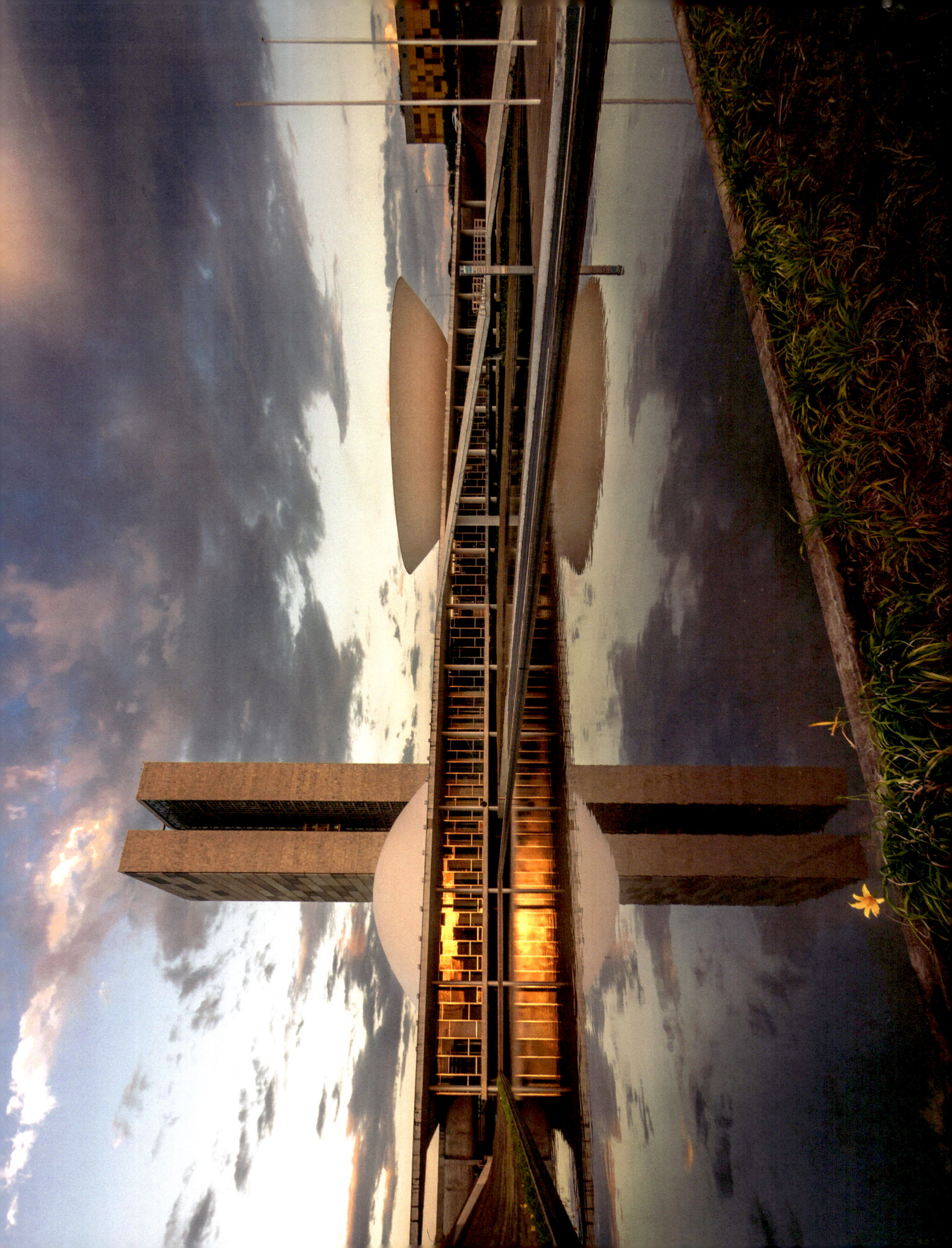

OPPOSITE:

National Congress, Brasília, Brazil

The seat of Brazil's federal legislature was designed by Oscar Niemeyer. The concave dome sits atop the Chamber of Deputies (lower house) and the convex one crowns the Federal Senate (upper house). The building was completed in 1960, the same year that Brasília was officially founded to replace Rio de Janeiro with a more central capital.

RIGHT:

Dom Bosco Sanctuary, Brasília

The patron saint of Brasília is Italian Catholic priest Don Bosco, who in 1883 had a dream in which he saw an extraordinary city in this location. Dedicated to the saint, this 1970 church by Carlos Alberto Naves blends abrupt Modernist forms with Gothic arched windows filled with brilliant blue glass.

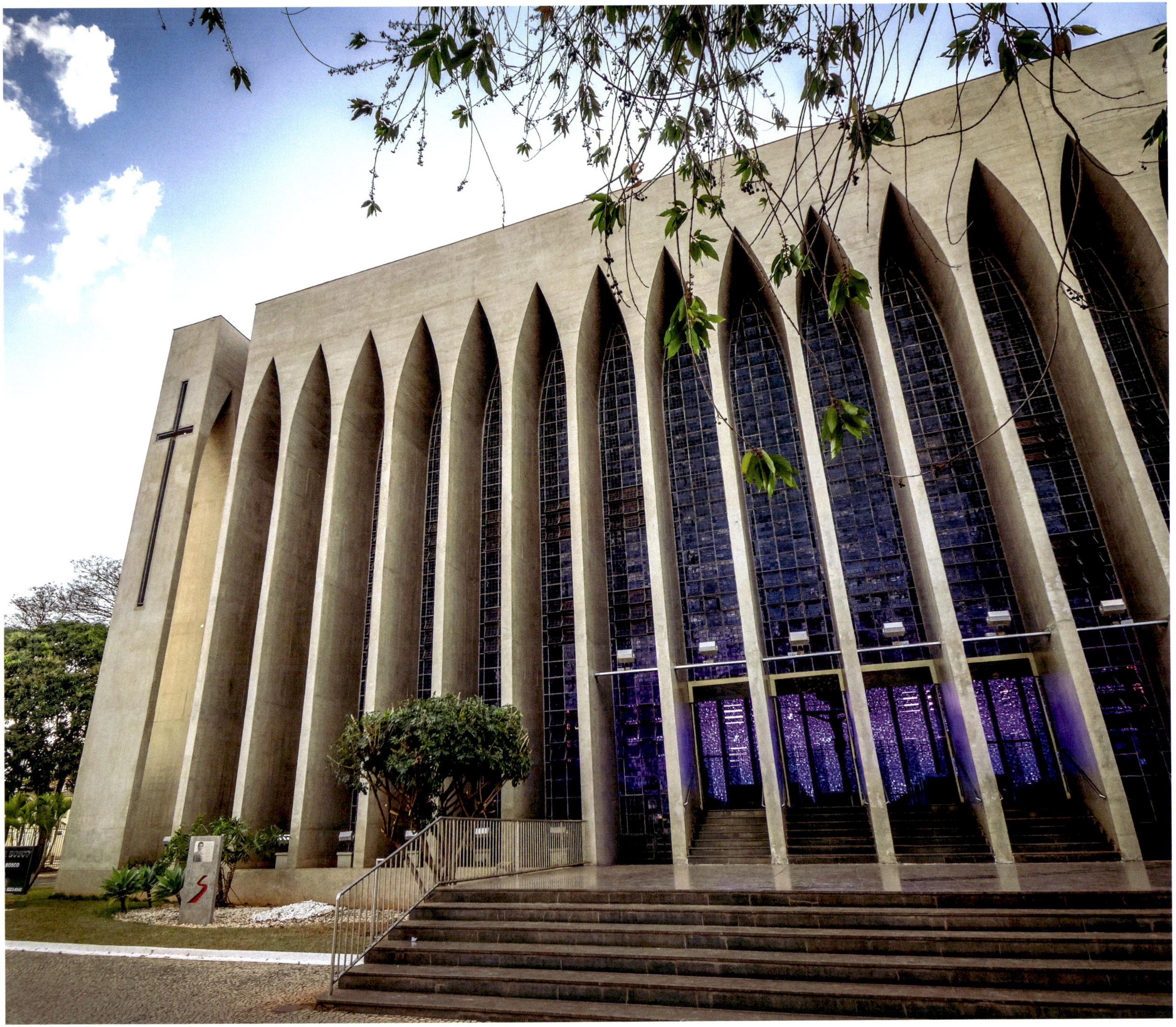

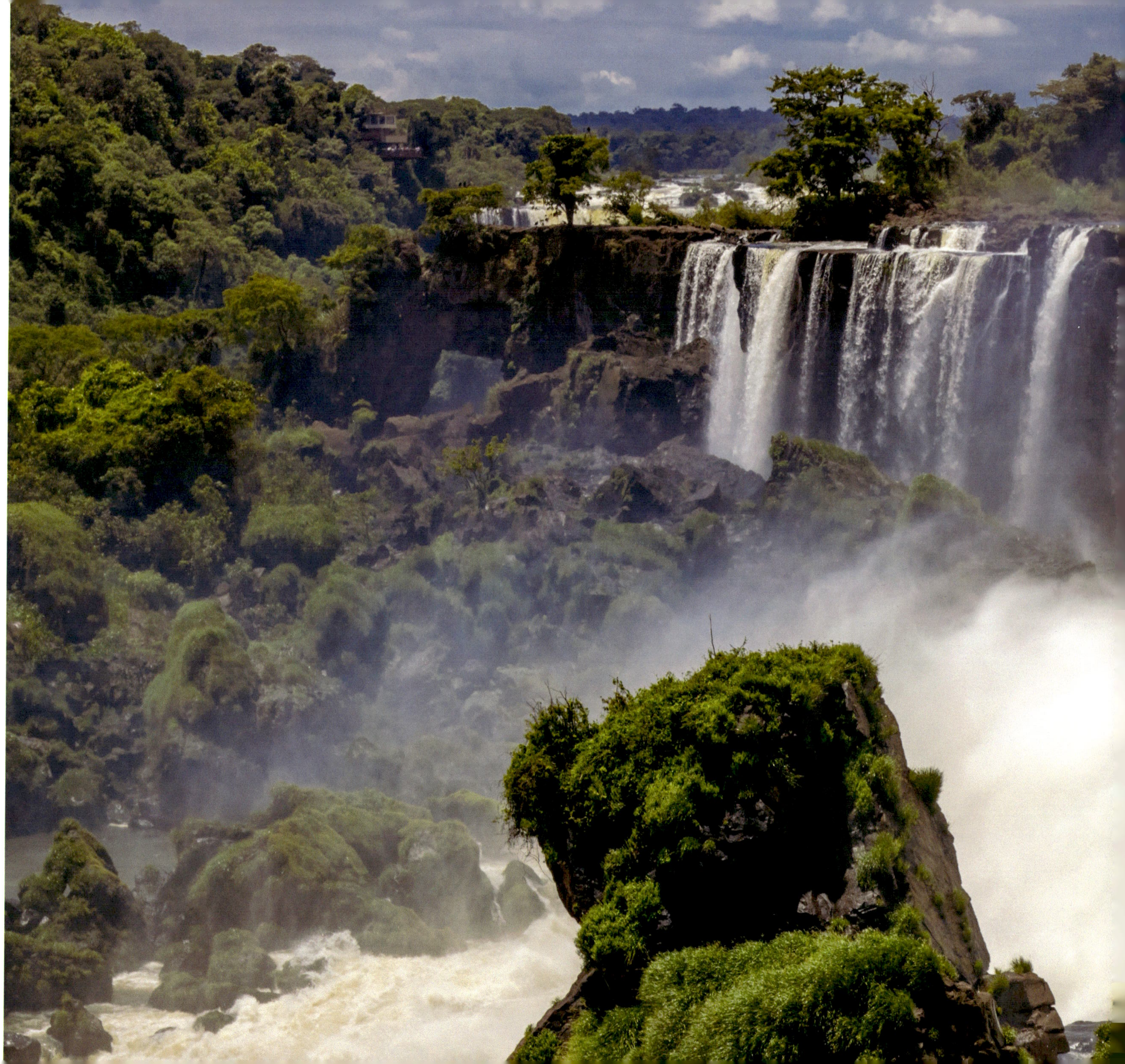

Iguaçu Falls, Brazil–Argentina
On the Iguaçu River, on the border between Brazil and Argentina, lies this immense horseshoe-shaped waterfall system, nearly 3km (1.7 miles) wide. There are up to 300 separate cataracts with a maximum height of 82m (269ft). The word 'Iguaçu' ('Iguazu' over the border in Argentina) comes from the Guaraní or Tupi words for 'big water'.

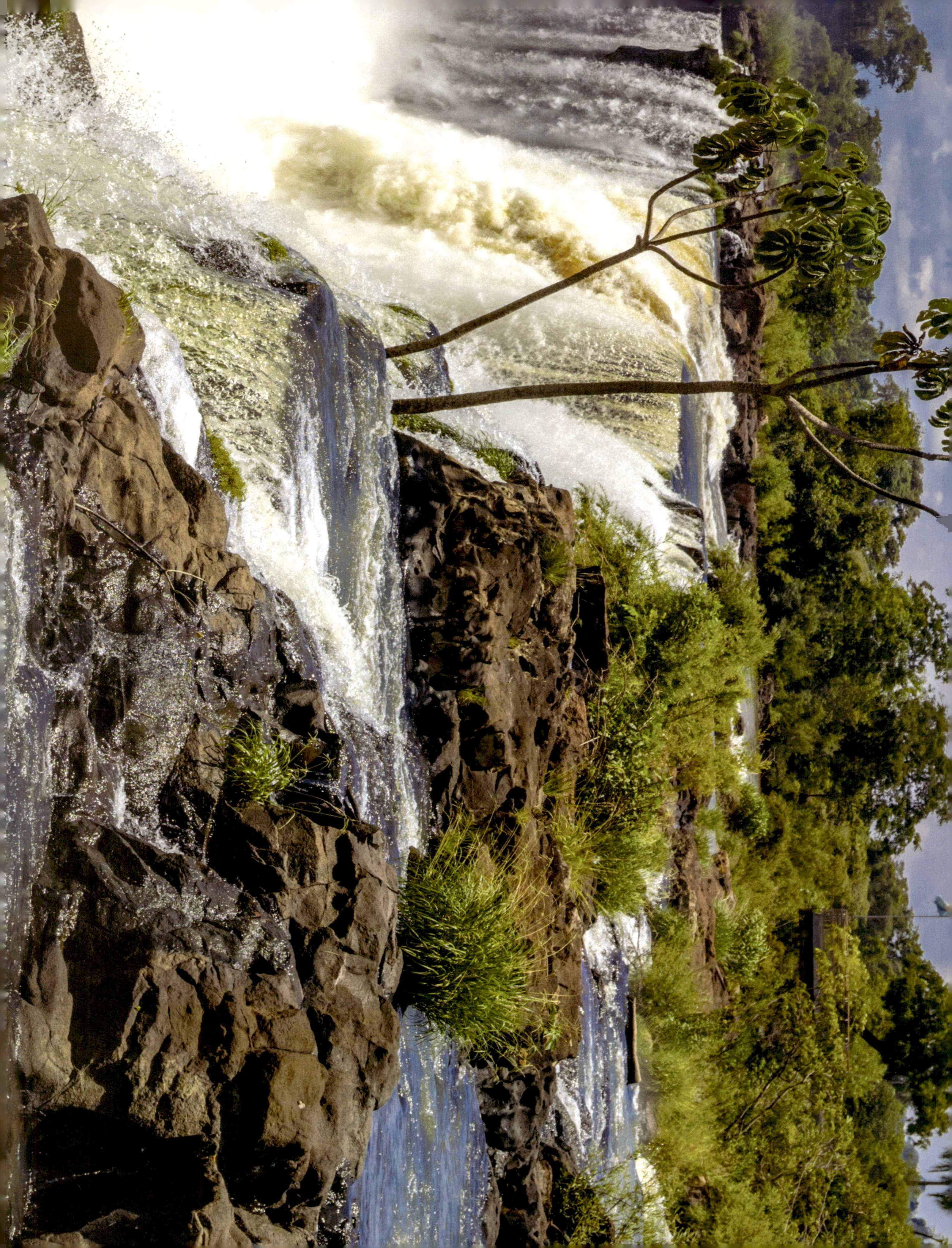

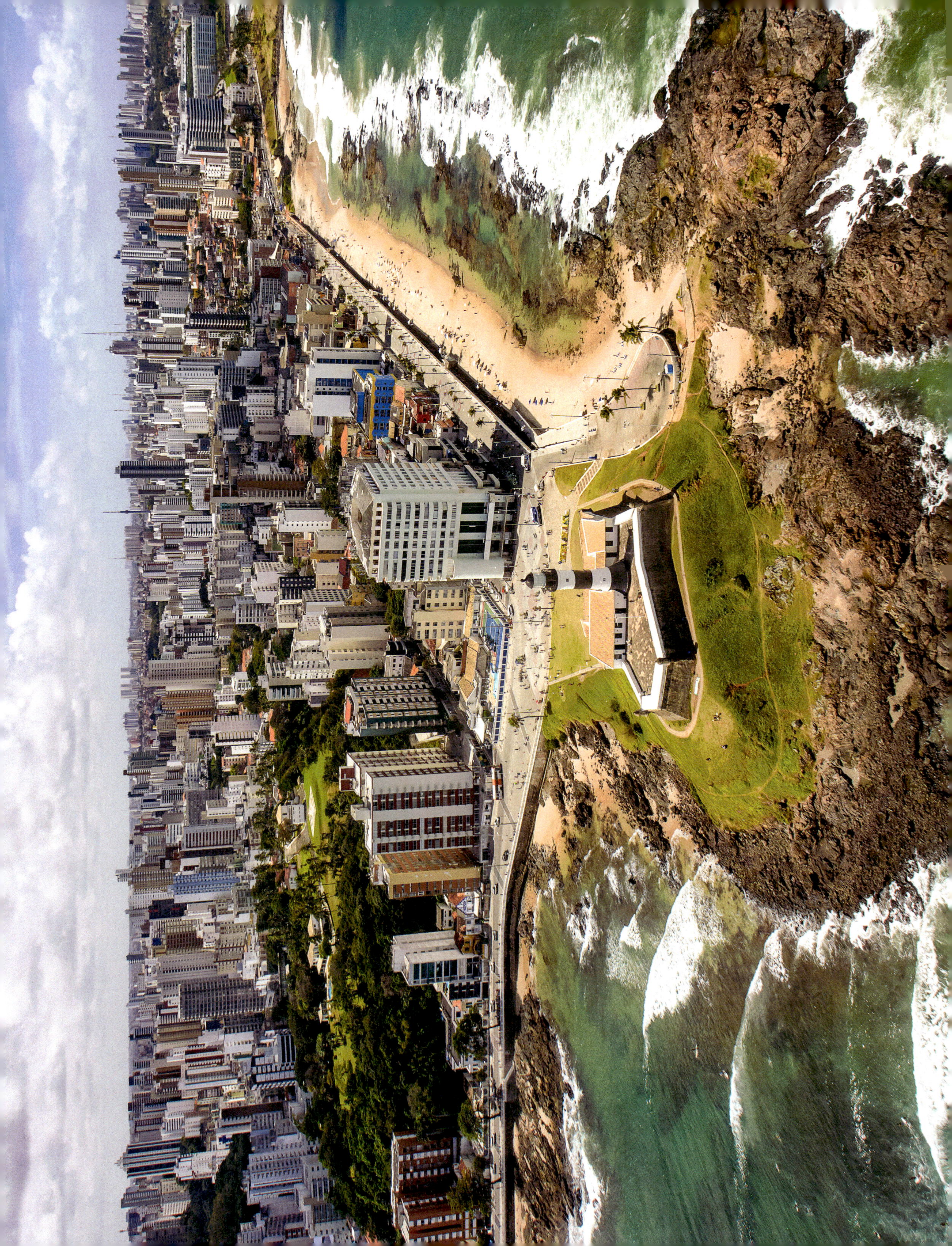

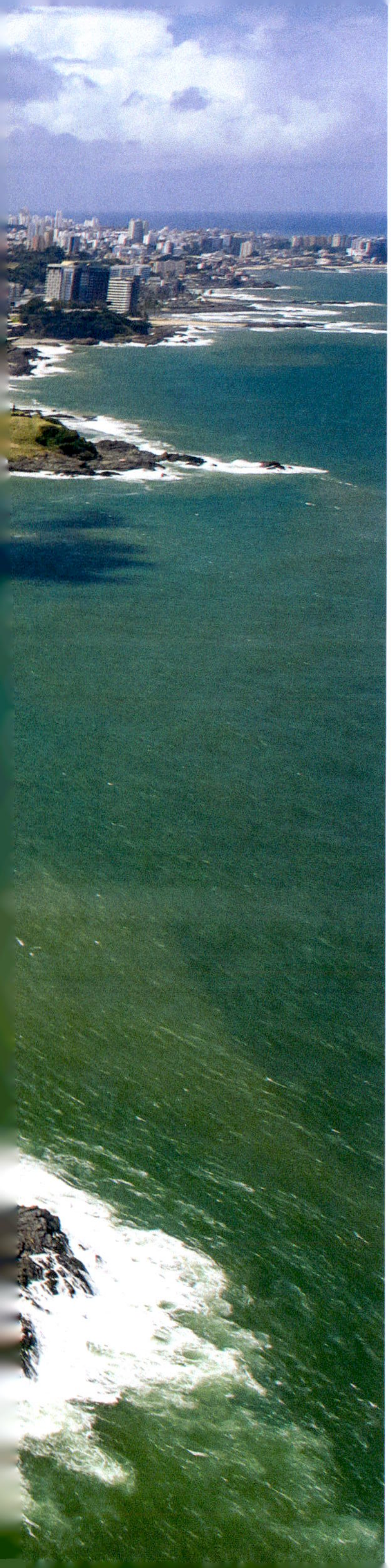

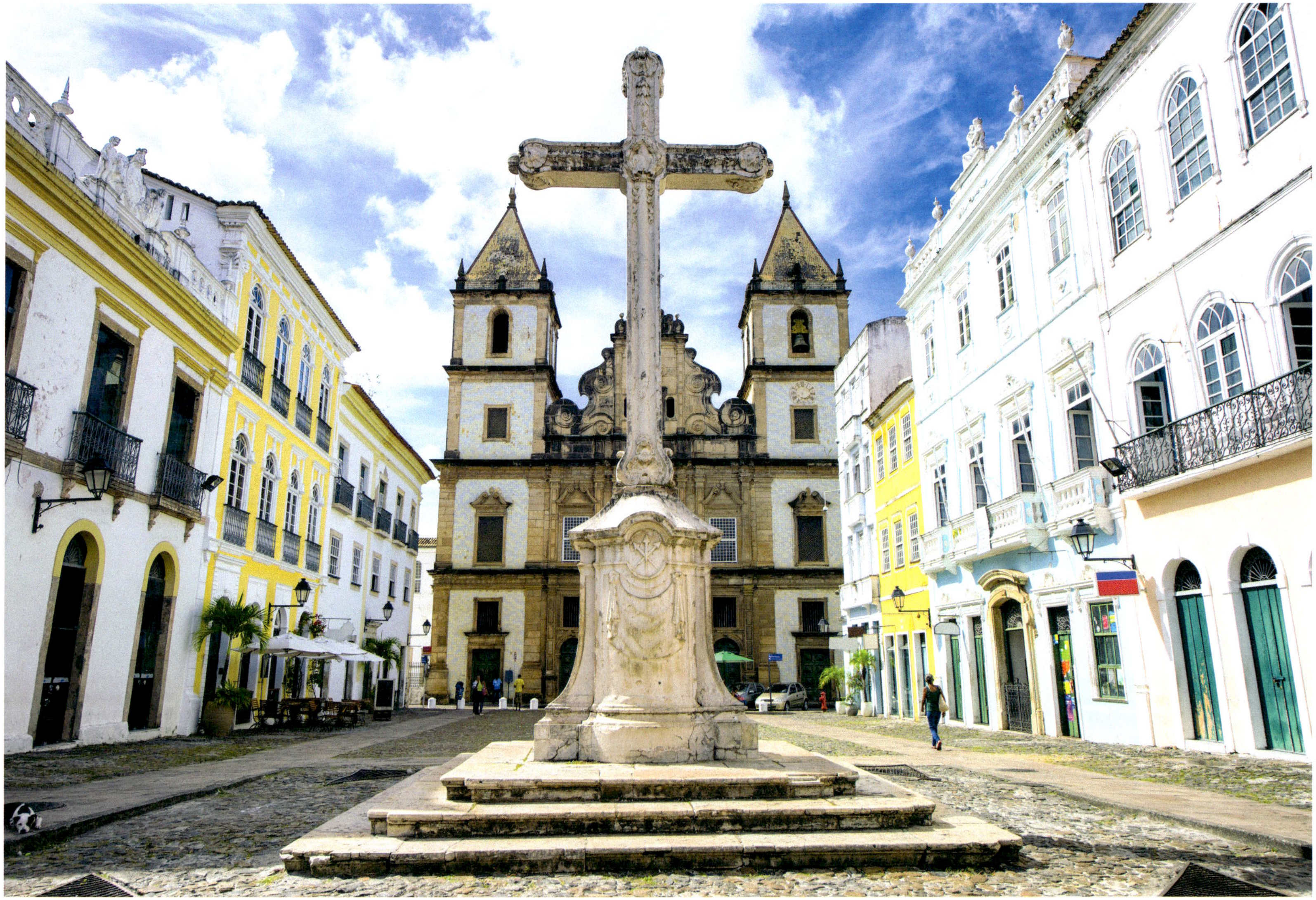

LEFT:

Barra Lighthouse, Salvador, Brazil

An 1839 lighthouse stands on the southwesternmost point of the city of Salvador, the former colonial capital. The lighthouse is inside Santo Antônio da Barra fort, built in 1702 by the Portuguese to protect the Baía de Todos os Santo, the key bay of Bahia, from which the state takes its name.

ABOVE:

Praça Anchieta, Pelourinho, Salvador

In Salvador's historic centre, this square is known for its marble cross, imported from Lisbon in 1807 and dedicated to São Francisco de Xavier, the city's patron saint. Lining the square are eighteenth-century colonial-style townhouses, known as *sobrados*, and the church of São Francisco, completed in 1723.

RIGHT:
Pantanal,
Mato Grosso, Brazil
The world's largest tropical wetland at up to 195,000 sq km (75,000 sq miles), the Pantanal stretches into Paraguay and Bolivia. It lies in a vast depression with heavy runoff from the surrounding uplands. One of the most common aquatic plants here is water hyacinth (*Pontederia crassipes*), which grows exceptionally fast and forms large floating mats.

OPPOSITE:
Copacabana Beach,
Rio de Janeiro, Brazil
This famous beach stretches 4km (2.5 miles) along the Atlantic Coast. Its promenade features a *calçada portuguesa* ('Portuguese pavement'), made of small stone tesserae. Completed in 1970, the pavement was designed by Brazilian landscape architect Roberto Burle Marx.

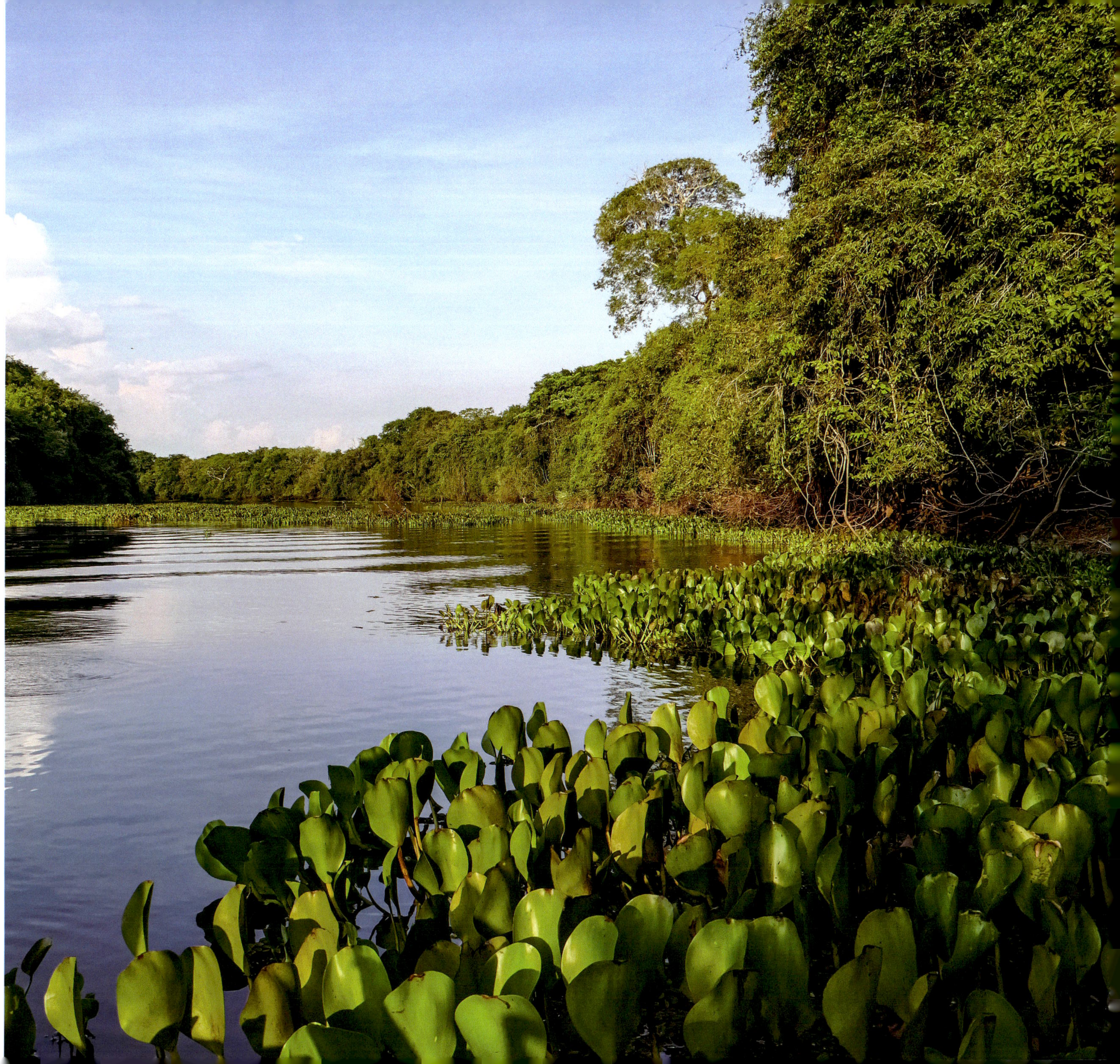

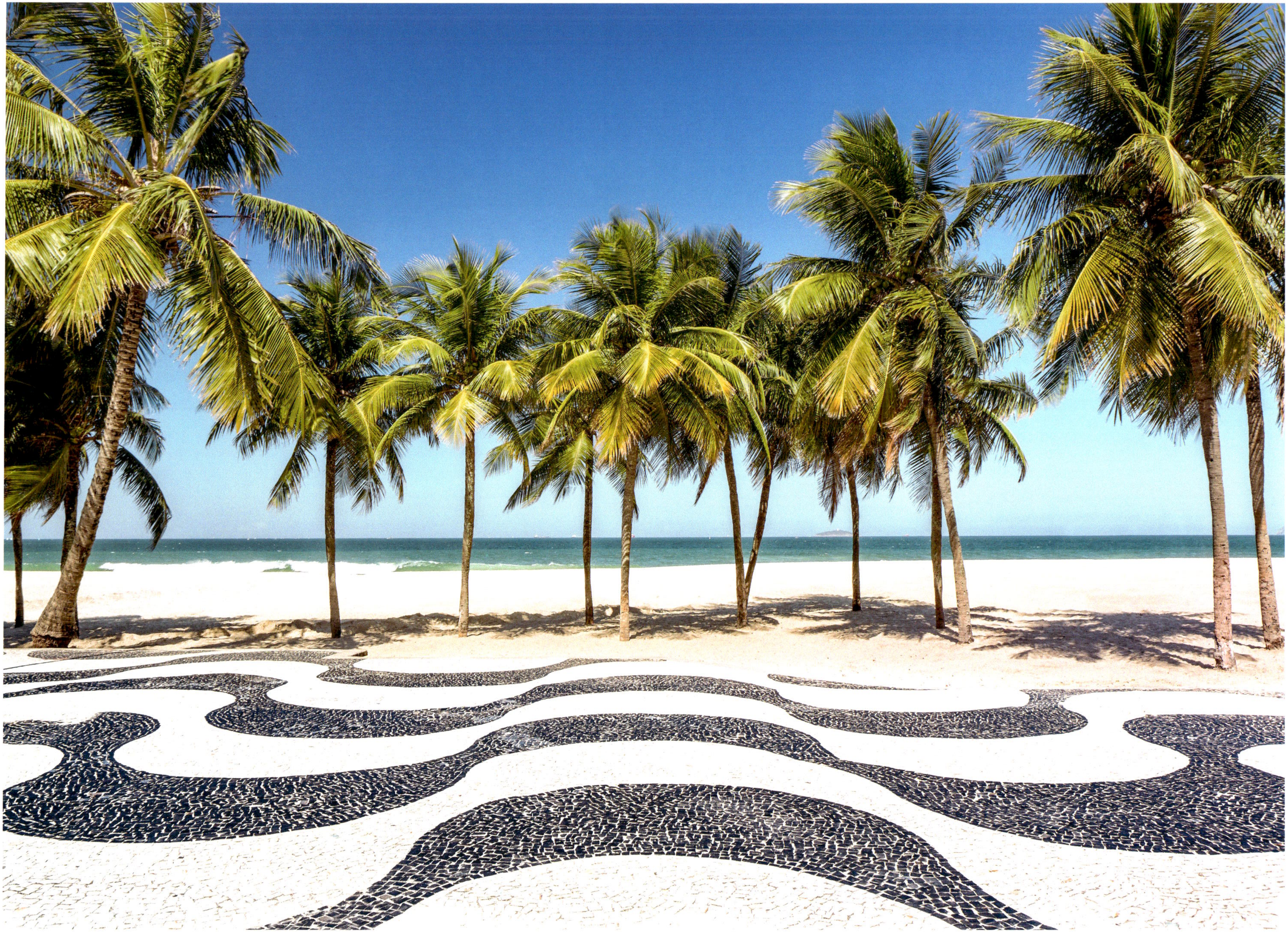

RIGHT:
Rio Carnival, Rio de Janeiro, Brazil
The world's largest carnival, with up to 2 million people per day, the Rio Carnival has been celebrated since 1723. During the Samba School Parade, the top samba schools process on elaborately decorated floats, with teams of dancers and drummers. Samba music and dance originated in Bahia's Afro-Brazilian community in the late nineteenth century and early twentieth century.

OPPOSITE:
***Capoeiristas*, Ibirapuera Park, São Paulo**
Probably with its roots in Angola, this Afro-Brazilian martial art is both dance-like and spiritual. Often performed to the music of *berimbaus* and *pandeiros*, it involves evasions, kicks, headbutts, cartwheels and *ginga*, a rocking, back-and-forth dance step.

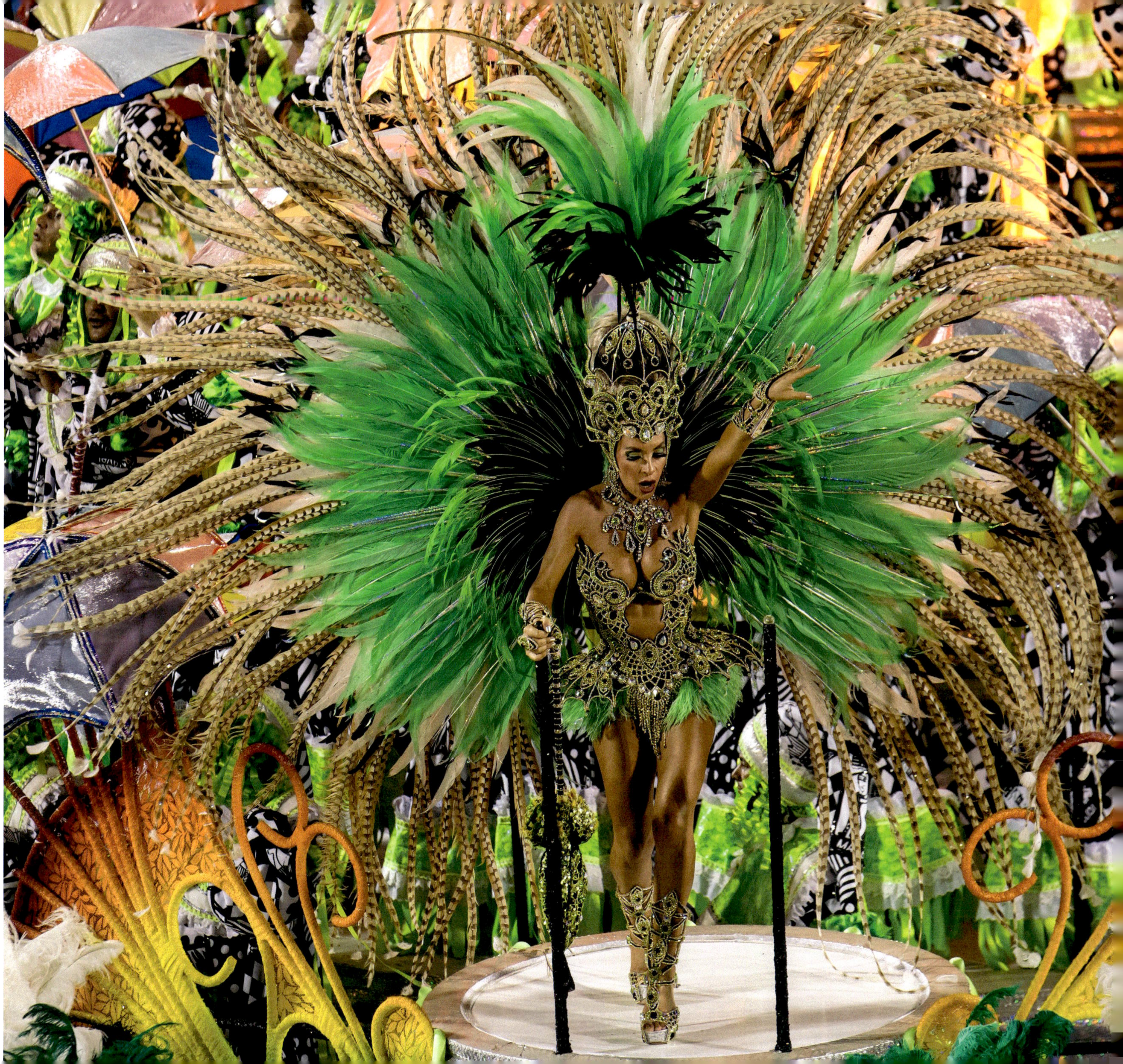

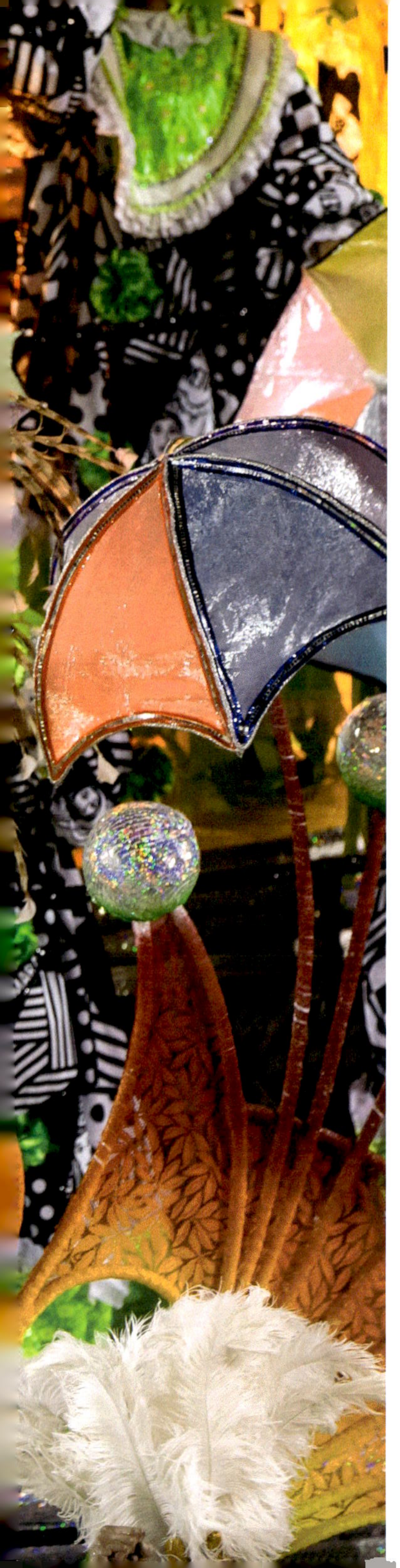

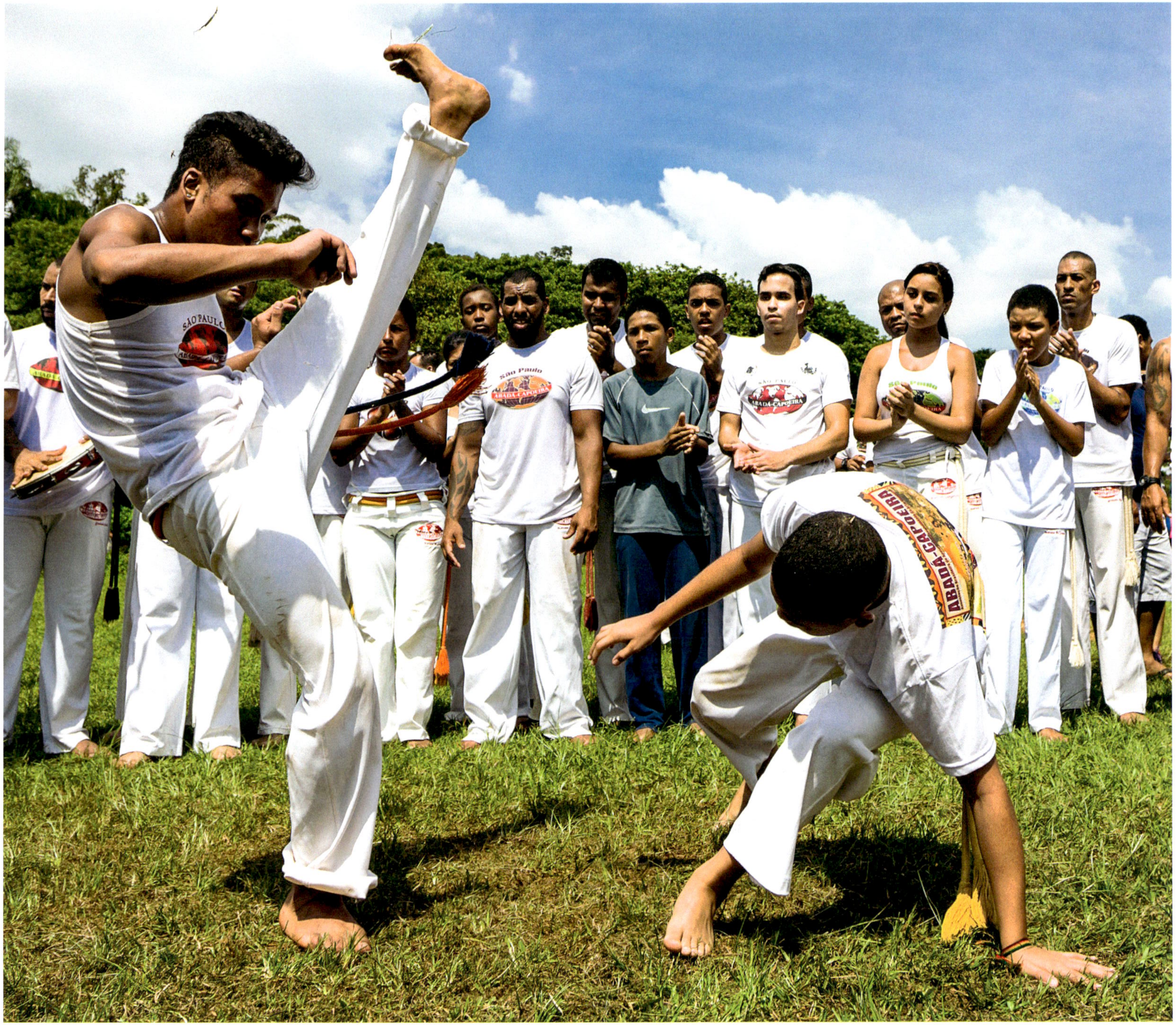
ABADÁ-CAPOEIRA

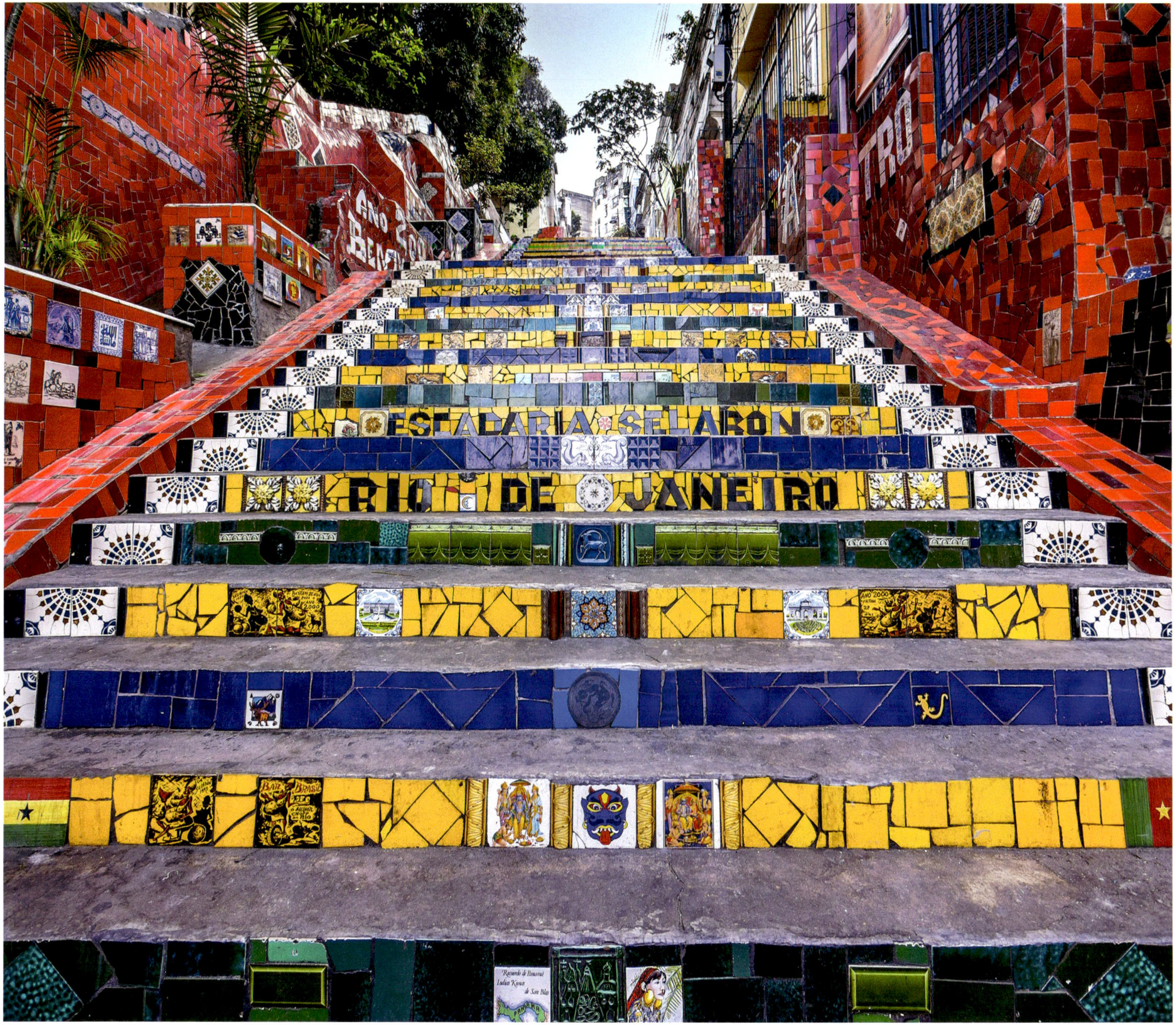
ESCADARIA SELARON
RIO DE JANEIRO

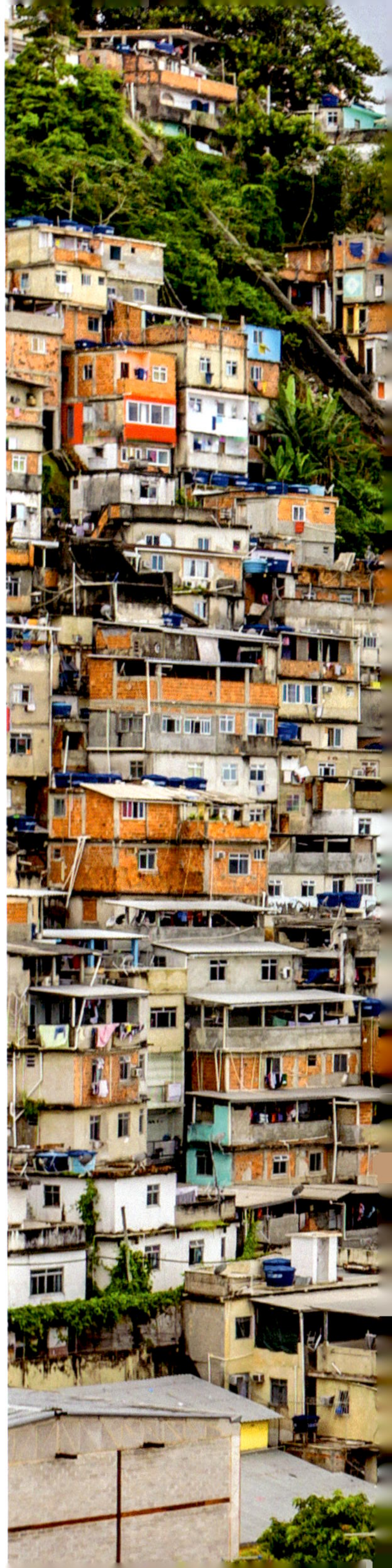

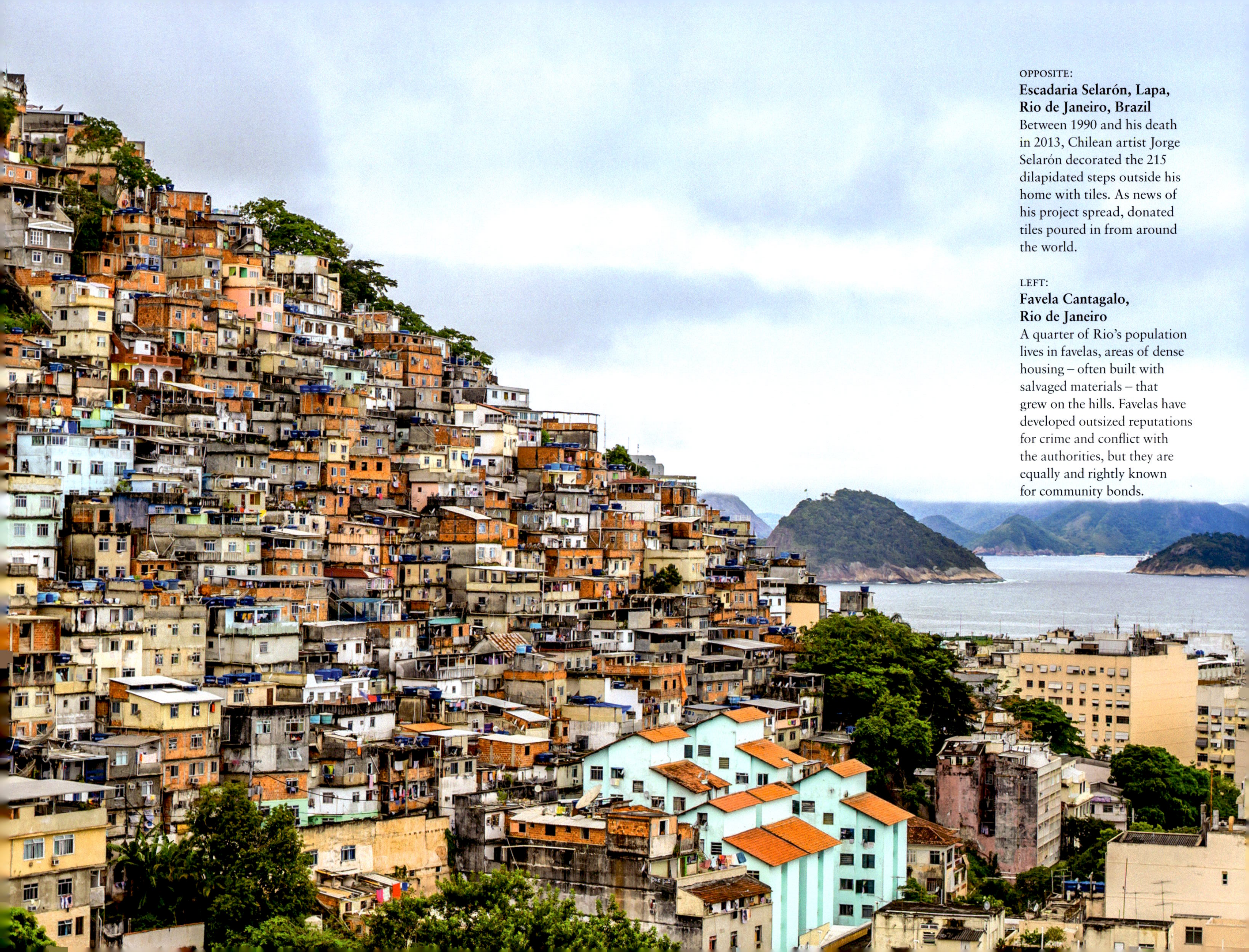

OPPOSITE:
Escadaria Selarón, Lapa, Rio de Janeiro, Brazil
Between 1990 and his death in 2013, Chilean artist Jorge Selarón decorated the 215 dilapidated steps outside his home with tiles. As news of his project spread, donated tiles poured in from around the world.

LEFT:
Favela Cantagalo, Rio de Janeiro
A quarter of Rio's population lives in favelas, areas of dense housing – often built with salvaged materials – that grew on the hills. Favelas have developed outsized reputations for crime and conflict with the authorities, but they are equally and rightly known for community bonds.

ALL PHOTOGRAPHS:
Chapada Diamantina, Brazil
This dramatically eroded portion of the Espinhaço Mountains is a place of canyons and waterfalls. Three Brazilian biomes converge here: the dry *caatinga* shrubland, the *cerrado* savanna and the lush Atlantic Forest. Lava lizards thrive in exposed, rocky areas, with their flattened body ideal for slipping into crevices.

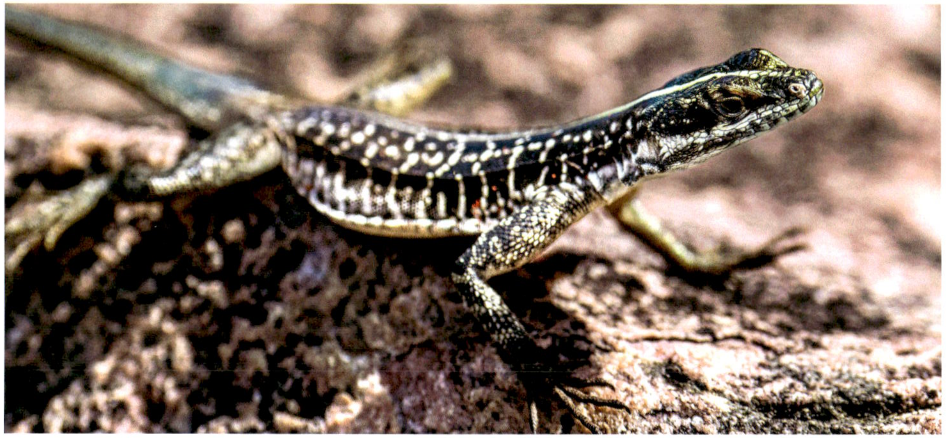

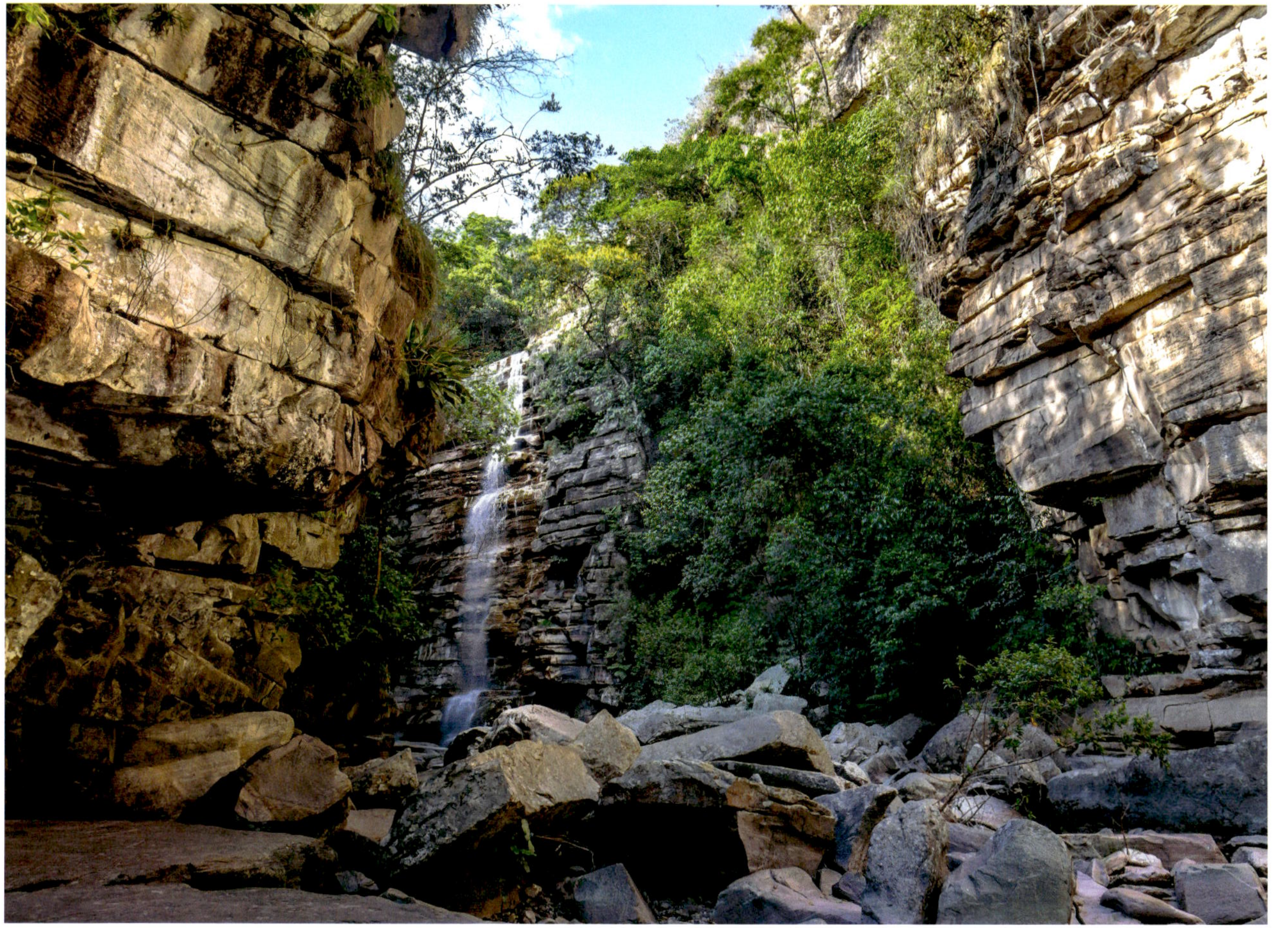

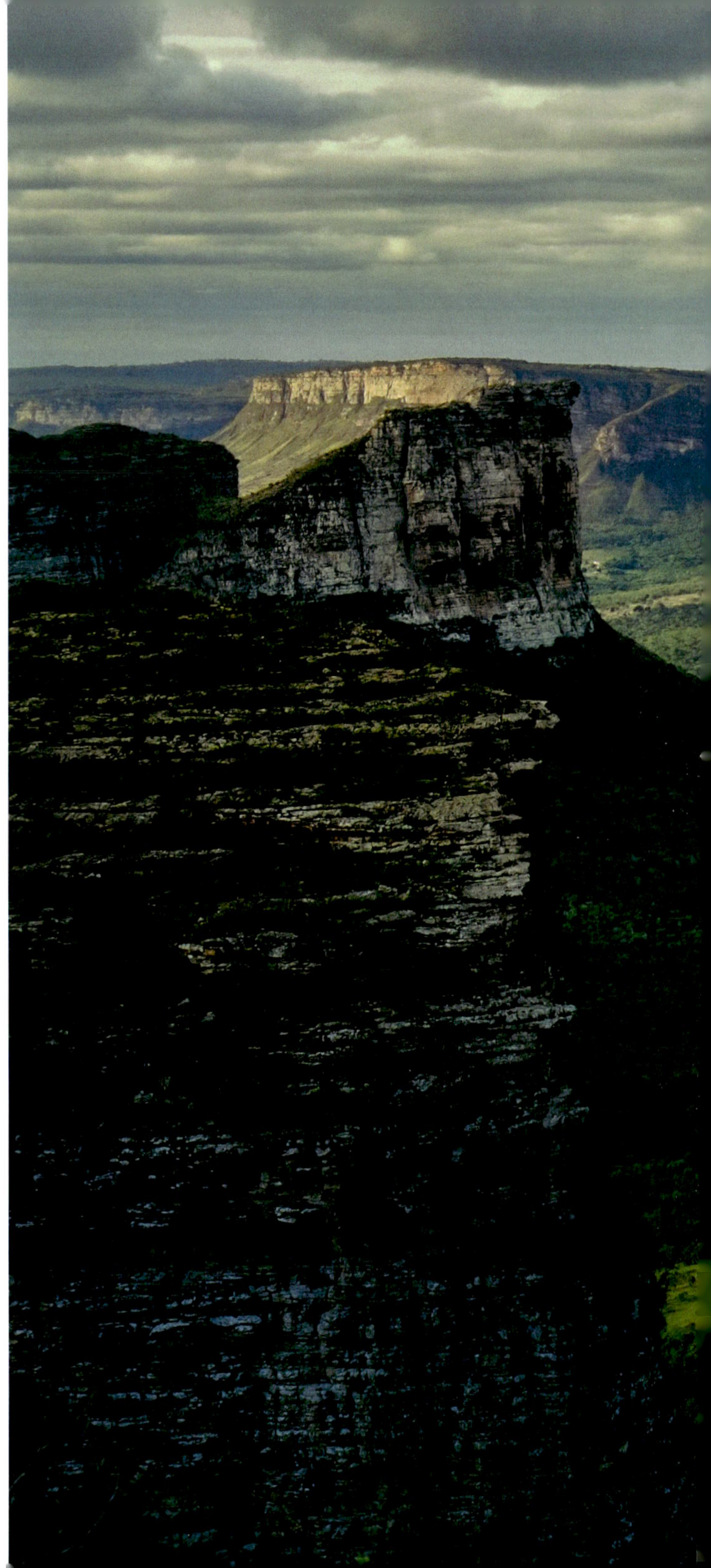

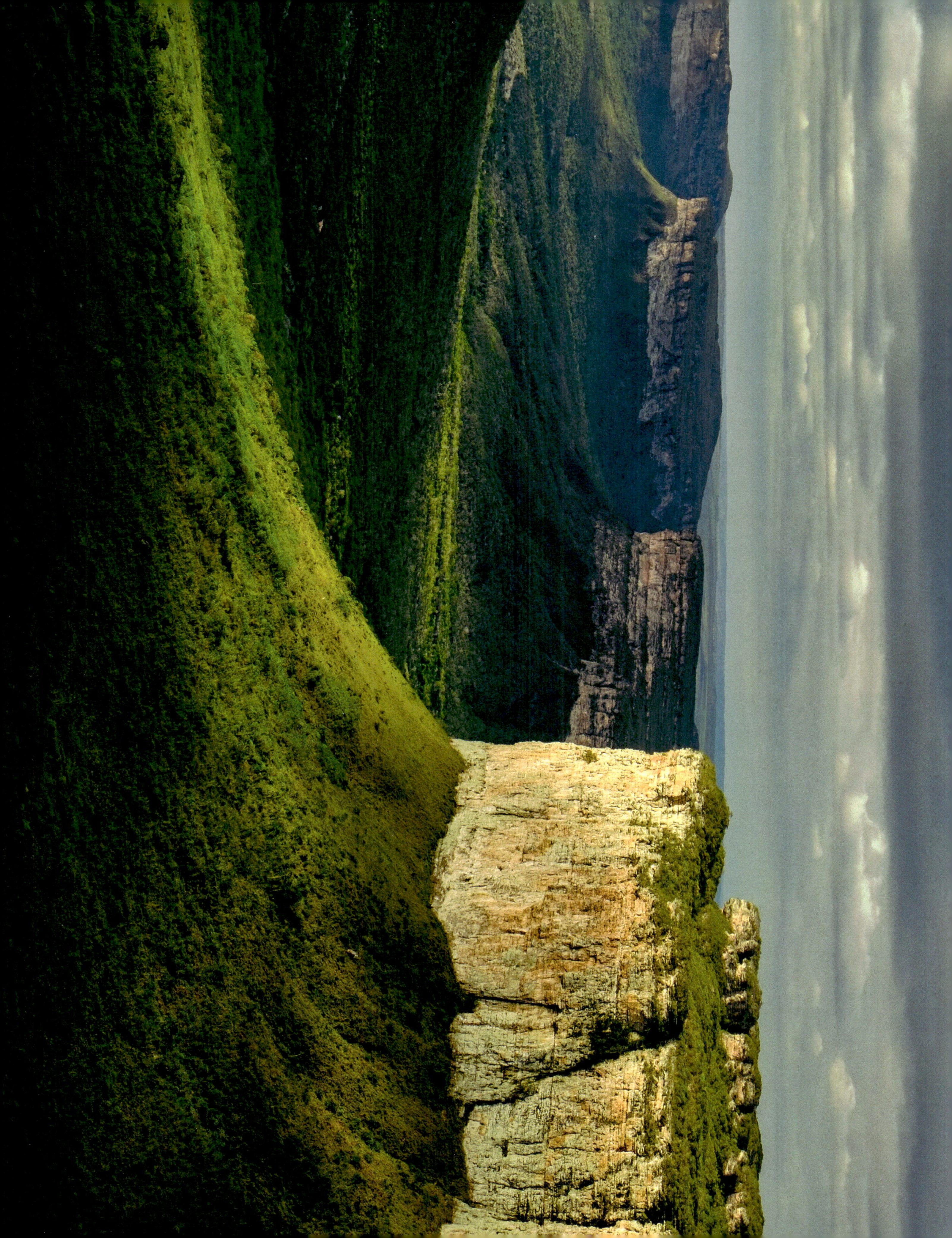

RIGHT:
**Ilha Grande,
Rio de Janeiro, Brazil**
This island is cloaked with one of the most unspoilt portions of Brazil's Atlantic Forest. When Europeans arrived in Brazil, this moist broadleaf forest covered more than 1 million sq km (390,000 sq miles) along the coast and far inland, but over 85 per cent of this area has gone. Endangered brazilwood trees can still be found here.

OPPOSITE:
**Círio de Nazaré,
Belém, Brazil**
Dedicated to Our Lady of Nazareth, this Catholic festival brings 2 million people to Bélem on the second Sunday in October. During the main procession, pilgrims pull a rope, around 400m (1300ft) long, attached to a statue of Our Lady, while others carry heavy crosses as an act of devotion.

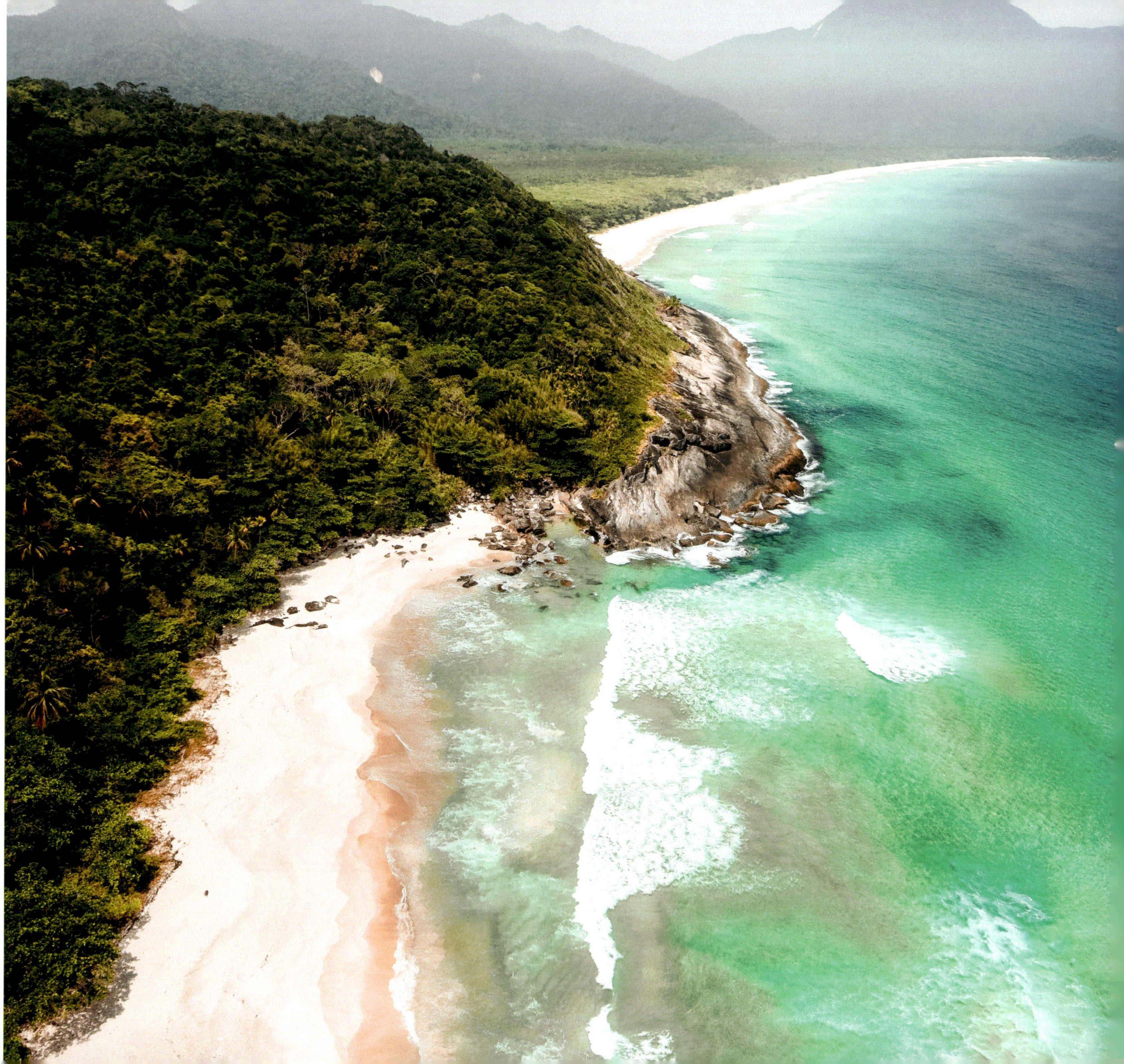

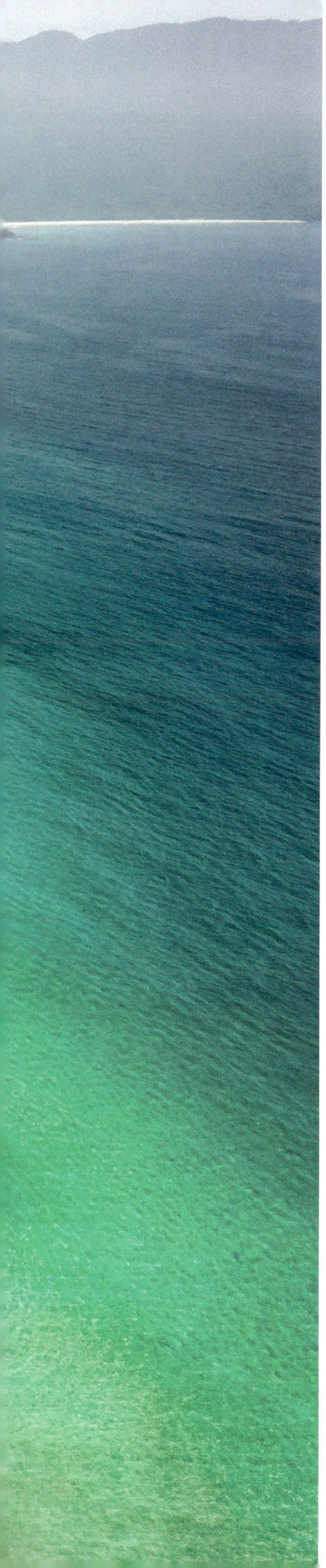

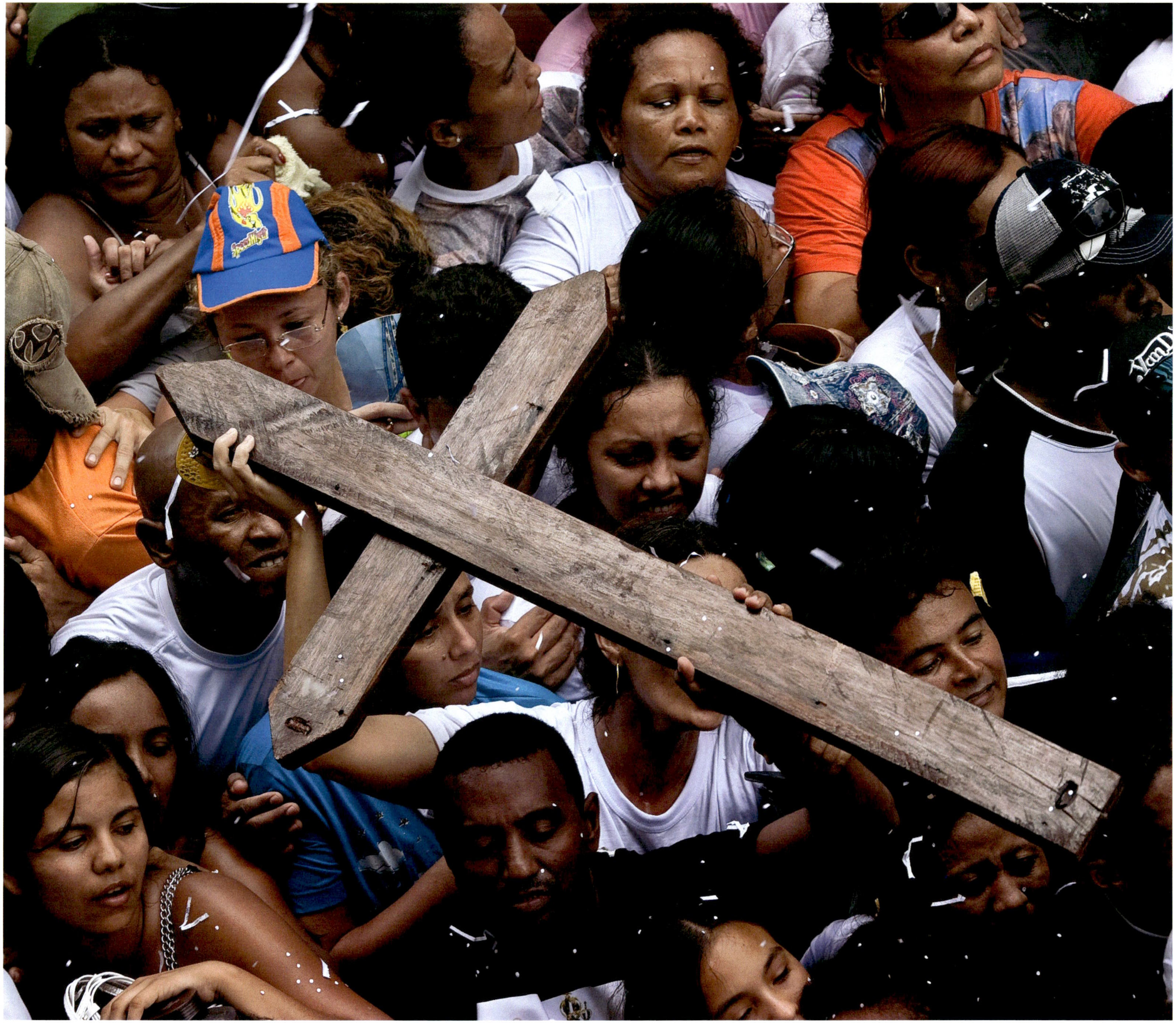

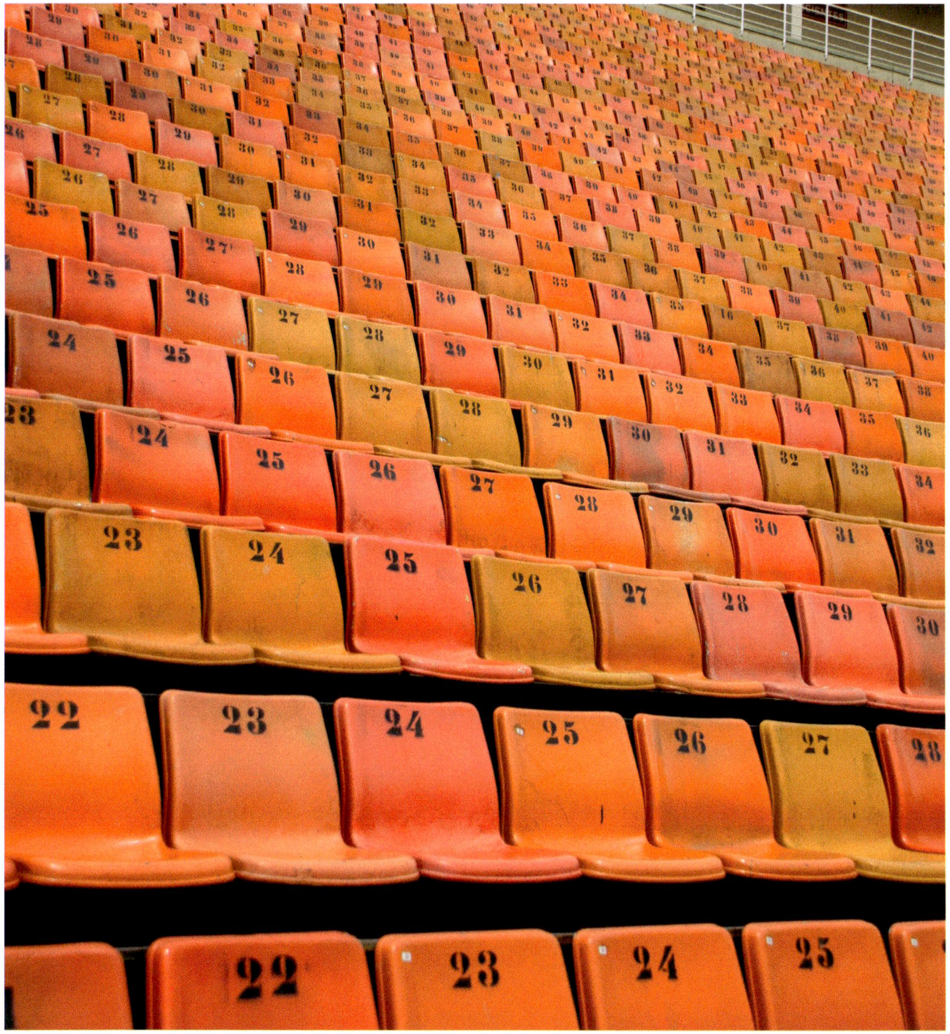

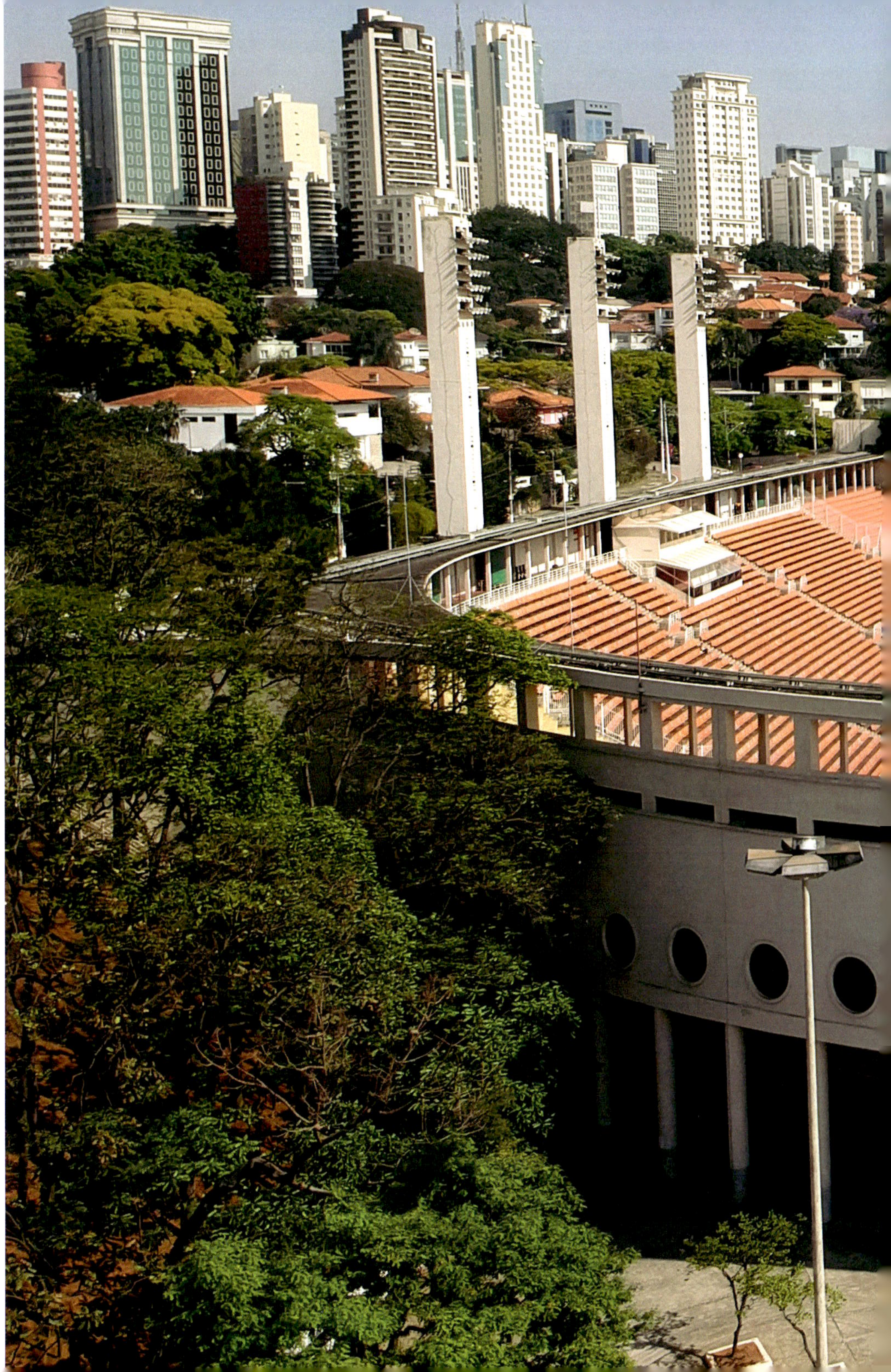

BOTH PHOTOGRAPHS:

Pacaembu Stadium, São Paulo, Brazil

This Art Deco stadium, completed in 1940, hosted six matches of the 1950 World Cup, in which Uruguay beat Brazil into second place. The stadium is frequently used for matches of São Paulo state's Big 4 clubs: Corinthians, Palmeiras, São Paulo and Santos. At the time of writing (in 2026), the south stand was being demolished and replaced by a five-storey building.

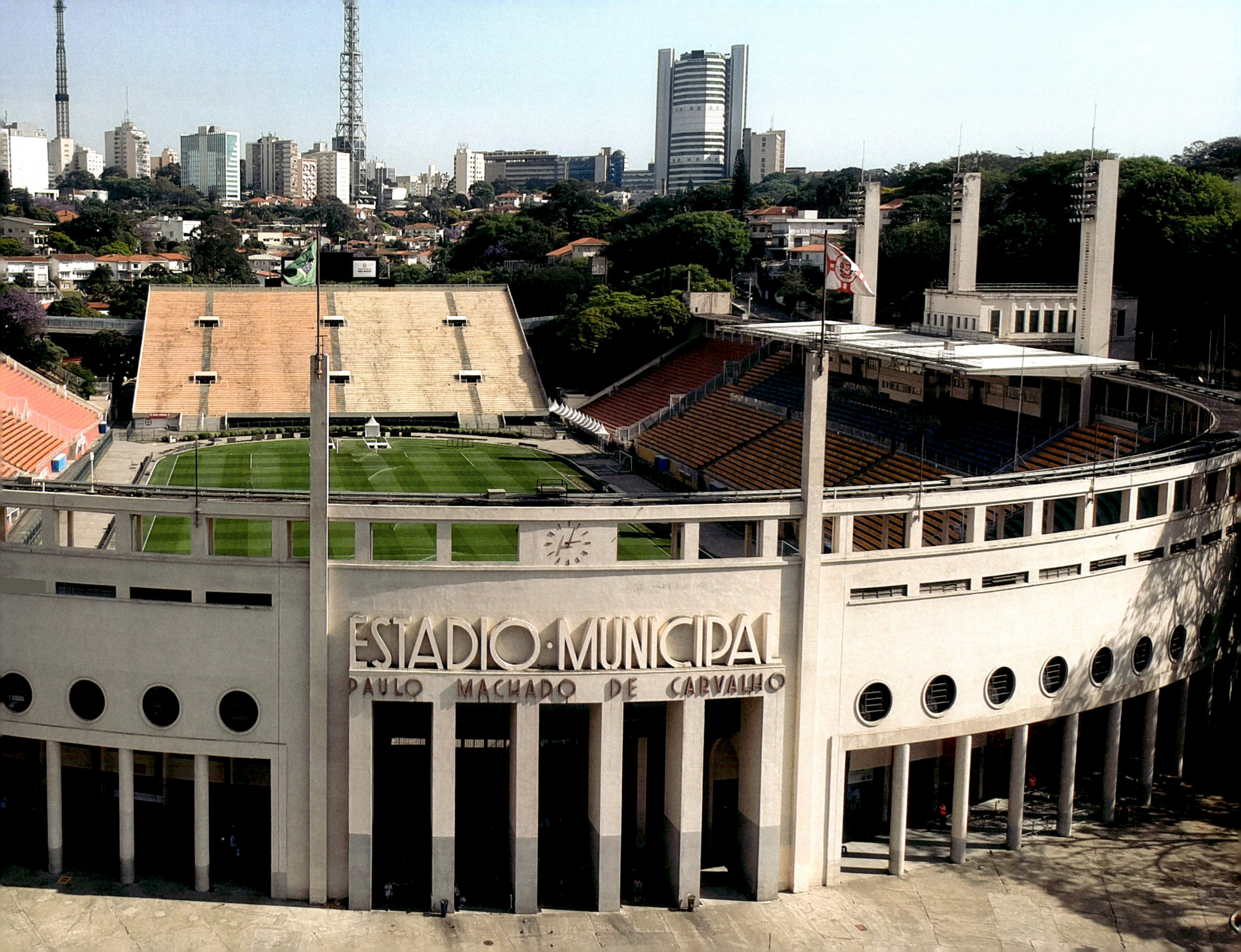
ESTADIO·MUNICIPAL
PAULO MACHADO DE CARVALHO

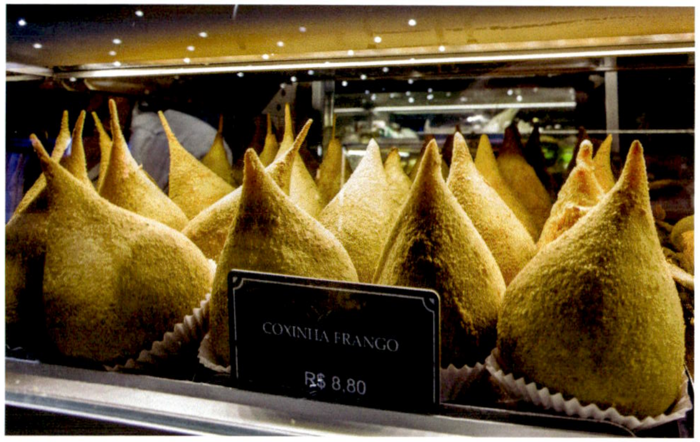

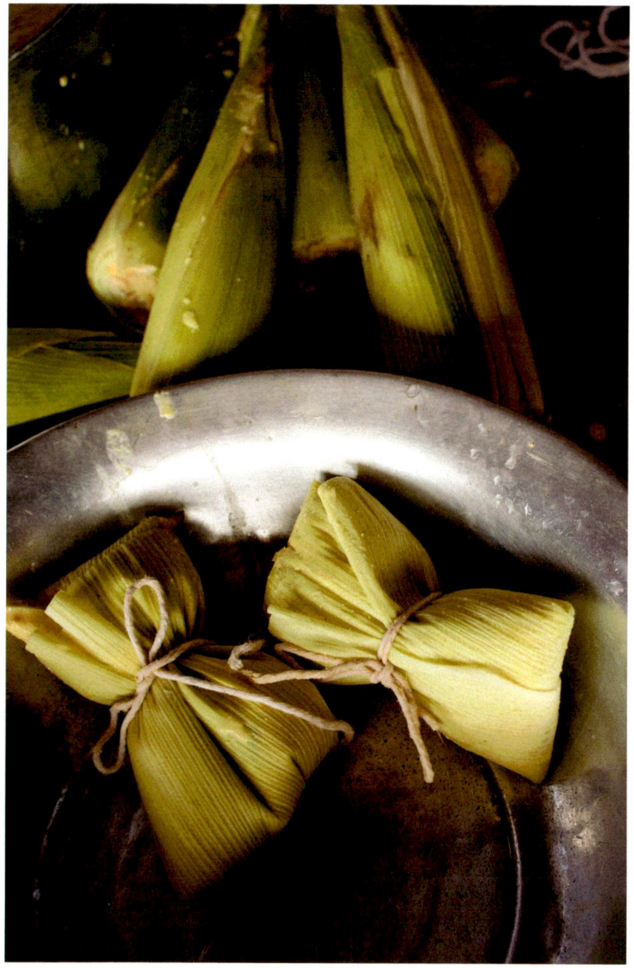

LEFT TOP:
***Coxinhas*, Brazil**
Possibly originating from the city of Limeira in the nineteenth century, this popular snack is made of chopped chicken, cheese and seasonings, wrapped in dough and breadcrumbs, shaped into a teardrop and fried.

LEFT BOTTOM:
***Pamonhas*, Brazil**
These snacks are made of ground sweetcorn wrapped in corn husks. Savoury versions include cheese, sausage or peppers, while sweet *pamonhas* contain coconut milk and sugar.

RIGHT:
Nossa Senhora dos Remédios, Paraty, Brazil
Completed in 1873, this church holds a gallery on its upper floor, with works by Brazilian artists including Djanira and Anita Malfatti.

OPPOSITE:
Anavilhanas Archipelago, Amazonas, Brazil
A tributary of the Amazon, the Rio Negro flows around an archipelago of over 400 islands. Dark, acidic and low in nutrients, the Negro is the world's largest blackwater river. While the water is home to the vulnerable Amazonian manatee and Amazon river dolphin, the islands host *igapó*, a blackwater-flooded forest ecosystem.

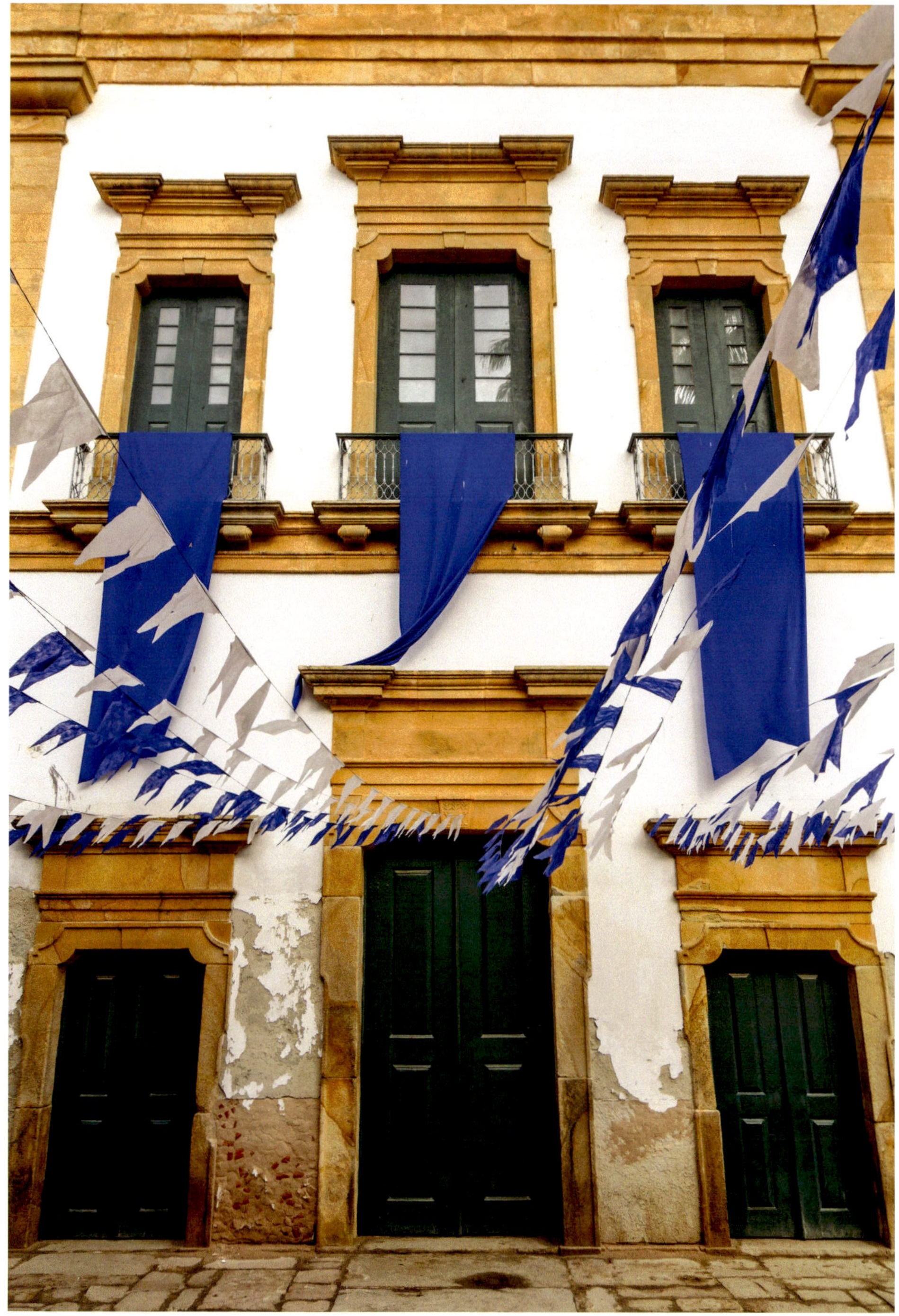

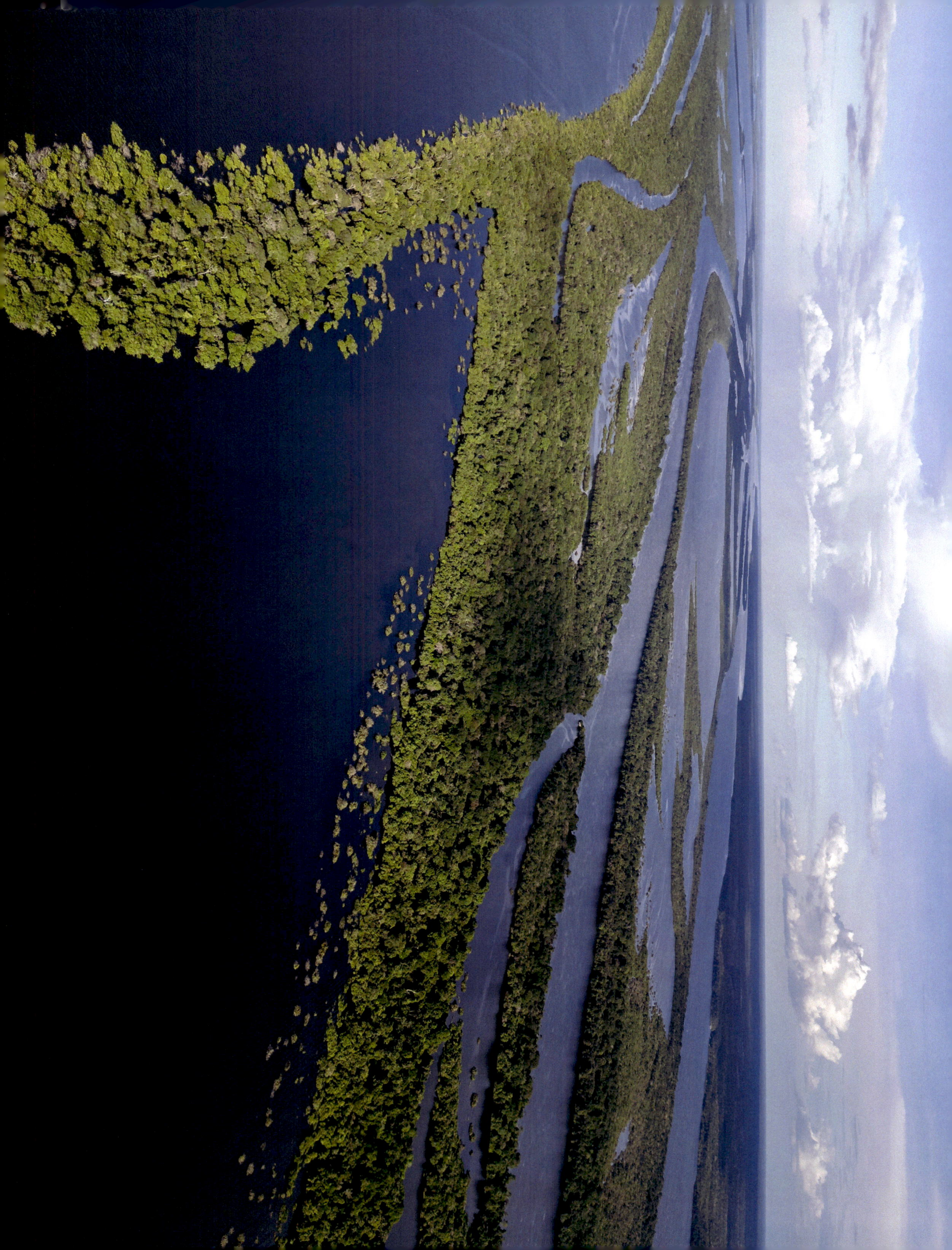

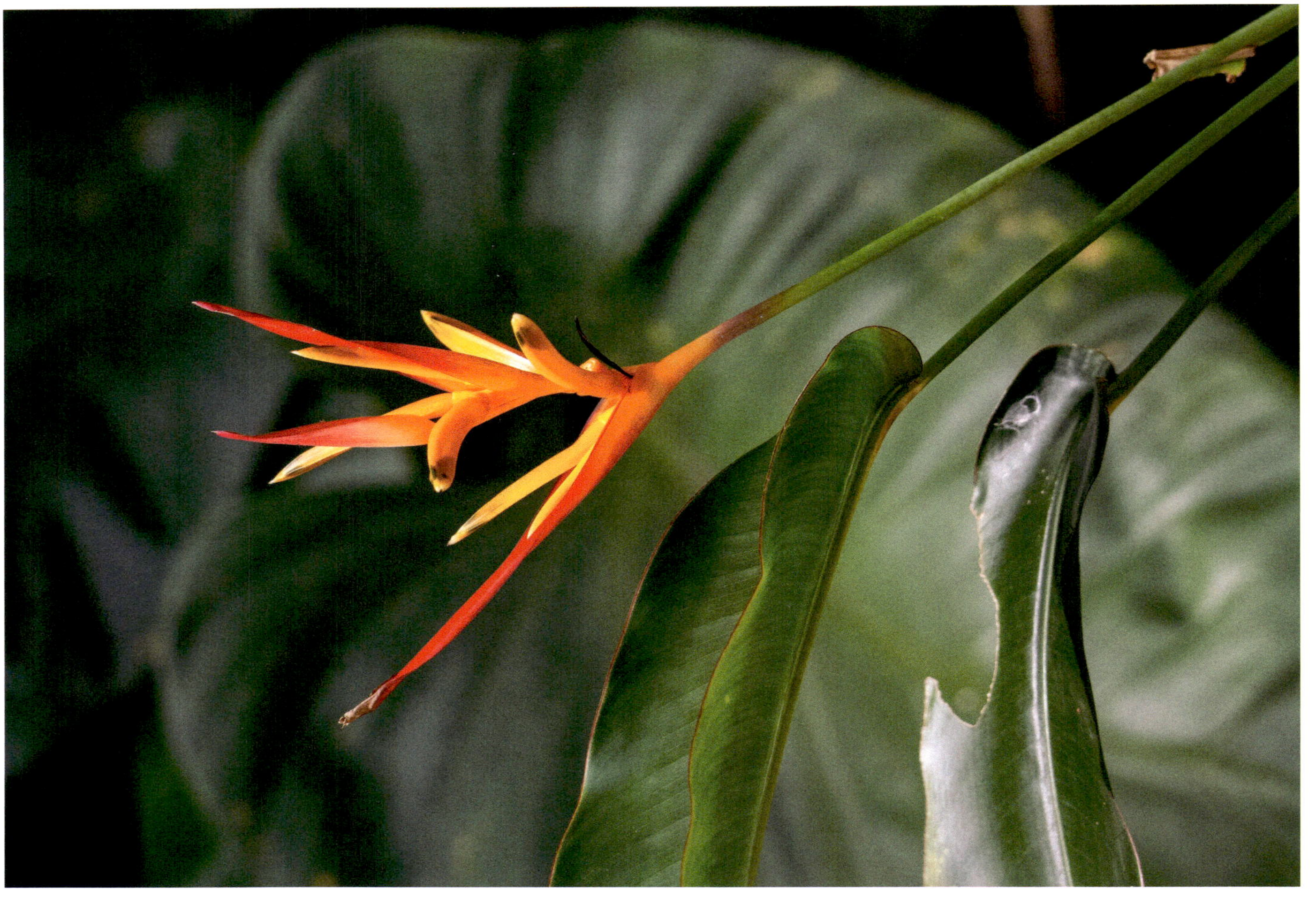

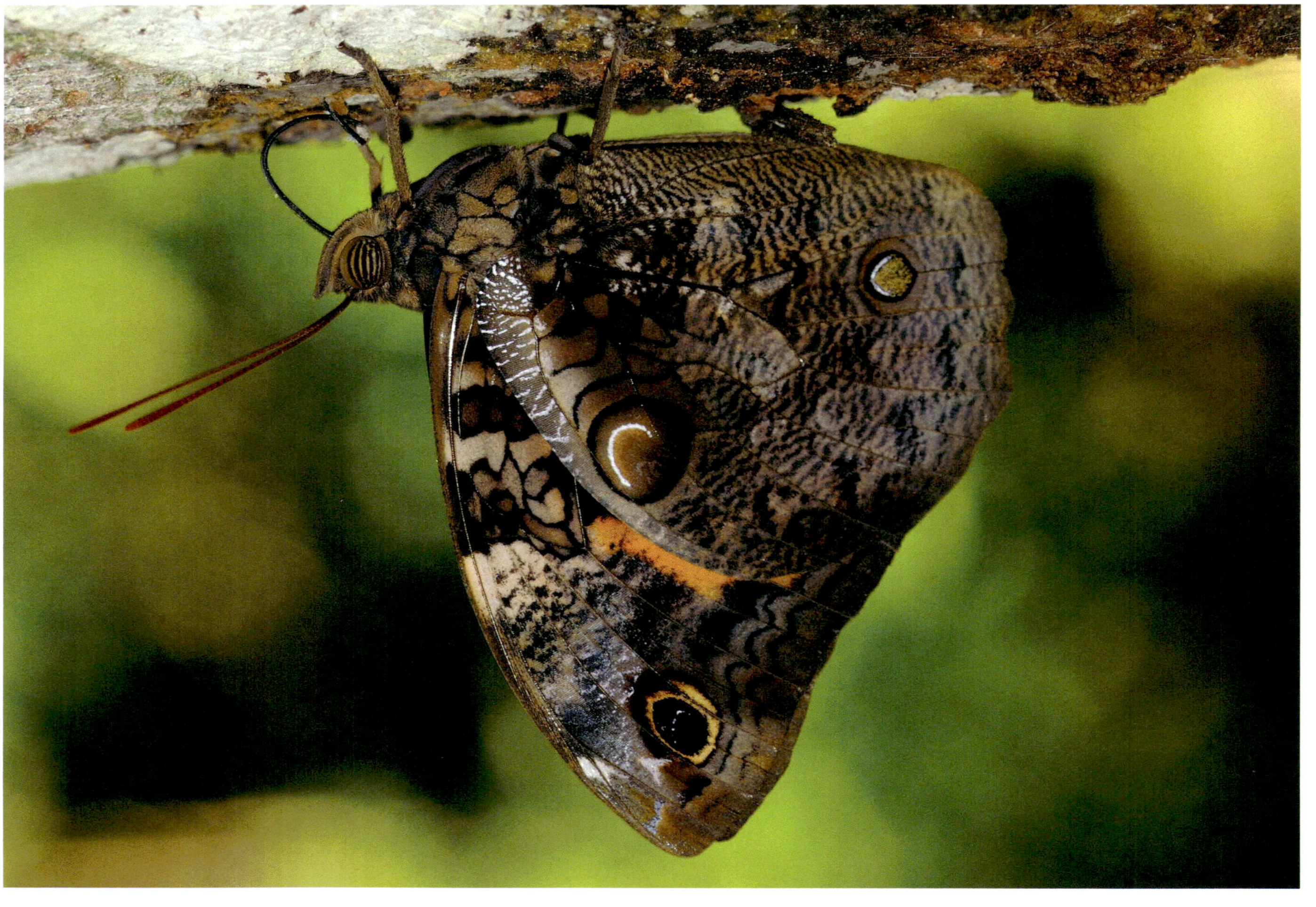

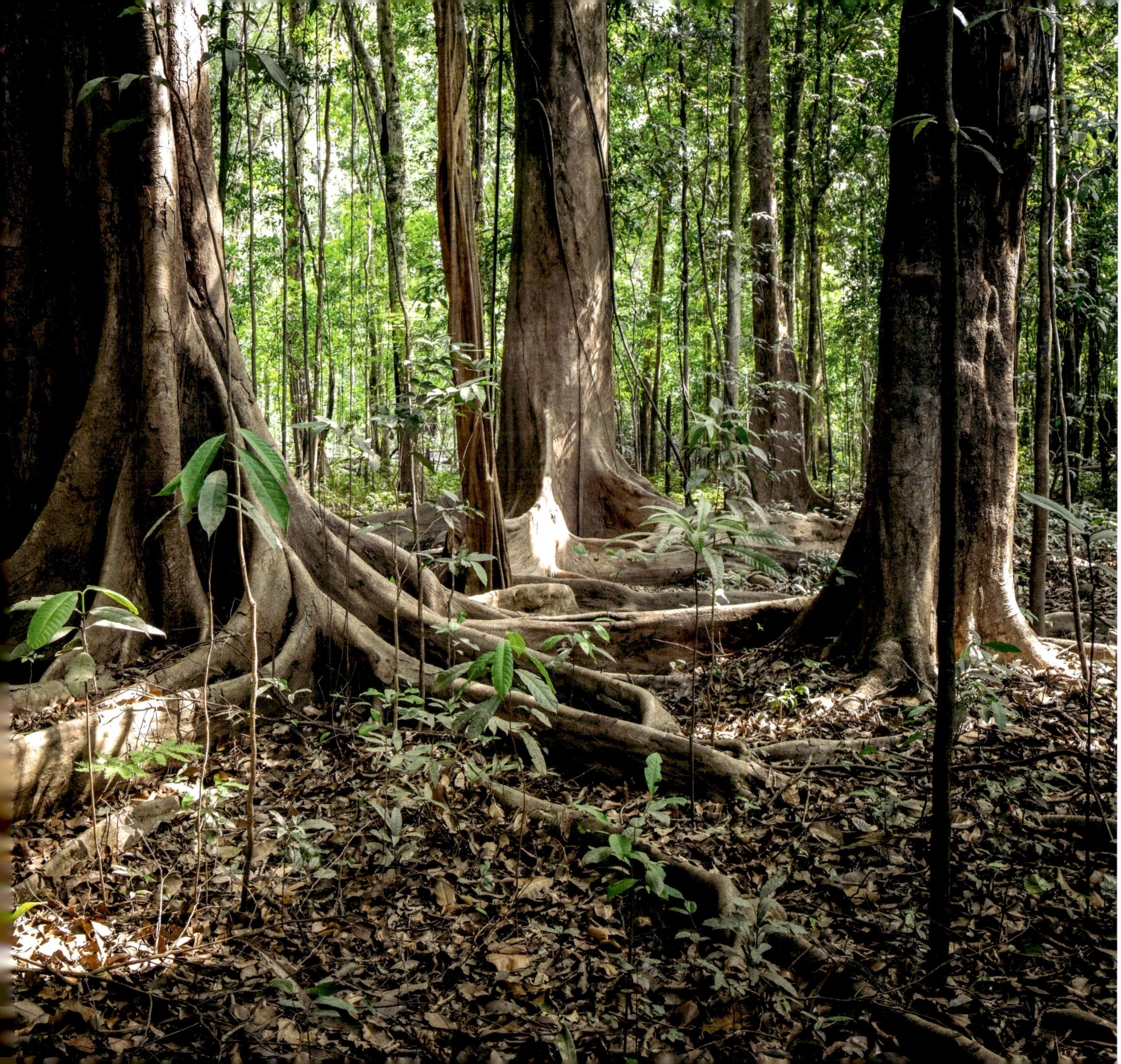

ALL PHOTOGRAPHS:
Amazon Rainforest, Brazil
The most biodiverse region on the planet, the Amazon is home to up to 50,000 species of plants, including more than 20 in just the *Heliconia* genus (pictured opposite right). Some estimates suggest there are over 3500 butterfly species in the rainforest, including the tamarind owl (pictured opposite left). It relies on its huge eyespots to frighten away predators – which fear it is a much larger creature – as it feeds on tree sap and fermented fruit.

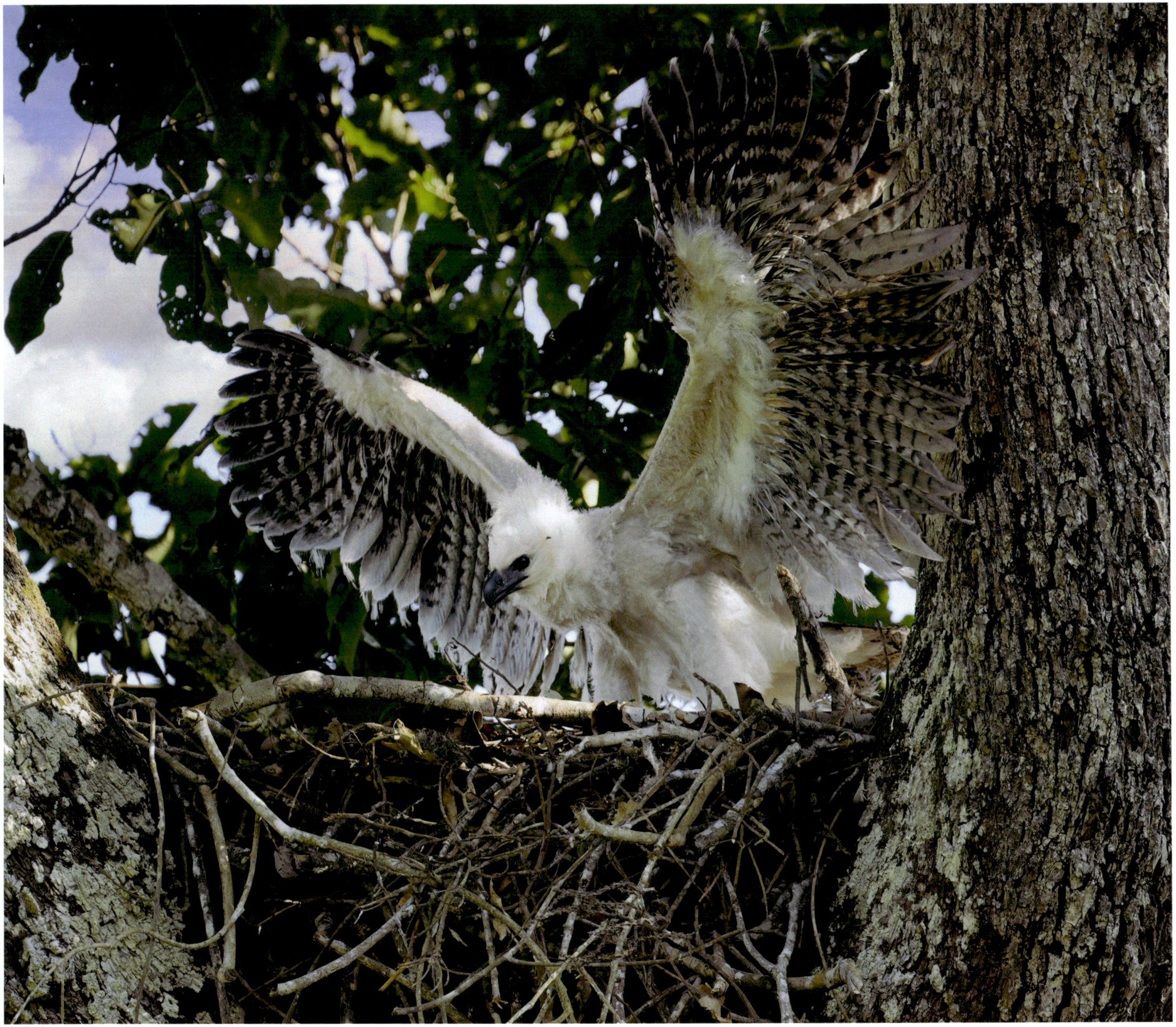

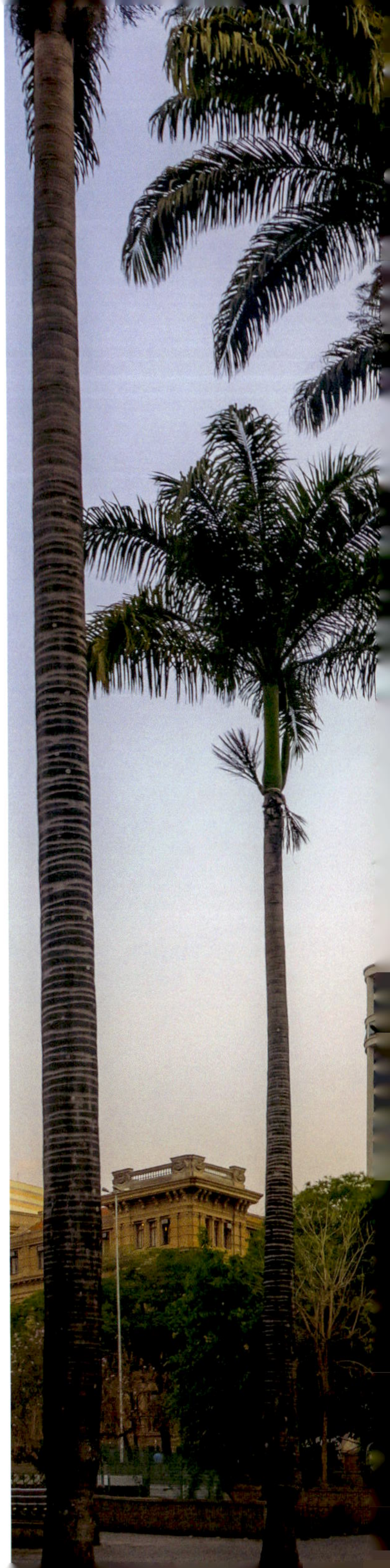

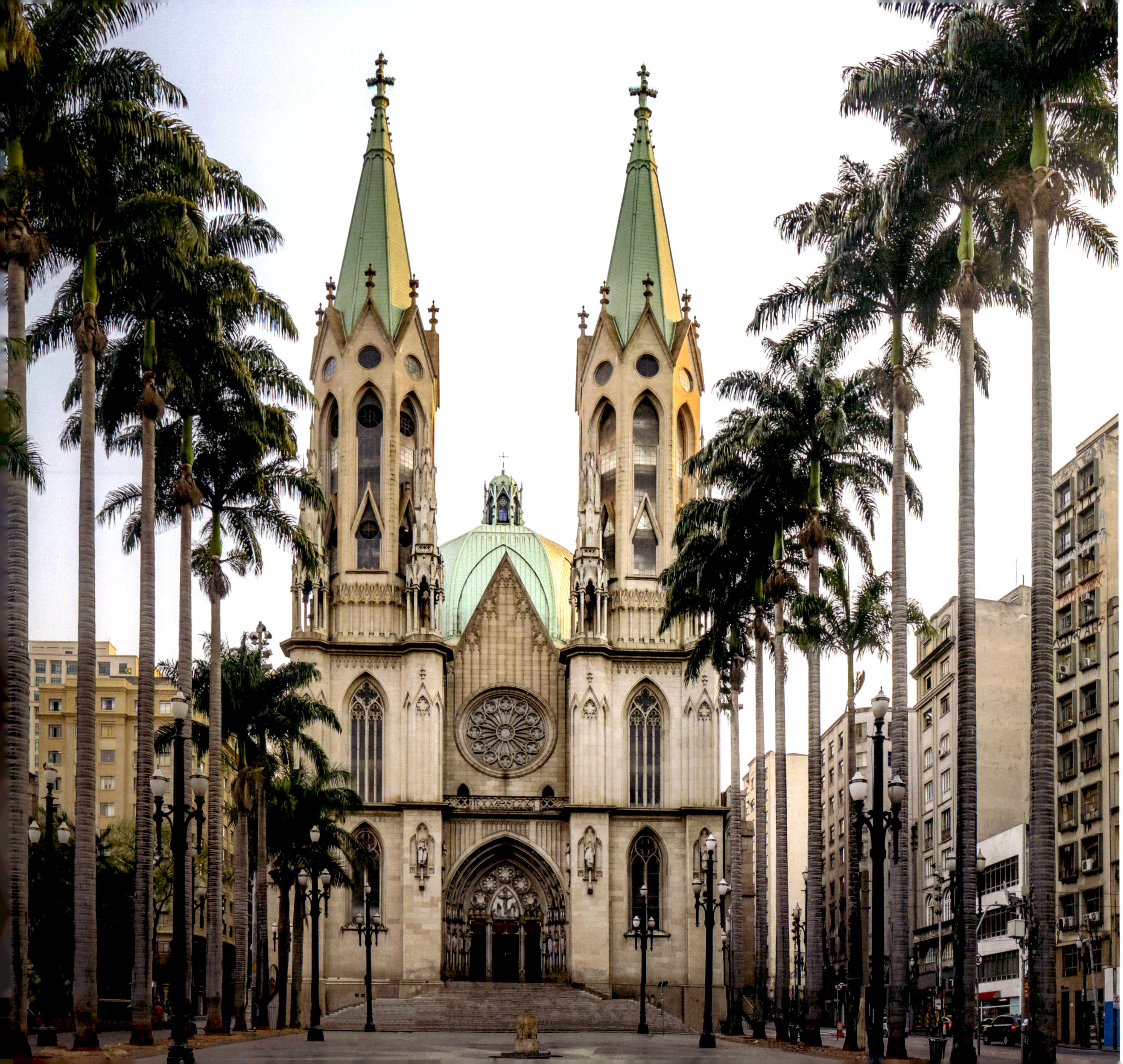

OPPOSITE:

Harpy Eagle, Amazon Rainforest, Brazil

With a wingspan of up to 224cm (88in), this eagle is the Amazon's largest bird of prey and the apex predator of the canopy and emergent layer. It feeds mainly on tree-dwelling mammals, including sloths and monkeys. This chick, just four months old, will continue to be fed by its parents until it is at least a year old.

LEFT:

Sé Cathedral, São Paulo, Brazil

Built between 1913 and 1954, this is São Paulo's largest Catholic church. While constructed mainly in the Gothic Revival style, with soaring spires and pointed arches, the cathedral also boasts a Renaissance Revival dome. Details of the exterior's carvings celebrate Brazilian flora, including pineapples and coffee branches.

RIGHT:
São Paulo Museum of Art, Brazil
With an exceptional collection of European, Brazilian, African and Asian art, this museum is housed in a landmark 1968 building by Italian-born Brazilian Modernist architect Lina Bo Bardi. The reinforced concrete structure, with its brilliant red details, was designed to embrace rationalism and escape pretension.

OPPOSITE:
Beco de Batman, São Paulo
The area around Rua Gonçalo Afonso and Rua Medeiros de Albuquerque earned its name in the 1980s after an anonymous graffiti artist decorated a wall with the DC Comics character. The neighbourhood has become known for its ever-changing street art by Brazilian and international artists.

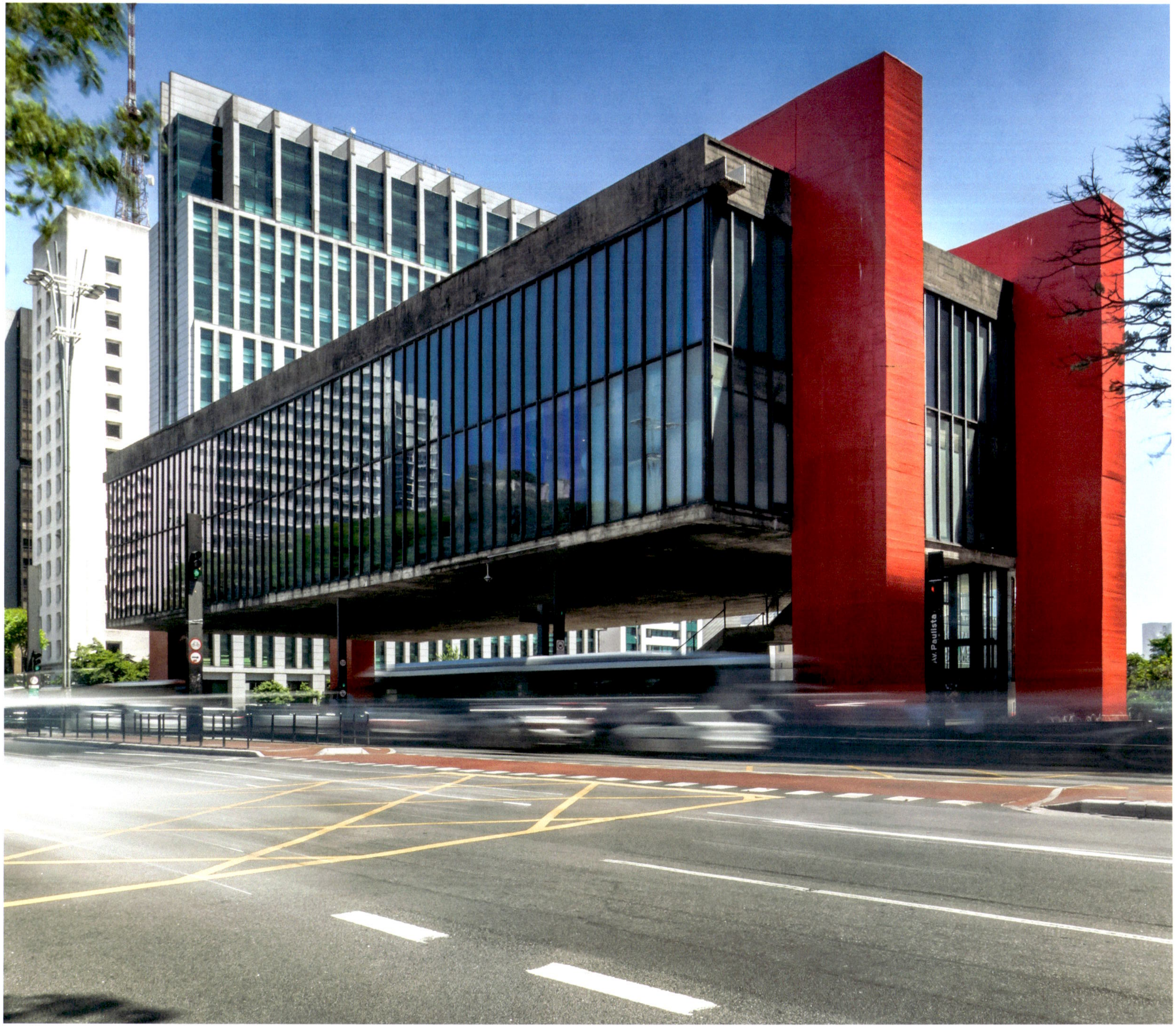

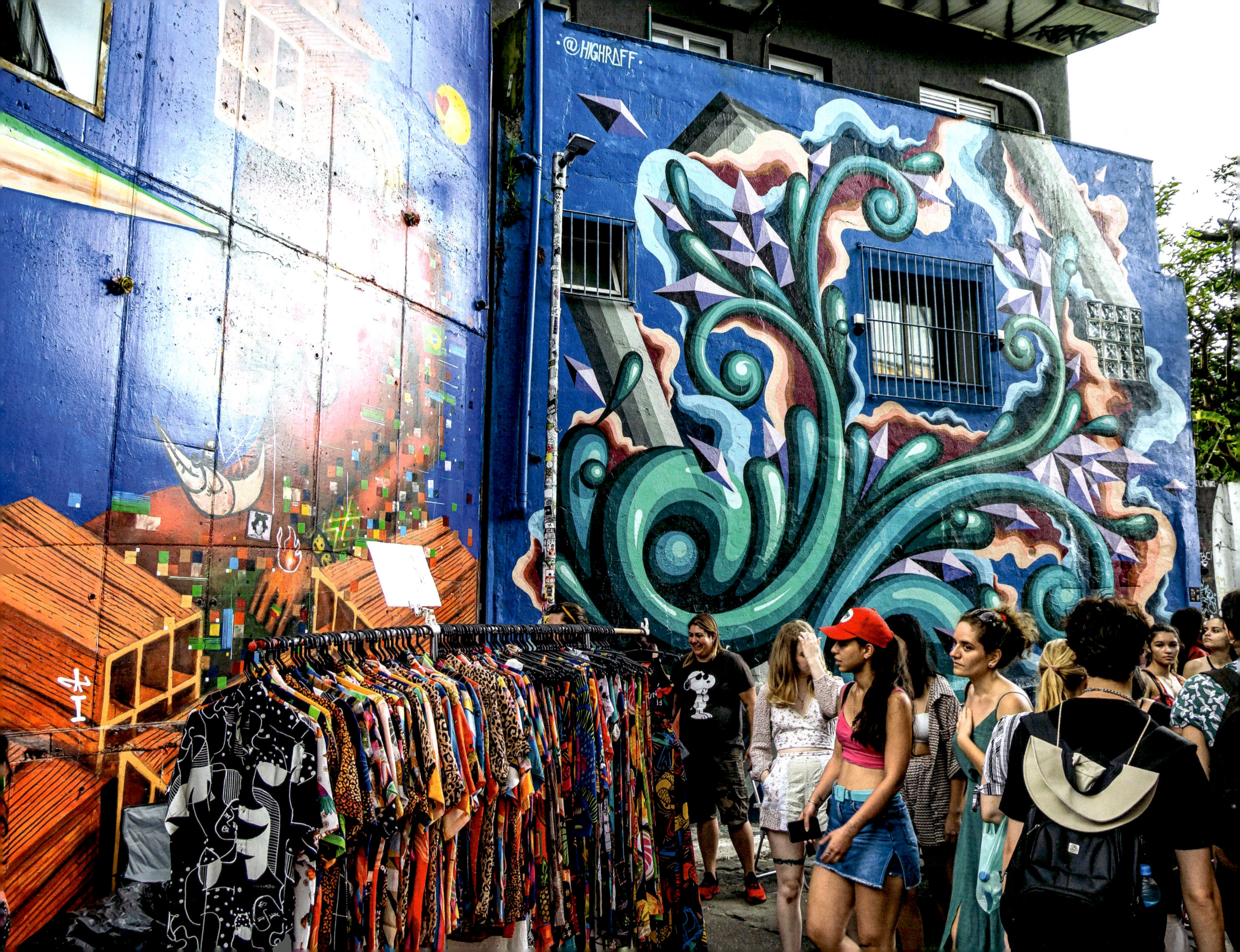
@HIGHRAFF

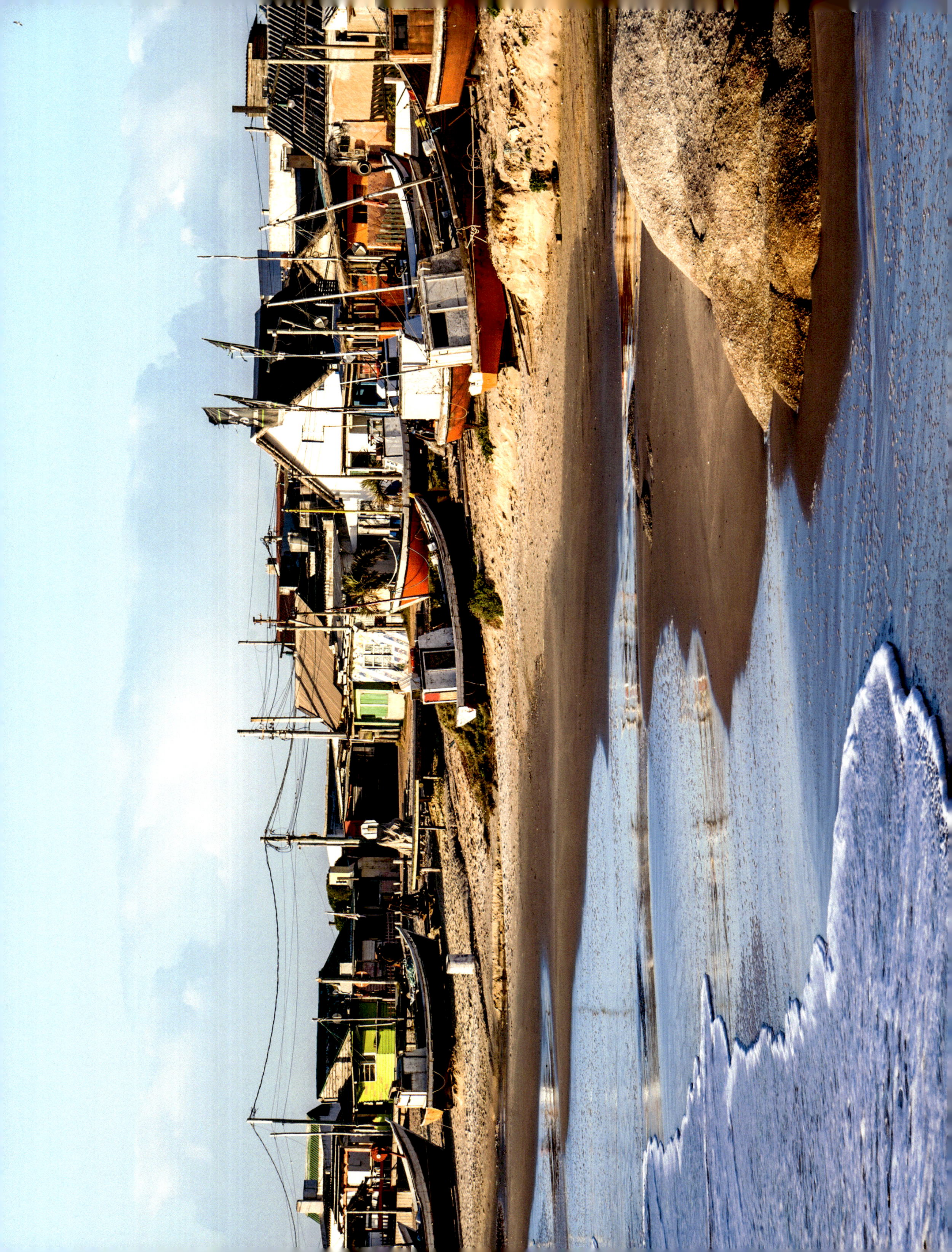

Uruguay and Paraguay

Both once part of the Spanish Viceroyalty of the Río de la Plata, Uruguay and Paraguay chose similar post-independence names. Both names have their roots in the Guaraní language spoken by many – or, in Paraguay's case, nearly all – of their inhabitants. Uruguay's name comes from the Río Uruguay (possibly meaning 'bird river'), while Paraguay's name comes from the Río Paraguay (which may mean 'river that gives birth to the sea'). Although the two countries do not share a land border, since Argentina and Brazil jut between them, they do share a river system: the Paraguay flows into the Paraná, which joins the Uruguay to form the wide Río de la Plata estuary. Some might say that this is where the similarities between the two modern countries end. Uruguay is one of South America's wealthiest nations when measured by gross domestic product per capita. In terms of wealth per person, only Guyana is better off, due to its oil boom. Known for its political stability, Uruguay has a diversified economy and – on a continent with high income inequality within nations – it has relatively low inequality and South America's lowest poverty rate. In contrast, landlocked Paraguay relies on the aforementioned river system to access the Atlantic Ocean, a disadvantage that has contributed to its slower economic development. Yet Paraguay is a country to watch, since in recent years its poverty rate has shrunk dramatically and its economy has grown due to manufacturing, construction and exports of beef, soya beans and hydroelectricity.

OPPOSITE:
Punta del Diablo, Uruguay
On the Atlantic Coast, the fishing village of Punta del Diablo is increasingly popular with surfers and sandboarders. Behind the growing resort is the Laguna Negra, visited by birds such as roseate spoonbills, great egrets and storks. Guinea pigs and greater rheas can be spotted in the surrounding grassland.

RIGHT:
Colonia del Sacramento, Uruguay
Founded by the Portuguese in 1680, this city switched hands between Spain, Portugal and, later, Brazil an inordinate number of times before becoming part of independent Uruguay in 1828. The city's historic centre is a UNESCO World Heritage Site for its seventeenth- to nineteenth-century stone buildings.

FAR RIGHT:
Palacio Salvo, Montevideo, Uruguay
At the heart of this photograph is the central dome of Palacio Salvo, an eclectic mixed-use building completed in 1928. It was designed by the ambitious Italian architect Mario Palanti, who used a similiar design for Palacio Barolo (see pages 198–9) in Buenos Aires.

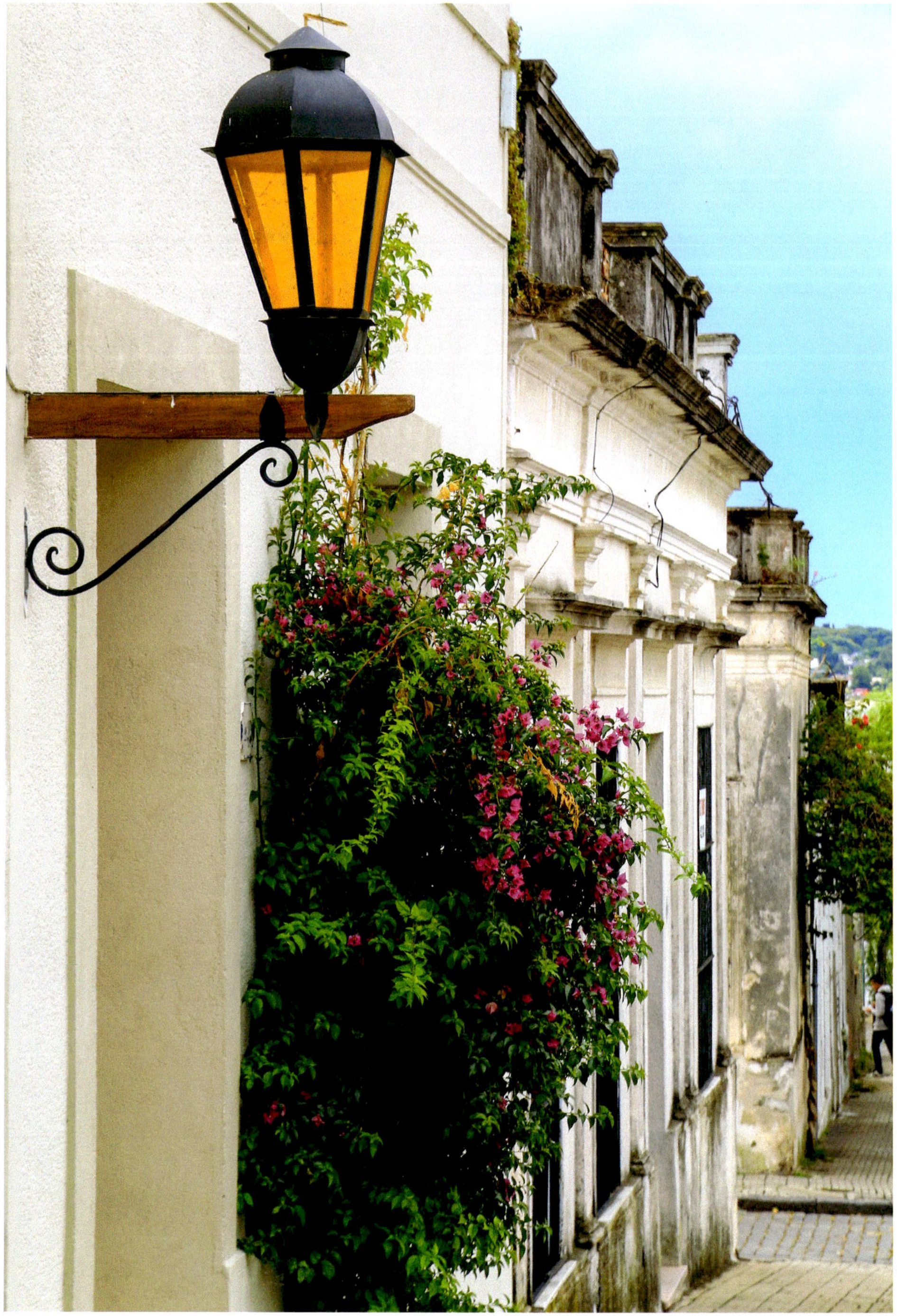

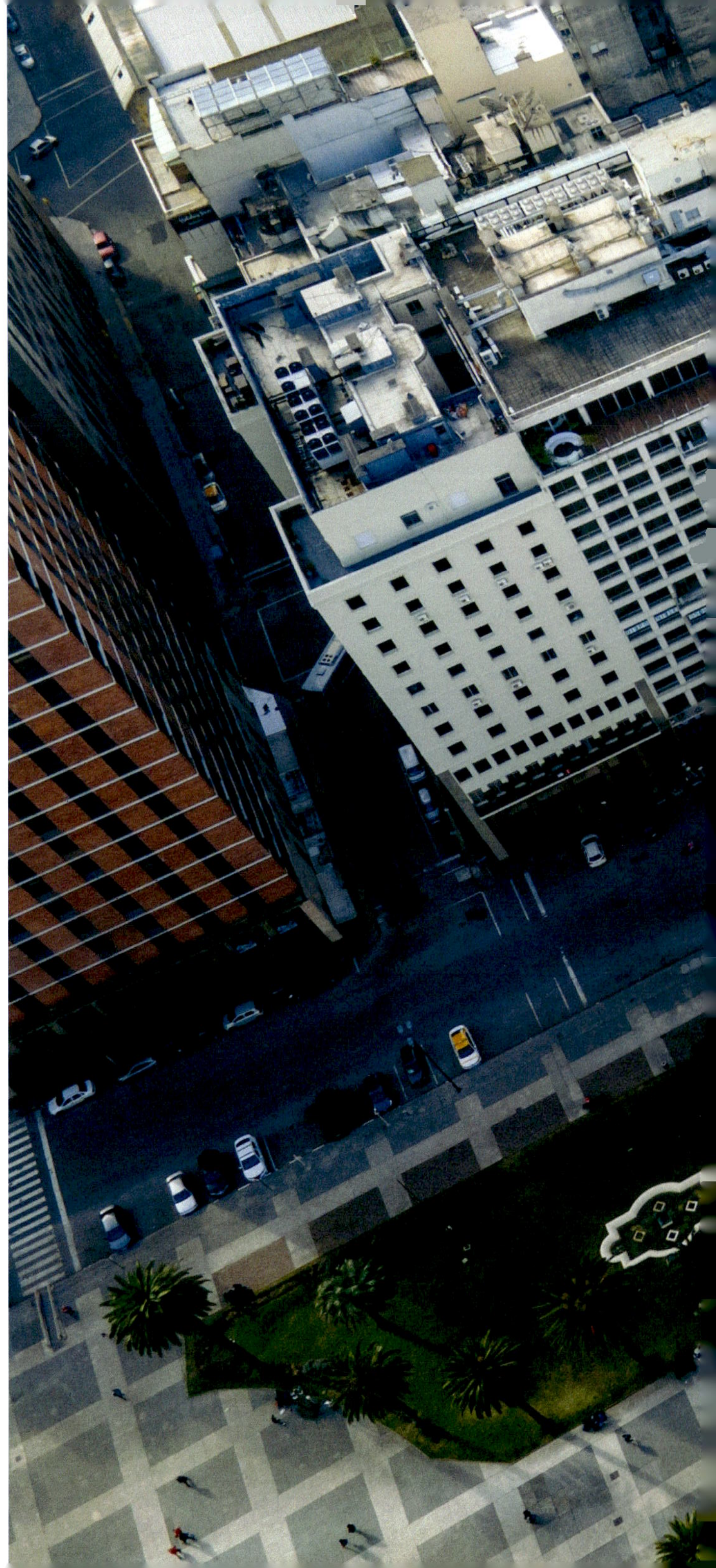

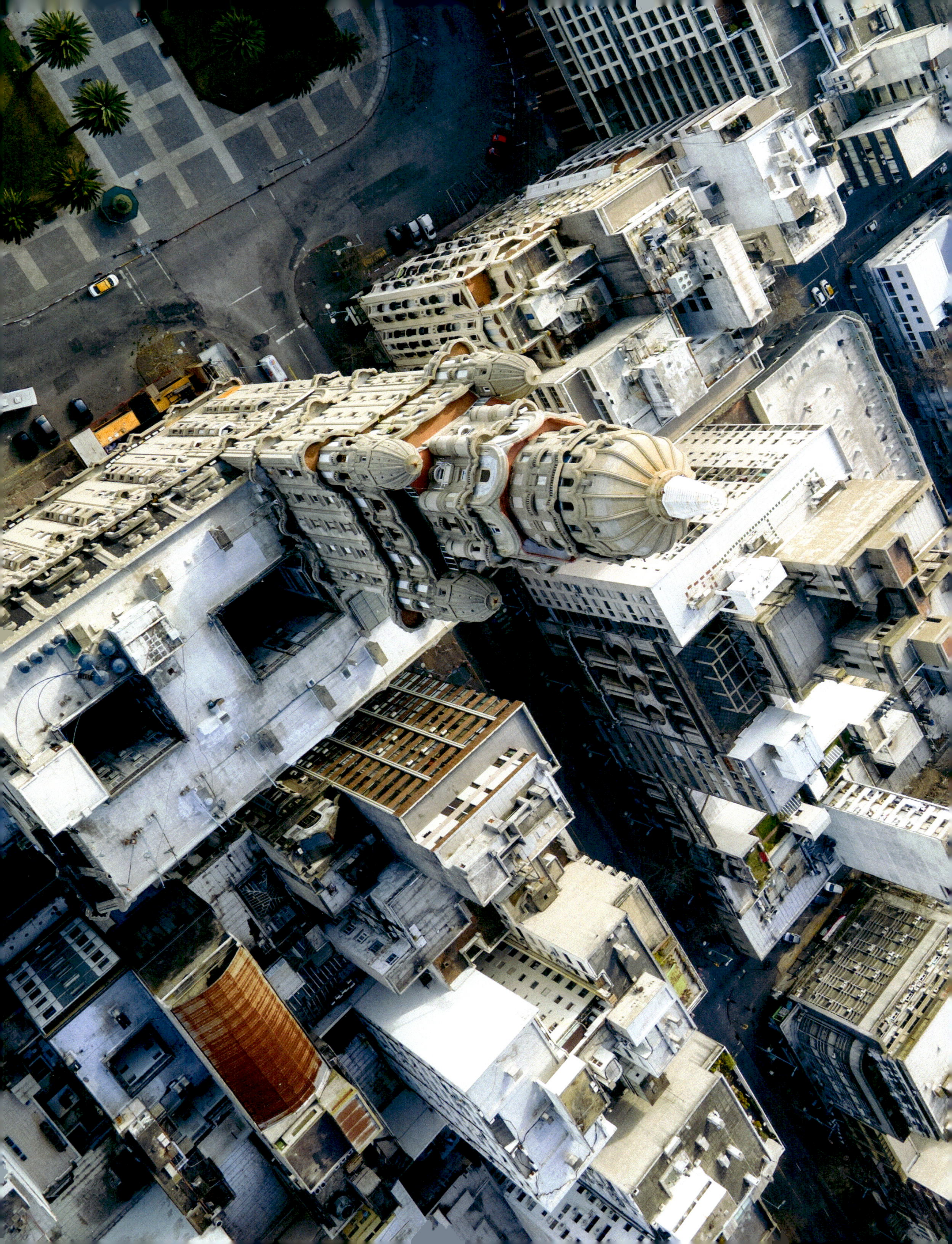

RIGHT ALL IMAGES:
***Parilladas*,**
Mercado del Puerto, Montevideo, Uruguay
Built as a covered marketplace in 1868, this venue now hosts traditional Uruguayan restaurants including several *parilladas*, where meat is barbecued over wood fires. The meat includes lightly seasoned beef, particularly sirloin and ribeye steaks, as well as sausages and sweetbreads. Essential sides include salads, a glass of Uruguayan Tannat wine and *chimichurri* sauce (containing parsley, oregano, chilli, garlic, olive oil and red wine vinegar or lemon juice).

OPPOSITE:
Mercado Agrícola, Montevideo
Inspired by Paris's Les Halles, this cast-iron market hall was completed in 1912. Ubiquitous vegetables that were native to South America include several pictured here: tomatoes, green and yellow beans, courgettes and chilli peppers. In 1493, Christopher Columbus and his crew carried the first chilli peppers to Europe, where they were soon a wild success in Spain and Portugal.

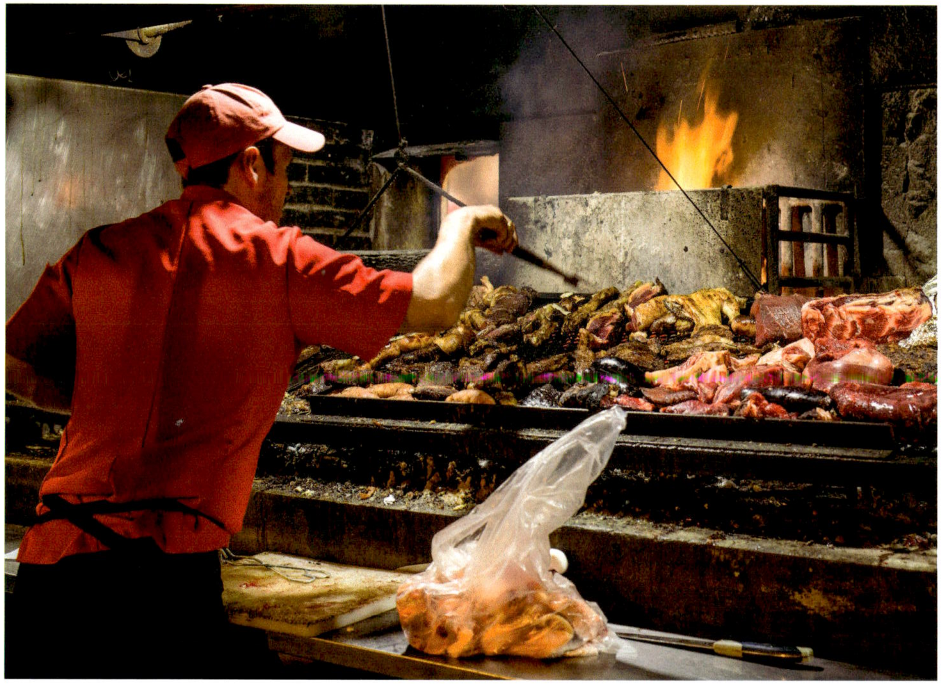

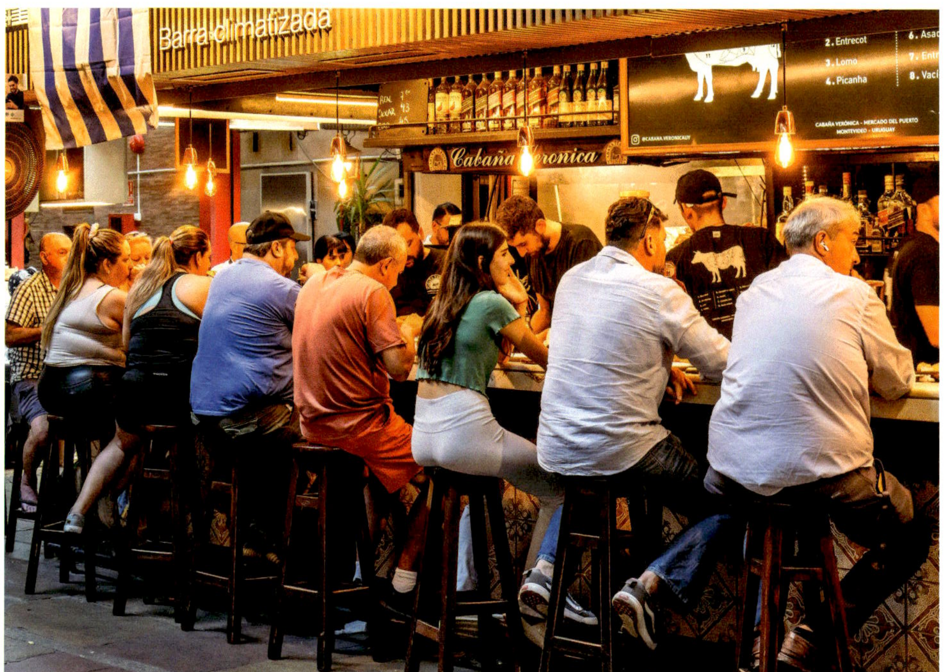

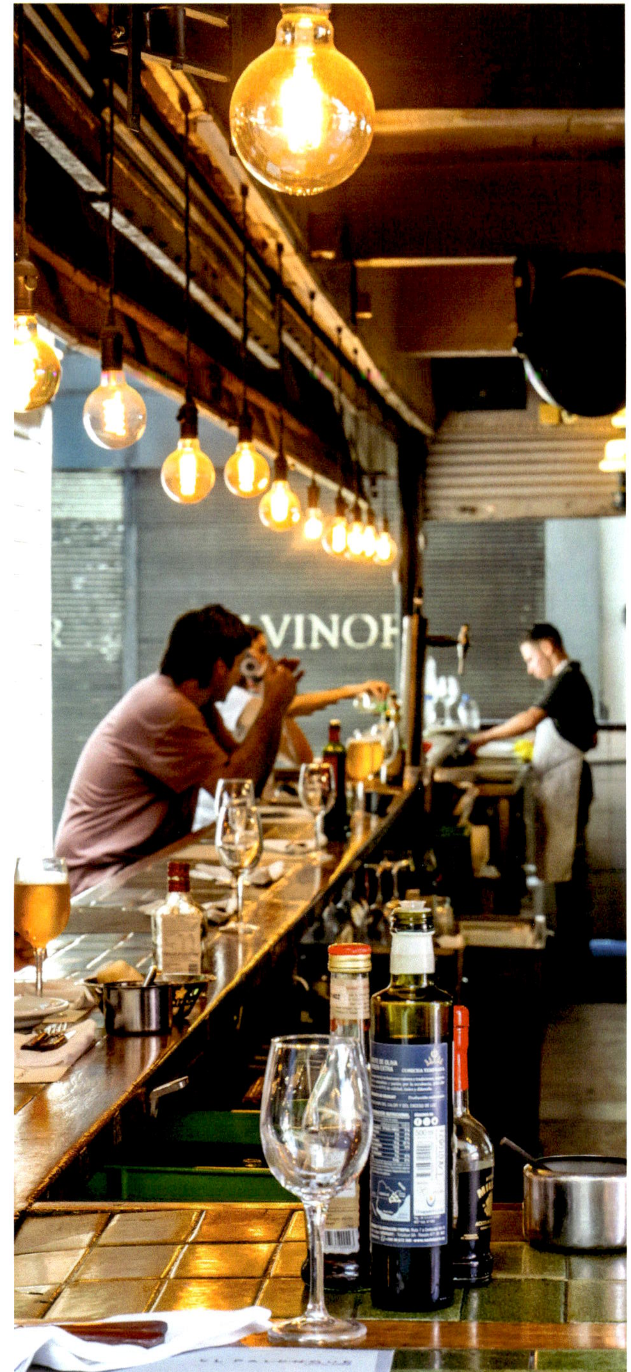

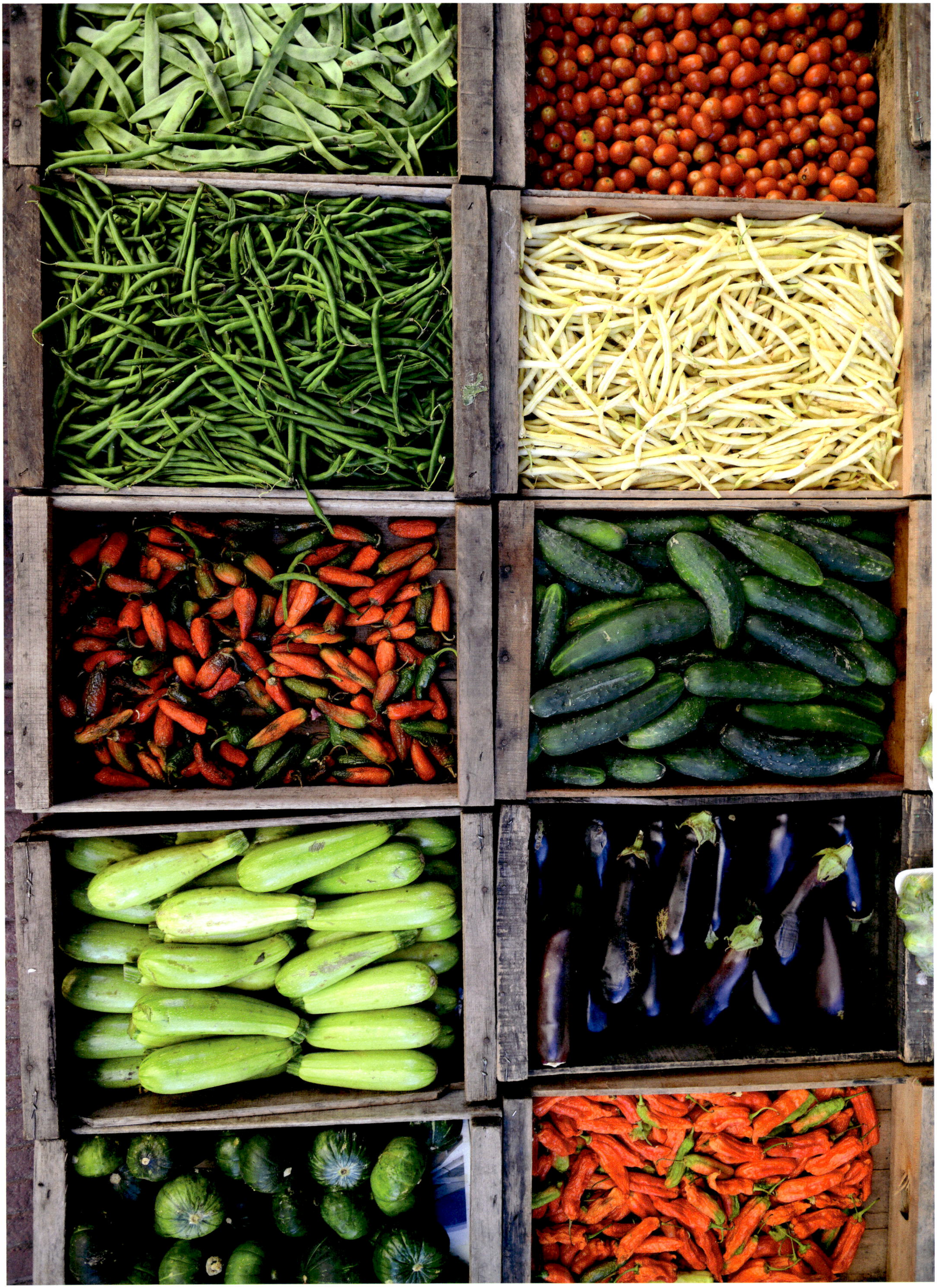

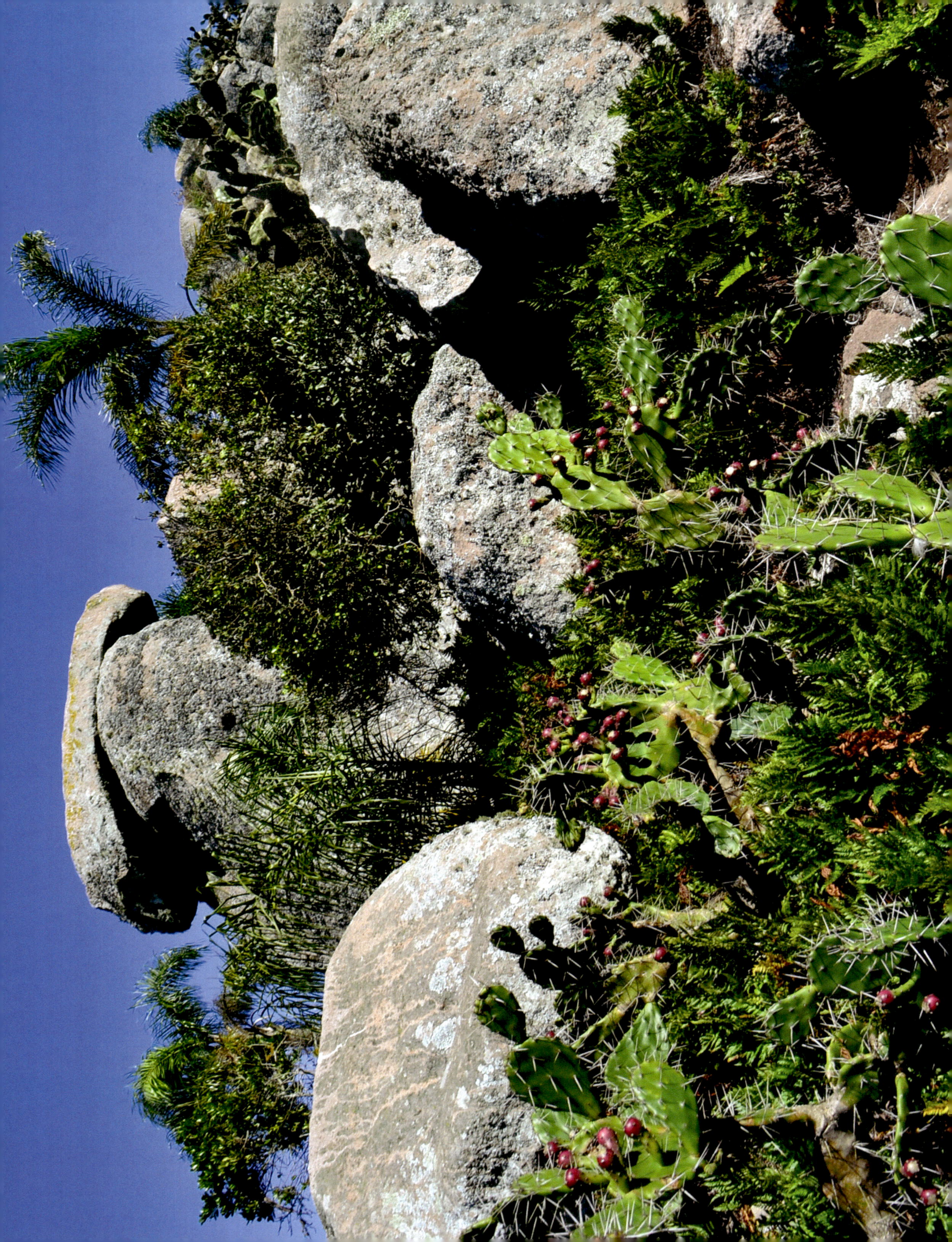

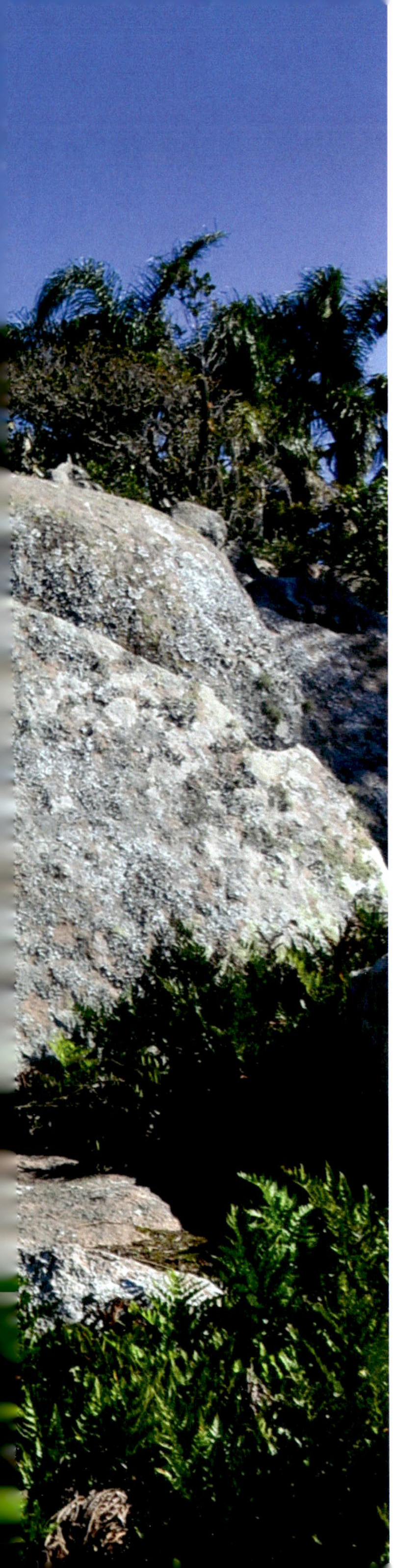

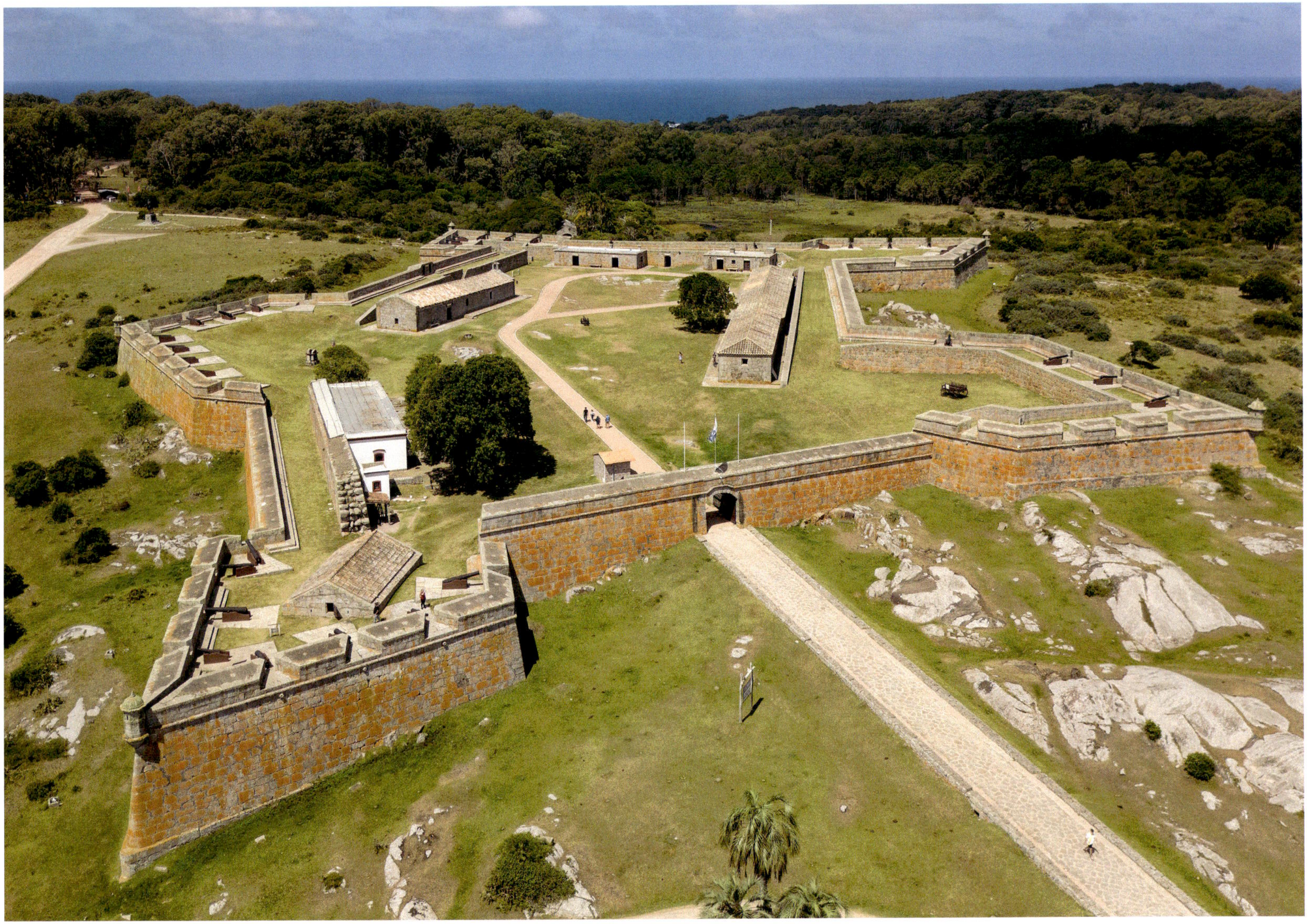

LEFT:
Cerro Picudo, Rocha, Uruguay
A short and easy hike from Fortaleza San Miguel, this hill offers views of the rice paddies of the plains, as well as the surrounding forest. Here are found native trees including queen palms, tarumás, arrayáns and talas.

ABOVE:
Fortaleza Santa Teresa, Rocha
Completed in the late eighteenth century by the Spanish but begun by the Portuguese, this fort controlled the route through the marshes to the coast. In the shape of an irregular pentagon with five bastions, the fort has walls up to 11.5m (38ft) high.

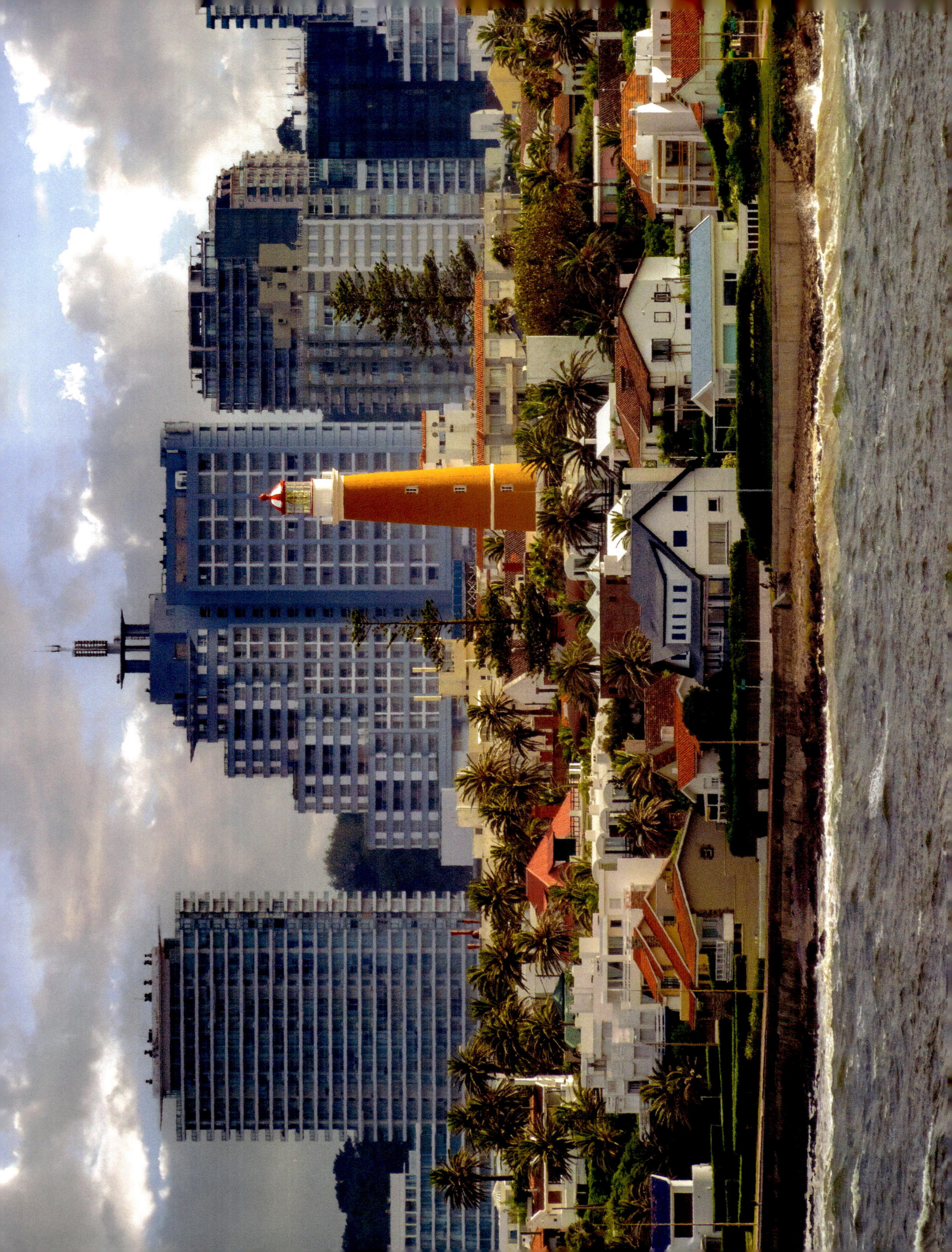

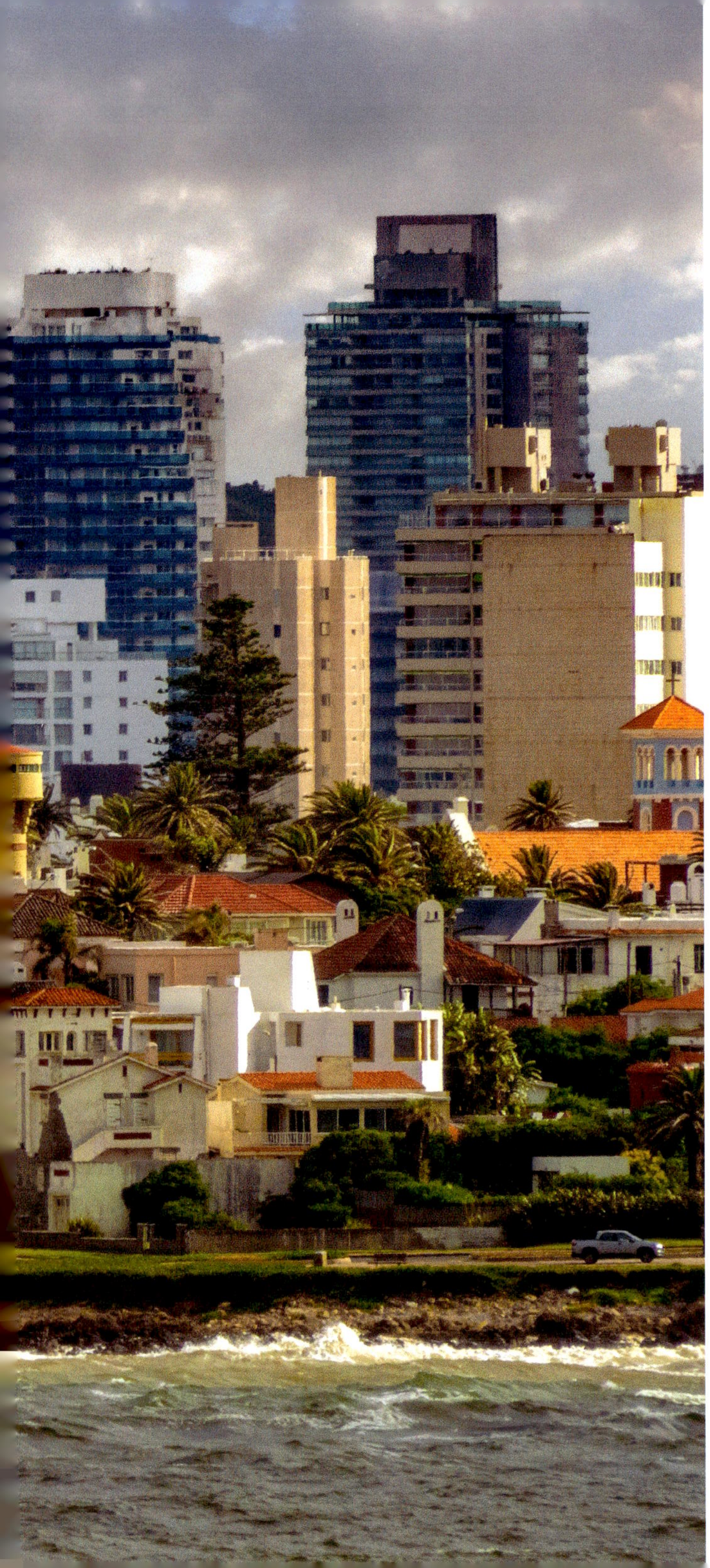

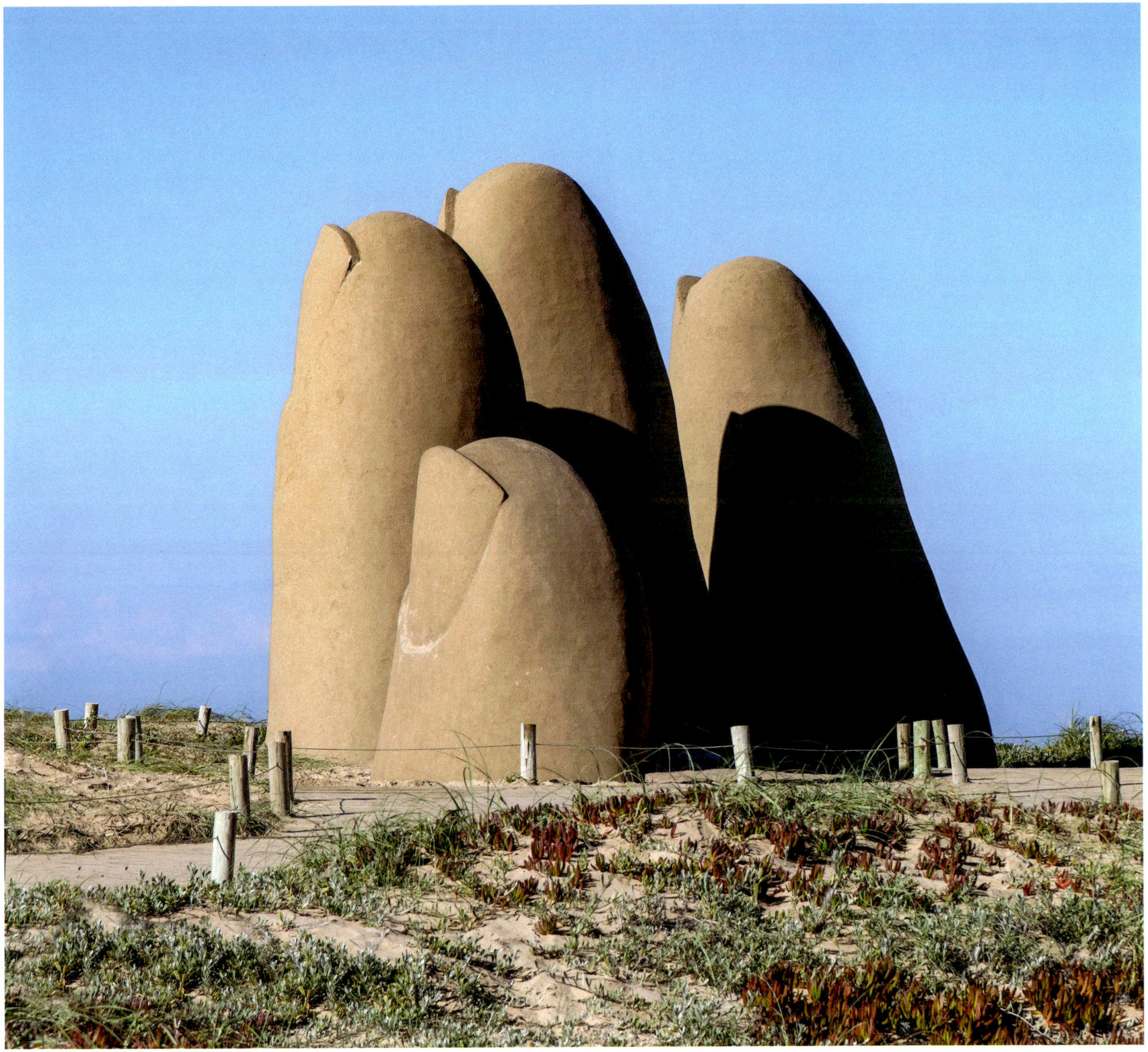

LEFT:

Punta del Este, Uruguay

The fashionable, upscale resort of Punta del Este lies at the point where the Río de la Plata estuary meets the Atlantic. In the city's Península neighbourhood, which juts southwest in the direction of Argentina, is an 1860s lighthouse.

ABOVE:

***La Mano*, Playa Brava, Punta del Este**

Erected in 1982, this statue is by Chilean sculptor Mario Irarrázabal. His concept was to show a hand 'drowning' in the sand, serving as a warning visitors that the waves at this beach are better suited to surfing than swimming.

RIGHT:
Solís Theatre, Montevideo, Uruguay
Opened in 1856, this Neoclassical theatre was desiged by Italian architect Carlo Zucchi. With its horseshoe shape and tiered boxes, the interior resembles classic Italian opera houses such as Milan's La Scala. The theatre was named after explorer Juan Díaz de Solís, who was probably the first European to reach this region, in 1516.

OPPOSITE:
Fiesta de la Patria Gaucha, Tacuarembó, Uruguay
Refreshing his horses in a break between events, this rider is taking part in Uruguay's annual festival of gaucho skills and culture. The heyday of cowboys known as gauchos, who were often of mixed Spanish and Indigenous or African descent, began in the seventeenth century. Today, the heroic, wild gaucho remains a key part of Uruguayan identity.

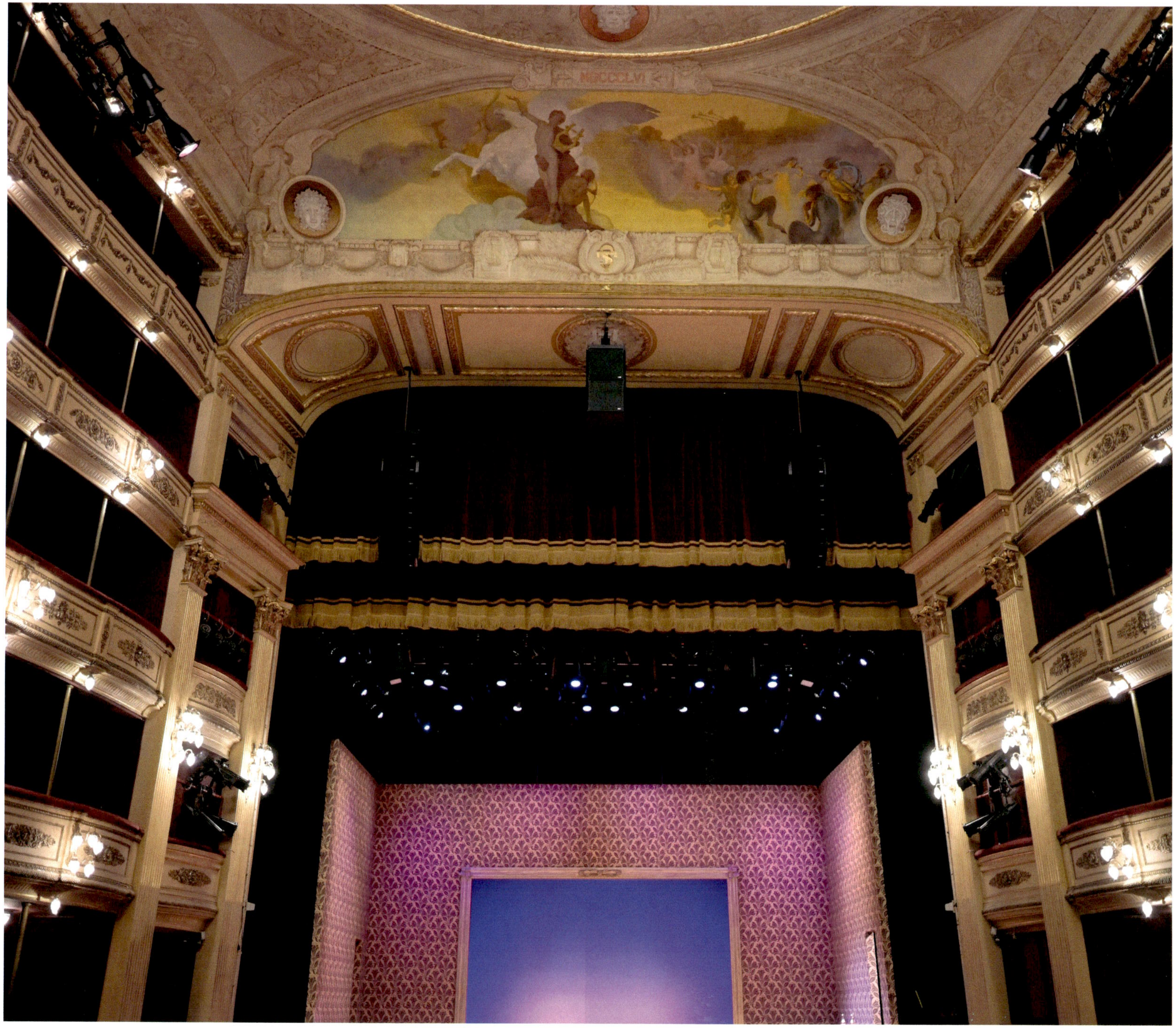

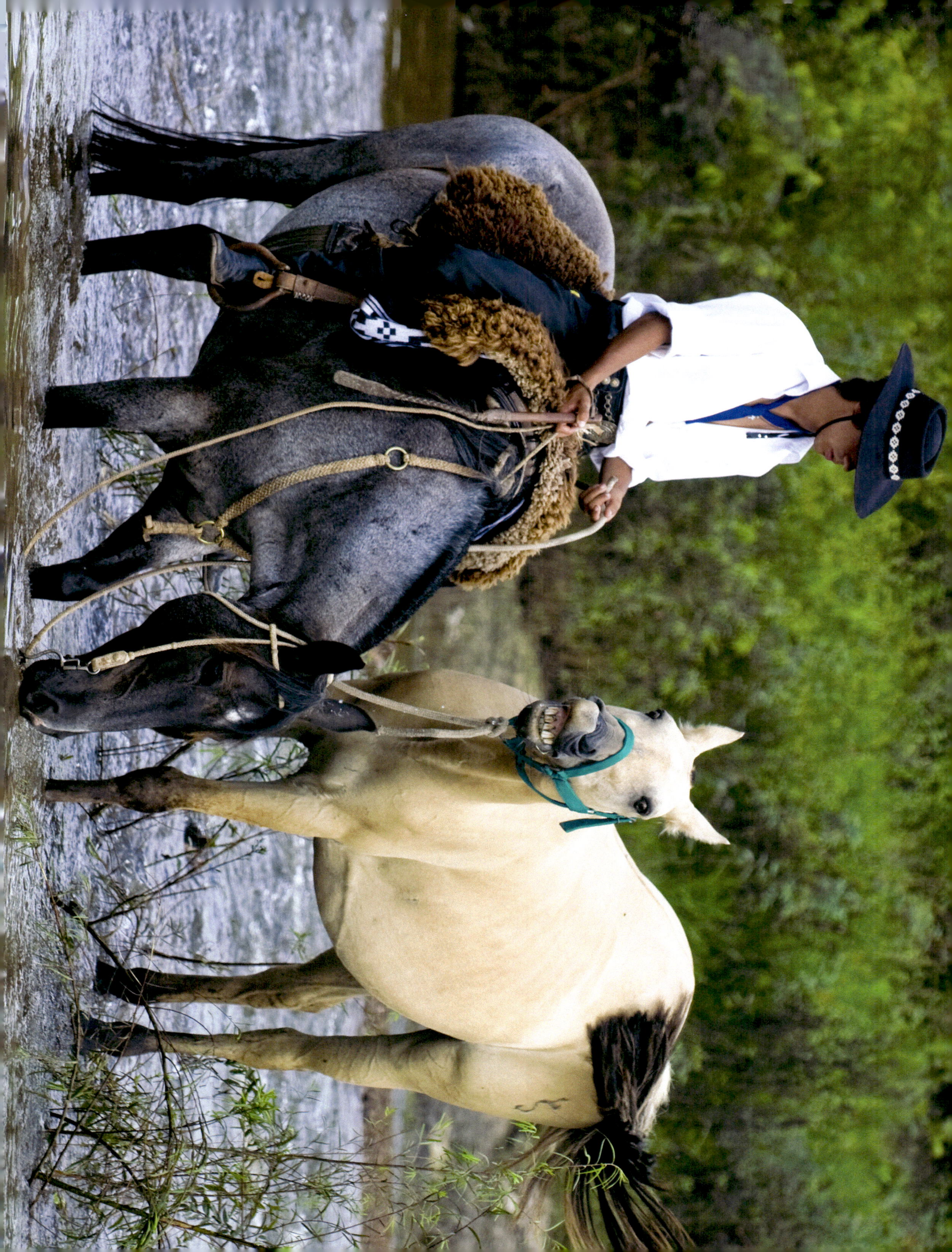

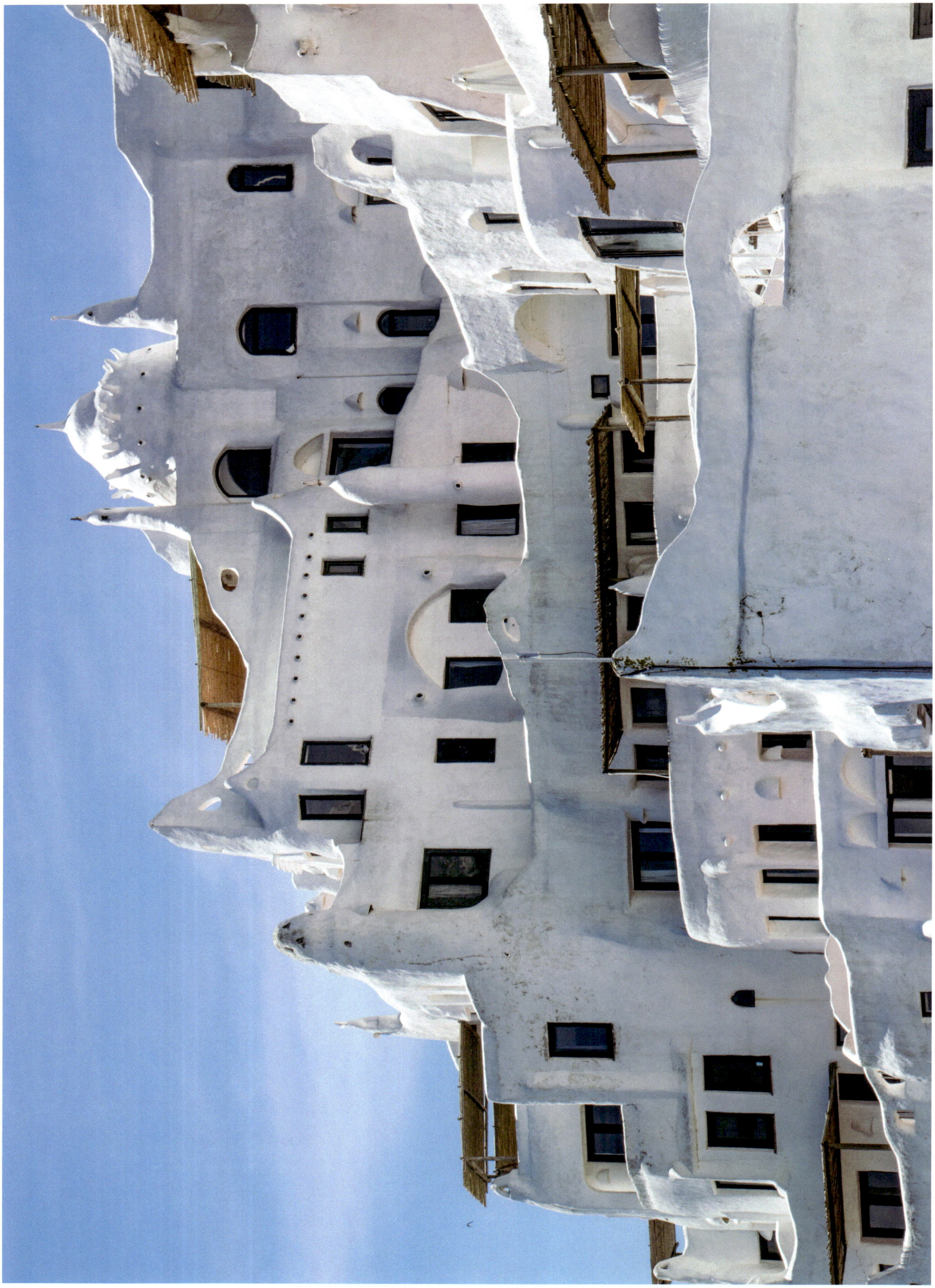

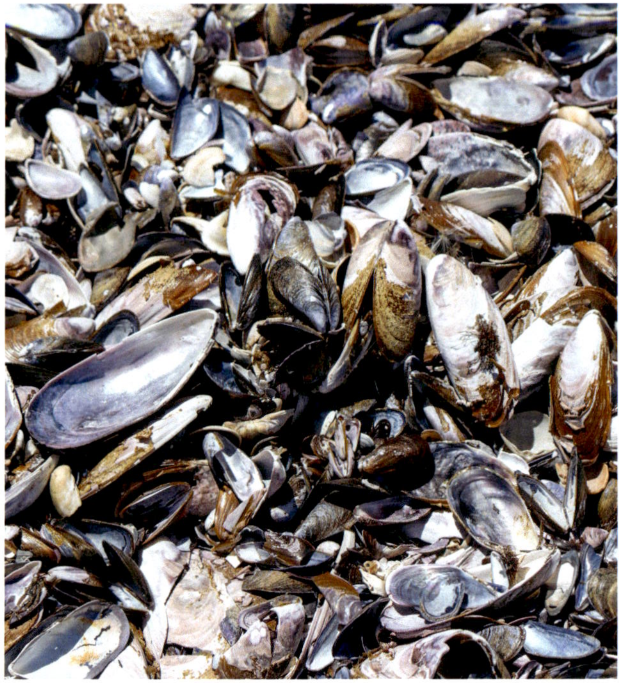

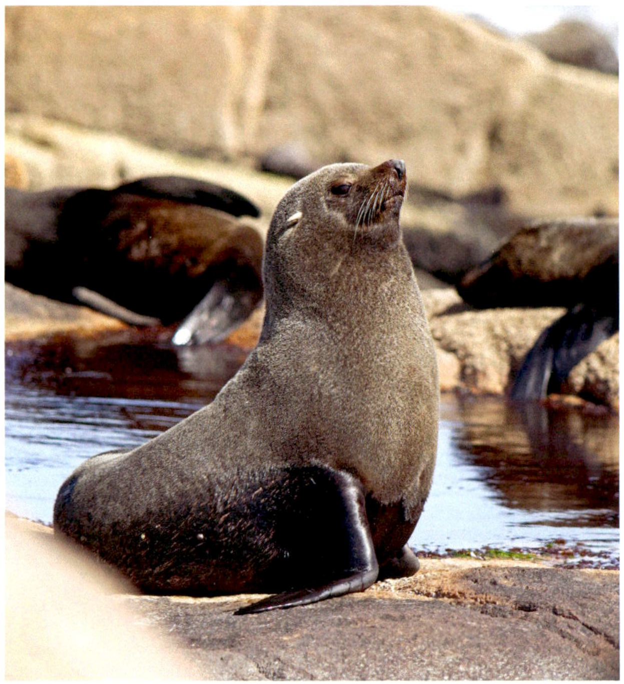

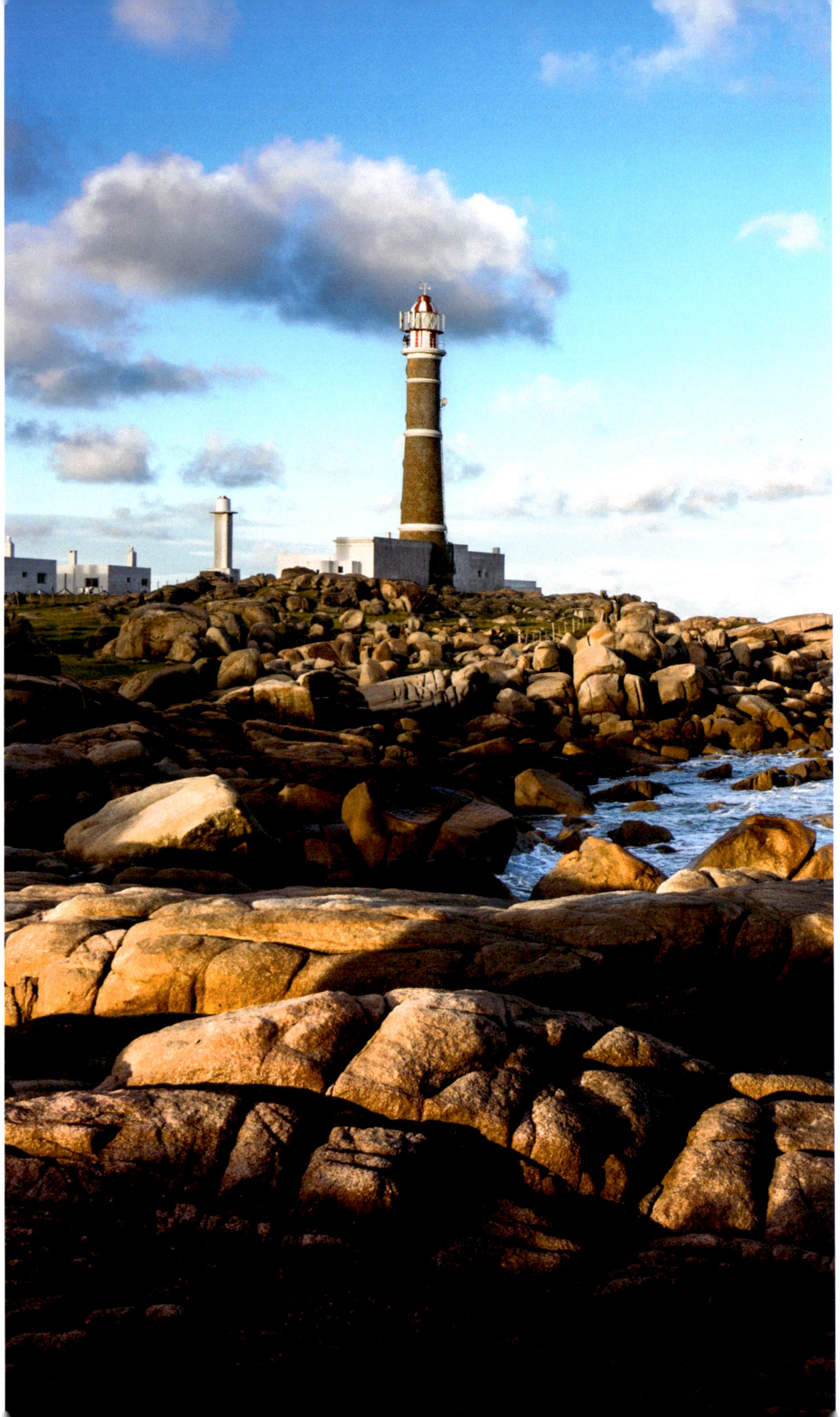

OPPOSITE:
Casapueblo, Punta Ballena, Uruguay
Begun in 1958, this building was constructed as a home and workshop by Uruguayan artist Carlos Páez Vilaró. He was inspired by the houses on Greece's Santorini, as well as the mud nests of rufous hornero ovenbirds from eastern South America. Today, the on-site museum holds a collection of the artist's work, as well as information about his son, Carlos Páez Rodríguez, a survivor of Flight 571, which crashed in the Andes in 1972, as depicted in the 1993 English-language movie *Alive*, the Spanish-language 1976 *Survive!* and the 2023 movie *Society of the Snow*.

LEFT ALL PHOTOGRAPHS:
Cabo Polonio, Uruguay
Home to an 1881 lighthouse, the off-grid village of Cabo Polonio is attached to the mainland only by a tombolo of wind-blown sand and can only be reached by four-wheel drive across the dunes. The surrounding rocky coast and islands are home to large colonies of South American sea lions (pictured) and South American fur seals, while rodents called tuco-tucos scurry across the dunes.

RIGHT:
Danza de la Botella, Asunción, Paraguay
This Paraguayan folk dance is traditionally performed by women wearing nineteenth-century rural costumes. The women dance, very carefully, to Paraguayan polka music, which has more complex rhythms than European polkas. Dancers learn to add more bottles as they grow in skill, with some managing 10 or 11.

OPPOSITE:
National Pantheon of the Heroes, Asunción, Paraguay
Begun in 1863 but not completed until 1936, this Neoclassical building houses the remains of famous Paraguayans, including Carlos Antonio López, who was the country's first president from 1844 to 1862. The stained-glass windows showcase the colours of the national flag.

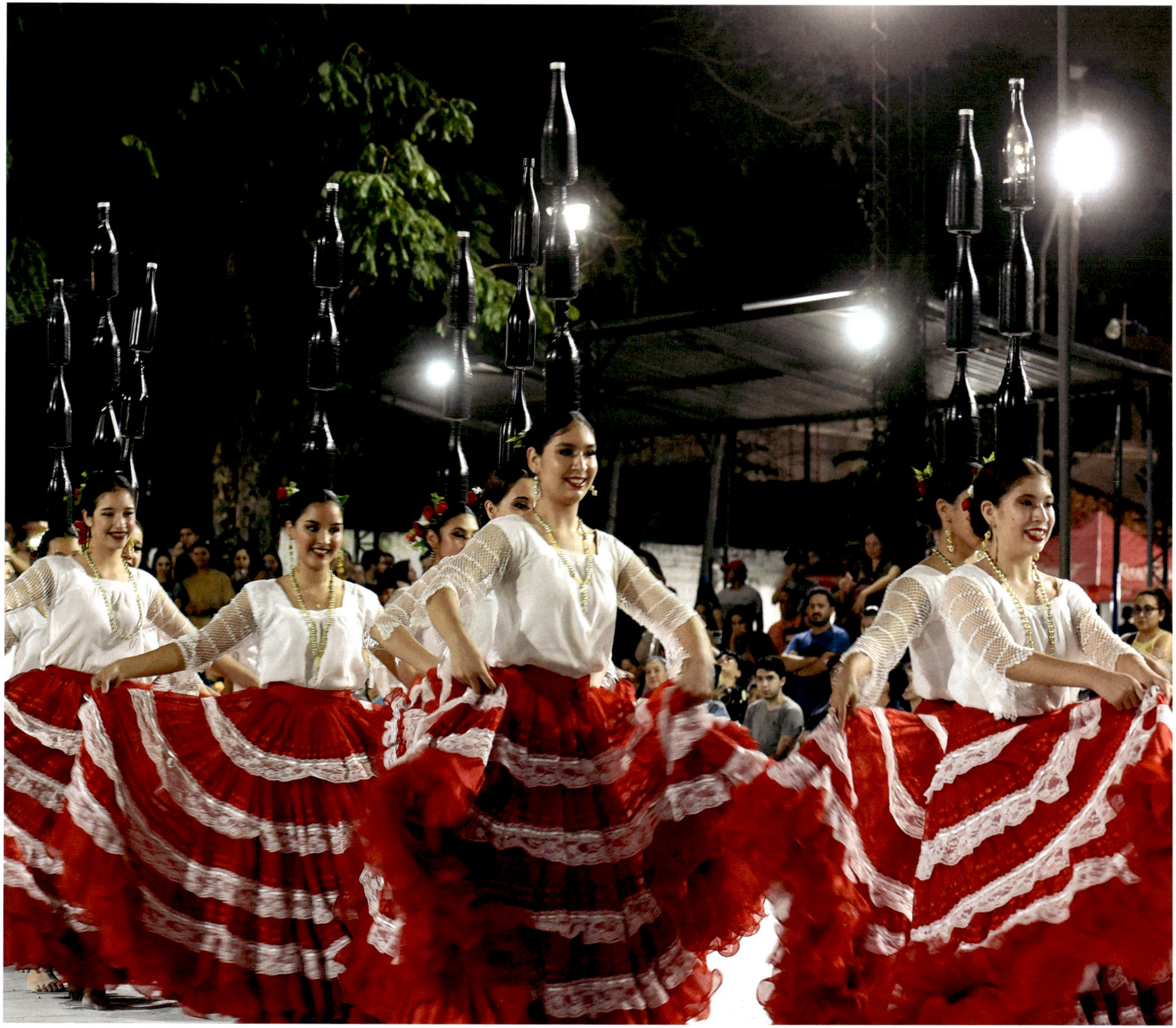

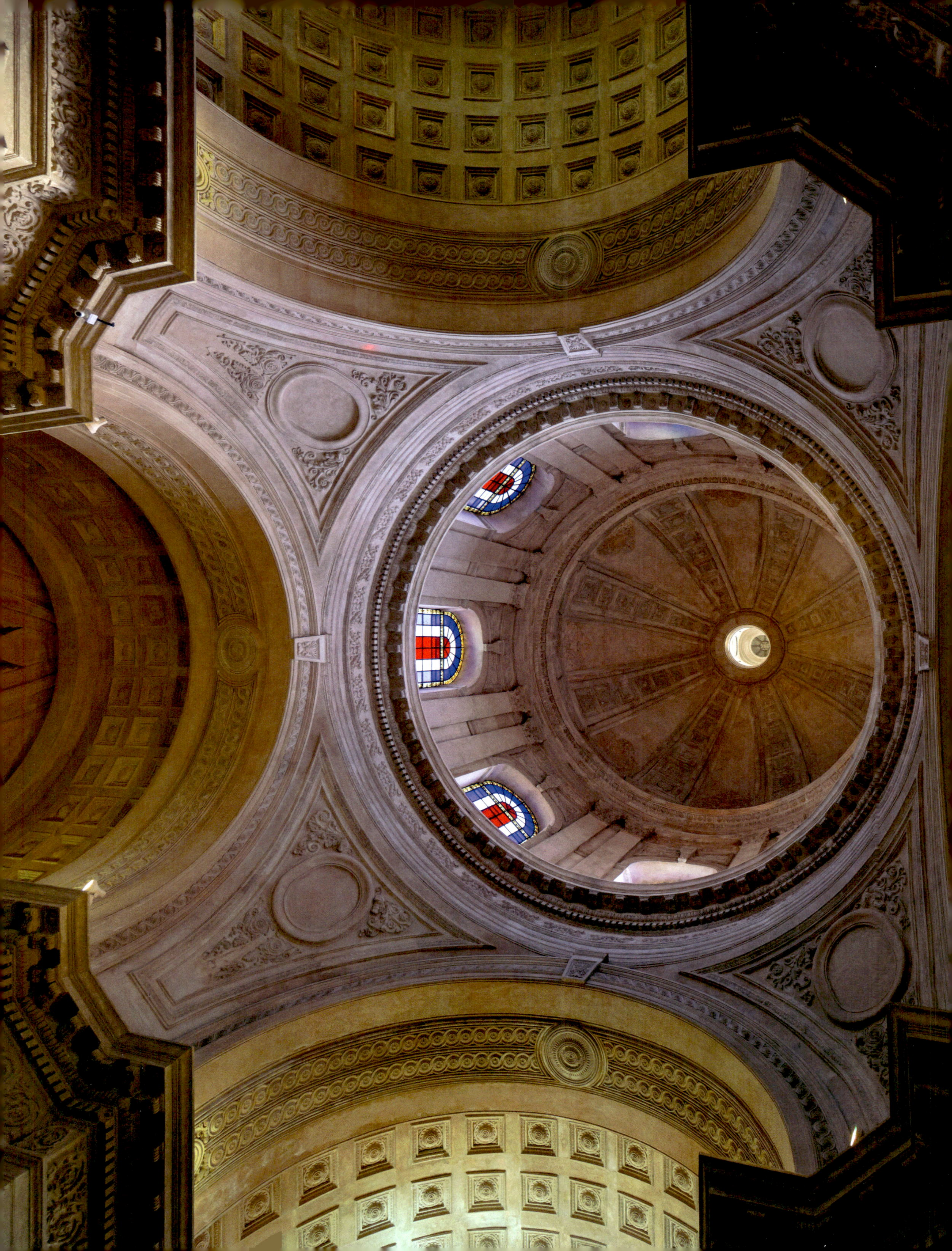

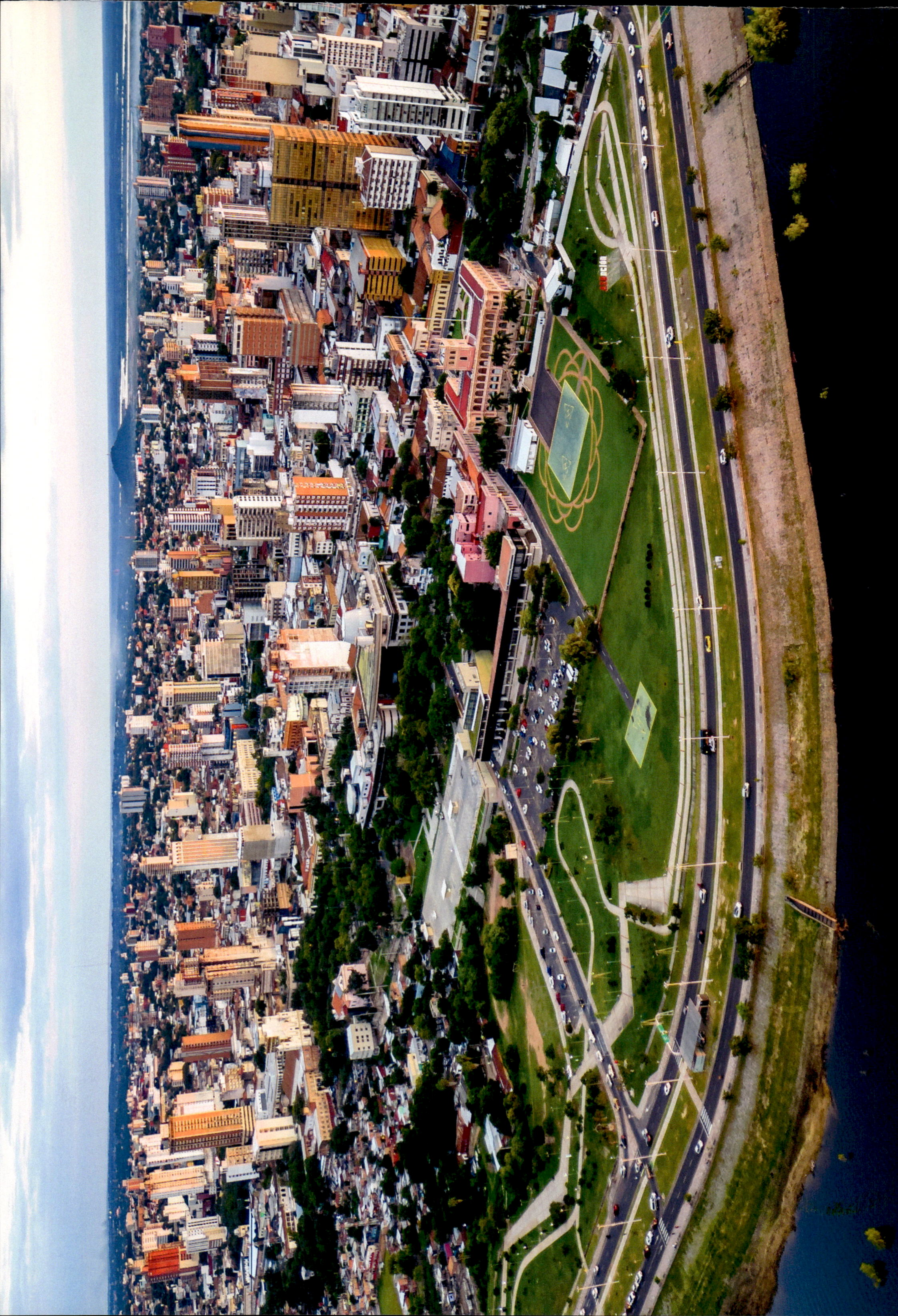

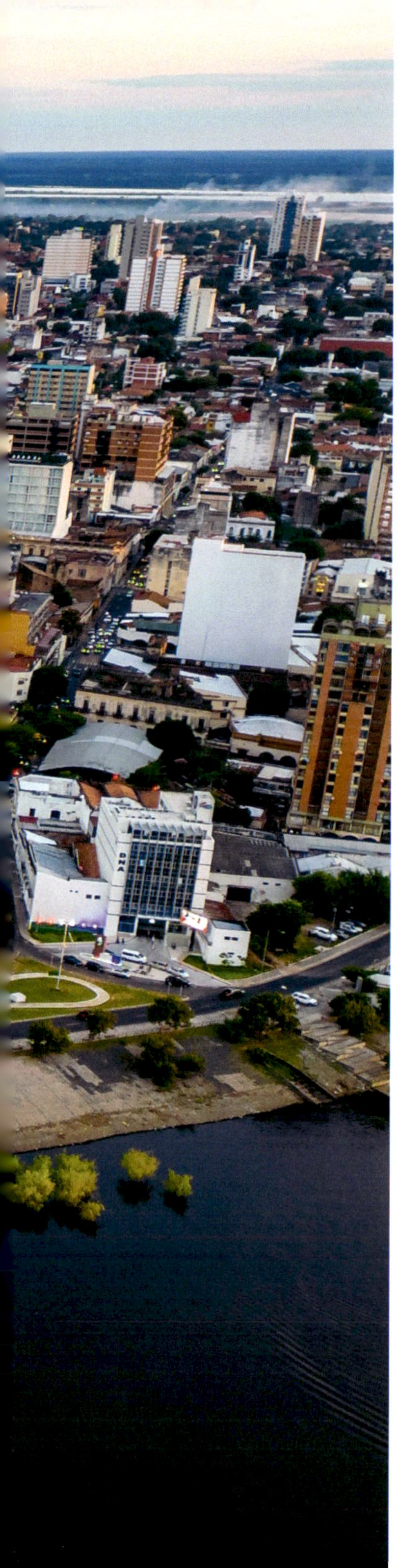

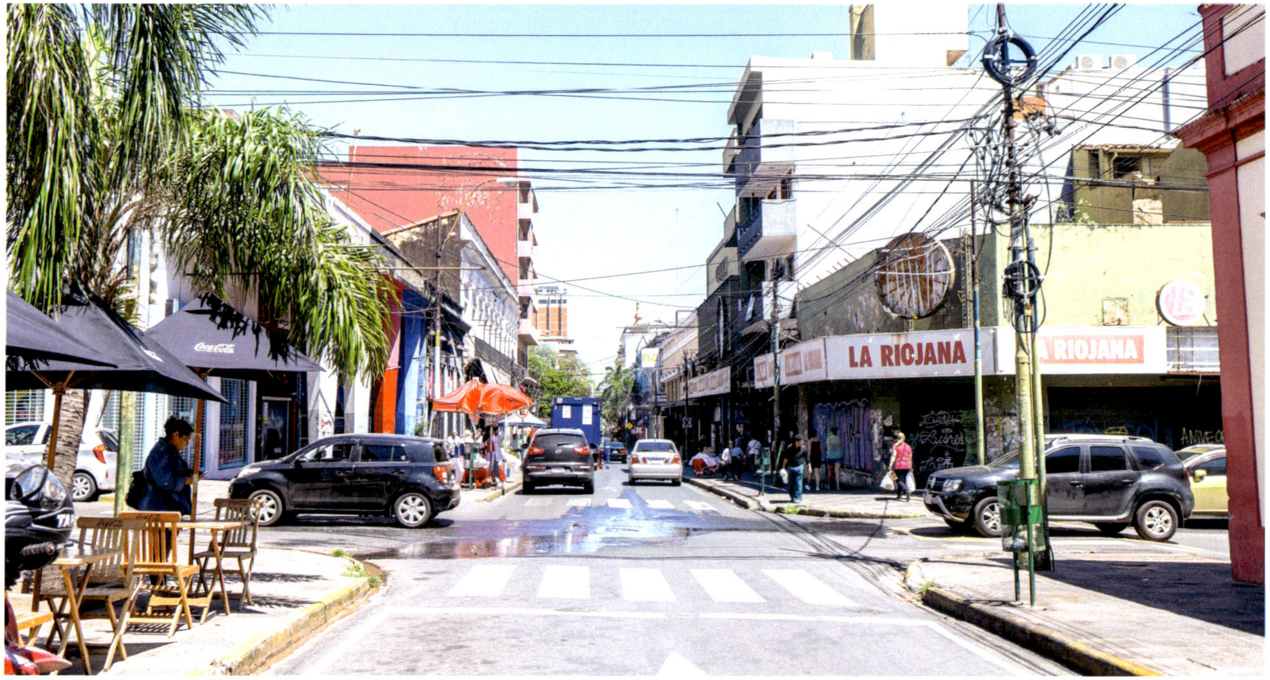

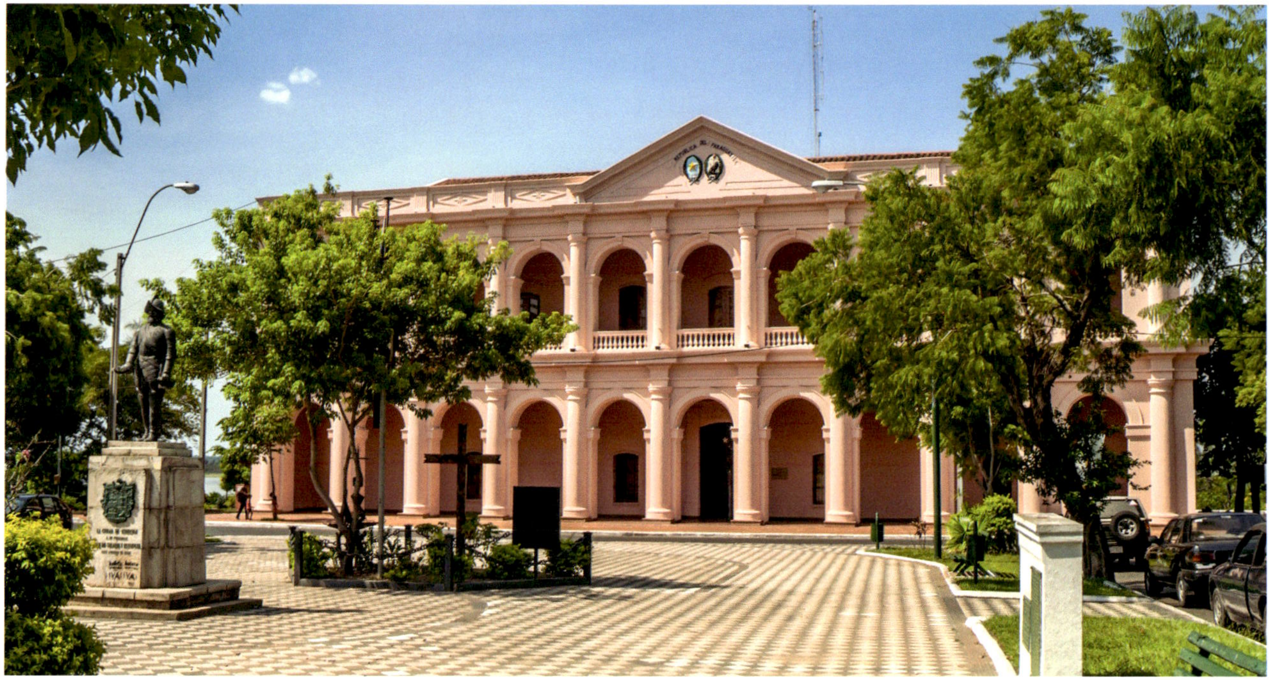

FAR LEFT AND LEFT TOP:

Asunción, Paraguay

Paraguay's capital and largest city is home to more than 3 million people. It lies on the eastern bank of the Paraguay River, a vital transport route from the landlocked country to the Atlantic Coast at the Río de la Plata. Since Asunción is located along the national border, the river flowing through the southern part of the city serves as the boundary between Paraguay and Argentina.

LEFT BOTTOM:

Cultural Centre of the Republic, Asunción

This history museum and event space is in the old Cabildo (council building), constructed in 1844. It holds *ñai'upo* pottery, a traditional technique involving hand-shaping black clay. Practised by women in areas like Yaguarón, Itá and Tobatí, the technique was passed down from pre-colonial times.

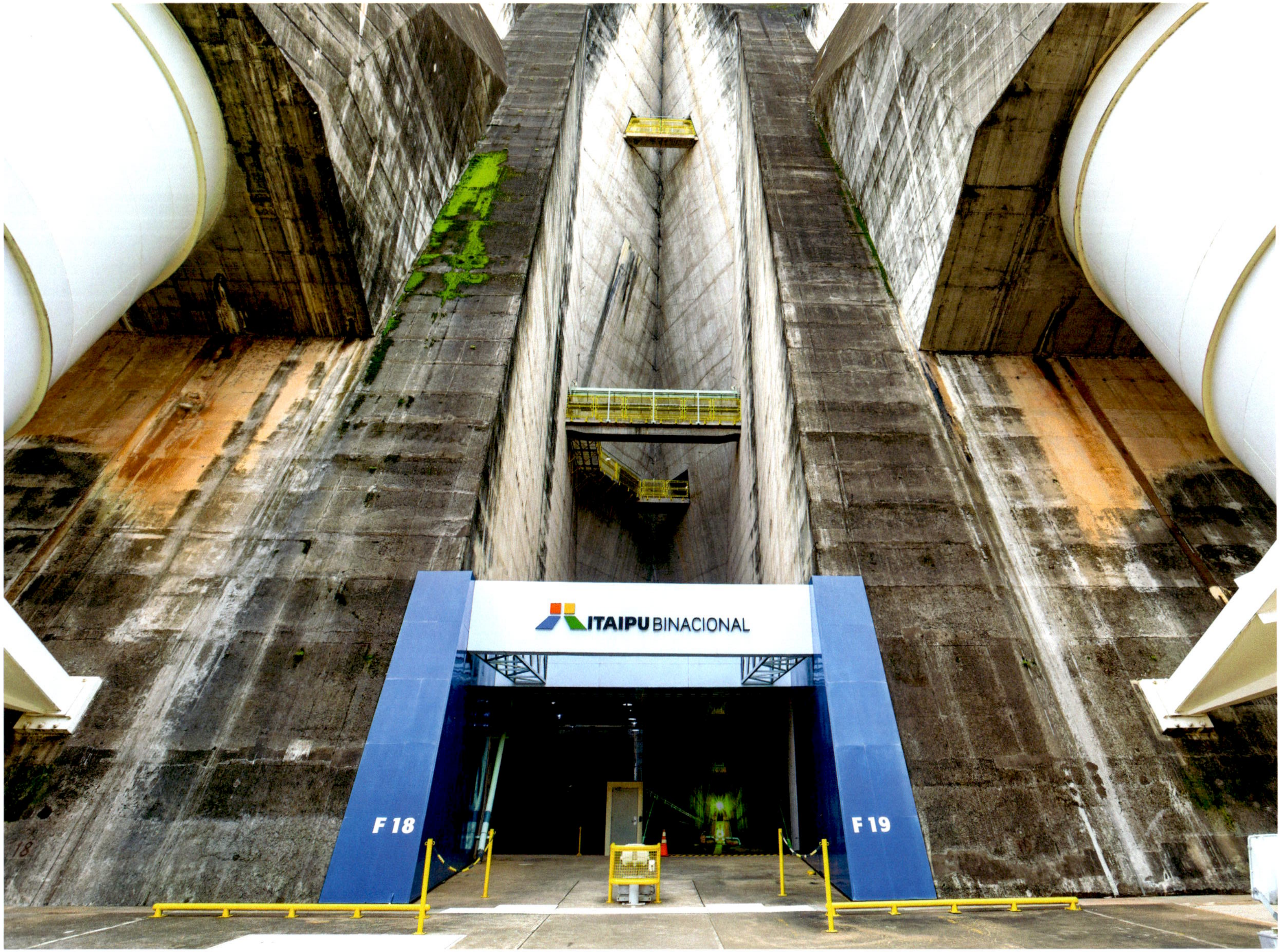

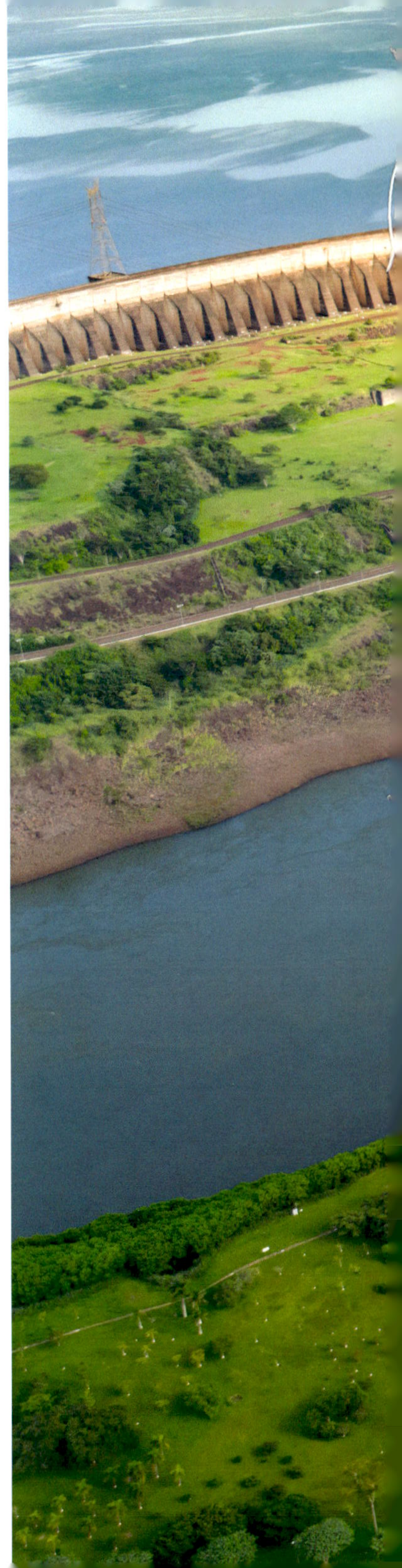

BOTH PHOTOGRAPHS:

Itaipu Dam, Paraná River, Paraguay–Brazil

Completed in 1984, this hydroelectric dam is the world's second largest producer of electricity after China's Three Gorges, producing up to 89 terawatt-hours per year. As Paraguay does not use all of its allocated share of the output, it sells its surplus to Brazil.

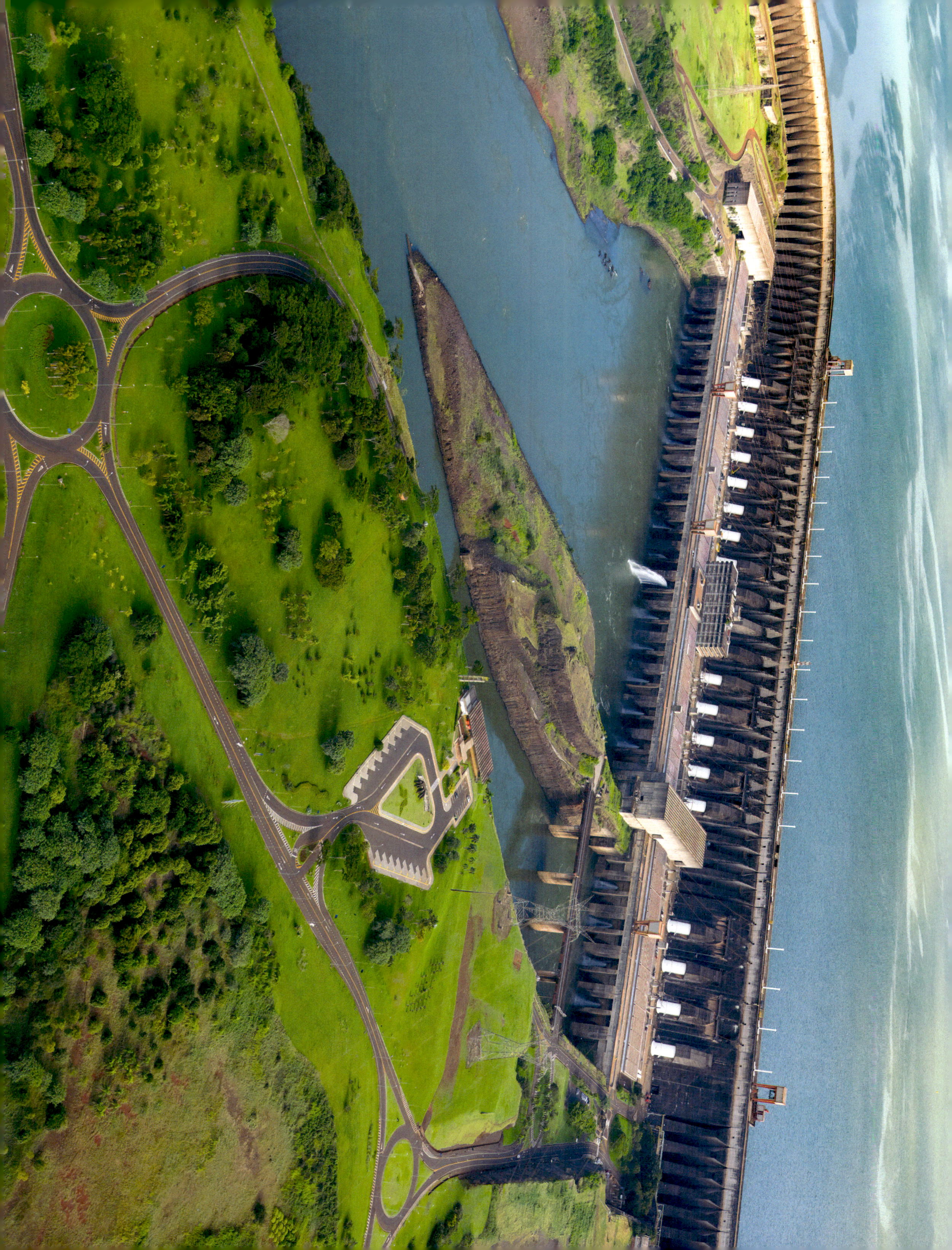

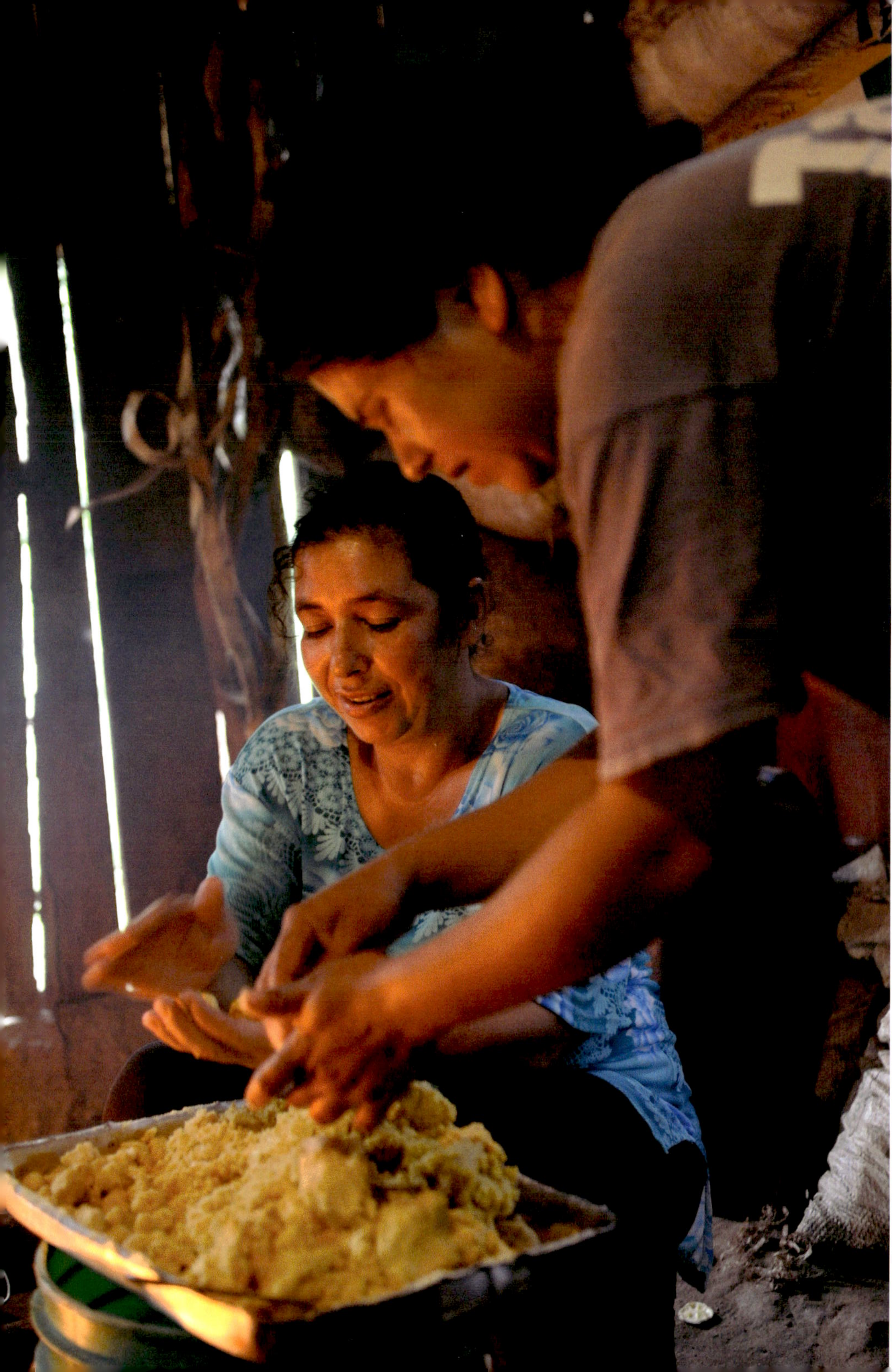

LEFT:
Preparing *Vori Vori*, Caaguazú, Paraguay
These women are preparing little balls made of cornmeal, cheese and fatty broth. The balls will then be added to soup and cooked briefly in its hot stock. In the Guaraní language, one way to express abundance is to repeat a word, so *vori vori* means 'lots of little balls', with *vori* coming from the Spanish word *bolita* ('little ball').

RIGHT AND OPPOSITE:
Templo San Buenaventura, Yaguarón, Paraguay
This jewel of Franciscan colonial architecture was built from wood and adobe in the seventeenth and eighteenth centuries. While the exterior is utilitarian, with a freestanding bell tower, the interior is fabulously carved and painted in a breathtaking blend of Catholic faith and Guaraní craft.

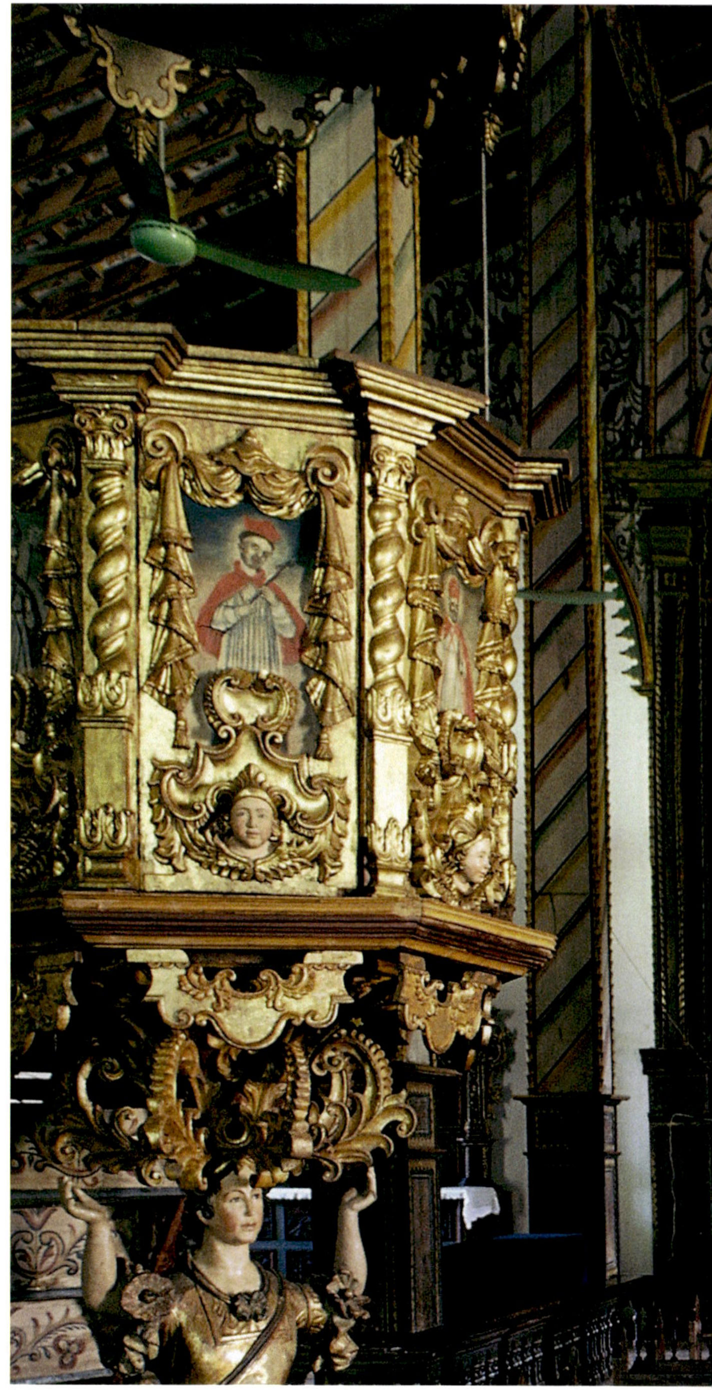

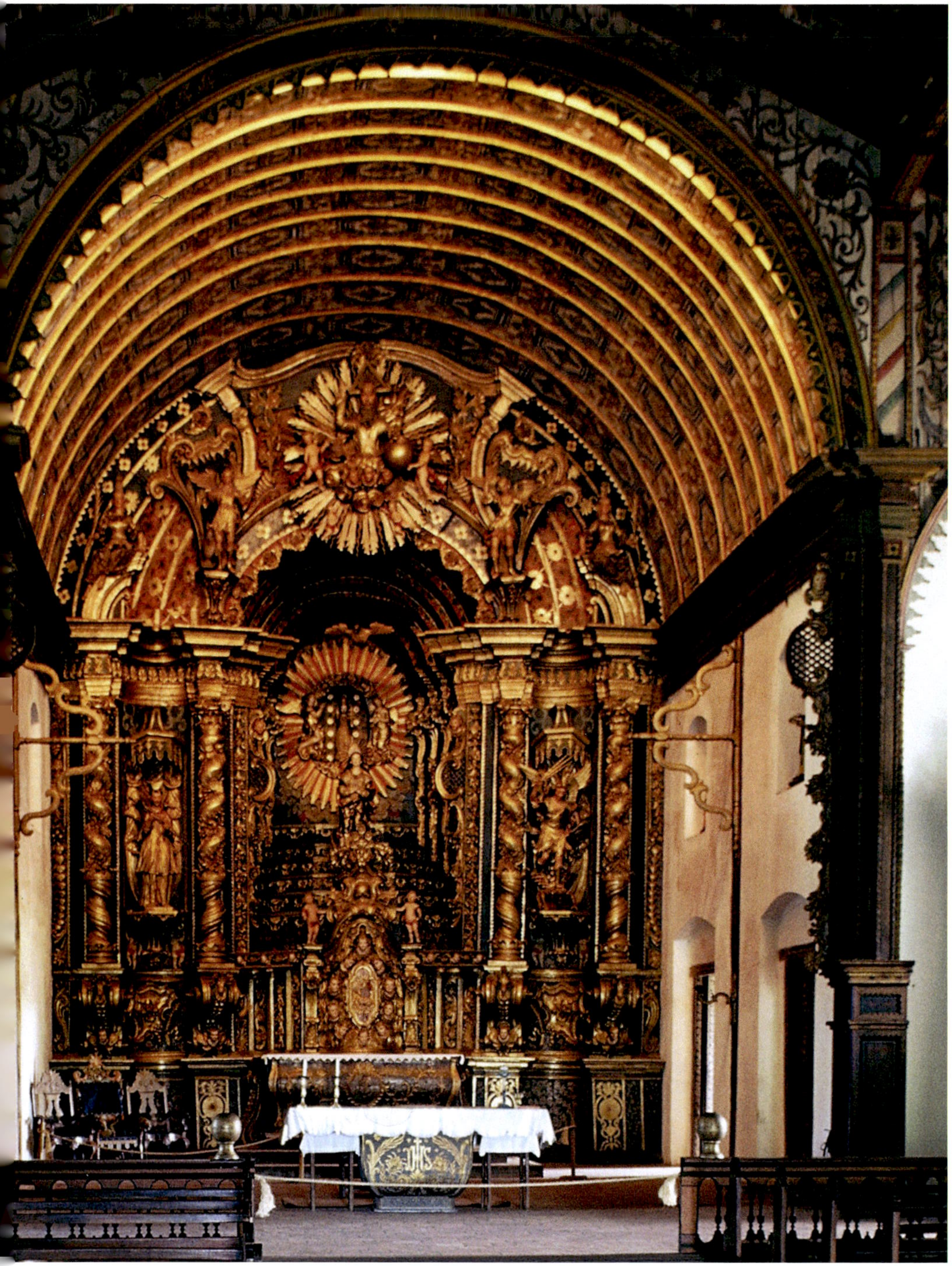

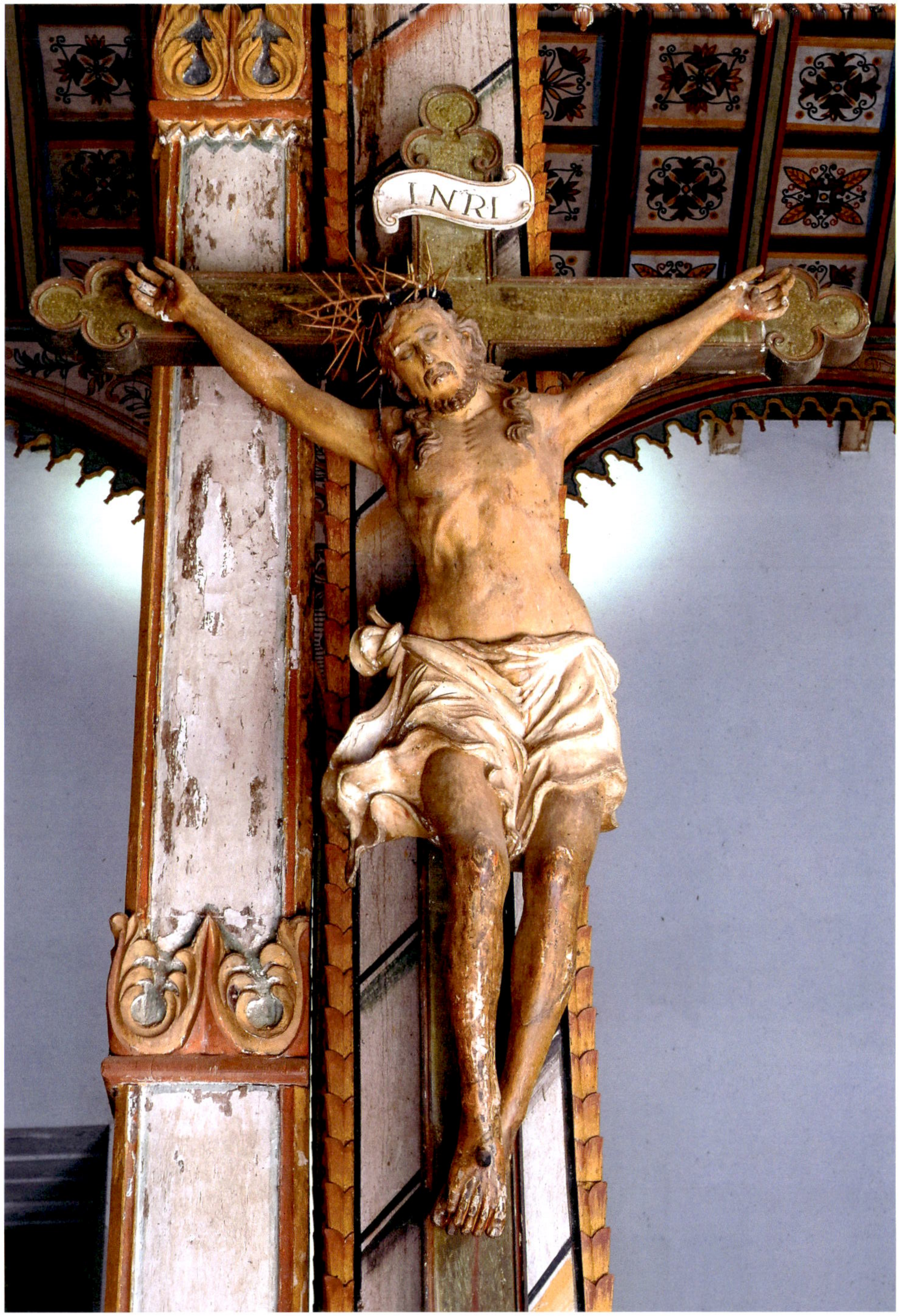
INRI

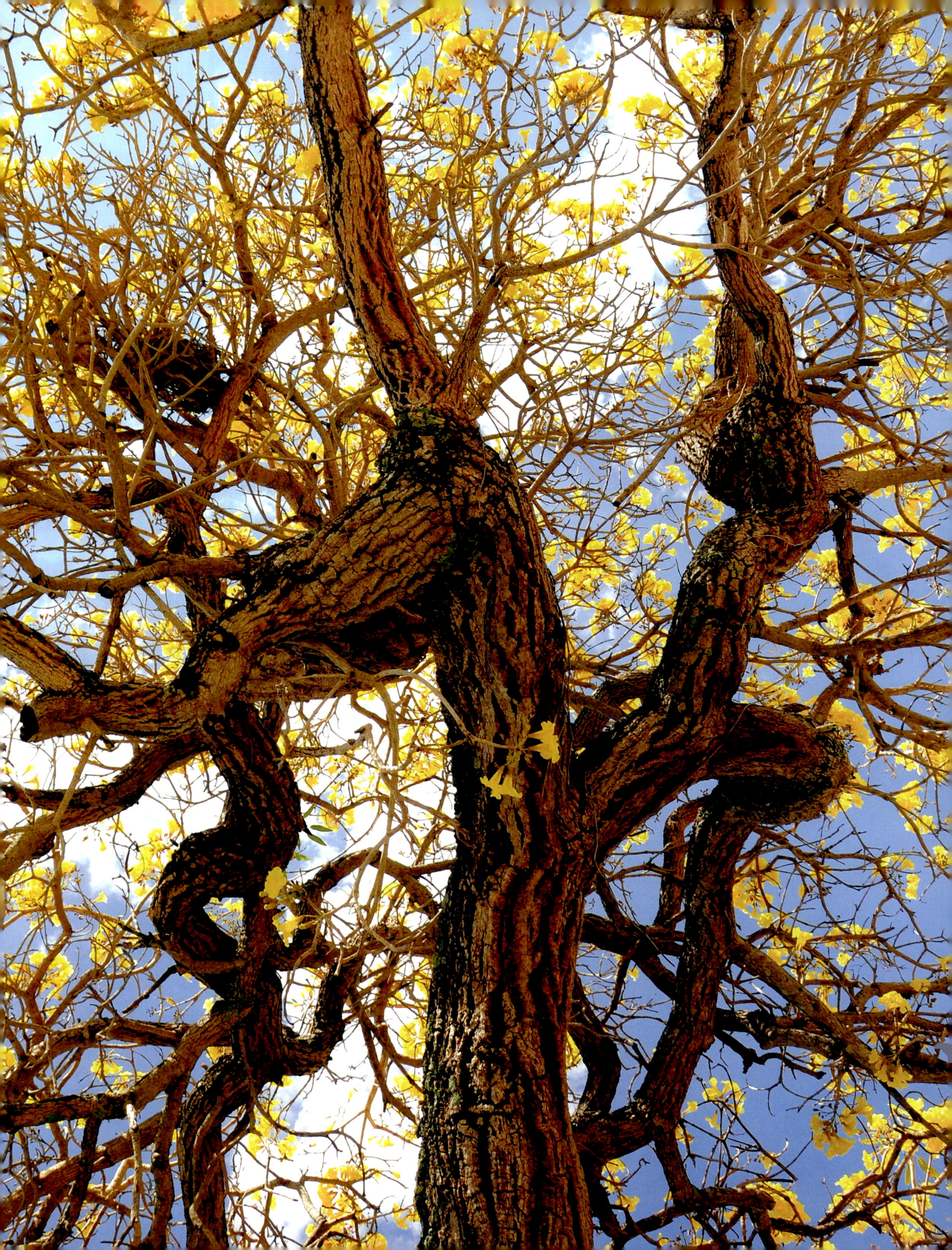

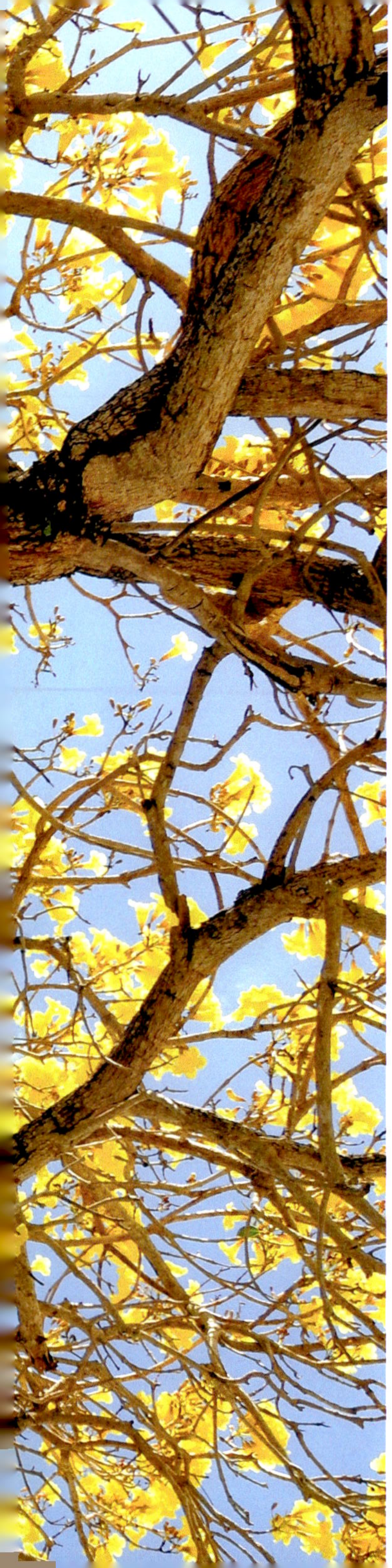

LEFT:
Trumpet Tree, Paraguay
The trumpet tree briefly sheds its leaves in the dry season, triggering the blooming of its trumpet-shaped flowers, creating an arresting golden display for pollinators and humans alike.

RIGHT TOP:
Pampas Fox, Paraguay
A canid called a zorro rather than a true fox, this species is found across the vast grassland known as the Pampas, as well as in forest and scrubland. It eats small animals, fruit and carrion.

RIGHT MIDDLE:
Six-banded Armadillo, Paraguay
Unlike three-banded armadillos, this species' armour does not allow it to roll into a ball, so it flees into its burrow when threatened.

RIGHT BOTTOM:
Margay, Paraguay
This wildcat, with a head and body length of up to 79cm (31 in), lives in forests, where it spends most of its life in trees, chasing birds and monkeys.

FAR RIGHT:
Bare-throated Bellbird, Paraguay
The national bird of Paraguay, this species is known for the male's loud call, which sounds like a hammer hitting an anvil. The 'Pájaro Campana' folk song, played on the harp, mimics the call.

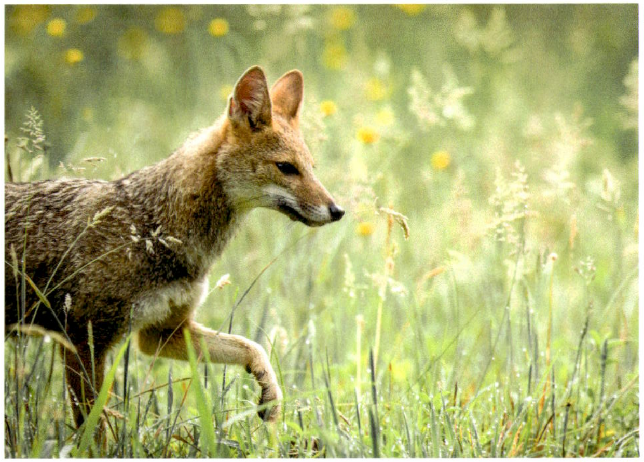

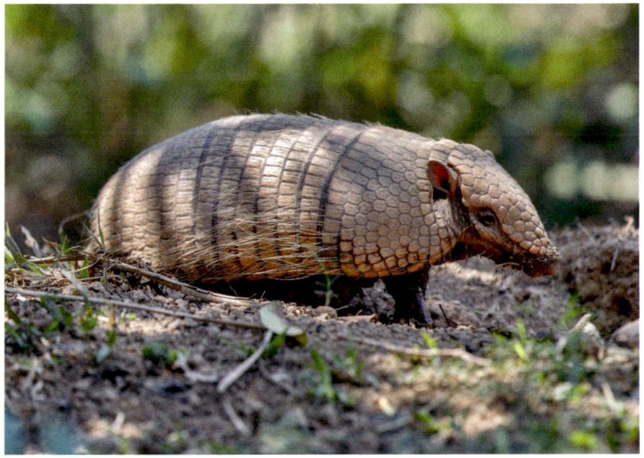

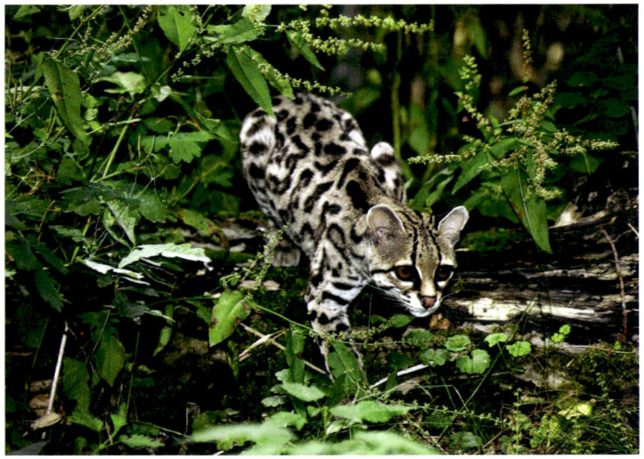

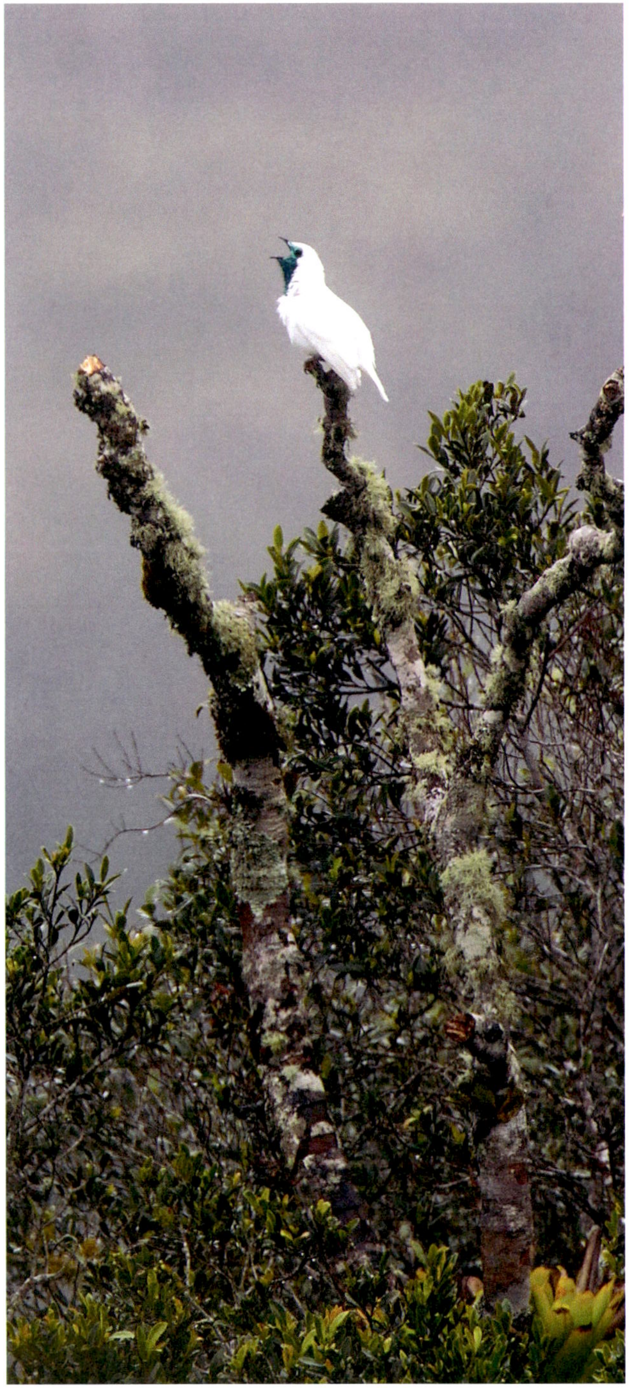

RIGHT:
Rolling Cigars, Asunción, Paraguay
Tobacco was probably first cultivated in the Andes region around 6000 years ago. By the early twentieth century, tobacco was a key export for Paraguay, but today cotton and soya beans are preferred cash crops.

OPPOSITE LEFT TOP:
La Recova Market, Asunción
This handicrafts market is a good place to find Guaraní-style cotton or palm leaf mats and bags, often woven on backstrap looms.

OPPOSITE LEFT BOTTOM:
Traditional Hats, Limpio
Woven from *karanda'y* palm fibres, hats are a key traditional craft, with distinct regional styles, such as the *piri* from Limpio.

OPPOSITE RIGHT TOP:
Leatherwork, Atyrá
Atyrá is a centre for artisan leatherwork, including bags, saddles and footwear made using natural dyes and stitched by hand.

OPPOSITE RIGHT BOTTOM:
***Ñandutí*, Itauguá**
Ñandutí (meaning 'spider web' in Guaraní) is a traditional needle lace. While lace making was brought to Paraguay by Spanish settlers, it soon incorporated Guaraní colours and motifs, including local flowers and animals.

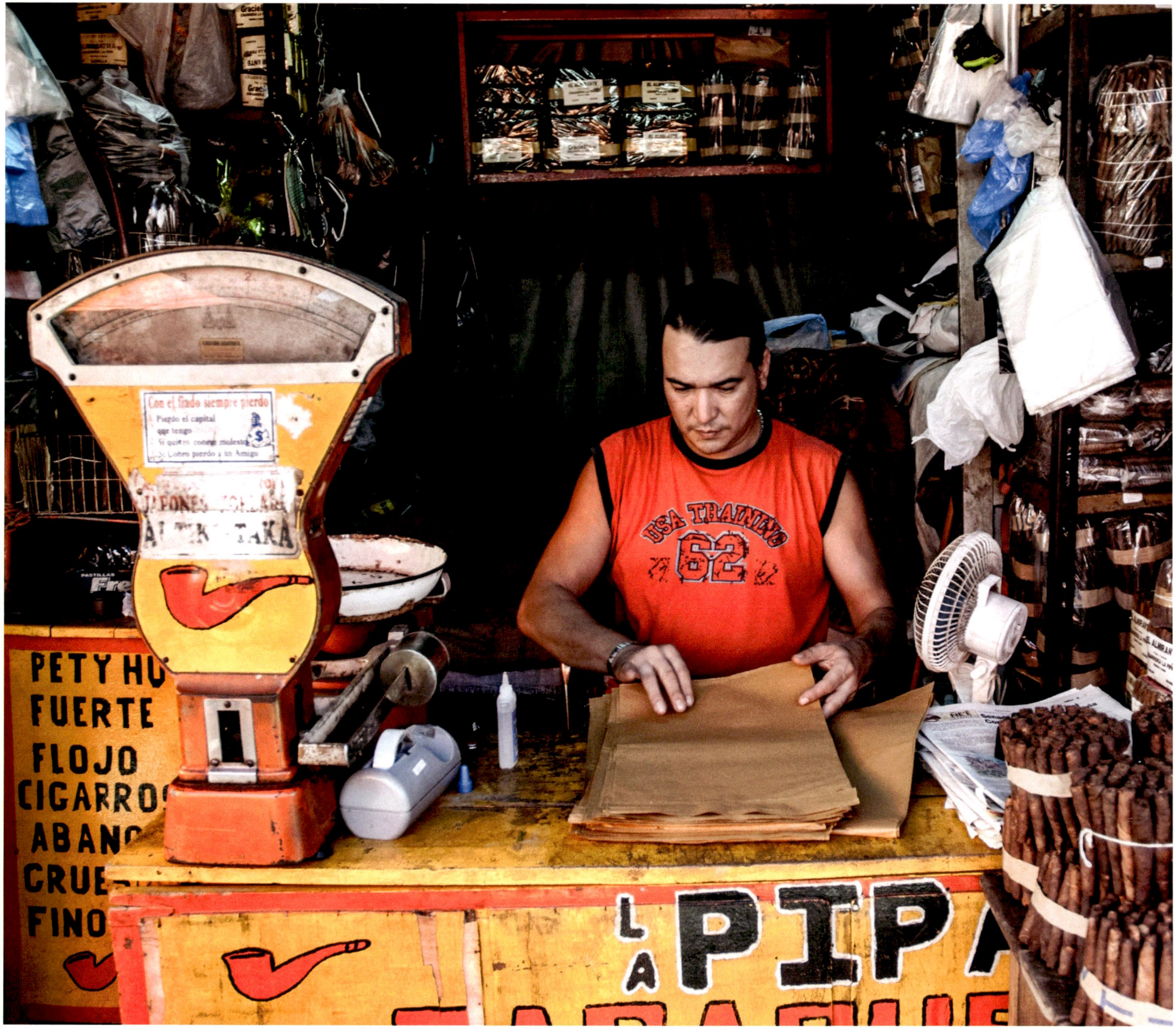

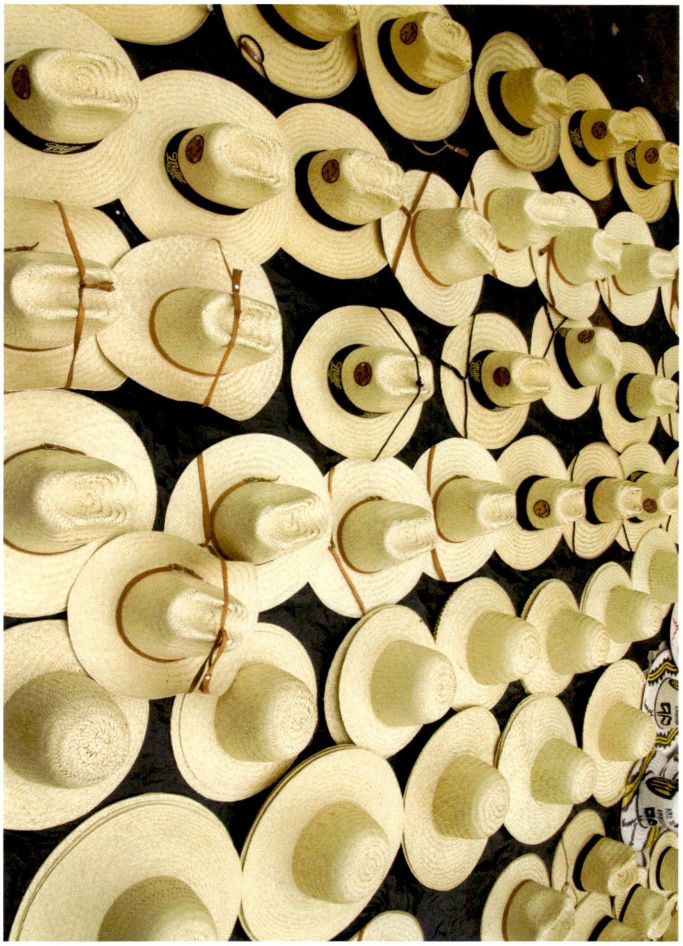

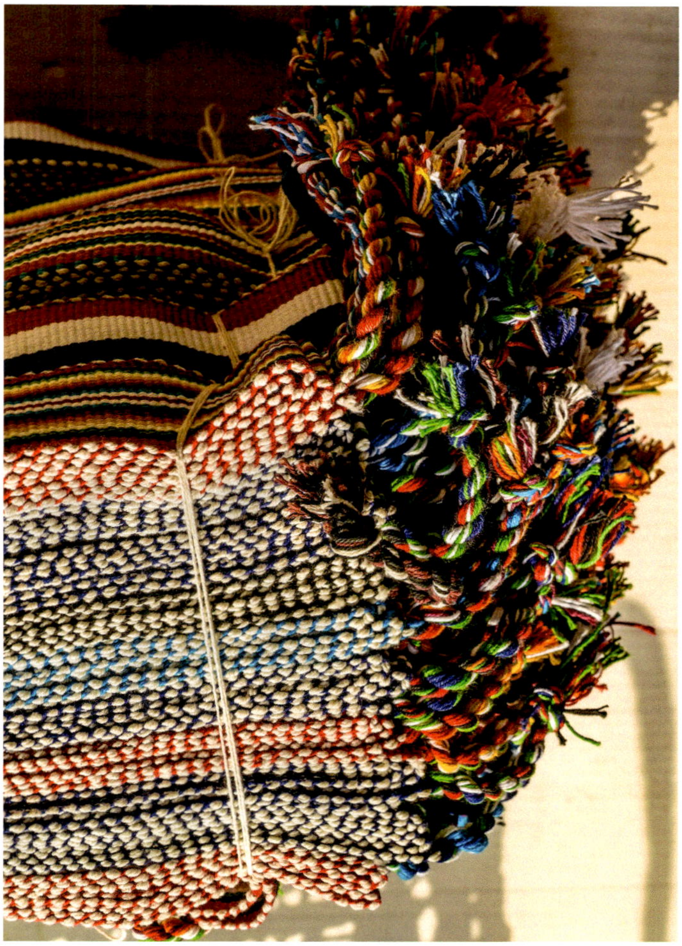

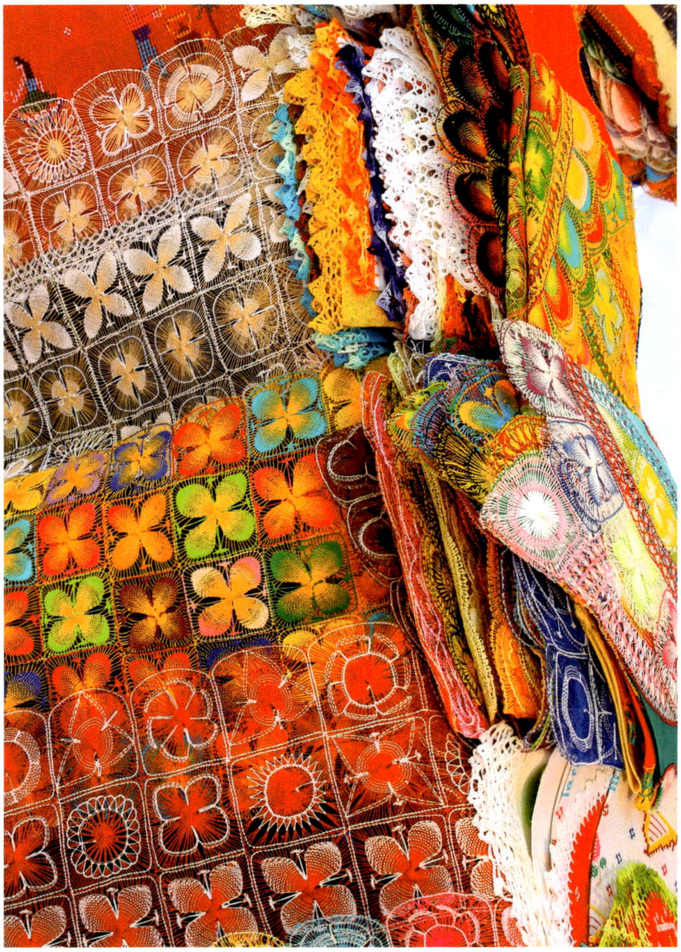

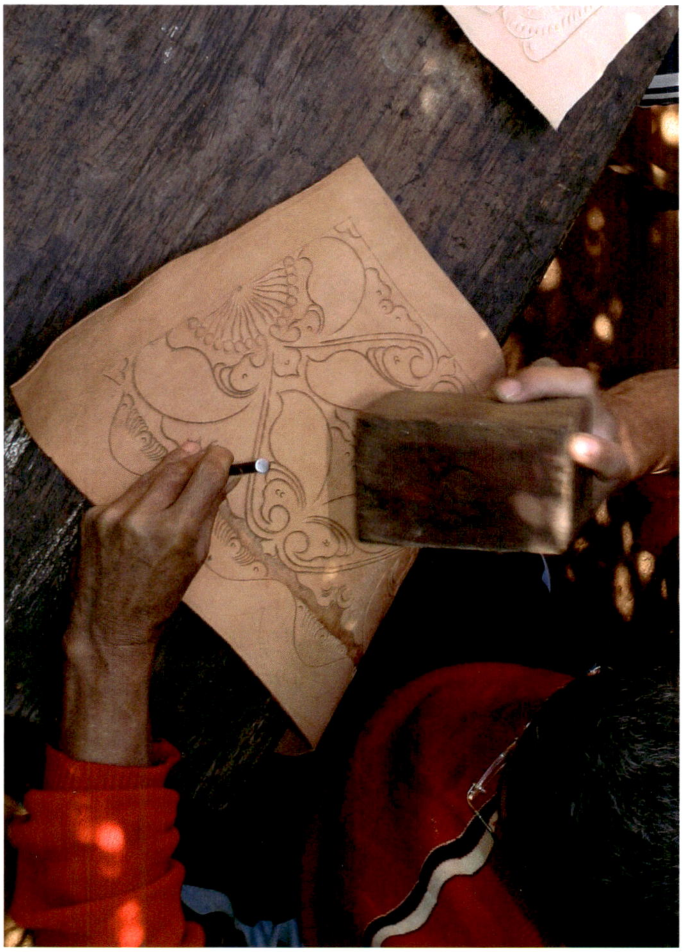

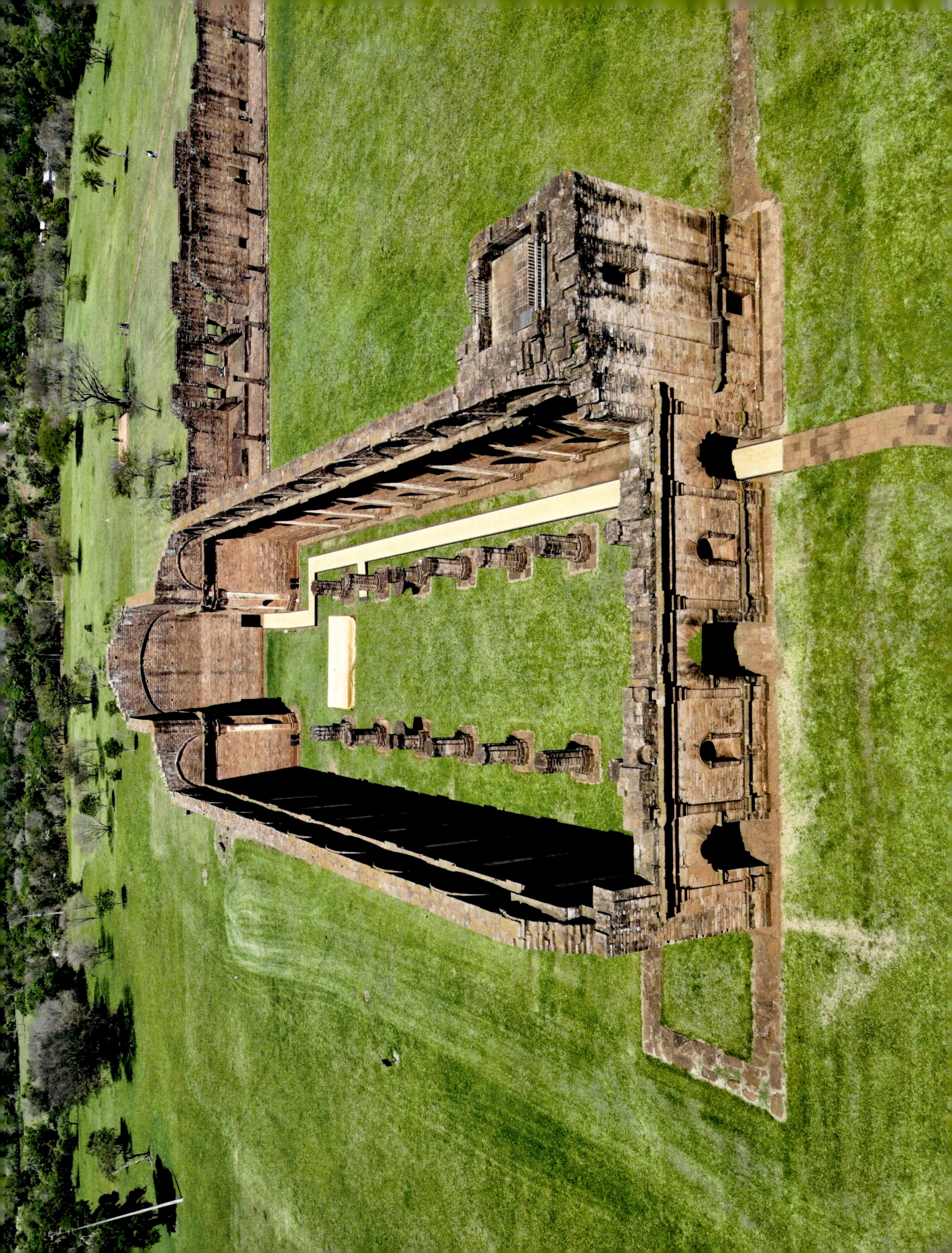

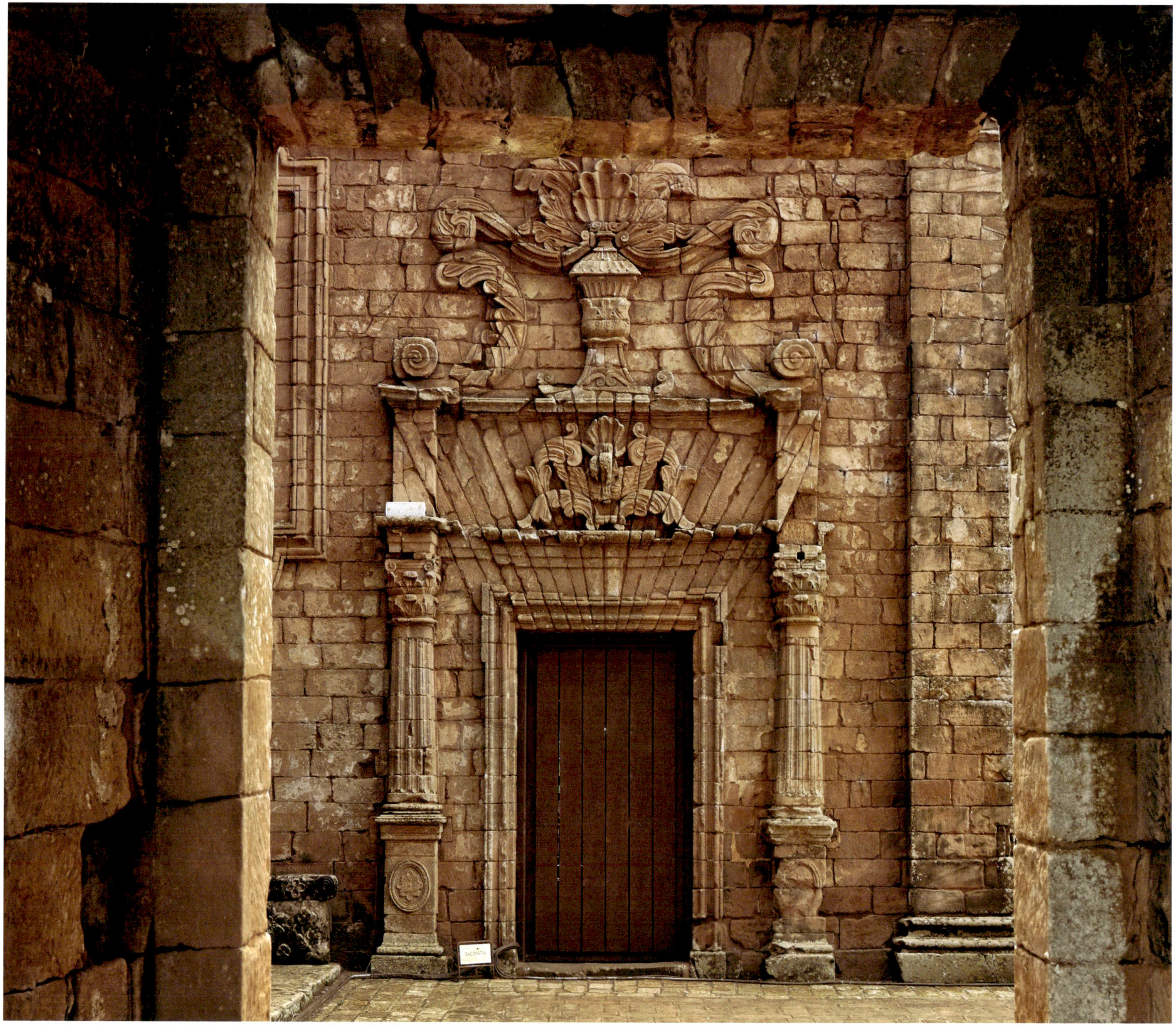

OPPOSITE:

Jesús de Tavarangue, Itapúa, Paraguay

This Jesuit 'reduction' church was begun in 1760 but not complete when the Jesuits were expelled from Paraguay in 1767. Both religious and secular groups established reduction communities across the country, where Guaraní peoples were housed and taught Catholicism and European cultural practices. While some argue the Jesuit reductions protected local people from slavery, they were also places of disease, abuse and forced indoctrination.

LEFT:

Santísima Trinidad de Paraná, Itapúa

After the Jesuits were expelled, this reduction, founded in 1706, was left to fall into ruin. Today, visitors can walk among the remaining buildings, which blend European Baroque architecture with intricate carvings by the mission's Guaraní inhabitants.

RIGHT TOP:
***Samu'ũ* Tree,**
Alto Paraná, Paraguay
The trunk of a *Ceiba speciosa* tree is studded with thorns that prevent herbivorous mammals from climbing the trunk to eat the bark, leaves or flowers. The flowers are pollinated by hummingbirds and bats, while the seeds are dispersed by the wind.

RIGHT BOTTOM:
Paraguay Caiman Lizard,
Pantanal, Alto Paraguay
Up to 1.2m (4ft) long, this semi-aquatic lizard is found in the Pantanal wetlands. It uses its powerful jaws to crack the shells of snails, clams and crabs. An excellent climber, it often basks on branches overhanging the water.

FAR RIGHT:
Monday Falls, Alto Paraná
Around 45m (148ft) high and 120m (390ft) wide, this waterfall lies on the Monday River, a tributary of the Paraná. 'Monday' means 'stolen river' in Guaraní. The surrounding forest is semi-deciduous, part of the Alto Paraná Atlantic forests ecoregion.

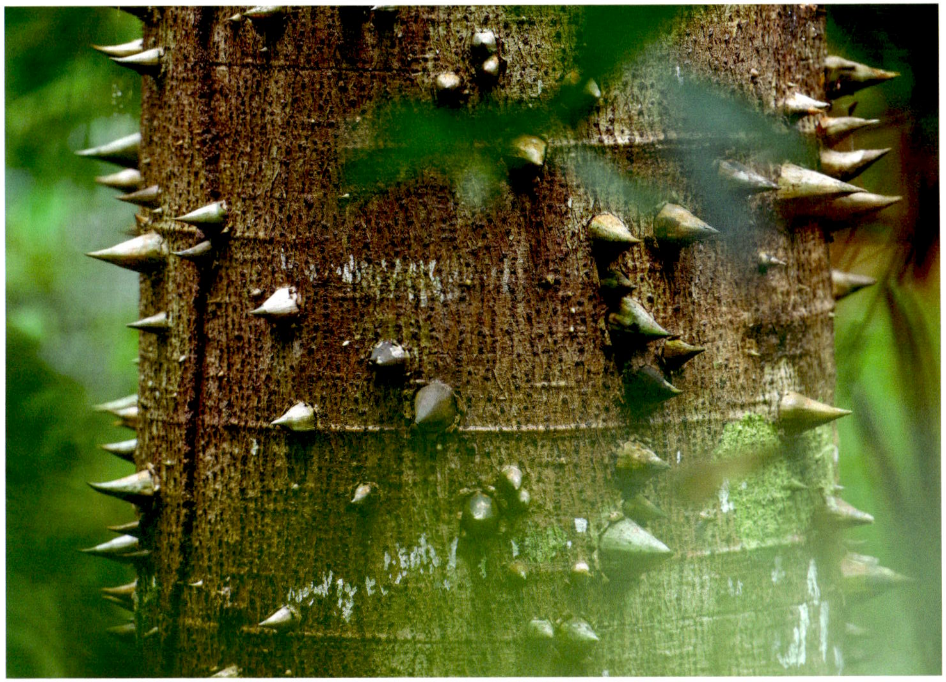

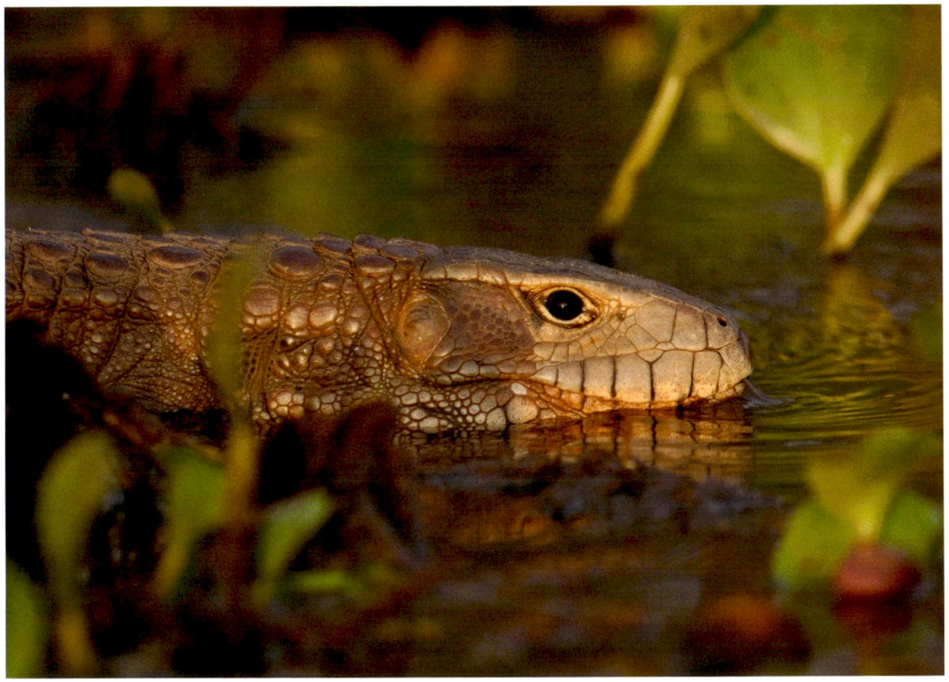

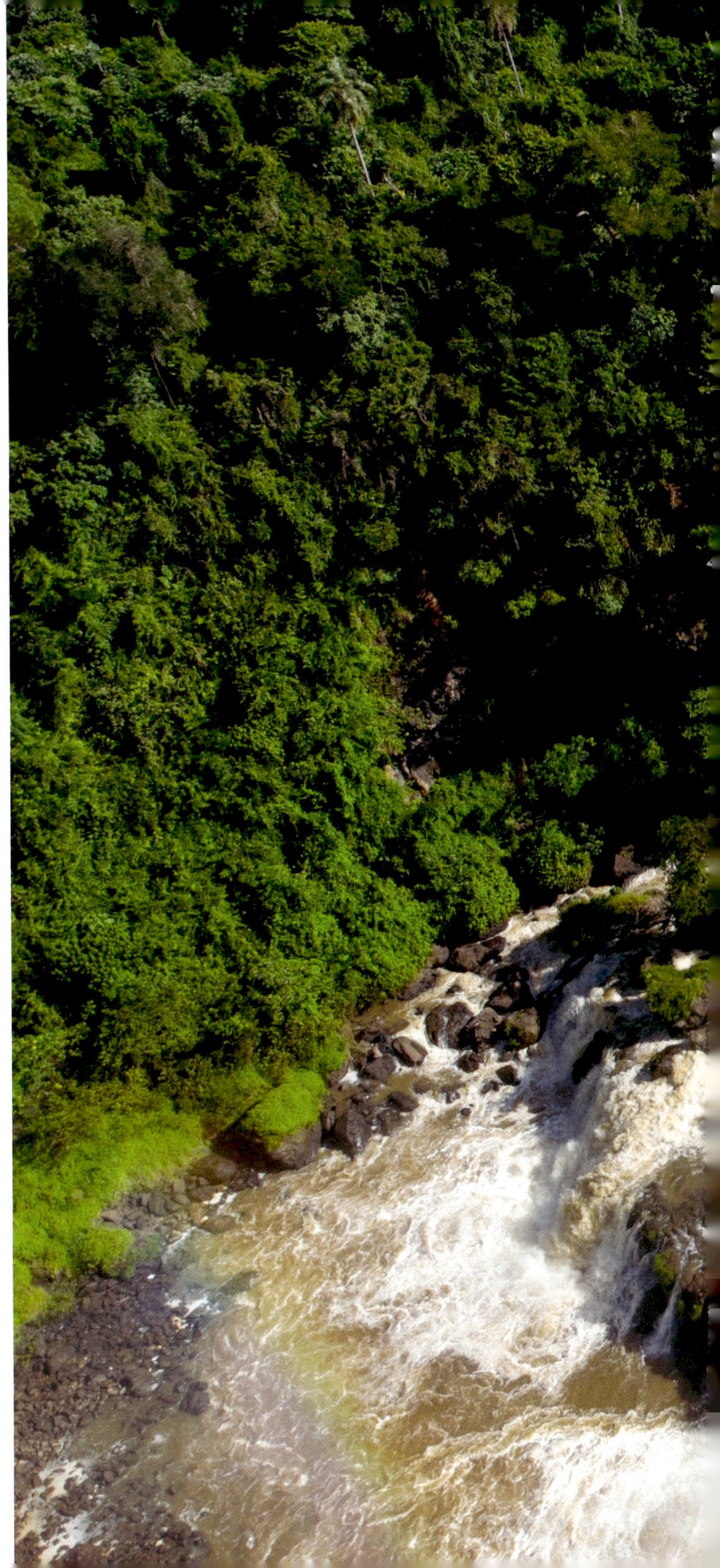

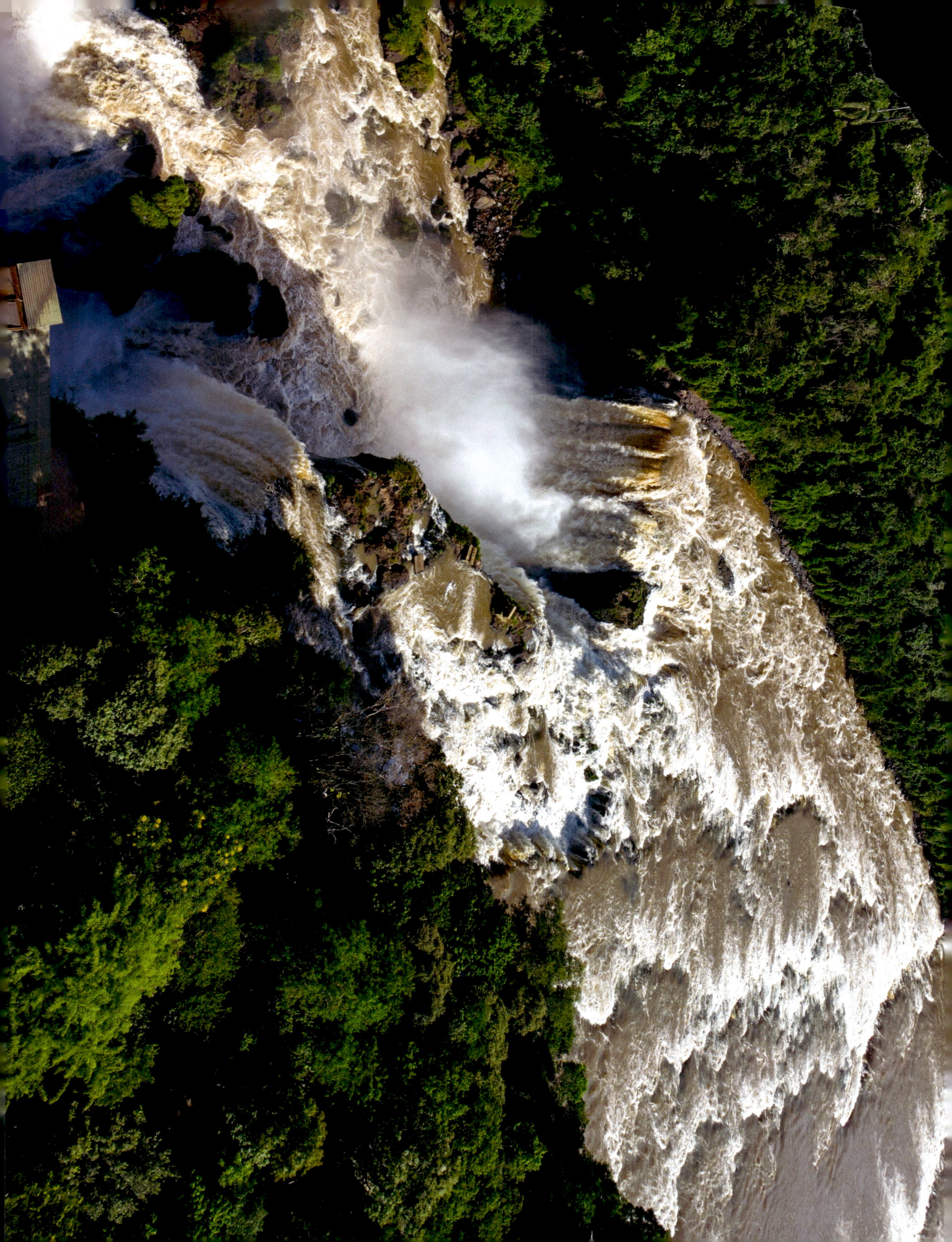

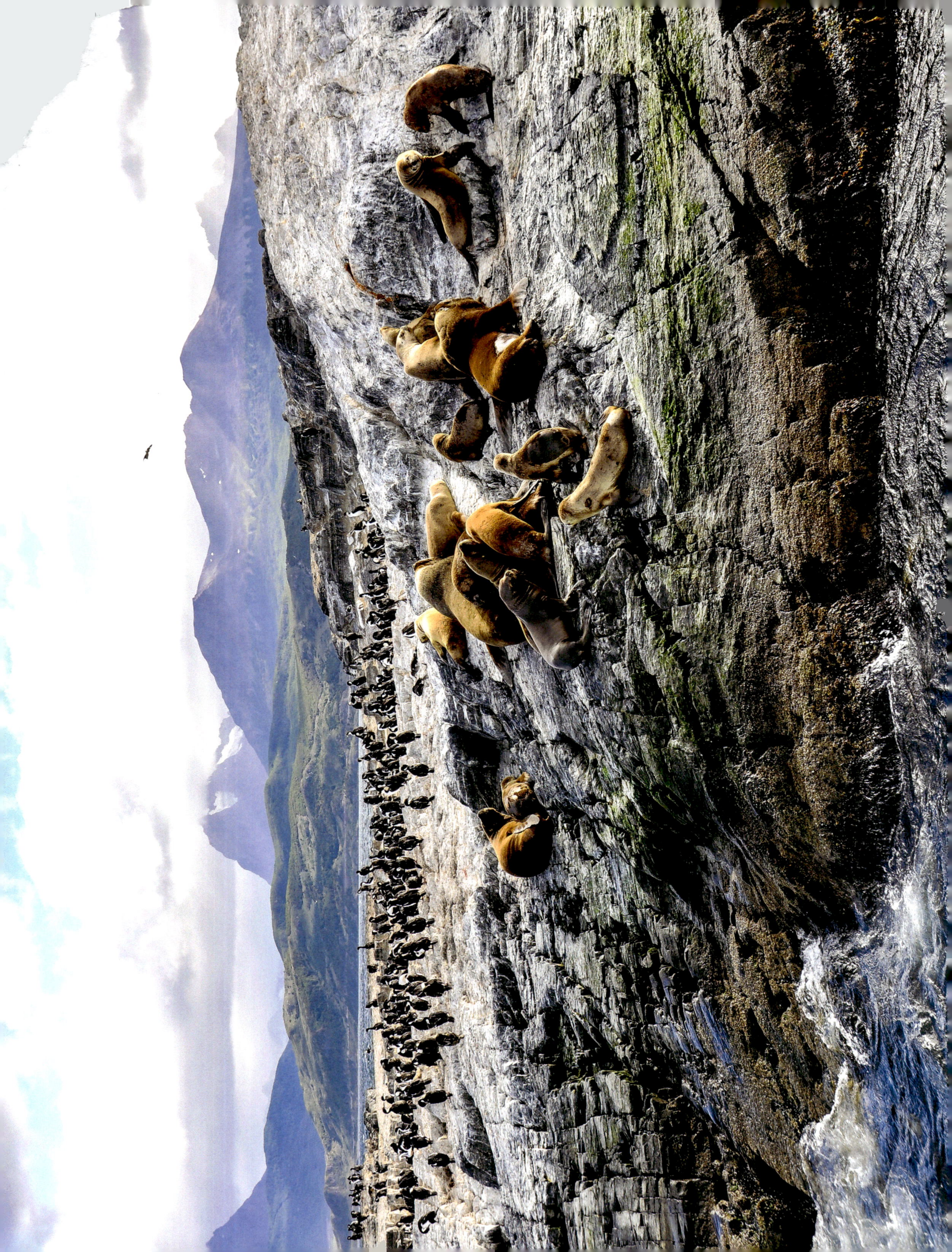

Argentina and Chile

This is a region of extraordinary geographical extremes and landmarks. In Argentina's Southern Andes towers the continent's highest mountain: Aconcagua (6967m; 22,858ft). Just over the border in Chile is the world's highest volcano, Ojos del Salado (6893m; 22,615ft). In fact, nine of the 10 highest peaks outside Asia lie in the Southern Andes, which form the border between Chile and Argentina. Just as the mountains and volcanoes of the Andes were made by violent tectonic activity, so too was the continent's lowest point: eastern Argentina's Laguna del Carbón, 105m (344ft) below sea level, which lies in a graben (a land depression between two faults). Back on the western side of the continent, caught in the rain shadows of the Andes and the Chilean Coastal Range, Chile's Atacama is the world's driest non-polar desert, where some weather stations have never recorded rain. Yet straddling the Chile–Argentina border is the Southern Patagonian Ice Field, the southern hemisphere's largest extrapolar body of ice, holding 4300 cu km (1030 cu miles) of water. Ice has left an indelible mark on Chile's geography, carving deep fjords through the southern and western coasts. This erosion was in part responsible for making Chile the South American country with the most islands: 43,000. South America's largest island is Isla Grande de Tierra del Fuego, shared by Chile and Argentina, which covers 47,992 sq km (18,530 sq miles). The Argentine portion of the island boasts Ushuaia, which with a latitude of 54° 48' 7" south, is considered the world's southernmost city.

OPPOSITE:
Isla de los Lobos, Beagle Channel, Ushuaia, Argentina
Named after Charles Darwin's ship, the HMS *Beagle*, this channel runs through the Tierra del Fuego Archipelago, providing a route between the Atlantic and Pacific Oceans. South American fur seals and South American sea lions can be seen resting on its islands, which are also breeding sites for Magellanic and southern rockhopper penguins.

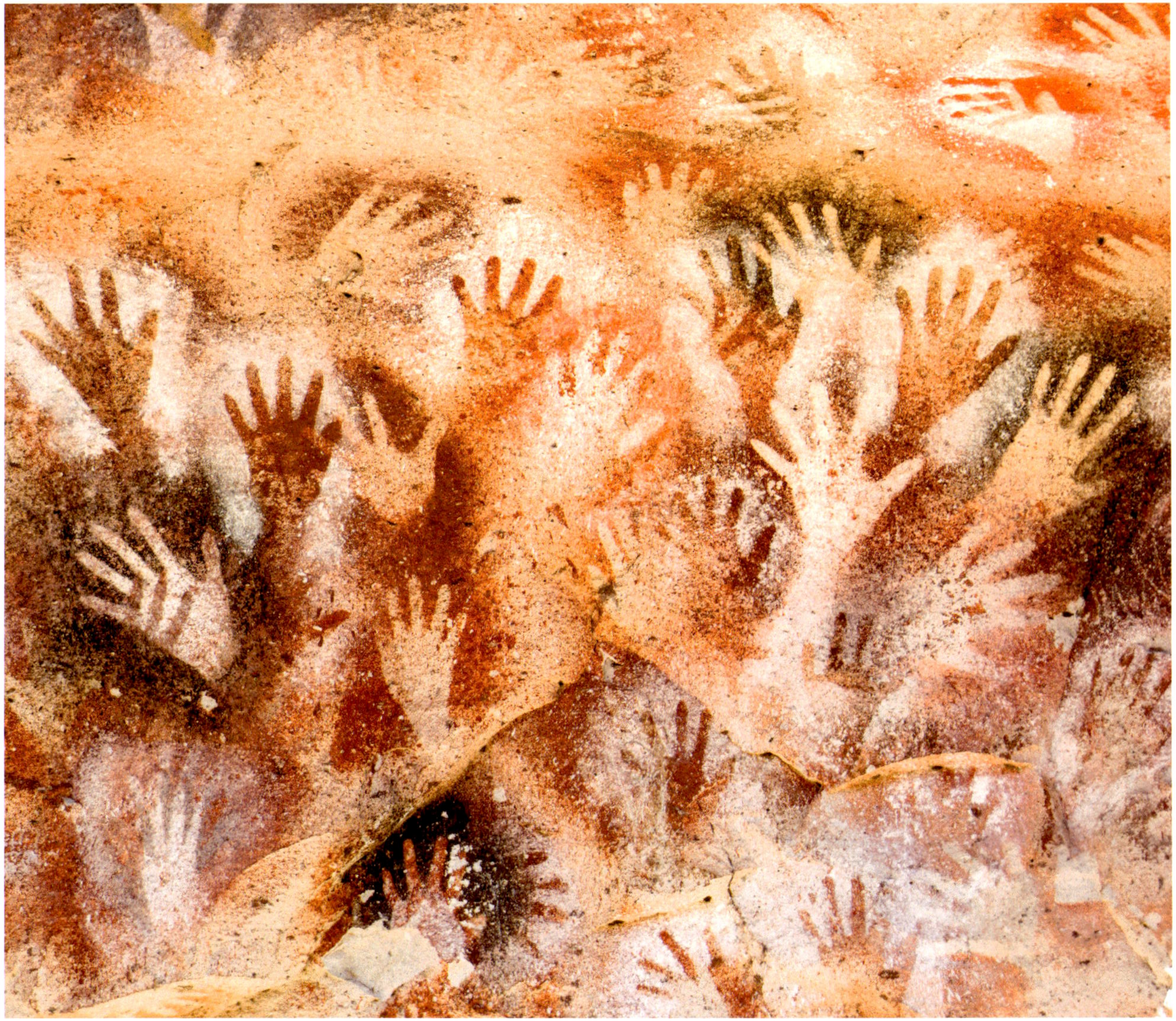

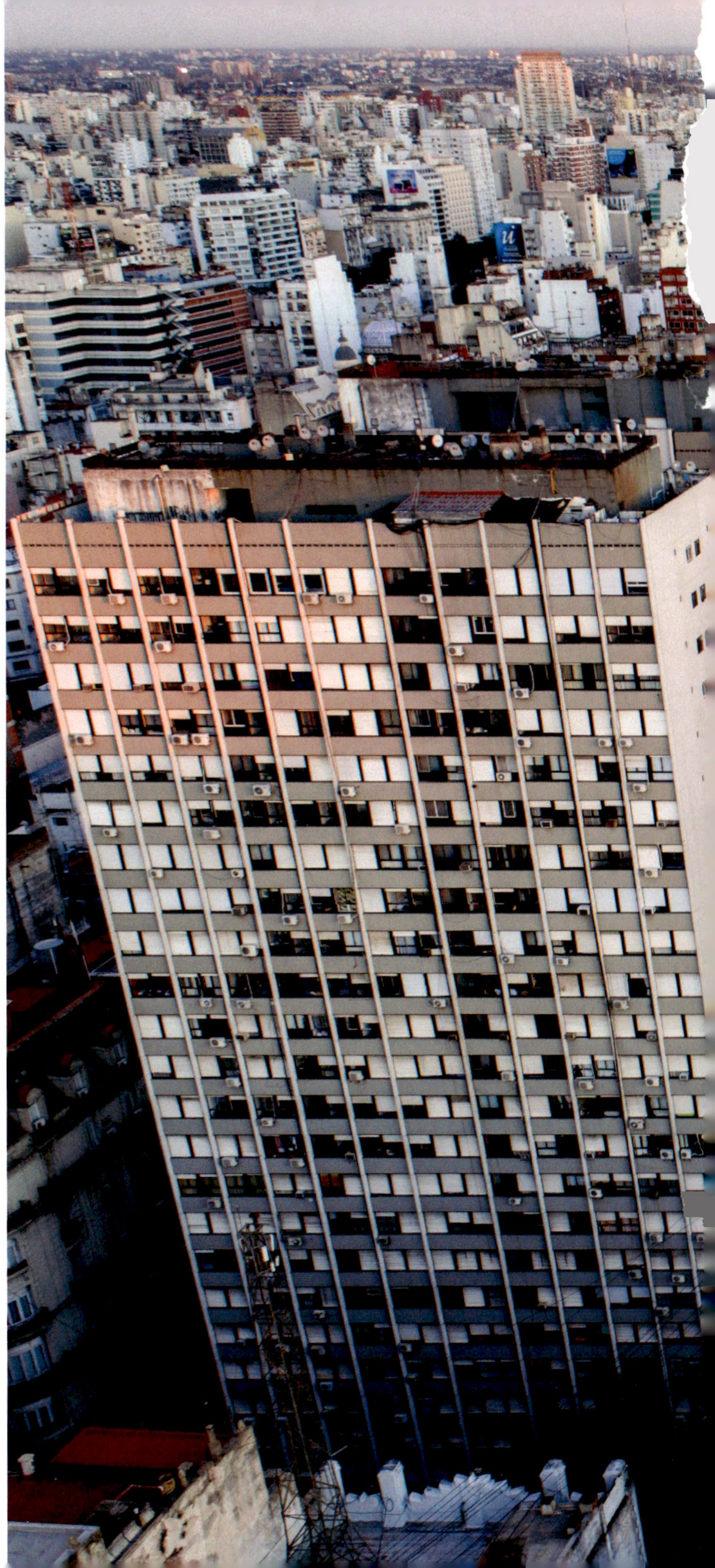

ABOVE:

Cueva de las Manos, Santa Cruz, Argentina

The 'Cave of the Hands' features hundreds of hand paintings made between 7300 BCE and 700 CE. These were created by holding a paint-filled bone pipe with the painter's dominant hand, then blowing paint over the other hand. As can be seen, the rate of right- and left-handedness was similar then and now.

RIGHT:

Palacio Barolo, Buenos Aires, Argentina

In the centre foreground of this photograph stands Palacio Barolo, which was the tallest building in Buenos Aires between its completion, in 1923, and 1936. The office building's design by Italian architect Mario Palanti incorporates Art Nouveau, Art Deco and Gothic Revival features.

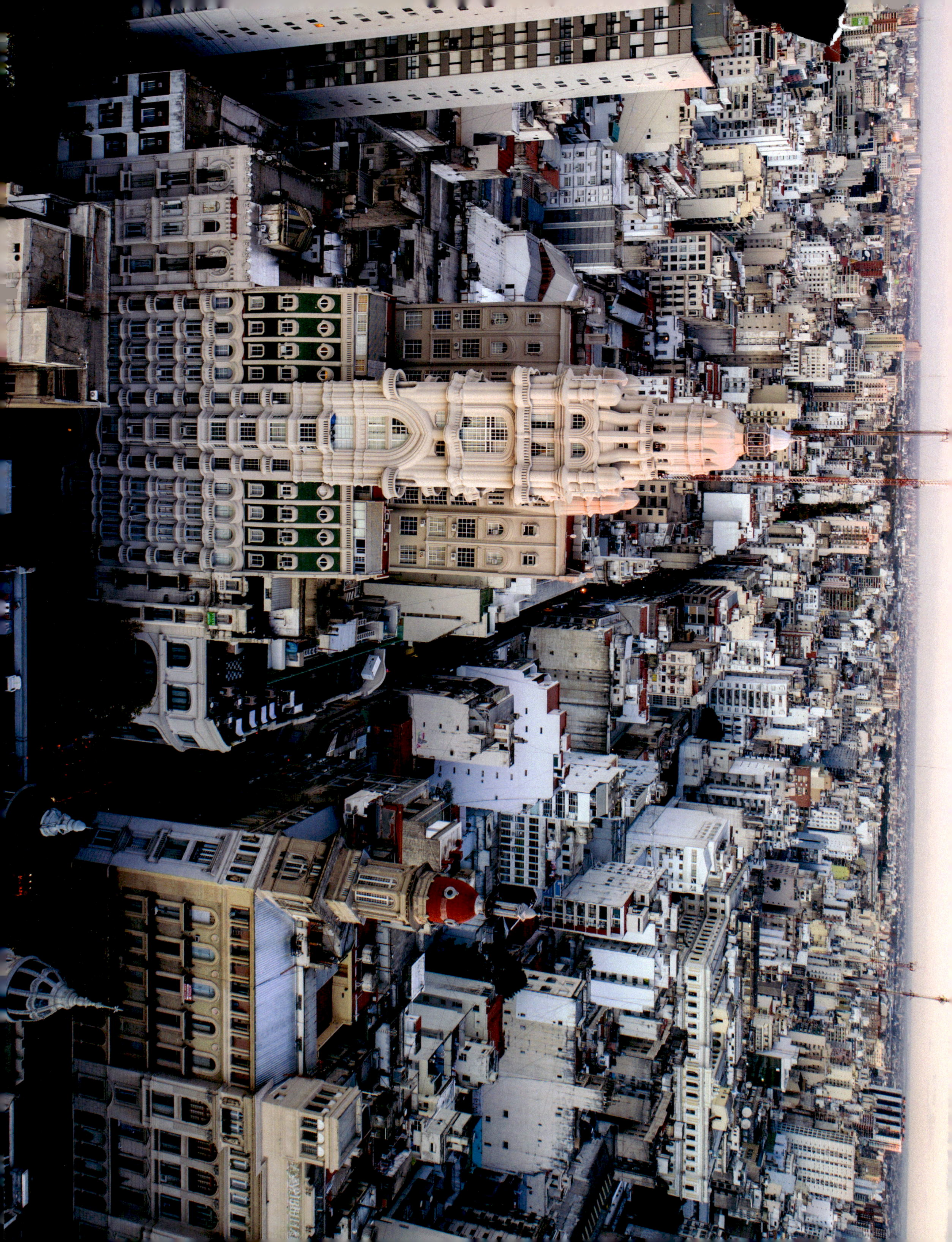

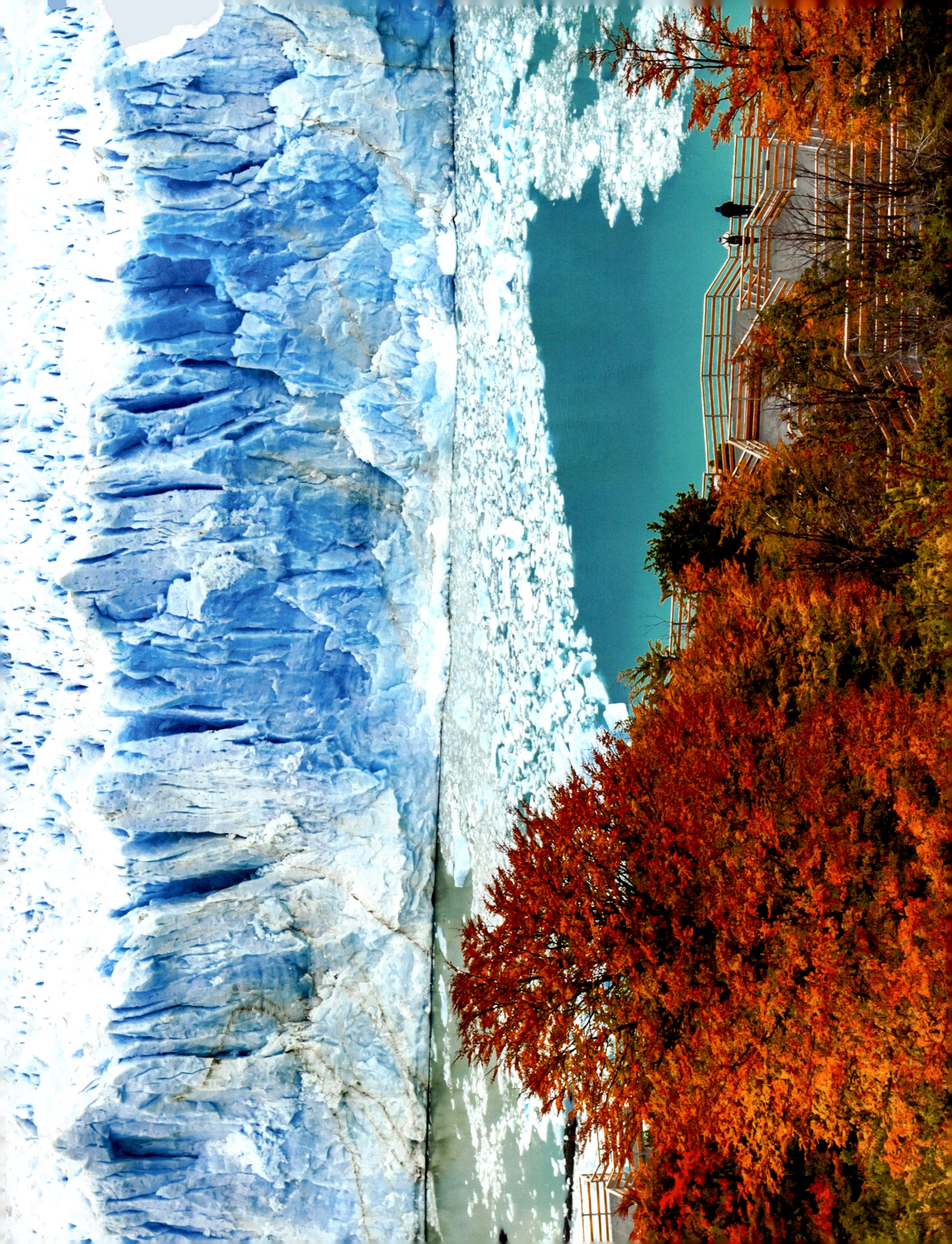

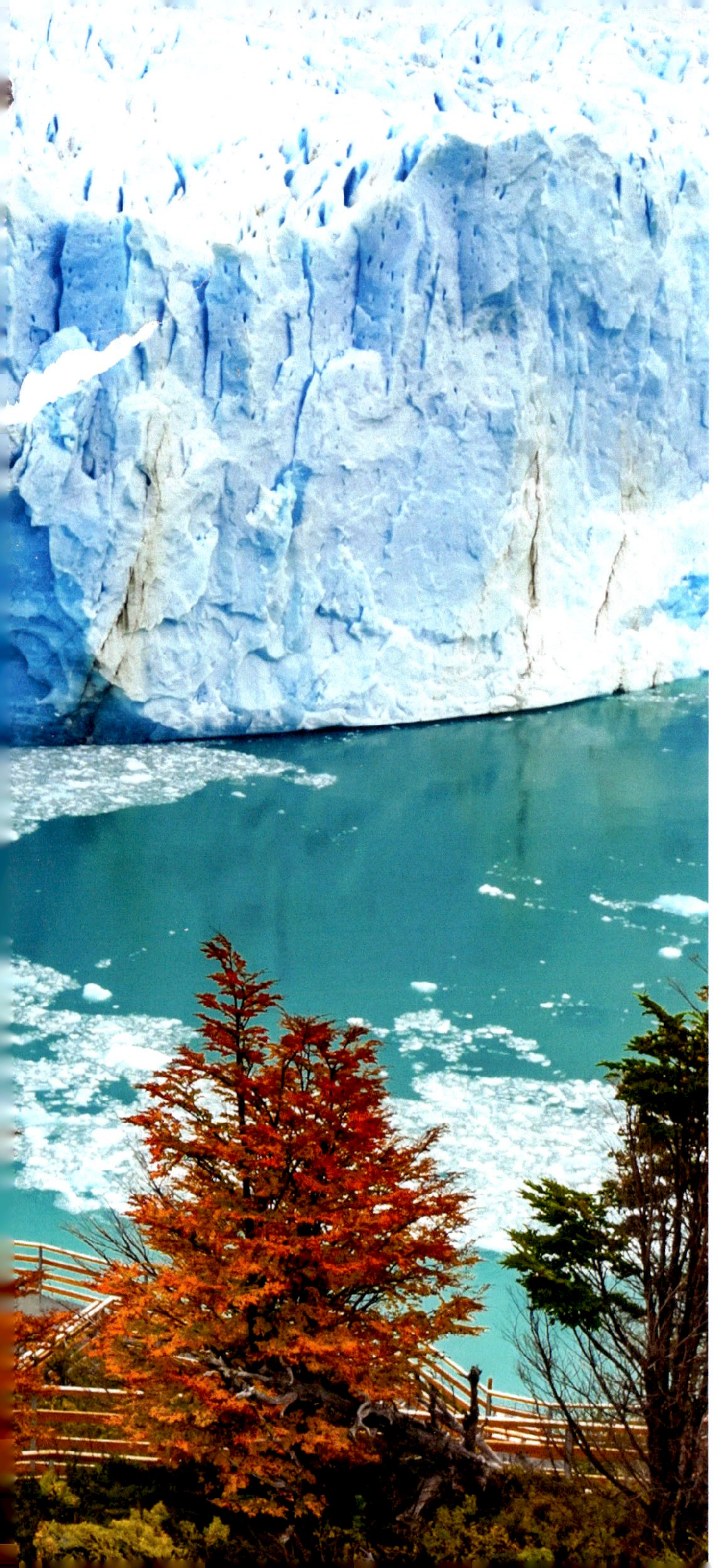

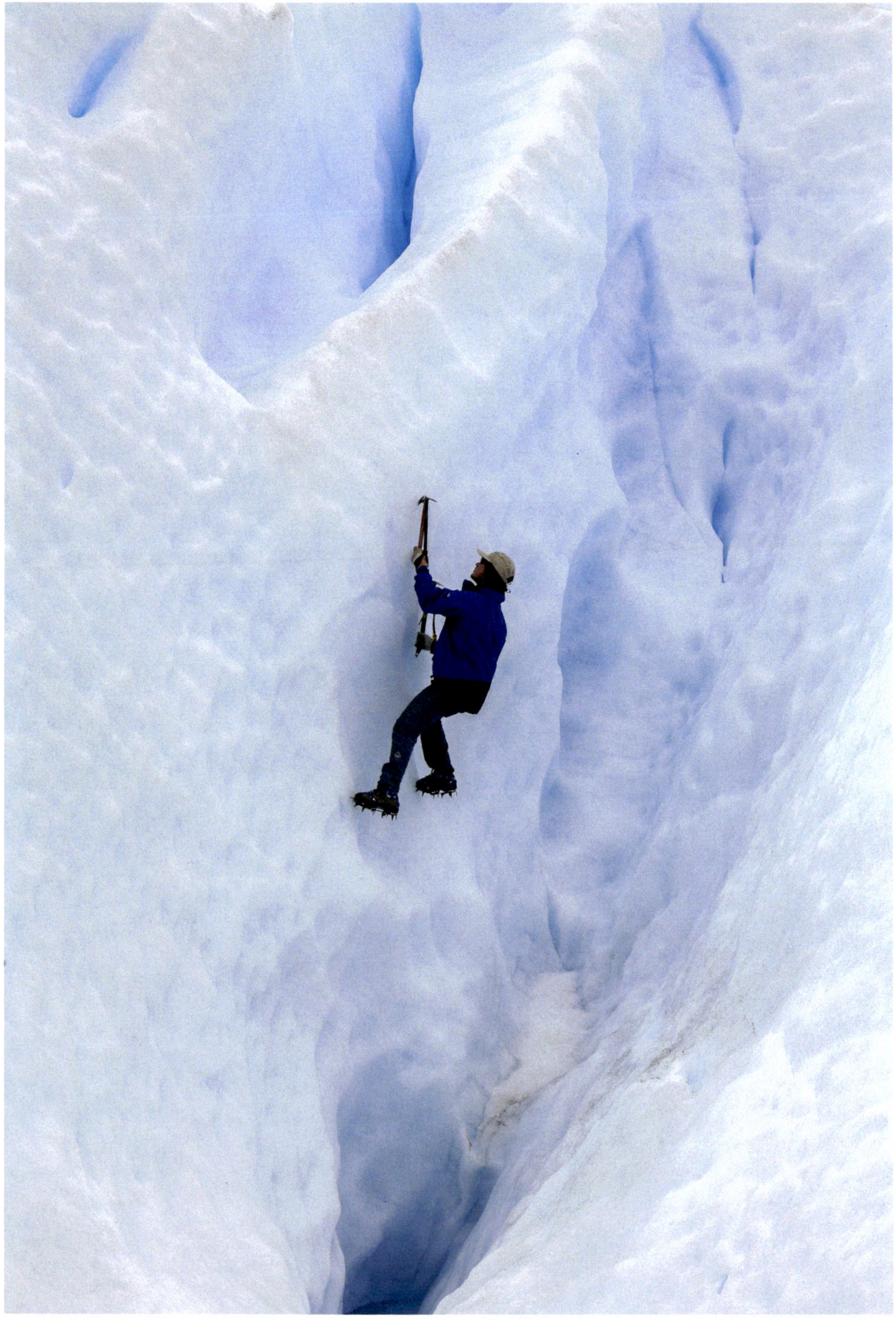

LEFT AND FAR LEFT:
Perito Moreno Glacier, Los Glaciares National Park, Argentina
Around 30km (19 miles) long, this glacier is one of 48 fed by the Southern Patagonian Ice Field, which lies high in the Andes on the border of Argentina and Chile. The vast ice field covers an area of 16,480 sq km (6360 sq miles).

OVERLEAF LEFT:
Basilica y Convento de San Francisco, Salta, Argentina
This basilica's heavily ornamented Italianate façade was completed in 1872. One of the exterior's most unusual features is the archways' faux curtains made of stucco.

OVERLEAF RIGHT:
Salta, Argentina
With its Spanish-style architecture, cobbled streets and pretty plazas, Salta's historic centre resembles an Andalusian town. In addition to people of Spanish descent, Salta's population includes a large Italian community as well as Wichí, Qulla and Guarani peoples.

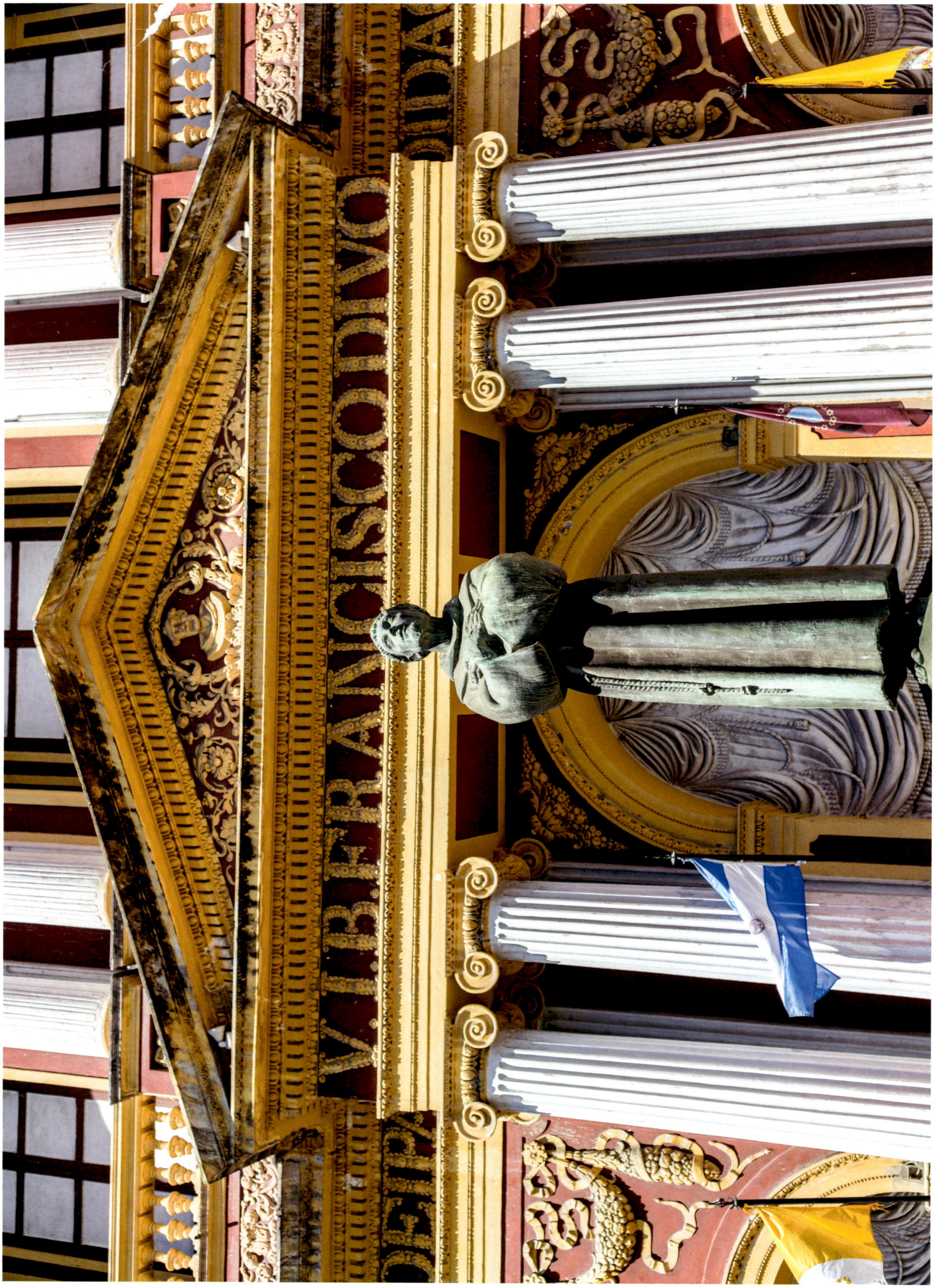

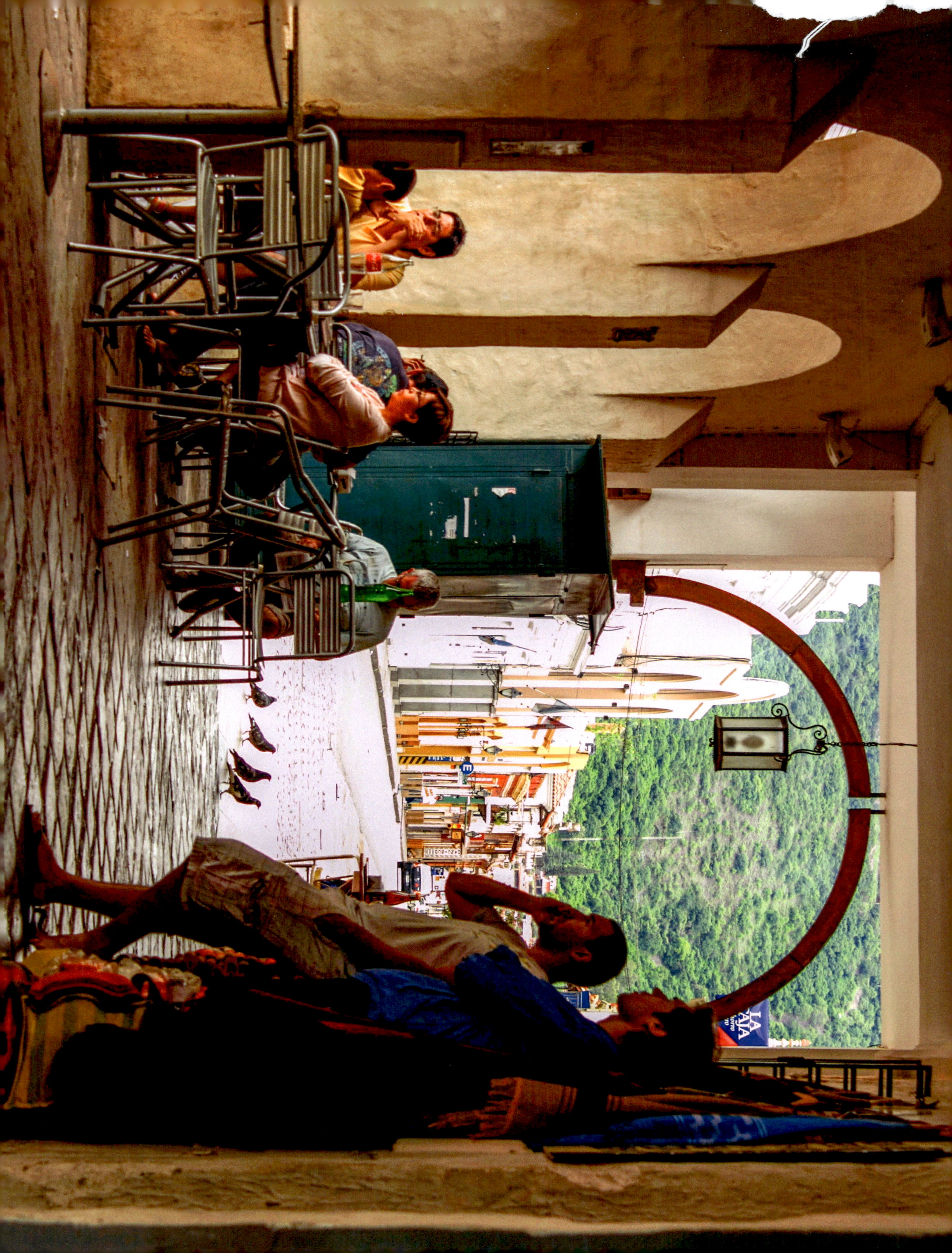

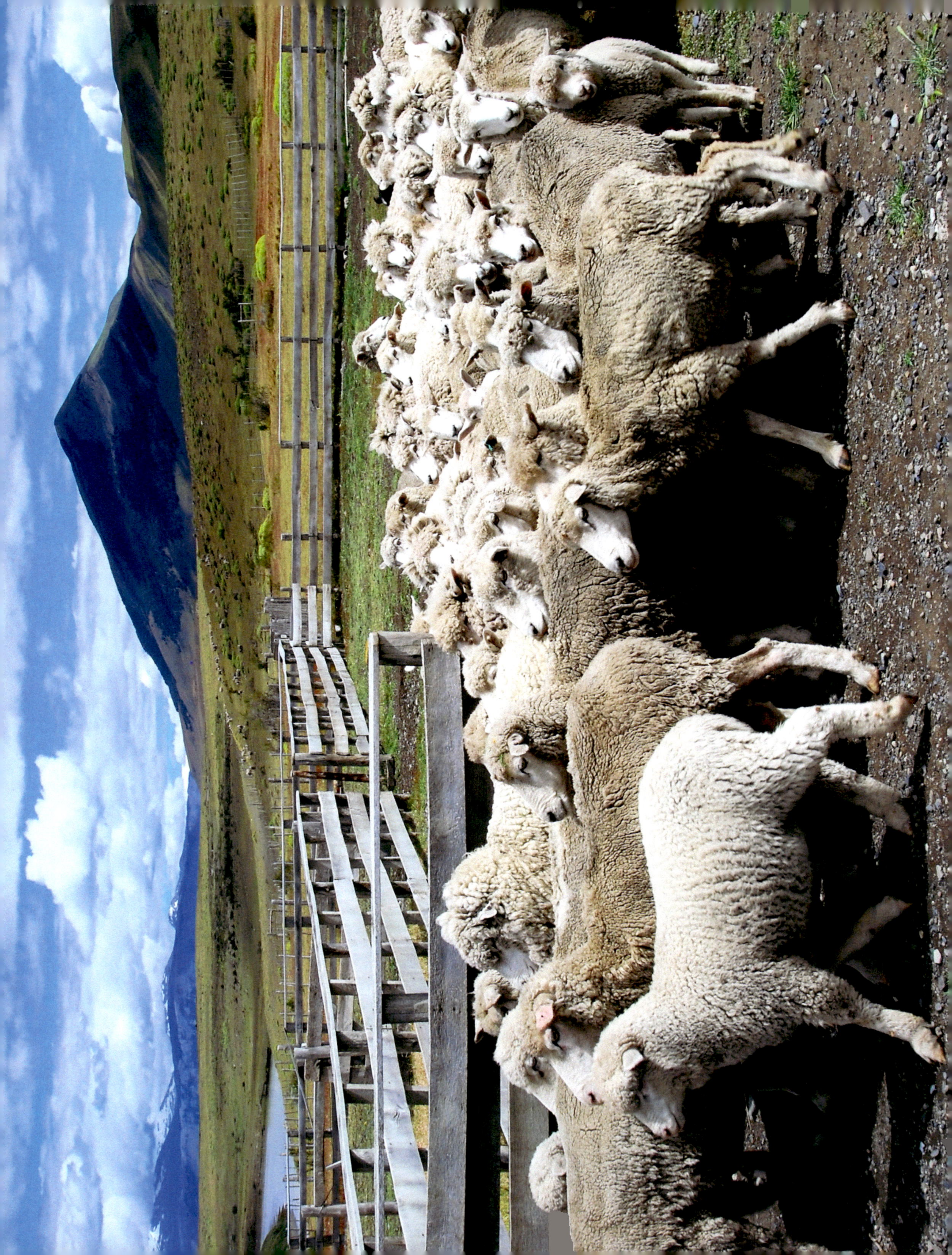

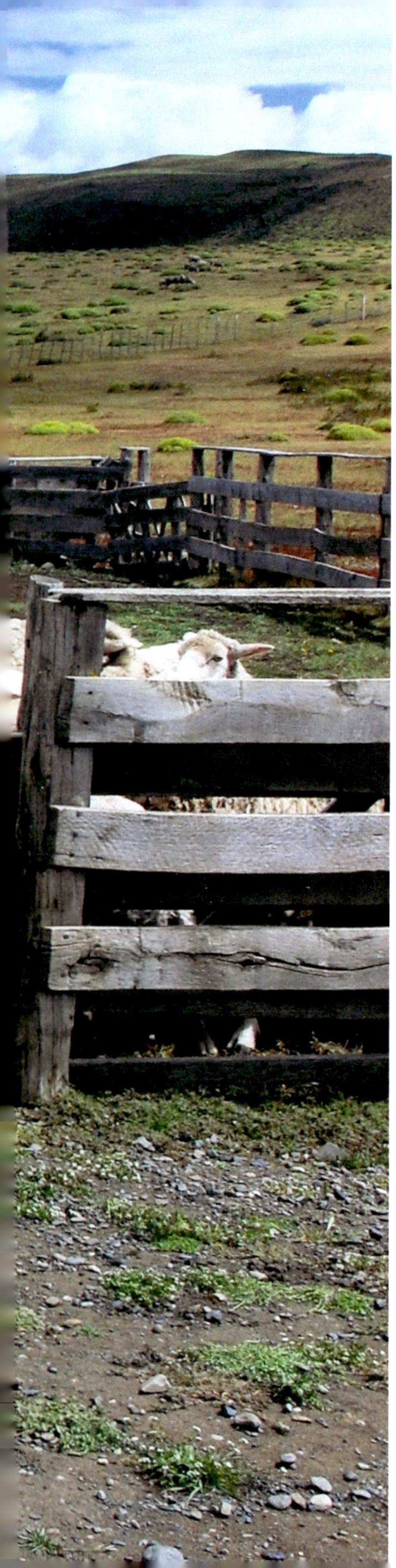

LEFT:
***Estancia*, Patagonia, Argentina**
In the late nineteenth and early twentieth centuries, sheep farming boomed on the Patagonian grasslands, attracting immigrants from as far afield as the UK. Plenty of sheep *estancias* remain, but now account for a small fraction of the region's exports.

RIGHT TOP:
La Bombonera, Buenos Aires, Argentina
Completed in 1940, this iconic stadium soon gained the nickname Bombonera due to its resemblance to a chocolate box. It is the home ground of Boca Juniors football team, winners of 22 major international titles.

RIGHT BOTTOM LEFT:
Brewing *Mate*, Argentina
First drunk by the Guaraní and Tupi peoples, *mate* is Argentina's national drink. It is made by steeping caffeine-rich *Ilex paraguariensis* leaves in hot water, then drunk using a filtered metal straw called a *bombilla*.

RIGHT BOTTOM RIGHT:
***Asado*, Argentina**
A traditional Argentine barbecue consists of beef, chicken, chorizo, *morcilla* (black sausage) and *molleja* (sweetbread) cooked by an *asador* over a charcoal fire.

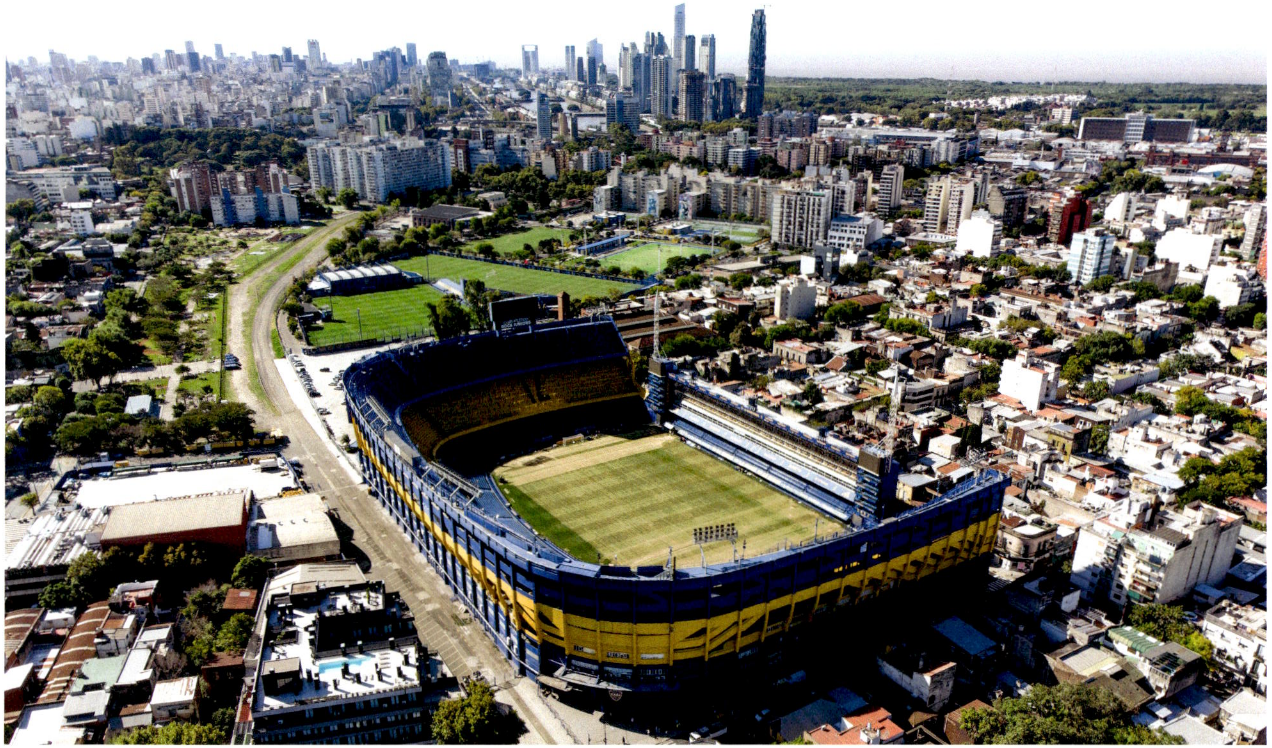

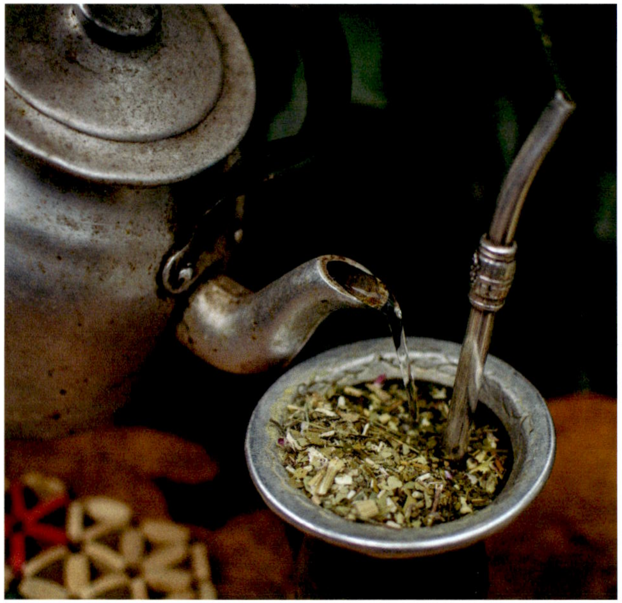

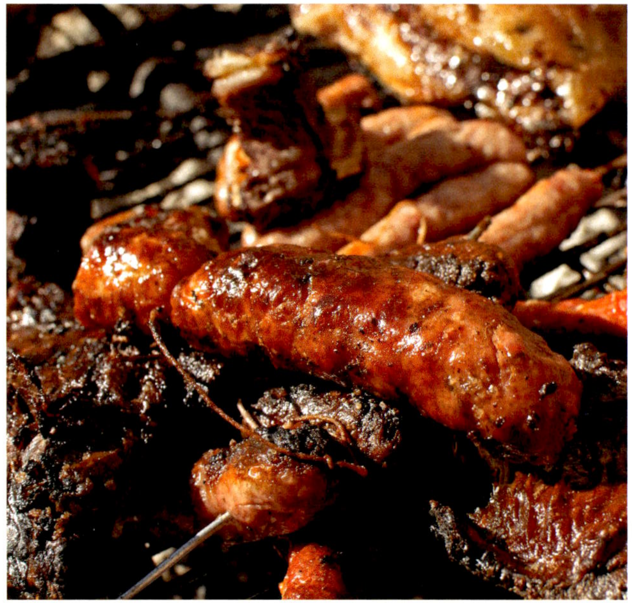

RIGHT:

Tango Dancers, Buenos Aires, Argentina

Tango was born in the 1880s in the bars of ports on the Río de la Plata, on the Argentina–Uruguay border. The dance has both European and African roots, with a key influence the Candombe dances performed by descendants of enslaved Africans.

OPPOSITE:

El Caminito, La Boca, Buenos Aires

This brightly painted, vibrant neighbourhood inspired the famous tango song 'Caminito', written in 1926. This is the place to see tango dancers perform, both on the street and in dedicated clubs, and to visit Italian *bodegóns* (traditional restaurants).

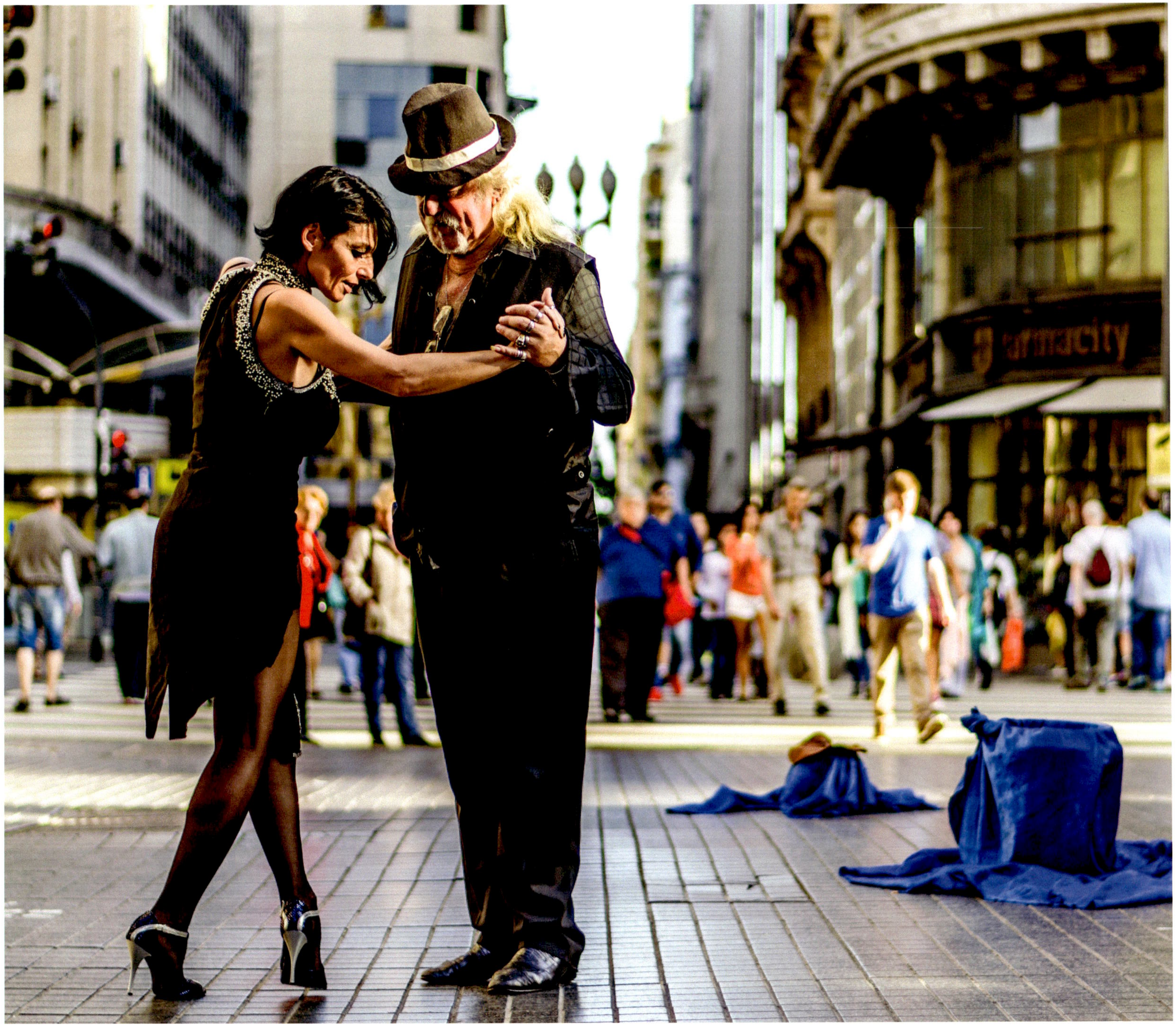

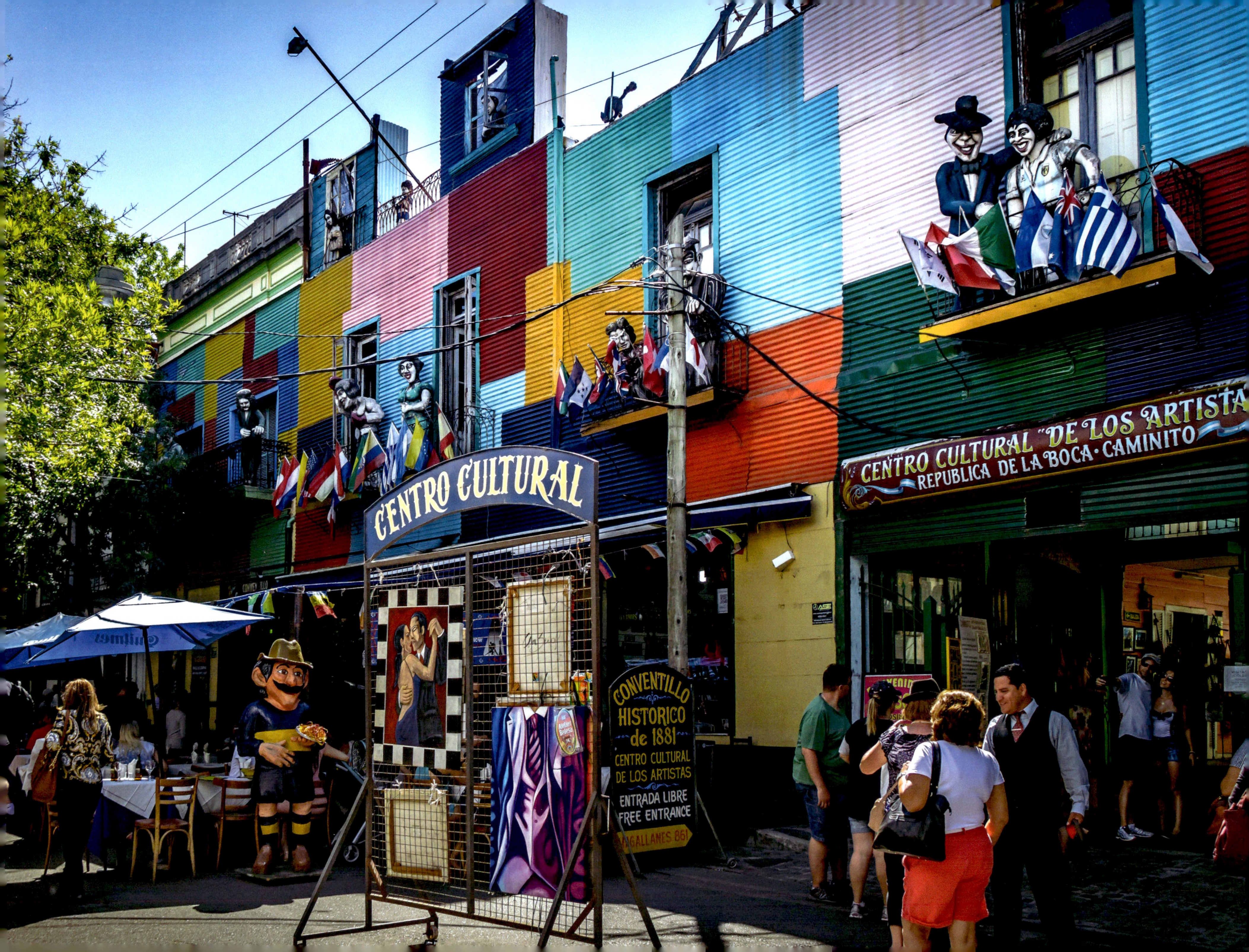
CENTRO CULTURAL
CENTRO CULTURAL "DE LOS ARTISTA
REPUBLICA DE LA BOCA · CAMINITO
CONVENTILLO
HISTORICO
de 1881
CENTRO CULTURAL
DE LOS ARTISTAS
ENTRADA LIBRE
FREE ENTRANCE

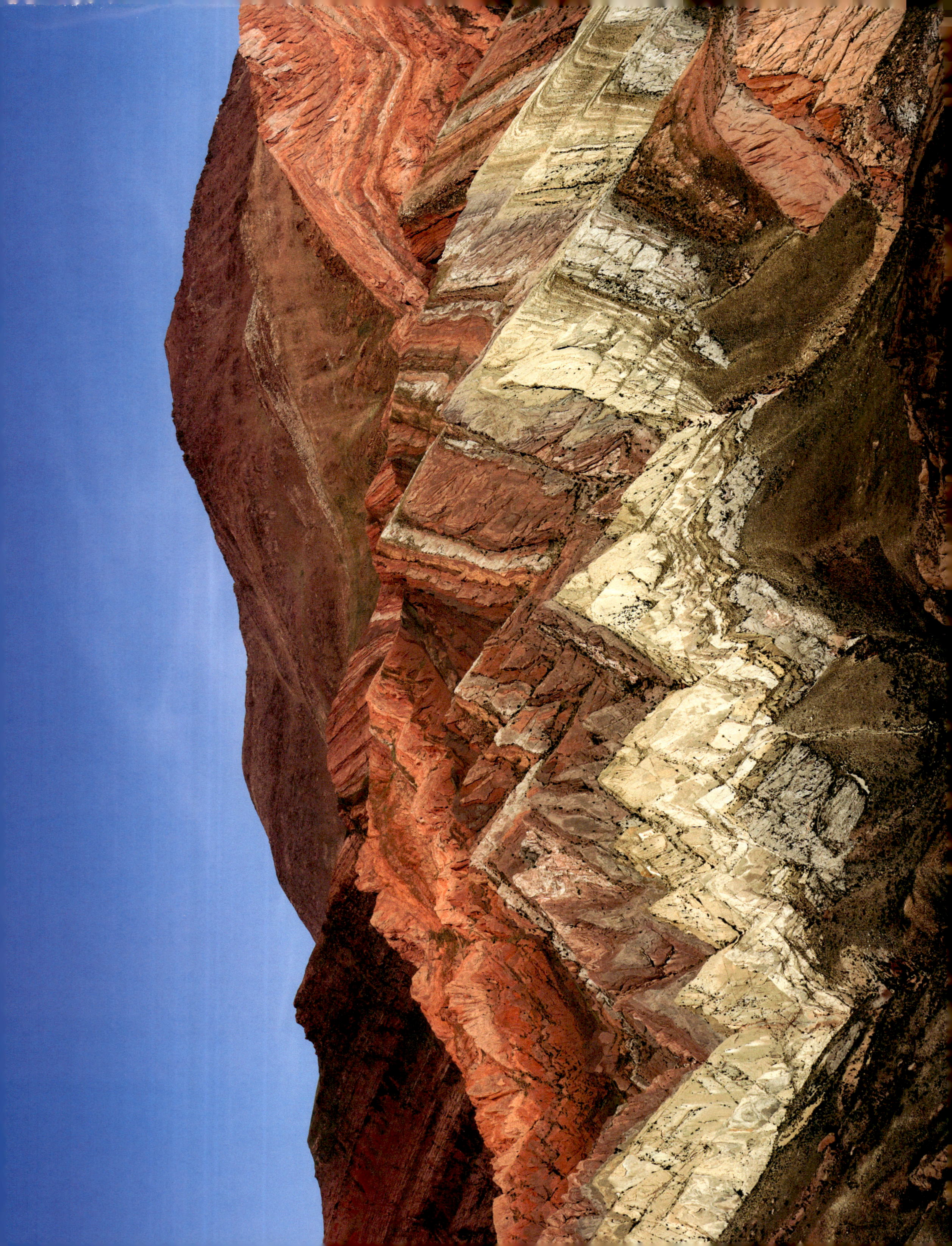

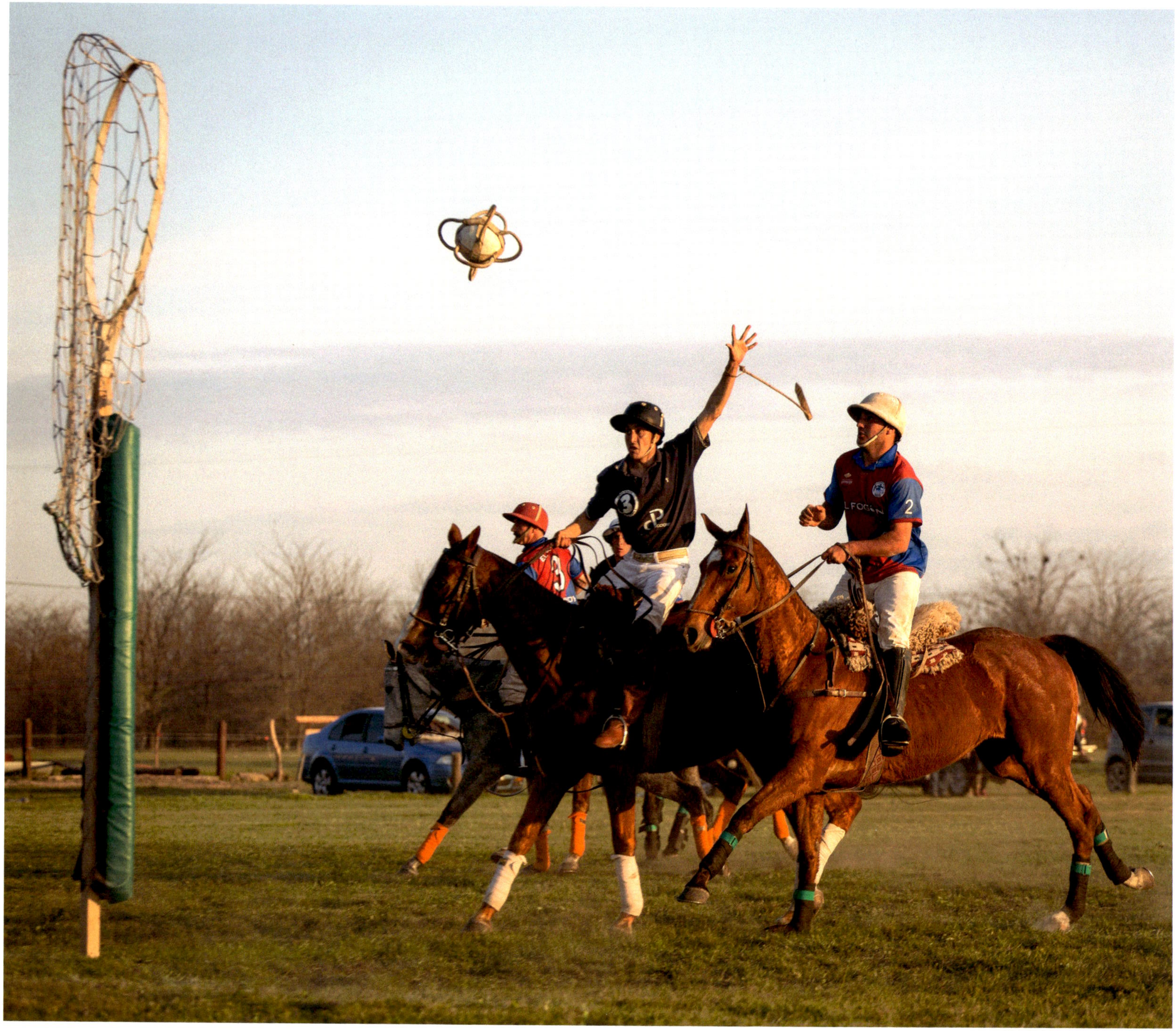

OPPOSITE:

Serranía de Hornocal, Jujuy, Argentina

The colours of this vivid hillside were created by layers of different minerals, including red iron oxides, as the limestone formed in the shallows and intertidal zone of an inland sea. The layers were later folded and tipped by the collision of the Nazca and South American plates, forming the Andes.

LEFT:

Playing *Pato*, Día de la Tradición, Argentina

Argentina's national sport, *pato* has Indigenous roots and grew wildly popular among the region's gauchos, or cowboys. It involves teams of horseriders throwing a ball through a ring. Matches are often played on 10 November, the birthday of nineteenth-century poet José Hernández, who wrote the beloved poem 'El Gaucho Martín Fierro'.

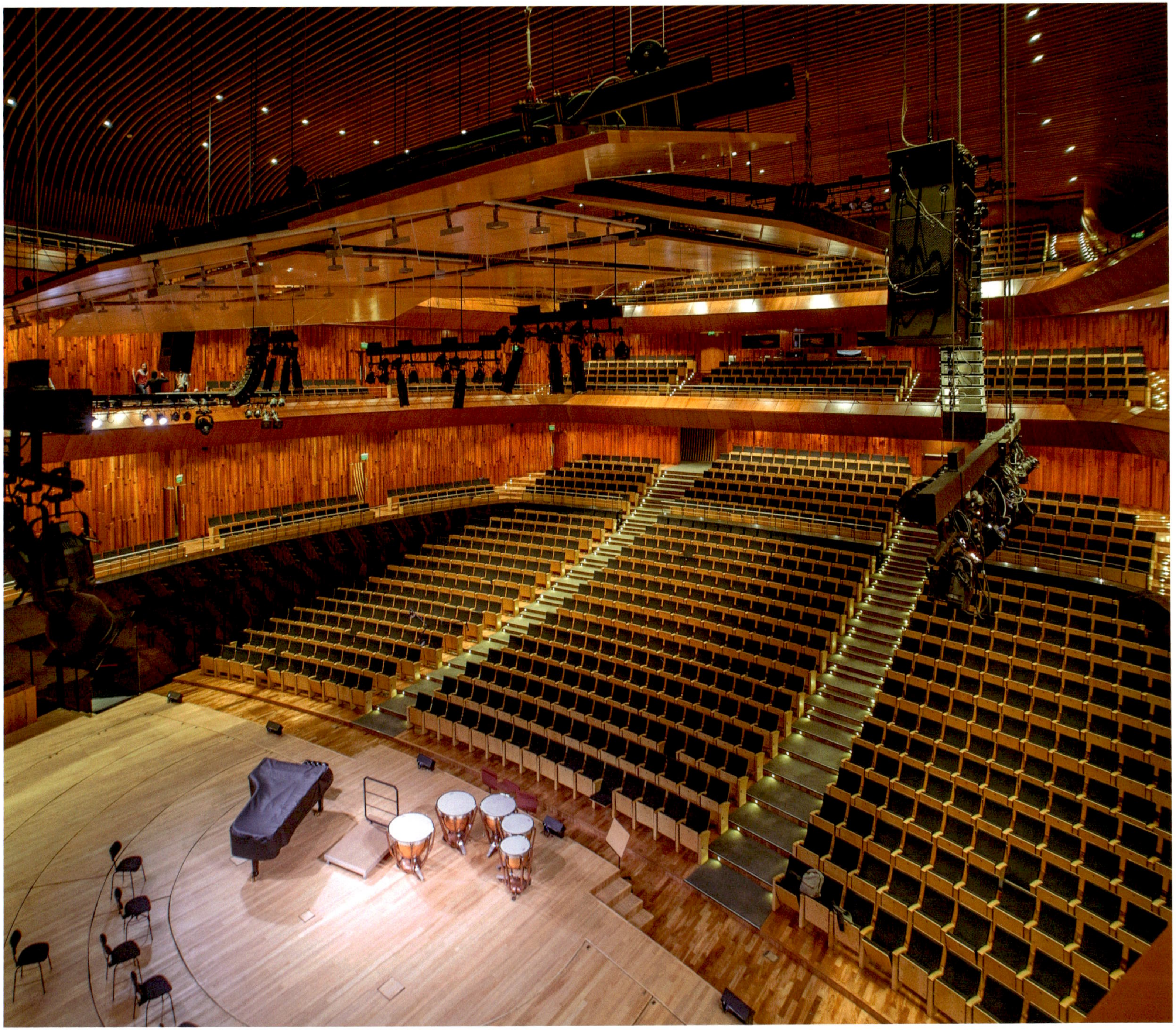

RIGHT:

Libertad Palace, Buenos Aires, Argentina
Also called the Domingo Faustino Sarmiento Cultural Centre, this is South America's largest cultural centre. Housed in the 1928 Central Post Office, once home to the offices of the Perón administration, the centre has six concert halls and auditoriums, as well as dozens of event spaces and galleries.

OPPOSITE:

Lanín Volcano, Lanín National Park, Argentina
In northern Patagonia, this park protects a region of lakes and temperate forest, where trees such as the lenga beech and monkey-puzzle abound. On the border between Chile and Argentina, the dormant stratovolcano Lanín rises to 3747m (12,293ft).

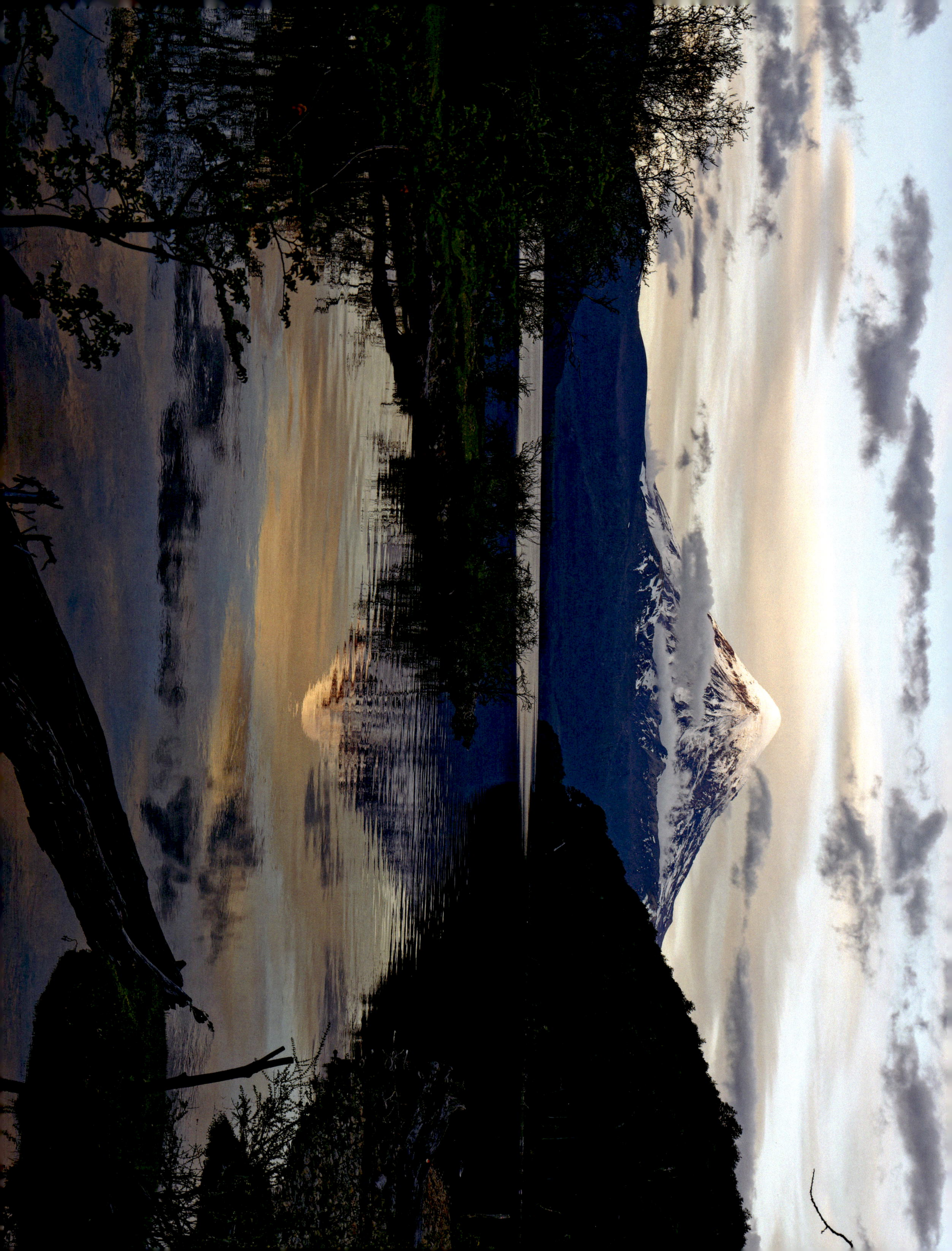

RIGHT:
Teleférico de Santiago, Santiago, Chile
Offering dizzying views of the city and mountains, this cable car ascends the capital's San Cristóbal Hill. The city lies in the Santiago Basin, flanked to the west by the Chilean Coastal Range and to the north, east and south by the Andes and its spurs.

OPPOSITE LEFT:
Ascensor Artillería, Valparaíso, Chile
Sixteen of Valparaíso's historic funiculars are still in use, ascending the port's many steep hills. Opened in 1893, Ascensor Artillería takes two minutes to climb 80m (260ft) with a slope of 27 degrees.

OPPOSITE RIGHT TOP:
Valle Nevado, Chile
From June to October, skiers and snowboarders flock to the Valle Nevado, in the foothills of the Andes, a hair-raising drive east from Santiago. The upscale resort is part of the Three Valleys ski destination.

OPPOSITE RIGHT BOTTOM:
King Penguins, Pinguino Rey Nature Reserve, Tierra del Fuego, Chile
Up to 1m (3.3ft) tall, the king penguin breeds on subantarctic islands. It dives as deep as 300m (980ft) for fish, squid and krill.

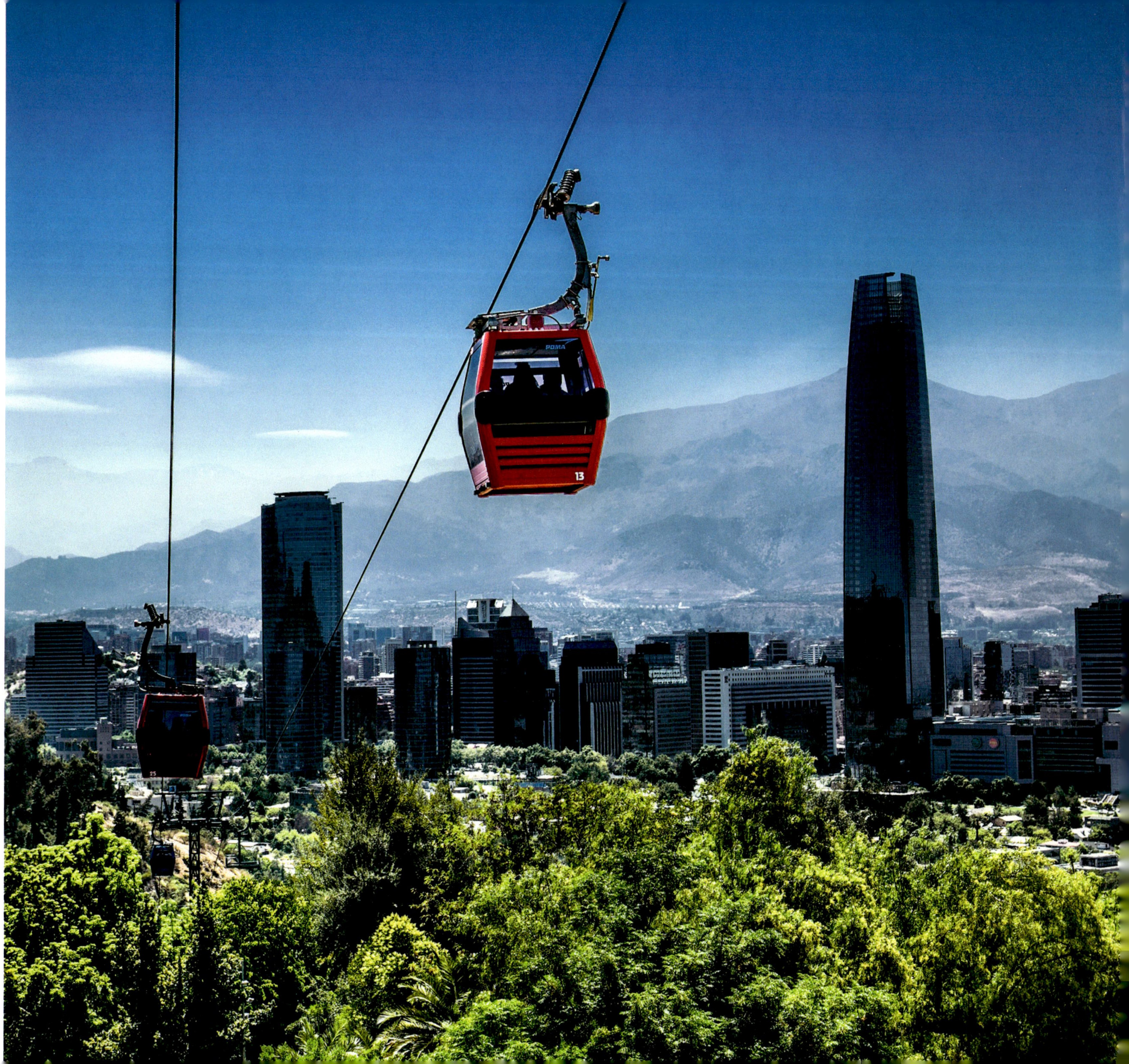

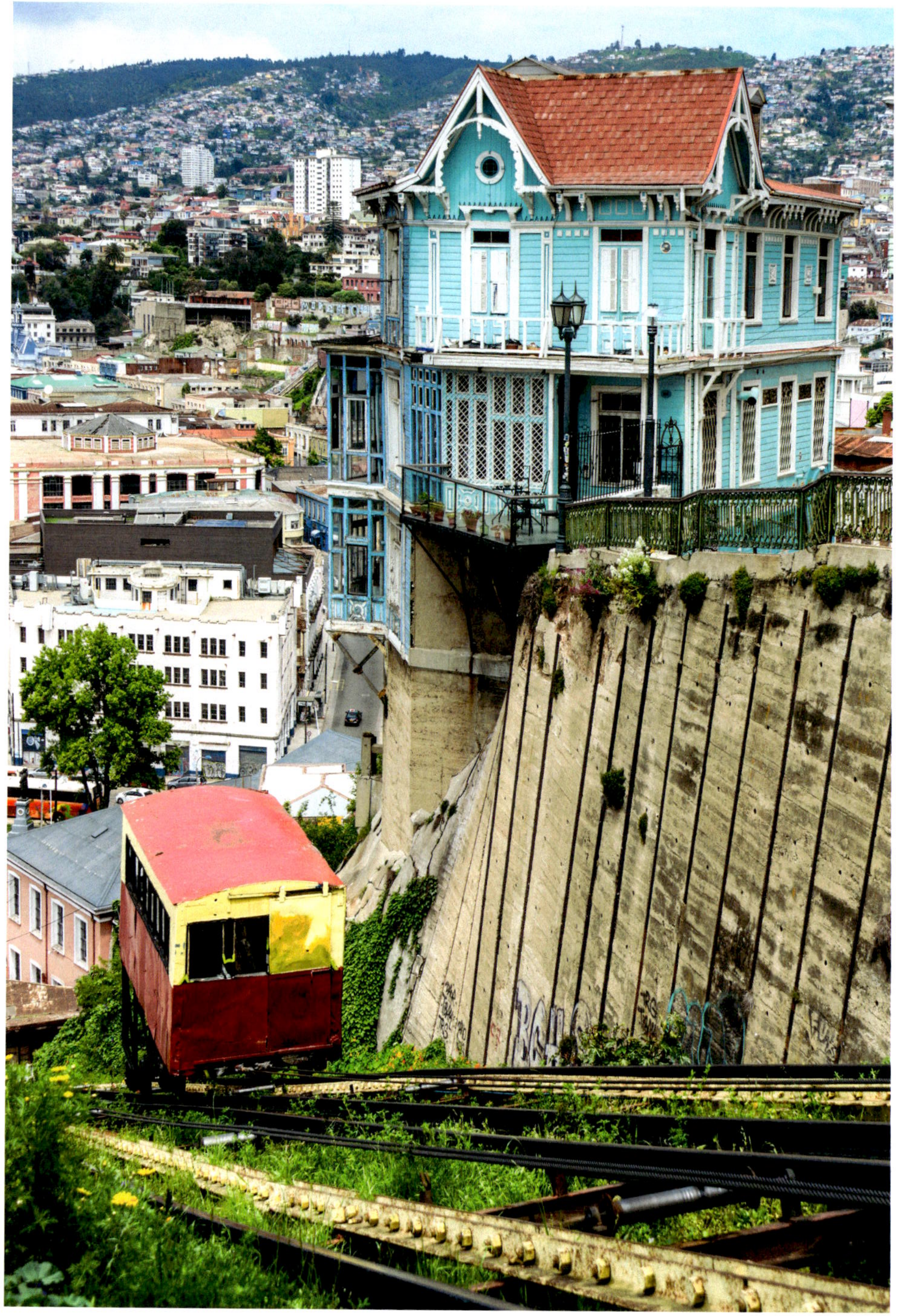

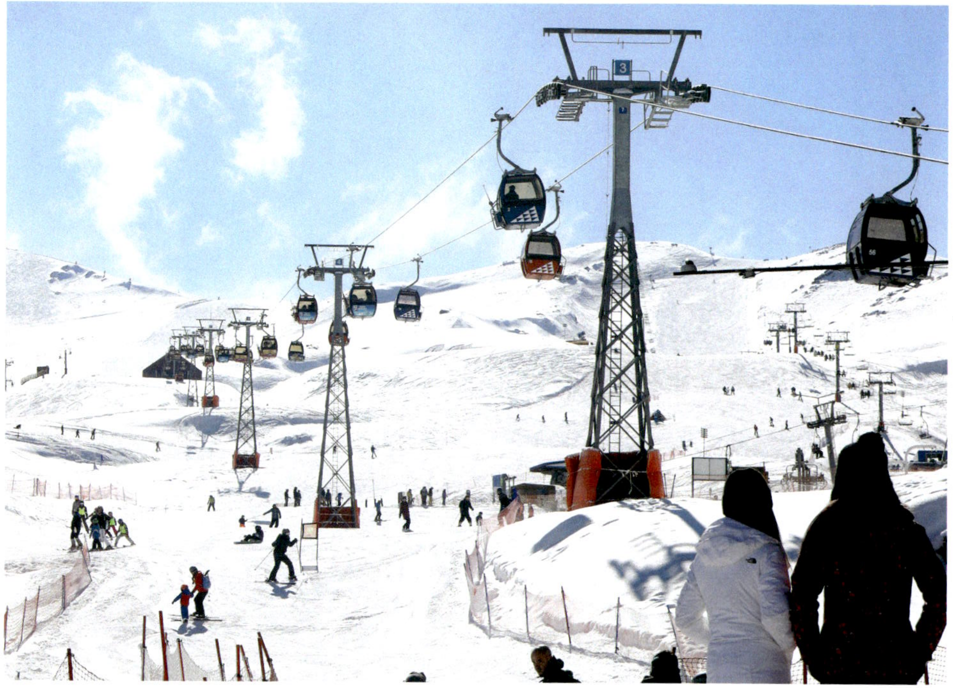

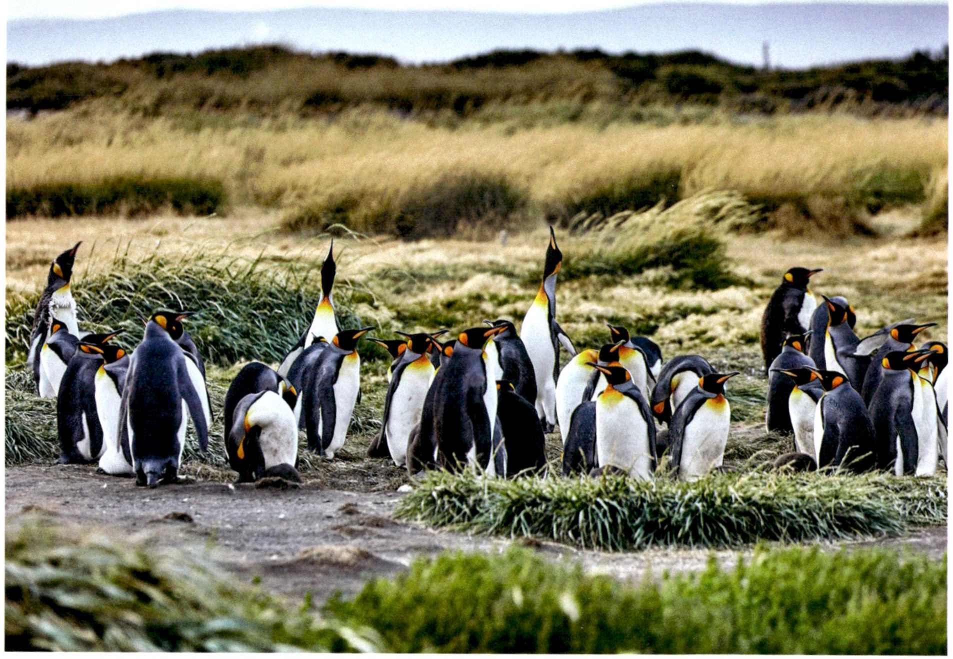

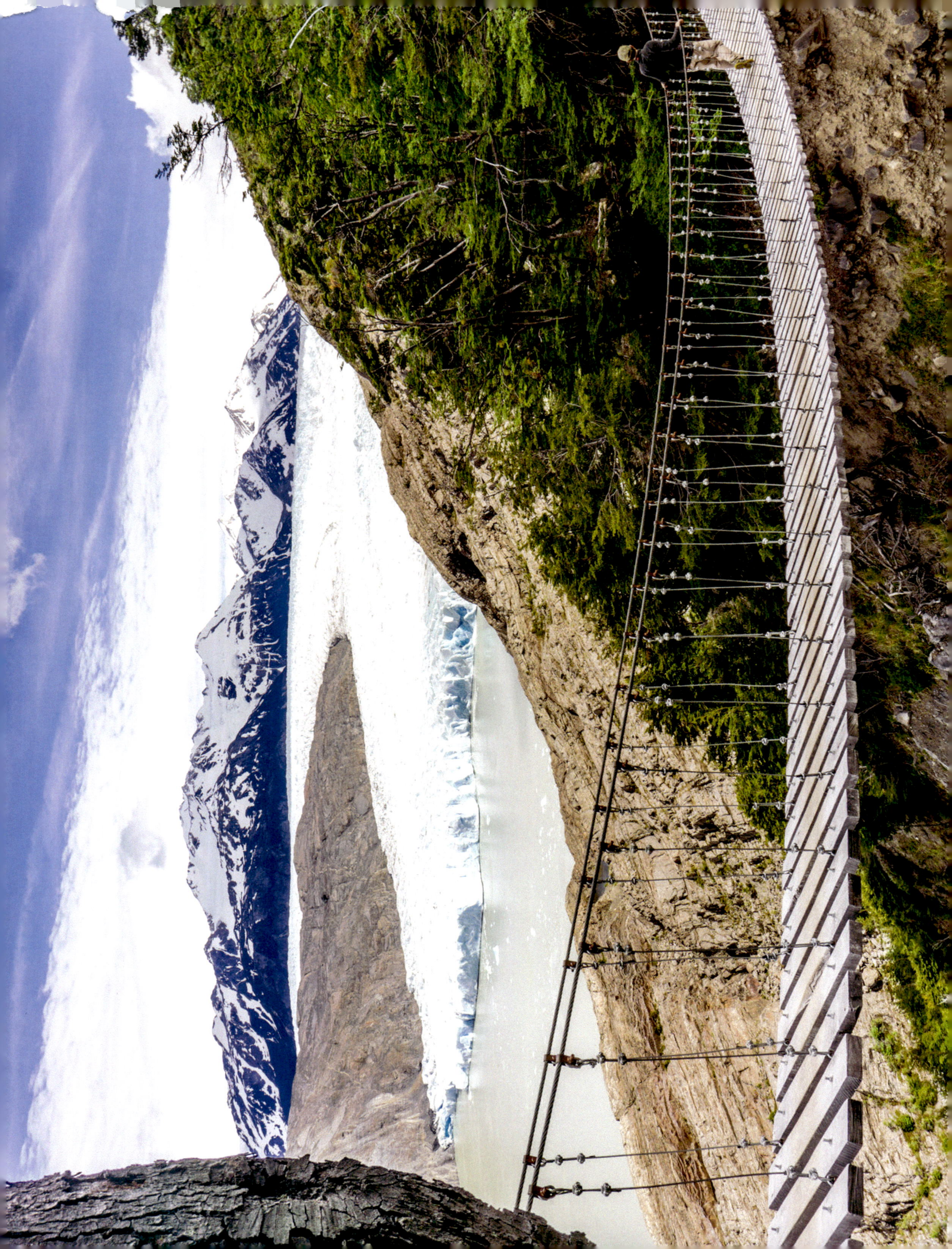

OPPOSITE:

Grey Glacier, Torres del Paine National Park, Chile
Hikers on the five-day W Circuit are rewarded with panoramic views of Grey Glacier. Around 28km (17 miles) long, the glacier descends from the Southern Patagonian Ice Field and calves into Lago Grey. The lake was named by British explorers for its silt-laden grey waters.

RIGHT:

Cuernos del Paine, Torres del Paine National Park
The centrepiece of this national park is the jagged granite Cuernos del Paine, which rise to 2600m (8530ft). In Spanish, *cuernos* means horns, while *paine* means blue in the local Tehuelche language, due to the area's blue lakes. The highest peak, Cuerno Principal, was first climbed in 1968.

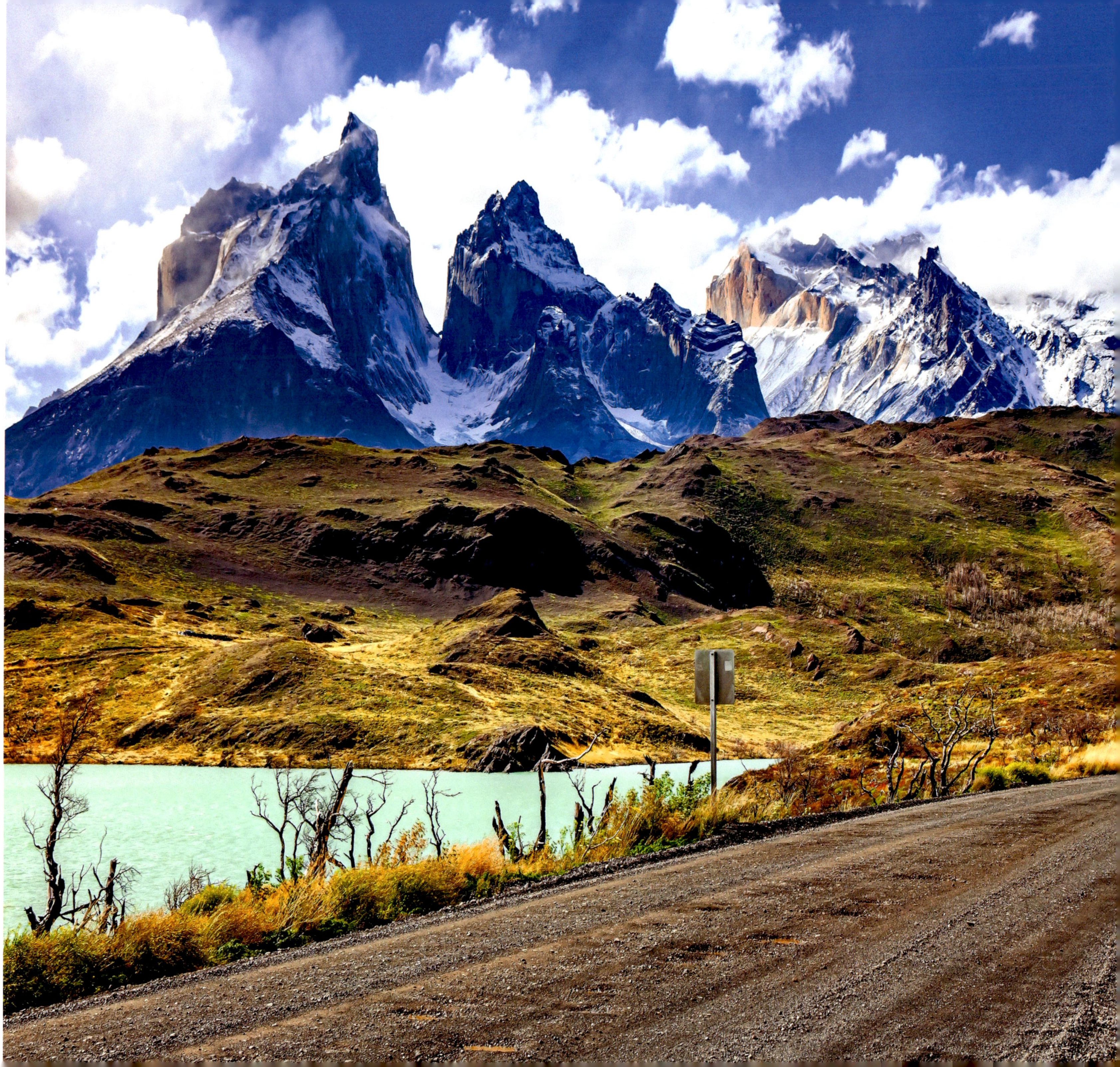

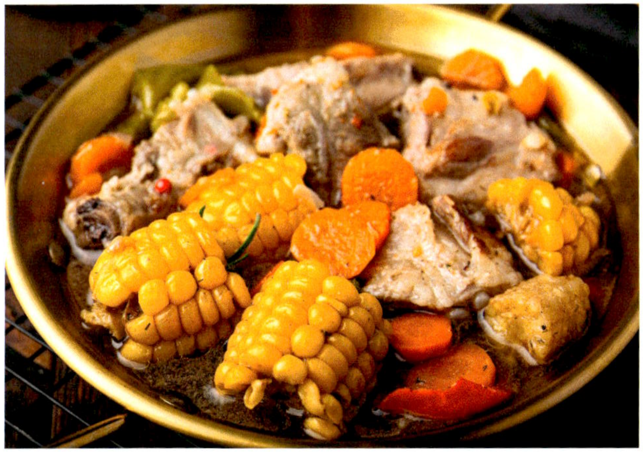

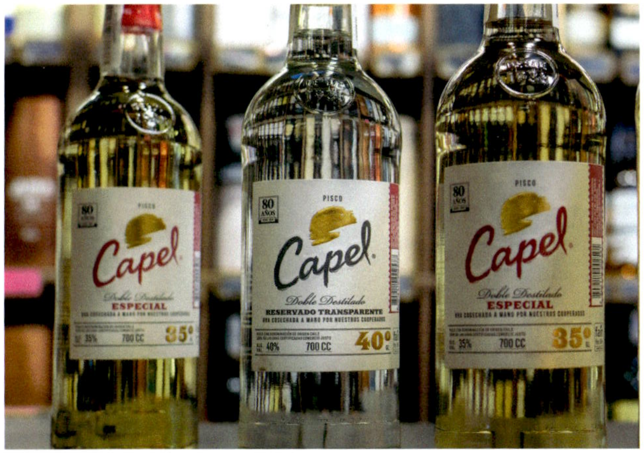
PISCO
Capel
Doble Destilado
ESPECIAL
700 CC
35°
RESERVADO TRANSPARENTE
40°

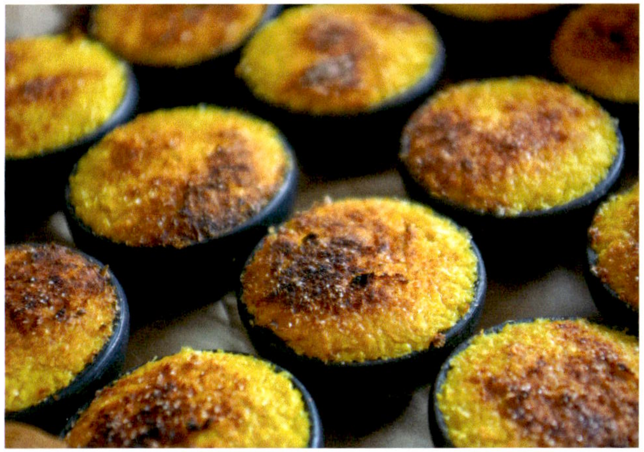

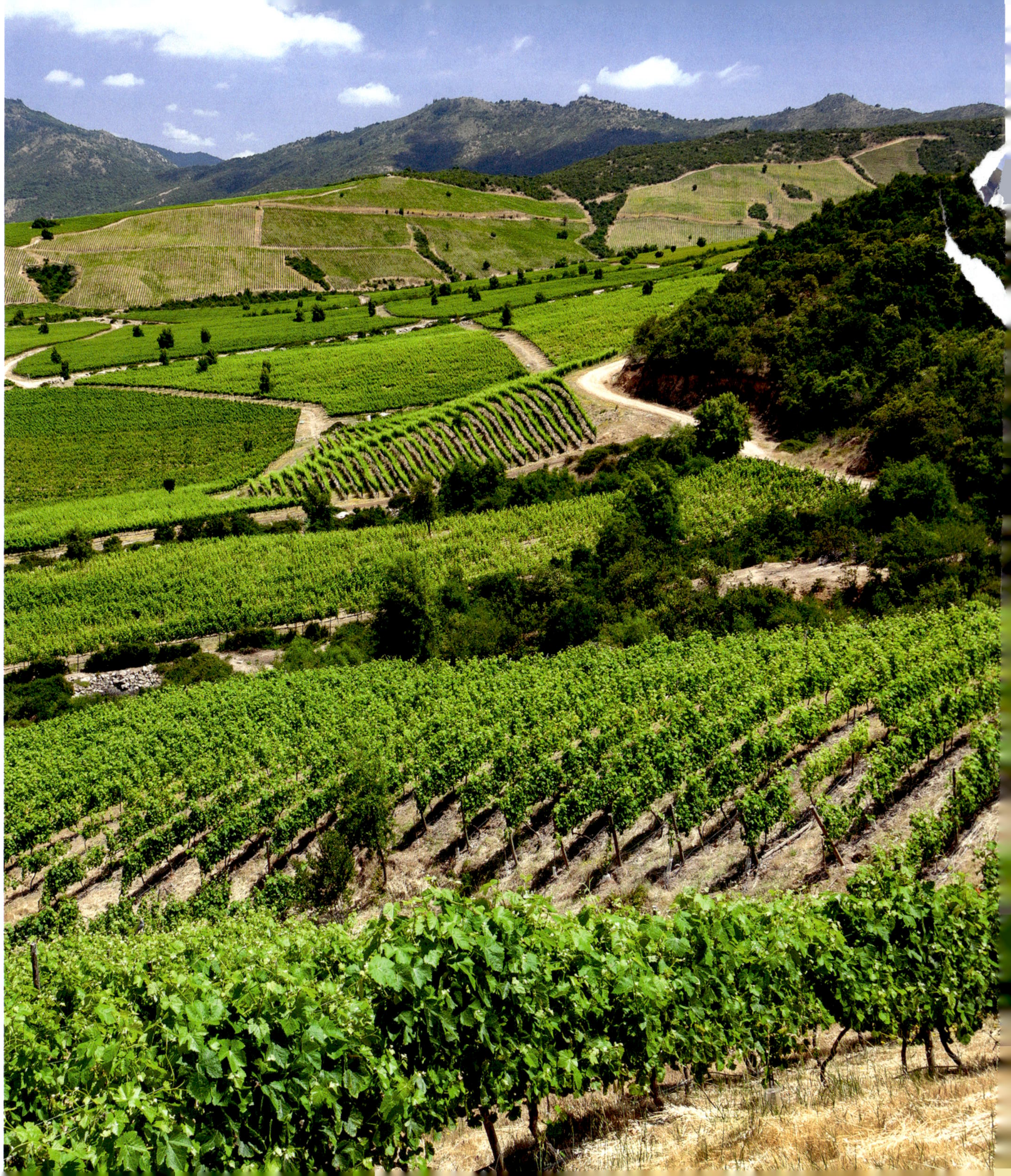

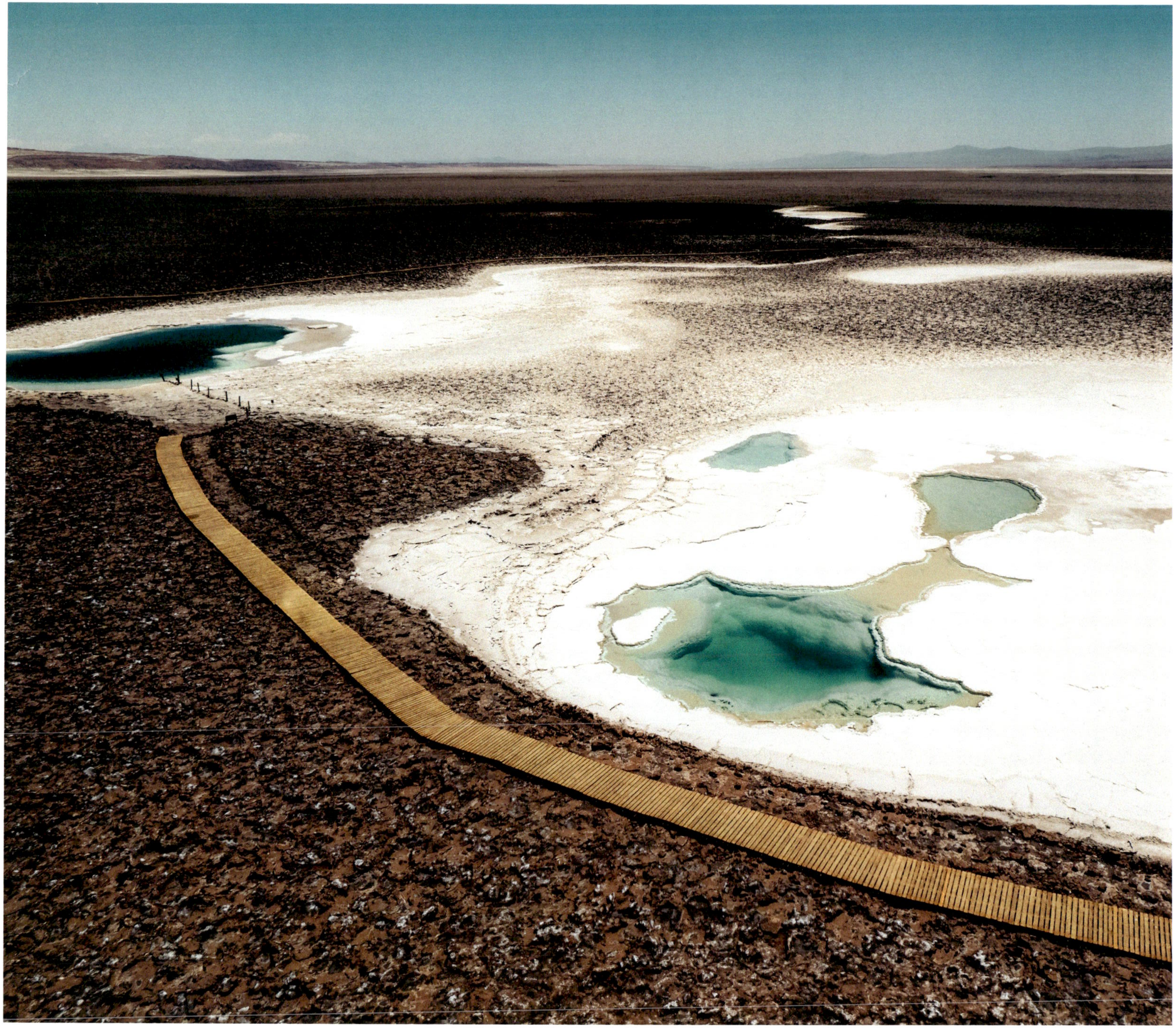

OPPOSITE LEFT TOP:
Cazuela de Cerdo
While *cazuela* (stew cooked in a clay pot) is eaten throughout Chile, hearty pork stew is a favourite in the cooler south. It often includes potato, squash and corn on the cob.

OPPOSITE LEFT MIDDLE:
Pisco, Elqui Valley, Chile
The national drink of Chile, *pisco* is a grape brandy first made by sixteenth- or seventeenth-century Spanish settlers. It is often used to make a *piscola*, containing *pisco* and cola.

OPPOSITE LEFT BOTTOM:
Pastel de Choclo, Chile
This traditional dish has a gratin topping of ground sweetcorn and basil, sprinkled with sugar to caramelize, baked over a filling of minced beef, onions, hard-boiled eggs, olives and raisins.

OPPOSITE RIGHT:
Colchagua Valley, Chile
The heart of Chile's wine-growing region, Colchagua Valley is renowned for its full-bodied, rich reds made from Carménère and Cabernet Sauvignon grapes.

LEFT:
Baltinache Lagoons, Atacama Desert, Chile
In the world's driest non-polar desert, saltwater pools pock a vast salt flat. Salt and other minerals have collected in this closed desert basin due to runoff from the Andes and intense evaporation.

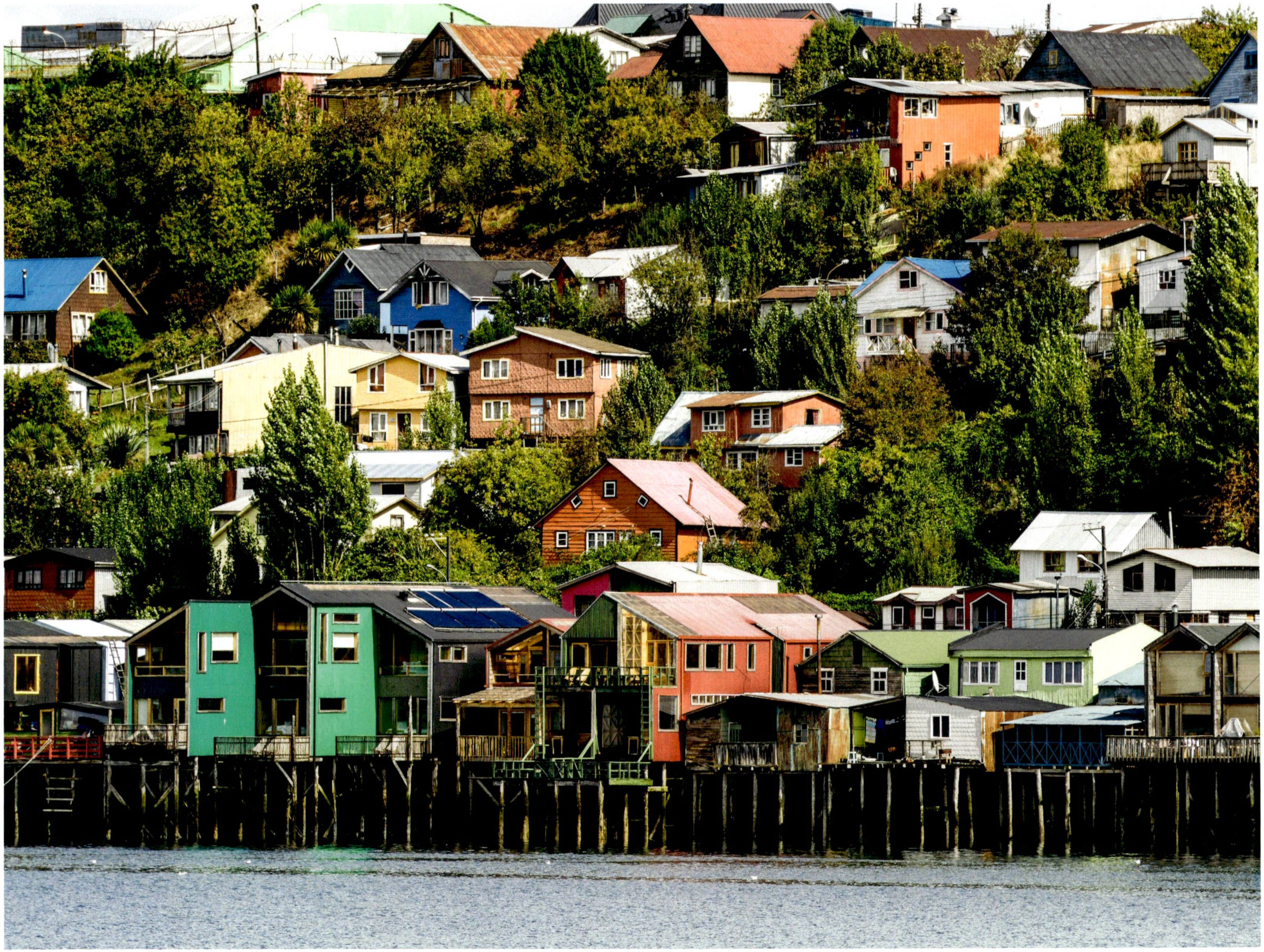

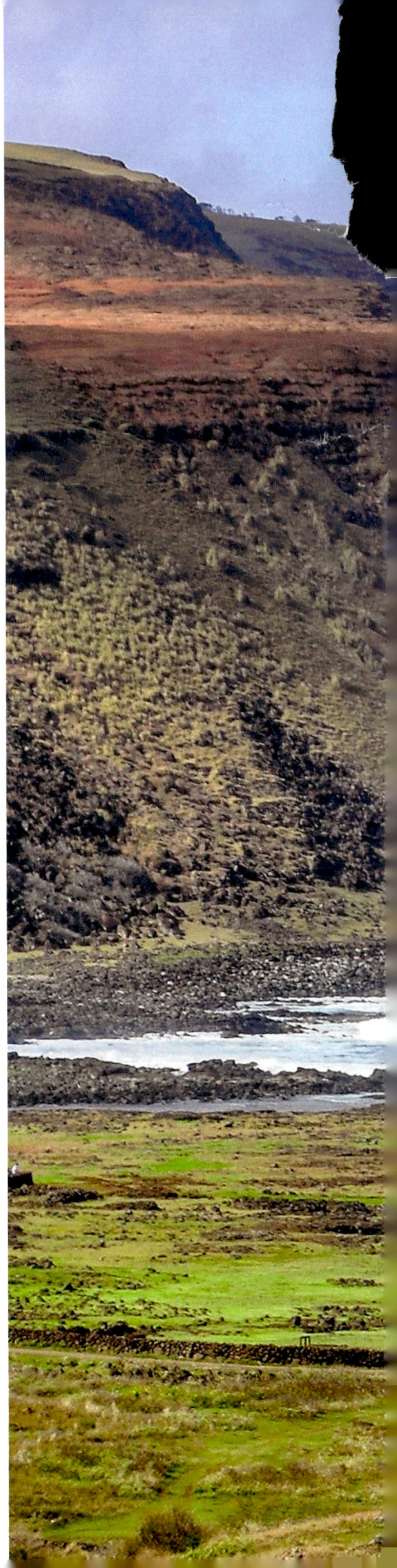

ABOVE:
Castro, Chiloé Island, Chile
Separated from central mainland Chile by the Chacao Channel, Chiloé Island is known for its blend of Spanish, Huilliche and Chono culture and architecture. In the island's largest city of Castro, wooden stilt houses called *palafitos* hug the shore.

RIGHT:
***Moai*, Easter Island, Chile**
Around 3512km (2182 miles) west of mainland Chile, Easter Island is known for its monolithic stone statues, called *moai*. Representing deified ancestors, these were carved by the Rapa Nui people between 1250 and 1500 CE.

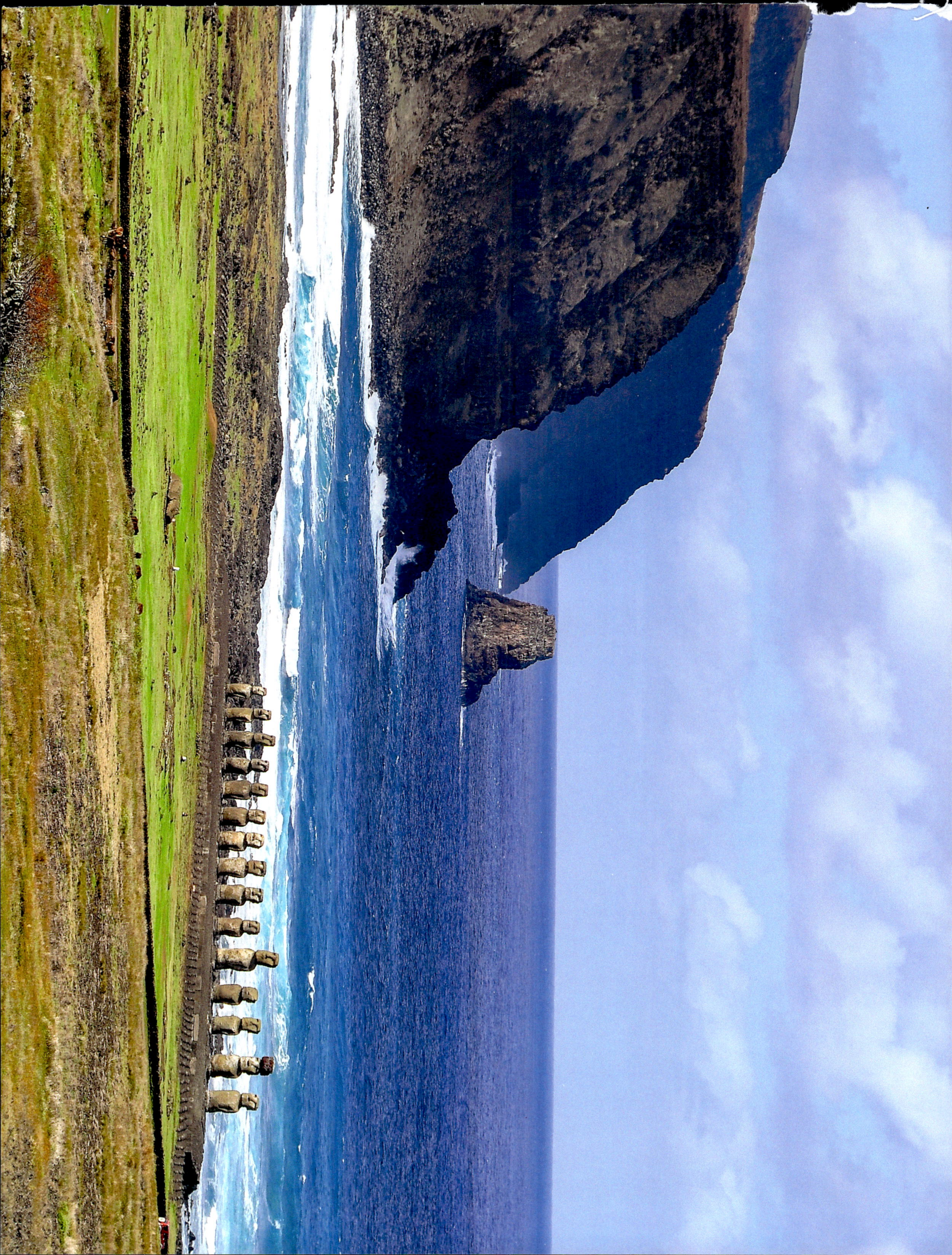

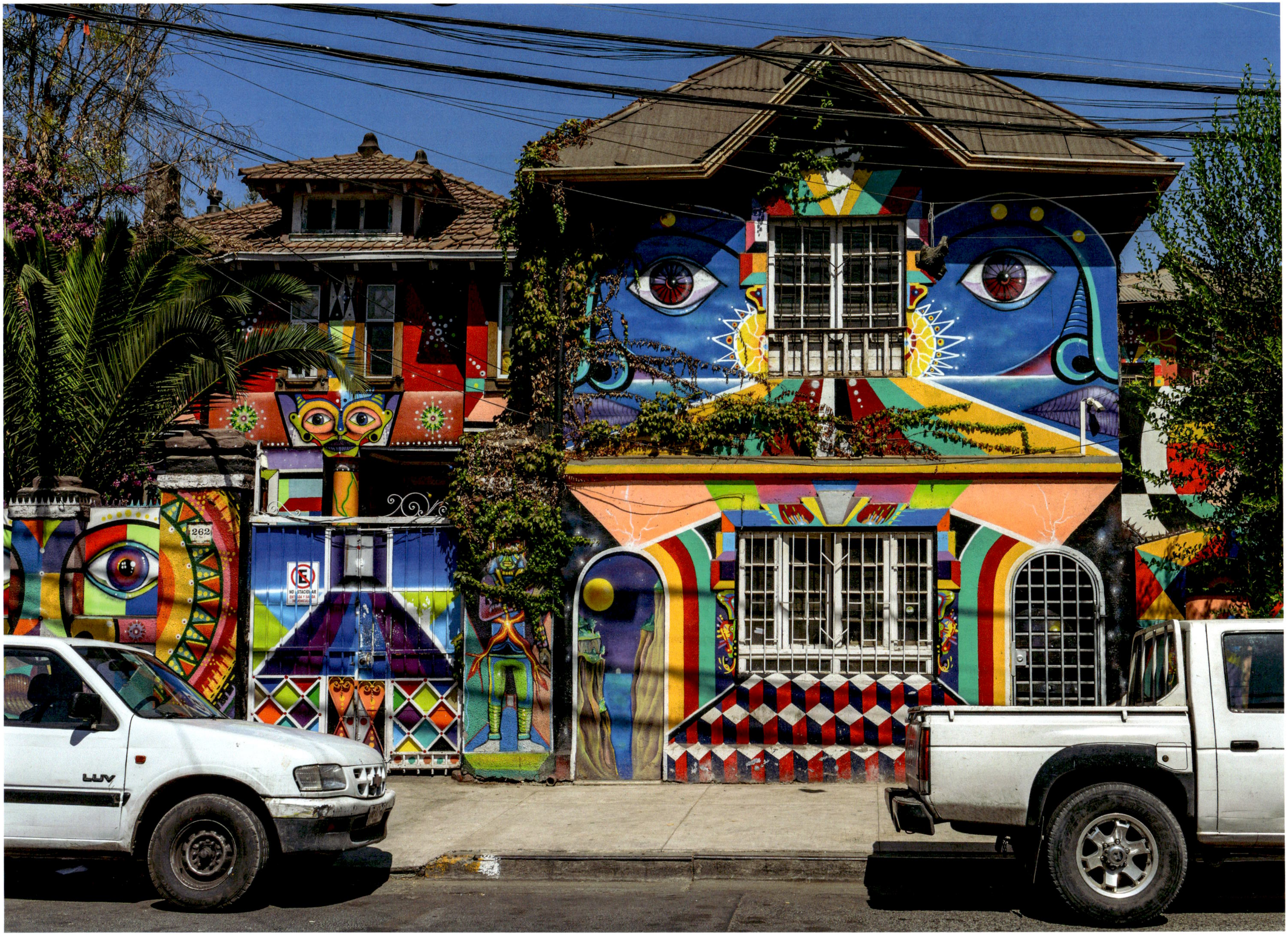
262
LUV

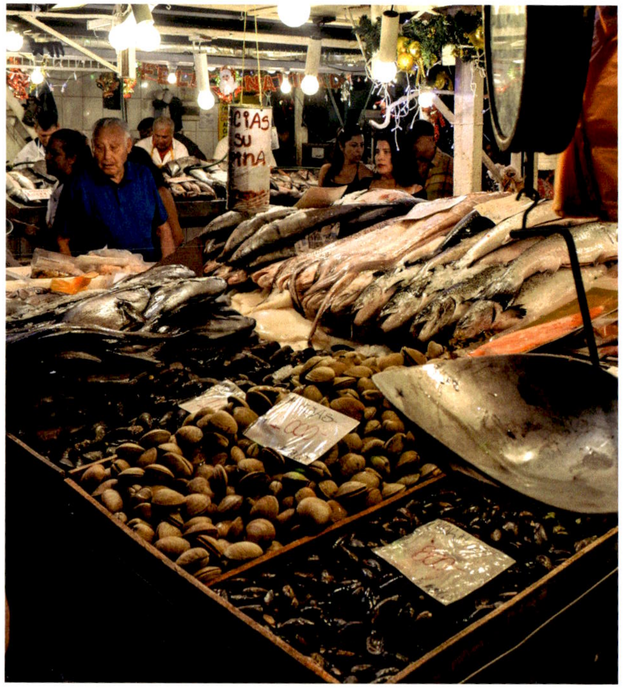

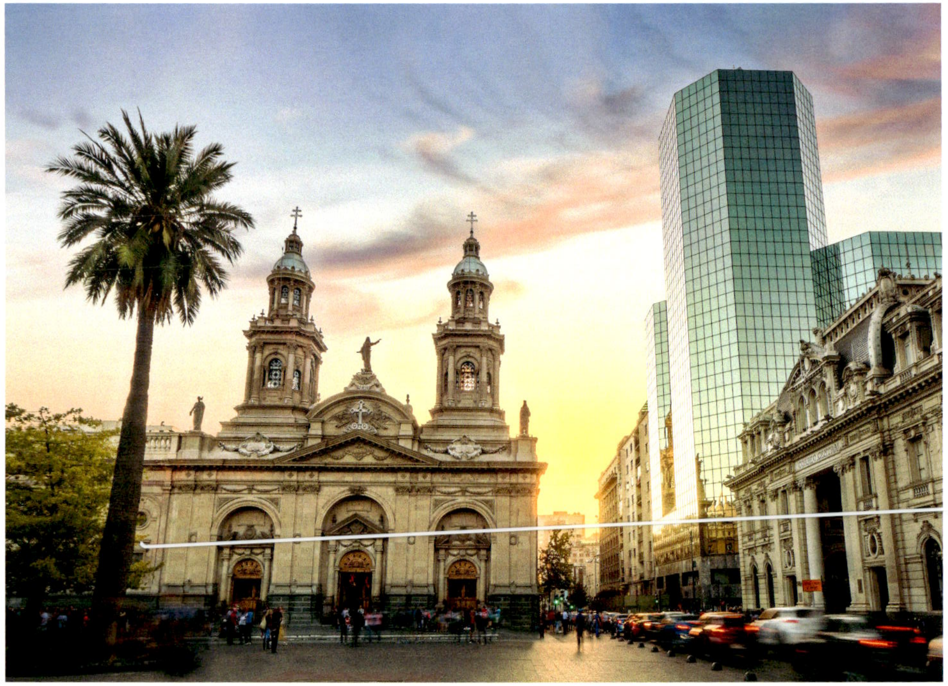

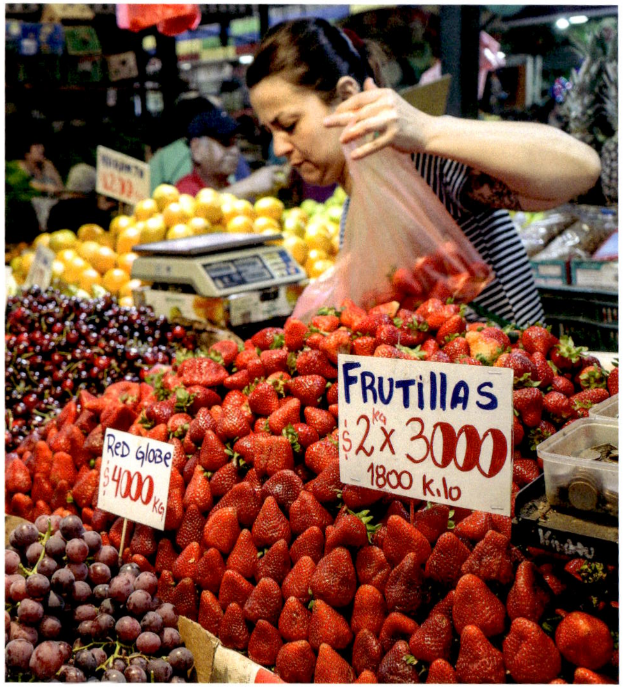

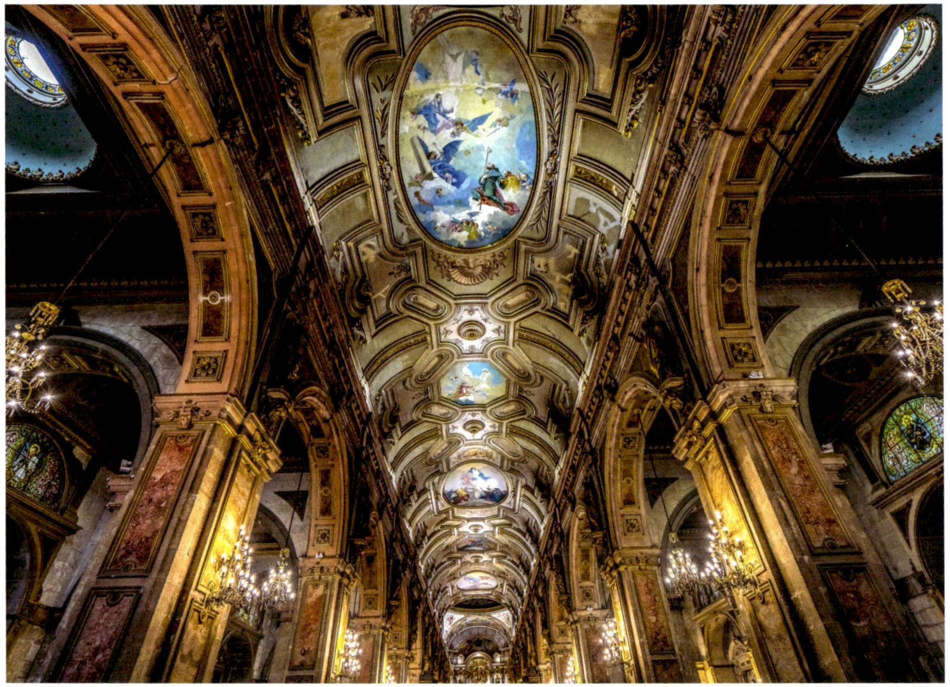

OPPOSITE:
Bellavista, Santiago, Chile
The Bellavista neighbourhood is known for its galleries, boutiques and jewellery stores that sell lapis lazuli from Chile's Coquimbo region. The barrio has long been home to many of Chile's artists and writers, including the twentieth-century poet Pablo Neruda.

FAR LEFT TOP AND BOTTOM:
Mercado Central, Santiago
Renowned particularly for its fish and seafood stalls and restaurants, Santiago's central market is housed in a cast-iron building dating from 1872.

LEFT TOP AND BOTTOM:
Metropolitan Cathedral, Santiago
Built between 1748 and 1906, the current cathedral replaced several earlier iterations destroyed by earthquakes and fire. The exterior showcases the Neoclassical style of eighteenth-century Italian architect Joaquín Toesca. In the late nineteenth century, the interior's ceiling was remodelled with ornate Tuscan touches.

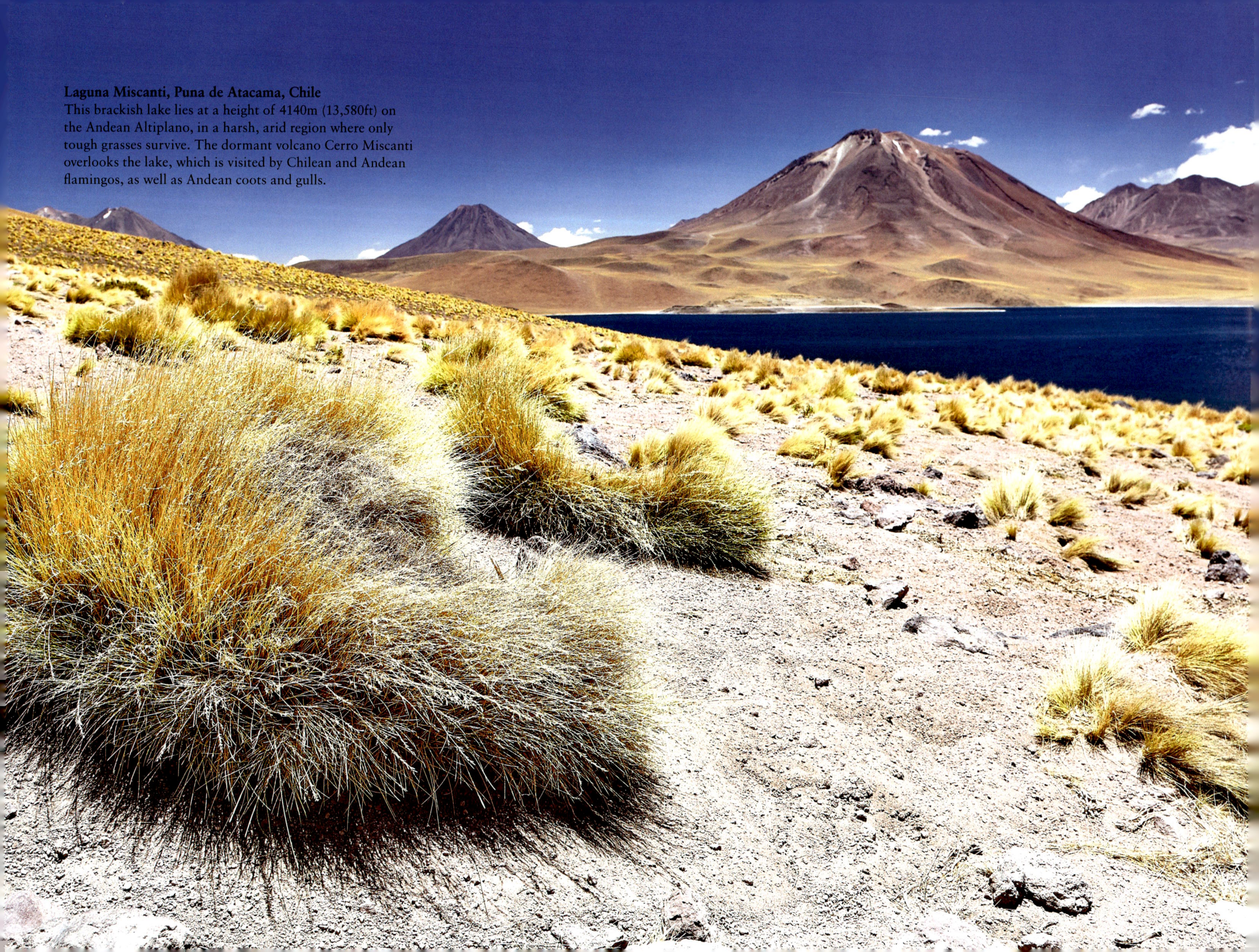

Laguna Miscanti, Puna de Atacama, Chile
This brackish lake lies at a height of 4140m (13,580ft) on the Andean Altiplano, in a harsh, arid region where only tough grasses survive. The dormant volcano Cerro Miscanti overlooks the lake, which is visited by Chilean and Andean flamingos, as well as Andean coots and gulls.

Index